The American Intellectual Tradition

The American Intellectual Tradition

A Sourcebook
Volume II: 1865 to the Present
THIRD EDITION

Edited by

DAVID A. HOLLINGER

University of California, Berkeley

and

CHARLES CAPPER

University of North Carolina, Chapel Hill

New York   Oxford
OXFORD UNIVERSITY PRESS
1997

Oxford University Press

Oxford   New York
Athens   Auckland   Bangkok
Bogota   Bombay   Buenos Aires   Calcutta
Cape Town   Dar es Salaam   Delhi
Florence   Hong Kong   Istanbul   Karachi
Kuala Lumpur   Madras   Madrid   Melbourne
Mexico City   Nairobi   Paris   Singapore
Taipei   Tokyo   Toronto
and associated companies in
Berlin   Ibadan

Published by Oxford University Press, Inc.,
198 Madison Avenue, New York, New York 10016

Oxford is a registered trademark of Oxford University Press

Library of Congress Cataloging-in-Publication Data
The American intellectual tradition : a sourcebook / edited by David
A. Hollinger and Charles Capper. — 3rd ed.
p. cm.   Includes bibliographical references.
Contents: v. 1. 1630–1865 — v. 2. 1865 to the present.
ISBN 0-19-509724-6 (cl : v. 1). — ISBN 0-19-509725-4 (pa : v. 1).
ISBN 0-19-509726-2 (cl : v. 2). — ISBN 0-19-509727-0 (pa : v. 2).
1. United States—Intellectual life—Sources.
I. Hollinger, David A.   II. Capper, Charles.
E169.1.A47218   1997
973—dc20   96-25901

1 3 5 7 9 8 6 4 2

Printed in the United States of America
on acid-free paper

For Henry F. May

Contents

Part Three   To Extend Democracy and To Formulate the Modern

Part Four   *Exploring Diversity and Postmodernity*

Preface

If a tradition is a family of disagreements, the American intellectual tradition is a very extended family. Its members include arguments inspired by the interests and ideals of a variety of communities within the United States as well as arguments concerned with the national community itself. The family also embraces arguments responsive to Western, if not universal, issues in philosophy, science, religion, politics, literature, and the arts. Some of the most influential members of this family are intensely aware of their European ancestry, whereas others have married into European families, and still others remain always preoccupied with the family's Americanness. The family is currently quite content with its extended state; its diverse and contested character is often a source of pride. But not everyone is agreed on just what makes it a family to begin with. And the family is divided, if not confused, over exactly which of its members ought to supervise the education of its young. What disagreements are primary? How should the tradition be structured to ensure its continuation and critical revision? What specific artifacts of discourse have played the greatest role historically in developing the American intellectual tradition?

Answers to these questions are necessarily implied by any sourcebook for the study of American intellectual history. In deciding what to include in this collection, we have been aware of the dynamism and diversity of our subject as well as highly conscious of the differing constructions of it offered by various scholars. We have sought the advice of numerous colleagues and accordingly have designed *The American Intellectual Tradition* to make available to students many of the documents now routinely assigned by teachers of this subject in colleges and universities throughout the United States. Hence these volumes are chiefly practical devices, not outlines of a systematic, comprehensive interpretation of American intellectual history. Yet certain priorities have shaped these volumes, and it is appropriate to make them explicit.

The American Intellectual Tradition is frankly intellectual in orientation. Most of the documents it contains are the result of someone's effort to make an analysis and to persuade others of the correctness of that analysis. Although these documents express "attitudes" and embody "ideas," we have been more sensitive to their status as arguments. Hence most of our selections are of the genres classically associated with purposive discourse: sermon, address, letter, treatise, and essay. We have tried to identify pieces of argumentation that became prominent points of reference for contemporaries or for Americans of later generations. In so doing, we have necessarily been drawn again and again to the work of men and women normally regarded as intellectual leaders: people who were relatively effective at making arguments.

Arguments can be addressed to an infinite number of issues, but the writings in this book respond to issues that have persistently generated extensive intellectual discussion. The bulk of our selections concern the theoretical basis for religious, scientific, artistic, political, social, and economic practice. Because the United States is above all a polity, the American family of disagreements includes a high proportion of arguments concerning the basis of politics. Because the public culture of America has often been caught up in the distinctive ethos of Protestant Christianity, many of our selections—especially in Volume I—are directed to religious issues. Because modern America has been a peculiarly science-preoccupied civilization, many of the selections in Volume II address the character of the scientific enterprise and debate the implications of scientific knowledge.

In order to give these issues historical shape, we have organized the documents around general themes or movements, which we address briefly in the introduction preceding each main section. Were this a textbook rather than a sourcebook, we would have attempted to indicate the entire structure of discourse surrounding the texts we discuss; here we can do no more than hint at this, leaving it to the instructor to fill in the missing arguments and counterarguments. In framing our selections, we have also tried to avoid what seems to us a failing in many previous anthologies: the packaging of each source as an example of a particular doctrine or movement. Throughout we have emphasized that most intellectual works are dynamic and mul-tifaceted and therefore have meaning in more than one frame of reference. With this in mind, we have written headnotes that highlight the dense internal content of each document as well as the setting in which it was produced.

It is easy to list the names of historically significant American thinkers whose work does not appear in these volumes. Yet, we have resisted the impulse to reduce the length of our selections in order to make room for a greater number of authors. The multiplication of texts by cutting them into mere snippets might have enabled us to more effectively register the social and cultural diversity of American intellec-tual leadership. Every ideological persuasion and identity group might then find its representative listed in the table of contents. The plural and contested character of the American intellectual tradition might then be acknowledged even more com-pellingly than is acknowledged by the selections we have decided to include. But the reducing of texts to brief excerpts has a great cost. The rhetorical and discursive power that helped draw attention to a text in the first place can be easily lost. Ten-sions within a text can be silenced, rendering the authors more univocal than they were. Although we have sometimes printed only a brief selection from a longer work, most of the documents found in *The American Intellectual Tradition* are complete, or nearly complete, essays, addresses, or chapters of books. We hope that what this sourcebook offers in the depth of its selections will compensate for what it lacks in the range of its inclusions.

Yet this range is greater in the third edition of *The American Intellectual Tradition* than it was in the second (1993) and the first (1989). In dropping some selections and adding new ones, we have been guided by the advice of colleagues who have used the earlier editions in teaching. We have also tried to take account of recent scholarship that assigns new historical significance to certain authors.

The chronologies at the end of each volume list almost as many European textual and sociopolitical events as American ones, reflecting our awareness that American intellectual history is bound up with the larger history of Europe, and indeed that of most of the world. The United States stands intellectually in much the same relation to Europe as Great Britain does: British intellectuals help consti-tute the discourse of Europe while simultaneously perpetuating and revising their own national tradition. The same can be said of intellectuals in Russia, Spain, Germany, or France, as well as of those in the United States. Moreover, national cultures are sites of differing international significance at different times. In the seventeenth century, for example, the discourse of an extended Europe went forward without much attention to what was being said in British North America, but in the twentieth century the United States became a major site for this discourse.

Students using this sourcebook can learn more about the authors of these selections, and about the issues being addressed, from the hundreds of thematic and biographical articles in Richard W. Fox and James T. Kloppenberg, eds., *A Companion to American Thought* (Cambridge, Mass., 1995). Students in need of a basic introduction to what is meant by "intellectual history" may be helped by Stefan Collini, et al., "What Is Intellectual History" in Juliet Gardiner, ed., *What Is History Today?* (London, 1988, 105–19. Those interested in contemporary debates about methodological questions in the study of intellectual history can turn to recent issues of the *Intellectual History Newsletter,* edited by Casey Blake at Indiana University. Students eager to explore the theoretical issues that most sharply divide intellectual historians from one another can examine the critical exchange between David A. Hollinger and David Harlan in the *American Historical Review,* 94 (June 1989), 581–626, and the overview essay by Martin Jay, "The Textual Approach to Intellectual History," in Jay's *Force Fields: Between Intellectual History and Cultural Critique* (New York, 1993), 158–16, 220–22.

For advice regarding this sourcebook, we wish to thank the following individuals: Patrick Allitt of Emory University; Joyce Appleby of the University of California, Los Angeles; Robert C. Bannister of Swarthmore College; Thomas Bender of New York University; Fred Beuttler of the University of Chicago; Casey Nelson Blake of Indiana University; Ruth H. Bloch of the University of California, Los Angeles; Eileen Boris of Howard University; Paul Boyer of the University of Wisconsin–Madison; Howard Brick of the University of Oregon; E. Wayne Carp of Pacific Lutheran University; Kenneth Cmiel of the University of Iowa; Charles Lloyd Cohen of the University of Wisconsin–Madison; George Cotkin of California State Polytechnic University at San Luis Obispo; David Brion Davis of Yale University; John P. Diggins of the City University of New York; Elizabeth Faue of Wayne State University; Richard Wightman Fox of Boston University; George M. Fredrickson of Stanford University; James B. Gilbert of the University of Maryland; Samuel Haber of the University of California, Berkeley; Thomas L. Haskell of Rice University; Hugh Hawkins of Amherst College; David Hoeveler of the University of Wisconsin—Milwaukee; E. Brooks Holifield of Emory University; James Hoopes of Babson College; Daniel Horowitz of Smith College; Daniel Walker Howe of Oxford University; David Johnson of Portland State University; John F. Kasson of the University of North Carolina at Chapel Hill; Linda K. Kerber of the University of Iowa; James T. Kloppenberg of Brandeis University; Lloyd S. Kramer of the University of North Carolina at Chapel Hill; Bruce Kuklick of the University of Pennsylvania; Ralph Luker of Antioch College; Henry F. May of the University of California, Berkeley; Donald B. Meyer of Wesleyan University; Robert Moates Miller of the University of North Carolina at Chapel Hill; Jill Morawski of Wesleyan University; Michael O'Brien of Miami University; Lewis Perry of Vanderbilt University; Mark Pittenger of the University of Colorado; Daniel T. Rodgers of Princeton University; Dorothy Ross of the Johns Hopkins University; Joan Shelly Rubin of the State University College of New York at Brockport; Barbara Sicherman of Trinity University;

Daniel Singal of Hobart and William Smith Colleges; Wilson Smith of the University of California, Davis; John W. Stewart of Princeton Theological Seminary; James Turner of the University of Michigan; Robert Westbrook of the University of Rochester; Daniel Wilson of Muhlenberg College; Rosemarie Zagarri of George Mason University; and members of the Berkeley Graduate Intellectual History Group. Some of these colleagues would have preferred a somewhat different table of contents, but without their counsel *The American Intellectual Tradition* would be less representative of current teaching practice.

For assistance in preparing this sourcebook we wish to thank Sonja Amadae, Eri Combest, and Jonathan Young. We also wish to express our appreciation for the advice and assistance of Nancy Lane of Oxford University Press. For technical assistance in the preparation of Volume II, we wish to thank Diana Wear.

The editors have worked closely at every stage of the preparation of *The American Intellectual Tradition,* but responsibility for Volume I belongs to Charles Capper and for Volume II to David Hollinger.

Berkeley, Calif.   D. A. H.
Chapel Hill, N.C.   C. C.
February 1996

Part One

Toward a Secular Culture

Introduction

William James recognized that the life of the mind during his own time was becoming increasingly secular. The Bible, which had for so long been uniquely privileged as a foundation for knowledge and morals, came to be approached more critically, especially in the light of modern science. James did not lament this historic transformation; on the contrary, he welcomed it. Yet he was concerned that the scientific spirit of the age would intimidate people into giving up cherished beliefs about God that might, after all, remain plausible even in the wake of such discoveries as evolution, thermodynamics, and the multiple authorship of various books of the Bible. When James wrote "The Will to Believe" in 1897, he sought to vindicate the individual soul's right to retain aspects of the Protestant heritage not actually proven false by the advancement of secular learning. James himself was an eminent man of science; his defense of religious belief can remind us that many late nineteenth-century American intellectuals were extremely conscious of a tension between religious tradition and scientific innovation.

Not all the documents in Part One manifest this tension as vividly as does James's "The Will to Believe," but these documents do display a tendency, if not a determination, to ground argument in naturalistic and humanistic premises. Even Josiah Royce's overtly biblical "The Problem of Job" did not suggest that scriptural authority enhances an idea's claim to truth. Rather, it was to logical analysis and humane instincts that Royce appealed in arguing for the justness of God's decision to permit the suffering of innocent persons. Royce's orientation can be contrasted with that of the theologian Charles Hodge. The latter's defense of biblical authority opens Part One and can serve as a reminder of the centrality of the Bible to the intellectual life in the United States through the Civil War.

Although the persistence of religious concern amid secular initiatives is a vital theme in the intellectual history of the United States during the late nineteenth and early twentieth century, these secular initiatives are appropriately central to Part One of this collection. Elizabeth Cady Stanton drew on an individualism she termed Protestant, but the free-thinking Stanton vindicated the rights of women largely on the basis of an Enlightenment-inspired tradition of universal human rights. Henry Adams's meditations on "the dynamo and the virgin" culminated not in religious inspiration but in the scientific measurement of its force. Indeed, the most general and pervasive of the secular initiatives of this era was the effort to install "scientific method" as the chief agency by which culture was to be constituted. This initiative is exemplified best by Charles Peirce's argument for the supremacy of scientific method but is manifest in most of the selections in Part One. "Realism" in literature and the arts was allied with the movement for a more scientific culture, as is made clear by William Dean Howells's plea for a literature that would tell the "truth" about people's actual lives rather than idealize them to suit a parochial moral agenda. More distant yet from the literary culture of idealization and uplift was George

Santayana, who called it "genteel" and complained that its overbearingly Protestant sensibility dominated philosophy, as well as literature and the arts.

Gilded Age thinkers often hoped that social science might provide a new, solid foundation for organizing and governing their society, but they disagreed on just what principles were "scientific." The selections from William Graham Sumner and Lester Frank Ward—both of whom were critics of inherited religious ideas—typify the debate between conservative and liberal assessments of the political implications of Darwinian science. Sumner and Ward also partook of the period's interest in explaining social phenomena historically, often with reference to the operation of putative natural laws. This interest is represented in the selection from Charlotte Perkins Gilman, which explains in terms of evolutionary history the subordinate social position of women.

Recommendations for Further Reading

Laurence R. Veysey, *The Emergence of the American University* (Chicago, 1965); R. Jackson Wilson, *In Quest of Community: Social Philosophy in the United States, 1860–1920* (New York, 1968); Howard Mumford Jones, *The Age of Energy: Varieties of American Experience, 1865–1915* (New York, 1973); William R. Hutchison, *The Modernist Impulse in American Protestantism* (Cambridge, 1976); Daniel Walker Howe, ed., *Victorian America* (Philadelphia, 1976); Alexandra Oleson and John Voss, eds., *The Organization of Knowledge in America, 1860–1920* (Baltimore, 1979); T. J. Jackson Lears, *No Place of Grace: Antimodernism and the Transformation of American Culture* (New York, 1981); Alan Trachtenberg, *The Incorporation of America: Culture and Society in the Gilded Age* (New York, 1982); Lewis Perry, *Intellectual Life in America: A History* (New York, 1984); James Turner, *Without God, Without Creed: The Origins of Unbelief in America* (Baltimore, 1985); Bruce Kuklick, *Churchmen and Philosophers: From Jonathan Edwards to John Dewey* (New Haven, 1985); Thomas Bender, *New York Intellect: A History of Intellectual Life in New York City from 1750 to the Beginnings of Our Own Time* (New York, 1987); Lawrence W. Levine, *Highbrow/Lowbrow: The Emergence of Cultural Hierarchy* (Cambridge, 1988); Cynthia Eagle Russett, *Sexual Science: The Victorian Construction of Womanhood* (Cambridge, 1989); Samuel Haber, *The Quest for Authority and Honor in the American Professions, 1750–1900* (Chicago, 1991); George Cotkin, *Reluctant Modernism* (Boston, 1992); Mark Pittenger, *American Socialists and Evolutionary Thought, 1870–1920* (Madison, 1993); James Livingston, *Pragmatism and the Political Economy of Cultural Revolution, 1850–1940* (Chapel Hill, 1994); David E. Shi, *Facing Facts: Realism in American Thought and Culture, 1850–1920* (New York, 1995); Gillis J. Harp, *Positivist Republic: Auguste Comte and the Reconstruction of American Liberalism, 1865–1920* (State College, Pa., 1995).

CHARLES HODGE

Selection from *Systematic Theology*
1872

Before the explosive growth of modern universities during the last quarter of the nineteenth century, theological seminaries were home to a number of the most learned and accomplished intellectuals in the United States. One of the most creative and influential of these seminarians was the Presbyterian divine Charles Hodge (1797–1878). Although Hodge is most remembered for his anti-Darwinian tract, *What Is Darwinism?* (New York, 1874), he was the author of eleven other books and was the chief editor of one of nineteenth-century America's most sophisticated journals, *The Biblical Repertory and Princeton Review,* to which Hodge himself contributed more than ninety articles, many of which were book length. Hodge boasted on his retirement that not a single new idea had been introduced at the Princeton Theological Seminary during his sixty-seven years there as a student and professor. This flippant, provocatively reactionary remark has badly damaged Hodge's reputation in the twentieth century. He was orthodox, to be sure, and appeared to be all the more rigidly so in the 1870s, but in the context of American theological disputation he had been, for most of his career, a centrist: He steered a middle course between revivalism and transcendentalism, between denominational exclusiveness and ecumenical unification, and between a number of other conflicting impulses. Moreover, Hodge was critically engaged with the latest scholarship from Europe, especially in fields related to biblical scholarship. In a culture to which the Bible was truly central, Hodge was for half a century both a preeminent interpreter of scripture and a trainer of entire synods of preachers. In the selection from his *Systematic Theology* reprinted here, Hodge defends biblical authority and tries to convey the character of theological work by comparing it with the practice of natural science. It was partly on the basis of the strict views of "induction" displayed here that Hodge rejected Darwin as "unscientific."

Hodge's role in the Darwinian controversy is dealt with by R. Jackson Wilson, ed., *Darwinism and the American Intellectual,* 2nd ed. (Chicago, 1989). For a brief biography of Hodge, see the introduction to Mark Noll, ed., *Charles Hodge: The Way of Life* (New York, 1987), 1–44. Noll has also edited a valuable anthology that includes several of Hodge's works: Mark Noll, ed., *The Princeton Theology, 1812–1921* (Grand Rapids, 1983). For a detailed study of Hodge's career as a biblical scholar during his most creative, pre–Civil War years, see John William Stewart, "The Tethered Theology: Biblical Criticism, Common Sense Philosophy, and the Princeton Theologians, 1812–1860" (Ph.D. diss., University of Michigan, 1990). For an important study of the perspectives on secular learning developed by Hodge's generation of American religious thinkers, see James Turner, *Without God, Without Creed: The Origins of Unbelief in America* (Baltimore, 1985).

IN every science there are two factors: facts and ideas; or, facts and the mind. Science is more than knowledge. Knowledge is the persuasion of what is true on adequate evidence. But the facts of astronomy, chemistry, or history do not constitute the science of those departments of knowledge. Nor does the mere orderly arrangement of facts amount to science. Historical facts arranged in chronological order, are mere annals. The philosophy of history supposes those facts to be understood in their causal relations. In every department the man of science is assumed to understand the laws by which the facts of experience are determined; so that he not only knows the past, but can predict the future. The astronomer can foretell the relative position of the heavenly bodies for centuries to come. The chemist can tell with certainty what will be the effect of certain chemical combinations. If, therefore, theology be a science, it must include something more than a mere knowledge of facts. It must embrace an exhibition of the internal relation to those facts, one to another, and each to all. It must be able to show that if one be admitted, others cannot be denied.

The Bible is no more a system of theology, than nature is a system of chemistry or of mechanics. We find in nature the facts which the chemist or the mechanical philosopher has to examine, and from them to ascertain the laws by which they are determined. So the Bible contains the truths which the theologian has to collect, authenticate, arrange, and exhibit in their internal relation to each other. This constitutes the difference between biblical and systematic theology. The office of the former is to ascertain and state the facts of Scripture. The office of the latter is to take those facts, determine their relation to each other and to other cognate truths, as well as to vindicate them and show their harmony and consistency. This is not an easy task, or one of slight importance.

It may naturally be asked, why not take the truths as God has seen fit to reveal them, and thus save ourselves the trouble of showing their relation and harmony?

The answer to this question is, in the first place, that it cannot be done. Such is the constitution of the human mind that it cannot help endeavoring to systematize and reconcile the facts which it admits to be true. In no department of knowledge have men been satisfied with the possession of a mass of undigested facts. And the students of the Bible can as little be expected to be thus satisfied. There is a necessity, therefore, for the construction of systems of theology. Of this the history of the Church affords abundant proof. In all ages and among all denominations, such systems have been produced.

Second, A much higher kind of knowledge is thus obtained, than by the mere accumulation of isolated facts. It is one thing, for example, to know that oceans, continents, islands, mountains, and rivers exist on the face of the earth; and a much higher thing to know the causes which have determined the distribution of land and water on the surface of our globe; the configuration of the earth; the effects of that configuration on climate, on the races of plants and animals, on commerce, civilization, and the destiny of nations. It is by determining these causes that geography has been raised from a collection of facts to a highly important and elevated science. In like manner, without the knowledge of the laws of attraction and motion, astronomy would be a

Source: Charles Hodge, *Systematic Theology* (New York: Charles Scribner's Sons, 1872), I, 1–4, 10–17.

confused and unintelligible collection of facts. What is true of other sciences is true of theology. We cannot know what God has revealed in his Word unless we understand, at least in some good measure, the relation in which the separate truths therein contained stand to each other. It cost the Church centuries of study and controversy to solve the problem concerning the person of Christ; that is, to adjust and bring into harmonious arrangement all the facts which the Bible teaches on that subject.

Third, We have no choice in this matter. If we would discharge our duty as teachers and defenders of the truth, we must endeavor to bring all the facts of revelation into systematic order and mutual relation. It is only thus that we can satisfactorily exhibit their truth, vindicate them from objections, or bring them to bear in their full force on the minds of men.

Fourth, Such is evidently the will of God. He does not teach men astronomy or chemistry, but He gives them the facts out of which those sciences are constructed. Neither does He teach us systematic theology, but He gives us in the Bible the truths which, properly understood and arranged, constitute the science of theology. As the facts of nature are all related and determined by physical laws, so the facts of the Bible are all related and determined by the nature of God and of his creatures. And as He wills that men should study his works and discover their wonderful organic relation and harmonious combination, so it is his will that we should study his Word, and learn that, like the stars, its truths are not isolated points, but systems, cycles, and epicycles, in unending harmony and grandeur. Besides all this, although the Scriptures do not contain a system of theology as a whole, we have in the Epistles of the New Testament, portions of that system wrought out to our hands. These are our authority and guide.

Every science has its own method, determined by its peculiar nature. This is a matter of so much importance that it has been erected into a distinct department. Modern literature abounds in works on Methodology, *i. e.*, on the science of method. They are designed to determine the principles which should control scientific investigations. If a man adopts a false method, he is like one who takes a wrong road which will never lead him to his destination. The two great comprehensive methods are the *à priori* and the *à posteriori*. The one argues from cause to effect, the other from effect to cause. The former was for ages applied even to the investigation of nature. Men sought to determine what the facts of nature must be from the laws of mind or assumed necessary laws. Even in our own day we have had Rational Cosmogonies, which undertake to construct a theory of the universe from the nature of absolute being and its necessary modes of development. Every one knows how much it cost to establish the method of induction on a firm basis, and to secure a general recognition of its authority. According to this method, we begin with collecting well-established facts, and from them infer the general laws which determine their occurrence. From the fact that bodies fall toward the centre of the earth, has been inferred the general law of gravitation, which we are authorized to apply far beyond the limits of actual experience. This inductive method is founded upon two principles: First, That there are laws of nature (forces) which are the proximate causes of natural phenomena. Secondly, That those laws are uniform; so that we are certain that the same causes, under the same circumstances, will produce the same effects. There may be diversity of opinion as to the nature of these laws. They may be assumed to be forces inherent in matter; or, they may be regarded as uniform modes of divine operation; but in any event there must be some cause for the phenomena which we perceive around us, and that cause must be uniform and permanent. On these principles all the inductive sciences are founded; and by them the investigations of natural philosophers are guided.

The same principle applies to metaphysics as to physics; to psychology as well as to natural science. Mind has its laws as well as matter, and those laws, although of a different kind, are as permanent as those of the external world. . . .

The Bible is to the theologian what nature is to the man of science. It is his store-house of facts; and his method of ascertaining what the Bible teaches, is the same as that which the natural philosopher adopts to ascertain what nature teaches. In the first place, he comes to his task with all the assumptions above mentioned. He must assume the validity of those laws of belief which God has impressed upon our nature. In these laws are included some which have no direct application to the natural sciences. Such, for example, as the essential distinction between right and wrong; that nothing contrary to virtue can be enjoined by God; that it cannot be right to do evil that good may come; that sin deserves punishment, and other similar first truths, which God has implanted in the constitution of all moral beings, and which no objective revelation can possibly contradict. These first principles, however, are not to be arbitrarily assumed. No man has a right to lay down his own opinions, however firmly held, and call them "first truths of reason," and make them the source or test of Christian doctrines. Nothing can rightfully be included under the category of first truths, or laws of belief, which cannot stand the tests of universality and necessity, to which many add self-evidence. But self-evidence is included in universality and necessity, in so far, that nothing which is not self-evident can be universally believed, and what is self-evident forces itself on the mind of every intelligent creature.

In the second place, the duty of the Christian theologian is to ascertain, collect, and combine all the facts which God has revealed concerning himself and our relation to Him. These facts are all in the Bible. This is true, because everything revealed in nature, and in the constitution of man concerning God and our relation to Him, is contained and authenticated in Scripture. It is in this sense that "the Bible, and the Bible alone, is the religion of Protestants." It may be admitted that the truths which the theologian has to reduce to a science, or, to speak more humbly, which he has to arrange and harmonize, are revealed partly in the external works of God, partly in the constitution of our nature, and partly in the religious experience of believers; yet lest we should err in our inferences from the works of God, we have a clearer relevation of all that nature reveals, in his word; and lest we should misinterpret our own consciousness and the laws of our nature, everything that can be legitimately learned from that source will be found recognized and authenticated in the Scriptures; and lest we should attribute to the teaching of the Spirit the operations of our own natural affections, we find in the Bible the norm and standard of all genuine religious experience. The Scriptures teach not only the truth, but what are the effects of the truth on the heart and conscience, when applied with saving power by the Holy Ghost.

In the third place, the theologian must be guided by the same rules in the collection of facts, as govern the man of science.

1. This collection must be made with diligence and care. It is not an easy work. There is in every department of investigation great liability to error. Almost all false

theories in science and false doctrines in theology are due in a great degree to mistakes as to matters of fact. A distinguished naturalist said he repeated an experiment a thousand times before he felt authorized to announce the result to the scientific world as an established fact.

2. This collection of facts must not only be carefully conducted, but also comprehensive, and if possible, exhaustive. An imperfect induction of facts led men for ages to believe that the sun moved round the earth, and that the earth was an extended plain. In theology a partial induction of particulars has led to like serious errors. . . .

Illustrations without end might be given of the necessity of a comprehensive induction of facts to justify our doctrinal conclusions. These facts must not be willfully denied or carelessly overlooked, or unfairly appreciated. We must be honest here, as the true student of nature is honest in his induction. Even scientific men are sometimes led to suppress or to pervert facts which militate against their favorite theories; but the temptation to this form of dishonesty is far less in their case, than in that of the theologian. The truths of religion are far more important than those of natural science. They come home to the heart and conscience. They may alarm the fears or threaten the hopes of men, so that they are under strong temptation to overlook or pervert them. If, however, we really desire to know what God has revealed we must be conscientiously diligent and faithful in collecting the facts which He has made known, and in giving them their due weight. If a geologist should find in a deposit of early date implements of human workmanship, he is not allowed to say they are natural productions. He must either revise his conclusion as to the age of the deposit, or carry back to an earlier period the existence of man. There is no help for it. Science cannot make facts; it must take them as they are. In like manner, if the Bible asserts that Christ's death was a satisfaction to justice, the theologian is not allowed to merge justice into benevolence in order to suit his theory of the atonement. If the Scriptures teach that men are born in sin, we cannot change the nature of sin, and make it a tendency to evil and not really sin, in order to get rid of difficulty. If it be a Scriptual fact that the soul exists in a state of conscious activity between death and the resurrection, we must not deny this fact or reduce this conscious activity to zero, because our anthropology teaches that the soul has no individuality and no activity without a body. We must take the facts of the Bible as they are, and construct our system so as to embrace them all in their integrity.

In the fourth place, in theology as in natural science, principles are derived from facts, and not impressed upon them. The properties of matter, the laws of motion, of magnetism, of light, etc., are not framed by the mind. They are not laws of thought. They are deductions from facts. The investigator sees, or ascertains by observation, what are the laws which determine material phenomena; he does not invent those laws. His speculations on matters of science unless sustained by facts, are worthless. It is no less unscientific for the theologian to assume a theory as to the nature of virtue, of sin, of liberty, of moral obligation, and then explain the facts of Scripture in accordance with his theories. His only proper course is to derive his theory of virtue, of sin, of liberty, of obligation, from the facts of the Bible. He should remember that his business is not to set forth his system of truth (that is of no account), but to ascertain and exhibit what is God's system, which is a matter of the greatest moment. If he cannot believe what the facts of the Bible assume to be true, let him say so. Let the sacred writers have their doctrine, while he has his own. To this ground a large class of modern exegetes and theologians, after a long struggle, have actually come. They give what they regard as the doctrines of the Old Testament; then those of the Evangelists; then those of the Apostles; and then their own. This is fair. So long, however, as the binding authority of Scripture is acknowledged, the temptation is very strong to press the facts of the Bible into accordance with our preconceived theories. If a man be persuaded that certainty in acting is inconsistent with liberty of action; that a free agent can always act contrary to any amount of influence (not destructive of his liberty) brought to bear upon him, he will inevitably deny that the Scriptures teach the contrary, and thus be forced to explain away all facts which prove the absolute control of God over the will and volitions of men. If he hold that sinfulness can be predicated only of intelligent, voluntary action in contravention of law, he must deny that men are born in sin, let the Bible teach what it may. If he believes that ability limits obligation, he must believe independently of the Scriptures, or in opposition to them, it matters not which, that men are able to repent, believe, love God perfectly, to live without sin, at any, and all times, without the least assistance from the Spirit of God. If he deny that the innocent may justly suffer penal evil for the guilty, he must deny that Christ bore our sins. If he deny that the merit of one man can be the judicial ground of the pardon and salvation of other men, he must reject the Scriptural doctrine of justification. It is plain that complete havoc must be made of the whole system of revealed truth, unless we consent to derive our philosophy from the Bible, instead of explaining the Bible by our philosophy. If the Scriptures teach that sin is hereditary, we must adopt a theory of sin suited to that fact. If they teach that men cannot repent, believe, or do anything spirtually good, without the supernatural aid of the Holy Spirit, we must make our theory of moral obligation accord with that fact. If the Bible teaches that we bear the guilt of Adam's first sin, that Christ bore our guilt, and endured the penalty of the law in our stead, these are facts with which we must make our principles agree. It would be easy to show that in every department of theology,—in regard to the nature of God, his relation to the world, the plan of salvation, the person and work of Christ, the nature of sin, the operations of divine grace, men, instead of taking the facts of the Bible, and seeing what principles they imply, what philosophy underlies them, have adopted their philosophy independently of the Bible, to which the facts of the Bible are made to bend. This is utterly unphilosophical. It is the fundamental principle of all sciences, and of theology among the rest, that theory is to be determined by facts, and not facts by theory. . . .

. . . All truth must be consistent. God cannot contradict himself. He cannot force us by the constitution of the nature which He has given us to believe one thing, and in his Word command us to believe the opposite. And second, All the truths taught by the constitution of our nature or by religious experience, are recognized and authenticated in the Scriptures. This is a safeguard and a limit. We cannot assume this or that principle to be intuitively true, or this or that conclusion to be demonstrably certain, and make them a standard to which the Bible must conform. What is self-evidently true, must be proved to be so, and is always recognized in the Bible as true. Whole systems of theologies are founded upon intuitions, so called, and if every man is at liberty to exalt his own intuitions, as men are accustomed to call their strong convictions, we should have as many theologies in the world as there are thinkers. The same remark is applicable to religious experience. There is no form of conviction more intimate and irresistible than that which arises from the inward teaching of the Spirit. All saving faith rests on his testimony or demonstrations (1 Cor. ii. 4). Believers have an unction from the Holy One, and they know the truth, and that no lie (or false doctrine) is of the truth. This inward teaching produces a conviction which no sophistries can obscure, and no arguments can shake. It is founded on consciousness, and you might as well argue a man out of a belief of his existence, as out of confidence that what he is thus taught of God is true. Two things, however, are to be borne in mind. First, That this inward teaching or demonstration of the Spirit is confined to truths objectively revealed in the Scriptures. It is given, says the Apostle, in order that we may know things gratuitously given, *i. e.,* revealed to us by God in his word (1 Cor. ii. 10–16). It is not, therefore, a revelation of new truths, but an illumination of the mind, so that it apprehends the truth, excellence, and glory of things already revealed. And second, This experience is depicted in the Word of God. The Bible gives us not only the facts concerning God, and Christ, ourselves, and our relation to our Maker and Redeemer, but also records the legitimate effects of those truths on the minds of believers. So that we cannot appeal to our own feelings or inward experience, as a ground or guide, unless we can show that it agrees with the experience of holy men as recorded in the Scriptures.

Although the inward teaching of the Spirit, or religious experience, is no substitute for an external revelation, and is no part of the rule of faith, it is, nevertheless, an invaluable guide in determining what the rule of faith teaches. The distinguishing feature of Augustinianism as taught by Augustin himself, and by the purer theologians of the Latin Church throughout the Middle Ages, which was set forth by the Reformers, and especially by Calvin and the Geneva divines, is that the inward teaching of the Spirit is allowed its proper place in determining our theology. The question is not first and mainly, What is true to the understanding, but what is true to the renewed heart? The effort is not to make the assertions of the Bible harmonize with the speculative reason, but to subject our feeble reason to the mind of God as revealed in his Word, and by his Spirit in our inner life. It might be easy to lead men to the conclusion that they are responsible only for their voluntary acts, if the appeal is made solely to the understanding. But if the appeal be made to every man's, and especially to every Christian's inward experience, the opposite conclusion is reached. We are convinced of the sinfulness of states of mind as well as of voluntary acts, even when those states are not the effect of our own agency, and are not subject to the power of the will. We are conscious of being sold under sin; of being its slaves; of being possessed by it as a power or law, immanent, innate, and beyond our control. Such is the doctrine of the Bible, and such is the teaching of our religious consciousness when under the influence of the Spirit of God. The true method in theology requires that the facts of religious experience should be accepted, as facts, and when duly authenticated by Scripture, be allowed to interpret the doctrinal statements of the Word of God. So legitimate and powerful is this inward teaching of the Spirit, that it is no uncommon thing to find men having two theologies,—one of the intellect, and another of the heart. The one may find expression in creeds and systems of divinity, the other in their prayers and hymns. It would be safe for a man to resolve to admit into his theology nothing which is not sustained by the devotional writings of true Christians of every denomination. It would be easy to construct from such writings, received and sanctioned by Romanists, Lutherans, Reformed, and Remonstrants, a system of Pauline or Augustinian theology, such as would satisfy any intelligent and devout Calvinist in the world.

　　The true method of theology is, therefore, the inductive, which assumes that the

Bible contains all the facts or truths which form the contents of theology, just as the facts of nature are the contents of the natural sciences. It is also assumed that the relation of these Biblical facts to each other, the principles involved in them, the laws which determine them, are in the facts themselves, and are to be deduced from them, just as the laws of nature are deduced from the facts of nature. In neither case are the principles derived from the mind and imposed upon the facts, but equally in both departments, the principles or laws are deduced from the facts and recognized by the mind.

CHARLES PEIRCE

"The Fixation of Belief"
1877

With this essay of 1877, Charles Peirce (1839–1914) began a series of articles on which much of his fame as a philosopher came to be based. Here he only introduced the topic of this series—"the logic of science"—but in so doing managed to (a) articulate a largely *social* vision of the scientific enterprise, according to which the community rather than the individual knower is the primary agent of cognitive progress; (b) direct the method of science against not only beliefs about nature, but against the entire panorama of inherited beliefs, especially and explicitly *religious* beliefs; (c) assert that open, honest inquiry is decidedly superior *morally* to pious loyalty to an inherited faith; and (d) argue, in what would eventually be recognized as a "pragmatic" mode, that true belief is simply a *habit* that can remain stable, a "fixed opinion."

Peirce's life and work are discussed cogently by R. Jackson Wilson, "Charles Sanders Peirce: The Community of Inquiry," in Wilson's *In Quest of Community: Social Philosophy in the United States, 1860–1920* (New York, 1968), 32–59. An excellent biography is Joseph Brent, *Charles Sanders Peirce: A Life* (Bloomington, 1993). For a more technical, philosophically rigorous study, see Murray G. Murphey, *The Development of Peirce's Philosophy* (Cambridge, Mass., 1961). For a lucid account of Peirce's work in relation to his contemporaries in the Harvard milieu, see Bruce Kuklick, *The Rise of American Philosophy: Cambridge, Massachusetts, 1960–1930* (New Haven, 1977), esp. 104–26. Peirce is a central figure in a history of philosophy of mind in New England: James Hoopes, *Consciousness in New England: From Puritanism and Ideas to Psychoanalysis and Semiotic* (Baltimore, 1989). Detailed studies of Peirce—and of other American philosophers—appear regularly in *The Transactions of the Charles S. Peirce Society*. Authoritative texts of all of Peirce's major works are being published by the Indiana University Press, *The Writings of Charles S. Peirce: A Chronological Edition* (Bloomington, 1982–   ). A readable account of Peirce's thought and of his troubled life is that by Josiah Lee Auspitz, "The Greatest Living American Philosopher," *Commentary* (December 1983), 51–64. A critical overview of recent Peirce scholarship is David Marr, "Signs of C. S. Peirce," *American Literary History* (Winter 1995), 681–699.

Few persons care to study logic, because everybody conceives himself to be proficient enough in the art of reasoning already. But I observe that this satisfaction is limited to one's own ratiocination, and does not extend to that of other men.

We come to the full possession of our power of drawing inferences the last of all our faculties, for it is not so much a natural gift as a long and difficult art. The history of its practice would make a grand subject for a book. The medieval schoolman, following the Romans, made logic the earliest of a boy's studies after grammar, as being very easy. So it was as they understood it. Its fundamental principle, according to them, was, that all knowledge rests on either authority or reason; but that whatever is deduced by reason depends ultimately on a premise derived from authority. Accordingly, as soon as a boy was perfect in the syllogistic procedure, his intellectual kit of tools was held to be complete.

To Roger Bacon, that remarkable mind who in the middle of the thirteenth century was almost a scientific man, the schoolmen's conception of reasoning appeared only an obstacle to truth. He saw that experience alone teaches anything—a proposition which to us seems easy to understand, because a distinct conception of experience has been handed down to us from former generations; which to him also seemed perfectly clear, because its difficulties had not yet unfolded themselves. Of all kinds of experience, the best, he thought, was interior illumination, which teaches many things about Nature which the external senses could never discover such as the transubstantiation of bread.

Four centuries later, the more celebrated Bacon, in the first book of his "Novum Organum," gave his clear account of experience as something which must be open to verification and re-examination. But, superior as Lord Bacon's conception is to earlier notions, a modern reader who is not in awe of his grandiloquence is chiefly struck by the inadequacy of his view of scientific procedure. That we have only to make some crude experiments, to draw up briefs of the results in certain blank forms, to go through these by rule, checking off everything disproved and setting down the alternatives, and that thus in a few years physical science would be finished up—what an idea! "He wrote on science like a Lord Chancellor," indeed.

The early scientists, Copernicus, Tycho Brahe, Kepler, Galileo, and Gilbert, had methods more like those of their modern brethren. Kepler undertook to draw a curve through the places of Mars; and his greatest service to science was in impressing on men's minds that this was the thing to be done if they wished to improve astronomy; that they were not to content themselves with inquiring whether one system of epicycles was better than another but that they were to sit down by the figures and find out what the curve, in truth, was. He accomplished this by his incomparable energy and courage, blundering along in the most inconceivable way (to us), from one irrational hypothesis to another, until, after trying twenty-two of these, he fell, by the mere exhaustion of his invention, upon the orbit which a mind well furnished with the weapons of modern logic would have tried almost at the outset.

In the same way, every work of science great enough to be remembered for a few generations affords some exemplification of the defective state of the art of reasoning of the time when it was written; and each chief step in science has been a lesson in logic. It was so when Lavoisier and his contemporaries took up the study of Chemistry. The old chemist's maxim had been, "Lege, lege, lege, labora, ora, et relege." Lavoisier's method was not to read and pray, not to dream that some long and complicated chemical

Source: *Popular Science Monthly* 12 (November 1877): 1–15.

process would have a certain effect, to put it into practice with dull patience, after its inevitable failure to dream that with some modification it would have another result, and to end by publishing the last dream as a fact: his way was to carry his mind into his laboratory, and to make of his alembics and cucurbits instruments of thought, giving a new conception of reasoning as something which was to be done with one's eyes open, by manipulating real things instead of words and fancies.

The Darwinian controversy is, in large part, a question of logic. Mr. Darwin proposed to apply the statistical method to biology. The same thing has been done in a widely different branch of science, the theory of gases. Though unable to say what the movement of any particular molecule of gas would be on a certain hypothesis regarding the constitution of this class of bodies, Clausius and Maxwell were yet able, by the application of the doctrine of probabilities, to predict that in the long run such and such a proportion of the molecules would, under given circumstances, acquire such and such velocities; that there would take place, every second, such and such a number of collisions, etc.; and from these propositions they were able to deduce certain properties of gases, especially in regard to their heat-relations. In like manner, Darwin, while unable to say what the operation of variation and natural selection in every individual case will be, demonstrates that in the long run they will adapt animals to their circumstances. Whether or not existing animal forms are due to such action, or what position the theory ought to take, forms the subject of a discussion in which questions of fact and questions of logic are curiously interlaced.

The object of reasoning is to find out, from the consideration of what we already know, something else which we do not know. Consequently, reasoning is good if it be such as to give a true conclusion from true premises, and not otherwise. Thus, the question of validity is purely one of fact and not of thinking. A being the premises and B being the conclusion, the question is, whether these facts are really so related that if A is B is. If so, the inference is valid; if not, not. It is not in the least the question whether, when the premises are accepted by the mind, we feel an impulse to accept the conclusion also. It is true that we do generally reason correctly by nature. But that is an accident; the true conclusion would remain true if we had no impulse to accept it; and the false one would remain false, though we could not resist the tendency to believe in it.

We are, doubtless, in the main logical animals, but we are not perfectly so. Most of us, for example, are naturally more sanguine and hopeful than logic would justify. We seem to be so constituted that in the absence of any facts to go upon we are happy and self-satisfied; so that the effect of experience is continually to counteract our hopes and aspirations. Yet a lifetime of the application of this corrective does not usually eradicate our sanguine disposition. Where hope is unchecked by any experience, it is likely that our optimism is extravagant. Logicality in regard to practical matters is the most useful quality an animal can possess, and might, therefore, result from the action of natural selection; but outside of these it is probably of more advantage to the animal to have his mind filled with pleasing and encouraging visions, independently of their truth; and thus, upon unpractical subjects, natural selection might occasion a fallacious tendency of thought.

That which determines us, from given premises, to draw one inference rather than another, is some habit of mind, whether it be constitutional or acquired. The habit is good or otherwise, according as it produces true conclusions from true premises or not; and an inference is regarded as valid or not, without reference to the truth or falsity of its conclusion specially, but according as the habit which determines it is such as to produce true conclusions in general or not. The particular habit of mind which governs this or that inference may be formulated in a proposition whose truth depends on the validity of the inferences which the habit determines; and such a formula is called a *guiding principle* of inference. Suppose, for example, that we observe that a rotating disk of copper quickly comes to rest when placed between the poles of a magnet, and we infer that this will happen with every disk of copper. The guiding principle is, that what is true of one piece of copper is true of another. Such a guiding principle with regard to copper would be much safer than with regard to many other substances—brass, for example.

A book might be written to signalize all the most important of these guiding principles of reasoning. It would probably be, we must confess, of no service to a person whose thought is directed wholly to practical subjects, and whose activity moves along thoroughly beaten paths. The problems which present themselves to such a mind are matters of routine which he has learned once for all to handle in learning his business. But let a man venture into an unfamiliar field, or where his results are not continually checked by experience, and all history shows that the most masculine intellect will ofttimes lose his orientation and waste his efforts in directions which bring him no nearer to his goal, or even carry him entirely astray. He is like a ship on the open sea, with no one on board who understands the rules of navigation. And in such a case some general study of the guiding principles of reasoning would be sure to be found useful.

The subject could hardly be treated, however, without being first limited; since almost any fact may serve as a guiding principle. But it so happens that there exists a division among facts, such that in one class are all those which are absolutely essential as guiding principles, while in the other are all those which have any other interests as object of research. This division is between those which are necessarily taken for granted in asking whether a certain conclusion follows from certain premises, and those which are not implied in that question. A moment's thought will show that a variety of facts are already assumed when the logical question is first asked. It is implied, for instance, that there are such states of mind as doubt and belief—that a passage from one to the other is possible, the object of thought remaining the same, and that this transition is subject to some rules which all minds are alike bound by. As these are facts which we must already know before we can have any clear conception of reasoning at all, it cannot be supposed to be any longer of much interest to inquire into their truth or falsity. On the other hand, it is easy to believe that those rules of reasoning which are deduced from the very idea of the process are the ones which are the most essential; and, indeed, that so long as it conforms to these it will, at least, not lead to false conclusions from true premises. In point of fact, the importance of what may be deduced from the assumptions involved in the logical question turns out to be greater than might be supposed, and this for reasons which it is difficult to exhibit at the outset. The only one which I shall here mention is, that conceptions which are really products of logical reflections, without being readily seen to be so, mingle with our ordinary thoughts, and are frequently the causes of great confusion. This is the case, for example, with the conception of quality. A quality as such is never an object of observation. We can see that a thing is blue or green, but the quality of being blue and the quality of being green are not things which we see; they are products of logical reflections. The truth is, that common-sense, or thought as it first emerges above the level of the narrowly practical, is deeply imbued with that bad logical quality to which the epithet *metaphysical* is commonly applied; and nothing can clear it up but a severe course of logic.

We generally know when we wish to ask a question and when we wish to pronounce a judgment, for there is a dissimiliarity between the sensation of doubting and that of believing.

But this is not all which distinguishes doubt from belief. There is a practical difference. Our beliefs guide our desires and shape our actions. The Assassins, or followers of the Old Man of the Mountain, used to rush into death at his least command, because they believed that obedience to him would insure everlasting felicity. Had they doubted this, they would not have acted as they did. So it is with every belief, according to its degree. The feeling of believing is a more or less sure indication of there being established in our nature some habit which will determine our actions. Doubt never has such an effect.

Nor must we overlook a third point of difference. Doubt is an uneasy and dissatisfied state from which we struggle to free ourselves and pass into the state of belief; while the latter is a calm and satisfactory state which we do not wish to avoid, or to change to a belief in anything else. On the contrary, we cling tenaciously, not merely to believing, but to believing just what we do believe.

Thus, both doubt and belief have positive effects upon us, though very different ones. Belief does not make us act at once, but puts us into such a condition that we shall behave in a certain way, when the occasion arises. Doubt has not the least effect of this sort, but stimulates us to action until it is destroyed. This reminds us of the irritation of a nerve and the reflex action produced thereby; while for the analogue of belief, in the nervous system, we must look to what are called nervous associations— for example, to that habit of the nerves in consequence of which the smell of a peach will make the mouth water.

The irritation of doubt causes a struggle to attain a state of belief. I shall term this struggle *inquiry,* though it must be admitted that this is sometimes not a very apt designation.

The irritation of doubt is the only immediate motive for the struggle to attain belief. It is certainly best for us that our beliefs should be such as may truly guide our actions so as to satisfy our desires; and this reflection will make us reject any belief which does not seem to have been so formed as to insure this result. But it will only do so by creating a doubt in the place of that belief. With the doubt, therefore, the struggle begins, and with the cessation of doubt it ends. Hence, the sole object of inquiry is the settlement of opinion. We may fancy that this is not enough for us, and that we seek not merely an opinion, but a true opinion. But put this fancy to the test, and it proves groundless; for as soon as a firm belief is reached we are entirely satisfied, whether the belief be false or true. And it is clear that nothing out of the sphere of our knowledge can be our object, for nothing which does not affect the mind can be a motive for a mental effort. The most that can be maintained is, that we seek for a belief that we shall *think* to be true. But we think each one of our beliefs to be true, and, indeed, it is mere tautology to say so.

That the settlement of opinion is the sole end of inquiry is a very important proposition. It sweeps away, at once, various vague and erroneous conceptions of proof. A few of these may be noticed here.

1. Some philosophers have imagined that to start an inquiry it was only necessary to utter or question or set it down on paper, and have even recommended us to begin our studies with questioning everything! But the mere putting of a proposition into the interrogative form does not stimulate the mind to any struggle after belief. There must be a real and living doubt, and without all this discussion is idle.

2. It is a very common idea that a demonstration must rest on some ultimate and absolutely indubitable propositions. These, according to one school, are first principles of a general nature; according to another, are first sensations. But, in point of fact, an inquiry, to have that completely satisfactory result called demonstration, has only to start with propositions perfectly free from all actual doubt. If the premises are not in fact doubted at all, they cannot be more satisfactory that they are.

3. Some people seem to love to argue a point after all the world is fully convinced of it. But no further advance can be made. When doubt ceases, mental action on the subject comes to an end; and, if it did go on, it would be without a purpose.

If the settlement of opinion is the sole object of inquiry, and if belief is of the nature of a habit, why should we not attain the desired end, by taking any answer to a question, which we may fancy, and constantly reiterating it to ourselves, dwelling on all which may conduce to that belief, and learning to turn with contempt and hatred from anything which might disturb it? This simple and direct method is really pursued by many men. I remember once being entreated not to read a certain newspaper lest it might change my opinion upon free-trade. "Lest I might be entrapped by its fallacies and misstatements," was the form of expression. "You are not," my friend said, "a special student of political economy. You might, therefore, easily be deceived by fallacious arguments upon the subject. You might, then, if you read this paper, be led to believe in protection. But you admit that free-trade is the true doctrine; and you do not wish to believe what is not true." I have often known this system to be deliberately adopted. Still oftener, the instinctive dislike of an undecided state of mind, exaggerated into a vague dread of doubt, makes men cling spasmodically to the views they already take. The man feels that, if he only holds to his belief without wavering, it will be entirely satisfactory. Nor can it be denied that a steady and immovable faith yields great peace of mind. It may, indeed, give rise to inconveniences, as if a man should resolutely continue to believe that fire would not burn him, or that he would be eternally damned if he received his *ingesta* otherwise than through a stomach-pump. But then the man who adopts this method will not allow that its inconveniences are greater than its advantages. He will say, "I hold steadfastly to the truth and the truth is always wholesome." And in many cases it may very well be that the pleasure he derives from his calm faith overbalances any inconveniences resulting from its deceptive character. Thus, if it be true that death is annihilation, then the man who believes that he will certainly go straight to heaven when he dies, provided he have fulfilled certain simple observances in this life, has a cheap pleasure which will not be followed by the least disappointment. A similar consideration seems to have weight with many persons in religious topics, for we frequently hear it said, "Oh, I could not believe so-and-so, because I should be wretched if I did." When an ostrich buries its head in the sand as danger approaches, it very likely takes the happiest course. It hides the danger, and then calmly says there is no danger; and, it feels perfectly sure there is none, why should it raise its head to see? A man may go through life, systematically keeping out of view all that might cause a change in his opinions, and if he only succeeds—basing his method, as he does, on two fundmental psychological laws—I do not see what can be said against his doing so. It would be an egotistical impertinence to object that his procedure is irrational, for that only amounts to saying that his method of settling belief is not ours. He does not propose to himself to be rational, and indeed, will often talk with scorn of man's weak and illusive reason. So let him think as he pleases.

But this method of fixing belief, which may be called the method of tenacity, will be unable to hold its ground in practice. The social impulse is against it. The man who adopts it will find that other men think differently from him, and it will be apt to occur to him in some saner moment that their opinions are quite as good as his own, and this will shake his confidence in his belief. This conception, that another man's thought or sentiment may be equivalent to one's own, is a distinctly new step, and a highly important one. It arises from an impulse too strong in man to be suppressed, without danger of destroying the human species. Unless we make ourselves hermits, we shall necessarily influence each other's opinions; so that the problem becomes how to fix belief, not in the individual merely, but in the community.

Let the will of the state act, then, instead of that of the individual. Let an institution be created which shall have for its object to keep correct doctrines before the attention of the people, to reiterate them perpetually, and to teach them to the young; having at the same time power to prevent contrary doctrines from being taught, advocated, or expressed. Let all possible causes of a change of mind be removed from men's apprehensions. Let them be kept ignorant, lest they should learn of some reason to think otherwise than they do. Let their passions be enlisted, so that they may regard private and unusual opinions with hatred and horror. Then, let all men who reject the established belief be terrified into silence. Let the people turn out and tar-and-feather such men, or let inquisitions be made into the manner of thinking of suspected persons, and, when they are found guilty of forbidden beliefs, let them be subjected to some signal punishment. When complete agreement could not otherwise be reached, a general massacre of all who have not thought in a certain way has proved a very effective means of settling opinion in a country. If the power to do this be wanting, let a list of opinions be drawn up, to which no man of the least independence of thought can assent, and let the faithful be required to accept all these propositions, in order to segregate them as radically as possible from the influence of the rest of the world.

This method has, from the earliest times, been one of the chief means of upholding correct theological and political doctrines, and of preserving their universal or catholic character. In Rome, especially, it has been practiced from the days of Numa Pompilius to those of Pius Nonus. This is the most perfect example in history; but wherever there is a priesthood—and no religion has been without one—this method has been more or less made use of. Wherever there is artistocracy, or a guild, or any association of a class of men whose interests depend or are supposed to depend on certain propositions, there will be inevitably found some traces of this natural product of social feeling. Cruelties always accompany this system; and when it is consistently carried out, they become atrocities of the most horrible kind in the eyes of any rational man. Nor should this occasion surprise, for the officer of a society does not feel justified in surrendering the interests of that society for the sake of mercy, as he might his own private interests. It is natural, therefore, that sympathy and fellowship should thus produce a most ruthless power.

In judging this method of fixing belief, which may be called the method of authority, we must, in the first place, allow its immeasurable mental and moral superiority to the method of tenacity. Its success is proportionally greater; and in fact it has over and over again worked the most majestic results. The mere structures of stone which it has caused to be put together—in Siam, for example, in Egypt, and in Europe—have many of them a sublimity hardly more than rivaled by the greatest works of Nature. And, except the geological epochs, there are no periods of time so vast as those which are measured by some of these organized faiths. If we scrutinize the matter closely, we shall find that there has not been one of their creeds which has remained always the same; yet the change is so slow as to be imperceptible during one person's life, so that individual belief remains sensibly fixed. For the mass of mankind, then, there is perhaps no better method than this. If it is their highest impulse to be intellectual slaves, then slaves they ought to remain.

But no institution can undertake to regulate opinions upon every subject. Only the most important ones can be attended to, and on the rest men's minds must be left to the action of natural causes. This imperfection will be no source of weakness so long as men are in such a state of culture that one opinion does not influence another—that is, so long as they cannot put two and two together. But in the most priest-ridden states some individuals will be found who are raised above that condition. These men possess a wider sort of social feeling; they see that men in other countries and in other ages have held to very different doctrines from those which they themselves have been brought up to believe; and they cannot help seeing that it is the mere accident of their having been taught as they have, and of their having been surrounded with the manners and associations they have, that has caused them to believe as they do and not far differently. And their candor cannot resist the reflection that there is no reason to rate their own views at a higher value than those of other nations and other centuries; and this gives rise to doubts in their minds.

They will further perceive that such doubts as these must exist in their minds with reference to every belief which seems to be determined by the caprice either of themselves or of those who originated the popular opinions. The willful adherence to a belief, and the arbitrary forcing of it upon others, must, therefore, both be given up and a new method of settling opinons must be adopted, which shall not only produce an impulse to believe, but shall also decide what proposition it is which is to be believed. Let the action of natural preferences be unimpeded, then, and under their influence let men conversing together and regarding matters in different lights, gradually develop beliefs in harmony with natural causes. This method resembles that by which conceptions of art have been brought to maturity. The most perfect example of it is to be found in the history of metaphysical philosophy. Systems of this sort have not usually rested upon observed facts, at least not in any great degree. They have been chiefly adopted because their fundamental propositions seemed "agreeable to reason." This is an apt expression; it does not mean that which agrees with experience, but that which we find ourselves inclined to believe. Plato, for example, finds it agreeable to reason that the distances of the celestial spheres from one another should be proportional to the different lengths of strings which produce harmonious chords. Many philosophers have been led to their main conclusions by considerations like this; but this is the lowest and least developed form which the method takes, for it is clear that another man might find Kepler's [earlier] theory, that the celestial spheres are proportional to the inscribed and circumscribed spheres of the different regular solids, more agreeable to *his* reason. But the shock of opinions will soon lead men to rest on preferences of a far more universal nature. Take, for example, the doctrine that man only acts selfishly—that is, from the consideration that acting in one way will afford him more pleasure than acting in another. This rests on no fact in the world, but it has had a wide acceptance as being the only reasonable theory.

This method is far more intellectual and respectable from the point of view of reason than either of the others which we have noticed. But its failure has been the most manifest. It makes of inquiry something similar to the development of taste; but taste, unfortunately, is always more or less a matter of fashion, and accordingly, metaphysicians have never come to any fixed agreement, but the pendulum has swung backward and forward between a more material and a more spiritual philosophy, from the earliest times to the latest. And so from this, which has been called the *a priori* method, we are driven, in Lord Bacon's phrase, to a true induction. We have examined into this *a priori* method as something which promised to deliver our opinions from their accidental and capricious element. But development, while it is a process which eliminates the effect of some casual circumstances, only magnifies that of others. This method, therefore, does not differ in a very essential way from that of authority. The government may not have lifted its finger to influence my convictions; I may have been left outwardly quite free to choose, we will say, between monogamy and polygamy, and appealing to my conscience only, I may have concluded that the latter practice is in itself licentious. But when I come to see that the chief obstacle to the spread of Christianity among a people of as high culture as the Hindoos has been a conviction of the immorality of our way of treating women, I cannot help seeing that, though governments do not interfere, sentiments in their development will be very greatly determined by accidental causes. Now, there are some people, among whom I must suppose that my reader is to be found, who, when they see that any belief of theirs is determined by any circumstance extraneous to the facts, will from that moment not merely admit in words that that belief is doubtful, but will experience a real doubt of it, so that it ceases to be a belief.

To satisfy our doubts, therefore, it is necessary that a method should be found by which our beliefs may be caused by nothing human, but by some external permanency—by something upon which our thinking has no effect. Some mystics imagine that they have such a method in a private inspiration from on high. But that is only a form of the method of tenacity, in which the conception of truth as something public is not yet developed. Our external permanency would not be external, in our sense, if it was restricted in its influence to one individual. It must be something which affects, or might affect, every man. And, though these affections are necessarily as various as are individual conditions, yet the method must be such that the ultimate conclusion of every man shall be the same. Such is the method of science. Its fundamental hypothesis, restated in more familiar language, is this: There are real things, whose characters are entirely independent of our opinions about them; whose realities affect our senses according to regular laws, and, though our sensations are as different as our relations to the objects, yet, by taking advantage of the laws of perception, we can ascertain by reasoning how things really are, and any man, if he have sufficient experience and reason enough about it, will be led to the one true conclusion. The new conception here involved is that of reality. It may be asked how I know that there are any realities. If this hypothesis is the sole support of my method of inquiry, my method of inquiry must not be used to support my hypothesis. The reply is this: 1. If investigation cannot be regarded as proving that there are real things, it at least does not lead to a contrary conclusion; but the method and the conception on which it is based remain ever in harmony. No doubts of the method, therefore, necessarily arise from its practice, as is the case with all the others. 2. The feeling which gives rise to any method of fixing belief is a dissatisfaction at two repungant propositions. But here already is a vague concession that there is some *one* thing to which a proposition should conform. Nobody, therefore, can really doubt that there are realities, or, if he did, doubt would not be a source of dissatisfaction. The hypothesis, therefore, is one which every mind admits. So that the social impulse does not cause me to doubt it. 3. Everybody uses the scientific method about a great many things, and only ceases to use it when he does not know how to apply it. 4. Experience of the method has not led me to doubt it, but, on the contrary, scientific investigation has had the most wonderful triumphs in the way of settling opinion. These afford the explanation of my not doubting the method or the hypothesis which it supposes; and not having any doubt, nor believing that anybody else whom I could influence has, it would be the merest babble for me to say more about it. If there be anybody with a living doubt upon the subject, let him consider it.

To describe the method of scientific investigation is the object of this series of papers. At present I have only room to notice some points of contrast between it and other methods of fixing belief.

This is the only one of the four methods which presents any distinction of a right and a wrong way. If I adopt the method of tenacity and shut myself out from all influences, whatever I think necessary to doing this is necessary according to that method. So with the method of authority: the state may try to put down heresy by means which, from a scientific point of view, seems very ill-calculated to accomplish its purposes; but the only test *on that method* is what the state thinks, so that it cannot pursue the method wrongly. So with the *a priori* method. The very essence of it is to think as one is inclined to think. All metaphysicians will be sure to do that, however they may be inclined to judge each other to be perversely wrong. The Hegelian system recognizes every natural tendency of thought as logical, although it is certain to be abolished by counter-tendencies. Hegel thinks there is a regular system in the succession of these tendencies, in consequence of which, after drifting one way and the other for a long time, opinion will at last go right. And it is true that metaphysicians get the right ideas at last; Hegel's system of Nature represents tolerably the science of that day; and one may be sure that whatever scientific investigation has put out of doubt will presently receive *a priori* demonstration on the part of the metaphysicians. But with the scientific method the case is different. I may start with known and observed facts to proceed to the unknown; and yet the rules which I follow in doing so may not be such as investigation would approve. The test of whether I am truly following the method is not an immediate appeal to my feelings and purposes, but, on the contrary, itself involves the application of the method. Hence it is that bad reasoning as well as good reasoning is possible; and this fact is the foundation of the practical side of logic.

It is not to be supposed that the first three methods of settling opinion present no advantage whatever over the scientific method. On the contrary, each has some peculiar convenience of its own. The *a priori* method is distinguished for its comfortable conclusions. It is the nature of the process to adopt whatever belief we are inclined to, and there are certain flatteries to one's vanities which we all believe by nature, until we are awakened from our pleasing dream by rough facts. The method of authority will always govern the mass of mankind; and those who wield the various forms of organized force in the state will never be convinced that dangerous reasoning ought not to be suppressed in some way. If liberty of speech is to be untrammeled from the grosser forms of constraint, then uniformity of opinion will be secured by a moral terrorism to which the respectability of society will give its thorough approval. Following the method of authority is the path of peace. Certain non-conformities are permitted; certain others (considered unsafe) are forbidden. These are different in different countries and in different ages; but, wherever you are let it be known that you seriously hold a tabooed belief, and you may be perfectly sure of being treated with a cruelty no less brutal but more refined than hunting you like a wolf. Thus, the greatest intellectual benefactors of mankind have never dared, and dare not now, to utter the whole of their thought; and thus a shade of *prima facie* doubt is cast upon every proposition which is considered essential to the security of society. Singularly enough, the persecution does not all come from without; but a man torments himself and is oftentimes most distressed at finding himself believing propositions which he has been brought up to regard with aversion. The peaceful and sympathetic man will, therefore, find it hard to resist the temptation to submit his opinions to authority. But most of all I admire the method of tenacity for its strength, simplicity, and directness. Men who pursue it are distinguished for their decision of character, which becomes very easy with such a mental rule. They do not waste time in trying to make up their minds to what they want, but, fastening like lightning upon whatever alternative comes first, they hold to it to the end, whatever happens, without an instant's irresolution. This is one of the splendid qualities which generally accompany brilliant, unlasting success. It is impossible not to envy the man who can dismiss reason, although we know how it must turn out at last.

Such are the advantages which the other methods of settling opinions have over scientific investigation. A man should consider well of them; and then he should consider that, after all, he wishes his opinions to coincide with the fact, and that there is no reason why the results of these three methods should do so. To bring about this effect is the prerogative of the method of science. Upon such considerations he has to make his choice—a choice which is far more than the adoption of any intellectual opinion, which is one of the ruling decisions of his life, to which when once made he is bound to adhere. The force of habit will sometimes cause a man to hold on to old beliefs, after he is in a condition to see that they have no sound basis. But reflection upon the state of the case will overcome these habits, and he ought to allow reflection full weight. People sometimes shrink from doing this, having an idea that beliefs are wholesome which they cannot help feeling rest on nothing. But let such persons suppose an analogous though different case from their own. Let them ask themselves what they would say to a reformed Mussulman who should hesitate to give up his old notions in regard to the relations of the sexes; or to a reformed Catholic who should still shrink from the Bible. Would they not say that these persons ought to consider the matter fully, and clearly understand the new doctrine, and then ought to embrace it in its entirety? But, above all, let it be considered that what is more wholesome than any particular belief, is integrity of belief; and that to avoid looking into the support of any belief from a fear that it may turn out rotten is quite as immoral as it is disadvantageous. The person who confesses that there is such a thing as truth, which is distinguished from falsehood simply by this, that if acted on it will carry us to the point we aim at and not astray, and then though convinced of this, dares not know the truth and seeks to avoid it, is in a sorry state of mind, indeed.

Yes, the other methods do have their merits: a clear logical conscience does cost something—just as any virtue, just as all that we cherish, costs us dear. But, we should not desire it to be otherwise. The genius of a man's logical method should be loved and reverenced as his bride, whom he has chosen from all the world. He need not condemn the others; on the contrary, he may honor them deeply, and in doing so he only honors her the more. But she is the one that he has chosen, and he knows that he was right in making that choice. And having made it, he will work and fight for her, and will not complain that there are blows to take, hoping that there may be as many and as hard to give, and will strive to be the worthy knight and champion of her from the blaze of whose splendors he draws his inspiration and his courage.

WILLIAM DEAN HOWELLS

"Pernicious Fiction"
1887

Perhaps no single individual was more central to the literary culture of the United States of the late nineteenth and early twentieth centuries than William Dean Howells (1837–1920). Accomplished and supremely influential as novelist, critic, and editor, Howells was at once an old-fashioned moralist—a figure in what came to be patronized as "the genteel tradition"—and a "realist." The piece of 1887 reprinted here expresses both features of Howells's sensibility. Howells displays acute concern for the moral effects of literature on the reader, yet at the same time he insists, in the realist's mode, on "truth" as the ultimate standard for "any work of the imagination." Howells was not prepared to consider the possibility that truth might sometimes conflict with morality or with beauty, but his ideals of morality and beauty were liberal enough to enable him in good conscience to sponsor Mark Twain, Hamlin Garland, Frank Norris, and other writers whose challenge to gentility was deeper than Howells's own.

This responsiveness on Howells's part is the focal point of a chapter ("Literary Hospitality") in Larzer Ziff, *The American 1890s: Life and Times of a Lost Generation* (New York, 1966), 24–49. A solid biography is Kenneth S. Lynn, *William Dean Howells: An American Life* (New York, 1971). For a splendid portrait of the literary culture of which Howells was the center, see Henry F. May, *The End of American Innocence: A Study of the First Years of Our Time, 1912–1917* (New York, 1959); republished with a new afterward by May and with a forward by David A. Hollinger, New York, 1993), 3–117. For examples of the finest writing to come out of the critics to Howells's cultural "right," the men May calls "custodians of culture," see William Crary Brownell's *French Traits* (New York, 1888) and *British Prose Masters* (1909), and Charles Eliot Norton's *Historical Studies of Church-Building in the Middle Ages: Venice, Siena, Florence* (1880). For Norton's career, see James Turner, *Charles Eliot Norton: A Biography* (New York, 1996). Howells's relationship with Mark Twain is discussed in Henry Nash Smith, *Mark Twain: The Development of a Writer* (Cambridge, 1962), which remains the most penetrating and sensitive study of the late-Victorian tension between the "gentility" and "reality" felt by both Twain and Howells.

It must have been a passage from Vernon Lee's *Baldwin,* claiming for the novel an indefinitely vast and subtle influence on modern character, which provoked the following suggestive letter from one of our readers:

—, — Co., Md., Sept. 18, 1886.

"Dear Sir,—With regard to article IV, in the Editor's Study in the September *Harper,* allow me to say that I have very grave doubts as to the whole list of magnificent things that you seem to think novels have done for the race, and can witness in myself many evil things which they have done for me. Whatever in my mental make-up is wild and visionary, whatever is untrue, whatever is injurious, I can trace to the perusal of some work of fiction. Worse than that, they beget such high-strung and supersensitive ideas of life that plain industry and plodding perseverance are despised, and matter-of-fact poverty, or everyday, commonplace distress, meets with no sympathy, if indeed noticed at all, by one who has wept over the impossibly accumulated sufferings of some gaudy hero or heroine.

"Hoping you will pardon the liberty I have taken in addressing you, I remain,
"Most respectfully yours,

We are not sure that we have the controversy with the writer which he seems to suppose, and we should perhaps freely grant the mischievous effects which he says novel-reading has wrought upon him, if we were not afraid that he had possibly reviewed his own experience with something of the inaccuracy we find in his report of our opinions. By his confession he is himself proof that Vernon Lee is right in saying, "The modern human being has been largely fashioned by those who have written about him, and most of all by the novelist," and there is nothing in what he urges to conflict with her claim that "the chief use of the novel" is "to make the shrewd and tolerant a little less shrewd and tolerant, and to make the generous and austere a little more skeptical and easy-going." If he will look more closely at these postulates, we think he will see that in the one she deals with the effect of the novel in the past, and in the other with its duty in the future. We still think that there "is sense if not final wisdom" in what she says, and we are quite willing to acknowledge something of each in our correspondent.

But novels are now so fully accepted by every one pretending to cultivated taste— and they really form the whole intellectual life of such immense numbers of people, without question of their influence, good or bad, upon the mind—that it is refreshing to have them frankly denounced, and to be invited to revise one's ideas and feelings in regard to them. A little honesty, or a great deal of honesty, in this quest will do the novel, as we hope yet to have it, and as we have already begun to have it, no harm; and for our own part we will confess that we believe fiction in the past to have been largely injurious, as we believe the stage play to be still almost wholly injurious, through its falsehood, its folly, its wantonness, and its aimlessness. It may be safely assumed that most of the novel-reading which people fancy is an intellectual pastime is the emptiest dissipation, hardly more related to thought or the wholesome exercise of the mental faculties than opium-eating; in either case the brain is drugged, and left weaker and crazier for the debauch. If this may be called the negative result of the fiction habit, the

Source: Harper's Magazine 74 (April 1887): 824–26.

positive injury that most novels work is by no means so easily to be measured in the case of young men whose character they help so much to form or deform, and the women of all ages whom they keep so much in ignorance of the world they misrepresent. Grown men have little harm from them, but in the other cases, which are the vast majority, they hurt because they are not true—not because they are malevolent, but because they are idle lies about human nature and the social fabric, which it behooves us to know and to understand, that we may deal justly with ourselves and with one another. One need not go so far as our correspondent, and trace to the fiction habit "whatever is wild and visionary, whatever is untrue, whatever is injurious," in one's life; bad as the fiction habit is, it is probbly not responsible for the whole sum of evil in its victims, and we believe that if the reader will use care in choosing from this fungus-growth with which the fields of literature teem every day, he may nourish himself as with the true mushroom, at no risk from the poisonous species.

The tests are very plain and simple, and they are perfectly infallible. If a novel flatters the passions, and exalts them above the principles, it is poisonous; it may not kill, but it will certainly injure; and this test will alone exclude an entire class of fiction, of which eminent examples will occur at all. Then the whole spawn of so-called unmoral romances, which imagine a world where the sins of sense are unvisited by the penalties following, swift or slow, but inexorably sure, in the real world, are deadly poison: these do kill. The novels that merely tickle our prejudices and lull our judgment, or that coddle our sensibilities, or pamper our gross appetite for the marvellous, are not so fatal, but they are innutritious, and clog the soul with un-wholesome vapors of all kinds. No doubt they too help to weaken the mental fibre, and make their readers indifferent to "plodding perseverance and plain industry," and to "matter-of-fact poverty and commonplace distress."

Without taking them too seriously, it still must be owned that the "gaudy hero and heroine" are to blame for a great deal of harm in the world. That heroine long taught by example, if not precept, that Love, or the passion or fancy she mistook for it, was the chief interest of a life which is really concerned with a great many other things; that it was lasting in the way she knew it; that it was worthy of every sacrifice, and was altogether a finer thing than prudence, obedience, reason; that love alone was glorious and beautiful, and these were mean and ugly in comparison with it. More lately she has begun to idolize and illustrate Duty, and she is hardly less mischievous in this new rôle, opposing duty, as she did love, to prudence, obedience, and reason. The stock hero, whom, if we met him, we could not fail to see was a most deplorable person, has undoubtedly imposed himself upon the victims of the fiction habit as admirable. With him, too, love was and is the great affair, whether in its old romantic phase of chivalrous achievement or manifold suffering for love's sake, or its more recent development of the "virile," the bullying, and the brutal, or its still more recent agonies of self-sacrifice, as idle and useless as the moral experiences of the insane asylums. With his vain posturings and his ridiculous splendor he is really a painted barbarian, the prey of his passions, and his delusions, full of obsolete ideals, and the motives and ethics of a savage, which the guilty author of his being does his best—or his worst—in spite of his own light and knowledge, to foist upon the reader as something generous and noble. We are not merely bringing this charge against that sort of fiction which is beneath literature and outside of it, "the shoreless lakes of ditch-water," whose miasms fill the air below the empyrean where the great ones sit; but we are accusing the work of some of the most famous, who have, in this instance or in that, sinned against the truth, which can alone exalt and purify men. We do not say that they have constantly done so, or even commonly done so; but that they have done so at all marks them as of the past, to be read with the due historical allowance for their epoch and their conditions. For we believe that, while inferior writers will and must continue to imitate them in their foibles and their errors, no one hereafter will be able to achieve greatness who is false to humanity, either in its facts or its duties. The light of civilization has already broken even upon the novel, and no conscientious man can now set about painting an image of life without perpetual question of the verity of his work, and without feeling bound to distinguish so clearly that no reader of his may be misled, between what is right and what is wrong, what is noble and what is base, what is health and what is perdition, in the actions and the characters he portrays.

The fiction that aims merely to entertain—the fiction that is to serious fiction as the opéra bouffe, the ballet, and the pantomime are to the true drama—need not feel the burden of this obligation so deeply; but even such fiction will not be gay or trivial to any reader's hurt, and criticism will hold it to account if it passes from painting to teaching folly.

More and more not only the criticism which prints its opinions, but the infinitely vaster and powerfuler criticism which thinks and feels them merely, will make this demand. For our own part we confess that we do not care to judge any work of the imagination without first of all applying this test to it. We must ask ourselves before we ask anything else, Is it true?—true to the motives, the impulses, the principles that shape the life of actual men and women? This truth, which necessarily includes the highest morality and the highest artistry—this truth given, the book *cannot* be wicked and cannot be weak; and without it all graces of style and feats of invention and cunning of construction are so many superfluities of naughtiness. It is well for the truth to have all these, and shine in them, but for falsehood they are merely meretricious, the bedizenment of the wanton; they atone for nothing, they count for nothing. But in fact they come naturally of truth, and grace it without solicitation; they are added unto it. In the whole range of fiction we know of no *true* picture of life—that is, of human nature—which is not also a masterpiece of literature, full of divine and natural beauty. It may have no touch or tint of this special civilization or of that; it had *better* have this local color well ascertained; but the truth is deeper and finer than aspects, and if the book is true to what men and women know of one another's souls it will be true enough, and it will be great and beautiful. It is the conception of literature as something apart from life, superfinely aloof, which makes it really unimportant to the great mass of mankind, without a message or a meaning for them; and it is the notion that a novel may be false in its portrayal of causes and effects that makes literary art contemptible even to those whom it amuses, that forbids them to regard the novelist as a serious or right-minded person. If they do not in some moment of indignation cry out against all novels, as our correspondent does, they remain besotted in the fume of the delusions purveyed to them, with no higher feeling for the author than such maudlin affection as the *habitué* of an opium-joint perhaps knows for the attendant who fills his pipe with the drug.

WILLIAM GRAHAM SUMNER

"Sociology"
1881

When William Graham Sumner (1840–1910) hailed sociology as a science of nature ready to stand next to physics and biology, he spoke for a host of nineteenth-century intellectuals eager to bring human affairs within the scope of science. But Sumner placed a politically conservative construction on the new science of society; this construction contrasted sharply with the outlook of some other enthusiasts for this new "science," including, for example, Lester Frank Ward, author of the essay that follows Sumner's selection. In this essay of 1881, Sumner interprets as scientific facts the doctrines of Thomas Malthus, David Ricardo, and other economists of the "classical," laissez-faire persuasion. Sumner attacks as scientifically naive the reformers of his own day who proposed to regulate in the public interest the economic activities of individuals. Arguing that "hard work and self-denial" are "the only two things" that really promote human progress, Sumner holds that one's chief mission in life ought to be "to accumulate capital." Sumner acknowledged that this mission involved conflict, while many of his fellow conservatives believed social progress a more harmonious process.

Although Sumner has often been called a social Darwinist, this term exaggerates Sumner's affinities with Darwin and minimizes his ties to the British discipline of political economy that was well developed before Darwin. For a detailed treatment, see Donald C. Bellomy, "'Social Darwinism' Revisited," *Perspectives in American History*, 1 n.s. (1984), 1–129. Many scholars find the concept of "social Darwinism" misleading. For a helpful discussion of the difficulties with the term and for a judicious review of recent scholarship, see the preface to the second edition of Robert C. Bannister, *Social Darwinism: Science and Myth in Anglo-American Social Thought* (Philadelphia, 1989), xi–xxxi. This book also offers (97–113) a valuable account of Sumner's intellectual development. For an exhaustive and perspicacious critique of the historiography of Darwinism, including the question of social Darwinism, see Antonello La Vergata, "Images of Darwin: A Historiographic Overview," in David Kohn, ed., *The Darwinian Heritage* (Princeton, 1985), 901–72.

... Let us ... endeavor to define the field of sociology. Life in society is the life of a human society on this earth. Its elementary conditions are set by the nature of human beings and the nature of the earth. We have already become familiar, in biology, with the transcendent importance of the fact that life on earth must be maintained by a struggle against nature, and also by a competition with other forms of life. In the latter fact biology and sociology touch. Sociology is a science which deals with one range of phenomena produced by the struggle for existence, while biology deals with another. The forces are the same, acting on different fields and under different conditions. The sciences are truly cognate. Nature contains certain materials which are capable of satisfying human needs, but those materials must, with rare and mean exceptions, be won by labor, and must be fitted to human use by more labor. As soon as any number of human beings are struggling each to win from nature the material goods necessary to support life, and are carrying on this struggle side by side, certain social forces come into operation. The prime condition of this society will lie in the ratio of its numbers to the supply of materials within its reach. For the supply at any moment attainable is an exact quantity, and the number of persons who can be supplied is arithmetically limited. If the actual number present is very much less than the number who might be supported, the condition of all must be ample and easy. Freedom and facility mark all social relations under such a state of things. If the number is larger than that which can be supplied, the condition of all must be one of want and distress, or else a few must be well provided, the other being proportionately still worse off. Constraint, anxiety, possibly tyranny and repression, mark social relations. It is when the social pressure due to an unfavorable ratio of population to land becomes intense that the social forces develop increased activity. Division of labor, exchange, higher social organization, emigration, advance in the arts, spring from the necessity of contending against the harsher conditions of existence which are continually reproduced as the population surpasses the means of existence on any given status.

The society with which we have to deal does not consist of any number of men. An army is not a society. A man with his wife and his children constitutes a society, for its essential parts are all present, and the number more or less is immaterial. A certain division of labor between the sexes is imposed by nature. The family as a whole maintains itself better under an organization with division of labor than it could if the functions were shared so far as possible. From this germ the development of society goes on by the regular steps of advancement to higher organization, accompanied and sustained by improvements in the arts. The increase of population goes on according to biological laws which are capable of multiplying the species beyond any assignable limits, so that the number to be provided for steadily advances and the status of ease and abundance gives way to a status of want and constraint. Emigration is the first and simplest remedy. By winning more land the ratio of population to land is once more rendered favorable. It is to be noticed, however, that emigration is painful to all men. To the uncivilized man, to emigrate means to abandon a mass of experiences and traditions which have been won by suffering, and to go out to confront new hardships and perils. To the civilized man migration means cutting off old ties of kin and country. The earth has been peopled by man at the cost of this suffering.

On the side of the land also stands the law of the diminishing return as a limitation.

Source: William Graham Sumner, *Collected Essays in Political and Social Science* (New York: Holt, 1885). Footnotes omitted.

More labor gets more from the land, but not proportionately more, hence, if more men are to be supported, there is need not of a proportionate increase of labor, but of a disproportionate increase of labor. The law of population, therefore, combined with the law of the diminishing returns, constitutes the great underlying condition of society. Emigration, improvements in the arts, in morals, in education, in political organization, are only stages in the struggle of man to meet these conditions, to break their force for a time, and to win room under them for ease and enlargement. Ease and enlargement mean either power to support more men on a given stage of comfort or power to advance the comfort of a given number of men. Progress is a word which has no meaning save in view of the laws of population and the diminishing return, and it is quite natural that anyone who fails to understand those laws should fall into doubt which way progress points, whether towards wealth or poverty. The laws of population and the diminishing return, in their combination, are the iron spur which has driven the race on to all which it has ever achieved, and the fact that population ever advances, yet advances against a barrier which resists more stubbornly at every step of advance, unless it is removed to a new distance by some conquest of man over nature, is the guarantee that the task of civilization will never be ended, but that the need for more energy, more intelligence, and more virtue will never cease while the race lasts. If it were possible for an increasing population to be sustained by proportionate increments of labor, we should all still be living in the original home of the race on the spontaneous products of the earth. Let him, therefore, who desires to study social phenomena first learn the transcendent importance for the whole social organization, industrial, political, and civil, of the ratio of population to land.

We have noticed that the relations involved in the struggle for existence are twofold. There is first the struggle of individuals to win the means of subsistence from nature, and secondly there is the competition of man with man in the effort to win a limited supply. The radical error of the socialists and sentimentalists is that they never distinguish these two relations from each other. They bring forward complaints which are really to be made, if at all, against the author of the universe for the hardships which man has to endure in his struggle with nature. The complaints are addressed, however, to society; that is, to other men under the same hardships. The only social element, however, is the competition of life, and when society is blamed for the ills which belong to the human lot, it is only burdening those who have successfully contended with those ills with the further task of conquering the same ills over again for somebody else. Hence liberty perishes in all socialistic schemes, and the tendency of such schemes is to the deterioration of society by burdening the good members and relieving the bad ones. The law of the survival of the fittest was not made by man and cannot be abrogated by man. We can only, by interfering with it, produce the survival of the unfittest. If a man comes forward with any grievance against the order of society so far as this is shaped by human agency, he must have patient hearing and full redress; but if he addresses a demand to society for relief from the hardships of life, he asks simply that somebody else should get his living for him. In that case he ought to be left to find out his error from hard experience.

The sentimental philosophy starts from the first principle that nothing is true which is disagreeable, and that we must not believe anything which is "shocking," no matter what the evidence may be. There are various stages of this philosophy. It touches on one side the intuitional philosophy which proves that certain things must exist by proving that man needs them, and it touches on the other side the vulgar socialism which affirms that the individual has a right to whatever he needs, and that this right is good against his fellow men. To this philosophy in all its grades the laws of population and the diminishing return have always been very distasteful. The laws which entail upon mankind an inheritance of labor cannot be acceptable to any philosophy which maintains that man comes into the world endowed with natural rights and an inheritor of freedom. It is a death-blow to any intuitional philosophy to find out, as an historical fact, what diverse thoughts, beliefs, and actions man has manifested, and it requires but little actual knowledge of human history to show that the human race has never had any ease which it did not earn, or any freedom which it did not conquer. Sociology, therefore, by the investigations which it pursues, dispels illusions about what society is or may be, and gives instead knowledge of facts which are the basis of intelligent effort by man to make the best of his circumstances on earth. Sociology, therefore, which can never accomplish anything more than to enable us to make the best of our situation, will never be able to reconcile itself with those philosophies which are trying to find out how we may arrange things so as so satisfy any ideal of society.

The competition of life has taken the form, historically, of a struggle for the possession of the soil. In the simpler states of society the possession of the soil is tribal, and the struggles take place between groups, producing the wars and feuds which constitute almost the whole of early history. On the agricultural stage the tribal or communal possession of land exists as a survival, but it gives way to private property in land whenever the community advances and the institutions are free to mold themselves. The agricultural stage breaks up tribal relations and encourages individualization. This is one of the reasons why it is such an immeasurable advance over the lower forms of civilization. It sets free individual energy, and while the social bond gains in scope and variety, it also gains in elasticity, for the solidarity of the group is broken up and the individual may work out his own ends by his own means, subject only to the social ties which lie in the natural conditions of human life. It is only on the agricultural stage that liberty as civilized men understand it exists at all. The poets and sentimentalists, untaught to recognize the grand and world-wide cooperation which is secured by the free play of individual energy under the great laws of the social order, bewail the decay of early communal relations and exalt the liberty of the primitive stages of civilization. These notions all perish at the first touch of actual investigation. The whole retrospect of human history runs downwards towards beast-like misery and slavery to the destructive forces of nature. The whole history has been one series of toilsome, painful, and bloody struggles, first to find out where we were and what were the conditions of greater ease, and then to devise means to get relief. Most of the way the motives of advance have been experience of suffering and instinct. It is only in the most recent years that science has undertaken to teach without and in advance of suffering, and as yet science has to fight so hard against tradition that its authority is only slowly winning recognition. The institutions whose growth constitutes the advance of civilization have their guarantee in the very fact that they grew and became established. They suited man's purpose better than what went before. They are all imperfect, and all carry with them incidental ills, but each came to be because it was better than what went before, and each of which has perished, perished because a better one supplanted it.

It follows once and for all that to turn back to any defunct institution or organization because existing institutions are imperfect is to turn away from advance and is to retrograde. The path of improvement lies forwards. Private property in land, for instance, is an institution which has been developed in the most direct and legitimate manner. It may give way at a future time to some other institution which will grow up by imperceptible stages out of the efforts of men to contend successfully with existing evils, but the grounds for private property in land are easily perceived, and it is safe to say that no *a priori* scheme of state ownership or other tenure invented *en bloc* by any philosopher and adopted by legislative act will ever supplant it. To talk of any such thing is to manifest a total misconception of the facts and laws which it is the province of sociology to investigate. The case is less in magnitude but scarcely less out of joint with all correct principle when it is proposed to adopt a unique tax on land, in a country where the rent of land is so low that any important tax on land exceeds it, and therefore becomes indirect, and where also political power is in the hands of small landowners, who hold, without ever having formulated it, a doctrine of absolute property in the soil such as is not held by any other landowners in the world.

Sociology must exert a most important influence on political economy. Political economy is the science which investigates the laws of the material welfare of human societies. It is not its province to teach individuals how to get rich. It is a social science. It was the first branch of sociology which was pursued by man as a science. It is not strange that when the industrial organization of society was studied apart from the organism of which it forms a part it was largely dominated over by arbitrary dogmatism, and that it should have fallen into disrepute as a mere field of opinion, and of endless wrangling about opinions for which no guarantees could be given. The rise of a school of "historical" economists is itself a sign of a struggle towards a positive and scientific study of political economy, in its due relations to other social sciences, and this sign loses none of its significance in spite of the crudeness and extravagance of the opinions of the historical economists, and in spite of their very marked tendency to fall into dogmatism and hobby-riding. Political economy is thrown over-board by all groups and persons whenever it becomes troublesome. When it got in the way of Mr. Gladstone's land-bill he relegated it, by implication, to the planet Saturn, to the great delight of all the fair-traders, protectionists, soft-money men, and others who had found it in the way of their devices. What political economy needs in order to emerge from the tangle in which it is now involved, and to win a dignified and orderly development, is to find its field and its relations to other sciences fairly defined within the wider scope of sociology. Its laws will then take their place not as arbitrary or broken fragments, but in due relation to other laws. Those laws will win proof and establishment from this relation.

For instance, we have plenty of books, some of them by able writers, in which the old-fashioned Malthusian doctrine of population and the Ricardian law of rent are disputed because emigration, advance in the arts, etc., can offset the action of those laws or because those laws are not seen in action in the United States. Obviously no such objections ever could have been raised if the laws in question had been understood or had been put in their proper bearings. The Malthusian law of population and the Ricardian law of rent are cases in which by rare and most admirable acumen powerful thinkers perceived two great laws in particular phases of their action. With wider information it now appears that the law of population breaks the barriers of Malthus' narrower formulae and appears as a great law of biology. The Ricardian law of rent is only a particular application of one of the great conditions of production. We have before us not special dogmas of political economy, but facts of the widest significance for the whole social development of the race. To object that these facts may be set aside by migration or advance in the arts is nothing to the purpose, for this is only altering the constants in the equation, which does not alter the form of the curve, but only its position relatively to some standard line. Furthermore, the laws themselves indicate that they have a maximum point for any society, or any given stage of the arts, and a condition of under-population, or of an extractive industry below its maximum, is just as consistent with the law as a condition of over-population and increasing distress. Hence inferences as to the law of population drawn from the status of an under-populated country are sure to be fallacious. In like manner arguments drawn from American phenomena in regard to rent and wages, when rent and wages are as yet only very imperfectly developed here, lead to erroneous conclusions. It only illustrates the unsatisfactory condition of political economy, and the want of strong criticism in it, that such arguments can find admission to its discussions and disturb its growth.

It is to the pursuit of sociology and the study of the industrial organization in combination with the other organizations of society that we must look for the more fruitful development of political economy. We are already in such a position with sociology that a person who has gained what we now possess of that science will bring to bear upon economic problems a sounder judgment and a more correct conception of all social relations than a person who may have read a library of the existing treatises on political economy. The essential elements of political economy are only corollaries or special cases of sociological principles. One who has command of the law of the conservation of energy as it manifests itself in society is armed at once against socialism, protectionism, paper money, and a score of other economic fallacies. The sociological view of political economy also includes whatever is sound in the dogmas of the "historical school" and furnishes what that school is apparently groping after.

As an illustration of the light which sociology throws on a great number of political and social phenomena which are constantly misconstrued, we may notice the differences in the industrial, political, and civil organizations which are produced all along at different stages of the ratio of population to land.

When a country is under-populated newcomers are not competitors, but assistants. If more come they may produce not only new quotas, but a surplus besides, to be divided between themselves and all who were present before. In such a state of things land is abundant and cheap. The possession of it confers no power or privilege. No one will work for another for wages when he can take up new land and be his own master. Hence it will pay no one to own more land than he can cultivate by his own labor, or with such aid as his own family supplies. Hence, again, land bears little or no rent; there will be no landlords living on rent and no laborers living on wages, but only a middle class of yeoman farmers. All are substantially on an equality, and democracy becomes the political form, because this is the only state of society in which the dogmatic assumption of equality, on which democracy is based, is realized as a fact. The same effects are powerfully reenforced by other facts. In a new and under-populated country the industries which are most profitable are the extractive industries. The characteristic of these, with the exception of some kinds of mining, is that they call for only a low organization of labor and small amount of capital. Hence they allow the workman to become speedily his own master, and they educate him to freedom, independence, and self-reliance. At the same time, the social groups being only vaguely marked off from each other, it is easy to pass from one class of occupations, and consequently from one social grade, to another. Finally, under the same circumstances education, skill, and superior training have but inferior value compared with what they have in densely populated countries.

The advantages lie, in an under-populated country, with the coarser, unskilled, manual occupations, and not with the highest developments of science, literature, and art.

If now we turn for comparison to cases of over-population we see that the struggle for existence and the competition of life are intense where the pressure of population is great. This competition draws out the highest achievements. It makes the advantages of capital, education, talent, skill, and training tell to the utmost. It draws out the social scale upwards and downwards to great extremes and produces aristocratic social organizations in spite of all dogmas of equality. Landlords, tenants (i.e., capitalist employers), and laborers are the three primary divisions of any aristocratic order, and they are sure to be developed whenever land bears rent and whenever tillage requires the application of large capital. At the same time liberty has to undergo curtailment. A man who has a square mile to himself can easily do as he likes, but a man who walks Broadway at noon or lives in a tenement-house finds his power to do as he likes limited by scores of considerations for the rights and feelings of his fellowmen. Furthermore, organization with subordination and discipline is essential in order that the society as a whole may win a support from the land. In an over-populated country the extremes of wealth and luxury are presented side by side with the extremes of poverty and distress. They are equally the products of an intense social pressure. The achievements of power are highest, the rewards of prudence, energy, enterprise, foresight, sagacity, and all other industrial virtues is greatest; on the other hand, the penalties of folly, weakness, error, and vice are most terrible. Pauperism, prostitution, and crime are the attendants of a state of society in which science, art, and literature reach their highest developments. Now it is evident that over-population and under-population are only relative terms. Hence as time goes on any under-populated nation is surely moving forward towards the other status, and is speedily losing its natural advantages which are absolute, and also that relative advantage which belongs to it if it is in neighborly relations with nations of dense population and high civilization; viz., the chance to borrow and assimilate from them the products, in arts and science, of high civilization without enduring the penalties of intense social pressure.

We have seen that if we should try by any measures of arbitrary interference and assistance to relieve the victims of social pressure from the calamity of their position we should only offer premiums to folly and vice and extend them further. We have also seen that we must go forward and meet our problems. We cannot escape them by running away. If then it be asked what the wit and effort of man can do to struggle with the problems offered by social pressure, the answer is that he can do only what his instinct has correctly and surely led him to do without any artificial social organization of any kind, and that is, by improvements in the arts, in science, in morals, in political institutions, to widen and strengthen the power of man over nature. The task of dealing with social ills is not a new task. People set about it and discuss it as if the human race had hitherto neglected it, and as if the solution of the problem was to be something new in form and substance, different from the solution of all problems which have hitherto engaged human effort. In truth, the human race has never done anything else but struggle with the problem of social welfare. That struggle constitutes history, or the life of the human race on earth. That struggle embraces all minor problems which occupy attention here, save those of religion, which reaches beyond this world and finds it objects beyond this life. Every successful effort to widen the power of man over nature is a real victory over poverty, vice, and misery, taking things in general and in the long run. It would be hard to find a single instance of a direct assault by positive effort upon poverty, vice, and misery which has not either failed or, if it has not failed directly and entirely, has not entailed other evils greater than the one which it removed. The only two things which really tell on the welfare of man on earth are hard work and self-denial (in technical language, labor and capital), and these tell most when they are brought to bear directly upon the effort to earn an honest living, to accumulate capital, and to bring up a family of children to be industrious and self-denying in their turn. I repeat that this is the way to work for the welfare of man on earth; and what I mean to say is that the common notion that when we are going to work for the social welfare of man we must adopt a great dogma, organize for the realization of some great scheme, have before us an abstract ideal, or otherwise do anything but live honest and industrious lives, is a great mistake. From the standpoint of the sociologist pessimism and optimism are alike impertinent. To be an optimist one must forget the frightful sanctions which are attached to the laws of right living. To be a pessimist one must overlook the education and growth which are the product of effort and self-denial. In either case one is passing judgment on what is inevitably fixed, and on which the approval or condemnation of man can produce no effect. The facts and laws are, once and for all, so, and for us men that is the end of the matter. The only persons for whom there would be any sense in the question whether life is worth living are primarily the yet unborn children, and secondarily the persons who are proposing to found families. For these latter the question would take a somewhat modified form: Will life be worth living for children born of me? This question is, unfortunately, not put to themselves by the appropriate persons as it would be if they had been taught sociology. The sociologist is often asked if he wants to kill off certain classes of troublesome and burdensome persons. No such inference follows from any sound sociological doctrine, but it is allowed to infer, as to a great many persons and classes, that it would have been better for society, and would have involved no pain to them, if they had never been born.

In further illustration of the interpretation which sociology offers of phenomena which are often obscure, we may note the world-wide effects of the advances in the arts and sciences which have been made during the last hundred years. These improvements have especially affected transportation and communication; that is, they have lessened the obstacles of time and space which separate the groups of mankind from each other and have tended to make the whole human race a single unit. The distinction between over-populated and under-populated countries loses its sharpness, and all are brought to an average. Every person who migrates from Europe to America affects the comparative status of the two continents. He lessens the pressure in the country he leaves and increases it in the country to which he goes. If he goes to Minnesota and raises wheat there, which is carried back to the country he left as cheap food for those who have not emigrated, it is evident that the bearing upon social pressure is twofold. It is evident, also, that the problem of social pressure can no longer be correctly studied if the view is confined either to the country of immigration or the country of emigration, but that it must embrace both. It is easy to see, therefore, that the ratio of population to land with which we have to deal is only in peculiar and limited cases that ratio as it exists in England, Germany, or the United States. It is the ratio as it exists in the civilized world, and every year that passes, as our improved arts break down the barriers between different parts of the earth, brings us nearer to the state of things where all the population of Europe, America, Australasia, and South Africa must be considered in relation to all the land of the same territories, for all that territory will be available for all that population, no matter what the proportion may be in which the population is distributed over the various portions of the territory. The British Islands may become one great manufacturing city. Minnesota, Texas, and Australia may not have five persons to the square mile. Yet all will eat the meat of Texas and the wheat of Minnesota and wear the wool of Australia manufactured on the looms of England. That all will enjoy the maximum of food and raiment under that state of things is as clear as anything possibly can be which is not yet an accomplished fact. We are working towards it by all our instincts of profit and improvement. The greatest obstacles are those which come from prejudices, traditions, and dogmas, which are held independently of any observation of facts or any correct reasoning, and which set the right hand working against the left. For instance, the Mississippi Valley was, a century ago, as unavailable to support the population of France and Germany as if it had been in the moon. The Mississippi Valley is now nearer to France and Germany than the British Islands were a century ago, reckoning distance by the only true standard; viz., difficulty of communication. It is a fair way of stating it to say that the improvements in transportation of the last fifty years have added to France and Germany respectively a tract of land of the very highest fertility, equal in area to the territory of those states, and available for the support of their population. The public men of those countries are now declaring that this is a calamity, and are devising means to counteract it.

The social and political effects of the improvements which have been made must be very great. It follows from what we have said about the effects of intense social pressure and high competition that the effect of thus bringing to bear on the great centers of population the new land of outlying countries must be to relieve the pressure in the oldest countries and at the densest centers. Then the extremes of wealth and poverty, culture and brutality, will be contracted and there will follow a general tendency towards an average equality which, however, must be understood only within very broad limits. Such is no doubt the meaning of the general tendency towards equality, the decline of aristocratic institutions, the rise of the proletariat, and the ambitious expansion, in short, which is characteristic of modern civilized society. It would lead me too far to follow out of this line of speculation as to the future, but two things ought to be noticed in passing. (1) There are important offsets to the brilliant promise which there is for mankind in a period during which, for the whole civilized world, there will be a wide margin of ease between the existing population and the supporting power of the available land. These offsets consist in the effects of ignorance, error, and folly— the same forces which have always robbed mankind of half what they might have enjoyed on earth. Extravagant governments, abuses of public credit, wasteful taxation, legislative monopolies and special privileges, juggling with currency, restrictions on trade, wasteful armaments on land and sea, and other follies in economy and statecraft, are capable of wasting and nullifying all the gains of civilization. (2) The old classical civilization fell under an irruption of barbarians from without. It is possible that our new civilization may perish by an explosion from within. The sentimentalists have been preaching for a century notions of rights and equality, of the dignity, wisdom, and power of the proletariat, which have filled the minds of ignorant men with impossible dreams. The thirst for luxurious enjoyment has taken possession of us all. It is the dark side of the power to foresee a possible future good with such distinctness as to make it a motive of energy and persevering industry—a power which is distinctly modern. Now the thirst for luxurious enjoyment, when brought into connection with the notions of rights, of power, and of equality, and dissociated from the notions of industry and economy, produces the notion that a man is robbed of his rights if he has not everything that he wants, and that he is deprived of equality if he sees anyone have more than he has, and that he is a fool if, having the power of the State in his hands, he allows this state of things to last. Then we have socialism, communism, and nihilism; and the fairest conquests of civilization, with all their promise of solid good to man, on the sole conditions of virtue and wisdom, may be scattered to the winds in a war of classes, or trampled underfoot by a mob which can only hate what it cannot enjoy.

It must be confessed that sociology is yet in a tentative and inchoate state. All that we can affirm with certainty is that social phenomena are subject to law, and that the natural laws of the social order are in their entire character like the laws of physics. We can draw in grand outline the field of sociology and forsee the shape that it will take and the relations it will bear to other sciences. We can also already find the standpoint which it will occupy, and, if a figure may be allowed, although we still look over a wide landscape largely enveloped in mist, we can see where the mist lies and define the general features of the landscape, subject to further corrections. . . . We are face to face with an issue no less grand than this: Shall we, in our general social policy, pursue the effort to realize more completely that constitutional liberty for which we have been struggling throughout modern history, or shall we return to the mediaeval device of functionaries to regulate procedure and to adjust interests? Shall we try to connect with liberty an equal and appropriate responsibility as its essential complement and corrective, so that a man who gets his own way shall accept his own consequences, or shall we yield to the sentimentalism which, after preaching an unlimited liberty, robs those who have been wise out of pity for those who have been foolish? Shall we accept the inequalities which follow upon free competition as the definition of justice, or shall we suppress free competition in the interest of equality and to satisfy a baseless dogma of justice? Shall we try to solve the social entanglements which arise in a society where social ties are constantly becoming more numerous and more subtle, and where contract has only partly superseded custom and status, by returning to the latter, only hastening a more complete development of the former? These certainly are practical questions, and their scope is such that they embrace a great number of minor questions which are before us and which are coming up. It is to the science of society, which will derive true conceptions of society from the facts and laws of the social order, studied without prejudice or bias of any sort, that we must look for the correct answer to these questions. By this observation the field of sociology and the work which it is to do for society are sufficiently defined.

LESTER FRANK WARD

"Mind as a Social Factor"
1884

Lester Frank Ward (1841–1913) yielded to no one, including his great rival William Graham Sumner, in the degree of his devotion to science in general and to the particular task of developing a science of society. Ward associated such a science not with obedience to facts, but with the authority of human beings over their own destiny. In the essay of 1884 that follows, Ward insisted on the creative powers of the human mind. These powers, Ward declared, were ignored by the conservative laissez faire versions of social science that warned against meddling with nature. The order of nature is indeed dominated by natural selection, Ward granted, but our own species represents a new stage of evolution. Human beings make progress by protecting the weak rather than by a relentless competition in which only the fit survive; it is perfectly natural for human beings—with their distinctive mental powers—to cooperate, to reduce competition, and to alter through invention the setting in which they live. Let human beings be understood as active, Ward proposed, and the natural world as passive. Ward argued against the treating as "natural" of social arrangements that he—and most twentieth-century social theorists after him—understood to be contingent, changeable products of human action.

A writer of enormous energy, Ward left an imposing shelf of books including *Dynamic Sociology*, 2 vols. (New York, 1883), *Pure Sociology* (New York, 1903), *Applied Sociology* (New York, 1906), and *Glimpses of the Cosmos,* 6 vols. (New York, 1913).

For a study of Ward that emphasizes his commitment to secular science, see Robert C. Bannister, *Sociology and Scientism: The American Quest for Objectivity,* (Chapel Hill, 1987), 13–14. See also Gillis J. Harp, "Lester Ward: Comtean Whig," *Historical Reflections* 15 (1988), 523–42.

After many centurys of exclusive study of the soul the thinkers of the world turned their attention for some centuries more to the study of the intellect. During all this time, the true influence of mind as a social factor was left quite out of view. At last there rose up the scientific philosophy which essayed to explain the nature of mind. Its dependence upon organisation in general and upon brain in particular was proved by scientific experimentation, and the domain of metaphysics became that of psychology. Mind was shown to be a function of body and psychology became a department of biology. Man has now taken his true position in the animal world as a product of development. Brain, which alone raises him above other animals, has been developed in the same manner as the other anatomical characters. The brain is the organ of the mind, its physical seat and cause. Mind is therefore a natural product of evolution, and its achievements are to be classed and studied along with all other natural phenomena. Such is the scientific conception of mind.

The modern scientist places all objects in the midst of an infinite series of antecedents and consequents. Organic forms as well as inorganic must take their places in this series—the animal no less than the plant, the man no less than the beast. Mind itself is a link of this endless chain. Its activities consist in the transmission of the properties of its antecedents to its consequents. The quantity of force in the universe is constant. No power can increase or diminish it. All attempts on the part of the creatures of this constant and unchangeable force to modify its normal effects are not less vain because such creatures happen to have acquired the faculty of observing the changes going on in nature.

The protracted study of nature's processes leads to admiration of them, and the belief has become prevalent that they are not only unalterable but also in some way necessarily beneficent. Nature has made great progress in developing organised beings and is assumed to be still working in this direction. The natural method is always the true method, and to find it out is the aim of all scientific investigation. Out of this earnest and laudable strife to discover the true method of nature has grown, logically enough, the assumption that when found it must be something of great worth. It is commonly supposed that the highest wisdom of man is to learn and then to follow the ways of nature. Those dissatisfied people who would improve upon the natural course of events are rebuked as meddlers with the unalterable. Their systems are declared utopian, their laws *bruta fulmina*. All efforts in this direction are held to be trifling and are stigmatised as so many ignorant attempts to nullify the immutable laws of nature.

This general mode of reasoning is carried into all departments of human life.

In government every attempt to improve the condition of the state is condemned and denounced. Curiously enough, here the claim is illogically made that such measures are harmful. In fact, unfortunately for the whole theory, they have often been proved to be so. But this, of course, proves their efficacy. This glaring inconsistency is, however, overlooked, and government is implored, not to adopt wise and successful measures, but to refrain from adopting any, to let society alone, and thus allow the laws of nature to work out their beneficent results.

In commerce and trade absolute freedom is insisted upon. Free trade is the watchword of this entire school. The laws of trade, they maintain, are natural laws. As such they must be better than any human rules. And here again we find them insisting that regulation is injurious to trade, although it is at the same time declared to be nugatory.

Source: Mind 4 (October 1884): 563–73.

In social affairs these doctrines are carried to their extreme logical outcome. The laws of nature as they manifest themselves in society must be left wholly untouched. The passions of men will neutralise and regulate themselves. Competition can be depended upon to correct abuses. The seller must be allowed to exaggerate and misstate the nature of his wares. This has the effect to sharpen the wits of the buyer, and this develops the brain. To dilute, adulterate, or even poison food and medicine for personal gain is not objectionable, since the destruction thereby of a few unwary consumers only proves their unfitness to survive in society. As in general commerce, so in private business, competition must be free. If a dealer, by selling at a loss, can hold out until all his competitors have been driven from the field, in order then to recover more than his losses by the monopoly he will enjoy, his right to do this must not be questioned. It is under such conditions and by the aid of such discipline that man and society have developed.

Education must be that of experience. Knowledge must be gained by efforts to avoid the consequences of ignorance already felt. The intellectual development of the child must be an epitome of that of the race. It is thus only that nature operates, and surely nature is greater and wiser than man.

All schemes of social reform are unscientific. Public charities tend to bolster up unworthy elements in society that nature has declared unfit to survive. Temperance reforms tend only to abridge individual liberty—for even the liberty to destroy one's self should be respected. Philanthropy is zeal without knowledge, while humanitarianism is fanaticism.

This general class of views antedated by many years the publication by Spencer and Darwin of their fomulated doctrines of the "survival of the fittest" and "natural selection." But it cannot be denied that these doctrines, supported as they were by facts fresh from nature, have greatly strengthened this habit of thought. Nature's method is now much better known than formerly, and it is now well understood that an utterly soulless competition constitutes its fundamental characteristic. Surely man cannot go astray in following in the footsteps of nature. Let him learn from the animal world. He has descended from some of the humble stocks which he is now studying. Nature's plan has raised him from the condition of a beast to that of a rational being. It has created and developed society and civilisation. Unless tampered with by "reformers" all the operations of society would be competitive. Competition is the law of nature out of which progress results. Sociology, as its founder insisted, must be based on biology, and the true sociologist must understand this biologic law. Those who propose to apply methods to society which are opposed to the methods of nature are supposed to be ignorant of these fundamental truths are called empiricists, "meddlers," and "tinkers."

Such, I say, is the tenor and tendency of modern scientific thought. I do not say that all scientific men hold these views. I merely maintain that leading ones have formulated and inculcated them a natural deductions from the established facts of science, and that the public mind is rapidly assimilating them, while scarcely any attempts are being made to check their advance.[1]

Is there any way of answering these arguments? Can the *laissez faire* doctrine be successfully met? That all attempts to do this have been timidly made cannot be denied.

---

1. The social philosophy of Mr. Herbert Spencer possesses this tone throughout, and his disciples, particularly in America, delight in going even farther than their master. The most extreme statement of the *laissez faire* doctrine known to me is that of Prof. W. G. Sumner, in his recent work *Social Classes.*

That these have been few and feeble is equally certain. While there has existed in the minds of many rational persons a vague sense of some hidden fallacy in all this reasoning, none have felt competent to formulate their objections with sufficient clearness and force to warrant pitting them against the resistless stream of concurrent science and philosophy of the nineteenth century. There has, however, been developing of late a more or less marked apprehension with regard to the possible consequences of this mode of thought. The feeling is distinct in the best minds, and to a large extent in the public mind, that the tendency of modern ideas is nihilistic. It is clear that if they become universally accepted they must work stagnation in society. The *laissez faire* doctrine is a gospel of inaction, the scientific creed is struck with sterility, the policy of resigning all into the hands of Nature is a surrender.

But this recognition is by no means proof that the prevalent opinions are false. At best it can only suggest this on the ground that true doctrines should be progressive. But this would be a *petitio principii*. Nature is not optimistic, still less anthropocentric. For aught we know, the laws of nature are such as make a recognition of strict scientific truth a positive barrier to social advancement. The argument we have been considering must be refuted, if at all, by legitimate counter-argument.

The present attempt to meet some parts of this argument is made in full consciousness of its strength as a factor in modern thought and with due deference to the great names that stand committed to it. The scientific facts which its defenders have brought to its support are, in the main, incontestable. To answer by denying these would be to abjure science and deserve contempt. The method of nature has been correctly interpreted. The doctrines of the survival of the fittest and natural selection are perfectly true doctrines. The law of competition is the fundamental law. It is unquestionably true that progress, not only in primary organic development, but also in society, has resulted from the action of this law.

After conceding all this, the attempt, notwithstanding, to stem the tide of modern scientific thought must, indeed, seem a hopeless one. At the outset it must be frankly acknowledged that if the current views are unsound the fault is not chargeable to science. If there is any defect it must lie in the inferences drawn from the facts and not in the facts themselves. To what extent, then, is the *laissez faire* doctrine, as defined and popularly accepted, an inference? If the method of nature is correctly formulated by that doctrine, wherein lies the fallacy when it is applied to man and to society?

In order to grapple at once with the whole problem let me answer these questions by the open charge that the modern scientific philosophers fail to recognise the true value of the *psychic factor*. Just as the metaphysicians lost their bearings by an empty worship of mind and made philosophy a plaything, so the modern evolutionists have missed their mark by degrading mind to a level with mechanical force. They seem thus about to fling away the grand results that the doctrine of evolution cannot otherwise fail to achieve. Far be it from me to appeal to the prejudices of the enemies of science by casting opprobrium upon scientific deductions, but when I consider the tendencies which are now so unmistakable, and which are so certainly the consequence of the protracted study, on the part of leading scientists, of the unquestionable methods of nature, I think I can, though holding precisely opposite opinions, fully sympathise with Carlyle in characterising the philosophy of evolution as a "gospel of dirt."

But I need not longer dwell upon the blighting influence of this construction of the known laws of nature. Let us approach the kernel of the problem.

The *laissez faire* doctrine fails to recognise that, in the development of mind, a virtually *new power* was introduced into the world. To say that this has been done is no startling announcement. It is no more than has taken place many times in the course of the evolution of living and feeling beings out of the tenuous nebulae of space. For, while it is true that nature makes no leaps, while, so long as we consider their beginning, all the great steps in evolution are due to minute increments repeated through vast periods, still, when we survey the whole field, as we must do to comprehend the scheme, and contrast the extremes, we find that nature has been making a series of enormous strides, and reaching from one plane of development to another. It is these independent achievements of evolution that the true philosopher must study.

Not to mention the great steps in the cosmical history of the solar system and of the earth, we must regard the evolution of protoplasm, the "physical basis of life," as one of those gigantic strides which thenceforth completely revolutionised the surface of our planet. The development of the cell as the unit of organisation was another such stride. The origin of vertebrate life introduced a new element, and the birth of man wrought still another transformation. These are only a few of nature's revolutions. Many more will suggest themselves. And although, in no single one of these cases can it be said at what exact point the new essence commenced to exist, although the development of all these several expressions of Nature's method of concentrating her hitherto diffused forces was accomplished through an unbroken series of minute transitional increments continued through eons of time, still, it is not a whit less true that each of these grand products of evolution, when at length fully formed, constituted a new cosmic energy, and proceeded to stamp all future products and processes with a character hitherto wholly unknown upon the globe.

It is in this sense, and in this only, that I claim the development of mind—of the thinking, reasoning, inventing faculty of the human brain—as another, and one of the best marked, of the great cosmic strides that have characterised the course of evolution and belong to the legitimate methods of nature.

It is, for example, only to a limited extent and in the most general way that we can apply the same canons to the organic as to the inorganic world. It is usually, but falsely, supposed that the student of biology need know nothing of physics, the assumption being that they have nothing in common. While this error is fatal to all fundamental acquaintance with the laws of life, it well illustrates the immensity of the advance from one realm to the other. The same could be said, in varying degrees of obviousness, of every one of the ascending steps to which reference has been made. I freely admit that the theologians and metaphysicians commit the most fatal error in treating the soul, or mind, as independent of the body, but this enormous fallacy is scarcely greater than that of the modern evolutionist, who, finding out their dependence, ignores the *magnitude* of the step by which mind was made a property of body, and proceeds as though no new factor had entered into the world.

But all this may be regarded as mere generality. Let us come to something more specific.

It has always been a marvel to my comprehension that wise men and philosophers, when smitten with the specious logic of the *laissez faire* school, can close their eyes to the most obtrusive fact that civilisation presents. In spite of the influence of philosophy, all forms of which have thus far been negative and nihilistic, the human animal, with his growing intellect, has still ever realised the power that is vouchsafed through mind, and has ever exercised that power. Philosophy would have long since robbed him of it and caused his early extermination from the earth but for the persistence, through heredity, of the impulse to exercise in self-preservation every power in his possession; by which practice alone he first gained his ascendancy ages before philosophy began.

The great fact, then, to which I allude is that, in spite of all philosophy, whether mythologic, metaphysical, or naturalistic, declaring that man must and can do nothing, he *has,* from the very dawn of his intelligence, been transforming the entire surface of the planet he inhabits. No other animal performs anything comparable to what man performs. This is solely because no other possesses the developed psychic faculty.

If we analyse mind into its two departments, sense and intellect, we shall see that it is through this latter faculty that these results are accomplished. If we inquire more closely into the mode by which intellect operates, we shall find that it serves as a guiding power to those natural forces with which it is acquainted (and no others), directing them into channels of human advantage. If we seek for a single term by which to characterise with precision the nature of this process, we find this in *Invention.* The essential characteristic of all intellectual action is invention.

Glancing now at the *ensemble* of human achievement, which may be collectively called civilisation, we readily see that it is all the result of this inventive process. All practical art is merely the product of successful invention, and it requires no undue expansion of the term, nor extraordinary power of generalisation, to see in all human institutions only modified forms of arts, and true products of the intellectual, or inventive, faculty.

But what is the general result of all this? An entirely new dispensation has been given to the world. All the materials and forces of nature have been thus placed completely under the control of one of the otherwise least powerful of the creatures inhabiting the earth. He has only to know them in order to become their master. Nature has thus been made the servant of man. Thus only has man succeeded in peopling the entire globe while all other animals are restricted to narrow faunal areas. He has also peopled certain portions far more densely than any other species could have done, and he seems destined to continue multiplying his numbers for a long time yet in the future. But this quantitative proof is even less telling than the qualitative. When we confine our attention to the *élite* of mankind we do not need to have the ways specified in detail by which the powers of mind have exalted the intellectual being above all other products of creation. At the present moment the most dense and the most enlightened populations of the globe occupy what are termed temperate latitudes, which means latitudes in which for from three to five months each year vegetation ceases entirely, the waters are locked in ice, and the temperature frequently sinks far below the zero of the Fahrenheit thermometer. Imagine the thin-skinned, furless animal man subsisting in such a climate. Extinguish his fires, banish his clothing, blot out the habitations that deck the civilised landscape. How long would the puny race survive? But these are not products of nature, they are products of *art,* the wages of thought—fruits of the intellect.

When a well-clothed philosopher on a bitter winter's night sits in a warm room well lighted for his purpose and writes on paper with pen and ink in the arbitrary characters of a highly developed language the statement that civilisation is the result of natural laws, and that man's duty is to let nature alone so that untrammeled it may work out a higher civilisation, he simply ignores every circumstance of his existence and deliberately closes his eyes to every fact within the range of his faculties. If man had acted upon his theory there would have been no civilisation, and our philosopher would have remained a troglodyte.

But how shall we distinguish this human, or anthropic, method from the method of nature? Simply by reversing all the definitions. Art is the antithesis of nature. If we call one the natural method we must call the other the artificial method. If nature's process is rightly named natural selection, man's process is artificial selection. The survival of the fittest is simply the survival of the strong, which implies, and might as well be called, the destruction of the weak. And if nature progresses through the destruction of the weak, man progresses through the *protection* of the weak. This is the essential distinction.

In human society the psychic power has operated to secure the protection of the weak in two distinct ways: first, by increasing the supply of the necessities of life, and, secondly, by preventing the destruction of life through the enemies of man. The immediate instrumentality through which the first of these processes is carried on is art, the product of invention. The second process takes place through the establishment of positive institutions.

It is difficult to say which of these agencies has been most effective. Both were always indispensable, and therefore all comparison is unprofitable.

Art operates to protect the weak against adverse surroundings. It is directed against natural forces, chiefly physical. By thus defeating the destructive influences of the elements and hostile forms of life, and by forcing nature to yield an unnatural supply of man's necessities, many who would have succumbed from inability to resist these adverse agencies—the feebler members of society—were able to survive, and population increased and expanded. While no one openly denies this, there is a tendency either to ignore it in politico-economic discussions, or to deny its application to them as an answer to naturalistic arguments.

If, on the other hand, we inquire into the nature of human institutions, we shall perceive that they are of three kinds, tending to protect the weak in three ways, or ascending degrees. These three successively higher means through which this end is attained are, first, Justice, second, Morality, and third, Charity. These forms of action have been reached through the development, respectively, of the three corresponding sentiments: Equity, Beneficence, and Benevolence.

All of these altruistic sentiments are wholly unknown, or known only in the merest embryo, to all animals below man, and therefore no such means of protection exist among them. They are strictly human, or anthropic. Many evolutionists fail to recognise this. Some sociologists refuse to admit it. They look about and see so much injustice, immorality and rapacity that they are led to suppose that only natural methods are in operation in society. This is a great mistake. In point of fact, the keener the sense of justice the more conspicuous the diminishing number of violations of it come to appear, and conversely, the obviousness of injustice proves the general prevalence of justice. It is the same with morality and philanthropy.

If we consider the effect of these three codes of human conduct in the direction of enabling the weaker ones to survive we shall see that it has been immense. Out of the first has arisen government, the chief value and function of which has always been and still is such protection. Great systems of jurisprudence have been elaborated, engrossing the attention of a large portion of the population of enlightened as well as of barbaric states. To say that these have been failures because often weighted with grave defects is to misinterpret history and misunderstand society. No one could probably be found to gainsay that the moral law of society has exerted a salutary influence, yet its aim is strictly altruistic, opposed to the law of the survival of the fittest, and wholly in the direction of enabling those to survive who would not survive without its protection. Finally, the last sentiment to be developed, and doubtless the highest, is so universally recognised as peculiar to man that his very name has been given to it—the sentiment of *humanity*. Yet the mode of protecting the weak arising out of this sentiment is the one that has been most seriously called in question by the naturalistic school. It must be admitted that humanitarian institutions have done far less good than either juridical or ethical institutions. The sentiment itself is of recent origin, the product only of highly developed and greatly refined mental organisation. It exists to an appreciable degree only in a minute fraction of the most enlightened populations. It is rarely directed with judgment; no fixed, self-enforcing code of conduct, as in the other cases, having had time to take shape. The institutions established to enforce it are for the most part poorly supported, badly managed, and often founded on a total misconception of human nature and of the true mode of attaining the end in view. Hence they are specially open to attack. But if ever humanitarian sentiments become diffused throughout the body politic, become the object of deep study, as have those of justice and right, it may be confidently predicted that society will prove itself capable of caring for the most unfortunate of its members in a manner that shall not work demoralisation.

In all these ways man, through his intelligence, has laboured successfully to resist the law of nature. His success is conclusively demonstrated by a comparison of his condition with that of other species of animals. No other cause can be assigned for his superiority. How can the naturalistic philosophers shut their eyes to such obvious facts? Yet, what is their attitude? They condemn all attempts to protect the weak, whether by private or public methods. They claim that it deteriorates the race by enabling the unfit to survive and transmit their inferiority. This is true only in certain cases of hereditary diseases or mental deficiencies, which should be taken account of by man because they are not by nature. Nothing is easier than to show that the unrestricted competition of nature does not secure the survival of the fittest possible, but only of the actually fittest, and in every attempt man makes to obtain something fitter than this actual fittest he succeeds, as witness improved breeds of animals and grafts of fruits. Now, the human method of protecting the weak deals in some such way with men. It not only increases the number but improves the quality.

But "government," at least, must *laisser faire*. It must not "meddle" with natural laws. The laws of trade, business, social intercourse, are natural laws, immutable and indestructible. All interference with them is vain. The fallacy here is a *non sequitur*. It may be readily granted that these laws are immutable and indestructible. Were this not the case it would certainly be hopeless to interfere with their action. But every mechanical invention proves that nothing is easier than to interfere successfully with the operation of these uniform natural forces. They have only to be first thoroughly understood and then they are easily *controlled*. To *destroy* a force is one thing, to control its action is quite another. Those who talk in this way involve themselves in the most palpable inconsistency. They must not be allowed to stop where they do. They must go on and carry their strictures to a logical conclusion. They must deny to government the right to protect its citizens from injustice. This is a clear interference with the natural laws of society. They must deny to society the right to enforce its code of morals. Nothing is more unnatural. They must suppress the healing art which keeps the sick from dying as they do among animals. Nor is this all. They must condemn all interference with physical laws and natural forces. To dam a stream must be characterised as a "vain" attempt to overcome a natural law. The wind must be left free to blow where it will, and not be forced against the fan of a wind-mill. The vapour of heated water must be allowed to float off naturally into the air and not be pent up in a steam-boiler and thence conducted into the cylinder of a steam-engine. All these things and every other device of inventive man are so many attempts to "violate" the laws of nature, which is declared impossible.

What then remains of the *laissez faire* doctrine? Nothing but this: That it is useless, and may be dangerous, to attempt to control natural forces until their character is first well understood. This is a proposition which is true for every department of force, and does not involve the surrender of the whole domain of sociology after it has been demonstrated that society is a theatre of forces.

The truth thus comes forth from a rational study of nature and human society that social progress has been due only in very slight degree to natural evolution as accomplished through the survival of the fittest, and its chief success has resulted from the reduction of competition in the struggle for existence and the protection of the weaker members. Such competition, in so far as it has been permitted to operate, has tended to lower the standard of the fittest and to check advancement. It is not, of course, claimed that the natural method has even been fully overcome. It has always operated, and still operates, powerfully in many ways. It has been chiefly in the simpler departments of physical and mechanical phenomena that the psychic, or anthropic, method has superseded it. The inventive arts have been the result. Vital forces have yielded to some extent to the influence of mind in bringing about improved stocks of animals and vegetables, and even certain social laws have come under rational control through the establishment of institutions. Still, every step in this progress has been contested. It was not enough that the intellect was feeble and ill-fitted to grapple with such problems. It was not enough that ignorance of nature's laws should cause unnumbered failures. A still stronger barrier was presented by the intellect itself in the form of positive error embodied in philosophy. As already remarked, philosophy has always been negative and nihilistic, and has steadily antagonised the common sense of mankind. It is only quite recently that there has come into existence anything like a truly *positive* philosophy, i.e., a philosophy of *action*. . . .

ELIZABETH CADY STANTON

"The Solitude of Self"
1892

When the seventy-seven-year-old Elizabeth Cady Stanton (1815–1902) stepped down from the presidency of the National American Woman Suffrage Association in 1892, she sought to vindicate the rights of women on the grounds of "the solitude and personal responsibility" of each woman's "individual life." Stanton made other arguments as well—in "The Solitude of Self" and throughout her career—but in treating the political significance and psychological resources of the "self" she produced one of the most vivid and prophetic testimonials in the entire discourse of modern feminism. Stanton demanded equality for women in the life of the mind as well as the life of politics. She was a distinctively intellectual exemplar for American women and spoke beyond as well as within feminist circles on many issues of her time. Stanton gained notoriety as a freethinker and was openly critical of Christianity. In *The Woman's Bible* (1895), she boldly evaluated sections of the Old Testament in terms of the attitudes toward women promoted by these texts. Stanton's radical views on religious questions and her vocal support for birth control and for revised divorce laws made her an embarrassment to more conservative feminists. During the Progressive Era and the 1920s, American feminist leaders singled out the less controversial Susan B. Anthony as their movement's chief emblem and deliberately deemphasized Stanton's role in the winning of the vote for women.

A good biography is Lois W. Banner, *Elizabeth Cady Stanton: A Radical for Women's Rights* (Boston, 1980). See also the extensive introductory and editorial comments by Ellen Carol DuBois, ed., *Elizabeth Cady Stanton and Susan B. Anthony: Correspondence, Writings, Speeches* (New York, 1981). The version of "The Solitude of Self," reprinted here, follows DuBois's editing of the text.

The point I wish plainly to bring before you on this occasion is the individuality of each human soul; our Protestant idea, the right of individual conscience and judgment; our republican idea, individual citizenship. In discussing the rights of woman, we are to consider, first, what belongs to her as an individual, in a world of her own, the arbiter of her own destiny, an imaginary Robinson Crusoe, with her woman, Friday, on a solitary island. Her rights under such circumstances are to use all her faculties for her own safety and happiness.

Secondly, if we consider her as a citizen, as a member of a great nation, she must have the same rights as all others members, according to the fundamental principles of our Government.

Thirdly, viewed as a woman, an equal factor in civilization, her rights and duties are still the same—individual happiness and development.

Fourthly, it is only the incidental relations of life, such as mother, wife, sister, daughter, which may involve some special duties and training. . . .

The strongest reason for giving woman all the opportunities for higher education, for the full development of her faculties, her forces of mind and body; for giving her the most enlarged freedom of thought and action; a complete emancipation from all forms of bondage, of custom, dependence, superstition; from all the crippling influences of fear—is the solitude and personal responsibility of her own individual life. The strongest reason why we ask for woman a voice in the government under which she lives; in the religion she is asked to believe; equality in social life, where she is the chief factor; a place in the trades and professions, where she may earn her bread, is because of her birthright to self-sovereignty; because, as an individual, she must rely on herself. No matter how much women prefer to lean, to be protected and supported, nor how much men desire to have them do so, they must make the voyage of life alone, and for safety in an emergency, they must know something of the laws of navigation. To guide our own craft, we must be captain, pilot, engineer; with chart and compass to stand at the wheel; to watch the winds and waves, and know when to take in the sail, and to read the signs in the firmament over all. It matters not whether the solitary voyager is man or woman; nature, having endowed them equally, leaves them to their own skill and judgment in the hour of danger, and, if not equal to the occasion, alike they perish.

To appreciate the importance of fitting every human soul for independent action, think for a moment of the immeasurable solitude of self. We come into the world alone, unlike all who have gone before us, we leave it alone, under circumstances peculiar to ourselves. No mortal ever has been, no mortal ever will be like the soul just launched on the sea of life. There can never again be just such a combination of prenatal influences; never again just such environments as make up the infancy, youth and manhood of this one. Nature never repeats herself, and the possibilities of one human soul will never be found in another. No one has ever found two blades of ribbon grass alike, and no one will ever find two human beings alike. Seeing, then, what must be the infinite diversity in human character, we can in a measure appreciate the loss to a nation when any class of the people is uneducated and unrepresented in the government.

We ask for the complete development of every individual, first, for his own benefit and happiness. In fitting out an army, we give each soldier his own knapsack, arms, powder, his blanket, cup, knife, fork and spoon. We provide alike for all their individual necessities; then each man bears his own burden.

Source: *Woman's Column*, 1892.

Again, we ask complete individual development for the general good; for the consensus of the competent on the whole round of human interests, on all questions of national life; and here each man must bear his share of the general burden. It is sad to see how soon friendless children are left to bear their own burdens, before they can analyze their feelings; before they can even tell their joys and sorrows, they are thrown on their own resources. The great lesson that nature seems to teach us at all ages in self-dependence, self-protection, self-support. . . .

In youth our most bitter disappointments, our brightest hopes and ambitions, are known only to ourselves. Even our friendship and love we never fully share with another; there is something of every passion, in every situation, we conceal. Even so in our triumphs and our defeats. . . .

We ask no sympathy from others in the anxiety and agony of a broken friendship or shattered love. When death sunders our nearest ties, alone we sit in the shadow of our affliction. Alike amid the greatest triumphs and darkest tragedies of life, we walk alone. On the divine heights of human attainment, eulogized and worshipped as a hero or saint, we stand alone. In ignorance, poverty and vice, as a pauper or criminal, alone we starve or steal; alone we suffer the sneers and rebuffs of our fellows; alone we are hunted and hounded through dark courts and alleys, in by-ways and high-ways; alone we stand in the judgment seat; alone in the prison cell we lament our crimes and misfortunes; alone we expiate them on the gallows. In hours like these we realize the awful solitude of individual life, its pains, its penalties, its responsibilities, hours in which the youngest and most helpless are thrown on their own resources for guidance and consolation. Seeing, then, that life must ever be a march and a battle that each soldier must be equipped for his own protection, it is the height of cruelty to rob the individual of a single natural right.

To throw obstacles in the way of a complete education is like putting out the eyes; to deny the rights of property is like cutting off the hands. To refuse political equality is to rob the ostracized of all self-respect; of credit in the market place; of recompense in the world of work, of a voice in choosing those who make and administer the law, a choice in the jury before whom they are tried, and in the judge who decides their punishment. [Think of] . . . woman's position! Robbed of her natural rights, handicapped by law and custom at every turn, yet compelled to fight her own battles, and in the emergencies of life to fall back on herself for protection. . . .

The young wife and mother, at the head of some establishment, with a kind husband to shield her from the adverse winds of life, with wealth, fortune and position, has a certain harbor of safety, secure against the ordinary ills of life. But to manage a household, have a desirable influence in society, keep her friends and the affections of her husband, train her children and servants well, she must have rare common sense, wisdom, diplomacy, and a knowledge of human nature. To do all this, she needs the cardinal virtues and the strong points of character that the most successful statesman possesses. An uneducated woman trained to dependence, with no resources in herself, must make a failure of any position in life. But society says women do not need a knowledge of the world, the liberal training that experience in public life must give, all the advantages of collegiate education; but when for the lack of all this, the woman's happiness is wrecked, alone she bears her humiliation; and the solitude of the weak and the ignorant is indeed pitiable. In the wild chase for the prizes of life, they are ground to powder.

In age, when the pleasures of youth are passed, children grown up, married and gone, the hurry and bustle of life in a measure over, when the hands are weary of active service, when the old arm chair and the fireside are the chosen resorts, then men and women alike must fall back on their own resources. If they cannot find companionship in books, if they have no interest in the vital questions of the hour, no interest in watching the consummation of reforms with which they might have been identified, they soon pass into their dotage. The more fully the faculties of the mind are developed and kept in use, the longer the period of vigor and active interest in all around us continues. If, from a life-long participation in public affairs, a woman feels responsible for the laws regulating our system of education, the discipline of our jails and prisons, the sanitary condition of our private homes, public buildings and thoroughfares, an interest in commerce, finance, our foreign relations, in any or all these questions, her solitude will at least be respectable, and she will not be driven to gossip or scandal for entertainment.

The chief reason for opening to every soul the doors to the whole round of human duties and pleasures is the individual development thus attained, the resources thus provided under all circumstances to mitigate the solitude that at times must come to everyone.

. . . Inasmuch, then, as woman shares equally the joys and sorrows of time and eternity, is it not the height of presumption in man to propose to represent her at the ballot box and the throne of grace, to do her voting in the state, her praying in the church, and to assume the position of high priest at the family altar?

Nothing strengthens the judgment and quickens the conscience like individual responsibility. Nothing adds such dignity to character as the recognition of one's self-sovereignty; the right to an equal place, everywhere conceded—a place earned by personal merit, not an artificial attainment by inheritance, wealth, family and position. Conceding, then, that the responsibilities of life rest equally on man and woman, that their destiny is the same, they need the same preparation for time and eternity. The talk of sheltering woman from the fierce storms of life is the sheerest mockery, for they beat on her from every point of the compass, just as they do on man, and with more fatal results, for he has been trained to protect himself, to resist, and to conquer. Such are the facts in human experience, the responsibilities of individual sovereignty. Rich and poor, intelligent and ignorant, wise and foolish, virtuous and vicious, man and woman; it is ever the same, each soul must depend wholly on itself.

Whatever the theories may be of woman's dependence on man, in the supreme moments of her life, he cannot bear her burdens. Alone she goes to the gates of death to give life to every man that is born into the world; no one can share her fears, no one can mitigate her pangs; and if her sorrow is greater than she can bear, alone she passes beyond the gates into the vast unknown.

From the mountain-tops of Judea long ago, a heavenly voice bade his disciples, "Bear ye one another's burdens"; but humanity has not yet risen to that point of self-sacrifice; and if ever so willing, how few the burdens are that one soul can bear for another! . . .

So it ever must be in the conflicting scenes of life, in the long, weary march, each one walks alone. We may have many friends, love, kindness, sympathy and charity, to smooth our pathway in everyday life, but in the tragedies and triumphs of human experience, each mortal stands alone.

But when all artificial trammels are removed, and women are recognized as individuals, responsible for their own environments, thoroughly educated for all positions in life they may be called to fill; with all the resources in themselves that liberal thought and broad culture can give; guided by their own conscience and judgment, trained to self-protection, by a healthy development of the muscular system, and skill in the use of weapons and defence; and stimulated to self-support by a knowledge of the business world and the pleasure that pecuniary independence must ever give; when women are trained in this way, they will in a measure be fitted for those hours of solitude that come alike to all, whether prepared or otherwise. As in our extremity we must depend on ourselves, the dictates of wisdom point to complete individual development.

In talking of education, how shallow the argument that each class must be educated for the special work it proposes to do, and that all those faculties not needed in this special work must lie dormant and utterly wither for want of use, when, perhaps, these will be the very faculties needed in life's greatest emergencies! Some say, "Where is the use of drilling girls in the languages, the sciences, in law, medicine, theology. As wives, mothers, housekeepers, cooks, they need a different curriculum from boys who are to fill all positions. The chief cooks in our great hotels and ocean steamers are men. In our large cities, men run the bakeries; they make our bread, cake and pies. They manage the laundries; they are now considered our best milliners and dressmakers. Because some men fill these departments of usefulness, shall we regulate the curriculum in Harvard and Yale to their present necessities? If not, why this talk in our best colleges of a curriculum for girls who are crowding into the trades and professions, teachers in all our public schools, rapidly filling many lucrative and honorable positions in life?"

. . . Women are already the equals of men in the whole realm of thought, in art, science, literature and government. . . . The poetry and novels of the century are theirs, and they have touched the keynote of reform, in religion, politics and social life. They fill the editor's and professor's chair, plead at the bar of justice, walk the wards of the hospital, speak from the pulpit and the platform. Such is the type of womanhood that an enlightened public sentiment welcomes to-day, and such the triumph of the facts of life over the false theories of the past.

Is it, then, consistent to hold the developed woman of this day within the same narrow political limits as the dame with the spinning wheel and knitting needle occupied in the past? No, no! Machinery has taken the labors of woman as well as man on its tireless shoulders; the loom and the spinning wheel are but dreams of the past; the pen, the brush, the easel, the chisel, have taken their places, while the hopes and ambitions of women are essentially changed.

We see reason sufficient in the outer conditions of human beings for individual liberty and development, but when we consider the self-dependence of every human soul, we see the need of courage, judgment and the exercise of every faculty of mind and body, strengthened and developed by use, in woman as well as man.

Whatever may be said of man's protecting power in ordinary conditions, amid all the terrible disasters by land and sea, in the supreme moments of danger, alone woman must ever meet the horrors of the situation. The Angel of Death even makes no royal pathway for her. Man's love and sympathy enter only into the sunshine of our lives. In that solemn solitude of self, that links us with the immeasurable and the eternal, each soul lives alone forever. A recent writer says: "I remember once, in crossing the Atlantic, to have gone upon the deck of the ship at midnight, when a dense black cloud enveloped the sky, and the great deep was roaring madly under the lashes of demoniac winds. My feeling was not of danger or fear (which is a base surrender of the immortal soul) but of utter desolation and loneliness; a little speck of life shut in by a tremendous darkness. . . ."

And yet, there is a solitude which each and every one of us has always carried with him, more inaccessible than the ice-cold mountains, more profound than the midnight sea; the solitude of self. Our inner being which we call ourself, no eye nor touch of man or angel has ever pierced. It is more hidden than the caves of the gnome; the sacred adytum of the oracle; the hidden chamber of Eleusinian mystery, for to it only omniscience is permitted to enter.

Such is individual life. Who, I ask you, can take, dare take on himself the rights, the duties, the responsibilities of another human soul?

CHARLOTTE PERKINS GILMAN

Selection from *Women and Economics* 1898

So prominent in the history of feminist theory in America are the works of Charlotte Perkins Gilman (1860–1935) that she is often called the Marx and the Veblen of American feminism. The selection herein—from *Women and Economics,* 1898—displays the sweep and the conviction with which she addressed the evolutionary-historical matrix of women's condition. Gilman argues that women, once forced into relations of dependency by men, were "cut off from the direct action of natural selection, that mighty force which heretofore had acted on male and female alike with inexorable and beneficial effect," developing the strength, skill, endurance and courage that made the human species what it was to become. In her conception of the evolutionary process, Gilman was much influenced by Lester Frank Ward. Gilman was an economist and an evolutionary theorist and also an accomplished writer of fiction and verse. Her utopian novel *Herland* (New York, 1979) was first published serially in 1915. Her short story of 1892, "The Yellow Wallpaper," has inspired extensive critical attention.

For an interpretation of this story in relation to *Women and Economics,* see Walter Benn Michaels, *The Gold Standard and the Logic of Naturalism* (Berkeley, 1987), 3–28. Because so many of Gilman's scattered writings remained undiscovered until recently, a book essential to the study of her ideas is Gary Sharnhorst, *Charlotte Perkins Gilman: A Bibliography* (Metuchen, N.J. 1985). A good selection of her writings can be found in Ann J. Lane, ed., *The Charlotte Perkins Gilman Reader* (New York, 1980). For a biography, see Ann J. Lane, *To Herland and Beyond* (New York, 1990). Gilman's early years are the subject of a more detailed study, Mary A. Hill, *Charlotte Perkins Gilman: The Making of a Radical Feminist* (Philadelphia, 1980). Two important histories of early twentieth-century American feminist intellectuals are Rosalind Rosenberg, *Beyond Separate Spheres: Intellectual Roots of Modern Feminism* (New Haven, 1982); and Nancy F. Cott, *The Grounding of Modern Feminism* (New Haven, 1987).

Having seen the disproportionate degree of sex-distinction in humanity and its greater manifestation in the female than in the male, and having seen also the unique position of the human female as an economic dependant on the male of her species, it is not difficult to establish a relation between these two facts. The general law acting to produce this condition of exaggerated sex-development . . . is as follows: the natural tendency of any function to increase in power by use causes sex-activity to increase under the action of sexual selection. This tendency is checked in most species by the force of natural selection, which diverts the energies into other channels and developes race-activities. Where the female finds her economic environment in the male, and her economic advantage is directly conditioned upon the sex-relation, the force of natural selection is added to the force of sexual selection, and both together operate to develop sex-activity. In any animal species, free from any other condition, such a relation would have inevitably developed sex to an inordinate degree, as may be readily seen in the comparatively similar cases of those insects where the female, losing economic activity and modified entirely to sex, becomes a mere egg-sac, an organism with no powers of self-preservation, only those of race-preservation. With these insects the only race-problem is to maintain and reproduce the species, and such a condition is not necessarily evil; but with a race like ours, whose development as human creatures is but comparatively begun, it is evil because of its check to individual and racial progress. There are other purposes before us besides mere maintenance and reproduction.

It should be clear to any one accustomed to the working of biological laws that all the tendencies of a living organism are progressive in their development, and are held in check by the interaction of their several forces. Each living form, with its dominant characteristics, represents a balance of power, a sort of compromise. The size of earth's primeval monsters was limited by the tensile strength of their material. Sea monsters can be bigger, because the medium in which they move offers more support. Birds must be smaller for the opposite reason. The cow requires many stomachs of a liberal size, because her food is of low nutritive value; and she must eat large quantities to keep her machine going. The size of arboreal animals, such as monkeys or squirrels, is limited by the nature of their habitat: creatures that live in trees cannot be so big as creatures that live on the ground. Every quality of every creature is relative to its condition, and tends to increase or decrease accordingly; and each quality tends to increase in proportion to its use, and to decrease in proportion to its disuse. Primitive man and his female were animals, like other animals. They were strong, fierce, lively beasts; and she was as nimble and ferocious as he, save for the added belligerence of the males in their sex-competition. In this competition, he, like the other male creatures, fought savagely with his hairy rivals; and she, like the other female creatures, complacently viewed their struggles, and mated with the victor. At other times she ran about in the forest, and helped herself to what there was to eat as freely as he did.

There seems to have come a time when it occurred to the dawning intelligence of this amiable savage that it was cheaper and easier to fight a little female, and have it done with, than to fight a big male every time. So he instituted the custom of enslaving the female; and she, losing freedom, could no longer get her own food nor that of her young. The mother ape, with her maternal function well fulfilled, flees leaping through the forest,—plucks her fruits and nuts, keeps up with the movement of the tribe, her young one on her back or held in one strong arm. But the mother woman, enslaved,

Source: Charlotte Perkins Gilman, *Women and Economics* (Boston: Small, Maynard & Co., 1898), 58–75.

could not do this. Then man, the father, found that slavery had its obligations: he must care for what he forbade to care for itself, else it died on his hands. So he slowly and reluctantly shouldered the duties of his new position. He began to feed her, and not only that, but to express in his own person the thwarted uses of maternity: he had to feed the children, too. It seems a simple arrangement. When we have thought of it at all, we have thought of it with admiration. The naturalist defends it on the ground of advantage to the species through the freeing of the mother from all other cares and confining her unreservedly to the duties of maternity. The poet and novelist, the painter and sculptor, the priest and teacher, have all extolled this lovely relation. It remains for the sociologist, from a biological point of view, to note its effects on the constitution of the human race, both in the individual and in society.

When man began to feed and defend woman, she ceased proportionately to feed and defend herself. When he stood between her and her physical environment, she ceased proportionately to feel the influence of that environment and respond to it. When he became her immediate and all-important environment, she began proportionately to respond to this new influence, and to be modified accordingly. In a free state, speed was of as great advantage to the female as to the male, both in enabling her to catch prey and in preventing her from being caught by enemies; but, in her new condition, speed was a disadvantage. She was not allowed to do the catching, and it profited her to be caught by her new master. Free creatures, getting their own food and maintaining their own lives, develop an active capacity for attaining their ends. Parasitic creatures, whose living is obtained by the exertions of others, develop powers of absorption and of tenacity,—the powers by which they profit most. The human female was cut off from the direct action of natural selection, that mighty force which heretofore had acted on male and female alike with inexorable and beneficial effect, developing strength, developing skill, developing endurance, developing courage,—in a word, developing species. She now met the influence of natural selection acting indirectly through the male, and developing, of course, the faculties required to secure and obtain a hold on him. Needless to state that these faculties were those of sex-attraction, the one power that has made him cheerfully maintain, in what luxury he could, the being in whom he delighted. For many, many centuries she had no other hold, no other assurance of being fed. The young girl had a prospective value, and was maintained for what should follow; but the old woman, in more primitive times, had but a poor hold on life. She who could best please her lord was the favorite slave or favorite wife, and she obtained the best economic conditions.

With the growth of civilization, we have gradually crystallized into law the visible necessity for feeding the helpless female; and even old women are maintained by their male relatives with a comfortable assurance. But to this day—save, indeed, for the increasing army of women wage-earners, who are changing the face of the world by their steady advance toward economic independence—the personal profit of women bears but too close a relation to their power to win and hold the other sex. From the odalisque with the most bracelets to the débutante with the most bouquets, the relation still holds good,—woman's economic profit comes through the power of sex-attraction.

When we confront this fact boldly and plainly in the open market of vice, we are sick with horror. When we see the same economic relation made permanent, established by law, sanctioned and sanctified by religion, covered with flowers and incense and all accumulated sentiment, we think it innocent, lovely, and right. The transient trade we think evil. The bargain for life we think good. But the biological effect remains the same.

In both cases the female gets her food from the male by virtue of her sex-relationship to him. In both cases, perhaps even more in marriage because of its perfect acceptance of the situation, the female of genus homo, still living under natural law, is inexorably modified to sex in an increasing degree.

Followed in specific detail, the action of the changed environment upon women has been in given instances as follows: in the matter of mere passive surroundings she has been immediately restricted in her range. This one factor has an immense effect on man and animal alike. An absolutely uniform environment, one shape, one size, one color, one sound, would render life, if any life could be, one helpless, changeless thing. As the environment increases and varies, the development of the creature must increase and vary with it; for he acquires knowledge and power, as the material for knowledge and the need for power appear. In migratory species the female is free to acquire the same knowledge as the male by the same means, the same development by the same experiences. The human female has been restricted in range from the earliest beginning. Even among savages, she has a much more restricted knowledge of the land she lives in. She moves with the camp, of course, and follows her primitive industries in its vicinity; but the war-path and the hunt are the man's. He has a far larger habitat. The life of the female savage is freedom itself, however, compared with the increasing constriction of custom closing in upon the woman, as civilization advanced, like the iron torture chamber of romance. Its culmination is expressed in the proverb: "A woman should leave her home but three times,—when she is christened, when she is married, and when she is buried." Or this: "The woman, the cat, and the chimney should never leave the house." The absolutely stationary female and the wide-ranging male are distinctly human institutions, after we leave behind us such low forms of life as the gypsy moth, whose female seldom moves more than a few feet from the pupa moth. She has aborted wings, and cannot fly. She waits humbly for the winged male, lays her myriad eggs, and dies,—a fine instance of modification to sex.

To reduce so largely the mere area of environment is a great check to race-development; but it is not to be compared in its effects with the reduction in voluntary activity to which the human female has been subjected. Her restricted impression, her confinement to the four walls of the home, have done great execution, of course, in limiting her ideas, her information, her thought-processes, and power of judgment; and in giving a disproportionate prominence and intensity to the few things she knows about; but this is innocent in action compared with her restricted expression, the denial of freedom to act. A living organism is modified far less through the action of external circumstances upon it and its reaction thereto, than through the effect of its own exertions. Skin may be thickened gradually by exposure to the weather; but it is thickened far more quickly by being rubbed against something, as the handle of an oar or of a broom. To be surrounded by beautiful things has much influence upon the human creature: to make beautiful things has more. To live among beautiful surroundings and make ugly things is more directly lowering than to live among ugly surroundings and make beautiful things. What we do modifies us more than what is done to us. The freedom of expression has been more restricted in women than the freedom of impression, if that be possible. Something of the world she lived in she has seen from her barred windows. Some air has come through the purdah's folds, some knowledge has filtered to her eager ears from the talk of men. Desdemona learned somewhat of Othello. Had she known more, she might have lived longer. But in the ever-growing human impulse to create, the power and will to make, to do, to express one's new spirit in new forms,—here she has been utterly debarred. She might work as she had worked from the begining,—at the primitive labors of the household; but in the inevitable expansion of even those industries to professional levels we have striven to hold her back. To work with her own hands, for nothing, in direct body-service to her own family,—this has been permitted,—yes, compelled. But to be and do anything further from this she has been forbidden. Her labor has not only been limited in kind, but in degree. Whatever she has been allowed to do must be done in private and alone, the first-hand industries of savage times.

Our growth in industry has been not only in kind, but in class. The baker is not in the same industrial grade with the house-cook, though both make bread. To specialize any form of labor is a step up: to organize it is another step. Specialization and organization are the basis of human progress, the organic methods of social life. They have been forbidden to women almost absolutely. The greatest and most beneficent change of this century is the progress of women in these two lines of advance. The effect of this check in industrial development, accompanied as it was by the constant inheritance of increased racial power, has been to intensify the sensations and emotions of women, and to develop great activity in the lines allowed. The nervous energy that up to present memory has impelled women to labor incessantly at something, be it the veriest folly of fancy work, is one mark of this effect.

In religious development the same dead-line has held back the growth of women through all the races and ages. In dim early times she was sharer in the mysteries and rites; but, as religion developed, her place receded, until Paul commanded her to be silent in the churches. And she had been silent until to-day. Even now, with all the ground gained, we have but the beginnings—the slowly forced and disapproved beginnings—of religious equality for the sexes. In some nations, religion is held to be a masculine attribute exclusively, it being even questioned whether women have souls. An early Christian council settled that important question by vote, fortunately deciding that they had. In a church whose main strength has always been derived from the adherence of women, it would have been an uncomfortable reflection not to have allowed them souls. Ancient family worship ran in the male line. It was the son who kept the sacred grandfathers in due respect, and poured libations to their shades. When the woman married, she changed her ancestors, and had to worship her husband's progenitors instead of her own. This is why the Hindu and the Chinaman and many others of like stamp must have a son to keep them in countenance,—a deep-seated sex-prejudice, coming to slow extinction as women rise in economic importance.

It is painfully interesting to trace the gradual cumulative effect of these conditions upon women: first, the action of large natural laws, acting on her as they would act on any other animal; then the evolution of social customs and laws (with her position as the active cause), following the direction of mere physical forces, and adding heavily to them; then, with increasing civilization, the unbroken accumulation of precedent, burnt into each generation by the growing force of education, made lovely by art, holy by religion, desirable by habit; and, steadily acting from beneath, the unswerving pressure of economic necessity upon which the whole structure rested. These are strong modifying conditions, indeed.

The process would have been even more effective and far less painful but for one important circumstance. Heredity has no Salic law. Each girl child inherits from her father a certain increasing percentage of human development, human power, human tendency; and each boy as well inherits from his mother the increasing percentage of sex-development, sex-power, sex-tendency. The action of heredity has been to equalize what every tendency of environment and education made to differ. This has saved us from such a female as the gypsy moth. It has held up the woman, and held down the man. It has set iron bounds to our absurd effort to make a race with one sex a million years behind the other. But it has added terribly to the pain and difficulty of human life,—a difficulty and a pain that should have taught us long since that we were living on wrong lines. Each woman born, re-humanized by the current of race activity carried on by her father and re-womanized by her traditional position, has had to live over again in her own person the same process of restriction, repression, denial; the smothering "no" which crushed down all her human desires to create, to discover, to learn, to express, to advance. Each woman has had, on the other hand, the same single avenue of expression and attainment; the same one way in which alone she might do what she could, get what she might. All other doors were shut, and this one always open; and the whole pressure of advancing humanity was upon her. No wonder that young Daniel in the apocryphal tale proclaimed: "The king is strong! Wine is strong! But women are stronger!"

To the young man confronting life the world lies wide. Such powers as he has he may use, must use. If he chooses wrong at first, he may choose again, and yet again. Not effective or successful in one channel, he may do better in another. The growing, varied needs of all mankind call on him for the varied service in which he finds his growth. What he wants to be, he may strive to be. What he wants to get, he may strive to get. Wealth, power, social distinction, fame,—what he wants he can try for.

To the young woman confronting life there is the same world beyond, there are the same human energies and human desires and ambition within. But all that she may wish to have, all that she may wish to do, must come through a single channel and a single choice. Wealth, power, social distinction, fame,—not only these, but home and happiness, reputation, ease and pleasure, her bread and butter,—all, must come to her through a small gold ring. This is a heavy pressure. It has accumulated behind her through heredity, and continued about her through environment. It has been subtly trained into her through education, till she herself has come to think it a right condition, and pours its influence upon her daughter with increasing impetus. Is it any wonder that women are over-sexed? But for the constant inheritance from the more human male, we should have been queen bees, indeed, long before this. But the daughter of the soldier and the sailor, of the artist, the inventor, the great merchant, has inherited in body and brain her share of his development in each generation, and so stayed somewhat human for all her femininity.

All morbid conditions tend to extinction. One check has always existed to our inordinate sex-development,—nature's ready relief, death. Carried to its furthest excess, the individual has died, the family has become extinct, the nation itself has perished, like Sodom and Gomorrah. Where one function is carried to unnatural excess, others are weakened, and the organism perishes. We are familiar with this in individual cases,—at least, the physician is. We can see it somewhat in the history of nations. From younger races, nearer savagery, nearer the healthful equality of pre-human creatures, has come each new start in history. Persia was older than Greece, and its highly differentiated sexuality had produced the inevitable result of enfeebling the racial qualities. The Greek commander stripped the rich robes and jewels from his Persian captives, and showed their unmanly feebleness to his men. "You have such bodies as these to fight for such plunder as this," he said. In the country, among peasant classes, there is much less sex-distinction than in cities, where wealth enables the women to live in absolute idleness; and even the men manifest the same characteristics. It is from the country and the lower classes that the fresh blood pours into the cities, to be weakened in its turn by the influence of this unnatural distinction until there is none left to replenish the nation.

The inevitable trend of human life is toward higher civilization; but, while that civilization is confined to one sex, it inevitably exaggerates sex-distinction, until the increasing evil of this condition is stronger than all the good of the civiliation attained, and the nation falls. Civilization, be it understood, does not consist in the acquisition of luxuries. Social development is an organic development. A civilized State is one in which the citizens live in organic industrial relation. The more full, free, subtle, and easy that relation; the more perfect the differentiation of labor and exchange of product, with their correlative institutions,—the more perfect is that civilization. To eat, drink, sleep, and keep warm,—these are common to all animals, whether the animal couches in a bed of leaves or one of eiderdown, sleeps in the sun to avoid the wind or builds a furnace-heated house, lies in wait for game or orders a dinner at a hotel. These are but individual animal processes. Whether one lays an egg or a million eggs, whether one bears a cub, a kitten, or a baby, whether one broods its chickens, guards its litter, or tends a nursery full of children, these are but individual animal processes. But to serve each other more and more widely; to live only by such service; to develop special functions, so that we depend for our living on society's return for services that can be of no direct use to ourselves,—this is civilization, our human glory and race-distinction.

All this human progress has been accomplished by men. Women have been left behind, outside, below, having no social relation whatever, merely the sex-relation, whereby they lived. Let us bear in mind that all the tender ties of family are ties of blood, of sex-relationship. A friend, a comrade, a partner,—this is a human relative. Father, mother, son, daughter, sister, brother, husband, wife,—these are sex-relatives. Blood is thicker than water, we say. True. But ties of blood are not those that ring the world with the succeeding waves of progressive religion, art, science, commerce, education, all that makes us human. Man is the human creature. Woman has been checked, starved, aborted in human growth; and the swelling forces of race-development have been driven back in each generation to work in her through sex-functions alone.

This is the way in which the sexuo-economic relation has operated in our species, checking race-development in half of us, and stimulating sex-development in both.

JOSIAH ROYCE

"The Problem of Job"
1898

During most of the twentieth century the Idealist philosopher Josiah Royce (1855–1916) has been remembered in the terms proposed by his critics, especially his two great anti-Idealist colleagues at Harvard, William James and George Santayana. To these earthier-than-thou thinkers, Royce was a tender soul, looking always on the bright side, complacently aloof from the strivings and sufferings of real men and women. "The Problem of Job" (1898) lends credibility to this view of Royce, as it justifies the ghastliest of evils as part of God's perfect plan for the universe. But the piece also displays the directness, the relentlessness, and the vigor that led Royce's admirers to compare him to the reigning heavyweight champion of the world: He was the John L. Sullivan of philosophy. And it is the willingness of Job to argue with God, to demand rational answers, that most endears Job to Royce. Although Royce himself does not draw the comparison, his answer to the problem of evil is, in fact, widely at variance with the response provided in the Book of Job. There, God convinces Job that he deserves no answer at all. But Royce, voicing the more rationalist faith characteristic of the liberal Protestantism of his milieu, believes he can give good reasons why a loving and just God allowed Job to suffer and allowed Armenians to be massacred by Turks.

An irony of Royce's reputation is that while he was continually depicted as "soft" by his tougher-than-thou critics, he, rather than they, actually had been born in a California mining camp and had experienced at first-hand the toughness of frontier life often idealized by tenderfeet from the East. Royce wrote a narrative history of early California, and a novel about its violence, *The Feud at Oakfield Creek* (New York, 1887). But Royce's most influential works were systematic works of philosophy, including *The Religious Aspect of Philosophy* (Boston, 1885), *The Spirit of Modern Philosophy* (Boston, 1892), *The Philosophy of Loyalty* (New York, 1908), and *The Problem of Christianity* 2 vols. (New York, 1913).

Royce's philosophy as a whole is addressed in Bruce Kuklick, *Josiah Royce: An Intellectual Biography* (Indianapolis, 1972). A briefer, more accessible overview can be found in R. Jackson Wilson, *In Quest of Community: Social Philosophy in the United States, 1860–1920* (New York, 1968), 144–70. Two more recent biographies are John Clendenning, *The Life and Thought of Josiah Royce* (Madison, 1985), and Robert V. Hine, *Josiah Royce-From Grass Valley to Harvard* (Norman, Okla., 1991).

The general problem of evil has received, as is well known, a great deal of attention from the philosophers. Few of them, at least in European thought, have been as fearless in stating the issue as was the original author of Job. The solutions offered have, however, been very numerous. For our purposes they may be reduced to a few.

First, then, one may escape Job's paradox by declining altogether to view the world in teleological terms. Evils, such as death, disease, tempests, enemies, fires, are not, so one may declare, the works of God or of Satan, but are natural phenomena. Natural, too, are the phenomena of our desires, of our pains, sorrows and failures. No divine purpose rules or overrules any of these things. That happens to us, at any time, which must happen, in view of our natural limitations and of our ignorance. The way to better things is to understand nature better than we now do. For this view—a view often maintained in our day—there is no problem of evil, in Job's sense, at all. Evil there indeed is, but the only rational problems are those of natural laws. I need not here further consider this method, not of solving but of abolishing the problem before us, since my intent is, in this paper, to suggest the possibility of some genuinely teleological answer to Job's question. I mention this first view only to recognize, historically, its existence.

In the second place, one may deal with our problem by attempting any one, or a number, of those familiar and popular compromises between the belief in a world of natural law and the belief in a teleological order, which are all, as compromises, reducible to the assertion that the presence of evil in the creation is a relatively insignificant, and an inevitable, incident of a plan that produces sentient creatures subject to law. Writers who expound such compromises have to point out that, since a burnt child dreads the fire, pain is, on the whole, useful as a warning. Evil is a transient discipline whereby finite creatures learn their place in the system of things. Again, a sentient world cannot get on without some experience of suffering, since sentience means tenderness. Take away pain (so one still again often insists), take away pain, and we should not learn our share of natural truth. Pain is the pedagogue to teach us natural science. The contagious diseases, for instance, are useful in so far as they lead us in the end to study Bacteriology, and thus to get an insight into the life of certain beautiful creatures of God whose presence in the world we should otherwise blindly overlook! Moreover (to pass to still another variation of this sort of explanation), created beings obviously grow from less to more. First the lower, then the higher. Otherwise there could be no Evolution. And were there no evolution, how much of edifying natural science we should miss! But if one is evolved, if one grows from less to more, there must be something to make the stages of growth. Now evil is useful to mark the lower stages of evolution. If you are to be, first an infant, then a man, or first a savage, then a civilized being, there must be evils attendant upon the earlier stages of your life—evils that make growth welcome and conscious. Thus, were there no colic and croup, were there no tumbles and crying-spells in infancy, there would be no sufficient incentives to loving parents to hasten the growing robustness of their children, and no motives to impel the children to long to grow big! Just so, cannibalism is valuable as a mark of a lower grade of evolution. Had there been no cannibalism, we should realize less joyously than we do what a respectable thing it is to have become civilized! In brief, evil is, as it were, the dirt of the natural order, whose value is that, when you wash it off, you thereby learn the charm of the bath of evolution.

Source: Josiah Royce, *Studies of Good and Evil* (New York: Appleton, 1898), 1–28.

The foregoing are mere hints of familiar methods of playing about the edges of our problem, as children play barefoot in the shallowest reaches of the foam of the sea. In our poem, . . . the speeches ascribed to Elihu contain the most hints of some such way of defining evil, as a merely transient incident of the discipline of the individual. With many writers explanations of this sort fill much space. They are even not without their proper place in popular discussion. But they have no interest for whoever has once come into the presence of Job's problem as it is in itself. A moment's thought reminds us of their superficiality. Pain is useful as a warning of danger. If we did not suffer, we should burn our hands off. Yes, but this explanation of one evil presupposes another, and a still unexplained and greater evil, namely, the existence of the danger of which we need to be thus warned. No doubt it is well that the past sufferings of the Armenians should teach the survivors, say the defenseless women and children, to have a wholesome fear in future of Turks. Does that explain, however, the need for the existence, or for the murderous doings of the Turks? If I can only reach a given goal by passing over a given road, say of evolution, it may be well for me to consent to the toilsome journey. Does that explain why I was created so far from my goal? Discipline, toil, penalty, surgery, are all explicable as means to ends, if only it be presupposed that there exists, and that there is quite otherwise explicable, the necessity for the situations which involve such fearful expenses. One justifies the surgery, but not the disease; the toil, but not the existence of the need for the toil; the penalty, but not the situation which has made the penalty necessary, when one points out that evil is in so many cases medicinal or disciplinary or prophylactic—an incident of imperfect stages of evolution, or the price of a distant good attained through misery. All such explanations, I insist, trade upon borrowed capital. But God, by hypothesis, is no borrower. He produces his own capital of ends and means. Every evil is explained on the foregoing plan only by presupposing at least an equal, and often a greater and a preëxistent evil, namely, the very state of things which renders the first evil the only physically possible way of reaching a given goal. But what Job wants his judge to explain is not that evil A is a physical means of warding off some other greater evil B, in this cruel world where the waters wear away even the stones, and where hopes of man are so much frailer than the stones; but why a God who can do whatever he wishes chooses situations where such a heaped-up mass of evil means become what we should call physical necessitites to the ends now physically possible.

No real explanation of the presence of evil can succeed which declares evil to be a merely physical necessity for one who desires, in this present world, to reach a given goal. Job's business is not with physical accidents, but with the God who chose to make this present nature; and an answer to Job must show that evil is not a physical but a logical necessity—something whose non-existence would simply contradict the very essence, the very perfection of God's own nature and power. This talk of medicinal and disciplinary evil, perfectly fair when applied to our poor fate-bound human surgeons, judges, jailors, or teachers, becomes cruelly, even cynically trivial when applied to explain the ways of a God who is to choose, not only the physical means to an end, but the very *Physis* itself in which path and goal are to exist together. I confess, as a layman, that whenever, at a funeral, in the company of mourners who are immediately facing Job's own personal problem, and who are sometimes, to say the least, wide enough awake to desire not to be stayed with relative comforts, but to ask that terrible and uttermost question of God himself, and to require the direct answer—that whenever I say, in such company I have to listen to these half-way answers, to these superficial plashes in the wavelets at the water's edge of sorrow, while the black, unfathomed ocean of finite evil spreads out before our wide-opened eyes—well, at such times this trivial speech about useful burns and salutary medicines makes me, and I fancy others, simply and wearily heartsick. Some words are due to children at school, to peevish patients in the sick-room who need a little temporary quieting. But quite other speech is due to men and women when they are wakened to the higher reason of Job by the fierce anguish of our mortal life's ultimate facts. They deserve either our simple silence, or, if we are ready to speak, the speech of people who ourselves inquire as Job inquired.

A third method of dealing with our problem is in essence identical with the course which, in a very antiquated form, the friends of Job adopt. This method takes its best known expression in the doctrine that the presence of evil in the world is explained by the fact that the value of free will in moral agents logically involves, and so explains and justifies, the divine permission of the evil deeds of those finite beings who freely choose to sin, as well as the inevitable fruits of the sins. God creates agents with free will. He does so because the existence of such agents has of itself an infinite worth. Were there no free agents, the highest good could not be. But such agents, because they are free, can offend. The divine justice of necessity pursues such offenses with attendant evils. These evils, the result of sin, must, logically speaking, be permitted to exist, if God once creates the agents who have free will, and himself remains, as he must logically do, a just God. How much ill thus results depends upon the choice of the free agents, not upon God, who wills to have only good chosen, but of necessity must leave his free creatures to their own devices, so far as concerns their power to sin.

This view has the advantage of undertaking to regard evil as a logically necessary part of a perfect moral order, and not as a mere incident of an imperfectly adjusted physical mechanism. So dignified a doctrine, by virtue of its long history and its high theological reputation, needs here no extended exposition. I assume it as familiar, and pass at once to its difficulties. It has its share of truth. There is, I doubt not, moral free will in the universe. But the presence of evil in the world simply cannot be explained by free will alone. This is easy to show. One who maintains this view asserts, in substance, "All real evils are the results of the acts of free and finite moral agents." These agents may be angels or men. If there is evil in the city, the Lord has *not* done it, except in so far as his justice has acted in readjusting wrongs already done. Such ill is due to the deeds of his creatures. But hereupon one asks at once, in presence of any ill, "Who did this?" Job's friends answer: "The sufferer himself; his deed wrought his own undoing. God punishes only the sinner. Every one suffers for his own wrongdoing. Your ill is the result of your crime."

But Job, and all his defenders of innocence, must at once reply: "Empirically speaking, this is obviously, in our visible world, simply not true. The sufferer may suffer innocently. The ill is often undeserved. The fathers sin; the child, diseased from birth, degraded, or a born wretch, may pay the penalty. The Turk or the active rebel sins. Armenia's helpless women and babes cry in vain unto God for help."

Hereupon the reply comes, although not indeed from Job's friends: "Alas! it is so. Sin means suffering; but the innocent may suffer *for* the guilty. This, to be sure, is God's way. One cannot help it. It is so." But therewith the whole effort to explain evil as a logically necessary result of free will and of divine justice alone is simply abandoned. The unearned ills are not justly due to the free will that indeed partly caused them, but to God who declines to protect the innocent. God owes the Turk and the rebel their due. He also owes to his innocent creatures, the babes and the women, his shelter. He owes to the sinning father his penalty, but to the son, born in our visible world a lost soul from the womb, God owes the shelter of his almighty wing, and no penalty. Thus Job's cry is once more in place. The ways of God are not thus justified.

But the partisan of free will as the true explanation of ill may reiterate his view in a new form. He may insist that we see but a fragment. Perhaps the soul born here as if lost, or the wretch doomed to pangs now unearned, sinned of old, in some previous state of existence. Perhaps Karma is to blame. You expiate to-day the sins of your own former existences. Thus the Hindoos varied the theme of our familiar doctrine. This is what Hindoo friends might have said to Job. Well, admit even that, if you like; and what then follows? Admit that here or in former ages the free deed of every present sufferer earned as its penalty every ill, physical or moral, that appears as besetting just this sufferer to-day. Admit that, and what logically follows? It follows, so I must insist, that the moral world itself, which this free-will theory of the source of evil, thus abstractly stated, was to save, is destroyed in its very heart and center.

For consider. A suffers ill. B sees A suffering. Can B, the onlooker, help his suffering neighbor, A? Can he comfort him in any true way? No, a miserable comforter must B prove, like Job's friends, so long as B, believing in our present hypothesis, clings strictly to the logic of this abstract free-will explanation of the origin of evil. T A he says: "Well, you suffer for your own ill-doing. I therefore simply cannot relieve you. This is God's world of justice. If I tried to hinder God's justice from working in your case, I should at best only postpone your evil day. It would come, for God is just. You are hungry, thirsty, naked, sick, in prison. What can I do about it? All this is your own deed come back to you. God himself, although justly punishing, is not the author of this evil. You are the sole originator of the ill." "Ah!" so A may cry out, "but can you not give me light, insight, instruction, sympathy? Can you not at least teach me to become good?" "No," B must reply, if he is a logical believer in the sole efficacy of the private free will of each finite agent as the one source, under the divine justice, of that agent's ill: "No, if you deserved light or any other comfort, God, being just, would enlighten you himself, even If I absolutely refused. But if you do not deserve light, I should preach to you in vain, for God's justice would harden your heart against any such good fortune as I could offer you from without, even if I spoke with the tongues of men and of angels. Your free will is yours. No deed of mine could give you a good free will, for what I gave you from without would not be *your* free will at all. Nor can any one but you cause your free will to be this or that. A great gulf is fixed between us. You and I, as sovereign free agents, live in God's holy world in sin-tight compartments and in evil-tight compartments too. I cannot hurt you, nor you me. You are damned for your own sins, while all that I can do is to look out for my own salvation." This, I say, is the logically inevitable result of asserting that every ill, physical or moral, that can happen to any agent, is solely the result of that agent's own free will acting under the government of the divine justice. The only possible consequence would indeed be that we live, every soul of us, in separate, as it were absolutely fire-proof, free-will compartments, so that real coöperation as to good and ill is excluded. What more cynical denial of the reality of any sort of moral world could be imagined than is involved in this horrible thesis, which no sane partisan of the abstract and traditional free-will explanation of the source of evil will to-day maintain, precisely because no such partisan really knows or can know what his doctrine logically means, while still continuing to maintain it. Yet whenever one asserts with pious obscurity that "No harm can come to the righteous," one in fact implies, with logical necessity, just this cynical consequence.

There remains a fourth doctrine as to our problem. This doctrine is in essence the thesis of philosophical idealism, a thesis which I myself feel bound to maintain, and, so far as space here permits, to explain. The theoretical basis of this view, the philosophical reasons for the notion of the divine nature which it implies, I cannot here explain. That is another argument. But I desire to indicate how the view in question deals with Job's problem.

This view first frankly admits that Job's problem is, upon Job's presuppositions, simply and absolutely insoluble. Grant Job's own presupposition that God is a being other than this world, that he is its external creator and ruler, and then all solutions fail. God is then either cruel or helpless, as regards all real finite ill of the sort that Job endures. Job, moreover, is right in demanding a reasonable answer to his question. The only possible answer is, however, one that undertakes to develop what I hold to be the immortal soul of the doctrine of the divine atonement. The answer to Job is: God is not in ultimate essence another being than yourself. He is the Absolute Being. You truly are one with God, part of his life. He is the very soul of your soul. And so, here is the first truth: When you suffer, *your sufferings are God's sufferings,* not his external work, not his external penalty, not the fruit of his neglect, but identically his own personal woe. In you God himself suffers, precisely as you do, and has all your concern in overcoming this grief.

The true question then is: Why does God thus suffer? The sole possible, necessary, and sufficient answer is, Because without suffering, without ill, without woe, evil, tragedy, God's life could not be perfected. This grief is not a physical means to an external end. It is a logically necessary and eternal constituent of the divine life. It is logically necessary that the Captain of your salvation should be perfect through suffering. No outer nature compels him. He chooses this because he chooses his own perfect selfhood. He is perfect. His world is the best possible world. Yet all its finite regions know not only of joy but of defeat and sorrow, for thus alone, in the completeness of his eternity, can God in his wholeness be triumphantly perfect.

This I say, is my thesis. In the absolute oneness of God with the sufferer, in the concept of the suffering and therefore triumphant God, lies the logical solution of the problem of evil. The doctrine of philosophical idealism is, as regards its purely theoretical aspects, a fairly familiar metaphysical theory at the present time. One may, then, presuppose here as known the fact that, for reasons which I have not now to expound, the idealist maintains that there is in the universe but one perfectly real being, namely, the Absolute, that the Absolute is self-conscious, and that his world is essentially in its wholeness the fulfillment *in actu* of an all-perfect ideal. We ourselves exist as fragments of the absolute life, or better, as partial functions in the unity of the absolute and conscious process of the world. On the other hand, our existence and our individuality are not illusory, but are what they are in an organic unity with the whole life of the Absolute Being. This doctrine once presupposed, our present task is to inquire what case idealism can make for the thesis just indicated as its answer to Job's problem.

In endeavoring to grapple with the theoretical problem of the place of evil in a world that, on the whole, is to be conceived, not only as good, but as perfect, there is happily one essentially decisive consideration concerning good and evil which falls directly within the scope of our own human experience, and which concerns matters at once familiar and momentous as well as too much neglected in philosophy. When we use such words as good, evil, perfect, we easily deceive ourselves by the merely abstract meanings which we associate with each of the terms taken apart from the other. We forget the experiences from which the words have been abstracted. To these experiences we must return whenever we want really to comprehend the words. If we take the mere words, in their abstraction, it is easy to say, for instance, that if life has any evil in it at all, it must needs not be so perfect as life would be were there no evil in it whatever. Just so, speaking abstractly, it is easy to say that, in estimating life, one has to set the good over against the evil, and to compare their respective sums. It is easy to declare that, since we hate evil, wherever and just so far as we recognize it, our sole human interest in the world must be furthered by the removal of evil from the world. And thus viewing the case, one readily comes to say that if God views as not only good but perfect a world in which we find so much evil, the divine point of view must be very foreign to ours, so that Job's rebellious pessimism seems well in order, and Prometheus appears to defy the world-ruler in a genuinely humane spirit. Shocked, however, by the apparent impiety of this result, some teachers, considering divine matters, still misled by the same one-sided use of words, have opposed one falsely abstract view by another, and have strangely asserted that the solution must be in proclaiming that since God's world, the real world, in order to be perfect, must be without evil, what we men call evil must be a mere illusion—a mirage of the human point of view—a dark vision which God, who sees all truth, sees not at all. To God, so this view asserts, the eternal world in its wholeness is not only perfect, but has merely the perfection of an utterly transparent crystal, unstained by any color of ill. Only mortal error imagines that there is any evil. There is no evil but only good in the real world, and that is why God finds the world perfect, whatever mortals dream.

Now neither of these abstract views is my view. I consider them both the result of a thoughtless trust in abstract words. I regard evil as a distinctly real fact, a fact just as real as the most helpless and hopeless sufferer finds it to be when he is in pain. Furthermore, I hold that God's point of view is not foreign to ours. I hold that God willingly, freely, and consciously suffers in us when we suffer, and that our grief is his. And despite all this I maintain that the world from God's point of view fulfills the divine ideal and is perfect. And I hold that when we abandon the one-sided abstract ideas which the words good, evil, and perfect suggest, and when we go back to the concrete experiences upon which these very words are founded, we can see, even within the limits of our own experience, facts which make these very paradoxes perfectly intelligible, and even commonplace.

As for that essentially pernicious view, nowadays somewhat current amongst a certain class of gentle but inconsequent people—the view that all evil is *merely* an illusion and that there is no such thing in God's world—I can say of it only in passing that it is often advanced as an idealistic view, but that, in my opinion, it is false idealism. Good idealism it is to regard all finite experience as an appearance, a hint, often a very poor hint, of deeper truth. Good idealism it is to admit that man can err about truth that lies beyond his finite range of experience. And very good idealism it is to assert that all truth, and so all finite experience, exists in and for the mind of God, and nowhere outside of or apart from God. But it is not good idealism to assert that any facts which fall within the range of finite experience are, even while they are experienced, mere illusions. God's truth is inclusive, not exclusive. What you experience God experiences.

The difference lies only in this, that God sees in unity what you see in fragments. For the rest, if one said, "The source and seat of evil is only the error of mortal mind," one would but have changed the name of one's problem. If the evil were but the error, the error would still be the evil, and altering the name would not have diminished the horror of the evil of this finite world.

But I hasten from the false idealism to the true; from the abstractions to the enlightening insights of our life. As a fact, idealism does not say: The finite world is, as such, a mere illusion. A sound idealism says, whatever we experience is a fragment, and, as far as it goes, a genuine fragment of the truth of the divine mind. With this principle before us, let us consider directly our own experiences of good and of evil, to see whether they are as abstractly opposed to each other as the mere words often suggest. We must begin with the elementary and even trivial facts. We shall soon come to something deeper.

By good, as we mortals experience it, we mean something that, when it comes or is expected, we actively welcome, try to attain or keep, and regard with content. By evil in general, as it is in our experience, we mean whatever we find in any sense repugnant and intolerable. I use the words repugnant and intolerable because I wish to indicate that words for evil frequently, like the words for good, directly refer to our actions as such. Commonly and rightly, when we speak of evil, we make reference to acts of resistance, of struggle, of shrinking, of flight, of removal of ourselves from a source of mischief—acts which not only follow upon the experience of evil, but which serve to define in a useful fashion what we mean by evil. The opposing acts of pursuit and of welcome define what we mean by good. By the evil which we experience we mean precisely whatever we regard as something to be gotten rid of, shrunken from, put out of sight, of hearing, or of memory, eschewed, expelled, assailed, or otherwise directly or indirectly resisted. By good we mean whatever we regard as something to be welcomed, pursued, won, grasped, held, persisted in, preserved. And we show all this in our acts in presence of any grade of good or evil, sensuous, aesthetic, ideal, moral. To shun, to flee, to resist, to destroy, these are our primary attitudes towards ill; the opposing acts are our primary attitudes towards the good; and whether you regard us as animals or as moralists, whether it is a sweet taste, a poem, a virtue, or God that we look to as good, and whether it is a burn or a temptation, an outward physical fore, or a stealthy, inward, ideal enemy, that we regard as evil. In all our organs of voluntary movement, in all our deeds, in a turn of the eye, in a sigh, a groan, in a hostile gesture, in an act of silent contempt, we can show in endlessly varied ways the same general attitude of repugnance.

But man is a very complex creature. He has many organs. He performs many acts at once, and he experiences his performance of these acts in one highly complex life of consciousness. As the next feature of his life we all observe that he can at the same time shun one object and grasp at another. In this way he can have at once present to him a consciousness of good and a consciousness of ill. But so far in our account these sorts of experience appear merely as facts side by side. Man loves, and he *also* hates, loves this, and hates that, assumes an attitude of repugnance towards one object, while he welcomes another. So far the usual theory follows man's life, and calls it an experience of good and ill as mingled but exclusively and abstractly opposed facts. For such a view the final question as to the worth of a man's life is merely the question whether there are more intense acts of satisfaction and of welcome than of repugnance and disdain in his conscious life.

But this is by no means an adequate notion of the complexity of man's life, even as an animal. If every conscious act of hindrance, of thwarting, of repugnance, means just in so far an awareness of some evil, it is noteworthy that men can have and can show just such tendencies, not only towards external experiences, but towards their own acts. That is, men can be seen trying to thwart and to hinder even their own acts themselves, at the very moment when they note the occurrence of these acts. One can consciously have an impulse to do something, and at that very moment a conscious disposition to hinder or to thwart as an evil that very impulse. If, on the other hand, every conscious act of attainment, of pursuit, of reinforcement, involves the awareness of some good, it is equally obvious that once can show by one's acts a disposition to reinforce or to emphasize or to increase, not only the externally present gifts of fortune, but also one's own deeds, in so far as one observes them. And in our complex lives it is common enough to find ourselves actually trying to reinforce and to insist upon a situation which involves for us, even at the moment of its occurrence, a great deal of repugnance. In such cases we often act as if we felt the very thwarting of our own primary impulses to be so much of a conscious good that we persist in pursuing and reinforcing the very situation in which this thwarting and hindering of our own impulses is sure to arise.

In brief, as phenomena of this kind show, man is a being who can to a very great extent find a sort of secondary satisfaction in the very act of thwarting his own desires, and thus of assuring for the time his own dissatisfactions. On the other hand, man can to an indefinite degree find himself dissatisfied with his satisfaction and disposed to thwart, not merely his external enemies, but his own inmost impulses themselves. But I now affirm that in all such cases you cannot simply say that man is preferring the less of two evils, or the greater of two goods, as if the good and evil stood merely side by side in his experience. On the contrary, in such cases, man is not merely setting his acts or his estimates of good and evil side by side and taking the sum of each; but he is making his own relatively primary acts, impulses, desires, the objects of all sorts of secondary impulses, desires, and reflective observations. His whole inner state is one of tension: and he is either making a secondary experience of evil out of his estimate of a primary experience of good, as is the case when he at once finds himself disposed to pursue a given good and to thwart this pursuit as being an evil pursuit; or else he is making a secondary experience of good out of his primary experience of evil, as when he is primarily dissatisfied with his situation, but yet secondarily regards this very dissatisfaction as itself a desirable state. In this way man comes not only to love some things and also to hate other things, he comes to love his own hates and to hate his own loves in an endlessly complex hierarchy of superposed interests in his own interests.

Now it is easy to say that such states of inner tension, where our conscious lives are full of a warfare of the self with itself, are contradictory or absurd states. But it is easy to say this only when you dwell on the words and fail to observe the facts of experience. As a fact, not only our lowest but our highest states of activity are the ones which are fullest of this crossing, conflict, and complex interrelation of loves and hates, of attractions and repugnances. As a merely physiological fact, we begin no muscular act without at the same time initiating acts which involve the innervation of opposing sets of muscles, and these opposing sets of muscles hinder each other's freedom. Every sort of control of movement means the conflicting play of opposed muscular impulses. We do nothing simple, and we will no complex act without willing what involves a certain measure of opposition between the impulses or partial acts which go to make up the whole act. If one passes from single acts to long series of acts, one finds only the more obviously this interweaving of repugnance and of acceptance, of pursuit and of flight upon which every complex type of conduct depends.

One could easily at this point spend time by dwelling upon numerous and relatively trivial instances of this interweaving of conflicting motives as it appears in all our life. I prefer to pass such instances over with a mere mention. There is, for instance, the whole marvelous consciousness of play, in its benign and in its evil forms. In any game that fascinates, one loves victory and shuns defeat, and yet as a loyal supporter of the game scorns anything that makes victory certain in advance; thus as a lover of fair play preferring to risk the defeat that he all the while shuns, and partly thwarting the very love of victory that from moment to moment fires his hopes. There are, again, the numerous cases in which we prefer to go to places where we are sure to be in a considerable measure dissatisfied; to engage, for instance, in social functions that absorbingly fascinate us despite or even in view of the very fact that, as long as they continue, they keep us in a state of tension which makes us, amongst other things, long to have the whole occasion over. Taking a wider view, one may observe that the greater part of the freest products of the activity of civilization, in ceremonies, in formalities, in the long social drama of flight, of pursuit, of repartee, of contest and of courtesy, involve an elaborate and systematic delaying and hindering of elemental human desires, which we continually outwit, postpone and thwart, even while we nourish them. When students of human nature assert that hunger and love rule the social world, they recognize that the elemental in human nature is trained by civilization into the service of the highest demands of the Spirit. But such students have to recognize that the elemental rules the higher world only in so far as the elemental is not only cultivated, but endlessly thwarted, delayed, outwitted, like a constitutional monarch, who is said to be a sovereign, but who, while he rules, must not govern.

But I pass from such instances, which in all their universality are still, I admit, philosophically speaking trivial, because they depend upon the accidents of human nature. I pass from these instances to point out what must be the law, not only of human nature, but of every broader form of life as well. I maintain that this organization of life by virtue of the tension of manifold impulses and interests is not a mere accident of our imperfect human nature, but must be a type of the organization of every rational life. There are good and bad states of tension, there are conflicts that can only be justified when resolved into some higher form of harmony. But I insist that, in general, the only harmony that can exist in the realm of the spirit is the harmony that we possess when we thwart the present but more elemental impulse for the sake of the higher unity of experience; as when we rejoice in the endurance of the tragedies of life, because they show us the depth of life, or when we know that it is better to have loved and lost than never to have loved at all, or when we possess a virtue in the moment of victory over the tempter. And the reason why this is true lies in the fact that the more one's experience fulfills ideals, the more that experience presents to one, not of ignorance, but of triumphantly wealthy acquaintance with the facts of manifold, varied and tragic life, full of tension and thereby of unity. Now this is an universal and not merely human law. It is not those innocent of evil who are fullest of the life of God, but those who in their own case have experienced the triumph over evil. It is not those naturally ignorant of fear, or those who, like Siegfried, have never shivered, who possess the genuine experience of courage; but the brave are those who have fears, but control their fears.

Such know the genuine virtues of the hero. Were it otherwise, only the stupid could be perfect heroes.

To be sure it is quite false to say, as the foolish do, that the object of life is merely that we may "know life" as an irrational chaos of experiences of good and evil. But knowing the good in life is a matter which concerns the form, rather than the mere content of life. One who knows life wisely knows indeed much of the content of life; but he knows the good of life in so far as, in the unity of his experience, he finds the evil of his experience not abolished, but subordinated, and in so far relatively thwarted by a control which annuls its triumph even while experiencing its existence.

Generalizing the lesson of experience we may then say: It is logically impossible that a complete knower of truth should fail to know, to experience, to have present to his insight, the fact of actually existing evil. On the other hand, it is equally impossible for one to know a higher good than comes from the subordination of evil to good in a total experience. When one first loving, in an elemental way, whatever you please, himself hinders, delays, thwarts his elemental interest in the interest of some larger whole of experience, he not only knows more fact, but he possesses a higher good than would or could be present to one who was aware neither of the elemental impulse, nor of the thwarting of it in the tension of a richer life. The knowing of the good, in the higher sense, depends upon contemplating the overcoming and subordination of a less significant impulse, which survives even in order that it should be subordinated. Now this law, this form of the knowledge of the good, applies as well to the existence of moral as to that of sensuous ill. If moral evil were simply destroyed and wiped away from the external world, the knowledge of moral goodness would also be destroyed. For the love of moral good is the thwarting of lower loves for the sake of the higher organization. What is needed, then, for the definition of the divine knowledge of a world that in its wholeness is perfect, is not divine knowledge that shall ignore, wipe out and utterly make naught the existence of any ill, whether physical or moral, but a divine knowledge to which shall be present that love of the world as a whole which is fulfilled in the endurance of physical ill, in the subordination of moral ill, in the thwarting of impulses which survive even when subordinated, in the acceptance of repugnances which are still eternal, in the triumph over an enemy that endures even through its eternal defeat, and in the discovery that the endless tension of the finite world is included in the contemplative consciousness of the repose and harmony of eternity. To view God's nature thus is to view his nature as the whole idealistic theory views him, not as the Infinite One beyond the finite imperfections, but as the being whose unity determines the very constitution, the lack, the tension, and relative disharmony of the finite world.

The existence of evil, then, is not only consistent with the perfection of the universe, but is necessary for the very existence of that perfection. This is what we see when we no longer permit ourselves to be deceived by the abstract meanings of the words good and evil into thinking that these two opponents exist merely as mutually exclusive facts side by side in experience, but when we go back to the facts of life and perceive that all relatively higher good, in the trivial as in the more truly spiritual realm, is known only in so far as, from some higher reflective point of view, we accept as good the thwarting of an existent interest that is even thereby declared to be a relative ill, and love a tension of various impulses which even thereby involves, as the object of our love, the existence of what gives us aversion or grief. Now if the love of God is more inclusive than the love of man, even as the divine world of experience is richer than the human world, we can simply set no human limit to the intensity of conflict, to the tragedies of existence, to the pangs of finitude, to the degree of moral ill, which in the end is included in the life that God not only loves, but finds the fulfillment of the perfect ideal. If peace means satisfaction, acceptance of the whole of an experience as good, and if even we, in our weakness, can frequently find rest in the very presence of conflict and of tension, in the very endurance of ill in a good cause, in the hero's triumph over temptation, or in the mourner's tearless refusal to accept the lower comforts of forgetfulness, or to wish that the lost one's preciousness had been less painfully revealed by death—well, if even we know our little share of this harmony in the midst of the wrecks and disorders of life, what limit shall we set to the divine power to face this world of his own sorrows, and to find peace in the victory over all its ills.

But in the last expression I have pronounced the word that serves to link this theory as to the place of evil in a good world with the practical problem of every sufferer. Job's rebellion came from the thought that God, as a sovereign, is far off, and that, for his pleasure, his creature suffers. Our own theory comes to the mourner with the assurance: "Your suffering, just as it is in you, is God's suffering. No chasm divides you from God. He is not remote from you even in his eternity. He is here. His eternity means merely the completeness of his experience. But that completeness is inclusive. Your sorrow is one of the included facts." I do not say: "God sympathizes with you from without, would spare you if he could, pities you with helpless external pity merely as a father pities his children." I say: "God here sorrows, not *with* but *in* your sorrow. Your grief is identically his grief, and what you know as your loss, God knows as his loss, just in and through the very moment when you grieve."

But hereupon the sufferer perchance responds: "If this is God's loss, could he not have prevented it? To him are present in unity all the worlds; and yet he must lack just this for which I grieve." I respond: "He suffers here that he may triumph. For the triumph of the wise is no easy thing. Their lives are not light, but sorrowful. Yet they rejoice in their sorrow, not, to be sure, because it is mere experience, but because, for them, it becomes part of a strenuous whole of life. They wander and find their home even in wandering. They long, and attain through their very love of longing. Peace they find in triumphant warfare. Contentment they have most of all in endurance. Sovereignty they win in endless service. The eternal world contains Gethsemane."

Yet the mourners may still insist: "If my sorrow is God's, his triumph is not mine. Mine is the woe. His is the peace." But my theory is a philosophy. It proposes to be coherent. I must persist: "It is your fault that you are thus sundered from God's triumph. His experience in its wholeness cannot now be yours, for you just as you—this individual—are now but a fragment, and see his truth as through a glass darkly. But if you see his truth at all, through even the dimmest light of a glimmering reason, remember, that truth is in fact your own truth, your own fulfillment, the whole from which your life cannot be divorced, the reality that you mean even when you most doubt, the desire of your heart even when you are most blind, the perfection that you unconsciously strove for even when you were an infant, the complete Self apart from whom you mean nothing, the very life that gives your life the only value which it can have. In thought, if not in the fulfillment of thought, in aim if not in attainment of aim, in aspiration if not in the presence of the revealed fact, you can view God's triumph and peace as your triumph and peace. Your defeat will be no less real than it is, nor will you falsely call your evil a mere illusion. But you will see not only the grief but the truth, your truth, your rescue, your triumph."

Well, to what ill-fortune does not just such reasoning apply? I insist: our conclusion is essentially universal. It discounts any evil that experience may contain. All the horrors of the natural order, all the concealments of the divine plan by our natural ignorance, find their general relation to the unity of the divine experience indicated in advance by this account of the problem of evil.

"Yes," one may continue, "ill-fortune you have discovered, but how about moral evil? What if the sinner now triumphantly retorts: 'Aha! So my will is God's will. All then is well with me.'" I reply: What I have said disposes of moral ill precisely as definitely as of physical ill. What the evil will is to the good man, whose goodness depends upon its existence, but also upon the thwarting and the condemnation of its aim, just such is the sinner's will to the divine plan. God's will, we say to the sinner, is your will. Yes, but it is your will thwarted, scorned, over-come, defeated. In the eternal world you are seen, possessed, present, but your damnation is also seen including and thwarting you. Your apparent victory in this world stands simply for the vigor of your impulses. God will you not to triumph. And that is the use of you in the world—the use of evil generally—to be hated but endured, to be triumphed over through the very fact of your presence, to be willed down even in the very life of which you are a part.

But to the serious moral agent we say: What you mean when you say that evil in this temporal world ought not to exist, and ought to be suppressed, is simply what God means by seeing that evil ought to be and is endlessly thwarted, endured, but subordinated. In the natural world you are the minister of God's triumph. Your deed is his. You can never clean the world of evil: but you can subordinate evil. The justification of the presence in the world of the morally evil becomes apparent to us mortals only in so far as this evil is overcome and condemned. It exists only that it may be cast down. Courage, then, for God works in you. In the order of time you embody in outer acts what is for him the truth of his eternity.

WILLIAM JAMES

"The Will to Believe"
1897

Of the host of late-nineteenth-century American intellectuals preoccupied with the relation of religion to science, William James (1842–1910) was uniquely creative and influential. This preoccupation informed his work as a psychologist, philosopher, and popular lecturer and essayist. Although "The Will to Believe" of 1897, which follows, was his most concentrated and widely quoted monument to this preoccupation with the destiny of religion in an age of science, his most probing and detailed exploration of religion was *The Varieties of Religious Experience* (New York, 1902). We also remember James for *The Principles of Psychology* (New York, 1890), and for *Pragmatism* (New York, 1907), a selection from which opens Part Two.

For an interpretation of James's entire career as a response to the apparent conflict between religion and science, see David A. Hollinger, "William James and the Culture of Inquiry," in Hollinger's *In the American Province: Studies in the History and Historiography of Ideas* (Bloomington, Ind., 1985), 3–22. In "The Will to Believe," James insisted that science had yet to show the falsity of the essentials of religious belief. He argued further that the actual direction taken by science was influenced by the desires and expectations of the inquirers themselves. Many scientists had come to regard religion as a "dead hypothesis," James complained, and were thus not likely to produce evidence to support its validity. "The Will to Believe" is best read in relation to James's foil, an agnostic classic published twenty years before by the British mathematician W. K. Clifford: "The Ethics of Belief," *Contemporary Review* 29 (1877, 289–309. Clifford was concerned with the social consequences of belief, whereas the more socially complacent James addressed the spiritual anxieties of the individual soul. Clifford told horror stories about frauds, fakers, and dupes and preached the duty of critically scrutinizing all beliefs; James lamented the believer's intimidation by scientific authority and defended the right to resist cognitive tyranny. As James himself latter acknowledged, his primary concern in this essay is less with the will than with the legitimacy of relying upon it; a better title might have substituted *right* for "will." A good sampling of the most recent scholarship on James by philosophers, historians, and literary scholars can be found in Ruth Anna Putnam, ed., *The Cambridge Companion to William James* (Cambridge, 1997). For additional comments on James and more bibliographical suggestions, see the headnote to James's "What Pragmatism Means."

In the recently published *Life* by Leslie Stephen of his brother, Fitz-James, there is an account of a school to which the latter went when he was a boy. The teacher, a certain Mr. Guest, used to converse with his pupils in this wise: "Gurney, what is the difference between justification and sanctification?—Stephen, prove the omnipotence of God!" etc. In the midst of our Harvard freethinking and indifference we are prone to imagine that here at your good old orthodox College conversation continues to be somewhat upon this order; and to show you that we at Harvard have not lost all interest in these vital subjects, I have brought with me to-night something like a sermon on justification by faith to read to you,—I mean an essay in justification *of* faith, a defence of our right to adopt a believing attitude in religious matters, in spite of the fact that our merely logical intellect may not have been coerced. 'The Will to Believe,' accordingly, is the title of my paper.

I have long defended to my own students the lawfulness of voluntarily adopted faith; but as soon as they have got well imbued with the logical spirit, they have as a rule refused to admit my contention to be lawful philosophically, even though in point of fact they were personally all the time chock-full of some faith or other themselves. I am all the while, however, so profoundly convinced that my own position is correct, that your invitation has seemed to me a good occasion to make my statements more clear. Perhaps your minds will be more open than those with which I have hitherto had to deal. I will be as little technical as I can, though I must begin by setting up some technical distinctions that will help us in the end.

Let us give the name of *hypothesis* to anything that may be proposed to our belief; and just as the electricians speak of live and dead wires, let us speak of any hypothesis as either *live* or *dead*. A live hypothesis is one which appeals as a real possibility to him to whom it is proposed. If I ask you to believe in the Mahdi, the notion makes no electric connection with your nature,—it refuses to scintillate with any credibility at all. As an hypothesis it is completely dead. To an Arab, however (even if he be not one of the Mahdi's followers), the hypothesis is among the mind's possibilities: it is alive. This shows that deadness and liveness in an hypothesis are not intrinsic properties, but relations to the individual thinker. They are measured by his willingness to act. The maximum of liveness in an hypothesis means willingness to act irrevocably. Practically, that means belief; but there is some believing tendency wherever there is willingness to act at all.

Next, let us call the decision between two hypotheses an *option*. Options may be of several kinds. They may be—1, *living* or *dead;* 2, *forced* or *avoidable;* 3, *momentous* or *trivial;* and for our purposes we may call an option a *genuine* option when it is of the forced, living, and momentous kind.

1. A living option is one in which both hypotheses are live ones. If I say to you: "Be a theosophist or be a Mohammedan," it is probably a dead option, because for you neither hypothesis is likely to be alive. But if I say: "Be an agnostic or be a Christian," it is otherwise: trained as you are, each hypothesis makes some appeal, however small, to your belief.

2. Next, if I say to you: "Choose between going out with your umbrella or without it," I do not offer you a genuine option, for it is not forced. You can easily avoid it by not going out at all. Similarly, if I say, "Either love me or hate me," "Either call my theory true or call it false," your option is avoidable. You may remain indifferent to me,

Source: William James, *The Will to Believe* (New York: Longman's, 1897), 1–31.

neither loving nor hating, and you may decline to offer any judgment as to my theory. But if I say, "Either accept this truth or go without it," I put on you a forced option, for there is no standing place outside of the alternative. Every dilemma based on a complete logical disjunction, with no possibility of not choosing, is an option of this forced kind.

3. Finally, if I were Dr. Nansen and proposed to you to join my North Pole expedition, your option would be momentous; for this would probably be your only similar opportunity, and your choice now would either exclude you from the North Pole sort of immortality altogether or put at least the chance of it into your hands. He who refuses to embrace a unique opportunity loses the prize as surely as if he tried and failed. *Per contra,* the option is trivial when the opportunity is not unique, when the stake is insignificant, or when the decision is reversible if it later prove unwise. Such trivial options abound in the scientific life. A chemist finds an hypothesis live enough to spend a year in its verification: he believes in it to that extent. But if his experiments prove inconclusive either way, he is quit for his loss of time, no vital harm being done.

It will facilitate our discussion if we keep all these distinctions well in mind.

The next matter to consider is the actual psychology of human opinion. When we look at certain facts, it seems as if our passional and volitional nature lay at the root of all our convictions. When we look at others, it seems as if they could know nothing when the intellect had once said its say. Let us take the latter facts up first.

Does it not seem preposterous on the very face of it to talk of our opinions being modifiable at will? Can our will either help or hinder our intellect in its perceptions of truth? Can we, by just willing it, believe that Abraham Lincoln's existence is a myth, and that the portraits of him in *McClure's Magazine* are all of some one else? Can we, by any effort of our will, or by any strength of wish that it were true, believe ourselves well and about when we are roaring with rheumatism in bed, or feel certain that the sum of the two one-dollar bills in our pocket must be a hundred dollars? We can *say* any of these things, but we are absolutely impotent to believe them; and of just such things is the whole fabric of the truths that we do believe in made up,—matters of fact, immediate or remote, as Hume said, and relations between ideas, which are either there or not there for us if we see them so, and which if not there cannot be put there by any action of our own.

In Pascal's *Thoughts* there is a celebrated passage known in literature as Pascal's wager. In it he tries to force us into Christianity by reasoning as if our concern with truth resembled our concern with the stakes in a game of chance. Translated freely his words are these: You must either believe or not believe what God is—which will you do? Your human reason cannot say. A game is going on between you and the nature of things which at the day of judgment will bring out either heads or tails. Weigh what your gains and your losses would be if you should stake all you have on heads, or God's existence: if you win in such case, you gain eternal beatitude; if you lose, you lose nothing at all. If there were an infinity of chances, and only one for God in this wager, still you ought to stake your all on God; for though you surely risk a finite loss by this procedure, any finite loss is reasonable, even a certain one is reasonable, if there is but the possibility of infinite gain. Go, then, and take holy water, and have masses said; belief will come and stupefy your scruples,—*Cela vous fera croire et vous abêtira.* Why should you not? At bottom, what have you to lose?

You probably feel that when religious faith expresses itself thus, in the language of the gaming-table, it is put to its last trumps. Surely Pascal's own personal belief in masses and holy water had far other springs; and this celebrated page of his is but an argument for others, a last desperate snatch at a weapon against the hardness of the unbelieving heart. We feel that a faith in masses and holy water adopted willfully after such a mechanical calculation would lack the inner soul of faith's reality; and if we were ourselves in the place of the Deity, we would probably take particular pleasure in cutting off believers of this pattern from their infinite reward. It is evident that unless there be some pre-existing tendency to believe in masses and holy water, the option offered to the will by Pascal is not a living option. Certainly no Turk ever took to masses and holy water on its account; and even to us Protestants these means of salvation seem such foregone impossibilities that Pascal's logic, invoked for them specifically, leaves us unmoved. As well might the Mahdi write to us, saying, "I am the Expected One whom God has created in his effulgence. You shall be infinitely happy if you confess me; otherwise you shall be cut off from the light of the sun. Weigh, then, your infinite gain if I am genuine against your finite sacrifice if I am not!" His logic would be that of Pascal; but he would vainly use it on us, for the hypothesis he offers us is dead. No tendency to act on it exists in us to any degree.

The talk of believing by our volition seems, then, from one point of view, simply silly. From another point of view it is worse than silly, it is vile. When one turns to the magnificent edifice of the physical sciences, and sees how it was reared; what thousands of disinterested moral lives of men lie buried in its mere foundations; what patience and postponement, what choking down of preference, what submission to the icy laws of outer fact are wrought into its very stones and mortar; how absolutely impersonal it stands in its vast augustness,—then how besotted and contemptible seems every little sentimentalist who comes blowing his voluntary smoke-wreaths, and pretending to decide things from out of his private dream! Can we wonder if those bred in the rugged and manly school of science should feel like spewing such subjectivism out of their mouths? The whole system of loyalties which grow up in the schools of science go dead against its toleration; so that it is only natural that those who have caught the scientific fever should pass over to the opposite extreme, and write sometimes as if the incorruptibly truthful intellect ought positively to prefer bitterness and unacceptableness to the heart in its cup.

> It fortifies my soul to know
> That, though I perish, Truth is so—

sings Clough, while Huxley exclaims: "My only consolation lies in the reflection that, however bad our posterity may become, so far as they hold by the plain rule of not pretending to believe what they have no reason to believe, because it may be to their advantage so to pretend [the word 'pretend' is surely here redundant], they will not have reached the lowest depth of immorality." And that delicious *enfant terrible* Clifford writes: "Belief is desecrated when given to unproved and unquestioned statements for the solace and private pleasure of the believer. . . . Whoso would deserve well of his fellows in this matter will guard the purity of his belief with a very fanaticism of jealous care, lest at any time it should rest on an unworthy object, and catch a stain which can never be wiped away. . . . If [a] belief has been accepted on insufficient evidence [even though the belief be true, as Clifford on the same page explains] the pleasure is a stolen one. . . . It is sinful because it is stolen in defiance of our duty to mankind. That duty is to guard ourselves from such beliefs as from a pestilence which may shortly master our own body and then spread to the rest of the town. . . . It is wrong always, everywhere, and for every one, to believe anything upon insufficient evidence."

All this strikes one as healthy, even when expressed, as by Clifford, with somewhat too much of robustious pathos in the voice. Free-will and simple wishing do seem, in the matter of our credences, to be only fifth wheels to the coach. Yet if any one should thereupon assume that intellectual insight is what remains after wish and will and sentimental preference have taken wing, or that pure reason is what then settles our opinions, he would fly quite as directly in the teeth of the facts.

It is only our already dead hypotheses that our willing nature is unable to bring to life again. But what has made them dead for us is for the most part a previous action of our willing nature of an antagonistic kind. When I say 'willing nature,' I do not mean only such deliberate volitions as may have set up habits of belief that we cannot now escape from,—I mean all such factors of belief as fear and hope, prejudice and passion, imitation and partisanship, the circumpressure of our caste and set. As a matter of fact we find ourselves believing, we hardly know how or why. Mr. Balfour gives the name of 'authority' to all those influences, born of the intellectual climate, that make hypotheses possible or impossible for us, alive or dead. Here in this room, we all of us believe in molecules and the conservation of energy, in democracy and necessary progress, in Protestant Christianity and the duty of fighting for 'the doctrine of the immortal Monroe,' all for no reasons worthy of the name. We see into these matters with no more inner clearness, and probably with much less, than any disbeliever in them might possess. His unconventionality would probably have some grounds to show for its conclusions; but for us, not insight, but the *prestige* of the opinions, is what makes the spark shoot from them and light up our sleeping magazines of faith. Our reason is quite satisfied, in nine hundred and ninety-nine cases out of every thousand of us, if it can find a few arguments that will do to recite in case our credulity is criticised by some one else. Our faith is faith in some one else's faith, and in the greatest matters this is most the case. Our belief in truth itself, for instance, that there is a truth, and that our minds and it are made for each other,—what is it but a passionate affirmation of desire, in which our social system backs us up? We want to have a truth; we want to believe that our experiments and studies and discussions must put us in a continually better and better position towards it; and on this line we agree to fight out our thinking lives. But if a pyrrhonistic sceptic asks us *how we know* all this, can our logic find a reply? No! certainly it cannot. It is just one volition against another,—we willing to go in for life upon a trust or assumption which he, for his part, does not care to make.

As a rule we disbelieve all facts and theories for which we have no use. Clifford's cosmic emotions find no use for Christian feelings. Huxley belabors the bishops because there is no use for sacerdotalism in his scheme of life. Newman, on the contrary, goes over to Romanism, and finds all sorts of reasons good for staying there, because a priestly system is for him an organic need and delight. Why do so few 'scientists' even look at the evidence for telepathy, so called? Because they think, as a leading biologist, now dead, once said to me, that even if such a thing were true, scientists ought to band together to keep it suppressed and concealed. It would undo the uniformity of Nature and all sorts of other things without which scientists cannot carry on their pursuits. But if this very man had been shown something which as a scientist he might *do* with telepathy, he might not only have examined the evidence, but even have found it good enough. This very law which the logicians would impose upon us—if I may give the name of logicians to those who would rule out our willing nature here—is based on nothing but their own natural wish to exclude all elements for which they, in their professional quality of logicians, can find no use.

Evidently, then, our non-intellectual nature does influence our convictions. There are passional tendencies and volitions which run before and others which come after belief, and it is only the latter that are too late for the fair; and they are not too late when the previous passional work has been already in their own direction. Pascal's argument, instead of being powerless, then seems a regular clincher, and is the last stroke needed to make our faith in masses and holy water complete. The state of things is evidently far from simple; and pure insight and logic, whatever they might do ideally, are not the only things that really do produce our creeds.

Our next duty, having recognized this mixed-up state of affairs, is to ask whether it be simply reprehensible and pathological, or whether, on the contrary, we must treat it as a normal element in making up our minds. The thesis I defend is, briefly stated, this: *Our passional nature not only lawfully may, but must, decide an option between proposi-tions, whenever it is a genuine option that cannot by its nature be decided on intellectual grounds; for to say, under such circumstances, "Do not decide, but leave the question open,"* *is itself a passional decision,—just like deciding yes or no,—and is attended with the same risk of losing the truth.* The thesis thus abstractly expressed will, I trust, soon become quite clear. But I must first indulge in a bit more of preliminary work.

It will be observed that for the purposes of this discussion we are on 'dogmatic' ground,—ground, I mean, which leaves systematic philosophical scepticism altogether out of account. The postulate that there is truth, and that it is the destiny of our minds to attain it, we are deliberately resolving to make, though the sceptic will not make it. We part company with him, therefore, absolutely, at this point. But the faith that truth exists, and that our minds can find it, may be held in two ways. We may talk of the *empiricist* way and of the *absolutist* way of believing in truth. The absolutists in this matter say that we not only can attain to knowing truth, but we can *know when* we have attained to knowing it; while the empiricists think that although we may attain it, we cannot infallibly know when. To *know* is one thing, and to know for certain *that* we know is another. One may hold to the first being possible without the second; hence the empiricists and the absolutists, although neither of them is a sceptic in the usual philosophic sense of the term, show very different degrees of dogmatism in their lives.

If we look at the history of opinions, we see that the empiricist tendency has largely prevailed in science, while in philosophy the absolutist tendency has had everything its own way. The characteristic sort of happiness, indeed, which philosophies yield has mainly consisted in the conviction felt by each successive school or system that by it bottom-certitude had been attained. "Other philosophies are collections of opinions, mostly false; *my* philosophy gives standing-ground forever,"—who does not recognize in this the key-note of every system worthy of the name? A system, to be a system at all, must come as a *closed* system, reversible in this or that detail, perchance, but in its essential features never!

Scholastic orthodoxy, to which one must always go when one wishes to find per-fectly clear statement, has beautifully elaborated this absolutist conviction in a doctrine which it calls that of 'objective evidence.' If, for example, I am unable to doubt that I now exist before you, that two is less than three, or that if all men are mortal then I am mortal too, it is because these things illumine my intellect irresistibly. The final ground of this objective evidence possessed by certain propositions is the *adaequatio intellectûs nostri cum rê*. The certitude it brings involves an *aptitudinem ad extorquendum certum assensum* on the part of the truth envisaged, and on the side of the subject a *quietem in cognitione,* when once the object is mentally received, that leaves no possibility of doubt behind; and in the whole transaction nothing operates but the *entitas ipsa* of the object and the *entitas ipsa* of the mind. We slouchy modern thinkers dislike to talk in Latin,—indeed, we dislike to talk in set terms at all; but at bottom our own state of mind is very much like this whenever we uncritically abandon ourselves: You believe in objective evidence, and I do. Of some things we feel that we are certain: we know, and we know that we do know. There is something that gives a click inside of us, a bell that strikes twelve, when the hands of our mental clock have swept the dial and meet over the meridian hour. The greatest empiricists among us are only empiricists on reflection: when left to their instincts, they dogmatize like infallible popes. When the Cliffords tell us how sinful it is to be Christians on such 'insufficient evidence,' insufficiency is really the last thing they have in mind. For them the evidence is absolutely sufficient, only it makes the other way. They believe so completely in an antichristian order of the universe that there is no living option: Christianity is a dead hypothesis from the start.

But now, since we are all such absolutists by instinct, what in our quality of students of philosophy ought we to do about the fact? Shall we espouse and indorse it? Or shall we treat it as a weakness of our nature from which we must free ourselves, if we can?

I sincerely believe that the latter course is the only one we can follow as reflective men. Objective evidence and certitude are doubtless very fine ideals to play with, but where on this moonlit and dream-visited planet are they found? I am, therefore, myself a complete empiricist so far as my theory of human knowledge goes. I live, to be sure, by the practical faith that we must go on experiencing and thinking over our experience, for only thus can our opinions grow more true; but to hold any one of them—I absolutely do not care which—as if it never could be reinterpretable or corrigible, I believe to be a tremendously mistaken attitude, and I think that the whole history of philosophy will bear me out. There is but one indefectibly certain truth, and that is the truth that pyrrhonistic scepticism itself leaves standing,—the truth that the present phenomenon of consciousness exists. That, however, is the bare starting-point of knowledge, the mere admission of a stuff to be philosophized about. The various philosophies are but so many attempts at expressing what this stuff really is. And if we repair to our libraries what disagreement do we discover! Where is a certainly true answer found? Apart from abstract propositions of comparison (such as two and two are the same as four), propositions which tell us nothing by themselves about concrete reality, we find no proposition ever regarded by any one as evidently certain that has not either been called a falsehood, or at least had its truth sincerely questioned by some one else. The transcending of the axioms of geometry, not in play but in earnest, by certain of our contemporaries (as Zöllner and Charles H. Hinton), and the rejection of the whole Aristotelian logic by the Hegelians, are striking instances in point.

No concrete test of what is really true has ever been agreed upon. Some make the criterion external to the moment of perception, putting it either in revelation, the *con-*

sensus gentium, the instincts of the heart, or the systematized experience of the race. Others make the perceptive moment its own test,—Descartes, for instance, with his clear and distinct ideas guaranteed by the veracity of God; Reid with his 'common-sense;' and Kant with his forms of synthetic judgment *a priori.* The inconceivability of the opposite; the capacity to be verified by sense; the possession of complete organic unity or self-relation, realized when a thing is its own other,—are standards which, in turn, have been used. The much lauded objective evidence is never triumphantly there; it is a mere aspiration or *Grenzbegriff,* marking the infinitely remote ideal of our thinking life. To claim that certain truths now possess it, is simply to say that when you think them true and they *are* true, then their evidence is objective, otherwise it is not. But practically one's conviction that the evidence one goes by is of the real objective brand, is only one more subjective opinion added to the lot. For what a contradictory array of opinions have objective evidence and absolute certitude been claimed! The world is rational through and through,—its existence is an ultimate brute fact; there is a personal God,— a personal God is inconceivable; there is an extra-mental physical world imme-diately known,—the mind can only know its own ideas; a moral imperative exists,—obligation is only the resultant of desires; a permanent spiritual principle is in every one,—there are only shifting states of mind; there is an endless chain of causes,—there is an absolute first cause; an eternal necessity,—a freedom; a purpose,—no purpose; a primal One,—a primal Many; a universal continuity,—an essential discontinuity in things; an infinity,—no infinity. There is this,—there is that; there is indeed nothing which some one has not thought absolutely true, while his neighbor deemed it abso-lutely false; and not an absolutist among them seems ever to have considered that the trouble may all the time be essential, and that the intellect, even with truth directly in its grasp, may have no infallible signal for knowing whether it be truth or no. When, indeed, one remembers that the most striking practical application to life of the doctrine of objective certitude has been the conscientious labors of the Holy Office of the Inqui-sition, one feels less tempted than ever to lend the doctrine a respectful ear.

But please observe, now, that when as empiricists we give up the doctrine of objec-tive certitude, we do not thereby give up the quest or hope of truth itself. We still pin our faith on its existence, and still believe that we gain an ever better position towards it by systematically continuing to roll up experiences and think. Our great difference from the scholastic lies in the way we face. The strength of his system lies in the principles, the origin, the *terminus a quo* of his thought; for us the strength is in the outcome, the upshot, the *terminus ad quem.* Not where it comes from but what it leads to is to decide. It matters not to an empiricist from what quarter an hypothesis may come to him: he may have acquired it by fair means or by foul; passion may have whispered or accident suggested it; but if the total drift of thinking continues to confirm it, that is what he means by its being true.

One more point, small but important, and our preliminaries are done. There are two ways of looking at our duty in the matter of opinion,—ways entirely different, and yet ways about whose difference the theory of knowledge seems hitherto to have shown very little concern. *We must know the truth;* and *we must avoid error,*—these are our first and great commandments as would-be knowers; but they are not two ways of stating an identical commandment, they are two separable laws. Although it may indeed happen that when we believe the truth *A,* we escape as an incidental consequence from believing the falsehood B, it hardly ever happens that by merely disbelieving B we necessarily believe A. We may in escaping B fall into believing other falsehoods, C or D, just as bad as B; or we may escape B by not believing anything at all, not even A.

Believe truth! Shun error!—these, we see, are two materially different laws; and by choosing between them we may end by coloring differently our whole intellectual life. We may regard the chase for truth as paramount, and the avoidance of error as secondary; or we may, on the other hand, treat the avoidance of error as more imperative, and let truth take its chance. Clifford, in the instructive passage which I have quoted, exhorts us in the latter course. Believe nothing, he tells us, keep your mind in suspense forever, rather than by closing it on insufficient evidence incur the awful risk of believing lies. You, on the other hand, may think that the risk of being in error is a very small matter when compared with the blessings of real knowledge, and be ready to be duped many times in your investigation rather than postpone indefinitely the chance of guessing true. I myself find it impossible to go with Clifford. We must remember that these feelings of our duty about either truth or error are in any case only expressions of our passional life. Biologically considered, our minds are as ready to grind out falsehood as veracity, and he who says, "Better go without belief forever than believe a lie!" merely shows his own preponderant private horror of becoming a dupe. He may be critical of many of his desires and fears, but this fear he slavishly obeys. He cannot imagine any one questioning its binding force. For my own part, I have also a horror of being duped; but I can believe that worse things than being duped may happen to a man in this world: so Clifford's exhortation has to my ears a thoroughly fantastic sound. It is like a general informing his soldiers that it is better to keep out of battle forever than to risk a single wound. Not so are victories either over enemies or over nature gained. Our errors are surely not such awfully solemn things. In a world where we are so certain to incur them in spite of all our caution, a certain lightness of heart seems healthier than this excessive nervousness on their behalf. At any rate, it seems the fittest thing for the empiricist philosopher.

And now, after all this introduction, let us go straight at our question. I have said, and now repeat it, that not only as a matter of fact do we find our passional nature influencing us in our opinions, but that there are some options between opinions in which this influence must be regarded both as an inevitable and as a lawful determinant of our choice.

I fear here that some of you my hearers will begin to scent danger, and lend an inhospitable ear. Two first steps of passion you have indeed had to admit as necessary,— we must think so as to avoid dupery, and we must think so as to gain truth; but the surest path to those ideal consummations, you will probably consider, is from now onwards to take no further passional step.

Well, of course, I agree as far as the facts will allow. Wherever the option between losing truth and gaining it is not momentous, we can throw the chance of *gaining truth* away, and at any rate save ourselves from any chance of *believing falsehood*, by not making up our minds at all till objective evidence has come. In scientific questions, this is almost always the case; and even in human affairs in general, the need of acting is seldom so urgent that a false belief to act on is better than no belief at all. Law courts, indeed, have to decide on the best evidence attainable for the moment, because a judge's duty is to make law as well as to ascertain it, and (as a learned judge once said to me) few cases are worth spending much time over: the great thing is to have them decided on *any* acceptable principle, and got out of the way. But in our dealings with objective nature we obviously are recorders, not makers, of the truth; and decisions for the mere sake of deciding promptly and getting on to the next business would be wholly out of place. Throughout the breadth of physical nature facts are what they are quite independently of us, and seldom is there any such hurry about them that the risks of being duped by believing a premature theory need be faced. The questions here are always trivial options, the hypotheses are hardly living (at any rate not living for us spectators), the choice between believing truth or falsehood is seldom forced. The attitude of sceptical balance is therefore the absolutely wise one if we would escape mistakes. What difference, indeed, does it make to most of us whether we have or have not a theory of the Röntgen rays, whether we believe or not in mind-stuff, or have a conviction about the causality of conscious states? It makes no difference. Such options are not forced on us. On every account it is better not to make them, but still keep weighing reasons *pro et contra* with an indifferent hand.

I speak, of course, here of the purely judging mind. For purposes of discovery such indifference is to be less highly recommended, and science would be far less advanced than she is if the passionate desires of individuals to get their own faiths confirmed had been kept out of the game. See for example the sagacity which Spencer and Weismann now display. On the other hand, if you want an absolute duffer in an investigation, you must, after all, take the man who has no interest whatever in its results: he is the warranted incapable, the positive fool. The most useful investigator, because the most sensitive observer, is always he whose eager interest in one side of the question is balanced by an equally keen nervousness lest he become deceived. Science has organized this nervousness into a regular *technique*, her so-called method of verification; and she has fallen so deeply in love with the method that one may even say she has ceased to care for truth by itself at all. It is only truth as technically verified that interests her. The truth of truths might come in merely affirmative form, and she would decline to touch it. Such truth as that, she might repeat with Clifford, would be stolen in defiance of her duty to mankind. Human passions, however, are stronger than technical rules. "Le cœur a ses raisons," as Pascal says, "que la raison ne connaît pas;" and however indifferent to all but the bare rules of the game the umpire, the abstract intellect, may be, the concrete players who furnish him the materials to judge of are usually, each one of them, in love with some pet 'live hypothesis' of his own. Let us agree, however, that wherever there is no forced option, the dispassionately judicial intellect with no pet hypothesis, saving us, as it does, from dupery at any rate, ought to be our ideal.

The question next arises: Are there not somewhere forced options in our speculative questions, and can we (as men who may be interested at least as much in positively gaining truth as in merely escaping dupery) always wait with impunity till the coercive evidence shall have arrived? It seems *a priori* improbable that the truth should be so nicely adjusted to our needs and powers as that. In the great boarding-house of nature, the cakes and the butter and the syrup seldom come out so even and leave the plates so clean. Indeed, we should view them with scientific suspicion if they did.

Moral questions immediately present themselves as questions whose solution cannot wait for sensible proof. A moral question is a question not of what sensibly exists, but of what is good, or would be good if it did exist. Science can tell us what exists; but to compare the *worths*, both of what exists and of what does not exist, we must consult not science, but what Pascal calls our heart. Science herself consults her heart when she lays it down that the infinite ascertainment of fact and correction of false belief are the supreme goods for man. Challenge the statement, and science can only repeat it oracularly, or else prove it by showing that such ascertainment and correction bring man all sorts of other goods which man's heart in turn declares. The question of having moral beliefs at all or not having them is decided by our will. Are our moral preferences true or false, or are they only odd biological phenomena, making things good or bad for *us*, but in themselves indifferent? How can your pure intellect decide? If your heart does not *want* a world of moral reality, your head will assuredly never make you believe in one. Mephistophelian scepticism, indeed, will satisfy the head's play-instincts much better than any rigorous idealism can. Some men (even at the student age) are so naturally cool-hearted that the moralistic hypothesis never has for them any pungent life, and in their supercilious presence the hot young moralist always feels strangely ill at ease. The appearance of knowingness is on their side, of *naïveté* and gullibility on his. Yet, in the inarticulate heart of him, he clings to it that he is not a dupe, and that there is a realm in which (as Emerson says) all their wit and intellectual superiority is no better than the cunning of a fox. Moral scepticism can no more be refuted or proved by logic than intellectual scepticism can. When we stick to it that there *is* truth (be it of either kind), we do so with our whole nature, and resolve to stand or fall by the results. The sceptic with his whole nature adopts the doubting attitude; but which of us is the wiser. Omniscience only knows.

Turn now from these wide questions of good to a certain class of questions of fact, questions concerning personal relations, states of mind between one man and another. *Do you like me or not?*—for example. Whether you do or not depends, in countless instances, on whether I meet you half-way, am willing to assume that you must like me, and show you trust and expectation. The previous faith on my part in your liking's existence is in such cases what makes your liking come. But if I stand aloof, and refuse to budge an inch until I have objective evidence, until you shall have done something apt, as the absolutists say, *ad extorquendum assensum meum,* ten to one your liking never comes. How many women's hearts are vanquished by the mere sanguine insistence of some man that they *must* love him! he will not consent to the hypothesis that they cannot. The desire for a certain kind of truth here brings about that special truth's existence; and so it is in innumerable cases of other sorts. Who gains promotions, boons, appointments, but the man in whose life they are seen to play the part of live hypotheses, who discounts them, sacrifices other things for their sake before they have come, and takes risks for them in advance? His faith acts on the powers above him as a claim, and creates its own verification.

A social organism of any sort whatever, large or small, is what it is because each member proceeds to his own duty with a trust that the other members will simultaneously do theirs. Wherever a desired result is achieved by the co-operation of many independent persons, its existence as a fact is a pure consequence of the precursive faith in one another of those immediately concerned. A government, an army, a commercial system, a ship, a college, an athletic team, all exist on this condition, without which not only is nothing achieved, but nothing is even attempted. A whole train of passengers (individually brave enough) will be looted by a few highwaymen, simply because the latter can count on one another, while each passenger fears that if he makes a movement of resistance, he will be shot before any one else backs him up. If we believed that the whole car-full would rise at once with us, we should each severally rise, and train-robbing would never even be attempted. There are, then, cases where a fact cannot come at all unless a preliminary faith exists in its coming. *And where faith in a fact can help create the fact,* that would be an insane logic which should say that faith running ahead of scientific evidence is the 'lowest kind of immorality' into which a thinking being can fall. Yet such is the logic by which our scientific absolutists pretend to regulate our lives!

In truths dependent on our personal action, then, faith based on desire is certainly a lawful and possibly an indispensable thing.

But now, it will be said, these are all childish human cases, and have nothing to do with great cosmical matters, like the question of religious faith. Let us then pass on to that. Religions differ so much in their accidents that in discussing the religious question we must make it very generic and broad. What then do we now mean by the religious hypothesis? Science says things are; morality says some things are better than other things; and religion says essentially two things.

First, she says that the best things are the more eternal things, the overlapping things, the things in the universe that throw the last stone, so to speak, and say the final word. "Perfection is eternal,"—this phrase of Charles Secrétan seems a good way of putting this first affirmation of religion, an affirmation which obviously cannot yet be verified scientifically at all.

The second affirmation of religion is that we are better off even now if we believe her first affirmation to be true.

Now, let us consider what the logical elements of this situation are *in case the religious hypothesis in both its branches be really true.* (Of course, we must admit that possibility at the outset. If we are to discuss the question at all, it must involve a living option. If for any of you religion be a hypothesis that cannot, by any living possibility be true, then you need go no farther. (I speak to the 'saving remnant' alone.) So proceeding, we see, first, that religion offers itself as a *momentous* option. We are supposed to gain, even now, by our belief, and to lose by our non-belief, a certain vital good. Secondly, religion is a *forced* option, so far as that good goes. We cannot escape the issue by remaining sceptical and waiting for more light, because, although we do avoid error in that way *if religion be untrue,* we lose the good, *if it be true,* just as certainly as if we positively chose to disbelieve. It is as if a man should hesitate indefinitely to ask a certain woman to marry him because he was not perfectly sure that she would prove an angel after he brought her home. Would he not cut himself off from that particular angel-possibility as decisively as if he went and married some one else? Scepticism, then, is not avoidance of option; it is option of a certain particular kind of risk. *Better risk loss of truth than chance of error,*—that is your faith-vetoer's exact position. He is actively playing his stake as much as the believer is; he is backing the field against the religious hypothesis, just as the believer is backing the religious hypothesis against the field. To preach scepticism to us as a duty until 'sufficient evidence' for religion be found, is tantamount therefore to telling us, when in presence of the religious hypothesis, that to yield to our fear of its being error is wiser and better than to yield to our hope that it may be true. It is not intellect against all passions, then; it is only intellect with one passion laying down its law. And by what, forsooth, is the supreme wisdom of this passion warranted? Dupery for dupery, what proof is there that dupery through hope is so much worse than dupery through fear? I, for one, can see no proof; and I simply refuse obedience to the scientist's command to imitate his kind of option, in a case where my own stake is important enough to give me the right to choose my own form of risk. If religion be true and the evidence for it be still insufficient, I do not wish, by putting your extinguisher upon my nature (which feels to me as if it had after all some business in this matter), to forfeit my sole chance in life of getting upon the winning side,—that chance depending, of course, on my willingness to run the risk of acting as if my passional need of taking the world religiously might be prophetic and right.

All this is on the supposition that it really may be prophetic and right, and that, even to us who are discussing the matter, religion is a live hypothesis which may be true. Now, to most of us religion comes in a still further way that makes a veto on our active faith even more illogical. The more perfect and more eternal aspect of the universe is represented in our religions as having personal form. The universe is no longer a mere *It* to us, but a *Thou,* if we are religious; and any relation that may be possible from person to person might be possible here. For instance, although in one sense we are passive portions of the universe, in another we show a curious autonomy, as if we were small active centres on our own account. We feel, too, as if the appeal of religion to us were made to our own active good-will, as if evidence might be forever withheld from us unless we met the hypothesis half-way. To take a trivial illustration: just as a man who in a company of gentlemen made no advances, asked a warrant for every concession, and believed no one's word without proof, would cut himself off by such churlishness from all the social rewards that a more trusting spirit would earn,—so here, one who should shut himself up in snarling logicality and try to make the gods extort his recognition willy-nilly, or not get it at all, might cut himself off forever from his only opportunity of making the gods' acquaintance. This feeling, forced on us we know not whence, that by obstinately believing that there are gods (although not to do so would be so easy both for our logic and our life) we are doing the universe the deepest service we can, seems part of the living essence of the religious hypothesis. If the hypothesis *were* true in all its parts, including this one, then pure intellectualism, with its veto on our making willing advances, would be an absurdity; and some participation of our sympathetic nature would be logically required. I, therefore, for one, cannot see my way to accepting the agnostic rules for truth-seeking, or wilfully agree to keep my willing nature out of the game. I cannot do so for this plain reason, that *a rule of thinking which would absolutely prevent me from acknowledging certain kinds of truth if those kinds of truth were really there, would be an irrational rule.* That for me is the long and short of the formal logic of the situation, no matter what the kinds of truth might materially be.

I confess I do not see how this logic can be escaped. But sad experience makes me fear that some of you may still shrink from radically saying with me, *in abstracto,* that we have the right to believe at our own risk any hypothesis that is live enough to tempt our will. I suspect, however, that if this is so, it is because you have got away from the abstract logical point of view altogether, and are thinking (perhaps without realizing it) of some particular religious hypothesis which for you is dead. The freedom to 'believe what we will' you apply to the case of some patent superstition; and the faith you think of is the faith defined by the schoolboy when he said, "Faith is when you believe something that you know ain't true." I can only repeat that this is misapprehension. *In concreto,* the freedom to believe can only cover living options which the intellect of the individual cannot by itself resolve; and living options never seem absurdities to him who has them to consider. When I look at the religious question as it really puts itself to concrete men, and when I think of all the possibilities which both practically and theoretically it involves, then this command that we shall put a stopper on our heart, instincts, and courage, and *wait*—acting of course meanwhile more or less as if religion were *not* true[1]—till doomsday, or till such time as our intellect and senses working together may have raked in evidence enough,—this command, I say, seems to me the queerest idol ever manufactured in the philosophic cave. Were we scholastic absolutists, there might be more excuse. If we had an infallible intellect with its objective certitudes, we might feel ourselves disloyal to such a perfect organ of knowledge in not trusting to it exclusively, in not waiting for its releasing word. But if we are empiricists, if we believe that no bell in us tolls to let us know for certain when truth is in our grasp, then it seems a piece of idle fantasticality to preach so solemnly our duty of waiting for the bell. Indeed we *may* wait if we will,—I hope you do not think that I am denying that,—but if we do so, we do so at our peril as much as if we believed. In either case we *act*, taking our life in our hands. No one of us ought to issue vetoes to the other, nor should we bandy words of abuse. We ought, on the contrary, delicately and pro- foundly to respect one another's mental freedom: then only shall we bring about the intellectual republic; then only shall we have that spirit of inner tolerance without which all our outer tolerance is soulless, and which is empiricism's glory; then only shall we live and let live, in speculative as well as in practical things.

I began by a reference to Fitz-James Stephen; let me end by a quotation from him. "What do you think of yourself? What do you think of the world? . . . These are ques- tions with which all must deal as it seems good to them. They are riddles of the Sphinx, and in some way or other we must deal with them. . . . In all important transactions of life we have to take a leap in the dark. . . . If we decide to leave the riddles unanswered, that is a choice; if we waver in our answer, that, too, is a choice: but whatever choice we make, we make it at our peril. If a man chooses to turn his back altogether on God and the future, no one can prevent him; no one can show beyond reasonable doubt that he is mistaken. If a man thinks otherwise and acts as he thinks, I do not see that any one can prove that *he* is mistaken. Each must act as he thinks best; and if he is wrong, so much the worse for him. We stand on a mountain pass in the midst of whirling snow and blinding mist, through which we get glimpses now and then of paths which may be deceptive. If we stand still we shall be frozen to death. If we take the wrong road we shall be dashed to pieces. We do not certainly know whether there is any right one. What must we do? 'Be strong and of a good courage.' Act for the best, hope for the best, and take what comes. . . . If death ends all, we cannot meet death better."

1 Since belief is measured by action, he who forbids us to believe religion to be true, necessarily also forbids us to act as we should if we did believe it to be true. The whole defence of religious faith hinges upon action. If the action required or inspired by the religious hypothesis is in no way different from that dictated by the naturalistic hypothesis, then religious faith is a pure superfluity, better pruned away, and controversy about its legitimacy is a piece of idle trifling, unworthy of serious minds. I myself believe, of course, that the religious hypothesis gives to the world an expression which specifically determines our reactions, and makes them in a large part unlike what they might be on a purely naturalistic scheme of belief.

HENRY ADAMS

"The Dynamo and the Virgin"
1907

Henry Adams (1838–1918), grandson of President John Quincy Adams and great-grandson of President John Adams, wrote his autobiography in the third person and attributed to himself the humble role of seeker of education. In the chapter from *The Education of Henry Adams* (Boston 1918; limited edition 1907) reprinted here, Adams presents himself with characteristic artifice: He is a "pupil," instructed by scientists and by experience, here viewing a dynamo in an exhibition hall in 1900. He contemplates the virtually infinite power of the dynamo and meditates on its historical significance. The "Langley" to which Adams refers is an astronomer friend, Samuel Langley, who accompanied Adams to the Paris exhibition of 1900, the setting for this scene of the *Education*. Adams's references to 1893 and to Chicago invoke exhibits at the Chicago World's Fair, where Adams's interest in "force" had been stimulated as reported in an earlier chapter of the *Education*.

Adams's fascination with the culture of medieval Europe—as seen in his comments on "the Virgin"—was the impetus behind another of his great works, *Mont-Saint Michel and Chartres* (New York, 1913). His fascination with the culture of the United States, also seen in his musings about American obliviousness to Venus as well as to the Virgin, was expressed in many of his works, including his formidable *History of the United States of America During the Administrations of Thomas Jefferson and James Madison,* 9 vols. (New York, 1889–91).

One of the most studied of all American intellectuals, Adams is the subject of countless books, of which one of the most helpful remains J. C. Levenson, *The Mind and Art of Henry Adams* (Stanford, 1957). A one-volume abridgment of a standard, three-volume biography is Ernest Samuels, *Henry Adams* (Cambridge, Mass., 1989). An even more accessible introduction to Adams's work is David R. Contosta, *Henry Adams and the American Experiment* (Boston, 1980). For a discussion of Adams in relation to the medievalist, antimodern enthusiasms of the turn of the century, see T. J. Jackson Lears, *No Place of Grace: Antimodernism and the Transformation of American Culture, 1880–1920* (New York, 1982), 262–97.

UNTIL THE GREAT EXPOSITION of 1900 closed its doors in November, Adams haunted it, aching to absorb knowledge, and helpless to find it. He would have liked to know how much of it could have been grasped by the best informed man in the world. While he was thus meditating chaos, Langley came by, and showed it to him. At Langley's behest, the Exhibition dropped its superfluous rags and stripped itself to the skin, for Langley knew what to study, and why, and how; while Adams might as well have stood outside in the night, staring at the Milky Way. Yet Langley said nothing new, and taught nothing that one might not have learned from Lord Bacon, three hundred years before; but though one should have known the Advancement of Science as well as one knew the Comedy of Errors, the literary knowledge counted for nothing until some teacher should show how to apply it. Bacon took a vast deal of trouble in teaching King James I and his subjects, American or other, towards the years 1620, that true science was the development or economy of forces; yet an elderly American in 1900 knew neither the formula nor the forces; or even so much as to say to himself that his historical business in the Exposition concerned only the economics or developments of force since 1893, when he began the study at Chicago.

Nothing in education is so astonishing as the amount of ignorance it accumulates in the form of inert facts. Adams had looked at most of the accumulations of art in the storehouses called Art Museums; yet he did not know how to look at the art-exhibits of 1900. He had studied Karl Marx and his doctrines of history with profound attention, yet he could not apply them at Paris. Langley, with the ease of a great master of experiment, threw out of the field every exhibit that did not reveal a new application of force, and naturally threw out, to begin with, almost the whole art-exhibit. Equally, he ignored almost the whole industrial exhibit. He led his pupil directly to the forces. His chief interest was in new motors to make his air-ship feasible, and he taught Adams the astonishing complexities of the new Daimler motor, and of the automobile, which, since 1893, had become a night-mare at a hundred kilometers an hour, almost as destructive as the electric tram which was only ten years older; and threatening to become as terrible as the locomotive steam-engine itself, which was almost exactly Adams's own age.

Then he showed his scholar the great hall of dynamos, and explained how little he knew about electricity or force of any kind, even of his own special sun, which spouted heat in inconceivable volume, but which, as far as he knew, might spout less or more, at any time, for all the certainty he felt in it. To him, the dynamo itself was but an ingenious channel for conveying somewhere the heat latent in a few tons of poor coal hidden in a dirty engine-house carefully kept out of sight; but to Adams the dynamo became a symbol of infinity. As he grew accustomed to the great gallery of machines, he began to feel the forty-foot dynamos as a moral force, much as the early Christians felt the Cross. The planet itself seemed less impressive, in its old-fashioned, deliberate, annual or daily revolution, than this huge wheel, revolving within arm's-length at some vertiginous speed, and barely murmuring,—scarcely humming an audible warning to stand a hair's-breadth further for respect of power,—while it would not wake the baby lying close against its frame. Before the end, one began to pray to it; inherited instinct taught the natural expression of man before silent and infinite force. Among the thousand symbols of ultimate energy, the dynamo was not so human as some, but it was the most expressive.

Yet the dynamo, next to the steam-engine, was the most familiar of exhibits. For

Source: Henry Adams, *The Education of Henry Adams: An Autobiography* (Boston: Houghton-Mifflin, 1918).

Adams's objects its values lay chiefly in its occult mechanism. Between the dynamo in the gallery of machines and the engine-house outside, the break of continuity amounted to abysmal fracture for a historian's objects. No more relation could he discover between the steam and the electric current than between the Cross and the cathedral. The forces were interchangeable if not reversible, but he could see only an absolute *fiat* in electricity as in faith. Langley could not help him. Indeed, Langley seemed to be worried by the same trouble, for he constantly repeated that the new forces were anarchical, and especially that he was not responsible for the new rays, that were little short of parricidal in their wicked spirit towards science. His own rays, with which he had doubled the solar spectrum, were altogether harmless and beneficient; but Radium denied its God— or, what was to Langley the same thing, denied the truths of his Science. The force was wholly new.

A historian who asked only to learn enough to be as futile as Langley or Kelvin, made rapid progress under this teaching, and mixed himself up in the tangle of ideas until he achieved a sort of Paradise of ignorance vastly consoling to his fatigued senses. He wrapped himself in vibrations and rays which were new, and he would have hugged Marconi and Branly had he met them, as he hugged the dynamo; while he lost his arithmetic in trying to figure out the equation between the discoveries and the economies of force. The economies, like the discoveries, were absolute, supersensual, occult; incapable of expression in horse-power. What mathematical equivalent could he suggest as the value of a Branly coherer? Frozen air, or the electric furnace had some scale of measurement, no doubt, if somebody could invent a thermometer adequate to the purpose; but X-rays had played no part whatever in man's consciousness, and the atom itself had figured only as a fiction of thought. In these seven years man had translated himself into a new universe which had no common scale of measurement with the old. He had entered a supersensual world, in which he could measure nothing except by chance collisions of movements imperceptible to his senses, perhaps even imperceptible to his instruments, but perceptible to each other, and so to some known ray at the end of the scale. Langley seemed prepared for anything, even for an indeterminable number of universes interfused,—physics stark mad in metaphysics.

Historians undertake to arrange sequences,—called stories, or histories—assuming in silence a relation of cause and effect. These assumptions, hidden in the depths of dusty libraries, have been astounding, but commonly unconscious and childlike; so much so, that if any captious critic were to drag them to light, historians would probably reply, with one voice, that they had never supposed themselves required to know what they were talking about. Adams, for one, had toiled in vain to find out what he meant. He had even published a dozen volumes of American history for no other purpose than to satisfy himself whether, by the severest process of stating, with the least possible comment, such facts as seemed sure, in such order as seemed rigorously consequent, he could fix for a familiar moment a necessary sequence of human movement. The result had satisfied him as little as at Harvard College. Where he saw sequence, other men saw something quite different, and no one saw the same unit of measure. He cared little about his experiments and less about his statesmen, who seemed to him quite as ignorant as himself and, as a rule, no more honest; but he insisted on a relation of sequence, and if he could not reach it by one method, he would try as many methods as science knew. Satisfied that the sequence of men led to nothing and that the sequence of their society could lead no further, while the mere sequence of time was artificial, and the sequence of thought was chaos, he turned at last to the sequence of force; and thus it happened that, after ten years' pursuit, he found himself lying in the Gallery of Machines at the Great Exposition of 1900, with his historical neck broken by the sudden irruption of force totally new.

Since no one else showed much concern, an elderly person without other cares, had no need to betray alarm. The year 1900 was not the first to upset schoolmasters. Copernicus and Galileo had broken many professional necks about 1600; Columbus had stood the world on its head towards 1500; but the nearest approach to the revolution of 1900 was that of 310, when Constantine set up the Cross. The rays that Langley disowned, as well as those which he fathered, were occult, supersensual, irrational; they were a revelation of mysterious energy like that of the Cross; they were what, in terms of mediæval science, were called immediate modes of the divine substance.

The historian was thus reduced to his last resources. Clearly if he was bound to reduce all these forces to a common value, this common value could have no measure but that of their attraction on his own mind. He must treat them as they had been felt; as convertible, reversible, interchangeable attractions on thought. He made up his mind to venture it; he would risk translating rays into faith. Such a reversible process would vastly amuse a chemist, but the chemist could not deny that he, or some of his fellow physicists, could feel the force of both. When Adams was a boy in Boston, the best chemist in the place had probably never heard of Venus except by way of scandal, or of the Virgin except as idolatry; neither had he heard of dynamos or automobiles or radium; yet his mind was ready to feel the force of all, though the rays were unborn and the women were dead.

Here opened another totally new education, which promised to be by far the most hazardous of all. The knife-edge along which he must crawl, like Sir Lancelot in the twelfth century, divided two kingdoms of force which had nothing in common but attraction. They were as different as a magnet is from gravitation, supposing one knew what a magnet was, or gravitation, or love. The force of the Virgin was still felt at Lourdes, and seemed to be as potent as X-rays; but in America neither Venus nor Virgin ever had value as force;—at most as sentiment. No American had ever been truly afraid of either.

This problem in dynamics gravely perplexed an American historian. The Woman had once been supreme; in France she still seemed potent, not merely as a sentiment but as a force; why was she unknown in America? for evidently America was ashamed of her, and she was ashamed of herself, otherwise they would not have strewn fig-leaves so profusely all over her. When she was a true force, she was ignorant of fig-leaves, but the monthly-magazine-made American female had not a feature that would have been recognised by Adam. The trait was notorious, and often humorous, but anyone brought up among Puritans knew that sex was sin. In any previous age, sex was strength. Neither art nor beauty was needed. Everyone, even among Puritans, knew that neither Diana of the Ephesians nor any of the oriental Goddesses was worshipped for her beauty. She was Goddess because of her force; she was the animated dynamo; she was reproduction—the greatest and most mysterious of all energies; all she needed was to be fecund. Singularly enough, not one of Adams's many schools of education had ever drawn his attention to the opening lines of Lucretius, though they were perhaps the finest in all Latin literature, where the poet invoked Venus exactly as Dante invoked the Virgin:

'Quae quoniam rerum naturam *sola* gubernas.'

The Venus of Epicurean philosophy survived in the Virgin of the Schools:—

'Donna, sei tanto grande, e tanto vali,
Che qual vuol grazia, e a te non ricorre,
Sua disianza vuol volar senz' ali.'

All this was to American thought as though it had never existed. The true American knew something of the facts, but nothing of the feelings; he read the letter but he never felt the law. Before this historical chasm, a mind like that of Adams felt itself helpless; he turned from the Virgin to the Dynamo as though he were a Branly coherer. On one side, at the Louvre and at Chartres, as he knew by the record of work actually done and still before his eyes, was the highest energy ever known to man, the creator of four-fifths of his noblest art, exercising vastly more attraction over the human mind than all the steam-engines and dynamos ever dreamed of; and yet this energy was unknown to the American mind. An American Virgin would never dare command; an American Venus would never dare exist.

The question, which to any plain American of the nineteenth century seemed as remote as it did to Adams, drew him almost violently to study, once it was posed; and on this point Langleys were as useless as though they were Herbert Spencers or dynamos. The idea survived only as art. There one turned as naturally as though the artist were himself a woman. Adams began to ponder, asking himself whether he knew of any American artist who had ever insisted on the power of sex, as every classic had always done; but he could think only of Walt Whitman; Bret Harte, as far as the magazines would let him venture; and one or two painters, for the flesh-tones. All the rest had used sex for sentiment, never for force; to them, Eve was a tender flower, and Herodias an unfeminine horror. American art, like the American language and American education was as far as possible sexless. Society regarded this victory over sex as its greatest triumph, and the historian readily admitted it, since the moral issue, for the moment, did not concern one who was studying the relations of unmoral force. He cared nothing for the sex of the dynamo until he could measure its energy. . . .

GEORGE SANTAYANA

"The Genteel Tradition in American Philosophy"
1913

One of the most incisive and influential constructions of American intellectual history ever written was contributed by a cosmopolitan philosopher who was born in Spain, died in Italy, and maintained a sardonic aloofness from American life even during his time in the United States. George Santayana (1863–1952) returned to his native Europe shortly after his lecture at Berkeley, which is reprinted here. "The Genteel Tradition in American Philosophy" was at once a grand narrative, in which were charted the destinies of Calvinism and Transcendentalism, and a critical portrait of a single academic department, the department of philosophy at Harvard, where Santayana taught from 1889 to 1912. Santayana associated the genteel tradition with his colleague Josiah Royce and linked the turn against it with another colleague, William James. Santayana's image of a country with two mentalities—one an inherited, feminine "Intellect" inhabiting a "colonial mansion" and the other a practical, masculine "Will" inhabiting a "sky-scraper"—was discussed by both popular and academic commentators on America throughout the twentieth century. Santayana was influential not only as a commentator on American culture but also as a metaphysician and an aesthetic theorist. *The Sense of Beauty* (New York, 1896) and *The Life of Reason*, 5 vols. (New York, 1905–6) were among the major works he completed while in the United States, but he retained a large American following attentive to *Scepticism and Animal Faith* (New York, 1923) and *Realms of Being*, 4 vols. (New York, 1927–40). A new, comprehensive edition of Santayana's works is now being published by the MIT Press.

In recent years Santayana has generated less attention from philosophers than from scholars in other disciplines. The two leading books on Santayana of the last decade have been written by professors of literature and religion, respectively: John McCormick, *George Santayana: A Biography* (New York, 1987), and Henry Samuel Levinson, *Santayana, Pragmatism, and the Spiritual Life* (Chapel Hill, 1992). See also the essay by the literary scholar, Frank Lentriccia, "Philosophers of Modernism at Harvard, circa 1900," *South Atlantic Quarterly* 89 (Fall 1990), 787–834.

LADIES AND GENTLEMEN,—The privilege of addressing you to-day is very welcome to me, not merely for the honour of it, which is great, nor for the pleasures of travel, which are many, when it is California that one is visiting for the first time, but also because there is something I have long wanted to say which this occasion seems particularly favourable for saying. America is still a young country, and this part of it is especially so; and it would have been nothing extraordinary if, in this young country, material preoccupations had altogether absorbed people's minds, and they had been too much engrossed in living to reflect upon life, or to have any philosophy. The opposite, however, is the case. Not only have you already found time to philosophise in California, as your society proves, but the eastern colonists from the very beginning were a sophisticated race. As much as in clearing the land and fighting the Indians they were occupied, as they expressed it, in wrestling with the Lord. The country was new, but the race was tried, chastened, and full of solemn memories. It was an old wine in new bottles; and America did not have to wait for its present universities, with their departments of academic philosophy, in order to possess a living philosophy—to have a distinct vision of the universe and definite convictions about human destiny.

Now this situation is a singular and remarkable one, and has many consequences, not all of which are equally fortunate. America is a young country with an old mentality: it has enjoyed the advantages of a child carefully brought up and thoroughly indoctrinated; it has been a wise child. But a wise child, an old head on young shoulders, always has a comic and an unpromising side. The wisdom is a little thin and verbal, not aware of its full meaning and grounds; and physical and emotional growth may be stunted by it, or even deranged. Or when the child is too vigorous for that, he will develop a fresh mentality of his own, out of his observations and actual instincts; and this fresh mentality will interfere with the traditional mentality, and tend to reduce it to something perfunctory, conventional, and perhaps secretly despised. A philosophy is not genuine unless it inspires and expresses the life of those who cherish it. I do not think the hereditary philosophy of America has done much to atrophy the natural activities of the inhabitants; the wise child has not missed the joys of youth or of manhood; but what has happened is that the hereditary philosophy has grown stale, and that the academic philosophy afterwards developed has caught the stale odour from it. America is not simply, as I said a moment ago, a young country with an old mentality: it is a country with two mentalities, one a survival of the beliefs and standards of the fathers, the other an expression of the instincts, practice, and discoveries of the younger generation. In all the higher things of the mind—in religion, in literature, in the moral emotions—it is the hereditary spirit that still prevails, so much so that Mr. Bernard Shaw finds that America is a hundred years behind the times. The truth is that one-half of the American mind, that not occupied intensely in practical affairs, has remained, I will not say high-and-dry, but slightly becalmed; it has floated gently in the back-water, while, alongside, in invention and industry and social organisation, the other half of the mind was leaping down a sort of Niagara Rapids. This division may be found symbolised in American architecture: a neat reproduction of the colonial mansion—with some modern comforts introduced surreptitiously—stands beside the sky-scraper. The American Will inhabits the sky-scraper; the American Intellect inhabits the colonial mansion. The one is the sphere of the American man; the other, at least predominantly,

Source: George Santayana, *Winds of Doctrine* (London: J. M. Dent & Co., 1913), 186–215.

of the American woman. The one is all aggressive enterprise; the other is all genteel tradition.

Now, with your permission, I should like to analyse more fully how this interesting situation has arisen, how it is qualified, and whither it tends. And in the first place we should remember what, precisely, that philosophy was which the first settlers brought with them into the country. In strictness there was more than one; but we may confine our attention to what I will call Calvinism, since it is on this that the current academic philosophy has been grafted. I do not mean exactly the Calvinism of Calvin, or even of Jonathan Edwards; for in their systems there was much that was not pure philosophy, but rather faith in the externals and history of revelation. Jewish and Christian revelation was interpreted by these men, however, in the spirit of a particular philosophy, which might have arisen under any sky, and been associated with any other religion as well as with Protestant Christianity. In fact, the philosophical principle of Calvinsim appears also in the Koran, in Spinoza, and in Cardinal Newman; and persons with no very distinctive Christian belief, like Carlyle or like Professor Royce, may be nevertheless, philosophically, perfect Calvinists. Calvinism, taken in this sense, is an expression of the agonised conscience. It is a view of the world which an agonised conscience readily embraces, if it takes itself seriously, as, being agonised, of course it must. Calvinism, essentially, asserts three things: that sin exists, that sin is punished, and that it is beautiful that sin should exist to be punished. The heart of the Calvinist is therefore divided between tragic concern at his own miserable condition, and tragic exultation about the universe at large. He oscillates between a profound abasement and a paradoxical elation of the spirit. To be a Calvinist philosophically is to feel a fierce pleasure in the existence of misery, especially of one's own, in that this misery seems to manifest the fact that the Absolute is irresponsible or infinite or holy. Human nature, it feels, is totally depraved: to have the instincts and motives that we necessarily have is a great scandal, and we must suffer for it; but that scandal is requisite, since otherwise the serious importance of being as we ought to be would not have been vindicated.

To those of us who have not an agonised conscience this system may seem fantastic and even unintelligible; yet it is logically and intently thought out from its emotional premises. It can take permanent possession of a deep mind here and there, and under certain conditions it can become epidemic. Imagine, for instance, a small nation with an intense vitality, but on the verge of ruin, ecstatic and distressful, having a strict and minute code of laws, that paints life in sharp and violent chiaroscuro, all pure righteousness and black abominations, and exaggerating the consequences of both perhaps to infinity. Such a people were the Jews after the exile, and again the early Protestants. If such a people is philosophical at all, it will not improbably be Calvinistic. Even in the early American communities many of these conditions were fulfilled. The nation was small and isolated; it lived under pressure and constant trial; it was acquainted with but a small range of goods and evils. Vigilance over conduct and an absolute demand for personal integrity were not merely traditional things, but things that practical sages, like Franklin and Washington, recommended to their countrymen, because they were virtues that justified themselves visibly by their fruits. But soon these happy results themselves helped to relax the pressure of external circumstances, and indirectly the pressure of the agonised conscience within. The nation became numerous; it ceased to be either ecstatic or distressful; the high social morality which on the whole it preserved took another colour; people remained honest and helpful out of good sense and good

will rather than out of scrupulous adherence to any fixed principles. They retained their
instinct for order, and often created order with surprising quickness; but the sanctity
of law, to be obeyed for its own sake, began to escape them; it seemed too unpractical
a notion, and not quite serious. In fact, the second and native-born American mentality
began to take shape. The sense of sin totally evaporated. Nature, in the words of Emerson, was all beauty and commodity; and while operating on it laboriously, and drawing
quick returns, the American began to drink in inspiration from it æsthetically. At the
same time, in so broad a continent, he had elbow-room. His neighbours helped more
than they hindered him; he wished their number to increase. Good will became the
great American virtue; and a passion arose for counting heads, and square miles, and
cubic feet, and minutes saved—as if there had been anything to save them for. How
strange to the American now that saying of Jonathan Edwards, that men are naturally
God's enemies! Yet that is an axiom to any intelligent Calvinist, though the words he
uses may be different. If you told the modern American that he is totally depraved, he
would think you were joking, as he himself usually is. He is convinced that he always
has been, and always will be, victorious and blameless.

Calvinism thus lost its basis in American life. Some emotional natures, indeed,
reverted in their religious revivals or private searchings of heart to the sources of the
tradition; for any of the radical points of view in philosophy may cease to be prevalent,
but none can cease to be possible. Other natures, more sensitive to the moral and literary
influences of the world, preferred to abandon parts of their philosophy, hoping thus to
reduce the distance which should separate the remainder from real life.

Meantime, if anybody arose with a special sensibility or a technical genius, he was
in great straits; not being fed sufficiently by the world, he was driven in upon his own
resources. The three American writers whose personal endowment was perhaps the
finest—Poe, Hawthorne, and Emerson—had all a certain starved and abstract quality.
They could not retail the genteel tradition; they were too keen, too perceptive, and too
independent for that. But life offered them little digestible material, nor were they
naturally voracious. They were fastidious, and under the circumstances they were
starved. Emerson, to be sure, fed on books. There was a great catholicity in his reading;
and he showed a fine tact in his comments, and in his way of appropriating what he
read. But he read transcendentally, not historically, to learn what he himself felt, not
what others might have felt before him. And to feed on books, for a philosopher or a
poet, is still to starve. Books can help him to acquire form, or to avoid pitfalls; they
cannot supply him with substance, if he is to have any. Therefore the genius of Poe and
Hawthorne, and even of Emerson, was employed on a sort of inner play, or digestion
of vacancy. It was a refined labour, but it was in danger of being morbid, or tinkling,
or self-indulgent. It was a play of intra-mental rhymes. Their mind was like an old
music-box, full of tender echoes and quaint fancies. These fancies expressed their personal genius sincerely, as dreams may; but they were arbitrary fancies in comparison
with what a real observer would have said in the premises. Their manner, in a word,
was subjective. In their own persons they escaped the mediocrity of the genteel tradition, but they supplied nothing to supplant it in other minds.

The churches, likewise, although they modified their spirit, had no philosophy to
offer save a new emphasis on parts of what Calvinism contained. The theology of Calvin,
we must remember, had much in it besides philosophical Calvinism. A Christian tenderness, and a hope of grace for the individual, came to mitigate its sardonic optimism;
and it was these evangelical elements that the Calvinistic churches now emphasised,

seldom and with blushes referring to hell-fire or infant damnation. Yet philosophic Calvinism, with a theory of life that would perfectly justify hell-fire and infant damnation if they happened to exist, still dominates the traditional metaphysics. It is an ingredient, and the decisive ingredient, in what calls itself idealism. But in order to see just what part Calvinism plays in current idealism, it will be necessary to distinguish the other chief element in that complex system, namely, transcendentalism.

Transcendentalism is the philosophy which the romantic era produced in Germany, and independently, I believe, in America also. Transcendentalism proper, like romanticism, is not any particular set of dogmas about what things exist; it is not a system of the universe regarded as a fact, or as a collection of facts. It is a method, a point of view, from which any world, no matter what it might contain, could be approached by a self-conscious observer. Transcendentalism is systemic subjectivism. It studies the perspectives of knowledge as they radiate from the self; it is a plan of those avenues of interference by which our ideas of things must be reached, if they are to afford any systematic or distant vistas. In other words, transcendentalism is the critical logic of science. Knowledge, it says, has a station, as in a watchtower; it is always seated here and now, in the self of the moment. The past and the future, things inferred and things conceived, lie around it, painted as upon a panorama. They cannot be lighted up save by some centrifugal ray of attention and present interest, by some active operation of the mind.

This is hardly the occasion for developing or explaining this delicate insight; suffice it to say, lest you should think later that I disparage transcendentalism, that as a method I regard it as correct and, when once suggested, unforgettable. I regard it as the chief contribution made in modern times to speculation. But it is a method only, an attitude we may always assume if we like and that will always be legitimate. It is no answer, and involves no particular answer, to the question: What exists; in what order is what exists produced; what is to exist in the future? This question must be answered by observing the object, and tracing humbly the movement of the object. It cannot be answered at all by harping on the fact that this object, if discovered, must be discovered by somebody, and by somebody who has an interest in discovering it. Yet the Germans who first gained the full transcendental insight were romantic people; they were more or less frankly poets; they were colossal egotists, and wished to make not only their own knowledge but the whole universe centre about themselves. And full as they were of their romantic isolation and romantic liberty, it occured to them to imagine that all reality might be a transcendental self and a romantic dreamer like themselves; nay, that it might be just their own transcendental self and their own romantic dreams extended indefinitely. Transcendental logic, the method of discovery for the mind, was to become also the method of evolution in nature and history. Transcendental method, so abused, produced transcendental myth. A conscientious critique of knowledge was turned into a sham system of nature. We must therefore distinguish sharply the transcendental grammar of the intellect, which is significant and potentially correct, from the various transcendental systems of the universe, which are chimeras.

In both its parts, however, transcendentalism had much to recommend it to American philosophers, for the transcendental method appealed to the individualistic and revolutionary temper of their youth, while transcendental myths enabled them to find a new status for their inherited theology, and to give what parts of it they cared to preserve some semblance of philosophical backing. This last was the use to which the transcendental method was put by Kant himself, who first brought it into vogue, before

the terrible weapon had got out of hand, and become the instrument of pure romanticism. Kant came, he himself, said, to remove knowledge in order to make room for
faith, which in his case meant faith in Calvinism. In other words, he applied the transcendental method to matters of fact, reducing them thereby to human ideas, in order
to give to the Calvinistic postulates of conscience a metaphysical validity. For Kant had
a genteel tradition of his own, which he wished to remove to a place of safety, feeling
that the empirical world had become too hot for it; and this play of safety was the region
of transcendental myth. I need hardly say how perfectly this expedient suited the needs
of philosophers in America, and it is no accident if the influence of Kant soon became
dominant here. To embrace this philosophy was regarded as a sign of profound metaphysical insight, although the most mediocre minds found no difficulty in embracing
it. In truth it was a sign of having been brought up in the genteel tradition, of feeling
it weak, and of wishing to save it.

But the transcendental method, in its way, was also sympathetic to the American
mind. It embodied, in a radical form, the spirit of Protestantism as distinguished from
its inherited doctrines; it was autonomous, undismayed, calmly revolutionary; it felt
that Will was deeper than Intellect; it focussed everything here and now, and asked all
things to show their credentials at the bar of the young self, and to prove their value
for this latest born moment. These things are truly American; they would be characteristic of any young society with a keen and discursive intelligence, and they are strikingly exemplified in the thought and in the person of Emerson. They constitute what
he called self-trust. Self-trust, like other transcendental attitudes, may be expressed in
metaphysical fables. The romantic spirit may imagine itself to be an absolute force,
evoking and moulding the plastic world to express its varying moods. But for a pioneer
who is actually a world-builder this metaphysical illusion has a partial warrant in historical fact; far more warrant than it could boast of in the fixed and articulated society
of Europe, among the moonstruck rebels and sulking poets of the romantic era. Emerson was a shrewd Yankee, by instinct on the winning side; he was a cheery, child-like
soul, impervious to the evidence of evil, as of everything that it did not suit his transcendental individuality to appreciate or to notice. More, perhaps, than anybody that
has ever lived, he practised the transcendental method in all its purity. He had no
system. He opened his eyes on the world every morning with a fresh sincerity, marking
how things seemed to him then, or what they suggested to his spontaneous fancy. This
fancy, for being spontaneous, was not always novel; it was guided by the habits and
training of his mind, which were those of a preacher. Yet he never insisted on his notions
so as to turn them into settled dogmas; he felt in his bones that they were myths.
Sometimes, indeed, the bad example of other transcendentalists, less true than he to
their method, or the pressing questions of unintelligent people, or the instinct we all
have to think our ideas final, led him to the very verge of system-making; but he stopped
short. Had he made a system out of his notion of compensation, or the over-soul, or
spiritual laws, the result would have been as thin and forced as it is in other transcendental systems. But he coveted truth; and he returned to experience, to history, to
poetry, to the natural science of his day, for new starting-points and hints toward fresh
transcendental musings.

To covet truth is a very distinguished passion. Every philosopher says he is pursuing the truth, but this is seldom the case. As Mr. Bertrand Russell has observed, one
reason why philosophers often fail to reach the truth is that often they do not desire to
reach it. Those who are genuinely concerned in discovering what happens to be true

are rather the men of science, the naturalists, the historians; and ordinarily they discover it, according to their lights. The truths they find are never complete, and are not always important; but they are integral parts of the truth, facts and circumstances that help to fill in the picture, and that no later interpretation can invalidate or afford to contradict. But professional philosophers are usually only apologists: that is, they are absorbed in defending some vested illusion or some eloquent idea. Like lawyers or detectives, they study the case for which they are retained, to see how much evidence or semblance of evidence they can gather for the defence, and how much prejudice they can raise against the witnesses for the prosecution; for they know they are defending prisoners suspected by the world, and perhaps by their own good sense, of falsification. They do not covet truth, but victory and the dispelling of their own doubts. What they defend is some system, that is, some view about the totality of things, of which men are actually ignorant. No system would have ever been framed if people had been simply interested in knowing what is true, whatever it may be. What produces systems is the interest in maintaining against all comers that some favourite or inherited idea of ours is sufficient and right. A system may contain an account of many things which, in detail, are true enough; but as a system, covering infinite possibilities that neither our experience nor our logic can prejudge, it must be a work of imagination and a piece of human soliloquy. It may be expressive of human experience, it may be poetical; but how should any one who really coveted truth suppose that it was true?

Emerson had no system; and his coveting truth had another exceptional consequence: he was detached, unworldly, contemplative. When he came out of the conventicle or the reform meeting, or out of the rapturous close atmosphere of the lecture-room, he heard Nature whispering to him: "Why so hot, little sir?" No doubt the spirit or energy of the world is what is acting in us, as the sea is what rises in every little wave; but it passes through us, and cry out as we may, it will move on. Our privilege is to have perceived it as it moves. Our dignity is not in what we do, but in what we understand. The whole world is doing things. We are turning in that vortex; yet within us is silent observation, the speculative eye before which all passes, which bridges the distances and compares the combatants. On this side of his genius Emerson broke away from all conditions of age or country and represented nothing except intelligence itself.

There was another element in Emerson, curiously combined with transcendentalism, namely, his love and respect for Nature. Nature, for the transcendentalist, is precious because it is his own work, a mirror in which he looks at himself and says (like a poet relishing his own verses), "What a genius I am! Who would have thought there was such stuff in me?" And the philosophical egotist finds in his doctrine a ready explanation of whatever beauty and commodity nature actually has. No wonder, he says to himself, that nature is sympathetic, since I made it. And such a view, one-sided and even fatuous as it may be, undoubtedly sharpens the vision of a poet and a moralist to all that is inspiriting and symbolic in the natural world. Emerson was particularly ingenuous and clear-sighted in feeling the spiritual uses of fellowship with the elements. This is something in which all Teutonic poetry is rich and which forms, I think, the most genuine and spontaneous part of modern taste, and especially of American taste. Just as some people are naturally enthralled and refreshed by music, so others are by landscape. Music and landscape make up the spiritual resources of those who cannot or dare not express their unfulfilled ideals in words. Serious poetry, profound religion (Calvinism, for instance), are the joys of an unhappiness that confesses itself; but when a genteel tradition forbids people to confess that they are unhappy, serious poetry and profound religion are closed to them by that; and since human life, in its depths, cannot then express itself openly, imagination is driven for comfort into abstract arts, where human circumstances are lost sight of, and human problems dissolve in a purer medium. The pressure of care is thus relieved, without its quietus being found in intelligence. To understand oneself is the classic form of consolation; to elude oneself is the romantic. In the presence of music or landscape human experience eludes itself; and thus romanticism is the bond between transcendental and naturalistic sentiment. The winds and clouds come to minister to the solitary ego.

Have there been, we may ask, any successful efforts to escape from the genteel tradition, and to express something worth expressing behind its back? This might well not have occurred as yet; but America is so precocious, it has been trained by the genteel tradition to be so wise for its years, that some indications of a truly native philosophy and poetry are already to be found. I might mention the humorists, of whom you here in California have had your share. The humorists, however, only half escape the genteel tradition; their humour would lose its savour if they had wholly escaped it. They point to what contradicts it in the facts; but not in order to abandon the genteel tradition, for they have nothing solid to put in its place. When they point out how ill many facts fit into it, they do not clearly conceive that this militates against the standard, but think it a funny perversity in the facts. Of course, did they earnestly respect the genteel tradition, such an incongruity would seem to them sad, rather than ludicrous. Perhaps the prevalence of humour in America, in and out of season, may be taken as one more evidence that the genteel tradition is present pervasively, but everywhere weak. Similarly in Italy, during the Renaissance, the Catholic tradition could not be banished from the intellect, since there was nothing articulate to take its place; yet its hold on the heart was singularly relaxed. The consequence was that humorists could regale themselves with the foibles of monks and of cardinals, with the credulity of fools, and the bogus miracles of the saints; not intending to deny the theory of the church, but caring for it so little at heart that they could find it infinitely amusing that it should be contradicted in men's lives and that no harm should come of it. So when Mark Twain says, "I was born of poor but dishonest parents," the humor depends on the parody of the genteel Anglo-Saxon convention that it is disreputable to be poor; but to hint at the hollowness of it would not be amusing if it did not remain at bottom one's habitual conviction.

The one American writer who has left the genteel tradition entirely behind is perhaps Walt Whitman. For this reason educated Amercians find him rather an unpalatable person, who they sincerely protest ought not to be taken for a representative of their culture; and he certainly should not, because their culture is so genteel and traditional. But the foreigner may sometimes think otherwise, since he is looking for what may have arisen in America to express, not the polite and conventional American mind, but the spirit and the inarticulate principles that animate the community, on which its own genteel mentality seems to sit rather lightly. When the foreigner opens the pages of Walt Whitman, he thinks that he has come at last upon something representative and original. In Walt Whitman democracy is carried into psychology and morals. The various sights, moods, and emotions are given each one vote; they are declared to be all free and equal, and the innumerable commonplace moments of life are suffered to speak like the others. Those moments formerly reputed great are not excluded, but they are made to march in the ranks with their companions—plain foot-soldiers and servants of the hour. Nor does the refusal to discriminate stop there; we must carry our principle further down, to the animals, to inanimate nature, to the cosmos as a whole. Whitman became a pantheist; but his pantheism, unlike that of the Stoics and of Spinoza, was unintellectual, lazy, and self-indulgent; for he simply felt jovially that everything real was good enough, and that he was good enough himself. In him Bohemia rebelled against the genteel tradition; but the reconstruction that alone can justify revolution did not ensue. His attitude, in principle, was utterly disintegrating; his poetic genius fell back to the lowest level, perhaps, to which it is possible for poetic genius to fall. He reduced his imagination to a passive sensorium for the registering of impressions. No element of construction remained in it, and therefore no element of penetration. But his scope was wide; and his lazy, desultory apprehension was poetical. His work, for the very reason that it is so rudimentary, contains a beginning, or rather many beginnings, that might possibly grow into a noble moral imagination, a worthy filling for the human mind. An American in the nineteenth century who completely disregarded the genteel tradition could hardly have done more.

But there is another distinguished man, lately lost to this country, who has given some rude shocks to this tradition and who, as much as Whitman, may be regarded as representing the genuine, the long silent American mind—I mean William James. He and his brother Henry were as tightly swaddled in the genteel tradition as any infant geniuses could be, for they were born before 1850, and in a Swedenborgian household. Yet they burst those bands almost entirely. The ways in which the two brothers freed themselves, however, are interestingly different. Mr. Henry James has done it by adopting the point of view of the outer world, and by turning the genteel American tradition, as he turns everything else, into a subject-matter for analysis. For him it is a curious habit of mind, intimately comprehended, to be compared with other habits of mind, also well known to him. Thus he has overcome the genteel tradition in the classic way, by understanding it. With William James too this infusion of worldly insight and European sympathies was a potent influence, especially in his earlier days; but the chief source of his liberty was another. It was his personal spontaneity, similar to that of Emerson, and his personal vitality, similar to that of nobody else. Convictions and ideas came to him, so to speak, from the subsoil. He had a prophetic sympathy with the dawning sentiments of the age, with the moods of the dumb majority. His scattered words caught fire in many parts of the world. His way of thinking and feeling represented the true America, and represented in a measure the whole ultra-modern, radical world. Thus he eluded the genteel tradition in the romantic way, by continuing it into its opposite. The romantic mind, glorified in Hegel's dialectic (which is not dialectic at all, but a sort of tragic-comic history of experience), is always rendering its thoughts unrecognisable through the infusion of new insights, and through the insensible transformation of the moral feeling that accompanies them, till at last it has completely reversed its old judgments under cover of expanding them. Thus the genteel tradition was led a merry dance when it fell again into the hands of a genuine and vigorous romanticist like William James. He restored their revolutionary force to its neutralised elements, by picking them out afresh, and emphasising them separately, according to his personal predilections.

For one thing, William James kept his mind and heart wide open to all that might seem, to polite minds, odd, personal, or visionary in religion and philosophy. He gave a sincerely respectful hearing to sentimentalists, mystics, spiritualists, wizards, cranks, quacks, and impostors—for it is hard to draw the line, and James was not willing to draw it prematurely. He thought, with his usual modesty, that any of these might have something to teach him. The lame, the halt, the blind, and those speaking with tongues could come to him with the certainty of finding sympathy; and if they were not healed, at least they were comforted, that a famous professor should take them so seriously; and they began to feel that after all to have only one leg, or one hand, or one eye, or to have three, might be in itself no less beauteous than to have just two, like the stolid majority. Thus William James became the friend and helper of those groping, nervous, half-educated, spiritually disinherited, passionately hungry individuals of which America is full. He became, at the same time, their spokesman and representative before the learned world; and he made it a chief part of his vocation to recast what the learned world has to offer, so that as far as possible it might serve the needs and interests of these people.

Yet the normal practical masculine American, too, had a friend in William James. There is a feeling abroad now, to which biology and Darwinism lend some colour, that theory is simply an instrument for practice, and intelligence merely a help toward material survival. Bears, it is said, have fur and claws, but poor naked man is condemned to be intelligent, or he will perish. This feeling William James embodied in that theory of thought and of truth which he called pragmatism. Intelligence, he thought, is no miraculous, idle faculty, by which we mirror passively any or everything that happens to be true, reduplicating the real world to no purpose. Intelligence has its roots and its issue in the context of events; it is one kind of practical adjustment, an experimental act, a form of vital tension. It does not essentially serve to picture other parts of reality, but to connect them. This view was not worked out by William James in its psychological and historical details; unfortunately he developed it chiefly in controversy against its opposite, which he called intellectualism, and which he hated with all the hatred of which his kind heart was capable. Intellectualism, as he conceived it, was pure pedantry; it impoverished and verbalised everthing, and tied up nature in red tape. Ideas and rules that may have been occasionally useful it put in the place of the full-blooded irrational movement of life which had called them into being; and these abstractions, so soon obsolete, it strove to fix and to worship for ever. Thus all creeds and theories and all formal precepts sink in the estimation of the pragmatist to a local and temporary grammar of action; a grammar that must be changed slowly by time, and may be changed quickly by genius. To know things as a whole, or as they are eternally, if there is anything eternal in them, is not only beyond our powers, but would prove worthless, and perhaps even fatal to our lives. Ideas are not mirrors, they are weapons; their function is to prepare us to meet events, as future experience may unroll them. Those ideas that disappoint us are false ideas; those to which events are true are true themselves.

This may seem a very utilitarian view of the mind; and I confess I think it a partial one, since the logical force of beliefs and ideas, their truth or falsehood as assertions, has been overlooked altogether, or confused with the vital force of the material processes which these ideas express. It is an external view only, which marks the place and conditions of the mind in nature, but neglects its specific essence; as if a jewel were defined as a round hole in a ring. Nevertheless, the more materialistic the pragmatist's theory of the mind is, the more vitalistic his theory of nature will have to become. If the intellect is a device produced in organic bodies to expedite their processes, these organic bodies must have interests and a chosen direction in their life; otherwise their life could not be expedited, nor could anything be useful to it. In other words—and this is a third point at which the philosophy of William James has played havoc with the genteel tradition, while ostensibly defending it—nature must be conceived anthropomorphically and in psychological terms. Its purposes are not to be static harmonies, self-unfolding destinies, the logic of spirit, the spirit of logic, or any other formal method and abstract law; its purposes are to be concrete endeavours, finite efforts of souls living in an environment which they transform and by which they, too, are affected. A spirit, the divine spirit as much as the human, as this new animism conceives it, is a romantic adventurer. Its future is undetermined. Its scope, its duration, and the quality of its life are all contingent. This spirit grows; it buds and sends forth feelers, sounding the depths around for such other centres of force or life as may exist there. It has a vital momentum, but no predetermined goal. It uses its past as a stepping-stone, or rather as a diving-board, but has an absolutely fresh will at each moment to plunge this way or that into the unknown. The universe is an experiment; it is unfinished. It has no ultimate or total nature, because it has no end. It embodies no formula or statable law; any formula is at best a poor abstraction, describing what, in some region and for some time, may be the most striking characteristic of existence; the law is a description *a posteriori* of the habit things have chosen to acquire, and which they may possibly throw off altogether. What a day may bring forth is uncertain; uncertain even to God. Omniscience is impossible; time is real; what had been omniscience hitherto might discover something more to-day. "There shall be news," William James was fond of saying with rapture, quoting from the unpublished poem of an obscure friend, "there shall be news in heaven!" There is almost certainly, he thought, a God now; there may be several gods, who might exist together, or one after the other. We might, by our conspiring sympathies, help to make a new one. Much in us is doubtless immortal; we survive death for some time in a recognisable form; but what our career and transformations may be in the sequel we cannot tell, although we may help to determine them by our daily choices. Observation must be continual if our ideas are to remain true. Eternal vigilance is the price of knowledge; perpetual hazard, perpetual experiment keep quick the edge of life.

This is, so far as I know, a new philosophical vista; it is a conception never before presented, although implied, perhaps, in various quarters, as in Norse and even Greek mythology. It is a vision radically empirical and radically romantic; and as William James himself used to say, the visions and not the arguments of a philosopher are the interesting and influential things about him. William James, rather too generously, attributed this vision to M. Bergson, and regarded him in consequence as a philosopher of the first rank, whose thought was to be one of the turning-points in history. M. Bergson had killed intellectualism. It was his book on creative evolution, said James with humorous emphasis, that had come at last to *"écraser l'infâme."* We may suspect, notwithstanding, that intellectualism, infamous and crushed, will survive the blow; and if the author of the Book of Ecclesiastes were now alive, and heard that there shall be news in heaven, he would doubtless say that there may possibly be news there, but that under the sun there is nothing new—not even radical empiricism or radical romanticism, which from the beginning of the world has been the philosophy of those who as yet had had little experience; for to the blinking little child it is not merely something in the world that is new daily, but everything is new all day.

I am not concerned with the rights and wrongs of that controversy; my point is only that William James, in this genial evolutionary view of the world, has given a rude shock to the genteel tradition. What! The world a gradual improvisation? Creation unpremeditated? God a sort of young poet or struggling artist? William James is an advocate of theism; pragmatism adds one to the evidences of religion; that is excellent.

But is not the cool abstract piety of the genteel getting more than it asks for? This empirical naturalistic God is too crude and positive a force; he will work miracles, he will answer prayers, he may inhabit distinct places, and have distinct conditions under which alone he can operate; he is a neighbouring being, whom we can act upon, and rely upon for specific aids, as upon a personal friend, or a physician, or an insurance company. How disconcerting! Is not this new theology a little like superstition? And yet how interesting, how exciting, if it should happen to be true! I am far from wishing to suggest that such a view seems to me more probable than conventional idealism or than Christian orthodoxy. All three are in the region of dramatic system-making and myth to which probabilities are irrelevant. If one man says the moon is sister to the sun, and another that she is his daughter, the question is not which notion is more probable, but whether either of them is at all expressive. The so-called evidences are devised afterwards, when faith and imagination have prejudged the issue. The force of William James's new theology, or romantic cosmology, lies only in this: that it has broken the spell of the genteel tradition, and enticed faith in a new direction, which on second thoughts may prove no less alluring than the old. The important fact is not that the new fancy might possibly be true—who shall know that?—but that it has entered the heart of a leading American to conceive and to cherish it. The genteel tradition cannot be dislodged by these insurrections; there are circles to which it is still congenial, and where it will be preserved. But it has been challenged and (what is perhaps more insidious) it has been discovered. No one need be browbeaten any longer into accepting it. No one need be afraid, for instance, that his fate is sealed because some young prig may call him a dualist; the pint would call the quart a dualist, if you tried to pour the quart into him. We need not be afraid of being less profound, for being direct and sincere. The intellectual world may be traversed in many directions; the whole has not been surveyed; there is a great career in it open to talent. That is a sort of knell, that tolls the passing of the genteel tradition. Something else is now in the field; something else can appeal to the imagination, and be a thousand times more idealistic than academic idealism, which is often simply a way of white-washing and adoring things as they are. The illegitmate monopoly which the genteel tradition had established over what ought to be assumed and what ought to be hoped for has been broken down by the first-born of the family, by the genius of the race. Henceforth there can hardly be the same peace and the same pleasure in hugging the old properties. Hegel will be to the next generation what Sir William Hamilton was to the last. Nothing will have been disproved, but everything will have been abandoned. An honest man has spoken, and the cant of the genteel tradition has become harder for young lips to repeat.

With this I have finished such a sketch as I am here able to offer you of the genteel tradition in American philosophy. The subject is complex, and calls for many an excursus and qualifying footnote; yet I think the main outlines are clear enough. The chief fountains of this tradition were Calvinism and transcendentalism. Both were living fountains; but to keep them alive they required, one an agonised conscience, and the other a radical subjective criticism of knowledge. When these rare metaphysical preoccupations disappeared—and the American atmosphere is not favourable to either of them—the two systems ceased to be inwardly understood; they subsisted as sacred mysteries only; and the combination of the two in some transcendental system of the universe (a contradiction in principle) was doubly artificial. Besides, it could hardly be held with a single mind. Natural science, history, the beliefs implied in labour and invention, could not be disregarded altogether; so that the transcendental philosopher was condemned to a double allegiance, and to not letting his left hand know the bluff that his right hand was making. Nevertheless, the difficulty in bringing practical inarticulate convictions to expression is very great, and the genteel tradition has subsisted in the academic mind for want of anything equally academic to take its place.

The academic mind, however, has had its flanks turned. On the one side came the revolt of the Bohemian temperament, with its poetry of crude naturalism; on the other side came an impassioned empiricism, welcoming popular religious witnesses to the unseen, reducing science to an instrument of success in action, and declaring the universe to be wild and young, and not to be harnessed by the logic of any school.

This revolution, I should think, might well find an echo among you, who live in a thriving society, and in the presence of a virgin and prodigious world. When you transform nature to your uses, when you experiment with her forces, and reduce them to industrial agents, you cannot feel that nature was made by you or for you, for then these adjustments would have been pre-established. Much less can you feel it when she destroys your labour of years in a momentary spasm. You must feel, rather, that you are an offshoot of her life; one brave little force among her immense forces. When you escape, as you love to do, to your forests and your sierras, I am sure again that you do not feel you made them, or that they were made for you. They have grown, as you have grown, only more massively and more slowly. In their non-human beauty and peace they stir the sub-human depths and the superhuman possibilities of your own spirit. It is no transcendental logic that they teach; and they give no sign of any deliberate morality seated in the world. It is rather the vanity and superficiality of all logic, the needlessness of argument, the relativity of morals, the strength of time, the fertility of matter, the variety, the unspeakable variety, of possible life. Everything is measurable and conditioned, indefinitely repeated, yet, in repetition, twisted somewhat from its old form. Everywhere is beauty and nowhere permanence, everywhere an incipient harmony, nowhere an intention, nor a responsibility, nor a plan. It is the irresistible suasion of this daily spectacle, it is the daily discipline of contact with things, so different from the verbal discipline of the schools, that will, I trust, inspire the philosophy of your children. A Californian whom I had recently the pleasure of meeting observed that, if the philosophers had lived among your mountains their systems would have been different from what they are. Certainly, I should say, very different from what those systems are which the European genteel tradition has handed down since Socrates; for these systems are egotistical; directly or indirectly they are anthropocentric, and inspired by the conceited notion that man, or human reason, or the human distinction between good and evil, is the centre and pivot of the universe. That is what the mountains and the woods should make you at last ashamed to assert. From what, indeed, does the society of nature liberate you, that you find it so sweet? It is hardly (is it?) that you wish to forget your past, or your friends, or that you have any secret contempt for your present ambitions. You respect these, you respect them perhaps too much; you are not suffered by the genteel tradition to criticise or to reform them at all radically. No; it is the yoke of this genteel tradition itself that these primeval solitudes lift from your shoulders. They suspend your forced sense of your own importance not merely as individuals, but even as men. They allow you, in one happy moment, at once to play and to worship, to take yourselves simply, humbly, for what you are, and to salute the wild, indifferent, noncensorious infinity of nature. You are admonished that what you can do avails little materially, and in the end nothing. At the same time, through wonder and pleasure, you are taught speculation. You learn what you are really fitted to do, and where lie your natural dignity and joy, namely, in representing many things, without being them, and in letting your imagination, through sympathy, celebrate and echo their life. Because the peculiarity of man is that his machinery for reaction on external things has involved an imaginative transcript of these things, which is preserved and suspended in his fancy; and the interest and beauty of this inward landscape, rather than any fortunes that may await his body in the outer world, constitute his proper happiness. By their mind, its scope, quality, and temper, we estimate men, for by the mind only do we exist as men, and are more than so many storage-batteries for material energy. Let us therefore be frankly human. Let us be content to live in the mind.

Part Two

Social Progress and the Power of Intellect

Introduction

In an essay of 1917 reprinted herein, the young journalist Randolph Bourne denounced John Dewey for supporting American involvement in the Great War. The eminent philosopher had led contemporary American intellectuals to relinquish their independent critical voice, Bourne complained; no longer could these now-compromised intellectuals hope to be more than servants of the war administration of President Woodrow Wilson. This disagreement between Bourne and Dewey is one of the most famous episodes in the intellectual history of the first third of the twentieth century. This period—to which Part Two is devoted—is appropriately remembered for the fierceness of its conflicts over the proper responsibilities of intellectuals. And no one had done more than Dewey himself—one of whose contributions appears here—to convince men and women with intelligence and learning that the destiny of their society depended in large part on *them*. The systematic use of human intelligence and the proper education of the public could create, according to Dewey, a modern social order more responsive than any previous one to the vital needs of every individual. Bourne himself was something of a disciple of Dewey's and hence all the more troubled when Dewey himself interpreted differently than Bourne did the implications of ideals the two men shared. In a 1916 essay we find Bourne calling explicitly for the formation of a new "intelligentsia" with American society. W.E.B. Du Bois, too, was a prominent advocate of intellect as a guide to progressive social action, and not only by the black intellectuals he sought to inspire and to mobilize. In Part Two, Du Bois exemplifies, along with Dewey and Bourne, the socially conscious, critical exercise of the mind.

We often associate this confidence in the social value of intellect with the reform spirit that gave the Progressive Era its name. Rexford G. Tugwell's vindication of rational planning in the public interest illustrates the power of progressive ideals as late as the Great Depression. Yet not all believers in social progress made as much of the powers of intellect as did Dewey, Bourne, and Du Bois, nor did all celebrants of these powers find reform so promising an endeavor. In Part Two, Jane Addams and Meridel Le Sueur represent those reformers and revolutionaries who placed more emphasis on moral and social energies than on scientific inquiry, and Thorstein Veblen represents those analysts of society whose commitment to reform was ambiguous. Not everyone believed in "social progress." The reactionary John Crowe Ransom condemned in the name of inherited tradition most of the innovations then said to be "progressive." H. L. Mencken was as devoted to intellect as was any American of his generation, but he was scarcely a progressive: He yearned for an aristocracy to counteract the intellectual mediocrity fostered, Mencken believed, by the democratic sensibility promoted by the progressives.

Although Margaret Mead was not inclined to theorize about the responsibilities of intellectuals, she was highly self-conscious about the role that intellectuals—especially social scientists like herself—could play in improving society. Mead's fellow social scientist Thorstein Veblen had performed this role through an ironic and sarcastic description of the American leisure class, but Mead herself, speaking in a more moralistic voice, contrasted the failings of her own modern, American culture with the apparent successes of some primitive societies studied by anthropologists. The enlargement of social science's space in American intellectual life is a noteworthy feature of this period.

Mead and Veblen represent also a relativistic perspective on social norms that became popular among educated Americans throughout the period covered in Part Two. This perspective is also evident in Dewey's work and in the strictures against natural law offered by U.S. Supreme Court Justice Oliver Wendell Holmes, Jr. But perhaps the most powerful critic of absolute rules was William James, whose defense of pragmatism opens Part Two.

James is a suitable choice to open "Social Progress and the Power of Intellect" because he was both a social meliorist and an intellectual voluntarist. As a meliorist, he looked to the gradual improvement of the lives of human beings; as a voluntarist, he believed that truth was partly made by inquiring minds rather than merely uncovered when veils of illusion were removed. Both dispositions were manifest in James's pragmatism. James's specific philosophical doctrines were controversial, but in his devotion to active intellectual inquiry in the interests of human welfare, he was both an influence on and an emblem for the culture of many educated Americans during the early decades of the twentieth century.

Recommendations for Further Reading

Frederick J. Hoffman, *The 20s* (New York, 1955); Henry F. May, *The End of American Innocence: A Study of the First Years of Our Time* (New York, 1959); Daniel Aaron, *Writers on the Left* (New York, 1961); Christopher Lasch, *The New Radicalism in America: The Emergence of the Intellectual as a Social Type*, 1889–1963 (New York, 1965); Jean B. Quandt, *From the Small Town to the Great Community: The Social Thought of Progressive Intellectuals* (New Brunswick, N.J., 1970); Edward A. Purcell, Jr., *The Crisis of Democratic Theory: Scientific Naturalism and the Problem of Value* (Lexington, Ky., 1973); Richard Pells, *Radical Visions and American Dreams: Culture and Social Thought in the Depression Years* (New York, 1973); Morton G. White, *Social Thought in America: The Revolt Against Formalism*, 3rd. ed. (New York, 1976); Bruce Kuklick, *The Rise of American Philosophy: Cambridge, Massachusetts, 1860–1930* (New Haven, 1977); J. David Hoeveler, *The New Humanism: A Critique of Modern America, 1900–1940* (Charlottesville, Va., 1977); Fred H. Matthews, *Quest for an American Sociology: Robert E. Park and the Chicago School* (Montreal, 1977); Rosalind Rosenberg, *Beyond Separate Spheres: Intellectual Roots of Modern Feminism* (New Haven, 1982); Daniel J. Kevles, *In the Name of Eugenics: Genetics and the Uses of Human Heredity* (New York, 1985); James T. Kloppenberg, *Uncertain Victory: Social Democracy and Progressivism in European and American Thought, 1870–1920* (New York, 1986); Peter Novick, *That Noble Dream: The "Objectivity Question" and the American Historical Profession* (New York, 1988); Miles Orvell, *The Real Thing: Imitation and Authenticity in American Culture, 1880–1940* (Chapel Hill, 1989); Casey Nelson Blake, *The Beloved Community: The Cultural Criticism of Randolph Bourne, Van Wycke Brooks, Waldo Frank, & Lewis Mumford* (Chapel Hill, 1990); Daniel J. Wilson, *Science, Community, and the Transformation of American Philosophy, 1860–1930* (Chicago, 1990); Dorothy Ross, *The Origins of American Social Science* (New York, 1991); Susanne Klingenstein, *Jews in the American Academy, 1900–1940: The Dynamics of Intellectual Assimilation* (New Haven, 1991); Andrew Feffer, *The Chicago Pragmatists and American Progressivism* (Chicago, 1993); Thomas Bender, *Intellect and Public Life: Essays on the Social History of Academic Intellectuals in the United States* (Baltimore, 1993); Dorothy Ross, ed., *The Modernist Impulse in the Human Sciences, 1870–1930* (Baltimore, 1994); Mark C. Smith, *Social Science in the Crucible: The American Debate Over Objectivity and Purpose, 1918–1941* (Durham, 1994); Elizabeth Lundbeck, *The Psychiatric Persuasion: Knowledge, Gender, and Power in Modern America* (Princeton, 1994); John M. Jordan, *Machine-Age Ideology: Social Engineering & American Liberalism, 1911–1939* (Chapel Hill, 1994); Ann Douglas, *Terrible Honesty: Mongrel Manhattan in the 1920s* (New York, 1995).

WILLIAM JAMES

"What Pragmatism Means"
1907

William James (1842–1910) opened *Pragmatism* (New York, 1907) with an account of the "present dilemma of philosophy," according to which individuals were asked to choose between two obviously deficient alternatives: a "tender-minded" religious idealism and a "tough-minded" scientific materialism:

The Tender-minded	The Tough-minded
Rationalistic (going by "principles")	Empiricist (going by "facts")
Intellectualistic	Sensationalistic
Idealistic	Materialistic
Optimistic	Pessimistic
Religious	Irreligious
Free-willist	Fatalistic
Monistic	Pluralistic
Dogmatical	Skeptical

James offered pragmatism as a viable middle way. "What Pragmatism Means," which follows, is the second chapter of *Pragmatism*, directly following James's characterization of philosophy's dilemma. Here James projects his vision of an open, contingent universe within which people continually test and revise their store of "truths" against new experiences. Although James's arguments were used by readers in many different secular contexts, James himself reminds readers of the religious preoccupations that render philosophy's dilemma so troubling to him. He returns to religion near the end of the essay and defends pragmatism as a means of widening the search for God.

 The most comprehensive of recent studies of James is Gerald Myers, *William James* (New Haven, 1986). A more historical study, and one that takes account of the professional and institutional matrix of James's work, is Bruce Kuklick, *The Rise of American Philosophy: Cambridge, Massachusetts, 1860–1930* (New Haven, 1977). The most valuable resource for studying James remains Ralph Barton Perry, *The Thought and Character of William James,* 2 vols. (Boston, 1935), in which an extensive selection from James's correspondence appears along with Perry's interpretive narrative of James's development as a thinker. An account of James as a public intellectual is George Cotkin, *William James: Public Philosopher* (Baltimore, 1990). A fresh and engaging treatment of James in relation to his brother, the novelist Henry James, and the milieu they shared, is Ross Posnock, *The Trial of Curiosity: Henry James, William James, and the Challenge of Modernity* (New York, 1991). For additional comments of James, see the headnote to "The Will to Believe." For a discerning, critical assessment of recent scholarship on pragmatism, see James T. Kloppenberg, "Pragmatism: An Old Name for Some New Ways of Thinking?" *Journal of American History* LXXXIII (1996), 100–138.

Some years ago, being with a camping party in the mountains, I returned from a solitary ramble to find every one engaged in a ferocious metaphysical dispute. The *corpus* of the dispute was a squirrel—a live squirrel supposed to be clinging to one side of a tree-trunk; while over against the tree's opposite side a human being was imagined to stand. This human witness tries to get sight of the squirrel by moving rapidly round the tree, but no matter how fast he goes, the squirrel moves as fast in the opposite direction, and always keeps the tree between himself and the man, so that never a glimpse of him is caught. The resultant metaphysical problem is this: *Does the man go round the squirrel or not?* He goes round the tree, sure enough, and the squirrel is on the tree; but does he go round the squirrel? In the unlimited leisure of the wilderness, discussion had been worn threadbare. Every one had taken sides, and was obstinate; and the numbers on both sides were even. Each side, when I appeared, therefore appealed to me to make it a majority. Mindful of the scholastic adage that whenever you meet a contradiction you must make a distinction, I immediately sought and found one, as follows: "Which party is right," I said, "depends on what you *practically mean* by 'going round' the squirrel. If you mean passing from the north of him to the east, then to the south, and then to the west, and then to the north of him again, obviously the man does go round him, for he occupies these successive positions. But if on the contrary you mean being first in front of him, then on the right of him, then behind him, then on his left, and finally in front again, it is quite as obvious that the man fails to go round him, for by the compensating movements the squirrel makes, he keeps his belly turned towards the man all the time, and his back turned away. Make the distinction, and there is no occasion for any further dispute. You are both right and both wrong according as you conceive the verb 'to go round' in one practical fashion or the other."

Although one or two of the hotter disputants called my speech a shuffling evasion, saying they wanted no quibbling or scholastic hair-splitting, but meant just plain honest English "round," the majority seemed to think that the distinction had assuaged the dispute.

I tell this trivial anecdote because it is a pecularly simple example of what I wish now to speak of as *the pragmatic method.* The pragmatic method is primarily a method of settling metaphysical disputes that otherwise might be interminable. Is the world one or many?—fated or free?—material or spiritual?—here are notions either of which may or may not hold good of the world; and disputes over such notions are unending. The pragmatic method in such cases is to try to interpret each notion by tracing its respective practical consequences. What difference would it practically make to any one if this notion rather than that notion were true? If no practical difference whatever can be traced, then the alternatives mean practically the same thing, and all dispute is idle. Whenever a dispute is serious, we ought to be able to show some practical difference that must follow from one side or the other's being right.

A glance at the history of the idea will show you still better what pragmatism means. The term is derived from the same Greek word πράγμα, meaning action, from which our words "practice" and "practical" come. It was first introduced into philosophy by Mr. Charles Peirce in 1878. In an article entitled "How to Make Our Ideas Clear," in the *Popular Science Monthly* for January of that year Mr. Peirce, after pointing out that our beliefs are really rules for action, said that, to develop a thought's meaning, we need only determine what conduct it is fitted to produce: that conduct is for us its sole

Source: William James, *Pragmatism* (New York: Longman's 1907), 48–81.

significance. And the tangible fact at the root of all our thought-distinctions, however subtle, is that there is no one of them so fine as to consist in anything but a possible difference of practice. To attain perfect clearness in our thoughts of an object, then, we need only consider what conceivable effects of a practical kind the object may involve— what sensations we are to expect from it, and what reactions we must prepare. Our conception of these effects, whether immediate or remote, is then for us the whole of our conception of the object, so far as that conception has positive significance at all.

This is the principle of Peirce, the principle of pragmatism. It lay entirely unnoticed by any one for twenty years, until I, in an address before Professor Howison's Philosophical Union at the University of California, brought it forward again and made a special application of it to religion. By that date (1898) the times seemed ripe for its reception. The word "pragmatism" spread, and at present it fairly spots the pages of the philosophic journals. On all hands we find the "pragmatic movement" spoken of, sometimes with respect, sometimes with contumely, seldom with clear understanding. It is evident that the term applies itself conveniently to a number of tendencies that hitherto have lacked a collective name, and that it has "come to stay."

To take in the importance of Peirce's principle, one must get accustomed to applying it to concrete cases. I found a few years ago that Ostwald, the illustrious Leipzig chemist, had been making perfectly distinct use of the principle of pragmatism in his lectures on the philosophy of science, though he had not called it by that name.

"All realities influence our practice," he wrote me, "and that influence is their meaning for us. I am accustomed to put questions to my classes in this way: In what respects would the world be different if this alternative or that were true? If I can find nothing that would become different, then the alternative has no sense."

That is, the rival views mean practically the same thing, and meaning, other than practical, there is for us none. Ostwald in a published lecture gives this example of what he means. Chemists have long wrangled over the inner constitution of certain bodies called "tautomerous." Their properties seemed equally consistent with the notion that an instable hydrogen atom oscillates inside of them, or that they are instable mixtures of two bodies. Controversy raged, but never was decided. "It would never have begun," says Ostwald, "if the combatants had asked themselves what particular experimental fact could have been made different by one or the other view being correct. For it would then have appeared that no difference of fact could possibly ensue; and the quarrel was as unreal as if, theorizing in primitive times about the raising of dough by yeast, one party should have invoked a 'brownie,' while another insisted on an 'elf' as the true cause of the phenomenon."

It is astonishing to see how many philosophical disputes collapse into insignificance the moment you subject them to this simple test of tracing a concrete consequence. There can *be* no difference anywhere that doesn't *make* a difference elsewhere— no difference in abstract truth that doesn't express itself in a difference in concrete fact and in conduct consequent upon that fact, imposed on somebody, somehow, somewhere, and somewhen. The whole function of philosophy ought to be to find out what definite difference it will make to you and me, at definite instants of our life, if this world-formula or that world-formula be the true one.

There is absolutely nothing new in the pragmatic method. Socrates was an adept at it. Aristotle used it methodically. Locke, Berkeley, and Hume made momentous contributions to truth by its means. Shadworth Hodgson keeps insisting that realities are only what they are "known as." But these forerunners of pragmatism used it in fragments: they were preluders only. Not until in our time has it generalized itself, become conscious of a universal mission, pretended to a conquering destiny. I believe in that destiny, and I hope I may end by inspiring you with my belief.

Pragmatism represents a perfectly familiar attitude in philosophy, the empiricist attitude, but it represents it, as it seems to me, both in a more radical and in a less objectionable form that it has ever yet assumed. A pragmatist turns his back resolutely and once for all upon a lot of inveterate habits dear to professional philosophers. He turns away from abstraction and insufficiency, from verbal solutions, from bad *a priori* reasons, from fixed principles, closed systems, and pretended absolutes and origins. He turns towards concreteness and adequacy, towards facts, towards action and towards power. That means the empiricist temper regnant and the rationalist temper sincerely given up. It means the open air and possibilities of nature, as against dogma, artificiality, and the pretence of finality in truth.

At the same time it does not stand for any special results. It is a method only. But the general triumph of that method would mean an enormous change in what I called in my last lecture the "temperament" of philosophy. Teachers of the ultra-rationalistic type would be frozen out, much as the courtier type is frozen out in republics, as the ultramontane type of priest is frozen out in Protestant lands. Science and metaphysics would come much nearer together, would in fact work absolutely hand in hand.

Metaphysics has usually followed a very primitive kind of quest. You know how men have always hankered after unlawful magic, and you know what a great part in magic *words* have always played. If you have his name, or the formula of incantation that binds him, you can control the spirit, genie, afrite, or whatever the power may be. Solomon knew the names of all the spirits, and having their names, he held them subject to his will. So the universe has always appeared to the natural mind as a kind of enigma, of which the key must be sought in the shape of some illuminating or power-bringing word or name. That word names the universe's *principle,* and to possess it is after a fashion to possess the universe itself. "God," "Matter," "Reason," "the Absolute," "Energy," are so many solving names. You can rest when you have them. You are at the end of your metaphysical quest.

But if you follow the pragmatic method, you cannot look on any such word as closing your quest. You must bring out of each word its practical cash-value, set it at work within the stream of your experience. It appears less as a solution, then, than as a program for more work, and more particularly as an indication of the ways in which existing realities may be *changed.*

Theories thus become instruments, not answers to enigmas, in which we can rest. We don't lie back upon them, we move forward, and, on occasion, make nature over again by their aid. Pragmatism unstiffens all our theories, limbers them up and sets each one at work. Being nothing essentially new, it harmonizes with many ancient philosophic tendencies. It agrees with nominalism, for instance, in always appealing to particulars; with utilitarianism in emphasizing practical aspects; with positivism in its disdain for verbal solutions, useless questions and metaphysical abstractions.

All these, you see, are *anti-intellectualist* tendencies. Against rationalism as a pretension and a method pragmatism is fully armed and militant. But, at the outset, at least, it stands for no particular results. It has no dogmas, and no doctrines save its method. As the young Italian pragmatist Papini has well said, it lies in the midst of our theories, like a corridor in a hotel. Innumerable chambers open out of it. In one you may find a man writing an atheistic volume; in the next some one on his knees praying for faith and strength; in a third a chemist investigating a body's properties. In a fourth a system of idealistic metaphysics is being excogitated; in a fifth the impossibility of metaphysics is being shown. But they all own the corridor, and all must pass through it if they want a practicable way of getting into or out of their respective rooms.

No particular results then, so far, but only an attitude of orientation, is what the pragmatic method means. *The attitude of looking away from first things, principles, "categories," supposed necessities; and of looking towards last things, fruits, consequences, facts.*

So much for the pragmatic method! You may say that I have been praising it rather than explaining it to you, but I shall presently explain it abundantly enough by showing how it works on some familiar problems. Meanwhile the word pragmatism has come to be used in a still wider sense, as meaning also a certain *theory of truth.* . . .

One of the most successfully cultivated branches of philosophy in our time is what is called inductive logic, the study of the conditions under which our sciences have evolved. Writers on this subject have begun to show a singular unanimity as to what the laws of nature and elements of fact mean, when formulated by mathematicians, physicists and chemists. When the first mathematical, logical, and natural uniformities, the first *laws*, were discovered, men were so carried away by the clearness, beauty and simplification that resulted, that they believed themselves to have deciphered authentically the eternal thoughts of the Almighty. His mind also thundered and reverberated in syllogisms. He also thought in comic sections, squares and roots and ratios, and geometrized like Euclid. He made Kepler's laws for the planets to follow; he made velocity increase proportionally to the time in falling bodies; he made the law of the sines for light to obey when refracted; he established the classes, orders, families and genera of plants and animals, and fixed the distances between them. He thought the archetypes of all things, and devised their variations; and when we rediscover any one of these his wondrous institutions, we seize his mind in its very literal intention.

But as the sciences have developed further, the notion has gained ground that most, perhaps all, of our laws are only approximations. The laws themselves, moreover, have grown so numerous that there is no counting them; and so many rival formulations are proposed in all the branches of science that investigators have become accustomed to the notion that no theory is absolutely a transcript of reality, but that any one of them may from some point of view be useful. Their great use is to summarize old facts and to lead to new ones. They are only a man-made language, a conceptual shorthand, as some one calls them, in which we write our reports of nature; and languages, as is well known, tolerate much choice of expression and many dialects.

Thus human arbitrariness has driven divine necessity from scientific logic. If I mention the names of Sigwart, Mach, Ostwald, Pearson, Milhaud, Poincaré, Duhem, Ruyssen, those of you who are students will easily identify the tendency I speak of, and will think of additional names.

Riding now on the front of this wave of scientific logic Messrs. Schiller and Dewey appear with the pragmatistic account of what truth everywhere signifies. Everywhere, these teachers say, "truth" in our ideas and beliefs means the same thing that it means in science. It means, they say, nothing but this, *that ideas (which themseles are but parts of our experience) become true just in so far as they help us to get into satisfactory relation with other parts of our experience,* to summarize them and get about among them by conceptual short-cuts instead of following the interminable succession of particular phenomena. Any idea upon which we can ride, so to speak; any idea that will carry us prosperously from any one part of our experience to any other part, linking things satisfactorily, working securely, simplifying, saving labor; is true for just so much, true in so far forth, true *instrumentally*. This is the "instrumental" view of truth taught so successfully at Chicago, the view that truth in our ideas means their power to "work," promulgated so brilliantly at Oxford.

Messrs. Dewey, Schiller, and their allies, in reaching this general conception of all truth, have only followed the example of geologists, biologists and philologists. In the establishment of these other sciences, the successful stroke was always to take some simple process actually observable in operation—as denudation by weather, say, or variation from parental type, or change of dialect by incorporation of new words and pronunciations—and then to generalize it, making it apply to all times, and produce great results by summating its effects thorugh the ages.

The observable process which Schiller and Dewey particularly singled out for generalization is the familiar one by which any individual settles into *new opinions*. The process here is always the same. The individual has a stock of old opinions already, but he meets a new experience that puts them to a strain. Somebody contradicts them; or in a reflective moment he discovers that they contradict each other; or he hears of facts with which they are incompatible; or desires arise in him which they cease to satisfy. The result is an inward trouble to which his mind till then had been a stranger, and from which he seeks to escape by modifying his previous mass of opinions. He saves as much of it as he can, for in this matter of belief we are all extreme conservatives. So he tries to change first this opinion, and then that (for they resist change very variously), until at last some new idea comes up which he can graft upon the ancient stock with a minimum of disturbance of the latter, some idea that mediates between the stock and the new experience and runs them into one another most felicitously and expediently.

This new idea is then adopted as the true one. It preserves the older stock of truths with a minimum of modification, stretching them just enough to make them admit the novelty, but conceiving that in ways as familiar as the case leaves possible. An *outrée* explanation, violating all our preconceptions, would never pass for a true account of a novelty. We should scratch round industriously till we found something less excentric. The most violent revolutions in an individual's beliefs leave most of his old order standing. Time and space, cause and effect, nature and history, and one's own biography remain untouched. New truth is always a go-between, a smoother-over of transitions. It marries old opinion to new fact so as ever to show a minimum of jolt, a maximum of continuity. We hold a theory true just in proportion to its success in solving this "problem of maxima and minima." But success in solving this problem is eminently a matter of approximation. We say this theory solves it on the whole more satisfactorily than that theory; but that means more satisfactorily to ourselves, and individuals will emphasize their points of satisfaction differently. To a certain degree, therefore, everything here is plastic.

The point I now urge you to observe particularly is the part played by the older truths. Failure to take account of it is the source of much of the unjust criticism levelled against pragmatism. Their influence is absolutely controlling. Loyalty to them is the first principle—in most cases it is the only principle; for by far the most usual way of handling phenomena so novel that they would make for a serious rearrangement of our preconception is to ignore them altogether, or to abuse those who bear witness for them.

You doubtless wish examples of this process of truth's growth, and the only trouble is their superabundance. The simplest case of new truth is of course the mere numerical addition of new kinds of facts, or of new single facts of old kinds, to our experience—an addition that involves no alteration in the old beliefs. Day follows day, and its contents are simply added. The new contents themselves are not true, they simple *come* and *are*. Truth is *what we say about* them, and when we say that they have come, truth is satisfied by the plain additive formula.

But often the day's contents oblige a rearrangment. If I should now utter piercing shrieks and act like a maniac on this platform, it would make many of you revise your ideas as to the probable worth of my philosophy. "Radium" came the other day as part of the day's content, and seemed for a moment to contradict our ideas of the whole order of nature, that order having come to be identified with what is called the conservation of energy. The mere sight of radium paying heat away indefinitely out of its own pocket seemed to violate that conservation. What to think? If the radiations from it were nothing but an escape of unsuspected "potential" energy, pre-existent inside of the atoms, the principle of conservation would be saved. The discovery of "helium" as the radiation's outcome, opened a way to this belief. So Ramsay's view is generally held to be true, because, although it extends our old ideas of energy, it causes a minimum of alteration in their nature.

I need not multiply instances. A new opinion counts as "true" just in proportion as it gratifies the individual's desire to assimilate the novel in his experience to his beliefs in stock. It must both lean on old truth and grasp new fact; and its success (as I said a moment ago) in doing this, is a matter for the individual's appreciation. When old truth grows, then, by new truth's addition, it is for subjective reasons. We are in the process and obey the reasons. That new idea is truest which performs most felicitously its function of satisfying our double urgency. It makes itself true, gets itself classed as true, by the way it works; grafting itself then upon the ancient body of truth, which thus grows much as a tree grows by the activity of a new layer of cambium.

Now Dewey and Schiller proceed to generalize this observation and to apply it to the most ancient parts of truth. They also once were plastic. They also were called true for human reasons. They also mediated between still earlier truths and what in those days were novel observations. Purely objective truth, truth in whose establishment the function of giving human satisfaction in marrying previous parts of experience with newer parts play no rôle whatever, is nowhere to be found. The reasons why we call things true is the reason why they *are* true, for "to be true" *means* only to perform this marriage-function.

The trail of the human serpent is thus over everything. Truth independent; truth that we *find* merely; truth no longer malleable to human need; truth incorrigible, in a word; such truth exists indeed superabundantly—or is supposed to exist by rationalistically minded thinkers; but then it means only the dead heart of the living tree, and its being there means only that truth also has its paleontology, and its "prescription," and may grow stiff with years of veteran service and petrified in men's regard by sheer antiquity. But how plastic even the oldest truths nevertheless really are has been vividly shows in our day by the transformation of logical and mathematical ideas, a transformation which seems even to be invading physics. The ancient formulas are reinterpreted as special expressions of much wider principles, principles that our ancestors never got a glimpse of in their present shape and formulation.

Mr. Schiller still gives to all this view of truth the name of "Humanism," but, for this doctrine too, the name of pragmatism seems fairly to be in the ascendant, so I will treat it under the name of pragmatism in these lectures.

Such then would be the scope of pragmatism—first, a method and second, a genetic theory of what is meant by truth. . . .

You will probably be surprised to learn . . . that Messrs. Schiller's and Dewey's theories have suffered a hailstorm of contempt and ridicule. All rationalism has risen against them. In influential quarters Mr. Schiller, in particular, has been treated like an impudent schoolboy who deserves a spanking. I should not mention this but for the fact that it throws so much sidelight upon that rationalistic temper to which I have opposed the temper of pragmatism. Pragmatism is uncomfortable away from facts. Rationalism is comfortable only in the presence of abstractions. This pragmatist talk about truths in the plural, about their utility and satisfactoriness, about the success with which they "work," etc., suggests to the typical intellectualist mind a sort of coarse lame second-rate makeshift article of truth. Such truths are not real truth. Such tests are merely subjective. As against this, objective truth must be something non-utilitarian, haughty, refined, remote, august, exalted. It must be an absolute reality. It must be what we *ought* to think unconditionally. The conditioned ways in which we *do* think are so much irrelevance and matter for psychology. Down with psychology, up with logic, in all this question!

See the exquisite contrast of the types of mind! The pragmatist clings to facts and concreteness, observes truth at its work in particular cases, and generalizes. Truth, for him, becomes a class-name for all sorts of definite working-values in experience. For the rationalist it remains a pure abstraction, to the bare name of which we must defer. When the pragmatist undertakes to show in detail just *why* we must defer, the rationalist is unable to recognize the concretes from which his own abstraction is taken. He accuses us of *denying* truth; whereas we have only sought to trace exactly why people follow it and always ought to follow it. Your typical ultra-abstractionist fairly shudders at concreteness: other things equal, he positively prefers the pale and spectral. If the two universes were offered, he would always choose the skinny outline rather than the rich thicket of reality. It is so much purer, clearer, nobler.

I hope that as these lectures go on, the concreteness and closeness to facts of the pragmatism which they advocate may be what approves itself to you as its most satisfactory pecularity. It only follows here the example of the sister-sciences, interpreting the unobserved by the observed. It brings old and new harmoniously together. It converts the absolutely empty notion of a static relation of "correspondence" (what that may mean we must ask later) between our minds and reality, into that of a rich and active commerce (that any one may follow in detail and understand) between particular thoughts of ours, and the great universe of other experiences in which they play their parts and have their uses.

But enough of this at present. The justification of what I say must be postponed. I wish now to add a word in further explanation of the claim I made at our last meeting, that pragmatism may be a happy harmonizer of empiricist ways of thinking with the more religious demands of human beings.

Men who are strongly of the fact-loving temperament, you may remember me to have said, are liable to be kept at a distance by the small sympathy with facts which that philosophy from the present-day fashion of idealism offers them. It is far too intellectualistic. Old fashioned theism was bad enough, with its notion of God as an exalted monarch, made up of a lot of unintelligible or preposterous "attributes"; but, so long as it held strongly by the argument from design, it kept some touch with concrete realities. Since, however, Darwinsim has once for all displaced design from the minds of the "scientific," theism has lost that foothold; and some kind of an immanent or pantheistic deity working *in* things rather than above them is, if any, the kind recommended to our contemporary imagination. Aspirants to a philosophic religion turn, as a rule, more hopefully nowadays towards idealistic pantheism than towards the older dualistic theism, in spite of the fact that the latter still counts able defenders.

But, as I said in my first lecture, the brand of pantheism offered is hard for them to assimilate if they are lovers of facts, or empirically minded. It is the absolutistic brand, spurning the dust and reared upon pure logic. It keeps no connexion whatever with concreteness. Affirming the Absolute Mind, which is its substitute for God, to be the rational presupposition of all particulars of fact, whatever they may be, it remains supremely indifferent to what the particular facts in our world actually are. Be they what they may, the Absolute will father them. Like the sick lion in Esop's fable, all footprints lead into his den, but *nulla vestigia retrorsum*. You cannot redescend into the world of particulars by the Absolute's aid, or deduce any necessary consequences of detail important for your life from your idea of his nature. He gives you indeed the assurance that all is well with *Him,* and for his eternal way of thinking; but thereupon he leaves you to be finitely saved by your own temporal devices.

Far be it from me to deny the majesty of this conception, or its capacity to yield religious comfort to a most respectable class of minds. But from the human point of view, no one can pretend that it doesn't suffer from the faults of remoteness and abstractness. It is eminently a product of what I have ventured to call the rationalistic temper. It disdains empiricism's needs. It substitutes a pallid outline for the real world's richness. It is dapper, it is noble in the bad sense, in the sense in which to be noble is to be inapt for humble service. In this real world of sweat and dirt, it seems to me that when a view of things is "noble," that ought to count as a presumption against its truth, and as a philosophic disqualification. The prince of darkness may be a gentleman, as we are told he is, but whatever the God of earth and heaven is, he can surely be no gentleman. His menial services are needed in the dust of our human trials, even more than his dignity is needed in the empyrean.

Now pragmatism, devoted though she be to facts, has no such materialistic bias as ordinary empiricism labors under. Moreover, she has no objection whatever to the realizing of abstractions, so long as you get about among particulars with their aid and they actually carry you somewhere. Interested in no conclusions but those which our minds and our experiences work out together, she has no *a priori* prejudices against theology. *If theological ideas prove to have a value for concrete life, they will be true, for pragmatism, in the sense of being good for so much. For how much more they are true, will depend entirely on their relations to the other truths that also have to be acknowledged.*

What I said just now about the Absolute, of transcendental idealism, is a case in point. First, I called it majestic and said it yielded religious comfort to a class of minds, and then I accused it of remoteness and sterility. But so far as it affords such comfort, it surely is not sterile; it has that amount of value; it performs a concrete function. As a good pragmatist, I myself ought to call the Absolute true "in so far forth," then; and I unhesitatingly now do so.

But what does *true in so far forth* mean in this case? To answer, we need only apply the pragmatic method. What do believers in the Absolute mean by saying that their belief affords them comfort? They mean that since, in the Absolute finite evil is "overruled" already, we may, therefore, whenever we wish, treat the temporal as if it were potentially the eternal, be sure that we can trust its outcome, and, without sin, dismiss our fear and drop the worry of our finite responsibility. In short, they mean that we have a right ever and anon to take a moral holiday, to let the world wag in its own way, feeling that its issues are in better hands than ours and are none of our business.

The universe is a system of which the individual members may relax their anxieties occasionally, in which the don't-care mood is also right for men, and moral holidays in order—that, if I mistake not, is part, at least, of what the Absolute is "known-as," that is the great difference in our particular experiences which his being true makes, for us, that is his cash-value when he is pragmatically interpreted. Farther than that the ordinary lay-reader in philosophy who thinks favorably of absolute idealism does not venture to sharpen his conceptions. He can use the Absolute for so much, and so much is very precious. He is pained at hearing you speak incredulously of the Absolute, therefore, and disregards your criticism because they deal with aspects of the conception that he fails to follow.

If the Absolute means this, and means no more than this, who can possibly deny the truth of it? To deny it would be to insist that men should never relax, and that holidays are never in order.

I am well aware how odd it must seem to some of you to hear me say that an idea is "true" so long as to believe it is profitable to our lives. That it is *good,* for as much as it profits, you will gladly admit. If what we do by its aid is good, you will allow the idea itself to be good in so far forth, for we are the better for possessing it. But is it not a strange misuse of the word "truth," you will say, to call ideas also "true" for this reason?

To answer this difficulty fully is impossible at this stage of my account. You touch here upon the very central point of Messrs. Schiller's, Dewey's, and my own doctrine of truth, which I cannot discuss with detail until my sixth lecture. Let me now say only this, the truth is *one species of good,* and not, as is usually supposed, a category distinct from good, and co-ordinate with it. *The true is the name of whatever proves itself to be good in the way of belief, and good, too, for definite, assignable reasons.* Surely you must admit this, that if there were *no* good for life in true ideas, or if the knowledge of them were positively disadvantageous and false ideas the only useful ones, then the current notion that truth is divine and precious, and its pursuit a duty, could never have grown up or become a dogma. In a world like that, our duty would be to *shun* truth, rather. But in this world, just as certain foods are not only agreeable to our taste, but good for our teeth, our stomach, and our tissues; so certain ideas are not only agreeable to think about, or agreeable as supporting other ideas that we are fond of, but they are also helpful in life's practical struggles. If there be any life that it is really better we should lead, and if there be any idea which, if believed in, would help us to lead that life, then it would be really *better for us* to believe in that idea, *unless, indeed, belief in it incidentally clashed with other greater vital benefits.*

"What would be better for us to believe!" This sounds very like a definition of truth. It comes very near to saying "what we *ought* to believe"; and in *that* definition none of you would find any oddity. Ought we ever not to believe what it is *better for us* to believe? And can we then keep the notion of what is better for us, and what is true for us, permanently apart?

Pragmatism says no, and I fully agree with her. Probably you also agree, so far as the abstract statement goes, but with a suspicion that if we practically did believe everything that made for good in our own personal lives, we should be found indulging all kinds of fancies about this world's affairs, and all kinds of sentimental superstitions about a world hereafter. Your suspicion here is undoubtedly well founded, and it is evident that something happens when you pass from the abstract to the concrete that complicates the situation.

I said just now that what is better for us to believe is true *unless the belief incidentally clashes with some other vital benefit.* Now in real life what vital benefits is any particular belief of our most liable to clash with? What indeed except the vital benefits yielded by *other beliefs* when these prove incompatible with the first ones? In other words, the greatest enemy of any one of our truths may be the rest of our truths. Truths have once for all this desperate instinct of self-preservation and of desire to extinguish whatever contradicts them. My belief in the Absolute, based on the good it does me, must run the gauntlet of all my other beliefs. Grant that it may be true in giving me a moral holiday. Nevertheless, as I conceive it—and let me speak now confidentially, as it were, and merely in my own private person—it clashes with other truths of mine whose benefits I hate to give up on its account. It happens to be associated with a kind of logic of which I am the enemy, I find that it entangles me in metaphysical paradoxes that are inacceptable, etc., etc. But as I have enough trouble in life already without adding the trouble of carrying these intellectual inconsistencies, I personally just give up the Absolute. I just *take* my moral holidays; or else as a professional philosopher, I try to justify them by some other principle.

If I could restrict my notion of the Absolute to its bare holiday-giving value, it wouldn't clash with my other truths. But we cannot easily thus restrict our hypotheses. They carry supernumerary features, and these it is that clash so. My disbelief in the Absolute means then disbelief in those other supernumerary features, for I fully believe in the legitimacy of taking moral holidays.

You see by this what I meant when I called pragmatism a mediator and reconciler and said, borrowing the word from Papini, that she "unstiffens" our theories. She has in fact no prejudices whatever, no obstructive dogmas, no rigid canons of what shall count as proof. She is completely genial. She will entertain any hypothesis, she will consider any evidence. It follows that in the religious field she is at a great advantage both over positivistic empiricism, with its anti-theological bias, and over religious rationalism, with its exclusive interest in the remote, the noble, the simple, and the abstract in the way of conception.

In short, she widens the field of search for God. Rationalism sticks to logic and the empyrean. Empiricism sticks to the external senses. Pragmatism is willing to take anything, to follow either logic or the senses and to count the humblest and most personal experiences. She will count mystical experiences if they have practical consequences. She will take a God who lives in the very dirt of private fact—if that should seem a likely place to find him.

Her only test of probable truth is what works best in the way of leading us, what fits every part of life best and combines with the collectivity of experience's demands, nothing being omitted. If theological ideas should do this, if the notion of God, in particular, should prove to do it, how could pragmatism possibly deny God's existence? She could see no meaning in treating as "not true" a notion that was pragmatically so successful. What other kind of truth could there be, for her, than all this agreement with concrete reality?

OLIVER WENDELL HOLMES, JR.

"Natural Law"
1918

Oliver Wendell Holmes, Jr., (1841–1935) did more than any other American thinker to develop and popularize the insight that law is a living, changing part of culture, responsive to the shifting circumstances with which societies must cope. He argued along these lines as early as 1881, when he published his greatest work, *The Common Law,* but Holmes achieved broader influence during the Progressive Era and the 1920s while serving as a justice of the U.S. Supreme Court. Although Holmes was aloof from the reform movements of this era, his refusal to defend the vested interests of his upper-class milieu endeared him to younger, liberal intellectuals, who tended to exaggerate his "progressive" tendencies.

Holmes inspired many "legal realists" of the 1930s and was appreciated even by some of the "critical legal studies" scholars of the 1980s. For introductions to these movements, see Laura Kalman, *Legal Realism at Yale, 1927–1960* (Chapel Hill, 1986); and Roberto Unger, *The Critical Legal Studies Movement* (Cambridge, Mass., 1986). Holmes's most important theoretical essays, "Privilege, Malice, and Intent" (1894) and "The Path of the Law" (1896) are available in Holmes's *Collected Legal Papers* (Boston, 1920), from which is reprinted here the essay of 1918, "Natural Law." This brief piece expresses the historicist bent of Holmes's jurisprudence and displays the aphoristic style in which he often dealt with theoretical issues.

The most important study of Holmes's legal philosophy is Thomas C. Grey, "Holmes and Legal Pragmatism," *Stanford Law Review* 41 (1989), 787–870, although Grey is more concerned with extracting from Holmes the rudiments of a legal pragmatism suitable to our own time than to clarify Holmes's relationship with James, Dewey, and other pragmatists of Holmes's own generation. An earlier study that emphasizes Holmes's aristocratic biases, his distance from the more democratic Dewey, and his unwillingness to make commitments is Yosal Rogat, "The Judge as Spectator," *University of Chicago Law Review* 31 (1964), 213–56. The most reliable and comprehensive of the many biographies is G. Edward White, *Justice Oliver Wendell Holmes: Law and the Inner Self* (New York, 1994). The best starting point for the study of Holmes today is the collection of new essays edited by Robert W. Gordon, *The Legacy of Oliver Wendell Holmes, Jr.* (Stanford, 1992).

It is not enough for the knight of romance that you agree that his lady is a very nice girl—if you do not admit that she is the best that God ever made or will make, you must fight. There is in all men a demand for the superlative, so much so that the poor devil who has no other way of reaching it attains it by getting drunk. It seems to me that this demand is at the bottom of the philosopher's effort to prove that truth is absolute and of the jurist's search for criteria of universal validity which he collects under the head of natural law.

I used to say, when I was young, that truth was the majority vote of that nation that could lick all others. Certainly we may expect that the received opinion about the present war will depend a good deal upon which side wins (I hope with all my soul it will be mine), and I think that the statement was correct in so far as it implied that our test of truth is a reference to either a present or an imagined future majority in favor of our view. If, as I have suggested elsewhere, the truth may be defined as the system of my (intellectual) limitations, what gives it objectivity is the fact that I find my fellow man to a greater or less extent (never wholly) subject to the same *Can't Helps*. If I think that I am sitting at a table I find that the other persons present agree with me; so if I say that the sum of the angles of a triangle is equal to two right angles. If I am in a minority of one they send for a doctor or lock me up; and I am so far able to transcend the to me convincing testimony of my senses or my reason as to recognize that if I am alone probably something is wrong with my works.

Certitude is not the test of certainty. We have been cock-sure of many things that were not so. If I may quote myself again, property, friendship, and truth have a common root in time. One can not be wrenched from the rocky crevices into which one has grown for many years without feeling that one is attacked in one's life. What we most love and revere generally is determined by early associations. I love granite rocks and barberry bushes, no doubt because with them were my earliest joys that reach back through the past eternity of my life. But while one's experience thus makes certain preferences dogmatic for oneself, recognition of how they came to be so leaves one able to see that others, poor souls, may be equally dogmatic about something else. And this again means scepticism. Not that one's belief or love does not remain. Not that we would not fight and die for it if important—we all, whether we know it or not—are fighting to make the kind of a world that we should like—but that we have learned to recognize that others will fight and die to make a different world, with equal sincerity or belief. Deep-seated preferences can not be argued about—you can not argue a man into liking a glass of beer—and therefore, when differences are sufficiently far reaching we try to kill the other man rather than let him have his way. But that is perfectly consistent with admitting that, so far as appears, his grounds are just as good as ours.

The jurists who believe in natural law seem to me to be in that naïve state of mind that accepts what has been familiar and accepted by them and their neighbors as something that must be accepted by all men everywhere. No doubt it is true that, so far as we can see ahead, some arrangements and the rudiments of familiar institutions seem to be necessary elements in any society that may spring from our own and that would seem to us to be civilized—some form of permanent association between the sexes—some residue of property individually owned—some mode of binding oneself to specified future conduct—at the bottom of all, some protection for the person. But without

Source: Oliver Wendell Holmes, Jr., *Collected Legal Papers* (New York: Harcourt Brace Jovanovitch, 1952), 310–16. Copyright 1920, 1952 by Harcourt Brace Jovanovich, Inc. Reprinted by permission of the publisher.

speculating whether a group is imaginable in which all but the last of these might disappear and the last be subject to qualifications that most of us would abhor, the question remains as to the *Ought* of natural law.

It is true that beliefs and wishes have a transcendental basis in the sense that their foundation is arbitrary. You can not help entertaining and feeling them, and there is an end of it. As an arbitrary fact people wish to live, and we say with various degrees of certainty that they can do so only on certain conditions. To do it they must eat and drink. That necessity is absolute. It is a necessity of less degree but practically general that they should live in society. If they live in society, so far as we can see, there are further conditions. Reason working on experience does tell us, no doubt, that if our wish to live continues, we can do it only on those terms. But that seems to me the whole of the matter. I see no *a priori* duty to live with others and in that way, but simply a statement of what I must do if I wish to remain alive. If I do live with others they tell me that I must do and abstain from doing various things or they will put the screws on to me. I believe that they will, and being of the same mind as to their conduct I not only accept the rules but come in time to accept them with sympathy and emotional affirmation and begin to talk about duties and rights. But for legal purposes a right is only the hypostasis of a prophecy—the imagination of a substance supporting the fact that the public force will be brought to bear upon those who do things said to contravene it—just as we talk of the force of gravitation accounting for the conduct of bodies in space. One phrase adds no more than the other to what we know without it. No doubt behind these legal rights is the fighting will of the subject to maintain them, and the spread of his emotions to the general rules by which they are maintained; but that does not seem to me the same thing as the supposed *a priori* discernment of a duty or the assertion of a preëxisting right. A dog will fight for his bone.

The most fundamental of the supposed preëxisting rights—the right to life—is sacrificed without a scruple not only in war, but whenever the interest of society, that is, of the predominant power in the community, is thought to demand it. Whether that interest is the interest of mankind in the long run no one can tell, and as, in any event, to those who do not think with Kant and Hegel it is only an interest, the sanctity disappears. I remember a very tenderhearted judge being of opinion that closing a hatch to stop a fire and the destruction of a cargo was justified even if it was known that doing so would stifle a man below. It is idle to illustrate further, because to those who agree with me I am uttering commonplaces and to those who disagree I am ignoring the necessary foundations of thought. The *a priori* men generally call the dissentients superficial. But I do agree with them in believing that one's attitude on these matters is closely connected with one's general attitude toward the universe. Proximately, as has been suggested, it is determined largely by early associations and temperament, coupled with the desire to have an absolute guide. Men to a great extent believe what they want to—although I see in that no basis for a philosophy that tells us what we should want to want.

Now when we come to our attitude toward the universe I do not see any rational ground for demanding the superlative—for being dissatisfied unless we are assured that our truth is cosmic truth, if there is such a thing—that the ultimates of a little creature on this earth are the last word of the unimaginable whole. If a man sees no reason for believing that significance, consciousness and ideals are more than marks of the finite, that does not justify what has been familiar in French sceptics: getting upon a pedestal and professing to look with haughty scorn upon a world in ruins. The real conclusion is that the part can not swallow the whole—that our categories are not, or may not be, adequate to formulate what we cannot know. If we believe that we come out of the universe, not it out of us, we must admit that we do not know what we are talking about when we speak of brute matter. We do know that a certain complex of energies can wag its tail and another can make syllogisms. These are among the powers of the unknown, and if, as may be, it has still greater powers that we can not understand, as Fabre in his studies of instinct would have us believe, studies that gave Bergson one of the strongest strands for his philosophy and enabled Maeterlinck to make us fancy for a moment that we heard a clang from behind phenomena—if this be true, why should we not be content? Why should we employ the energy that is furnished to us by the cosmos to defy it and shake our fist at the sky? It seems to me silly.

That the universe has in it more than we understand, that the private soldiers have not been told the plan of the campaign, or even that there is one, rather than some vaster unthinkable to which every predicate is an impertinence, has no bearing upon our conduct. We still shall fight—all of us because we want to live, some, at least, because we want to realize our spontaneity and prove our powers, for the joy of it, and we may leave to the unknown the supposed final valuation of that which in any event has value to us. It is enough for us that the universe has produced us and has within it, as less than it, all that we believe and love. If we think of our existence not as that of a little god outside, but as that of a ganglion within, we have the infinite behind us. It gives us our only but our adequate significance. A grain of sand has the same, but what competent person supposes that he understands a grain of sand? That is as much beyond our grasp as man. If our imagination is strong enough to accept the vision of ourselves as parts inseverable from the rest, and to extend our final interest beyond the boundary of our skins, it justifies the sacrifice even of our lives for ends outside of ourselves. The motive, to be sure, is the common wants and ideals that we find in man. Philosophy does not furnish motives, but it shows men that they are not fools for doing what they already want to do. It opens to the forlorn hopes on which we throw ourselves away, the vista of the farthest stretch of human thought, the chords of a harmony that breathes from the unknown.

THORSTEIN VEBLEN

Selection from *The Theory of the Leisure Class* 1899

No evolutionary social theorist put Darwinian formulations to more critical uses than Thorstein Veblen (1857–1929). At once playful, angry, mordant, and ironic, Veblen sketched in *The Theory of the Leisure Class: An Economic Study of Institutions* (New York, 1899) a picture of the turn-of-the-century "new rich" that endures in American literature and political economy. In our selections from this book reprinted here, Veblen depicts people of this class as social parasites who only "retard the adaptation of human nature to the exigencies of modern industrial life." Veblen went on to write a number of other influential books, including *The Theory of Business Enterprise* (New York, 1904), *The Higher Learning in America* (New York, 1918), *The Place of Science in Modern Civilization* (New York, 1919), *The Engineers and the Price System* (1921), and *Absentee Ownership* (New York, 1923). Eager as he was to see intellectual men and women lead society, Veblen remained alienated from the prevailing academic culture of his own time. He bounced from faculty to faculty and died in a cabin in the wooded hills above Stanford University.

The most comprehensive study of his life and thought was written shortly after his death: Joseph Dorfmann, *Thorstein Veblen and His America* (New York, 1934). Perhaps the most succinct and penetrating introduction to Veblen's ideas is C. Wright Mills's introduction to the Mentor edition of *The Theory of the Leisure Class* (New York, 1953), vi–xix. For a provocative interpretation of Veblen in the context of modern social theory, see John P. Diggins, *The Bard of Savagery* (New York, 1978). See also the discussion of Veblen in relation to the development of the social sciences in the United States, in Dorothy Ross, *The Origins of American Social Science* (New York, 1991), 204–16. A helpful analysis of Veblen's rhetorical strategies is Clare Virginia Eby, "Thorstein Veblen and the Rhetoric of Authority," *American Quarterly* XLVI (1994), 139–73.

The life of man in society, just like the life of other species, is a struggle for existence, and therefore it is a process of selective adaptation. The evolution of social structure has been a process of natural selection of institutions. The progress which has been and is being made in human institutions and in human character may be set down, broadly, to a natural selection of the fittest habits of thought and to a process of enforced adaptation of individuals to an environment which has progressively changed with the growth of the community and with the changing institutions under which men have lived. Institutions are not only themselves the result of a selective and adaptive process which shapes the prevailing or dominant types of spiritual attitude and aptitudes; they are at the same time special methods of life and of human relations, and are therefore in their turn efficient factors of selection. So that the changing institutions in their turn make for a further selection of individuals endowed with the fittest temperament, and a further adaptation of individual temperament and habits to the changing environment through the formation of new institutions.

The forces which have shaped the development of human life and of social structure are no doubt ultimately reducible to terms of living tissue and material environment; but proximately, for the purpose in hand, these forces may best be stated in terms of an environment, partly human, partly non-human, and a human subject with a more or less definite physical and intellectual constitution. Taken in the aggregate or average, this human subject is more or less variable; chiefly, no doubt, under a rule of selective conservation of favourable variations. The selection of favourable variations is perhaps in great measure a selective conservation of ethnic types. In the life history of any community whose population is made up of a mixture of divers ethnic elements, one or another of several persistent and relatively stable types of body and of temperament rises into dominance at any given point. The situation, including the institutions in force at any given time, will favour the survival and dominance of one type of character in preference to another; and the type of man so selected to continue and to further elaborate the institutions handed down from the past will in some considerable measure shape these institutions in his own likeness. But apart from selection as between relatively stable types of character and habits of mind, there is no doubt simultaneously going on a process of selective adaptation of habits of thought within the general range of aptitudes which is characteristic of the dominant ethnic type or types. There may be a variation in the fundamental character of any population by selection between relatively stable types; but there is also a variation due to adaptation in detail within the range of the type, and to selection between specific habitual views regarding any given social relation or group of relations.

For the present purpose, however, the question as to the nature of the adaptive process—whether it is chiefly a selection between stable types of temperament and character, or chiefly an adaptation of men's habits of thought to changing circumstances—is of less importance than the fact that, by one method or another, institutions change and develop. Institutions must change with changing circumstances, since they are of the nature of an habitual method of responding to the stimuli which these changing circumstances afford. The development of these institutions is the development of society. The institutions are, in substance, prevalent habits of thought with respect to particular relations and particular functions of the individual and of the community;

Source: Thorstein Veblen, *The Theory of the Leisure Class: An Economic Study of Institutions* (New York: Macmillan, 1899), 188–213, 233–44.

and the scheme of life, which is made up of the aggregate of institutions in force at a given time or at a given point in the development of any society, may, on the psychological side, be broadly characterised as a prevalent spiritual attitude or a prevalent theory of life. As regards its generic features, this spiritual attitude or theory of life is in the last analysis reducible to terms of a prevalent type of character.

The situation of to-day shapes the institutions of to-morrow through a selective, coercive process, by acting upon men's habitual view of things, and so altering or fortifying a point of view or a mental attitude handed down from the past. The institutions—that is to say the habits of thought—under the guidance of which men live are in this way received from an earlier time; more or less remotely earlier, but in any event they have been elaborated in and received from the past. Institutions are products of the past process, are adapted to past circumstances, and are therefore never in full accord with the requirements of the present. In the nature of the case, this process of selective adaptation can never catch up with the progressively changing situation in which the community finds itself at any given time; for the environment, the situation, the exigencies of life which enforce the adaptation and exercise the selection, change from day to day; and each successive situation of the community in its turn tends to obsolescence as soon as it has been established. When a step in the development has been taken, this step itself constitutes a change of situation which requires a new adaptation; it becomes the point of departure for a new step in the adjustment, and so on interminably.

It is to be noted then, although it may be a tedious truism, that the institutions of to-day—the present accepted scheme of life—do not entirely fit the situation of to-day. At the same time, men's present habits of thought tend to persist indefinitely, except as circumstances enforce a change. These institutions which have so been handed down, these habits of thought, points of view, mental attitudes and aptitudes, or what not, are therefore themselves a conservative factor. This is the factor of social inertia, psychological inertia, conservatism.

Social structure changes, develops, adapts itself to an altered situation, only through a change in the habits of thought of the several classes of the community; or in the last analysis, through a change in the habits of thought of the individuals which make up the community. The evolution of society is substantially a process of mental adaptation on the part of individuals under the stress of circumstances which will no longer tolerate habits of thought formed under and conforming to a different set of circumstances in the past. For the immediate purpose it need not be a question of serious importance whether this adaptive process is a process of selection and survival of persistent ethnic types or a process of individual adaptation and an inheritance of acquired traits.

Social advance, especially as seen from the point of view of economic theory, consists in a continued progressive approach to an approximately exact "adjustment of inner relations to outer relations"; but this adjustment is never definitively established, since the "outer relations" are subject to constant change as a consequence of the progressive change going on in the "inner relations." But the degree of approximation may be greater or less, depending on the facility with which an adjustment is made. A readjustment of men's habits of thought to conform with the exigencies of an altered situation is in any case made only tardily and reluctantly, and only under the coercion exercised by a situation which has made the accredited views untenable. The readjustment of institutions and habitual views to an altered environment is made in response to pressure from without; it is of the nature of a response to stimulus. Freedom and facility of readjustment, that is to say capacity for growth in social structure, therefore depends in great measure on the degree of freedom with which the situation at any given time acts on the individual members of the community—the degree of exposure of the individual members to the constraining forces of the environment. If any portion or class of society is sheltered from the action of the environment in any essential respect, that portion of the community, or that class, will adapt its views and its scheme of life more tardily to the altered general situation; it will in so far tend to retard the process of social transformation. The wealthy leisure class is in such a sheltered position with respect to the economic forces that make for change and readjustment. And it may be said that the forces which make for a readjustment of institutions, especially in the case of a modern industrial community, are, in the last analysis, almost entirely of an economic nature.

Any community may be viewed as an industrial or economic mechanism, the structure of which is made up of what is called its economic institutions. These institutions are habitual methods of carrying on the life process of the community in contact with the material environment in which it lives. When given methods of unfolding human activity in this given environment have been elaborated in this way, the life of the community will express itself with some facility in these habitual directions. The community will make use of the forces of the environment for the purposes of its life according to methods learned in the past and embodied in these institutions. But as population increases, and as men's knowledge and skill in directing the forces of nature widen, the habitual methods of relation between the members of the group, and the habitual method of carrying on the life process of the group as a whole no longer give the same result as before; nor are the resulting conditions of life distributed and apportioned in the same manner or with the same effect among the various members as before. If the scheme according to which the life process of the group was carried on under the earlier conditions gave approximately the highest attainable result—under the circumstances—in the way of efficiency or facility of the life process of the group; then the same scheme of life unaltered will not yield the highest result attainable in this respect under the altered conditions. Under the altered conditions of population, skill, and knowledge, the facility of life as carried on according to the traditional scheme may not be lower than under the earlier conditions; but the chances are always that it is less than might be if the scheme were altered to suit the altered conditions.

The group is made up of individuals, and the group's life is the life of individuals carried on in at least ostensible severalty. The group's accepted scheme of life is the consensus of views held by the body of these individuals as to what is right, good, expedient, and beautiful in the way of human life. In the redistribution of the conditions of life that comes of the altered method of dealing with the environment, the outcome is not an equable change in the facility of life throughout the group. The altered conditions may increase the facility of life for the group as a whole, but the redistribution will usually result in a decrease of facility or fulness of life for some members of the group. An advance in technical methods, in population, or in industrial organisation will require at least some of the members of the community to change their habits of life, if they are to enter with facility and effect into the altered industrial methods; and in doing so they will be unable to live up to the received notions as to what are the right and beautiful habits of life.

Any one who is required to change his habits of life and his habitual relations to his fellow-men will feel the discrepancy between the method of life required of him by the newly arisen exigencies, and the traditional scheme of life to which he is accustomed. It is the individuals placed in this position who have the liveliest incentive to reconstruct the received scheme of life and are most readily persuaded to accept new standards; and it is through the need of the means of livelihood that men are placed in such a position. The pressure exerted by the environment upon the group, and making for a readjustment of the group's scheme of life, impinges upon the members of the group in the form of pecuniary exigencies; and it is owing to this fact—that external forces are in great part translated into the form of pecuniary or economic exigencies—it is owing to this fact that we can say that the forces which count toward a readjustment of institutions in any modern industrial community are chiefly economic forces; or more specifically, these forces take the form of pecuniary pressure. Such a readjustment as is here contemplated is substantially a change in men's views as to what is good and right, and the means through which a change is wrought in men's apprehension of what is good and right is in large part the pressure of pecuniary exigencies.

Any change in men's views as to what is good and right in human life makes its way but tardily at the best. Especially is this true of any change in the direction of what is called progress; that is to say, in the direction of divergence from the archaic position—from the position which may be accounted the point of departure at any step in the social evolution of the community. Retrogression, reapproach to a standpoint to which the race has been long habituated in the past, is easier. This is especially true in case the development away from this past standpoint has not been due chiefly to a substitution of an ethnic type whose temperament is alien to the earlier standpoint.

The cultural stage which lies immediately back of the present in the life history of Western civilisation is what has here been called the quasi-peaceable stage. At this quasi-peaceable stage the law of status is the dominant feature in the scheme of life. There is no need of pointing out how prone the men of to-day are to revert to the spiritual attitude of mastery and of personal subservience which characterises that stage. It may rather be said to be held in an uncertain abeyance by the economic exigencies of to-day, than to have been definitively supplanted by a habit of mind that is in full accord with these later-developed exigencies. The predatory and quasi-peaceable stages of economic evolution seem to have been of long duration in the life history of all the chief ethnic elements which go to make up the populations of the Western culture. The temperament and the propensities proper to those cultural stages have, therefore, attained such a persistence as to make a speedy reversion to the broad features of the corresponding psychological constitution inevitable in the case of any class or community which is removed from the action of those forces that make for a maintenance of the later-developed habits of thought.

It is a matter of common notoriety that when individuals, or even considerable groups of men, are segregated from a higher industrial culture and exposed to a lower cultural environment, or to an economic situation of a more primitive character, they quickly show evidence of reversion toward the spiritual features which characterise the predatory type; and it seems probable that the dolicho-blond type of European man is possessed of a greater facility for such reversion to barbarism than the other ethnic elements with which that type is associated in the Western culture. Examples of such a reversion on a small scale abound in the later history of migration and colonisation. Except for the fear of offending that chauvinistic patriotism which is so characteristic a feature of the predatory culture, and the presence of which is frequently the most striking mark of reversion in modern communities, the case of the American colonies might be cited as an example of such a reversion on an unusually large scale, though it was not a reversion of very large scope.

The leisure class is in great measure sheltered from the stress of those economic exigencies which prevail in any modern, highly organised industrial community. The exigencies of the struggle for the means of life are less exacting for this class than for any other; and as a consequence of this privileged position we should expect to find it one of the least responsive of the classes of society to the demands which the situation makes for a further growth of institutions and a readjustment to an altered industrial situation. The leisure class is the conservative class. The exigencies of the general economic situation of the community do not freely or directly impinge upon the members of this class. They are not required under penalty of forfeiture to change their habits of life and their theoretical views of the external world to suit the demands of an altered industrial technique, since they are not in the full sense an organic part of the industrial community. Therefore these exigencies do not readily produce, in the members of this class, that degree of uneasiness with the existing order which alone can lead any body of men to give up views and methods of life that have become habitual to them. The office of the leisure class in social evolution is to retard the movement and to conserve what is obsolescent. This proposition is by no means novel; it has long been one of the commonplaces of popular opinion.

The prevalent conviction that the wealthy class is by nature conservative has been popularly accepted without much aid from any theoretical view as to the place and relation of that class in the cultural development. When an explanation of this class conservatism is offered, it is commonly the invidious one that the wealthy class opposes innovation because it has a vested interest, of an unworthy sort, in maintaining the present conditions. The explanation here put forward imputes no unworthy motive. The opposition of the class to changes in the cultural scheme is instinctive, and does not rest primarily on an interested calculation of material advantages; it is an instictive revulsion at any departure from the accepted way of doing and of looking at things— a revulsion common to all men and only to be overcome by stress of circumstances. All change in habits of life and of thought is irksome. The difference in this respect between the wealthy and the common run of mankind lies not so much in the motive which prompts to conservatism as in the degree of exposure to the economic forces that urge a change. The members of the wealthy class do not yield to the demand for innovation as readily as other men because they are not constrained to do so.

This conservatism of the wealthy class is so obvious a feature that it has even come to be recognised as a mark of respectability. Since conservatism is a characteristic of the wealthier and therefore more reputable portion of the community, it has acquired a certain honorific or decorative value. It has become prescriptive to such an extent that an adherence to conservative views is comprised as a matter of course in our notions of respectability; and it is imperatively incumbent on all who would lead a blameless life in point of social repute. Conservatism, being an upper-class characteristic, is decorous; and conversely, innovation, being a lower-class phenomenon, is vulgar. The first and most unreflected element in that instinctive revulsion and reprobation with which we turn from all social innovators is this sense of the essential vulgarity of the thing. So that even in cases where one recognises the substantial merits of the case for which the innovator is spokesman—as may easily happen if the evils which he seeks to remedy are sufficiently remote in point of time or space or personal contact—still one cannot but be sensible of the fact that the innovator is a person with whom it is at least distasteful to be associated, and from whose social contact one must shrink. Innovation is bad form.

The fact that the usages, actions, and views of the well-to-do leisure class acquire the character of a prescriptive canon of conduct for the rest of society, gives added weight and reach to the conservative influence of that class. It makes it incumbent upon all reputable people to follow their lead. So that, by virtue of its high position as the avatar of good form, the wealthier class comes to exert a retarding influence upon social development far in excess of that which the simple numerical strength of the class would assign it. Its prescriptive example acts to greatly stiffen the resistance of all other classes against any innovation, and to fix men's affections upon the good institutions handed down from an earlier generation.

There is a second way in which the influence of the leisure class acts in the same direction, so far as concerns hindrance to the adoption of a conventional scheme of life more in accord with the exigencies of the time. This second method of upper-class guidance is not in strict consistency to be brought under the same category as the instinctive conservatism and aversion to new modes of thought just spoken of; but it may as well be dealt with here, since it has at least this much in common with the conservative habit of mind that it acts to retard innovation and the growth of social structure. The code of proprieties, conventionalities, and usages in vogue at any given time and among any given people has more or less of the character of an organic whole; so that any appreciable change in one point of the scheme involves something of a change or readjustment at other points also, if not a reorganisation all along the line. When a change is made which immediately touches only a minor point in the scheme, the consequent derangement of the structure of conventionalities may be inconspicuous; but even in such a case it is safe to say that some derangement of the general scheme, more or less far-reaching, will follow. On the other hand, when an attempted reform involves the suppression or thorough-going remodelling of an institution of first-rate importance in the conventional scheme, it is immediately felt that a serious derangement of the entire scheme would result; it is felt that a readjustment of the structure to the new form taken on by one of its chief elements would be a painful and tedious, if not a doubtful process.

In order to realise the difficulty which such a radical change in any one feature of the conventional scheme of life would involve, it is only necessary to suggest the suppression of the monogamic family, or of the agnatic system of consanguinity, or of private property, or of the theistic faith, in any country of the Western civilisation; or suppose the suppression of ancestor worship in China, or of the caste system in India, or of slavery in Africa, or the establishment of equality of the sexes in Mohammedan countries. It needs no argument to show that the derangement of the general structure of conventionalities in any of these cases would be very considerable. In order to effect such an innovation a very far-reaching alteration of men's habits of thought would be involved also at other points of the scheme than the one immediately in question. The aversion to any such innovation amounts to a shrinking from an essentially alien scheme of life.

The revulsion felt by good people at any proposed departure from the accepted methods of life is a familiar fact of everyday experience. It is not unusual to hear those persons who dispense salutary advice and admonition to the community express themselves forcibly upon the far-reaching pernicious effects which the community would suffer from such relatively slight changes as the disestablishment of the Anglican Church, an increased facility of divorce, adoption of female suffrage, prohibition of the manufacture and sale of intoxicating beverages, abolition or restriction of inheritance, etc. Any one of these innovations would, we are told, "shake the social structure to its base," "reduce society to chaos," "subvert the foundations of morality," "make life intolerable," "confound the order of nature," etc. These various locutions are, no doubt, of the nature of hyperbole; but, at the same time, like all overstatement, they are evidence of a lively sense of the gravity of the consequences which they are intended to describe. The effect of these and like innovations in deranging the accepted scheme of life is felt to be of much graver consequence than the simple alteration of an isolated item in a series of contrivances for the convenience of men in society. What is true in so obvious a degree of innovations of first-rate importance is true in a less degree of changes of a smaller immediate importance. The aversion to change is in large part an aversion to the bother of making the readjustment which any given change will necessitate; and this solidarity of the system of institutions of any given culture or of any given people strengthens the instinctive resistance offered to any change in men's habits of thought, even in matters which, taken by themselves, are of minor importance.

A consequence of this increased reluctance, due to the solidarity of human institutions, is that any innovation calls for a greater expenditure of nervous energy in making the necessary readjustment than would otherwise be the case. It is not only that a change in established habits of thought is distasteful. The process of readjustment of the accepted theory of life involves a degree of mental effort—a more or less protracted and laborious effort to find and to keep one's bearings under the altered circumstances. This process requires a certain expenditure of energy, and so presumes, for its successful accomplishment, some surplus of energy beyond that absorbed in the daily struggle for subsistence. Consequently it follows that progress is hindered by underfeeding and excessive physical hardship, no less effectually than by such a luxurious life as will shut out discontent by cutting off the occasion for it. The abjectly poor, and all those persons whose energies are entirely absorbed by the struggle for daily sustenance, are conservative because they cannot afford the effort of taking thought for the day after to-morrow; just as the highly prosperous are conservative because they have small occasion to be discontented with the situation as it stands to-day.

From this proposition it follows that the institution of a leisure class acts to make the lower classes conservative by withdrawing from them as much as it may of the means of sustenance, and so reducing their consumption, and consequently their available energy, to such a point as to make them incapable of the effort required for the learning and adoption of new habits of thought. The accumulation of wealth at the upper end of the pecuniary scale implies privation at the lower end of the scale. It is a commonplace that, wherever it occurs, a considerable degree of privation among the body of the people is a serious obstacle to any innovation.

This direct inhibitory effect of the unequal distribution of wealth is seconded by an indirect effect tending to the same result. As has already been seen, the imperative example set by the upper class in fixing the canons of reputability fosters the practice of conspicuous consumption. The prevalence of conspicuous consumption as one of the main elements in the standard of decency among all classes is of course not traceable wholly to the example of the wealthy leisure class, but the practice and the insistence on it are no doubt strengthened by the example of the leisure class. The requirements of decency in this matter are very considerable and very imperative; so that even among classes whose pecuniary position is sufficiently strong to admit a consumption of goods considerably in excess of the subsistence minimum, the disposable surplus left over after the more imperative physical needs are satisfied is not infrequently diverted to the purpose of a conspicuous decency, rather than to added physical comfort and fulness of life. Moreover, such surplus energy as is available is also likely to be expended in the acquisition of goods for conspicuous consumption or conspicuous hoarding. The result is that the requirements of pecuniary reputability tend (1) to leave but a scanty subsistence minimum available for other than conspicuous consumption, and (2) to absorb any surplus energy which may be available after the bare physical necessities of life have been provided for. The outcome of the whole is a strengthening of the general conservative attitude of the community. The institution of a leisure class hinders cultural development immediately (1) by the inertia proper to the class itself, (2) through its prescriptive example of conspicuous waste and of conservatism, and (3) indirectly through that system of unequal distribution of wealth and sustenance on which the institution itself rests.

To this is to be added that the leisure class has also a material interest in leaving things as they are. Under the circumstances prevailing at any given time this class is in a privileged position, and any departure from the existing order may be expected to work to the detriment of the class rather than the reverse. The attitude of the class, simply as influenced by its class interest, should therefore be to let well-enough alone. This interested motive comes in to supplement the strong instinctive bias of the class, and so to render it even more consistently conservative than it otherwise would be.

All this, of course, has nothing to say in the way of eulogy or deprecation of the office of the leisure class as an exponent and vehicle of conservatism or reversion in social structure. The inhibition which it exercises may be salutary or the reverse. Whether it is the one or the other in any given case is a question of casuistry rather than of general theory. There may be truth in the view (as a question of policy) so often expressed by the spokesmen of the conservative element, that without some such substantial and consistent resistance to innovation as is offered by the conservative well-to-do classes, social innovation and experiment would hurry the community into untenable and intolerable situations; the only possible result of which would be discontent and disastrous reaction. All this, however, is beside the present argument.

But apart from all deprecation, and aside from all question as to the indispensability of some such check on headlong innovation, the leisure class, in the nature of things, consistently acts to retard that adjustment to the environment which is called social advance or development. The characteristic attitude of the class may be summed up in the maxim: "Whatever is, is right"; whereas the law of natural selection, as applied to human institutions, gives the axiom: "Whatever is, is wrong." Not that the institutions of to-day are wholly wrong for the purposes of the life of to-day, but they are, always and in the nature of things, wrong to some extent. They are the result of a more or less inadequate adjustment of the methods of living to a situation which prevailed at some point in the past development; and they are therefore wrong by something more than the interval which separates the present situation from that of the past. "Right" and "wrong" are of course here used without conveying any reflection as to what ought or ought not to be. They are applied simply from the (morally colourless) evolutionary standpoint and are intended to designate compatibility or incompatibility with the effective evolutionary process. The institution of a leisure class, by force of class interest and instinct, and by precept and prescriptive example, makes for the perpetuation of the existing maladjustment of institutions, and even favours a reversion to a somewhat more archaic scheme of life; a scheme which would be still farther out of adjustment with the exigencies of life under the existing situation even than the accredited, obsolescent scheme that has come down from the immediate past.

But after all has been said on the head of conservation of the good old ways, it remains true that institutions change and develop. There is a cumulative growth of customs and habits of thought; a selective adaptation of conventions and methods of life. Something is to be said of the office of the leisure class in guiding this growth as well as in retarding it; but little can be said here of its relation to institutional growth except as it touches the institutions that are primarily and immediately of an economic character. These institutions—the economic structure—may be roughly distinguished into two classes or categories, according as they serve one or the other of two divergent purposes of economic life.

To adapt the classical terminology, they are institutions of acquisition or of production; or to revert to terms already employed in a different connection in earlier chapters, they are pecuniary or industrial institutions; or in still other terms, they are institutions serving either the invidious or the non-invidious economic interest. The former category have to do with "business," the latter with industry, taking the latter word in the mechanical sense. The latter class are not often recognised as institutions, in great part because they do not immediately concern the ruling class, and are, therefore, seldom the subject of legislation or of deliberate convention. When they do receive attention they are commonly approached from the pecuniary or business side; that being the side or phase of economic life that chiefly occupies men's deliberations in our time, especially the deliberations of the upper classes. These classes have little else than a business interest in things economic, and on them at the same time it is chiefly incumbent to deliberate upon the community's affairs.

The relation of the leisure (that is, propertied non-industrial) class to the economic process is a pecuniary relation—a relation of acquisition, not of production; of exploitation, not of serviceability. Indirectly their economic office may, of course, be of the utmost importance to the economic life process; and it is by no means here intended to depreciate the economic function of the propertied class or of the captains of industry. The purpose is simply to point out what is the nature of the relation of these classes to the industrial process and to economic institutions. Their office is of a parasitic character, and their interest is to divert what substance they may to their own use, and to retain whatever is under their hand. The conventions of the business world have grown up under the selective surveillance of this principle of predation or parasitism. They are conventions of ownership; derivatives, more or less remote, of the ancient predatory culture. But these pecuniary institutions do not entirely fit the situation of to-day, for they have grown up under a past situation differing somewhat from the present. Even for effectiveness in the pecuniary way, therefore, they are not as apt as might be. The changed industrial life requires changed methods of acquisition; and the pecuniary classes have some interest in so adapting the pecuniary institutions as to give them the best effect for acquisition of private gain that is compatible with the continuance of the industrial process out of which this gain arises. Hence there is a more or less consistent trend in the leisure-class guidance of institutional growth, answering to the pecuniary ends which shape leisure-class economic life.

The effect of the pecuniary interest and the pecuniary habit of mind upon the growth of institutions is seen in those enactments and conventions that make for security of property, enforcement of contracts, facility of pecuniary transactions, vested interests. Of such bearing are changes affecting bankruptcy and receiverships, limited liability, banking and currency, coalitions of labourers or employers, trusts and pools. The community's institutional furniture of this kind is of immediate consequence only to the propertied classes, and in proportion as they are propertied; that is to say, in proportion as they are to be ranked with the leisure class. But indirectly these conventions of business life are of the gravest consequence for the industrial process and for the life of the community. And in guiding the institutional growth in this respect, the pecuniary classes, therefore, serve a purpose of the most serious importance to the community, not only in the conservation of the accepted social scheme, but also in shaping the industrial process proper.

The immediate end of this pecuniary institutional structure and of its amelioration is the greater facility of peaceable and orderly exploitation; but its remoter effects far outrun this immediate object. Not only does the more facile conduct of business permit industry and extra-industrial life to go on with less perturbation; but the resulting elimination of disturbances and complications calling for an exercise of astute discrimination in everyday affairs acts to make the pecuniary class itself superfluous. As fast as pecuniary transactions are reduced to routine, the captain of industry can be dispensed with. This consummation, it is needless to say, lies yet in the indefinite future. The ameliorations wrought in favour of the pecuniary interest in modern institutions tend, in another field, to substitute the "soulless" joint-stock corporation for the captain, and so they make also for the dispensability of the great leisure-class function of ownership. Indirectly, therefore, the bent given to the growth of economic institutions by the leisure-class influence is of very considerable industrial consequence. . . .

The institution of a leisure class has an effect not only upon social structure but also upon the individual character of the members of society. So soon as a given proclivity or a given point of view has won acceptance as an authoritative standard or norm of life it will react upon the character of the members of the society which has accepted it as a norm. It will to some extent shape their habits of thought and will exercise a selective surveillance over the development of men's aptitudes and inclinations. This effect is wrought partly by a coercive, educational adaptation of the habits of all individuals, partly by a selective elimination of the unfit individuals and lines of descent. Such human material as does not lend itself to the methods of life imposed by the accepted scheme suffers more or less elimination as well as repression. The principles of pecuniary emulation and of industrial exemption have in this way been erected into canons of life, and have become coercive factors of some importance in the situation to which men have to adapt themselves.

These two broad principles of conspicuous waste and industrial exemption affect the cultural development both by guiding men's habits of thought, and so controlling the growth of institutions, and by selectively conserving certain traits of human nature that conduce to facility of life under the leisure-class scheme, and so controlling the effective temper of the community. The proximate tendency of the institution of a leisure class in shaping human character runs in the direction of spiritual survival and reversion. Its effect upon the temper of a community is of the nature of an arrested spiritual development. . . .

The constituency of the leisure class is kept up by a continual selective process, whereby the individuals and lines of descent that are eminently fitted for an aggressive pecuniary competition are withdrawn from the lower classes. In order to reach the upper levels the aspirant must have, not only a fair average complement of the pecuniary aptitudes, but he must have these gifts in such an eminent degree as to overcome very material difficulties that stand in the way of his ascent. Barring accidents, the *nouveaux arrivés* are a picked body.

This process of selective admission has, of course, always been going on; ever since the fashion of pecuniary emulation set in,—which is much the same as saying, ever since the institution of a leisure class was first installed. But the precise ground of selection has not always been the same, and the selective process has therefore not always given the same results. In the early barbarian, or predatory stage proper, the test of fitness was prowess, in the naïve sense of the word. To gain entrance to the class, the candidate must be gifted with clannishness, massiveness, ferocity, unscrupulousness, and tenacity of purpose. These were the qualities that counted toward the accumulation and continued tenure of wealth. The economic basis of the leisure class, then as later, was the possession of wealth; but the methods of accumulating wealth, and the gifts required for holding it, have changed in some degree since the early days of the predatory culture. In consequence of the selective process the dominant traits of the early barbarian leisure class were bold aggression, an alert sense of status, and a free resort to fraud. The members of the class held their place by tenure of prowess. In the later barbarian culture society attained settled methods of acquisition and possession under the quasi-peaceable régime of status. Simple aggression and unrestrained violence in great measure gave place to shrewd practise and chicanery, as the best approved method of accumulating wealth. A different range of aptitudes and propensities would then be conserved in the leisure class. Masterful aggression, and the coorelative massiveness, together with a ruthlessly consistent sense of status, would still count among the most splendid traits of the class. These have remained in our traditions as the typical "aristocratic virtues." But with these were associated an increasing complement of the less obtrusive pecuniary virtues; such as providence, prudence, and chicane. As time has gone on, and the modern peaceable stage of pecuniary culture has been approached, the last-named range of aptitudes and habits has gained in relative effectiveness for pecuniary ends, and they have counted for relatively more in the selective process under which admission is gained and place is held in the leisure class.

The ground of selection has changed, until the aptitudes which now qualify for admission to the class are the pecuniary aptitudes only. What remains of the predatory barbarian traits is the tenacity of purpose or consistency of aim which distinguished the successful predatory barbarian from the peaceable savage whom he supplanted. But this trait can not be said characteristically to distinguish the pecuniarily successful upper-class man from the rank and file of the industrial classes. The training and the selection to which the latter are exposed in modern industrial life give a similarly decisive weight to this trait. Tenacity of purpose may rather be said to distinguish both these classes from two others: the shiftless ne'er-do-well and the lower-class delinquent. In point of natural endowment the pecuniary man compares with the delinquent in much the same way as the industrial man compares with the good-natured shiftless dependent. The ideal pecuniary man is like the ideal delinquent in his unscrupulous conversion of goods and persons to his own ends, and in a callous disregard of the feelings and wishes of others and of the remoter effects of his actions; but he is unlike him in possessing a keener sense of status, and in working more consistently and farsightedly to a remoter end. The kinship of the two types of temperament is further shown in a proclivity to "sport" and gambling, and a relish of aimless emulation. The ideal pecuniary man also shows a curious kinship with the delinquent in one of the concomitant variations of the predatory human nature. The delinquent is very commonly of a superstitious habit of mind; he is a great believer in luck, spells, divination and destiny, and in omens and shamanistic ceremony. Where circumstances are favourable, this proclivity is apt to express itself in a certain servile devotional fervour and a punctilious attention to devout observances; it may perhaps be better characterised as devoutness than as religion. At this point the temperament of the delinquent has more in common with the pecuniary and leisure classes than with the industrial man or with the class of shiftless dependents.

Life in a modern industrial community, or in other words life under the pecuniary culture, acts by a process of selection to develop and conserve a certain range of aptitudes and propensities. The present tendency of this selective process is not simply a reversion to a given, immutable ethnic type. It tends rather to a modification of human nature differing in some respects from any of the types or variants transmitted out of the past. The objective point of the evolution is not a single one. The temperament which the evolution acts to establish as normal differs from any one of the archaic variants of human nature in its greater stability of aim—greater singleness of purpose and greater persistence in effort. So far as concerns economic theory, the objective point of the selective process is on the whole single to this extent; although there are minor tendencies of considerable importance diverging from this line of development. But apart from this general trend the line of development is not single. As concerns economic theory, the development in other respects runs on two divergent lines. So far as regards the selective conservation of capacities or aptitudes in individuals, these two lines may be called the pecuniary and the industrial. As regards the conservation of propensities, spiritual attitude, or animus, the two may be called the invidious or self-regarding and the non-invidious or economical. As regards the intellectual or cognitive bent of the two directions of growth, the former may be characterised as the personal standpoint, of conation, qualitative relation, status, or worth; the latter as the impersonal standpoint, of sequence, quantitative relation, mechanical efficiency, or use.

The pecuniary employments call into action chiefly the former of these two ranges of aptitudes and propensities, and act selectively to conserve them in the population. The industrial employments, on the other hand, chiefly exercise the latter range, and act to conserve them. An exhaustive psychological analysis will show that each of these two ranges of aptitudes and propensities is but the multiform expression of a given temperamental bent. By force of the unity or singleness of the individual, the aptitudes, animus, and interests comprised in the first-named range belong together as expressions of a given variant of human nature. The like is true of the latter range. The two may be conceived as alternative directions of human life, in such a way that a given individual inclines more or less consistently to the one or the other. The tendency of the pecuniary life is, in a general way, to conserve the barbarian temperament, but with the substitution of fraud and prudence, or administrative ability, in place of that predilection for physical damage that characterises the early barbarian. This substitution of chicane in place of devastation takes place only in an uncertain degree. Within the pecuniary employments the selective action runs pretty consistently in this direction, but the discipline of pecuniary life, outside the competition for gain, does not work consistently to the same effect. The discipline of modern life in the consumption of time and goods does not act unequivocally to eliminate the aristocratic virtues or to foster the bourgeois virtues. The conventional scheme of decent living calls for a considerable exercise of the earlier barbarian traits. . . .

From what has been said, it appears that the leisure-class life and the leisure-class scheme of life should further the conservation of the barbarian temperament; chiefly of the quasi-peaceable, or bourgeois, variant, but also in some measure of the predatory variant. In the absence of disturbing factors, therefore, it should be possible to trace a difference of temperament between the classes of society. The aristocratic and the bourgeois virtues—that is to say the destructive and pecuniary traits—should be found chiefly among the upper classes, and the industrial virtues—that is to say the peaceable traits—chiefly among the classes given to mechanical industry.

In a general and uncertain way this holds true, but the test is not so readily applied nor so conclusive as might be wished. There are several assignable reasons for its partial failure. All classes are in a measure engaged in the pecuniary struggle, and in all classes the possession of the pecuniary traits counts towards the success and survival of the individual. Wherever the pecuniary culture prevails, the selective process by which men's habits of thought are shaped, and by which the survival of rival lines of descent is decided, proceeds proximately on the basis of fitness for acquisition. Consequently, if it were not for the fact that pecuniary efficiency is on the whole incompatible with industrial efficiency, the selective action of all occupations would tend to the unmitigated dominance of the pecuniary temperament. The result would be the installation of what has been known as the "economic man," as the normal and definitive type of human nature. But the "economic man," whose only interest is the self-regarding one and whose only human trait is prudence, is useless for the purposes of modern industry.

The modern industry requires an impersonal, non-invidious interest in the work in hand. Without this the elaborate processes of industry would be impossible, and would, indeed, never have been conceived. This interest in work differentiates the workman from the criminal on the one hand, and from the captain of industry on the other. Since work must be done in order to the continued life of the community, there results a qualified selection favouring the spiritual aptitude for work, within a certain range of occupations. This much, however, is to be conceded, that even within the industrial occupations the selective elimination of the pecuniary traits is an uncertain process, and that there is consequently an appreciable survival of the barbarian temperament even within these occupations. On this account there is at present no broad distinction in this respect between the leisure-class character and the character of the common run of the population.

The whole question as to a class distinction in respect of spiritual make-up is also obscured by the presence, in all classes of society, of acquired habits of life that closely simulate inherited traits and at the same time act to develop in the entire body of the population the traits which they simulate. These acquired habits, or assumed traits of character, are not commonly of an aristocratic cast. The prescriptive position of the leisure class as the exemplar of reputability has imposed many features of the leisure-class theory of life upon the lower classes; with the result that there goes on, always and throughout society, a more or less persistent cultivation of these aristocratic traits. On this ground also these traits have a better chance of survival among the body of the people than would be the case if it were not for the precept and example of the leisure class. As one channel, and an important one, through which this transfusion of aristocratic views of life, and consequently more or less archaic traits of character, goes on, may be mentioned the class of domestic servants. These have their notions of what is good and beautiful shaped by contact with the master class and carry the preconceptions so acquired back among their low-born equals, and so disseminate the higher ideals abroad through the community without the loss of time which this dissemeination might otherwise suffer. The saying, "Like master, like man," has a greater significance than is commonly appreciated for the rapid popular acceptance of many elements of upper-class culture.

There is also a further range of facts that go to lessen class differences as regards the survival of the pecuniary virtues. The pecuniary struggle produces an underfed class, of large proportions. This underfeeding consists in a deficiency of the necessaries of life or of the necessaries of a decent expenditure. In either case the result is a closely enforced struggle for the means with which to meet the daily needs; whether it be the physical or the higher needs. The strain of self-assertion against odds takes up the whole energy of the individual; he bends his efforts to compass his own invidious ends alone, and becomes continually more narrowly self-seeking. The industrial traits in this way tend to obsolescence through disuse. Indirectly, therefore, by imposing a scheme of pecuniary decency and by withdrawing as much as may be of the means of life from the lower classes, the institution of a leisure class acts to conserve the pecuniary traits in the body of the population. The result is an assimilation of the lower classes to the type of human nature that belongs primarily to the upper classes only.

It appears, therefore, that there is no wide difference in temperament between the upper and the lower classes; but it appears also that the absence of such a difference is in good part due to the prescriptive example of the leisure class and to the popular acceptance of those broad principles of conspicuous waste and pecuniary emulation on which the institution of a leisure class rests. The institution acts to lower the industrial efficiency of the community and retard the adaptation of human nature to the exigencies of modern industrial life. . . .

W. E. B. DU BOIS

"Of the Sons of Master and Man"
1903

W.E.B. Du Bois (1868–1963) died in Africa, an expatriate, at almost the same moment that Martin Luther King, Jr., was delivering his "I Have a Dream" speech in front of the Lincoln Memorial, bringing to a climax one of the greatest civil rights demonstrations in American history. By 1963 Du Bois had largely been forgotten in the United States, although he had once been a prominent figure in the National Association for the Advancement of Colored People and had etched a formidable record as a historian, literary essayist, social critic, and editor. Even before the turn of the century, Du Bois had written two important books, one a history of the suppression of the African slave trade and the other a sociological study of the black population of Philadelphia. A fine anthology of work from all stages of Du Bois's career is Eric Sundquist, ed., *The Oxford W. E. B. Du Bois Reader* (New York 1996). Since Du Bois's death, his stature has grown steadily, and he is now, along with King, one of the most widely appreciated and carefully studied of all American intellectuals of the twentieth century, of any color.

One passage from Du Bois's early work that has become especially popular is worth quoting here, as it is widely regarded as an emblem for the morally and intellectually complex perspective that Du Bois brought to the question of what it means to be black in the United States. This passage appears in the early pages of his most enduring book, *The Souls of Black Folk: Essays and Sketches* (Chicago, 1903):

> After the Egyptian and Indian, the Greek and Roman, the Teuton and Mongolian, the Negro is a sort of seventh son, born with a veil, and gifted with second-sight in this American world,—a world which yields him no true self-consciousness, but only lets him see himself through the revelation of the other world. It is a peculiar sensation, this double-consciousness, this sense of always looking at one's self through the eyes of others, of measuring one's soul by the tape of a world that looks on in amused contempt and pity. One ever feels his twoness,—an American, a Negro; two souls, two thoughts, two unreconciled strivings; two warring ideals in one dark body, whose dogged strength alone keeps it from being torn asunder.

> The history of the American Negro is the history of this strife,—this longing to attain self-conscious manhood, to merge his double self into a better and true self. In this merging he wishes neither of the older selves to be lost. He would not Africanize America, for America has too much to teach the world and Africa. He would not bleach his Negro soul in a flood of white Americanism, for he knows that Negro blood has a message for the world. He simply wishes to make it possible for a man to be both a Negro and an American, without being cursed and spit upon by his fellows, without having the doors of Opportunity closed roughly in his face.

This prophetic passage could be a prologue to the chapter of *Souls of Black Folk* reprinted here, "Of the Sons of Master and Man." In this essay, Du Bois engages the social realities of black–white contact in the post-Emancipation South and outlines a political, economic, and cultural program considerably more ambitious than the program advocated and developed by Booker T. Washington, the most influential African-American of that period. In another famous chapter of *Souls of Black Folk*—"On Mr. Booker T. Washington and Others"—Du Bois criticized Washington's vision of a black–white partnership based on the acceptance of political inequality and on the economic tracking of blacks into agri cultural and industrial roles subordinate to white business interests. Washington's ideas are best approached through his own writings, however, rather than through Du Bois's representation of them. The most accessible of Washington's writings is his autobiography, *Up from Slavery* (New York, 1901). Du Bois's thought can also be profitably studied in relation to that of a clergyman often regarded as a founder of black nationalism, Alexander Crummell. See especially Crummell's collected addresses, *Africa and America* (Springfield, Mass., 1891).

Prominent among recent studies of Du Bois himself are Arnold Rampersad, *The Art and Imagination of W.E.B. Du Bois* (Cambridge, Mass., 1976,), Manning Marable, *W.E.B. Du Bois: Black Radical Democrat* (Boston, 1986), David Levering Lewis, *W.E.B. Du Bois: Biography of a Race, 1868–1919* (New York, 1993), and Shamoon Zamir, *Dark Voices: W.E.B. Du Bois and American Thought, 1888–1903* (Chicago, 1995). For an analysis of key issues in the study of the most productive years of Du Bois's career, see Thomas S. Holt, "The Political Uses of Alienation: W.E.B. Du Bois on Politics, Race, and Culture, 1903–1940," *American Quarterly.* XLII (1990), 301–23. For a fresh reading of Du Bois in relation to pragmatism, see Ross Posnock, "The Distinction of Du Bois: Aesthetics, Pragmatism, Politics," *American Literary History* VIII (Fall 1995), 500–524.

Life treads on life, and heart on heart;
We press too close in church and mart
To keep a dream or grave apart.
                    Mrs. Browning.

The world-old phenomenon of the contact of diverse races of men is to have new exemplification during the new century. Indeed, the characteristic of our age is the contact of European civilization with the world's undeveloped peoples. Whatever we may say of the results of such contact in the past, it certainly forms a chapter in human action not pleasant to look back upon. War, murder, slavery, extermination, and debauchery,—this has again and again been the result of carrying civilization and the blessed gospel to the isles of the sea and the heathen without the law. Nor does it altogether satisfy the conscience of the modern world to be told complacently that all this has been right and proper, the fated triumph of strength over weakness, of righteousness over evil, of superiors over inferiors. It would certainly be soothing if one could readily believe all this; and yet there are too many ugly facts for everything to be thus easily explained away. We feel and know that there are many delicate differences in race psychology, numberless changes that our crude social measurements are not yet able to follow minutely, which explain much of history and social development. At the same time, too, we know that these considerations have never adequately explained or excused the triumph of brute force and cunning over weakness and innocence.

It is, then, the strife of all honorable men of the twentieth century to see that in the future competition of races the survival of the fittest shall mean the triumph of the good, the beautiful, and the true; that we may be able to preserve for future civiliation all that is really fine and noble and strong, and not continue to put a premium on greed and impudence and cruelty. To bring this hope to fruition, we are compelled daily to turn more and more to a conscientious study of the phenomena of race-contact,—to a study frank and fair, and not falsified and colored by our wishes or our fears. And we have in the South as fine a field for such a study as the world affords,—a field, to be sure, which the average American scientist deems somewhat beneath his dignity, and which the average man who is not a scientist knows all about, but nevertheless a line of study which by reason of the enormous race complications with which God seems about to punish this nation must increasingly claim our sober attention, study, and thought, we must ask, what are the actual relations of whites and blacks in the South? and we must be answered, not by apology or fault-finding, but by a plain, unvarnished tale.

In the civilized life of to-day the contact of men and their relations to each other fall in a few main lines of action and communication: there is, first, the physical proximity of homes and dwelling-places, the way in which neighborhoods group themselves, and the contiguity of neighborhoods. Secondly, and in our age chiefest, there are the economic relations,—the methods by which individuals coöperate for earning a living, for the mutual satisfaction of wants, for the production of wealth. Next, there are the political relations, the coöperation in social control, in group government, in laying and paying the burden of taxation. In the fourth place there are the less tangible but highly important forms of intellectual contact and commerce, the interchange of ideas through conversation and conference, through periodicals and libraries; and, above all, the gradual formation for each community of that curious *tertium quid* which we call public

Source: W. E. B. Du bois, *The Souls of Black Folk* (Chicago, 1903).

opinion. Closely allied with this come the various forms of social contact in everyday life, in travel, in theatres, in house gatherings, in marrying and giving in marriage. Finally, there are the varying forms of religious enterprise, of moral teaching and benevolent endeavor. These are the principal ways in which men living in the same communities are brought into contact with each other. It is my present task, therefore, to indicate, from my point of view, how the black race in the South meet and mingle with the whites in these matters of everday life.

First, as to physical dwelling. It is usually possible to draw in nearly every Southern community a physical color-line on the map, on the one side of which whites dwell and on the other Negroes. The winding and intricacy of the geographical color line varies, of course, in different communities. I know some towns where a straight line drawn through the middle of the main street separates nine-tenths of the whites from nine-tenths of the blacks. In other towns the older settlement of whites has been encircled by a broad band of blacks; in still other cases little settlements or nuclei of blacks have sprung up amid surrounding whites. Usually in cities each street has its distinctive color, and only now and then do the colors meet in close proximity. Even in the country something of this segregation is manfiest in the smaller areas, and of course in the larger phenomena of the Black Belt.

All this segregation by color is largely independent of that natural clustering by social grades common to all communities. A Negro slum may be in dangerous proximity to a white residence quarter, while it is quite common to find a white slum planted in the heart of a respectable Negro district. One thing, however, seldom occurs: the best of the whites and the best of the Negroes almost never live in anything like close proximity. It thus happens that in nearly every Southern town and city, both whites and blacks see commonly the worst of each other. This is a vast change from the situation in the past, when, through the close contact of master and house-servant in the patriarchal big house, one found the best of both races in close contact and sympathy, while at the same time the squalor and dull round of toil among the field-hands was removed from the sight and hearing of the family. One can easily see how a person who saw slavery thus from his father's parlors, and sees freedom on the streets of a great city, fails to grasp or comprehend the whole of the new picture. On the other hand, the settled belief of the mass of the Negroes that the Southern white people do not have the black man's best interests at heart has been intensified in later years by this continual daily contact of the better class of blacks with the worst representatives of the white race.

Coming now to the economic relations of the races, we are on ground made familiar by study, much discussion, and no little philanthropic effort. And yet with all this there are many essential elements in the coöperation of Negroes and whites for work and wealth that are too readily overlooked or not thoroughly understood. The average American can easily conceive of a rich land awaiting development and filled with black laborers. To him the Southern problem is simply that of making efficient workingmen out of this material, by giving them the requisite technical skill and the help of invested capital. The problem, however, is by no means as simple as this, from the obvious fact that these workingmen have been trained for centuries as slaves. They exhibit, therefore, all the advantages and defects of such training; they are willing and good-natured, but not self-reliant, provident, or careful. If now the economic development of the South is to be pushed to the verge of exploitation, as seems probable, then we have a mass of working men thrown into relentless competition with the workingmen of the world, but handicapped by a training the very opposite to that of the modern self-reliant democratic laborer. What the black laborer needs is careful personal guidance, group leadership of men with hearts in their bosoms, to train them to foresight, carefulness, and honesty. Nor does it require any fine-spun theories of racial differences to prove the necessity of such group training after the brains of the race have been knocked out by two hundred and fifty years of assiduous education in submission, carelessness, and stealing. After Emancipation, it was the plain duty of some one to assume this group leadership and training of the Negro laborer. I will not stop here to inquire whose duty it was,—whether that of the white ex-master who has profited by unpaid toil, or the Northern philanthropist whose persistence brought on the crisis, or the National Government whose edict freed the bondmen; I will not stop to ask whose duty it was, but I insist it was the duty of some one to see that these workingmen were not left alone and unguided, without capital, without land, without skill, without economic organization, without even the bald protection of law, order, and decency,—left in a great land, not to settle down to slow and careful internal development, but destined to be thrown almost immediately into relentless and sharp competition with the best of modern workingmen under an economic system where every participant is fighting for himself, and too often utterly regardless of the rights or welfare of his neighbor.

For we must never forget that the economic system of the South to-day which has succeeded the old *régime* is not the same system as that of the old industrial North, of England, or of France, with their trades-unions, their restrictive laws, their written and unwritten commercial customs, and their long experience. It is, rather, a copy of that England of the early nineteenth century, before the factory acts,—the England that wrung pity from thinkers and fired the wrath of Carlyle. The rod of empire that passed from the hands of Southern gentlemen in 1865, partly by force, partly by their own petulance, has never returned to them. Rather it has passed to those men who have come to take charge of the industrial exploitation of the New South,—the sons of poor whites fired with a new thirst for wealth and power, thrifty and avaricious Yankees, shrewd and unscrupulous Jews. Into the hands of these men the Southern laborers, white and black, have fallen; and this to their sorrow. For the laborers as such there is in these new captains of industry neither love nor hate, neither sympathy nor romance; it is a cold question of dollars and dividends. Under such a system all labor is bound to suffer. Even the white laborers are not yet intelligent, thrifty, and well trained enough to maintain themselves against the powerful inroads of organized capital. The results among them, even, are long hours of toil, low wages, child labor, and lack of protection against usury and cheating. But among the black laborers all this is aggravated, first, by a race prejudice which varies from a doubt and distrust among the best element of whites to a frenzied hatred among the worst; and, secondly, it is aggravated, as I have said before, by the wretched economic heritage of the freedmen from slavery. With this training it is difficult for the freedman to learn to grasp the opportunities already opened to him, and the new opportunities are seldom given him, but go by favor to the whites.

Left by the best elements of the South with little protection or oversight, he has been made in law and custom the victim of the worst and most unscrupulous men in each community. The crop-lien system which is depopulating the fields of the South is not simply the result of shiftlessness on the part of Negroes, but is also the result of cunningly devised laws as to mortgages, liens, and misdemeanors, which can be made by conscienceless men to entrap and snare the unwary until escape is impossible, further toil a farce, and protest a crime. I have seen, in the Black Belt of Georgia, an ignorant, honest Negro buy and pay for a farm in installments three separate times, and then in the face of law and decency the enterprising Russian Jew who sold it to him pocketed money and deed and left the black man landless, to labor on his own land at thirty cents a day. I have seen a black farmer fall in debt to a white storekeeper, and that storekeeper go to his farm and strip it of every single marketable article,—mules, ploughs, stored crops, tools, furniture, bedding, clocks, looking-glass,—and all this without a warrant, without process of law, without a sheriff or officer, in the face of the law for homestead exemptions, and without rendering to a single responsible person any account or reckoning. And such proceedings can happen, and will happen, in any community where a class of ignorant toilers are placed by custom and race-prejudice beyond the pale of sympathy and race-brotherhood. So long as the best elements of a community do not feel in duty bound to protect and train and care for the weaker members of their group, they leave them to be preyed upon by these swindlers and rascals.

This unfortunate economic situation does not mean the hindrance of all advance in the black South, or the absence of a class of black landlords and mechanics who, in spite of disadvantages, are accumulating property and making good citizens. But it does mean that this class is not nearly so large as a fairer economic system might easily make it, that those who survive in the competition are handicapped so as to accomplish much less than they deserve to, and that, above all, the *personnel* of the successful class is left to chance and accident, and not to any intelligent culling or reasonable methods of selection. As a remedy for this, there is but one possible procedure. We must accept some of the race prejudice in the South as a fact,—deplorable in its intensity, unfortunate in results, and dangerous for the future, but nevertheless a hard fact which only time can efface. We cannot hope, then, in this generation, or for several generations, that the mass of the whites can be brought to assume that close sympathetic and self-sacrificing leadership of the blacks which their present situation so eloquently demands. Such leadership, such social teaching and example, must come from the blacks themselves. For some time men doubted as to whether the Negro could develop such leaders; but to-day no one seriously disputes the capability of individual Negroes to assimilate the culture and common sense of modern civilization, and to pass it on, to some extent at least, to their fellows. If this is true, then here is the path out of the economic situation, and here is the imperative demand for trained Negro leaders of character and intelligence,—men of skill, men of light and leading, college-bred men, black captains of industry, and missionaries of culture; men who thoroughly comprehend and know modern civilization, and can take hold of Negro communities and raise and train them by force of precept and example, deep sympathy, and the inspiration of common blood and ideals. But if such men are to be effective they must have some power,—they must be backed by the best public opinion of these communities, and able to wield for their objects and aims such weapons as the experience of the world has taught are indispensable to human progress.

Of such weapons the greatest, perhaps, in the modern world is the power of the ballot; and this brings me to a consideration of the third form of contact between whites and blacks in the South,—political activity.

In the attitude of the American mind toward Negro suffrage can be traced with unusual accuracy the prevalent conceptions of government. In the fifties we were near enough the echoes of the French Revolution to believe pretty thoroughly in universal suffrage. We argued, as we thought then rather logically, that no social class was so good, so true, and so disinterested as to be trusted wholly with the political destiny of its neighbors; that in every state the best arbiters of their own welfare are the persons directly affected; consequently that it is only by arming every hand with a ballot,—with the right to have a voice in the policy of the state,—that the greatest good to the greatest number could be attained. To be sure, there were objections to these arguments, but we thought we had answered them tersely and convincingly; if some one complained of the ignorance of voters, we answered, "Educate them." If another complained of their venality, we replied, "Disfranchise them or put them in jail." And, finally, to the men who feared demagogues and the natural perversity of some human beings we insisted that time and bitter experience would teach the most hardheaded. It was at this time that the question of Negro suffrage in the South was raised. Here was a defenceless people suddenly made free. How were they to be protected from those who did not believe in their freedom and were determined to thwart it? Not by force, said the North; not by government guardianship, said the South; then by the ballot, the sole and legitimate defence of a free people, said the Common Sense of the Nation. No one thought, at the time, that the ex-slaves could use the ballot intelligently or very effectively; but they did think that the possession of so great power by a great class in the nation would compel their fellows to educate this class to its intelligent use.

Meantime, new thoughts came to the nation: the inevitable period of moral retrogression and political trickery that ever follows in the wake of war overtook us. So flagrant became the political scandals that reputable men began to leave politics alone, and politics consequently became disreputable. Men began to pride themselves on having nothing to do with their own goverment, and to agree tacitly with those who regarded public office as a private perquisite. In this state of mind it became easy to wink at the suppression of the Negro vote in the South, and to advise self-respecting Negroes to leave politics entirely alone. The decent and reputable citizens of the North who neglected their own civic duties grew hilarious over the exaggerated importance with which the Negro regarded the franchise. Thus it easily happened that more and more the better class of Negroes followed the advice from abroad and the pressure from home, and took no further interest in politics, leaving to the careless and the venal of their race the exercise of their rights as voters. The black vote that still remained was not trained and educated, but further debauched by open and unblushing bribery, or force and fraud; until the Negro voter was thoroughly inoculated with the idea that politics was a method of private gain by disreputable means.

And finally, now, to-day, when we are awakening to the fact that the perpetuity of republican institutions on this continent depends on the purification of the ballot, the civic training of voters, and the raising of voting to the plane of a solemn duty which a patriotic citizen neglects to his peril and to the peril of his children's children,—in this day, when we are striving for a renaissance of civic virtue, what are we going to say to the black voter of the South? Are we going to tell him still that politics is a disreputable and useless form of human activity? Are we going to induce the best class of Negroes to take less and less interest in government, and to give up their right to take such an interest, without a protest? I am not saying a word against all legitimate efforts to purge the ballot of ignorance, pauperism, and crime. But few have pretended that the present movement for disfranchisement in the South is for such a purpose; it has been plainly and frankly declared in nearly every case that the object of the disfranchising laws is the elimination of the black man from politics.

Now, is this a minor matter which has no influence on the main question of the industrial and intellectual development of the Negro? Can we establish a mass of black laborers and artisans and landholders in the South who, by law and public opinion, have absolutely no voice in shaping the laws under which they live and work? Can the modern organization of industry, assuming as it does free democratic government and the power and ability of the laboring classes to compel respect for their welfare,—can this system be carried out in the South when half its laboring force is voiceless in the public councils and powerless in its own defence? To-day the black man of the South has almost nothing to say as to how much he shall be taxed, or how those taxes shall be expended; as to who shall execute the laws, and how they shall do it; as to who shall make the laws, and how they shall be made. It is pitiable that frantic efforts must be made at critical times to get lawmakers in some States even to listen to the respectful presentation of the black man's side of a current controversy. Daily the Negro is coming more and more to look upon law and justice, not as protecting safeguards, but as sources of humiliation and oppression. The laws are made by men who have little interest in him; they are executed by men who have absolutely no motive for treating the black people with courtesy or consideration; and, finally, the accused law-breaker is tried, not by his peers, but too often by men who would rather punish ten innocent Negroes than let one guilty one escape.

I should be the last one to deny the patent weaknesses and shortcomings of the Negro people; I should be the last to withhold sympathy from the white South in its efforts to solve its intricate social problems. I freely acknowledge that it is possible, and sometimes best, that a partially undeveloped people should be ruled by the best of their stronger and better neighbors for their own good, until such time as they can start and fight the world's battles alone. I have already pointed out how sorely in need of such economic and spiritual guidance the emancipated Negro was, and I am quite willing to admit that if the representatives of the best white Southern public opinion were the ruling and guiding powers in the South to-day the conditions indicated would be fairly well fulfilled. But the point I have insisted upon, and now emphasize again, is that the best opinion of the South to-day is not the ruling opinion. That to leave the Negro helpless and without a ballot to-day is to leave him, not to the guidance of the best, but rather to the exploitation and debauchment of the worst; that this is no truer of the South than of the North,—of the North than of Europe: in any land, in any country under modern free competition, to lay any class of weak and despised people, be they white, black, or blue, at the political mercy of their stronger, richer, and more resourceful fellows, is a temptation which human nature seldom has withstood and seldom will withstand.

Moreover, the political status of the Negro in the South is closely connected with the question of Negro crime. There can be no doubt that crime among Negroes has sensibly increased in the last thirty years, and that there has appeared in the slums of great cities a distinct criminal class among the blacks. In explaining this unfortunate development, we must note two things: (1) that the inevitable result of Emancipation was to increase crime and criminals, and (2) that the police system of the South was primarily designed to control slaves. As to the first point, we must not forget that under a strict slave system there can scarcely be such a thing as crime. But when these variously constituted human particles are suddenly thrown broadcast on the sea of life, some swim, some sink, and some hang suspended, to be forced up or down by the chance currents of a busy hurrying world. So great an economic and social revolution as swept the South in '63 meant a weeding out among the Negroes of the incompetents and vicious, the beginning of a differentiation of social grades. Now a rising group of people are not lifted bodily from the ground like an inert solid mass, but rather stretch upward like a living plant with its roots still clinging in the mould. The appearance, therefore, of the Negro criminal was a phenomenon to be awaited; and while it causes anxiety, it should not occasion surprise.

Here again the hope for the future depended peculiarly on careful and delicate dealing with these criminals. Their offences at first were those of laziness, carelessness, and impulse, rather than of malignity or ungoverned viciousness. Such misdemeanors needed discriminating treatment, firm but reformatory, with no hint of injustice, and full proof of guilt. For such dealing with criminals, white or black, the South had no machinery, no adequate jails or reformatories; its police system was arranged to deal with blacks alone, and tacitly assumed that every white man was *ipso facto* a member of that police. Thus grew up a double system of justice, which erred on the white side by undue leniency and the practical immunity of red-handed criminals, and erred on the black side by undue severity, injustice, and lack of discrimination. For, as I have said, the police system of the South was originally designed to keep track of all Negroes, not simply of criminals; and when the Negroes were freed and the whole South was convinced of the impossibility of free Negro labor, the first and almost universal device was to use the courts as a means of reënslaving the blacks. It was not then a question of crime, but rather one of color, that settled a man's conviction on almost any charge. Thus Negroes came to look upon courts as instruments of injustice and oppression, and upon those convicted in them as martyrs and victims.

When, now, the real Negro criminal appeared, and instead of petty stealing and vagrancy we began to have highway robbery, burglary, murder, and rape, there was a curious effect on both sides of the color-line: the Negroes refused to believe the evidence of white witnesses or the fairness of white juries, so that the greatest deterrent to crime, the public opinion of one's own social caste, was lost, and the criminal was looked upon as crucified rather than hanged. On the other hand, the whites, used to being careless as to the guilt or innocence of accused Negroes, were swept in moments of passion beyond law, reason, and decency. Such a situation is bound to increase crime, and has increased it. To natural viciousness and vagrancy are being daily added motives of revolt and revenge which stir up all the latent savagery of both races and make peaceful attention to economic development often impossible.

But the chief problem in any community cursed with crime is not the punishment of the criminals, but the preventing of the young from being trained to crime. And here again the peculiar conditions of the South have prevented proper precautions. I have seen twelve-year-old boys working in chains on the public streets of Atlanta, directly in front of the schools, in company with old and hardened criminals; and this indiscriminate mingling of men and women and children makes the chain-gangs perfect schools of crime and debauchery. The struggle for reformatories, which has gone on in Virginia, Georgia, and other States, is the one encouraging sign of the awakening of some communities to the suicidal results of this policy.

It is the public schools, however, which can be made, outside the homes, the greatest means of training decent self-respecting citizens. We have been so hotly engaged recently in discussing trade-schools and the higher education that the pitiable plight of the public-school system in the South has almost dropped from view. Of every five dollars spent for public education in the State of Georgia, the white schools get four dollars and the Negro one dollar; and even then the white public-school system, save in the cities, is bad and cries for reform. If this is true of the whites, what of the blacks? I am becoming more and more convinced, as I look upon the system of common-school training in the South, that the national government must soon step in and aid popular education in some way. To-day it has been only by the most strenuous efforts on the part of the thinking men of the South that the Negro's share of the school fund has not been cut down to a pittance in some half-dozen States; and that movement not only is not dead, but in many communities is gaining strength. What in the name of reason does this nation expect of a people, poorly trained and hard pressed in severe economic competition, without political rights, and with ludicrously inadequate common-school facilities? What can it expect but crime and listlessness, offset here and there by the dogged struggles of the fortunate and more determined who are themselves buoyed by the hope that in due time the country will come to its senses?

I have thus far sought to make clear the physical, economic, and political relations of the Negroes and whites in the South, as I have conceived them, including, for the reasons set forth, crime and education. But after all that has been said on these more tangible matters of human contact, there still remains a part essential to a proper description of the South which it is difficult to describe or fix in terms easily understood by strangers. It is, in fine, the atmosphere of the land, the thought and feeling, the thousand and one little actions which go to make up life. In any community or nation it is these little things which are most elusive to the grasp and yet most essential to any clear conception of the group life taken as a whole. What is thus true of all communities is peculiarly true of the South, where, outside of written history and outside of printed law, there has been going on for a generation as deep a storm and stress of human souls, as intense a ferment of feeling, as intricate a writhing of spirit, as ever a people experienced. Within and without the sombre veil of color vast social forces have been at work,—efforts for human betterment, movements toward disintegration and despair, tragedies and comedies in social and economic life, and a swaying and lifting and sinking of human hearts which have made this land a land of mingled sorrow and joy, of change and excitement and unrest.

The centre of this spiritual turmoil has ever been the millions of black freedmen and their sons, whose destiny is so fatefully bound up with that of the nation. And yet the casual observer visiting the South sees at first little of this. He notes the growing frequency of dark faces as he rides along,—but otherwise the days slip lazily on, the sun shines, and this little world seems as happy and contented as other worlds he has visited. Indeed, on the question of questions—the Negro problem—he hears so little that there almost seems to be a conspiracy of silence; the morning papers seldom mention it, and then usually in a far-fetched academic way, and indeed almost every one seems to forget and ignore the darker half of the land, until the astonished visitor is inclined to ask if after all there is any problem here. But if he lingers long enough there comes the awakening: perhaps in a sudden whirl of passion which leaves him gasping at its bitter intensity; more likely in a gradually dawning sense of things he had not at first noticed. Slowly but surely his eyes begin to catch the shadows of the color-line: here he meets crowds of Negroes and whites; then he is suddenly aware that he cannot discover a single dark face; or again at the close of a day's wandering he may find himself in some strange assembly, where all faces are tinged brown or black, and where he has the vague, uncomfortable feeling of the stranger. He realizes at last that silently, resistlessly, the world about flows by him in two great streams: they ripple on in the same sunshine, they approach and mingle their waters in seeming carelessness,—then they divide and flow wide apart. It is done quietly; no mistakes are made, or if one occurs, the swift arm of the law and of public opinion swings down for a moment, as when the other day a black man and a white woman were arrested for talking together on White-hall Street in Atlanta.

Now if one notices carefully one will see that between these two worlds, despite much physical contact and daily intermingling, there is almost no community of intel-lectual life or point of transference where the thoughts and feelings of one race can come into direct contact and sympathy with the thoughts and feelings of the other. Before and directly after the war, when all the best of the Negroes were domestic servants in the best of the white families, there were bonds of intimacy, affection, and sometimes blood relationship, between the races. They lived in the same home, shared in the family life, often attended the same church, and talked and conversed with each other. But the increasing civilization of the Negro since then has naturally meant the development of higher classes: there are increasing numbers of ministers, teachers, physicians, mer-chants, mechanics, and independent farmers, who by nature and training are the aris-tocracy and leaders of the blacks. Between them, however, and the best element of the whites, there is little or no intellectual commerce. They go to separate churches, they live in separate sections, they are strictly separated in all public gatherings, they travel separately, and they are beginning to read different papers and books. To most libraries, lectures, concerts, and museums, Negroes are either not admitted at all, or on terms peculiarly galling to the pride of the very classes who might otherwise be attracted. The daily paper chronicles the doings of the black world from afar with no great regard for accuracy; and so on, throughout the category of means for intellectual communica-tion,—schools, conferences, efforts for social betterment, and the like,—it is usually true that the very representatives of the two races, who for mutual benefit and welfare of the land ought to be in complete understanding and sympathy, are so far strangers that one side thinks all whites are narrow and prejudiced, and the other thinks educated Negroes dangerous and insolent. Moreover, in a land where the tyranny of public opin-ion and the intolerance of criticism is for obvious historical reasons so strong as in the South, such a situation is extremely difficult to correct. The white man, as well as the Negro, is bound and barred by the color-line, and many a scheme of friendliness and philanthropy, of broad-minded sympathy and generous fellowship between the two has dropped still-born because some busybody has forced the color-question to the front and brought the tremendous force of unwritten law against the innovators.

It is hardly necessary for me to add very much in regard to the social contact between the races. Nothing has come to replace that finer sympathy and love between some masters and house servants which the radical and more uncompromising drawing of the color-line in recent years has caused almost completely to disappear. In a world where it means so much to take a man by the hand and sit beside him, to look frankly into his eyes and feel his heart beating with red blood; in a world where a social cigar or a cup of tea together means more than legislative halls and magazine articles and speeches,—one can imagine the consequences of the almost utter absence of such social amenities between estranged races, whose separation extends even to parks and street-cars.

Here there can be none of that social going down to the people,—the opening of heart and hand of the best to the worst, in generous acknowledgment of a common humanity and a common destiny. On the other hand, in matters of simple almsgiving, where there can be no question of social contact, and in the succor of the aged and sick, the South, as if stirred by a feeling of its unfortunate limitations, is generous to a fault. The black beggar is never turned away without a good deal more than a crust, and a call for help for the unfortunate meets quick response. I remember, one cold winter, in Atlanta, when I refrained from contributing to a public relief fund lest Negroes should be discriminated against, I afterward inquired of a friend: "Were any black people receiving aid?" "Why," said he, "they were *all* black."

And yet this does not touch the kernel of the problem. Human advancement is not a mere question of almsgiving, but rather of sympathy and coöperation among classes who would scorn charity. And here is a land where, in the higher walks of life, in all the higher striving for the good and noble and true, the color-line comes to separate natural friends and co-workers; while at the bottom of the social group, in the saloon, the gambling-hell, and the brothel, that same line wavers and disappears.

I have sought to paint an average picture of real relations between the sons of master and man in the South. I have not glossed over matters for policy's sake, for I fear we have already gone too far in that sort of thing. On the other hand, I have sincerely sought to let no unfair exaggerations creep in. I do not doubt that in some Southern communities conditions are better than those I have indicated; while I am no less certain that in other communities they are far worse.

Nor does the paradox and danger of this situation fail to interest and perplex the best conscience of the South. Deeply religious and intensely democratic as are the mass of the whites, they feel acutely the false position in which the Negro problems place them. Such an essentially honest-hearted and generous people cannot cite the caste-levelling precepts of Christianity, or believe in equality of opportunity for all men, without coming to feel more and more with each generation that the present drawing of the color-line is a flat contradiction to their beliefs and professions. But just as often as they come to this point, the present social condition of the Negro stands as a menace and a portent before even the most open-minded: if there were nothing to charge against the Negro but his blackness or other physical peculiarities, they argue, the problem would be comparatively simple; but what can we say to his ignorance, shiftlessness, poverty, and crime? can a self-respecting group hold anything but the least possible fellowship with such persons and survive? and shall we let a mawkish sentiment sweep away the culture of our fathers or the hope of our children? The argument so put is of great strength, but it is not a whit stronger than the argument of thinking Negroes: granted, they reply, that the condition of our masses is bad; there is certainly on the one hand adequate historical cause for this, and unmistakable evidence that no small number have, in spite of tremendous disadvantages, risen to the level of American civilization. And when, by proscription and prejudice, these same Negroes are classed with and treated like the lowest of their people, simply *because* they are Negroes, such a policy not only discourages thrift and intelligence among black men, but puts a direct premium on the very things you complain of,—inefficiency and crime. Draw lines of crime, of incompetency, of vice, as tightly and uncompromisingly as you will, for these things must be proscribed; but a color-line not only does not accomplish this purpose, but thwarts it.

In the face of two such arguments, the future of the South depends on the ability of the representatives of these opposing views to see and appreciate and sympathize with each other's position,—for the Negro to realize more deeply than he does at present the need of uplifting the masses of his people, for the white people to realize more vividly than they have yet done the deadening and disastrous effect of a color-prejudice that classes Phillis Wheatley and Sam Hose in the same despised class.

It is not enough for the Negroes to declare that color-prejudice is the sole cause of their social condition, nor for the white South to reply that their social condition is the main cause of prejudice. They both act as reciprocal cause and effect, and a change in neither alone will bring the desired effect. Both must change, or neither can improve to any great extent. The Negro cannot stand the present reactionary tendencies and unreasoning drawing of the color-line indefinitely without discouragement and retrogression. And the condition of the Negro is ever the excuse for further discrimination. Only by a union of intelligence and sympathy across the color-line in this critical period of the Republic shall justice and right triumph,—

"That mind and soul according well,
May make one music as before,
But vaster."

JANE ADDAMS

"The Subjective Necessity of Social Settlements"
1892

Jane Addams (1860–1935) was one of the most influential and indefatigable social reformers in all American history. Although based in Chicago at Hull House—the settlement house she created to serve the needs of a poor, largely immigrant neighborhood—she helped to lead a host of national movements, including the 1912 presidential campaign of Theodore Roosevelt. Addams was the founding president of the Woman's International League for Peace and Freedom and in 1931 shared the Nobel Peace Prize. Addams wrote widely on the theory and practice of social reform and international reconciliation. In the selection that follows, she scrutinizes in a social and religious context the motives of men and women who, like herself, had devoted themselves to the improvement of society. "The Subjective Necessity of Social Settlements" was first delivered as an address to a conference of social workers in 1892, but it gained fame as a classic statement of reform commitment after 1910 when it appeared in Addams' most widely appreciated book, *Twenty Years qt* .
Hull-House.

"The Subjective Necessity of Social Settlements" is also a strong statement of the "social gospel," a movement in American Protestantism devoted to the vigorous application of Christian ethics to the contemporary social and economic world. For a more extensive expression of this outlook, see two books by the theologian Walter Rauschenbusch, *Christianity and the Social Crisis* (New York, 1908), and *A Theology for the Social Gospel* (New York, 1917). For differing historical perspectives on the social gospel, see Henry F. May, *Protestant Churches and Industrial America* (New York, 1949), and Susan Curtis, *A Consuming Faith: The Social Gospel and Modern American Culture* (Baltimore, 1991).

For Addams's life and work, see Alan Davis, *An American Heroine: The Life and Legend of Jane Addams* (New York, 1973). For an interpretation of Addams as the paradigmatic example of the intellectual as a reformer and critic, see Christopher Lasch, *The New Radicalism in America, 1889–1963: The Emergence of the Intellectual as a Social Type* (New York, 1965), 3–37. Lasch has also edited a collection of Addams's most important writings, *The Social Thought of Jane Addams* (Indianapolis, 1965). For a detailed study of Jane Addams's work with immigrants and of the ideology Addams and her coworkers shared, see Rivka Shpak Lissak, *Pluralism & Progressives: Hull House and the New Immigrants, 1890–1919* (Chicago, 1989).

... This paper is an attempt to analyze the motives which underlie a movement based, not only upon conviction, but upon genuine emotion, wherever educated young people are seeking an outlet for that sentiment of universal brotherhood, which the best spirit of our times is forcing from an emotion into a motive. These young people accomplish little toward the solution of this social problem, and bear the brunt of being cultivated into unnourished, oversensitive lives. They have been shut off from the common labor by which they live which is a great source of moral and physical health. They feel a fatal want of harmony between their theory and their lives, a lack of coördination between thought and action. I think it is hard for us to realize how seriously many of them are taking to the notion of human brotherhood, how eagerly they long to give tangible expression to the democratic ideal. These young men and women, longing to socialize their democracy, are animated by certain hopes which may be thus loosely formulated; that if in a democratic country nothing can be permanently achieved save through the masses of the people, it will be impossible to establish a higher political life than the people themselves crave; that it is difficult to see how the notion of a higher civic life can be fostered save through common intercourse; that the blessings which we associate with a life of refinement and cultivation can be made universal and must be made universal if they are to be permanent; that the good we secure for ourselves is precarious and uncertain, is floating in mid-air, until it is secured for all of us and incorporated into our common life. It is easier to state these hopes than to formulate the line of motives, which I believe to constitute the trend of the subjective pressure toward the Settlement. There is something primordial about these motives, but I am perhaps overbold in designating them as a great desire to share the race life. We all bear traces of the starvation struggle which for so long made up the life of the race. Our very organism holds memories and glimpses of that long life of our ancestors which still goes on among so many of our contemporaries. Nothing so deadens the sympathies and shrivels the power of enjoyment as the persistent keeping away from the great opportunities for helpfulness and a continual ignoring of the starvation struggle which makes up the life of at least half the race. To shut one's self away from that half of the race life is to shut one's self away from the most vital part of it; it is to live out but half the humanity to which we have been born heir and to use but half our faculties. We have all had longings for a fuller life which should include the use of these faculties. These longings are the physical complement of the "Intimations of Immortality," on which no ode has yet been written. To portray these would be the work of a poet, and it is hazardous for any but a poet to attempt it.

You may remember the forlorn feeling which occasionally seizes you when you arrive early in the morning a stranger in a great city: the stream of laboring people goes past you as you gaze through the plate-glass window of your hotel; you see hard work-ingmen lifting great burdens; you hear the driving and jostling of huge carts and your heart sinks with a sudden sense of futility. The door opens behind you and you turn to the man who brings you in your breakfast with a quick sense of human fellowship. You find yourself praying that you may never lose your hold on it all. A more poetic prayer would be that the great mother breasts of our common humanity, with its labor and suffering and its homely comforts, may never be withheld from you. You turn helplessly to the waiter and feel that it would be almost grotesque to claim from him the sympathy you crave because civilization has placed you apart, but you resent your

Source: Jane Addams, *Twenty Years at Hull-House* (New York: Macmillan, 1910), 91–100.

position with a sudden sense of snobbery. Literature is full of portrayals of these glimpses: they come to shipwrecked men on rafts; they overcome the differences of an incongruous multitude when in the presence of a great danger or when moved by a common enthusiasm. They are not, however, confined to such moments, and if we were in the habit of telling them to each other, the recital would be as long as the tales of children are, when they sit down on the green grass and confide to each other how many times they have remembered that they lived once before. If these childish tales are the stirring of inherited impressions, just so surely is the other the striving of inherited powers.

"It is true that there is nothing after disease, indigence and a sense of guilt, so fatal to health and to life itself as the want of a proper outlet for active faculties." I have seen young girls suffer and grow sensibly lowered in vitality in the first years after they leave school. In our attempt then to give a girl pleasure and freedom from care we succeed, for the most part, in making her pitifully miserable. She finds "life" so different from what she expected it to be. She is besotted with innocent little ambitions, and does not understand this apparent waste of herself, this elaborate preparation, if no work is provided for her. There is a heritage of noble obligation which young people accept and long to perpetuate. The desire for action, the wish to right wrong and alleviate suffering haunts them daily. Society smiles at it indulgently instead of making it of value to itself. The wrong to them begins even farther back, when we restrain the first childish desires for "doing good" and tell them that they must wait until they are older and better fitted. We intimate that social obligation begins at a fixed date, forgetting that it begins with birth itself. We treat them as children who, with strong-growing limbs, are allowed to use their legs but not their arms, or whose legs are daily carefully exercised that after a while their arms may be put to high use. We do this in spite of the protest of the best educators, Locke and Pestalozzi. We are fortunate in the meantime if their unused members do not weaken and disappear. They do sometimes. There are a few girls who, by the time they are "educated," forget their old childish desires to help the world and to play with poor little girls "who haven't play things." Parents are often inconsistent: they deliberately expose their daughters to knowledge of the distress in the world; they send them to hear missionary addresses on famines in India and China; they accompany them to lectures on the suffering in Siberia; they agitate together over the forgotten region of East London. In addition to this, from babyhood the altruistic tendencies of these daughters are persistently cultivated. They are taught to be self-forgetting and self-sacrificing, to consider the good of the whole before the good of the ego. But when all this information and culture show results, when the daughter comes back from college and begins to recognize her social claim to the "submerged tenth," and to evince a disposition to fulfill it, the family claim is strenuously asserted; she is told that she is unjustified, ill-advised in her efforts. If she persists, the family too often are injured and unhappy unless the efforts are called missionary and the religious zeal of the family carry them over their sense of abuse. When this zeal does not exist, the result is perplexing. It is a curious violation of what we would fain believe a fundamental law—that the final return of the deed is upon the head of the doer. The deed is that of exclusiveness and caution, but the return, instead of falling upon the head of the exclusive and cautious, falls upon a young head full of generous and unselfish plans. The girl loses something vital out of her life to which she is entitled. She is restricted and unhappy; her elders, meanwhile, are unconscious of the situation and we have all the elements of a tragedy.

We have in America a fast-growing number of cultivated young people who have no recognized outlet for their active faculties. They hear constantly of the great social maladjustment, but no way is provided for them to change it, and their uselessness hangs about them heavily. Huxley declares that the sense of uselessness is the severest shock which the human system can sustain, and that if persistently sustained, it results in atrophy of function. These young people have had advantages of college, of European travel, and of economic study, but they are sustaining this shock of inaction. They have pet phrases, and they tell you that the things that make us all alike are stronger than the things that make us different. They say that all men are united by needs and sympathies far more permanent and radical than anything that temporarily divides them and sets them in opposition to each other. If they affect art, they say that the decay in artistic expression is due to the decay in ethics, that art when shut away from the human interests and from the great mass of humanity is self-destructive. They tell their elders with all the bitterness of youth that if they expect success from them in business or politics or in whatever lines their ambition for them has run, they must let them consult all of humanity; that they must let them find out what the people want and how they want it. It is only the stronger young people, however, who formulate this. Many of them dissipate their energies in so-called enjoyment. Others not content with that, go on studying and go back to college for their second degrees; not that they are especially fond of study, but because they want something definite to do, and their powers have been trained in the direction of mental accumulation. Many are buried beneath this mental accumulation which lowered vitality and discontent. Walter Besant says they have had the vision that Peter had when he saw the great sheet let down from heaven, wherein was neither clean nor unclean. He calls it the sense of humanity. It is not philanthropy nor benevolence, but a thing fuller and wider than either of these.

This young life, so sincere in its emotion and good phrase and yet so undirected, seems to me as pitiful as the other great mass of destitute lives. One is supplementary to the other, and some method of communication can surely be devised. Mr. Barnett, who urged the first Settlement—Toynbee Hall, in East London—recognized this need of outlet for the young men of Oxford and Cambridge, and hoped that the Settlement would supply the communication. It is easy to see why the Settlement movement originated in England, where the years of education are more constrained and definite than they are here, where class distinctions are more rigid. The necessity of it was greater there, but we are fast feeling the pressure of the need and meeting the necessity for Settlements in America. Our young people feel nervously the need of putting theory into action, and respond quickly to the Settlement form of activity.

Other motives which I believe make toward the Settlement are the result of a certain renaissance going forward in Christianity. The impulse to share the lives of the poor, the desire to make social service, irrespective of propaganda, express the spirit of Christ, is as old as Christianity itself. We have no proof from the records themselves that the early Roman Christians, who strained their simple art to the point of grotesqueness in their eagerness to record a "good news" on the walls of the catacombs, considered this good news a religion. Jesus had no set of truths labeled Religious. On the contrary, his doctrine was that all truth is one, that the appropriation of it is freedom. His teaching had no dogma to mark it off from truth and action in general. He himself called it a revelation—a life. These early Roman Christians received the Gospel message, a command to love all men, with a certain joyous simplicity. The image of the Good Shepherd is blithe and gay beyond the gentlest shepherd of Greek mythology; the hart no longer pants, but rushes to the water brooks. The Christians looked for the continuous reve-lation, but believed what Jesus said, that this revelation, to be retained and made man-ifest, must be put into terms of action; that action is the only medium man has for receiving and appropriating truth; that the doctrine must be known through the will.

That Christianity has to be revealed and embodied in the line of social progress is a corollary to the simple proposition that man's action is found in his social relationships in the way in which he connects with his fellows; that his motives for action are the zeal and affection with which he regards his fellows. By this simple process was created a deep enthusiasm for humanity, which regarded man as at once the organ and the object of revelation; and by this process came about the wonderful fellowship, the true democracy of the early Church, that so captivates the imagination. The early Christians were pre-eminently nonresistant. They believed in love as a cosmic force. There was no inconoclasm during the minor peace of the Church. They did not yet denounce nor tear down temples, nor preach the end of the world. They grew to a mighty number but it never occurred to them, either in their weakness or in their strength, to regard other men for an instant as their foes or as aliens. The spectacle of the Christians loving all men was the most astounding Rome had ever seen. They were eager to sacrifice themselves for the weak, for children, and for the aged; they identified themselves with slaves and did not avoid the plague; they longed to share the common lot that they might receive the constant revelation. It was a new treasure which the early Christians added to the sum of all treasures, a joy hitherto unknown in the world—the joy of finding the Christ which lieth in each man, but which no man can unfold save in fellowship. A happiness ranging from the heroic to the pastoral enveloped them. They were to possess a revelation as long as life had new meaning to unfold, new action to propose.

I believe that there is a distinct turning among many young men and women toward this simple acceptance of Christ's message. They resent the assumption that Christianity is a set of ideas which belong to the religious consciousness, whatever that may be. They insist that it cannot be proclaimed and instituted apart from the social life of the community and that it must seek a simple and natural expression in the social organism itself. The Settlement movement is only one manifestation of that wider humanitarian movement which throughout Christendom, put pre-eminently in England, is endeav-oring to embody itself, not in a sect, but in society itself.

I believe that this turning, this renaissance of the early Christian humanitarianism, is going on in America, in Chicago, if you please, without leaders who write or philos-ophize, without much speaking, but with a bent to express in social service and in terms of action the spirit of Christ. Certain it is that spiritual force is found in the Settlement movement, and it is also true that this force must be evoked and must be called into play before the success of any Settlement is assured. There must be the overmastering belief that all that is noblest in life is common to men as men, in order to accentuate the likenesses and ignore the differences which are found among the people whom the Settlement constantly brings into juxtaposition. It may be true, as the Positivists insist, that the very religious fervor of man can be turned into love for his race, and his desire for a future life into content to live in the echo of his deeds; Paul's formula of seeking for the Christ which lieth in each man and founding our likenesses on him, seems a simpler formula to many of us.

In a thousand voices singing the Hallelujah Chorus in Handel's "Messiah," it is possible to distinguish the leading voices, but the differences of training and cultivation between them and the voices of the chorus, are lost in the unity of purpose and in the fact that they are all human voices lifted by a high motive. This is a weak illustration of what a Settlement attempts to do. It aims, in a measure, to develop whatever of social life its neighborhood may afford, to focus and give form to that life, to bring to bear upon it the results of cultivation and training; but it receives in exchange for the music of isolated voices the volume and strength of the chorus. It is quite impossible for me to say in what proportion or degree the subjective necessity which led to the opening of Hull-House combined the three trends: first, the desire to interpret democracy in social terms; secondly, the impulse beating at the very source of our lives, urging us to aid in the race progress; and, thirdly, the Christian movement toward humanitarianism. It is difficult to analyze a living thing; the analysis is at best imperfect. Many more motives may blend with the three trends; possibly the desire for a new form of social success due to the nicety of imagination, which refuses worldly pleasures unmixed with the joys of self-sacrifice; possibly a love of approbation, so vast that it is not content with the treble clapping of delicate hands, but wishes also to hear the brass notes from toughened palms, may mingle with these.

The Settlement, then, is an experimental effort to aid in the solution of the social and industrial problems which are engendered by the modern conditions of life in a great city. It insists that these problems are not confined to any one portion of a city. It is an attempt to relieve, at the same time, the overaccumulation at one end of society and the destitution at the other; but it assumes that this overaccumulation and destitution is most sorely felt in the things that pertain to social and educational privileges. From its very nature it can stand for no political or social propaganda. It must, in a sense, give the warm welcome of an inn to all such propaganda, if perchance one of them be found an angel. The one thing to be dreaded in the Settlement is that it lose its flexibility, its power of quick adaptation, its readiness to change its methods as its environment may demand. It must be open to conviction and must have a deep and abiding sense of tolerance. It must be hospitable and ready for experiment. It should demand from its residents a scientific patience in the accumulation of facts and the steady holding of their sympathies as one of the best instruments for that accumulation. It must be grounded in a philosophy whose foundation is on the solidarity of the human race, a philosophy which will not waver when the race happens to be represented by a drunken woman or an idiot boy. Its residents must be emptied of all conceit of opinion and all self-assertion, and ready to arouse and interpret the public opinion of their neighborhood. They must be content to live quietly side by side with their neighbors, until they grow into a sense of relationship and mutual interests. Their neighbors are held apart by differences of race and language which the residents can more easily overcome. They are bound to see the needs of their neighborhood as a whole, to furnish data for legislation, and to use their influence to secure it. In short, residents are pledged to devote themselves to the duties of good citizenship and to the arousing of the social energies which too largely lie dormant in every neighborhood given over to industrialism. They are bound to regard the entire life of their city as organic, to make an effort to unify it, and to protest against its overdifferentiation. . . .

JOHN DEWEY

"Philosophy and Democracy"
1918

The name of John Dewey (1859–1952) is appropriately remembered in relation to so many ideas and movements that his role in the history of American thought is less easily indicated in a sourcebook of this kind than is the role of perhaps any other thinker represented within these two covers. Dewey did creative work in philosophy and psychology as early as the mid-1880s, rose to national prominence in the Progressive Era as a theorist of educational and political reform, and went on during the 1920s and 1930s to publish almost a dozen influential books that renewed his standing as the preeminent liberal intellectual in the United States. In his ninetieth year he coauthored a treatise on epistemology, on which he worked while helping his new, young wife look after two Belgian orphans the Deweys had adopted at the end of World War II.

Dewey's prose was oblique, but he managed to convey an earnest and almost messianic faith in the powers of human intelligence. His contemporary, Justice Oliver Wendell Holmes, Jr., caught this quality when he observed that Dewey spoke as God would have spoken "had He been inarticulate but keenly desirous to tell you how it was."

The paper reprinted here is one of Dewey's most lucid and ambitious essays, in which he sets forth his vision of philosophy as a democratic, reforming practice. "Philosophy and Democracy" was delivered at the University of California at Berkeley in the same lecture series in which William James first introduced the concept of pragmatism and in which George Santayana criticized "the genteel tradition."

The most comprehensive and discerning book on Dewey is Robert Westbrook, *John Dewey and American Democracy* (Ithaca, 1991). Another highly valuable study is Steven C. Rockefeller, *John Dewey: Religious Faith and Democratic Humanism* (New York, 1991). The extent to which Dewey departed from his "pragmatic" forebears, Peirce and James, is emphasized in R. W. Sleeper, *The Necessity of Pragmatism: John Dewey's Conception of Philosophy* (New Haven, 1986). Dewey's perpetuation in a secular context of the sensibility of liberal Protestantism is traced in Bruce Kuklick, *Churchman and Philosophers: From Jonathan Edwards to John Dewey* (New Haven, 1985). Dewey's contributions as a theorist of liberalism are clarified in James T. Kloppenberg, *Uncertain Victory: Social Democracy and Progressivism in European and American Social Thought, 1870–1920* (New York, 1986). For a brief overview of Dewey's thought and career, see the introduction to David Sidorsky, ed., *John Dewey: The Essential Writings* (New York, 1977).

Why such a title as Philosophy and Democracy? Why Philosophy and Democracy, any more than Chemistry and Oligarchy, Mathematics and Aristocracy, Astronomy and Monarchy? Is not the concern of philosophy with truth, and can truth vary with political and social institutions any more than with degrees of latitude and meridians of longitude? Is there one ultimate reality for men who live where suffrage is universal and another and different reality where limited suffrage prevails? If we should become a socialistic republic next week would that modify the nature of the ultimates and absolutes with which philosophy deals any more than it would affect the principles of arithmetic or the laws of physics?

Such questions, I fancy, lurk in your minds when they are confronted by a title like that which is chosen. It is well that these questions should not be allowed to lurk in subconscious recesses, but should be brought out into the open. For they have to do with what is the first and last problem for a student of philosophy: The problem of what after all is the business and province of philosophy itself. What is it about? What is it after? What would it have to be possessed of in order to be satisfied? To such questions as these must the remarks be chiefly addressed, leaving the nominal and explicit subject of the relation of democracy to philosophy to figure for the most part as a corollary or even as a postscript.

If then we return to the imaginary interrogations with which we set out we shall find that a certain assumption underlies them—or rather two assumptions. One is that philosophy ranks as a science, that its business is with a certain body of fixed and finished facts and principles. Philosophy is viewed not as its etymology would lead us to expect as a form of love or desire, but as a form of knowledge, of apprehension and acknowledgment of a system of truths comparable in its independence of human wish and effort with the truths of physics. Such, I take it, is the first assumption. The second is that since the realities or truths to be known must be marked off from those of physics and mathematics in order that philosophy may be itself a distinctive form of knowledge, philosophy somehow knows reality more *ultimately* than do the other sciences. It approaches truth with an effort at a more comprehensive, a more completely total vision, and takes reality at a deeper and more fundamental level than do those subjects which orthodox philosophers have loved to call the *special* sciences. What they take piecemeal and therefore more or less erroneously (since a fragment arbitrarily torn from the organic whole is not truly a truth) philosophy takes *teres et rotundus*. What they take superficially, in, so to say, its appearance, philosophy takes at that deeper level where connections and relations within the whole are found.

Some such suppositions as these have, I think, been fostered by many philosophers. They are in the back of the minds of many students when they come to the study of philosophy. They are equally in the minds of many foes of philosophy who also compare philosophy with science, but only to contrast them—at the expense of philosophy. Philosophy, they say, is circular and disputatious; it settles nothing, for its schools are still divided much as they were in the times of the Greeks, engaged in arguing the same questions. Science is progressive; it settles some things and moves on to others. Philosophy moreover is sterile. Where are its works? Where are its concrete applications and living fruits? Hence they conclude that while philosophy is a form of knowledge or science, it is a pretentious and pseudo-form, an effort at a kind of knowledge which is impossible—impossible at all events to human minds.

Source: John Dewey, *Character and Events* (New York, 1929), Vol. 2, 841–855.

Yet every generation, no matter how great the advance of positive knowledge, nor how great the triumphs of the special sciences, shows in its day discontent with all these proved and ascertained results and turns afresh and with infinite hope to philosophy, as to a deeper, more complete and more final revelation. Something is lacking in even the most demonstrated of scientific truths which breeds dissatisfaction, and a yearning for something more conclusive and more mind-filling.

In the face of such perplexities as these there is, I think, another alternative, another way out. Put baldly, it is to deny that philosophy is in any sense whatever a form of knowledge. It is to say that we should return to the original and etymological sense of the word, and recognize that philosophy is a form of desire, of effort at action—a love, namely, of wisdom; but with the thorough proviso, not attached to the Platonic use of the word, that wisdom, whatever it is, is not a mode of science or knowledge. A philosophy which was conscious of its own business and province would then perceive that it is an intellectualized wish, an aspiration subjected to rational discriminations and tests, a social hope reduced to a working program of action, a prophecy of the future, but one disciplined by serious thought and knowledge.

These are statements at once sweeping and vague. Let us recur to the question of whether there is such a thing as a philosophy which is distinctively that of a social order, a distinctive type appropriate to a democracy or to a feudalism. Let us consider the matter not theoretically but historically. In point of fact, nobody would deny that there has been a German, a French, an English philosophy in a sense in which there have not been national chemistries or astronomies. Even in science there is not the complete impersonal detachment which some views of it would lead us to expect. There is difference in color and temper, in emphasis and preferred method characteristic of each people. But these differences are inconsiderable in comparison with those which we find in philosophy. There the differences have been differences in standpoint, outlook and ideal. They manifest not diversities of intellectual emphasis so much as incompatabilities of temperament and expectation. They are different ways of construing life. They indicate different practical ethics of life, not mere variations of intellectual assent. In reading Bacon, Locke, Descartes, Comte, Hegel, Schopenhauer, one says to oneself this could have proceeded only from England, or France, or Germany, as the case may be. The parallelisms with political history and social needs are obvious and explicit.

Take the larger divisions of thought. The conventional main division of philosophy is into ancient, medieval and modern. We may make a similar division in the history of science. But there the meaning is very different. We either mean merely to refer to the stage of ignorance and of knowledge found in certain periods, or we mean not science at all but certain phases of philosophy. When we take science proper, astronomy or geometry, we do not find Euclid especially Greek in his demonstrations. No, ancient, medieval, modern, express in philosophy differences of interest and of purpose characteristic of great civilizations, great social epochs, differences of religious and social desire and belief. They are applicable to philosophy only because economic, political and religious differences manifest themselves in philosophy in fundamentally the same ways that they are shown in other institutions. The philosophies embodied not colorless intellectual readings of reality, but men's most passionate desires and hopes, their basic beliefs about the sort of life to be lived. They started not from science, not from ascertained knowledge, but from moral convictions, and then resorted to the best knowledge and the best intellectual methods available in their day to give the form of demonstration to what was essentially an attitude of will, or a moral resolution to prize one mode of life more highly than another, and the wish to persuade other men that this was the wise way of living.

And this explains what is meant by saying that love of wisdom is not after all the same thing as eagerness for scientific knowledge. By wisdom we mean not systematic and proved knowledge of fact and truth, but a conviction about moral values, a sense for the better kind of life to be led. Wisdom is a moral term, and like every moral term refers not to the constitution of things already in existence, not even if that constitution be magnified into eternity and absoluteness. As a moral term it refers to a choice about something to be done, a preference for living this sort of life rather than that. It refers not to accomplished reality but to a desired future which our desires, when translated into articulate conviction, may help bring into existence.

There are those who think that such statements give away the whole case for philosophy. Many critics and foes of philosophy coming from the camp of science would doubtless claim they were admissions of the claims that philosophy has always been a false light, a pretentious ambition; and that the lesson is that philosophers should sit down in humility and accept the ascertainments of the special sciences, and not go beyond the task of weaving these statements into a more coherent fabric of expression. Others would go further and find in such statements a virtual confession of the futility of all philosophizing.

But there is another way of taking the matter. One might rather say that the fact that the collection purpose and desire of a given generation and people dominates its philosophy is evidence of the sincerity and vitality of that philosophy; that failure to employ the known facts of the period in support of a certain estimate of the proper life to lead would show lack of any holding and directing force in the current social ideal. Even wresting facts to a purpose, obnoxious as it is, testifies to a certain ardency in the vigor with which a belief about the right life to be led is held. It argues moral debility if the slave Epictetus and the Emperor Aurelius entertain just the same philosophy of life, even though both belong to the same Stoic school. "A community devoted to industrial pursuits, active in business and commerce, is not likely to see the needs and possibilities of life in the same way as a country with high esthetic culture and little enterprise in turning the energies of nature to mechanical account. A social group with a fairly continuous history will respond mentally to a crisis in a very different way from one which has felt the shock of distinct breaks." Different hues of philosophic thought are bound to result. Women have as yet made little contribution to philosophy. But when women who are not mere students of other persons' philosophy set out to write it, we cannot conceive that it will be the same in viewpoint or tenor as that composed from the standpoint of the different masculine experience of things. Institutions, customs of life, breed certain systematized predilections and aversions. The wise man reads historic philosophies to detect in them intellectual formulations of men's habitual purposes and cultivated wants, not to gain insight into the ultimate nature of things or information about the make-up of reality. As far as what is loosely called reality figures in philosophies, we may be sure that it signifies those selected aspects of the world which are chosen because they lend themselves to the support of men's judgment of the worthwhile life, and hence are most highly prized. In philosophy, "reality" is a term of value or choice.

To deny however that philosophy is in any essential sense a form of science or of knowledge, is not to say that philosophy is a mere arbitrary expression of wish or feeling or a vague suspiration after something, nobody knows what. All philosophy bears an intellectual impress because it is an effort to convince some one, perhaps the writer himself, of the reasonableness of some course of life which has been adopted from custom or instinct. Since it is addressed to man's intelligence, it must employ knowledge and established beliefs, and it must proceed in an orderly way, logically. The art of literature catches men unaware and employs a charm to bring them to a spot whence they see vividly and intimately some picture which embodies life in a meaning. But magic and immediate vision are denied the philosopher. He proceeds prosaically along the highway, pointing out recognizable landmarks, mapping the course, and labeling with explicit logic the stations reached. This means of course that philosophy must depend upon the best science of its day. It can intellectually recommend its judgments of value only as it can select relevant material from that which is recognized to be established truth, and can persuasively use current knowledge to drive home the reasonableness of its conception of life. It is this dependence upon the method of logical presentation and upon scientific subject matter which confers upon philosophy the garb, though not the form, of knowledge.

Scientific form is a vehicle for conveying a non-scientific conviction, but the carriage is necessary, for philosophy is not mere passion but a passion that would exhibit itself as a reasonable persuasion. Philosophy is therefore always in a delicate position, and gives the heathen and Philistine an opportunity to rage. It is always balancing between sophistry, or pretended and illegitimate knowledge, and vague, incoherent mysticism—not of necessity mysticism in its technical definition, but in that sense of the mysterious and misty which affects the popular meaning of the word. When the stress is too much on intellectual form, when the original moral purpose has lost its vitality, philosophy becomes learned and dialectical. When there is cloudy desire, unclarified and unsustained by the logical exhibition of attained science, philosophy becomes hortatory, edifying, sentimental, or fantastic and semi-magical. The perfect balance may hardly be attained by man, and there are few indeed who can, like Plato, even rhythmically alternate with artistic grace from one emphasis to the other. But what makes philosophy hard work and also makes its cultivation worth while, is precisely the fact that it assumes the responsibility for setting forth some ideal of a collective good life by the methods which the best science of the day employs in its quite different task, and with the use of the characteristic knowledge of its day. The philosopher fails when he avoids sophistry, or the conceit of knowledge, only to pose as a prophet of miraculous intuition or mystic revelation or a preacher of pious nobilities of sentiment.

Perhaps we can now see why it is that philosophers have so often been led astray into making claims for philosophy which when taken literally are practically insane in their inordinate scope, such as the claim that philosophy deals with some supreme and total reality beyond that with which the special sciences and arts have to do. Stated sincerely and moderately, the claim would take the form of pointing out that no knowledge as long as it remains just knowledge, just apprehension of fact and truth, is complete or satisfying. Human nature is such that it is impossible that merely finding out that things are thus and so can long content it. There is an instinctive uneasiness which forces men to go beyond any intellectual grasp or recognition, no matter how extensive. Even if a man had seen the whole existent world and gained insight into its hidden and complicated structure, he would after a few moments of ecstasy at the marvel thus revealed to him become dissatisfied to remain at that point. He would begin to ask himself what of it? What is it all about? What does it all mean? And by these questions he would not signify the absurd search for a knowledge greater than all knowledge, but would indicate the need for projecting even the completest knowledge upon a realm of another dimension—namely, the dimension of action. He would mean: What am I to do about it? What course of activity does this state of things require of me? What possibilities to be achieved by my own thought turned over into deed does it open up to me? What new responsibilities does this knowledge impose? To what new adventures does it invite? All knowledge in short makes a difference. It opens new perspectives and releases energy to new tasks. This happens anyway and continuously, philosophy or no philosophy. But philosophy tries to gather up the threads into a central stream of tendency, to inquire what more fundamental and general attitudes of response the trend of knowledge exacts of us, to what new fields of action it calls us. It is in this sense, a practical and moral sense, that philosophy can lay claim to the epithets of universal, basic and superior. Knowledge *is* partial and incomplete, any and all knowledge, till we have placed it in the context of a future which cannot be known, but only speculated about and resolved upon. It is, to use in another sense a favorite philosophical term, a matter of *appearance,* for it is not self-enclosed, but an indication of something to be done.

As was intimated at the outset, considerable has been said about philosophy, but nothing as yet about democracy. Yet, I hope, certain implications are fairly obvious. There has been, roughly speaking, a coincidence in the development of modern experimental science and of democracy. Philosophy has no more important question than a consideration of how far this may be mere coincidence, and how far it marks a genuine correspondence. Is democracy a comparatively superficial human expedient, a device of petty manipulation, or does nature itself, as that is uncovered and understood by our best contemporaneous knowledge, sustain and support our democratic hopes and aspirations? Or, if we choose to begin arbitrarily at the other end, if to construct democratic institutions is our aim, how then shall we construe and interpret the natural environment and natural history of humanity in order to get an intellectual warrant for our endeavors, a reasonable persuasion that our undertaking is not contradicted by what science authorizes us to say about the structure of the world? How shall we read what we call reality (that is to say the world of existence accessible to verifiable inquiry) so that we may essay our deepest political and social problems with a conviction that they are to a reasonable extent sanctioned and sustained by the nature of things? Is the world as an object of knowledge at odds with our purposes and efforts? Is it merely neutral and indifferent? Does it lend itself equally to all our social ideals, which means that it gives itself to none, but stays aloof, ridiculing as it were the ardor and earnestness with which we take our trivial and transitory hopes and plans? Or is its nature such that it is at least willing to coöperate, that it not only does not say us nay, but gives us an encouraging nod?

Is not this, you may ask, taking democracy too seriously? Why not ask the question about say presbyterianism or free verse? Well, I would not wholly deny the pertinency of similar questions about such movements. All deliberate action of mind is in a way an experiment with the world to see what it will stand for, what it will promote and what frustrate. The world is tolerant and fairly hospitable. It permits and even encourages all sorts of experiments. But in the long run some are more welcomed and assimilated than others. Hence there can be no difference save one of depth and scope between the questions of the relation of the world to a scheme of conduct in the form of church government or a form of art and that of its relation to democracy. If there be a difference, it is only because democracy is a form of desire and endeavor which reaches further and condenses into itself more issues.

This statement implies a matter of definition. What is meant by democracy? It can certainly be defined in a way which limits the issue to matters which if they bear upon philosophy at all affect it only in limited and technical aspects. Anything that can be said in the way of definition in the remaining space must be, and confessedly is, arbitrary. The arbitrariness may however, be mitigated by linking up the conception with the historic formula of the greatest liberal movement of history—the formula of liberty, equality and fraternity. In referring to this, we only exchange arbitrariness for vagueness. It would be hard indeed to arrive at any consensus of judgment about the meaning of any one of the three terms inscribed on the democratic banner. Men did not agree in the eighteenth century and subsequent events have done much to accentuate their differences. Do they apply purely politically, or do they have an economic meaning?—to refer to one great cleavage which in the nineteenth century broke the liberal movement into two factions, now opposed to one another as liberal and conservative were once opposed.

Let us then take frank advantage of the vagueness and employ the terms with a certain generosity and breadth. What does the demand for liberty imply for philosophy, when we take the idea of liberty as conveying something of decided moral significance? Roughly speaking, there are two typical ideas of liberty. One of them says that freedom is action in accord with the consciousness of fixed law; that men are free when they are rational, and they are rational when they recognize and consciously conform to the necessities which the universe exemplified. As Tolstoi says, even the ox would be free if it recognized the yoke about its neck and took the yoke for the law of its own action instead of engaging in a vain task of revolt which escapes no necessity but only turns it in the direction of misery and destruction. This is a noble idea of freedom embodied, both openly and disguisedly, in classic philosophies. It is the only view consistent with any form of absolutism whether materialistic or idealistic, whether it considers the necessary relations which form the universe to be physical in character or spiritual. It holds of any view which says that reality exists under the form of eternity, that it is, to use a technical term, a *simul totum,* an all at once and forever affair, no matter whether the all at once be of mathematical-physical laws and structures, or a comprehensive and exhaustive divine consciousness. Of such a conception one can only say that however noble, it is not one which is spontaneously congenial to the idea of liberty in a society which has set its heart on democracy.

A philosophy animated, be it unconsciously or consciously, by the strivings of men to achieve democracy will construe liberty as meaning a universe in which there is real uncertainty and contingency, a world which is not all in, and never will be, a world which in some respect is incomplete and in the making, and which in these respects may be made this way or that according as men judge, prize, love and labor. To such a philosophy any notion of a perfect or complete reality, finished, existing always the same without regard to the vicissitudes of time, will be abhorrent. It will think of time not as that part of reality which for some strange reason has not yet been traversed, but as a genuine field of novelty, of real and unpredictable increments to existence, a field for experimentation and invention. It will indeed recognize that there is in things a grain against which we cannot successfully go, but it will also insist that we cannot even discover what that grain is except as we make this new experiment and that fresh effort, and that consequently the mistake, the effort which is frustrated in direct exe-cution, is as true a constituent of the world as is the act which most carefully observes law. For it is the grain which is rubbed the wrong way which more clearly stands out. It will recognize that in a world where discovery is genuine, error is an inevitable ingredient of reality, and that man's business is not to avoid it—or to cultivate the illusion that it is mere appearance—but to turn it to account, to make it fruitful. Nor will such a philosophy be mealy-mouthed in admitting that where contingency is real and experiment is required, good fortune and bad fortune are facts. It will not construe all accomplishment in terms of merit and virtue, and all loss and frustration in terms of demerit and just punishment. Because it recognizes that contingency coöperates with intelligence in the realization of every plan, even the one most carefully and wisely thought out, it will avoid conceit and intellectual arrogance. It will not fall into the delusion that consciousness is or can be everything as a determiner of events. Hence it will be humbly grateful that a world in which the most extensive and accurate thought and reason can only take advantage of events is also a world which gives room to move about in, and which offers the delights of consummations that are new revelations, as well as those defeats that are admonishments to conceit.

The evident contrast of equality is inequality. Perhaps it is not so evident that inequality means practically inferiority and superiority. And that this relation works out practically in support of a régime of authority or feudal hierarchy in which each lower or inferior element depends upon, holds from, one superior from which it gets direction and to which it is responsible. Let one bear this idea fully in mind and he will see how largely philosophy has been committed to a metaphysics of feudalism. By this I mean it has thought of things in the world as occupying certain grades of value, or as having fixed degrees of truth, ranks of reality.

The traditional conception of philosophy to which I referred at the outset, which identifies it with insight into supreme reality or ultimate and comprehensive truth, shows how thoroughly philosophy has been committed to a notion that inherently some realities are superior to others, are better than others. Now any such philosophy inev-itably works in behalf of a régime of authority, for it is only right that the superior should lord it over the inferior. The result is that much of philosophy has gone to justifying the particular scheme of authority in religion or social order which happened to exist at a given time. It has become unconsciously an apologetic for the established order, because it has tried to show the rationality of this or that existent hierarchical grading of values and schemes of life. Or when it has questioned the established order it has been a revolutionary search for some rival principle of authority.

How largely indeed has historic philosophy been a search for an indefeasible seat of authority! Greek philosophy began when men doubted the authority of custom as a regulator of life; it sought in universal reason or in the immediate particular, in being or in flux, a rival source of authority, but one which as a rival was to be as certain and definite as ever custom had been. Medieval philosophy was frankly an attempt to rec-oncile authority with reason, and modern philosophy began when man doubting the authority of revelation began a search for some authority which should have all the weight, certainty and inerrancy previously ascribed to the will of God embodied in the divinely instituted church.

Thus for the most part the democratic practice of life has been at an immense intellectual disadvantage. Prevailing philosophies have unconsciously discountenanced it. They have failed to furnish it with articulation, with reasonableness, for they have at bottom been committed to the principle of a single, final and unalterable authority from which all lesser authorities are derived. The men who questioned the divine right of kings did so in the name of another absolute. The voice of the people was mythologized into the voice of God. Now a halo may be preserved about the monarch. Because of his distance, he can be rendered transcendentally without easy detection. But the people are too close at hand, too obviously empirical, to be lent to deification. Hence democracy has ranked for the most part as an intellectual anomaly, lacking philosophical basis and logical coherency, but upon the whole to be accepted because somehow or other it works better than other schemes and seems to develop a more kindly and humane set of social institutions. For when it has tried to achieve a philosophy it has clothed itself in an atomistic individualism, as full of defects and inconsistencies in theory as it was charged with obnoxious consequences when an attempt was made to act upon it.

Now whatever the idea of equality means for democracy, it means, I take it, that the world is not to be construed as a fixed order of species, grades or degrees. It means that every existence deserving the name of existence has something unique and irreplaceable about it, that it does not exist to illustrate a principle, to realize a universal or to embody a kind or class. As philosophy it denies the basic principle of atomistic individualism as truly as that of rigid feudalism. For the individualism traditionally associated with democracy makes equality quantitative, and hence individuality something external and mechanical rather than qualitative and unique.

In social and moral matters, equality does not mean mathematical equivalence. It means rather the inapplicability of considerations of greater and less, superior and inferior. It means that no matter how great the quantitative differences of ability, strength, position, wealth, such differences are negligible in comparison with something else—the fact of individuality, the manifestation of something irreplaceable. It means, in short, a world in which an existence must be reckoned with on its own account, not as something capable of equation with and transformation into something else. It implies, so to speak, a metaphysical mathematics of the incommensurable in which each speaks for itself and demands consideration on its own behalf.

If democratic equality may be construed as individuality, there is nothing forced in understanding fraternity as continuity, that is to say, as association and interaction without limit. Equality, individuality, tends to isolation and independence. It is centrifugal. To say that what is specific and unique can be exhibited and become forceful or actual only in relationship with other like beings is merely, I take it, to give a metaphysical version to the fact that democracy is concerned not with freaks or geniuses or heroes or divine leaders but with associated individuals in which each by intercourse with others somehow makes the life of each more distinctive.

All this, of course, is but by way of intimation. In spite of its form it is not really a plea for a certain kind of philosophizing. For if democracy be a serious, important choice and predilection it must in time justify itself by generating its own child of wisdom, to be justified in turn by its children, better institutions of life. It is not so much a question as to whether there will be a philosophy of this kind as it is of just who will be the philosophers associated with it. And I cannot conclude without mentioning the name of one through whom this vision of a new mode of life has already spoken with beauty and power—William James.

RANDOLPH BOURNE

"Trans-National America"
1916

"Twilight of Idols"
1917

In "Trans-National America" (1916), Randolph Bourne (1886–1918) condemned the Anglo-conformist ideology often associated with the figure of the melting pot and called instead for the dynamic mixing and mingling of diverse peoples in the interests of new cultural combinations. Bourne was the most influential of the handful of intellectuals who opposed the nativism dominant among Americans of Protestant Anglo-Saxon stock during the era of World War I. The ideal of cosmopolitanism to which Bourne gave voice was destined during the next several decades to serve as a rallying point for immigrant intellectuals as well as for antiprovincial WASPS like Bourne himself. This function of the cosmopolitan ideal is addressed in David A. Hollinger, "Ethnic Diversity, Cosmopolitanism, and the Emergence of the American Liberal Intelligentsia," in Hollinger's *In the American Province: Studies in the History and Historiography of Ideas* (Bloomington, Ind., 1985), 56–73.

Bourne's vision for America was slightly different from that of Horace Kallen, whose criticism of the "melting pot" helped to inspire Bourne's defense of cultural diversity. Kallen's "Democracy vs the Melting Pot," *Nation* (February 25, 1915), 218–20, looked to the United States as a broad canopy providing protection for immigrant groups expected to remain enduring, relatively autonomous presences in American life. But Bourne accepted a greater measure of cross-fertilization, and anticipated the development of a new, distinctive culture. For an influential study of Kallen's ideas, see Werner Sollors, "A Critique of Pure Pluralism," in Sacvan Bercovitch, ed., *Reconstructing American Literary History* (Cambridge, 1986), 250–79.

Bourne is also remembered for his vindication, during World War I, of the vocation of the intellectual as an independent critic of prevailing authorities. The most influential of Bourne's writings on this theme was "Twilight of Idols" (1917), the second Bourne essay reprinted here. This attack on John Dewey and other "pragmatic" and "instrumentalist" intellectuals for their support of the war opens and closes with invocations of another great pragmatist, William James. James offered some of the "poetic vision" that Bourne believed Dewey lacked. For a fair-minded account of the Dewey–Bourne disagreement that emphasizes Bourne's continued indebtedness to Dewey, see Robert B. Westbrook, *John Dewey and American Democracy* (Ithaca, 1991), esp. 202–12. For a careful study of Bourne and the other "Young America" critics of his generation, see Casey Nelson Blake, *Beloved Community: The Cultural Criticism of Randolph Bourne, Van Wyck Brooks, Waldo Frank, & Lewis Mumford* (Chapel Hill, 1991).

"Trans-National America"
1916

No reverberatory effect of the great war has caused American public opinion more solicitude than the failure of the "melting-pot."ᐟ The discovery of diverse nationalistic feelings among our great alien population has come to most people as an intense shock. It has brought out the unpleasant inconsistencies of our traditional beliefs. We have had to watch hard-hearted old Brahmins virtuously indignant at the spectacle of the immigrant refusing to be melted, while they jeer at patriots like Mary Antin who write about "our forefathers." We have had to listen to publicists who express themselves as stunned by the evidence of vigorous nationalistic and cultural movements in this country among Germans, Scandinavians, Bohemians, and Poles, while in the same breath they insist that the alien shall be forcibly assimilated to that Anglo-Saxon tradition which they unquestioningly label "American."

As the unpleasant truth has come upon us that assimilation in this country was proceeding on lines very different from those we had marked out for it, we found ourselves inclined to blame those who were thwarting our prophecies. The truth became culpable. We blamed the war, we blamed the Germans. And then we discovered with a moral shock that these movements had been making great headway before the war even began. We found that the tendency, reprehensible and paradoxical as it might be, has been for the national clusters of immigrants, as they became more and more firmly established and more and more prosperous, to cultivate more and more assiduously the literatures and cultural traditions of their homelands. Assimilation, in other words, instead of washing out the memories of Europe, made them more and more intensely real. Just as these clusters became more and more objectively American, did they become more and more German or Scandinavian or Bohemian or Polish.

To face the fact that our aliens are already strong enough to take a share in the direction of their own destiny, and that the strong cultural movements represented by the foreign press, schools, and colonies are a challenge to our facile attempts, is not, however, to admit the failure of Americanization. It is not to fear the failure of democracy. It is rather to urge us to an investigation of what Americanism may rightly mean. It is to ask ourselves whether our ideal has been broad or narrow—whether perhaps the time has not come to assert a higher ideal than the "melting-pot." Surely we cannot be certain of our spiritual democracy when, claiming to melt the nations within us to a comprehension of our free and democratic institutions, we fly into panic at the first sign of their own will and tendency. We act as if we wanted Americanization to take place only on our own terms, and not by the consent of the governed. All our elaborate machinery of settlement and school and union, of social and political naturalization, however, will move with friction just in so far as it neglects to take into account this strong and virile insistence that America shall be what the immigrant will have a hand

Source: Atlantic Monthly 118 (July 1916): 86–97.

in making it, and not what a ruling class, descendant of those British stocks which were the first permanent immigrants, decide that America shall be made. This is the condition which confronts us, and which demands a clear and general readjustment of our attitude and our ideal.

Mary Antin is right when she looks upon our foreign-born as the people who missed the Mayflower and came over on the first boat they could find. But she forgets that when they did come it was not upon other Mayflowers, but upon a "Maiblume," a "Fleur de Mai," a "Fior di Maggio," a "Majblomst." These people were not mere arrivals from the same family, to be welcomed as understood and long-loved, but strangers to the neighborhood, with whom a long process of settling down had to take place. For they brought with them their national and racial characters, and each new national quota had to wear slowly away the contempt with which its mere alienness got itself greeted. Each had to make its way slowly from the lowest strata of unskilled labor up to a level where it satisfied the accredited norms of social success.

We are all foreign-born or the descendants of foreign-born, and if distinctions are to be made between us they should rightly be on some other ground than indigenousness. The early colonists came over with motives no less colonial than the later. They did not come to be assimilated in an American melting-pot. They did not come to adopt the culture of the American Indian. They had not the smallest intention of "giving themselves without reservation" to the new country. They came to get freedom to live as they wanted to. They came to escape from the stifling air and chaos of the old world; they came to make their fortune in a new land. They invented no new social framework. Rather they brought over bodily the old ways to which they had been accustomed. Tightly concentrated on a hostile frontier, they were conservative beyond belief. Their pioneer daring was reserved for the objective conquest of material resources. In their folkways, in their social and political institutions, they were, like every colonial people, slavishly imitative of the mother-country. So that, in spite of the "Revolution," our whole legal and political system remained more English than the English, petrified and unchanging, while in England law developed to meet the needs of the changing times.

It is just this English-American conservatism that has been our chief obstacle to social advance. We have needed the new peoples—the order of the German and Scandinavian, the turbulence of the Slav and Hun—to save us from our own stagnation. I do not mean that the illiterate Slav is now the equal of the New Englander of pure descent. He is raw material to be educated, not into a New Englander, but into a socialized American. . . . Let us cease to think of ideals like democracy as magical qualities inherent in certain peoples. Let us speak, not of inferior races, but of inferior civilizations. We are all to educate and to be educated. These peoples in America are in a common enterprise. It is not what we are now that concerns us, but what this plastic next generation may become in the light of a new cosmopolitan ideal.

We are not dealing with static factors, but with fluid and dynamic generations. To contrast the older and the newer immigrants and see the one class as democratically motivated by love of liberty, and the other by mere money-getting, is not to illuminate the future. To think of earlier nationalities as culturally assimilated to America, while we picture the later as a sodden and resistive mass, makes only for bitterness and misunderstanding. There may be a difference between these earlier and these later stocks, but it lies neither in motive for coming nor in strength of cultural allegiance to the homeland. The truth is that no more tenacious cultural allegiance to the mother country has been shown by any alien nation than by the ruling class of Anglo-Saxon descendants in these American States. English snobberies, English religion, English literary styles, English literary reverences and canons, English ethics, English superiorities, have been the cultural food that we have drunk in from our mothers' breasts. The distinctively American spirit—pioneer, as distinguished from the reminiscently English—that appears in Whitman and Emerson and James, has had to exist on sufferance alongside of this other cult, unconsciously belittled by our cultural makers of opinion. No country has perhaps had so great indigenous genius which had so little influence on the country's traditions and expressions. The unpopular and dreaded German-American of the present day is a beginning amateur in comparison with those foolish Anglophiles of Boston and New York and Philadelphia whose reversion to cultural type sees uncritically in England's cause the cause of Civilization, and, under the guise of ethical independence of thought, carries along European traditions which are no more "American" than the German categories themselves. . . .

The non-English American can scarcely be blamed if he sometimes thinks of the Anglo-Saxon predominance in America as little more than a predominance of priority. The Anglo-Saxon was merely the first immigrant, the first to found a colony. He has never really ceased to be the descendant of immigrants, nor has he ever succeeded in transforming that colony into a real nation, with a tenacious, richly woven fabric of native culture. Colonials from the other nations have come and settled down beside him. They found no definite native culture which should startle them out of their colonialism, and consequently they looked back to their mother-country, as the earlier Anglo-Saxon immigrant was looking back to his. What has been offered the newcomer has been the chance to learn English, to become a citizen, to salute the flag. And those elements of our ruling classes who are responsible for the public schools, the settlements, all the organizations for amelioration in the cities, have every reason to be proud of the care and labor which they have devoted to absorbing the immigrant. His opportunities the immigrant has taken to gladly, with almost a pathetic eagerness to make his way in the new land without friction or disturbance. The common language has made not only for the necessary communication, but for all the amenities of life.

If freedom means the right to do pretty much as one pleases, so long as one does not interfere with others, the immigrant has found freedom, and the ruling element has been singularly liberal in its treatment of the invading hordes. But if freedom means a democratic coöperation in determining the ideals and purposes and industrial and social institutions of a country, then the immigrant has not been free, and the Anglo-Saxon element is guilty of just what every dominant race is guilty of in every European country: the imposition of its own culture upon the minority peoples. The fact that this imposition has been so mild and, indeed, semi-conscious does not alter its quality. And the war has brought out just the degree to which that purpose of "Americanizing," that is, "Anglo-Saxonizing," the immigrant has failed.

For the Anglo-Saxon now in his bitterness to turn upon the other peoples, talk about their "arrogance," scold them for not being melted in a pot which never existed, is to betray the unconscious purpose which lay at the bottom of his heart. It betrays too the possession of a racial jealousy similar to that of which he is now accusing the so-called "hyphenates." Let the Anglo-Saxon be proud enough of the heroic toil and heroic sacrifices which moulded the nation. But let him ask himself, if he had had to depend on the English descendants, where he would have been living to-day. To those of us who see in the exploitation of unskilled labor the strident red *leit-motif* of our civilization, the settling of the country presents a great social drama as the waves of immigration broke over it.

Let the Anglo-Saxon ask himself where he would have been if these races had not come? Let those who feel the inferiority of the non-Anglo-Saxon immigrant contemplate that region of the States which has remained the most distinctively American," the South. Let him ask himself whether he would really like to see the foreign hordes Americanized into such an Americanization. Let him ask himself how superior this native civilization is to the great "alien" states of Wisconsin and Minnesota, where Scandinavians, Poles, and Germans have self-consciously labored to preserve their traditional culture, while being outwardly and satisfactorily American. Let him ask himself how much more wisdom, intelligence, industry and social leadership has come out of these alien states than out of all the truly American ones. The South, in fact, while this vast Northern development has gone on, still remains an English colony, stagnant and complacent, having progressed culturally scarcely beyond the early Victorian era. It is culturally sterile because it has had no advantage of cross-fertilization like the Northern states. What has happened in states such as Wisconsin and Minnesota is that strong foreign cultures have struck root in a new and fertile soil. America has meant liberation, and German and Scandinavian political ideas and social energies have expanded to a new potency. The process has not been at all the fancied "assimilation" of the Scandinavian or Teuton. Rather has it been a process of their assimilation of us—I speak as an Anglo-Saxon. The foreign cultures have not been melted down or run together, made into some homogeneous Americanism, but have remained distinct but coöperating to the greater glory and benefit, not only of themselves but of all the native "Americanism" around them.

What we emphatically do not want is that these distinctive qualities should be washed out into a tasteless, colorless fluid of uniformity. Already we have far too much of this insipidity,—masses of people who are cultural half-breeds, neither assimilated Anglo-Saxons nor nationals of another culture. Each national colony in this country seems to retain in its foreign press, its vernacular literature, its schools, its intellectual and patriotic leaders, a central cultural nucleus. From this nucleus the colony extends out by imperceptible gradations to a fringe where national characteristics are all but lost. Our cities are filled with these half-breeds who retain their foreign names but have lost the foreign savor. This does not mean that they have actually been changed into New Englanders or Middle Westerners. It does not mean that they have been really Americanized. It means that, letting slip from them whatever native culture they had, they have substituted for it only the most rudimentary American—the American culture of the cheap newspaper, the "movies," the popular song, the ubiquitous automobile. The unthinking who survey this class call them assimilated, Americanized. The great American public school has done its work. With these people our institutions are safe. We may thrill with dread at the aggressive hyphenate, but this tame flabbiness is accepted as Americanization. The same moulders of opinion whose ideal is to melt the different races into Anglo-Saxon gold hail this poor product as the satisfying result of their alchemy.

Yet a truer cultural sense would have told us that it is not the self-conscious cultural nuclei that sap at our American life, but these fringes. It is not the Jew who sticks proudly to the faith of his fathers and boasts of that venerable culture of his who is dangerous to America, but the Jew who has lost the Jewish fire and become a mere elementary, grasping animal. It is not the Bohemian who supports the Bohemian schools in Chicago whose influence is sinister, but the Bohemian who has made money and has got into ward politics. Just so surely as we tend to disintegrate these nuclei of nationalistic culture do we tend to create hordes of men and women without a spiritual country, cultural outlaws, without taste, without standards but those of the mob. We sentence them to live on the most rudimentary planes of American life. The influences at the centre of the nuclei are centripetal. They make for the intelligence and the social values which mean an enhancement of life. And just because the foreign-born retains this expressiveness is he likely to be a better citizen of the American community. The influences at the fringe, however, are centrifugal, anarchical. They make for detached fragments of peoples. Those who came to find liberty achieve only license. They become the flotsam and jetsam of American life, the downward undertow of our civilization with its leering cheapness and falseness of taste and spiritual outlook, the absence of mind and sincere feeling which we see in our slovenly towns, our vapid moving pictures, our popular novels, and in the vacuous faces of the crowds on the city street. This is the cultural wreckage of our time, and it is from the fringes of the Anglo-Saxon as well as the other stocks that it falls. America has as yet no impelling integrating force. It makes too easily for this detritus of cultures. In our loose, free country, no constraining national purpose, no tenacious folk-tradition and folk-style hold the people to a line.

The war has shown us that not in any magical formula will this purpose be found. No intense nationalism of the European plan can be ours. But do we not begin to see a new and more adventurous ideal? Do we not see how the national colonies in America, deriving power from the deep cultural heart of Europe and yet living here in mutual toleration, freed from the age-long tangles of races, creeds, and dynasties, may work out a federated ideal? America is transplanted Europe, but a Europe that has not been disintegrated and scattered in the transplanting as in some Dispersion. Its colonies live here inextricably mingled, yet not homogeneous. They merge but they do not fuse.

America is a unique sociological fabric, and it bespeaks poverty of imagination not to be thrilled at the incalculable potentialities of so novel a union of men. To seek no other goal than the weary old nationalism,—belligerent, exclusive, inbreeding, the poison of which we are witnessing now in Europe,—is to make patriotism a hollow sham, and to declare that, in spite of our boastings, America must ever be a follower and not a leader of nations.

If we come to find this point of view plausible, we shall have to give up the search for our native "American" culture. With the exception of the South and that New England which, like the Red Indian, seems to be passing into solemn oblivion, there is no distinctively American culture. It is apparently our lot rather to be a federation of cultures. This we have been for half a century, and the war has made it ever more evident that this is what we are destined to remain. This will not mean, however, that there are not expressions of indigenous genius that could not have sprung from any other soil. Music, poetry, philosophy, have been singularly fertile and new. Strangely enough, American genius has flared forth just in those directions which are least understood of the people. If the American note is bigness, action, the objective as contrasted with the reflective life, where is the epic expression of this spirit? Our drama and our fiction, the peculiar fields for the expression of action and objectivity, are somehow exactly the fields of the spirit which remain poor and mediocre. American materialism is in some way inhibited from getting into impressive artistic form its own energy with which it bursts. Nor is it any better in architecture, the least romantic and subjective of all the arts. We are inarticulate of the very values which we profess to idealize. But in the finer forms—music, verse, the essay, philosophy—the American genius puts forth work equal to any of its contemporaries. Just in so far as our American genius has expressed the pioneer spirit, the adventurous, forward-looking drive of a colonial empire, is it representative of that whole America of the many races and peoples, and not of any partial or traditional enthusiasm. And only as that pioneer note is sounded can we really speak of the American culture. As long as we thought of Americanism in terms of the "melting-pot," our American cultural tradition lay in the past. It was something to which the new Americans were to be moulded. In the light of our changing ideal of Americanism, we must perpetrate the paradox that our American cultural tradition lies in the future. It will be what we all together make out of this incomparable opportunity of attacking the future with a new key.

Whatever American nationalism turns out to be, it is certain to become something utterly different from the nationalisms of twentieth-century Europe. This wave of reactionary enthusiasm to play the orthodox nationalistic game which is passing over the country is scarcely vital enough to last. We cannot swagger and thrill to the same national self-feeling. We must give new edges to our pride. We must be content to avoid the unnumbered woes that national patriotism has brought in Europe, and that fiercely heightened pride and self-consciousness. Alluring as this is, we must allow our imaginations to transcend this scarcely veiled belligerency. We can be serenely too proud to fight if our pride embraces the creative forces of civilization which armed contest nullifies. We can be too proud to fight if our code of honor transcends that of the schoolboy on the playground surrounded by his jeering mates. Our honor must be positive and creative, and not the mere jealous and negative protectiveness against metaphysical violations of our technical rights. When the doctrine is put forth that in one American flows the mystic blood of all our country's sacred honor, freedom, and prosperity, so that an injury to him is to be the signal for turning our whole nation into that clan-feud of horror and reprisal which would be war, then we find ourselves back among the musty schoolmen of the Middle Ages, and not in any pragmatic and realistic America of the twentieth century.

We should hold our gaze to what America has done, not what mediaeval codes of dueling she has failed to observe. We have transplanted European modernity to our soil, without the spirit that inflames it and turns all its energy into mutual destruction. Out of these foreign peoples there has somehow been squeezed the poison. An America, "hyphenated" to bitterness, is somehow non-explosive. For, even if we all hark back in sympathy to a European nation, even if the war has set every one vibrating to some emotional string twanged on the other side of the Atlantic, the effect has been one of almost dramatic harmlessness. . . .

The failure of the melting-pot, far from closing the great American democratic experiment, means that it has only just begun. Whatever American nationalism turns out to be, we see already that it will have a color richer and more exciting than our ideal has hitherto encompassed. In a world which has dreamed of internationalism, we find that we have all unawares been building up the first international nation. The voices which have cried for a tight and jealous nationalism of the European pattern are failing. From that ideal, however valiantly and disinterestedly it has been set for us, time and tendency have moved us further and further away. What we have achieved has been rather a cosmopolitan federation of national colonies, of foreign cultures, from whom the sting of devastating competition has been removed. America is already the world-federation in miniature, the continent where for the first time in history has been achieved that miracle of hope, the peaceful living side by side, with character substantially preserved, of the most heterogeneous peoples under the sun. Nowhere else has such contiguity been anything but the breeder of misery. Here, notwithstanding our tragic failures of adjustment, the outlines are already too clear not to give us a new vision and a new orientation of the American mind in the world.

It is for the American of the younger generation to accept this cosmopolitanism, and carry it along with self-conscious and fruitful purpose. In his colleges, he is already getting, with the study of modern history and politics, the modern literatures, economic geography, the privilege of a cosmopolitan outlook such as the people of no other nation of to-day in Europe can possibly secure. If he is still a colonial, he is no longer the colonial of one partial culture, but of many. He is a colonial of the world. Colonialism has grown into cosmopolitanism, and his mother-land is no one nation, but all who have anything life-enhancing to offer to the spirit. That vague sympathy which the France of ten years ago was feeling for the world—a sympathy which was drowned in the terrible reality of war—may be the modern American's, and that in a positive and aggressive sense. If the American is parochial, it is in sheer wantonness or cowardice. His provincialism is the measure of his fear of bogies or the defect of his imagination.

Indeed, it is not uncommon for the eager Anglo-Saxon who goes to a vivid American university to-day to find his true friends not among his own race but among the acclimatized German or Austrian, the acclimatized Jew, the acclimatized Scandinavian or Italian. In them he finds the cosmopolitan note. In these youths, foreign-born or the children of foreign-born parents, he is likely to find many of his old inbred morbid problems washed away. These friends are oblivious to the repressions of that tight little society in which he so provincially grew up. He has a pleasurable sense of liberation from the stale and familiar attitudes of those whose ingrowing culture has scarcely created anything vital for his America of to-day. He breathes a larger air. In his new enthusiasms for continental literature, for unplumbed Russian depths, for French clarity of thought, for Teuton philosophies of power, he feels himself citizen of a larger world. He may be absurdly superficial, his outward-reaching wonder may ignore all the stiller and homelier virtues of his Anglo-Saxon home, but he has at least found the clue to that international mind which will be essential to all men and women of good-will if they are ever to save this Western world of ours from suicide. His new friends have gone through a similar evolution. America has burned most of the baser metal also from them. Meeting now with this common American background, all of them may yet retain that distinctiveness of their native cultures and their national spiritual slants. They are more valuable and interesting to each other for being different, yet that difference could not be creative were it not for this new cosmopolitan outlook which America has given them and which they all equally possess.

A college where such a spirit is possible even to the smallest degree, has within itself already the seeds of this international intellectual world of the future. It suggests that the contribution of America will be an intellectual internationalism which goes far beyond the mere exchange of scientific ideas and discoveries and the cold recording of facts. It will be an intellectual sympathy which is not satisfied until it has got at the heart of the different cultural expressions, and felt as they feel. It may have immense preferences, but it will make understanding and not indignation its end. Such a sympathy will unite and not divide.

Against the thinly disguised panic which calls itself "patriotism" and the thinly disguised militarism which calls itself "preparedness" the cosmopolitan ideal is set. This does not mean that those who hold it are for a policy of drift. They, too, long passionately for an integrated and disciplined America. But they do not want one which is integrated only for domestic economic exploitation of the workers or for predatory economic imperialism among the weaker peoples. They do not want one that is integrated by coercion or militarism, or for the truculent assertion of a mediaeval code of honor and of doubtful rights. They believe that the most effective integration will be one which coördinates the diverse elements and turns them consciously toward working out together the place of America in the world-situation. They demand for integration a genuine integrity, a wholeness and soundness of enthusiasm and purpose which can only come when no national colony within our America feels that it is being discriminated against or that its cultural case is being prejudged. This strength of coöperation, this feeling that all who are here may have a hand in the destiny of America, will make for a finer spirit of integration than any narrow "Americanism" or forced chauvinism.

In this effort we may have to accept some form of that dual citizenship which meets with so much articulate horror among us. Dual citizenship we may have to recognize as the rudimentary form of that international citizenship to which, if our words mean anything, we aspire. We have assumed unquestioningly that mere participation in the political life of the United States must cut the new citizen off from all sympathy with his old allegiance. Anything but a bodily transfer of devotion from one sovereignty to another has been viewed as a sort of moral treason against the Republic. We have insisted that the immigrant whom we welcomed escaping from the very exclusive nationalism of his European home shall forthwith adopt a nationalism just as exclusive, just as narrow, and even less legitimate because it is founded on no warm traditions of his own. Yet a nation like France is said to permit a formal and legal dual citizenship even at the present time. Though a citizen of hers may pretend to cast off his allegiance in favor of some other sovereignty, he is still subject to her laws when he returns. Once a citizen, always a citizen, no matter how many new citizenships he may embrace. And such a dual citizenship seems to us sound and right. For it recognizes that, although the Frenchman may accept the formal institutional framework of his new country and indeed become intensely loyal to it, yet his Frenchness he will never lose. What makes up the fabric of his soul will always be of this Frenchness, so that unless he becomes utterly degenerate he will always to some degree dwell still in his native environment.

Indeed, does not the cultivated American who goes to Europe practice a dual citizenship, which, if not formal, is no less real? The American who lives abroad may be the least expatriate of men. If he falls in love with French ways and French thinking and French democracy and seeks to saturate himself with the new spirit, he is guilty of at least a dual spiritual citizenship. He may be still American, yet he feels himself through sympathy also a Frenchman. And he finds that this expansion involves no shameful conflict within him, no surrender of his native attitude. He has rather for the first time caught a glimpse of the cosmopolitan spirit. And after wandering about through many races and civilizations he may return to America to find them all here living vividly and crudely, seeking the same adjustment that he made. He sees the new peoples here with a new vision. They are no longer masses of aliens, waiting to be "assimilated," waiting to be melted down into the indistinguishable dough of Anglo-Saxonism. They are rather threads of living and potent cultures, blindly striving to weave themselves into a novel international nation, the first the world has seen. In an

Austria-Hungary or a Prussia the stronger of these cultures would be moving almost instinctively to subjugate the weaker. But in America those wills-to-power are turned in a different direction into learning how to live together.

Along with dual citizenship we shall have to accept, I think, that free and mobile passage of the immigrant between America and his native land again which now arouses so much prejudice among us. We shall have to accept the immigrant's return for the same reason that we consider justified our own flitting about the earth. To stigmatize the alien who works in America for a few years and returns to his own land, only perhaps to seek American fortune again, is to think in narrow nationalistic terms. It is to ignore the cosmopolitan significance of this migration. It is to ignore the fact that the returning immigrant is often a missionary to an inferior civilization.

This migratory habit has been especially common with the unskilled laborers who have been pouring into the United States in the last dozen years from every country in southeastern Europe. Many of them return to spend their earnings in their own country or to serve their country in war. But they return with an entirely new critical outlook, and a sense of the superiority of American organization to the primitive living around them. This continued passage to and fro has already raised the material standard of living in many regions of these backward countries. For these regions are thus endowed with exactly what they need, the capital for the exploitation of their natural resources, and the spirit of enterprise. America is thus educating these laggard peoples from the very bottom of society up, awaking vast masses to a new-born hope for the future. In the migratory Greek, therefore, we have not the parasitic alien, the doubtful American asset, but a symbol of that cosmopolitan interchange which is coming, in spite of all war and national exclusiveness.

Only America, by reason of the unique liberty of opportunity and traditional isolation for which she seems to stand, can lead in this cosmopolitan enterprise. Only the American—and in this category I include the migratory alien who has lived with us and caught the pioneer spirit and a sense of new social vistas—has the chance to become that citizen of the world. America is coming to be, not a nationality but a trans-nationality, a weaving back and forth, with the other lands, of many threads of all sizes and colors. Any movement which attempts to thwart this weaving, or to dye the fabric any one color, or disentangle the threads of the strands, is false to this cosmopolitan vision. I do not mean that we shall necessarily glut ourselves with the raw product of humanity. It would be folly to absorb the nations faster than we could weave them. We have no duty either to admit or reject. It is purely a question of expediency. What concerns us is the fact that the strands are here. We must have a policy and an ideal for an actual situation. Our question is, What shall we do with our America? How are you likely to get the more creative America—by confining our imaginations to the ideal of the melting-pot, or broadening them to some such cosmopolitan conception as I have been vaguely sketching?

The war has shown America to be unable, though isolated geographically and politically from a European world-situation, to remain aloof and irresponsible. She is a wandering star in a sky dominated by two colossal constellations of states. Can she not work out some position of her own, some life of being in, yet not quite of, this seething and embroiled European world? This is her only hope and promise. . . .

Is it a wild hope that the undertow of opposition to metaphysics in international relations, opposition to militarism, is less a cowardly provincialism than a groping for this higher cosmopolitan ideal? One can understand the irritated restlessness with which our proud pro-British colonists contemplate a heroic conflict across the seas in which they have no part. It was inevitable that our necessary inaction should evolve in their minds into the bogey of national shame and dishonor. But let us be careful about accepting their sensitiveness as final arbiter. Let us look at our reluctance rather as the first crude beginnings of assertion on the part of certain strands in our nationality that they have a right to a voice in the construction of the American ideal. Let us face realistically the America we have around us. Let us work with the forces that are at work. Let us make something of this trans-national spirit instead of outlawing it. Already we are living this cosmopolitan America. What we need is everywhere a vivid consciousness of the new ideal. Deliberate headway must be made against the survivals of the melting-pot ideal for the promise of American life.

We cannot Americanize America worthily by sentimentalizing and moralizing history. When the best schools are expressly renouncing the questionable duty of teaching patriotism by means of history, it is not the time to force shibboleth upon the immigrant. This form of Americanization has been heard because it appealed to the vestiges of our old sentimentalized and moralized patriotism. This has so far held the field as the expression of the new American's new devotion. The inflections of other voices have been drowned. They must be heard. We must see if the lesson of the war has not been for hundreds of these later Americans a vivid realization of their trans-nationality, a new consciousness of what America meant to them as a citizenship in the world. It is the vague historic idealisms which have provided the fuel for the European flame. Our American ideal can make no progress until we do away with this romantic gilding of the past.

All our idealisms must be those of future social goals in which all can participate, the good life of personality lived in the environment of the Beloved Community. No mere doubtful triumphs of the past, which redound to the glory of only one of our trans-nationalities, can satisfy us. It must be a future America, on which all can unite, which pulls us irresistibly toward it, as we understand each other more warmly.

To make real this striving amid dangers and apathies is work for a younger *intelligentsia* of America. Here is an enterprise of integration into which we can all pour ourselves, of a spiritual welding which should make us, if the final menace ever came, not weaker, but infinitely strong.

Twilight of Idols
1917

Where are the seeds of American promise? Man cannot live by politics alone, and it is small cheer that our best intellects are caught in the political current and see only the hope that America will find her soul in the remaking of the world. If William James were alive would he be accepting the war-situation so easily and complacently? Would he be chiding the over-stimulated intelligence of peace-loving idealists, and excommunicating from the ranks of liberal progress the pitiful remnant of those who struggle "above the battle?" I like to think that his gallant spirit would have called for a war to be gallantly played, with insistent care for democratic values at home, and unequivocal alliance with democratic elements abroad for a peace that should promise more than a mere union of benevolent imperialisms. I think of James now because the recent articles of John Dewey's on the war suggest a slackening in his thought for our guidance and stir, and the inadequacy of his pragmatism as a philosophy of life in this emergency. Whether James would have given us just that note of spiritual adventure which would make the national enterprise seem creative for an American future,—this we can never know. But surely that philosophy of Dewey's which we had been following so uncritically for so long, breaks down almost noisily when it is used to grind out interpretation for the present crisis. These articles on "Conscience and Compulsion," "The Future of Pacifism," "What America Will Fight For," "Conscription of Thought," which *The New Republic* has been printing, seem to me to be a little off-color. A philosopher who senses so little the sinister forces of war, who is so much more concerned over the excesses of the pacifists than over the excesses of military policy, who can feel only amusement at the idea that any one should try to conscript thought, who assumes that the war-technique can be used without trailing along with it the mob-fanaticisms, the injustices and hatreds, that are organically bound up with it, is speaking to another element of the younger intelligentsia than that to which I belong. Evidently the attitudes which war calls out are fiercer and more incalculable than Professor Dewey is accustomed to take into his hopeful and intelligent imagination, and the pragmatist mind, in trying to adjust itself to them, gives the air of grappling, like the pioneer who challenges the arid plains, with a power too big for it. It is not an arena of creative intelligence our country's mind is now, but of mob-psychology. The soldiers who tried to lynch Max Eastman showed that current patriotism is not a product of the will to remake the world. The luxuriant releases of explosive hatred for which peace apparently gives far too little scope cannot be wooed by sweet reasonableness, nor can they be the raw material for the creation of rare liberal political structures. All that can be done is to try to keep your country out of situations where such expressive releases occur. If you have willed the situation, however, or accepted it as inevitable, it is fatuous to protest against the gay debauch of hatred and fear and swagger that must mount and mount, until the

Source: Randolph Bourne, "Twilight of Idols," *The Seven Arts* 11 (October 1917):688–702.

heady and virulent poison of war shall have created its own anti-toxin of ruin and disillusionment. To talk as if war were anything else than such a poison is to show that your philosophy has never been confronted with the pathless and the inexorable, and that, only dimly feeling the change, it goes ahead acting as if it had not got out of its depth. Only a lack of practice with a world of human nature so raw-nerved, irrational, uncreative, as an America at war was bound to show itself to be, can account for the singular unsatisfactoriness of these latter utterances of Dewey. He did have one moment of hesitation just before the war began, when the war and its external purposes and unifying power seemed the small thing beside that internal adventure which should find our American promise. But that perspective has now disappeared, and one finds Dewey now untainted by skepticism as to our being about a business to which all our idealism should rally. That failure to get guaranties that this country's efforts would obligate the Allies to a democratic world-order Dewey blames on the defection of the pacifists, and then somehow manages to get himself into a "we" who "romantically," as he says, forewent this crucial link of our strategy. Does this easy identification of himself with undemocratically-controlled foreign policy mean that a country is democratic when it accepts what its government does, or that war has a narcotic effect on the pragmatic mind? For Dewey somehow retains his sense of being in the controlling class, and ignores those anxious questions of democrats who have been his disciples but are now resenters of the war.

What I come to is a sense of suddenly being left in the lurch, of suddenly finding that a philosophy upon which I had relied to carry us through no longer works. I find the contrast between the idea that creative intelligence has free functioning in wartime, and the facts of the inexorable situation, too glaring. The contrast between what liberals ought to be doing and saying if democratic values are to be conserved, and what the real forces are imposing upon them, strikes too sternly on my intellectual senses. I should prefer some philosophy of War as the grim and terrible cleanser to this optimism-haunted mood that continues unweariedly to suggest that all can yet be made to work for good in a mad and half-destroyed world. I wonder if James, in the face of such disaster, would not have abandoned his "moral equivalent of war" for an "immoral equivalent" which, in swift and periodic saturnalia, would have acted as vaccination against the sure pestilence of war.

Dewey's philosophy is inspiring enough for a society at peace, prosperous and with a fund of progressive good-will. It is a philosophy of hope, of clear-sighted comprehension of materials and means. Where institutions are at all malleable, it is the only clue for improvement. It is scientific method applied to "uplift." But this careful adaptation of means to desired ends, this experimental working out of control over brute forces and dead matter in the interests of communal life, depends on a store of rationality, and is effective only where there is strong desire for progress. It is precisely the school, the institution to which Dewey's philosophy was first applied, that is of all our institutions the most malleable. And it is the will to educate that has seemed, in these days, among all our social attitudes the most rationally motivated. It was education, and almost education alone, that seemed susceptible to the steady pressure of an "instrumental" philosophy. Intelligence really seemed about to come into conscious control of an institution, and that one the most potent in moulding the attitudes needed for a civilized society and the aptitudes needed for the happiness of the individual.

For both our revolutionary conceptions of what education means, and for the intellectual strategy of its approach, this country is immeasurably indebted to the influence of Professor Dewey's philosophy. With these ideas sincerely felt, a rational nation would have chosen education as its national enterprise. Into this it would have thrown its energy though the heavens fell and the earth rocked around it. But the nation did not use its isolation from the conflict to educate itself. It fretted for three years and then let war, not education, be chosen, at the almost unanimous behest of our intellectual class, from motives alien to our cultural needs, and for political ends alien to the happiness of the individual. But nations, of course, are not rational entities, and they act within their most irrational rights when they accept war as the most important thing the nation can do in the face of metaphysical menaces of imperial prestige. What concerns us here is the relative ease with which the pragmatist intellectuals, with Professor Dewey at the head, have moved out their philosophy, bag and baggage, from education to war. So abrupt a change in the direction of the national enterprise, one would have expected to cause more emotion, to demand more apologetics. His optimism may have told Professor Dewey that war would not materially demoralize our growth—would, perhaps, after all, be but an incident in the nation's life—but it is not easy to see how, as we skate toward the bankruptcy of war-billions, there will be resources available for educational enterprise that does not contribute directly to the war-technique. Neither is any passion for growth, for creative mastery, going to flourish among the host of militaristic values and new tastes for power that are springing up like poisonous mushrooms on every hand.

How could the pragmatist mind accept war without more violent protest, without a greater wrench? Either Professor Dewey and his friends felt that the forces were too strong for them, that the war had to be, and it was better to take it up intelligently than to drift blindly in; or else they really expected a gallant war, conducted with jealous regard for democratic values at home and a captivating vision of international democracy as the end of all the toil and pain. If their motive was the first, they would seem to have reduced the scope of possible control of events to the vanishing point. If the war is too strong for you to prevent, how is it going to be weak enough for you to control and mould to your liberal purposes? And if their motive was to shape the war firmly for good, they seem to have seriously miscalculated the fierce urgencies of it. Are they to be content, as the materialization of their hopes, with a doubtful League of Nations and the suppression of the I. W. W.? Yet the numbing power of the war-situation seems to have kept them from realizing what has happened to their philosophy. The betrayal of their first hopes has certainly not discouraged them. But neither has it roused them to a more energetic expression of the forces through which they intend to realize them. I search Professor Dewey's articles in vain for clues as to the specific working-out of our democratic desires, either nationally or internationally, either in the present or in the reconstruction after the war. No programme is suggested, nor is there feeling for present vague popular movements and revolts. Rather are the latter chided, for their own vagueness and impracticalities. Similarly, with the other prophets of instrumentalism who accompany Dewey into the war, democracy remains an unanalyzed term, useful as a call to battle, but not an intellectual tool, turning up fresh sod for the changing future. Is it the political democracy of a plutocratic America that we are fighting for, or is it the social democracy of the new Russia? Which do our rulers really fear more, the menace of Imperial Germany, or the liberating influence of a socialist Russia? In the application of their philosophy to politics, our pragmatists are sliding over this crucial question of ends. Dewey says our ends must be intelligently international rather than chauvinistic. But this gets us little distance along our way.

In this difficult time the light that has been in liberals and radicals has become darkness. If radicals spend their time holding conventions to attest their loyalty and stamp out the "enemies within," they do not spend it in breaking intellectual paths, or giving us shining ideas to which we can attach our faith and conscience. The spiritual apathy from which the more naive of us suffer, and which the others are so busy fighting, arises largely from sheer default of a clear vision that would melt it away. Let the motley crew of ex-socialists, and labor radicals, and liberals, and pragmatist philosophers, who have united for the prosecution of the war, present a coherent and convincing democratic programme, and they will no longer be confronted with the skepticism of the conscientious and the impossibilist. But when the emphasis is on technical organization, rather than organization of ideas, on strategy rather than desires, one begins to suspect that no programme is presented because they have none to present. This burrowing into war-technique hides the void where a democratic philosophy should be. Our intellectuals consort with war-boards in order to keep their minds off the question what the slow masses of the people are really desiring, or toward what the best hope of the country really drives. Similarly the blaze of patriotism on the part of the radicals serves the purpose of concealing the feebleness of their intellectual light.

Is the answer that clear formulation of democratic ends must be postponed until victory in the war is attained? But to make this answer is to surrender the entire case. For the support of the war by radicals, realists, pragmatists, is due—or so they say—to the fact that the war is not only saving the cause of democracy, but is immensely accelerating its progress. Well, what are those gains? How are they to be conserved? What do they lead to? How can we further them? Into what large idea of society do they group? To ignore these questions, and think only of the war-technique and its accompanying devotions, is to undermine the foundations of these people's own faith.

A policy of "win the war first" must be, for the radical, a policy of intellectual suicide. Their support of the war throws upon them the responsibility of showing inch by inch the democratic gains, and of laying out a charter of specific hopes. Otherwise they confess that they are impotent and that the war is submerging their expectations, or that they are not genuinely imaginative and offer little promise for future leadership.

It may seem unfair to group Professor Dewey with Mr. Spargo and Mr. Gompers, Mr. A. M. Simons, and the Vigilantes. I do so only because in their acceptance of the war, they are all living out that popular American "instrumental" philosophy which Professor Dewey has formulated in such convincing and fascinating terms. On an infinitely more intelligent plane, he is yet one with them in his confidence that the war is motivated by democratic ends and is being made to serve them. A high mood of confidence and self-righteousness moves them all, a keen sense of control over events that makes them eligible to discipleship under Professor Dewey's philosophy. They are all hostile to impossibilism, to apathy, to any attitude that is not a cheerful and brisk setting to work to use the emergency to consolidate the gains of democracy. Not, Is it being used? but, Let us make a flutter about using it! This unanimity of mood puts the resenter of war out of the arena. But he can still seek to explain why this philosophy which has no place for the inexorable should have adjusted itself so easily to the inexorable of war, and why, although a philosophy of the creative intelligence in using means toward ends, it should show itself so singularly impoverished in its present supply of democratic values.

What is the matter with the philosophy? One has a sense of having come to a sudden, short stop at the end of an intellectual era. In the crisis, this philosophy of intelligent control just does not measure up to our needs. What is the root of this inadequacy that is felt so keenly by our restless minds? Van Wyck Brooks has pointed out searchingly the lack of poetic vision in our pragmatist "awakeners." Is there something in these realistic attitudes that works actually against poetic vision, against concern for the quality of life as above machinery of life? Apparently there is. The war has revealed a younger intelligentsia, trained up in the pragmatic dispensation, immensely ready for the executive ordering of events, pitifully unprepared for the intellectual interpretation or the idealistic focussing of ends. The young men in Belgium, the officers' training corps, the young men being sucked into the councils at Washington and into war-organization everywhere, have among them a definite element, upon whom Dewey, as veteran philosopher, might well bestow a papal blessing. They have absorbed the secret of scientific method as applied to political administration. They are liberal, enlightened, aware. They are touched with creative intelligence toward the solution of political and industrial problems. They are a wholly new force in American life, the product of the swing in the colleges from a training that emphasized classical studies to one that emphasized political and economic values. Practically all this element, one would say, is lined up in service of the war-technique. There seems to have been a peculiar congeniality between the war and these men. It is as if the war and they have been waiting for each other. One wonders what scope they would have had for their intelligence without it. Probably most of them would have gone into industry and devoted themselves to sane reorganization schemes. What is significant is that it is the technical side of the war that appeals to them, not the interpretative or political side. The formulation of values and ideals, the production of articulate and suggestive thinking, had not, in their education, kept pace, to any extent whatever, with their technical aptitude. The result is that the field of intellectual formulation is very poorly manned by this younger intelligentsia. While they organize the war, formulation of opinion is left largely in the hands of professional patriots, sensational editors, archaic radicals. The intellectual work of this younger intelligentsia is done by the sedition-hunting Vigilantes, and by the saving remnant of older liberals. It is true, Dewey calls for a more attentive formulation of war-purposes and ideas, but he calls largely to deaf ears. His disciples have learned all too literally the instrumental attitude toward life, and, being immensely intelligent and energetic, they are making themselves efficient instruments of the war-technique, accepting with little question the ends as announced from above. That those ends are largely negative does not concern them, because they have never learned not to subordinate idea to technique. Their education has not given them a coherent system of large ideas, or a feeling for democratic goals. They have, in short, no clear philosophy of life except that of intelligent service, the admirable adaptation of means to ends. They are vague as to what kind of a society they want, or what kind of society America needs, but they are equipped with all the administrative attitudes and talents necessary to attain it.

To those of us who have taken Dewey's philosophy almost as our American religion, it never occurred that values could be subordinated to technique. We were instrumentalists, but we had our private utopias so clearly before our minds that the means fell always into its place as contributory. And Dewey, of course, always meant his philosophy, when taken as a philosophy of life, to start with values. But there was always that unhappy ambiguity in his doctrine as to just how values were created, and it became easier and easier to assume that just any growth was justified and almost any activity valuable so long as it achieved ends. The American, in living out this philosophy, has habitually confused results with product, and been content with getting somewhere without asking too closely whether it was the desirable place to get. It is now becoming plain that unless you start with the vividest kind of poetic vision, your instrumentalism is likely to land you just where it has landed this younger intelligentsia which is so happily and busily engaged in the national enterprise of war. You must have your vision and you must have your technique. The practical effect of Dewey's philosophy has evidently been to develop the sense of the latter at the expense of the former. Though he himself would develop them together, even in him there seems to be a flagging of values, under the influence of war. *The New Republic* honorably clamors for the Allies to subordinate military strategy to political ends, technique to demonstratic values. But war always undermines values. It is the outstanding lesson of the whole war that statesmen cannot be trusted to get this perspective right, that their only motto is, first to win and then grab what they can. The struggle against this statesman-like animus must be a losing one as long as we have not very clear and very determined and very revolutionary democratic ideas and programmes to challenge them with. The trouble with our situation is not only that values have been generally ignored in favor of technique, but that those who have struggled to keep values foremost, have been too bloodless and too near-sighted in their vision. The defect of any philosophy of "adaptation" or "adjustment," even when it means adjustment to changing, living experience, is that there is no provision for thought or experience getting beyond itself. If your ideal is to be adjustment to your situation, in radiant co-operation with reality, then your success is likely to be just that and no more. You never transcend anything. You grow, but your spirit never jumps out of your skin to go on wild adventures. If your policy as a publicist reformer is to take what you can get, you are likely to find that you get something less than you should be willing to take. Italy in the settlement is said to be demanding one hundred in order to get twenty, and this machiavellian principle might well be adopted by the radical. Vision must constantly outshoot technique, opportunist efforts usually achieve less even than what seemed obviously possible. An impossibilist élan that appeals to desire will often carry further. A philosophy of adjustment will not even make for adjustment. If you try merely to "meet" situations as they come, you will not even meet them. Instead you will only pile up behind you deficits and arrears that will some day bankrupt you.

We are in the war because an American Government practised a philosophy of adjustment, and an instrumentalism for minor ends, instead of creating new values and setting at once a large standard to which the nations might repair. An intellectual attitude of mere adjustment, of mere use of the creative intelligence to make your progress, must end in caution, regression, and a virtual failure to effect even that change which you so clear-sightedly and desirously see. This is the root of our dissatisfaction with much of the current political and social realism that is preached to us. It has everything good and wise except the obstreperous vision that would drive and draw all men into it.

The working-out of this American philosophy in our intellectual life then has meant an exaggerated emphasis on the mechanics of life at the expense of the quality of living. We suffer from a real shortage of spiritual values. A philosophy that worked when we were trying to get that material foundation for American life in which more impassioned living could flourish no longer works when we are faced with inexorable disaster and the hysterias of the mob. The note of complacency which we detect in the current expressions of this philosophy has a bad taste. The congruous note for the situation would seem to be, on the contrary, that of robust desperation,—a desperation that shall rage and struggle until new values come out of the travail, and we see some glimmering of our democratic way. In the creation of these new values, we may expect the old philosophy, the old radicalism, to be helpless. It has found a perfectly definite level, and there is no reason to think that it will not remain there. Its flowering appears in the technical organization of the war by an earnest group of young liberals, who direct their course by an opportunist programme of State-socialism at home and a league of benevolently-imperialistic nations abroad. At their best they can give us a government by prudent, enlightened college men instead of by politicians. At their best, they can abolish war by making everybody a partner in the booty of exploitation. That is all, and it is technically admirable. Only there is nothing in the outlook that touches in any way the happiness of the individual, the vivifying of the personality, the comprehension of social forces, the flair of art,—in other words, the quality of life. Our intellectuals have failed us as value-creators, even as value-emphasizers. The allure of the martial in war has passed only to be succeeded by the allure of the technical. The allure of fresh and true ideas, of free speculation, of artistic vigor, of cultural styles, of intelligence suffused by feeling, and feeling given fibre and outline by intelligence, has not come, and can hardly come, we see now, while our reigning philosophy is an instrumental one.

Whence can come this allure? Only from those who are thorough malcontents. Irritation at things as they are, disgust at the continual frustrations and aridities of American life, deep dissatisfaction with self and with the groups that give themselves forth as hopeful—out of such moods there might be hammered new values. The malcontents would be men and women who could not stomach the war, or the reactionary idealism that has followed in its train. They are quite through with the professional critics and classicists who have let cultural values die through their own personal ineptitude. Yet these malcontents have no intention of being cultural vandals, only to slay. They are not barbarians, but seek the vital and the sincere everywhere. All they want is a new orientation of the spirit that shall be modern, an orientation to accompany that technical orientation which is fast coming, and which the war accelerates. They will be harsh and often bad-tempered, and they will feel that the break-up of things is no time for mellowness. They will have a taste for spiritual adventure, and for sinister imaginative excursions. It will not be Puritanism so much as complacency that they will fight. A tang, a bitterness, an intellectual fibre, a verve, they will look for in literature, and their most virulent enemies will be those unaccountable radicals who are still morally servile, and are now trying to suppress all free speculation in the interests of nationalism. Something more mocking, more irreverent, they will constantly want. They will take institutions very lightly, indeed will never fail to be surprised at the seriousness with which good radicals take the stated offices and systems. Their own contempt will be scarcely veiled, and they will be glad if they can tease, provoke, irritate thought on any subject. These malcontents will be more or less of the American tribe of talent who used either to go immediately to Europe, or starved submissively at home. But these people will neither go to Europe, nor starve submissively. They are too much entangled emotionally in the possibilities of American life to leave it, and they have no desire whatever to starve. So they are likely to go ahead beating their heads at the wall until they are either bloody or light appears. They will give offense to their elders who cannot see what all the concern is about, and they will hurt the more middle-aged sense of adventure upon which the better integrated minds of the younger generation will have compromised. Optimism is often compensatory, and the optimistic mood in American thought may mean merely that American life is too terrible to face. A more skeptical, malicious, desperate, ironical mood may actually be the sign of more vivid and more stirring life fermenting in America today. It may be a sign of hope. That thirst for more of the intellectual "war and laughter" that we find Nietzsche calling us to may bring us satisfactions that optimism-haunted philosophies could never bring. Malcontentedness may be the beginning of the promise. That is why I evoked the spirit of William James, with its gay passion for ideas, and its freedom of speculation, when I felt the slightly pedestrian gait into which the war had brought pragmatism. It is the creative desire more than the creative intelligence that we shall need if we are ever to fly.

H. L. MENCKEN

"The National Letters"
1920

Whatever virtues H. L. Mencken (1880–1956) lacked, he certainly possessed in abundance the "intellectual audacity" and "aesthetic passion" he professed to find absent in American literature and in American life generally. This most iconoclastic of all major American journalists was a critic of democracy, which he thought conducive to social conformity and intellectual mediocrity. In the selection that follows, Mencken insists that the society would benefit from a "genuine aristocracy" permitting at least some people to tell the truth and to advance beyond their "responsibility to the general masses of men." Mencken enjoyed angering "the Boobsoisie," but in so doing he won an enormous following, and his name became an emblem for the revolt of the 1920s against Victorianism (or, as Mencken put it misleadingly, "Puritanism"). Mencken reached his widest audience as a newspaper columnist and as an essayist in the magazine *The American Mercury,* which he edited for many years. Yet Mencken was also an energetic amateur scholar and became famous for *The American Language* (New York, 1919). Mencken revised this study of the development of English in America through many editions and added a number of supplements, bearing witness to his extraordinary fascination with both language and America, until a stroke diminished his abilities in 1948.

Two excellent collections of Mencken's writings are those by Alastair Cooke, ed., *The Vintage Mencken* (New York, 1955), and a volume of Mencken's own favorite selections from his writings, *A Mencken Chrestomathy* (New York, 1949). Mencken has inspired dozens of biographical and critical studies; one lively and informative account is William Manchester, *Disturber of the Peace: The Life and Thought of H. L. Mencken,* 2nd ed. (Amherst, Mass., 1986). See also Fred C. Hobson, *H. L. Mencken: A Life* (New York, 1993). Although Mencken's public writings outraged many people, his diaries, published recently, generated a new round in the ongoing controversy over Mencken's tastes and prejudices. For a discerning discussion of the issues, see Louis D. Rubin, Jr., "The Mencken Mystery," *Sewanee Review* 99 (1991), 445–63.

. . . Our literature, despite several false starts that promised much, is chiefly remarkable, now as always, for its respectable mediocrity. Its typical great man, in our own time, has been Howells, as its typical great man a generation ago was Lowell, and two generations ago, Irving. Viewed largely, its salient character appears as a sort of timorous flaccidity, an amiable hollowness. In bulk it grows more and more formidable, in ease and decorum it makes undoubted progress, and on the side of mere technic, of the bald capacity to write, it shows an ever-widening competence. But when one proceeds from such agencies and externals to the intrinsic substance, to the creative passion within, that substance quickly reveals itself as thin and watery, and that passion fades to something almost puerile. In all that mass of suave and often highly diverting writing there is no visible movement toward a distinguished and singular excellence, a signal national quality, a ripe and stimulating flavor, or, indeed, toward any other describable goal. What one sees is simply a general irresolution, a pervasive superficiality. There is no sober grappling with fundamentals, but only a shy sporting on the surface; there is not even any serious approach, such as Whitman dreamed of, to the special experiences and emergencies of the American people. When one turns to any other national literature—to Russian literature, say, or French, or German or Scandanavian—one is conscious immediately of a definite attitude toward the primary mysteries of existence, the unsolved and ever-fascinating problems at the bottom of human life, and of a definite preoccupation with some of them, and a definite way of translating their challenge into drama. These attitudes and preoccupations raise a literature above mere poetizing and tale-telling; they give it dignity and importance; above all, they give it national character. But it is precisely here that the literature of America, and especially the later literature, is most colorless and inconsequential. As if paralyzed by the national fear of ideas, the democratic distrust of whatever strikes beneath the prevailing platitudes, it evades all resolute and honest dealing with what, after all, must be every healthy literature's elementary materials. One is conscious of no brave and noble earnestness in it, of no generalized passion for intellectual and spiritual adventure, of no organized determination to think things out. What is there is a highly self-conscious and insipid correctness, a bloodless respectability, a submergence of matter in manner—in brief, what is there is the feeble, uninspiring quality of German painting and English music. . . .

What ails [the prevailing literary culture] . . . is a dearth of intellectual audacity and of aesthetic passion. Running through it, and characterizing the work of almost every man and woman producing it, there is an unescapable suggestion of the old Puritan suspicion of the fine arts as such—of the doctrine that they offer fit asylum for good citizens only when some ulterior and superior purpose is carried into them. This purpose, naturally enough, most commonly shows a moral tinge. The aim of poetry, it appears, is to fill the mind with lofty thoughts—not to give it joy, but to give it a grand and somewhat gaudy sense of virtue. The essay is a weapon against the degenerate tendencies of the age. The novel, properly conceived, is a means of uplifting the spirit; its aim is to inspire, not merely to satisfy the low curiosity of man in man. The Puritan, of course, is not entirely devoid of æsthetic feeling. He has a taste for good form; he responds to style; he is even capable of something approaching a purely æsthetic emotion. But he fears this æsthetic emotion as an insinuating distraction from his chief

Source: The Vintage Mencken, by H. L. Mencken. Copyright 1920 by Alfred A. Knopf, Inc., and renewed 1948 by H. L. Mencken. Reprinted by permission of Alfred A. Knopf, Inc.

business in life: the sober consideration of the all-important problem of conduct. Art is a temptation, a seduction, a Lorelei, and the Good Man may safely have traffic with it only when it is broken to moral uses—in other words, when its innocence is pumped out of it, and it is purged of gusto. It is precisely this gusto that one misses in all the work of the New England school, and in all the work of the formal schools that derive from it. One observes in such a fellow as Dr. Henry Van Dyke an excellent specimen of the whole clan. He is, in his way, a genuine artist. He has a hand for pretty verses. He wields a facile rhetoric. He shows, in indiscreet moments, a touch of imagination. But all the while he remains a sound Presbyterian, with one eye on the devil. He is a Presbyterian first and an artist second, which is just as comfortable as trying to be a Presbyterian first and a chorus girl second. To such a man it must inevitably appear that a Molière, a Wagner, a Goethe or a Shakespeare was more than a little bawdy.

The criticism that supports this decaying caste of literary Brahmins is grounded almost entirely upon ethical criteria. You will spend a long while going through the works of such typical professors as More, Phelps, Boynton, Burton, Perry, Brownell and Babitt before ever you encounter a purely æsthetic judgment upon an æsthetic question. It is almost as if a man estimating daffodils should do it in terms of artichokes. Phelps' whole body of "we churchgoers" criticism—the most catholic and tolerant, it may be said in passing, that the faculty can show—consists chiefly of a plea for correctness, and particularly for moral correctness; he never gets very far from "the axiom of the moral law." Brownell argues eloquently for standards that would bind an imaginative author as tightly as a Sunday-school superintendent is bound by the Ten Commandments and the Mann Act. Sherman tries to save Shakespeare for the right-thinking by proving that he was an Iowa Methodist—a member of his local Chamber of Commerce, a contemner of Reds, an advocate of democracy and the League of Nations, a patriotic dollar-a-year-man during the Armada scare. Elmer More devotes himself, year in and year out, to denouncing the Romantic movement, *i.e.*, the effort to emancipate the artist from formulae and categories, and so make him free to dance with arms and legs. And Babbitt, to make an end, gives over his days and his nights to deploring Rousseau's anarchistic abrogation of "the veto power" over the imagination, leading to such "wrongness" in both art and life that it threatens "to wreck civilization." In brief, the alarms of schoolmasters. Not many of them deal specifically with the literature that is in being. It is too near to be quite nice. To More or Babbitt only death can atone for the primary offense of the artist. But what they preach nevertheless has its echoes contemporaneously, and those echoes, in the main, are woefully falsetto. I often wonder what sort of picture of These States is conjured up by foreigners who read, say, Crothers, Van Dyke, Babbitt, the later Winston Churchill, and the old maids of the Freudian suppression school. How can such a foreigner, moving in those damp, asthmatic mists, imagine such phenomena as Roosevelt, Billy Sunday, Bryan, the Becker case, the I. W. W., Newport, Palm Beach, the University of Chicago, Chicago itself—the whole, gross, glittering, excessively dynamic, infinitely grotesque, incredibly stupendous drama of American life? . . .

So far, the disease. As to the cause, I have delivered a few hints. I now describe it particularly. It is, in brief, a defect in the general culture of the country—one reflected, not only in the national literature, but also in the national political theory, the national attitude toward religion and morals, the national habit in all departments of thinking.

It is the lack of a civilized aristocracy, secure in its position, animated by an intelligent curiosity, skeptical of all facile generalizations, superior to the sentimentality of the mob, and delighting in the battle of ideas for its own sake.

The word I use, despite the qualifying adjective, has got itself meanings, of course, that I by no means intend to convey. Any mention of an aristocracy, to a public fed upon democratic fustian, is bound to bring up images of stockbrokers' wives lolling obscenely in opera boxes, or of haughty Englishmen slaughtering whole generations of grouse in an inordinate and incomprehensible manner, or of Junkers with tight waists elbowing American schoolmarms off the sidewalks of German beer towns, or of perfumed Italians coming over to work their abominable magic upon the daughters of breakfast-food and bathtub kings. Part of this misconception, I suppose, has its roots in the gaudy imbecilities of the yellow press, but there is also a part that belongs to the general American tradition, along with the oppression of minorities and the belief in political panaceas. Its depth and extent are constantly revealed by the naïve assumption that the so-called fashionable folk of the large cities—chiefly wealthy industrials in the interior-decorator and country-club stage of culture—constitute an aristocracy, and by the scarcely less remarkable assumption that the peerage of England is identical with the gentry—that is, that such men as Lord Northcliffe, Lord Iveagh and even Lord Reading are English gentlemen, and of the ancient line of the Percys.

Here, as always, the worshiper is the father of the gods, and no less when they are evil than when they are benign. The inferior man must find himself superiors, that he may marvel at his political equality with them, and in the absence of recognizable superiors *de facto* he creates superiors *de jure*. The sublime principle of one man, one vote must be translated into terms of dollars, diamonds, fashionable intelligence; the equality of all men before the law must have clear and dramatic proofs. Sometimes, perhaps, the thing goes further and is more subtle. The inferior man needs an aristocracy to demonstrate, not only his mere equality, but also his actual superiority. The society columns in the newspapers may have some such origin: they may visualize once more the accomplished journalist's understanding of the mob mind that he plays upon so skillfully, as upon some immense and cacophonous organ, always going *fortissimo*. What the inferior man and his wife see in the sinister revels of those amazing first families, I suspect, is often a massive witness to their own higher rectitude—to their relative innocence of cigarette-smoking, poodle-coddling, child-farming and the more abstruse branches of adultery—in brief, to their firmer grasp upon the immutable axioms of Christian virtue, the one sound boast of the nether nine-tenths of humanity in every land under the cross.

But this bugaboo aristocracy, as I hint, is actually bogus, and the evidence of its bogusness lies in the fact that it is insecure. One gets into it only onerously, but out of it very easily. Entrance is effected by dint of a long and bitter struggle, and the chief incidents of that struggle are almost intolerable humiliations. The aspirant must school and steel himself to sniffs and sneers; he must see the door slammed upon him a hundred times before ever it is thrown open to him. To get in at all he must show a talent for abasement—and abasement makes him timorous. Worse, that timorousness is not cured when he succeeds at last. On the contrary, it is made even more tremulous, for what he faces within the gates is a scheme of things made up almost wholly of harsh and often unintelligible taboos, and the penalty for violating even the least of them is swift and disastrous. He must exhibit exactly the right social habits, appetites and prejudices, public and private. He must harbor exactly the right political enthusiasms and indignations. He must have a hearty taste for exactly the right sports. His attitude toward the fine arts must be properly tolerant and yet not a shade too eager. He must read and like exactly the right books, pamphlets and public journals. He must put up at the right hotels when he travels. His wife must patronize the right milliners. He himself must stick to the right haberdashery. He must live in the right neighborhood. He must even embrace the right doctrines of religion. It would ruin him, for all opera box and society column purposes, to set up a plea for justice to the Bolsheviki, or even for ordinary decency. It would ruin him equally to wear celluloid collars, or to move to Union Hill, N. J., or to serve ham and cabbage at his table. And it would ruin him, too, to drink coffee from his saucer, or to marry a chambermaid with a gold tooth, or to join the Seventh Day Adventists. Within the boundaries of his curious order he is worse fettered than a monk in a cell. Its obscure conception of propriety, its nebulous notion that this or that is honorable, hampers him in every direction, and very narrowly. What he resigns when he enters, even when he makes his first deprecating knocking at the door, is every right to attack the ideas that happen to prevail within. Such as they are, he must accept them without question. And as they shift and change in response to great instinctive movements (or perhaps, now and then, to the punished but not to be for-gotten revolts of extraordinary rebels) he must shift and change with them, silently and quickly. To hang back, to challenge and dispute, to preach reforms and revolutions—these are crimes against the brummagen Holy Ghost of the order.

Obviously, that order cannot constitute a genuine aristocracy, in any rational sense. A genuine aristocracy is grounded upon very much different principles. Its first and most salient character is its interior security, and the chief visible evidence of that security is the freedom that goes with it—not only freedom in act, the divine right of the aristocrat to do what he jolly well pleases, so long as he does not violate the primary guarantees and obligations of his class, but also and more importantly freedom in thought, the liberty to try and err, the right to be his own man. It is the instinct of a true aristocracy, not to punish eccentricity by expulsion, but to throw a mantle of protection about it—to safeguard it from the suspicions and resentments of the lower orders. Those lower orders are inert, timid, inhospitable to ideas, hostile to changes, faithful to a few maudlin superstitions. All progress goes on on the higher levels. It is there that salient personalities, made secure by artificial immunities, may oscillate most widely from the normal track. It is within that entrenched fold, out of reach of the immemorial certainties of the mob, that extraordinary men of the lower orders may find their city of refuge, and breathe a clear air. This, indeed, is at once the hall-mark and the justification of an aristocracy—that it is beyond responsibility to the general masses of men, and hence superior to both their degraded longings and their no less degraded aversions. It is nothing if it is not autonomous, curious, venturesome, cou-rageous, and everything if it is. It is the custodian of the qualities that make for change and experiment; it is the class that organizes danger to the service of the race; it pays for its high prerogatives by standing in the forefront of the fray.

No such aristocracy, it must be plain, is now on view in the United States. The makings of one were visible in the Virginia of the later eighteenth century, but with Jefferson and Washington the promise died. In New England, it seems to me, there was never an aristocracy, either in being or in nascency: there was only a theocracy that degenerated very quickly into a plutocracy on the one hand a caste of sterile *Gelehrten* on the other—the passion for God splitting into a lust for dollars and a weakness for mere words. Despite the common notion to the contrary—a notion generated by confusing literacy with intelligence—New England has never shown the slightest sign of a genuine enthusiasm for ideas. It began its history as a slaughter-house of ideas, and it is to-day not easily distinguishable from a cold-storage plant. Its celebrated adventures in mysticism, once apparently so bold and significant, are now seen to have been little more than an elaborate hocus-pocus—respectable Unitarians shocking the peasantry and scaring the horned cattle in the fields by masquerading in the robes of Rosicrucians. The ideas that it embraced in those austere and far-off days were stale, and when it had finished with them they were dead: to-day one hears of Jakob Böhme almost as rarely as one hears of Allen G. Thurman. So in politics. Its glory is Abolition—an English invention, long under the interdict of the native plutocracy. Since the Civil War its six states have produced fewer political ideas, as political ideas run in the Republic, than any average county in Kansas or Nebraska. Appomattox seemed to be a victory for New England idealism. It was actually a victory for the New England plutocracy, and that plutocracy has dominated thought above the Housatonic ever since. The sect of professional idealists has so far dwindled that it has ceased to be of any importance, even as an opposition. When the plutocracy is challenged now, it is challenged by the proletariat.

Well, what is on view in New England is on view in all other parts of the nation, sometimes with ameliorations, but usually with the colors merely exaggerated. What one beholds, sweeping the eye over the land, is a culture that, like the national literature, is in three layers—the plutocracy on top, a vast mass of undifferentiated human blanks at the bottom, and a forlorn *intelligentsia* gasping out a precarious life beween. I need not set out at any length, I hope, the intellectual deficiencies of the plutocracy—its utter failure to show anything even remotely resembling the makings of an aristocracy. It is badly educated, it is stupid, it is full of low-caste superstitions and indignations, it is without decent traditions or informing vision; above all, it is extraordinarily lacking in the most elemental independence and courage. Out of this class comes the grotesque fashionable society of our big towns, already described. Imagine a horde of peasants incredibly enriched and with almost infinite power thrust into their hands, and you will have a fair picture of its habitual state of mind.

It shows all the stigmata of inferiority—moral certainty, cruelty, suspicion of ideas, fear. Never did it function more revealingly than in the late *pogrom* against the so-called Reds, i.e., against humorless idealists who, like Andrew Jackson, took the platitudes of democracy quite seriously. The machinery brought to bear upon these feeble and scattered fanatics would have almost sufficed to repel an invasion by the united powers of Europe. They were hunted out of their sweat-shops and coffee-houses as if they were so many Carranzas or Ludendorffs, dragged to jail to the tooting of horns, arraigned before quaking judges on unintelligible charges, condemned to deportation without the slightest chance to defend themselves, torn from their dependent families, herded into prison-ships, and then finally dumped in a snow waste, to be rescued and fed by the Bolsheviki. And what was the theory at the bottom of all these astounding proceedings? So far as it can be reduced to comprehensible terms it was much less a theory than a fear—a shivering, idiotic, discreditable fear of a mere banshee—an overpowering, paralyzing dread that some extra-eloquent Red, permitted to emit his balderdash unwhipped, might eventually convert a couple of courageous men, and that the courageous men, filled with indignation against the plutocracy, might take to the highroad, burn down a nail-factory or two, and slit the throat of some virtuous profiteer. . . .

Obviously, it is out of reason to look for any hospitality to ideas in a class so extravagantly fearful of even the most palpably absurd of them. Its philosophy is firmly grounded upon the thesis that the existing order must stand forever free from attack, and not only from attack, but also from mere academic criticism, and its ethics are as firmly grounded upon the thesis that every attempt at any such criticism is a proof of moral turpitude. Within its own ranks, protected by what may be regarded as the privilege of the order, there is nothing to take the place of this criticism. A few feeble platitudes by Andrew Carnegie and a book of moderate merit by John D. Rockefeller's press-agent constitute almost the whole of the interior literature of ideas. In other countries the plutocracy has often produced men of reflective and analytical habit, eager to rationalize its instincts and to bring it into some sort of relationship to the main streams of human thought. The case of David Ricardo at once comes to mind. There have been many others: John Bright, Richard Cobden, George Grote, and, in our own time, Walther von Rathenau. But in the United States no such phenomenon has been visible. There was a day, not long ago, when certain young men of wealth gave signs of an unaccustomed interest in ideas on the political side, but the most they managed to achieve was a banal sort of Socialism, and even this was abandoned in sudden terror when the war came, and Socialism fell under suspicion of being genuinely international—in brief, of being honest under the skin. Nor has the plutocracy of the country ever fostered an inquiring spirit among its intellectual valets and footmen, which is to say, among the gentlemen who compose headlines and leading articles for its newspapers. What chiefly distinguishes the daily press of the United States from the press of all other countries pretending to culture is not its lack of truthfulness or even its lack of dignity and honor, for these deficiencies are common to the newspapers everywhere, but its incurable fear of ideas, its constant effort to evade the discussion of fundamentals by translating all issues into a few elemental fears, its incessant reduction of all reflection to mere emotion. It is, in the true sense, never well-informed. It is seldom intelligent, save in the arts of the mob-master. It is never courageously honest. Held harshly to a rigid correctness of opinion by the plutocracy that controls it with less and less attempt at disguise, and menaced on all sides by censorships that it dare not flout, it sinks rapidly into formalism and feebleness. Its yellow section is perhaps its most respectable section, for there the only vestige of the old free journalist survives. In the more conservative papers one finds only a timid and petulant animosity to all questioning of the existing order, however urbane and sincere—a pervasive and ill-concealed dread that the mob now heated up against the orthodox hobgoblins may suddenly begin to unearth hobgoblins of its own, and so run amok. For it is upon the emotions of the mob, of course, that the whole comedy is played. Theoretically the mob is the repository of all political wisdom and virtue; actually it is the ultimate source of all political power. Even the plutocracy cannot make war upon it openly, or forget the least of its weaknesses. The business of keeping it in order must be done discreetly, warily, with delicate technique. In the main that business consists of keeping alive its deep-seated fears—of strange faces, of unfamiliar ideas, of unhackneyed gestures, of untested liberties and responsibilities. The one permanent emotion of the inferior man, as of all the simpler mammals, is fear—fear of the unknown, the complex, the inexplicable. What he wants beyond everything else is safety. His instincts incline him toward a society so organized that it will protect him at all hazards, and not only against perils to his hide but also against assaults upon his mind—against the need to grapple with unaccustomed problems, to weigh ideas, to think things out for himself, to scrutinize the platitudes upon which his everyday thinking is based. Content under kaiserism so long as it functions efficiently, he turns, when kaiserism falls, to some other and perhaps worse form of paternalism, bringing to his benign tyranny only the docile tribute of his pathetic allegiance. In America it is the newspaper that is his boss. From it he gets support for his elemental illusions. In it he sees a visible embodiment of his own wisdom and consequence. Out of it he draws fuel for his simple moral passion, his congenital suspicion of heresy, his dread of the unknown. And behind the newspaper stands the plutocracy, ignorant, unimaginative and timorous.

Thus at the top and at the bottom. Obviously, there is no aristocracy here. One finds only one of the necessary elements, and that only in the plutocracy, to wit, a truculent egoism. But where is intelligence? Where are ease and surety of manner? Where are enterprise and curiosity? Where, above all, is courage, and in particular, moral courage—the capacity for independent thinking, for difficult problems, for what Nietzsche called the joys of the labyrinth? As well look for these things in a society of half-wits. Democracy, obliterating the old aristocracy, has left only a vacuum in its place; in a century and a half it has failed either to lift up the mob to intellectual autonomy and dignity or to purge the plutocracy of its inherent stupidity and swinishness. It is precisely here, the first and favorite scene of the Great Experiment, that the culture of the individual has been reduced to the most rigid and absurd regimentation. It is precisely here, of all civilized countries, that eccentricity in demeanor and opinion has come to bear the heaviest penalties. The whole drift of our law is toward the absolute prohibition of all ideas that diverge in the slightest from the accepted platitudes, and behind that drift of law there is a far more potent force of growing custom, and under that custom there is a national philosophy which erects conformity into the noblest of virtues and the free functioning of personality into a captial crime against society.

But there remain the *intelligentsia*, the free spirits in the middle ground, neither as anæsthetic to ideas as the plutocracy on the one hand nor as much the slaves of emotion as the proletariat on the other. Have I forgotten them? I have not. But what actually reveals itself when this small brotherhood of the superior is carefully examined? What reveals itself, it seems to me, is a gigantic disappointment. Superficially, there are all the marks of a caste of learned and sagacious men—a great book-knowledge, a laudable diligence, a certain fine reserve and sniffishness, a plain consciousness of intellectual superiority, not a few gestures that suggest the aristocratic. But under the surface one quickly discovers that the whole thing is little more than play-acting, and not always very skillful. Learning is there, but not curiosity. A heavy dignity is there, but not much genuine self-respect. Pretentiousness is there, but not a trace of courage. Squeezed between the plutocracy on one side and the mob on the other, the *intelligentsia* face the eternal national problem of maintaining their position, of guarding themselves against challenge and attack, of keeping down suspicion. They have all the attributes of knowledge save the sense of power. They have all the qualities of an aristocracy save the capital qualities that arise out of a feeling of security, of complete independence, of absolute immunity to onslaught from above and below. In brief, the old bogusness hangs about them, as about the fashionable aristocrats of the society columns. They are safe so long as they are good, which is to say, so long as they neither aggrieve the plutocracy nor startle the proletariat. Immediately they fall into either misdemeanor all their apparent dignity vanishes, and with it all of their influence, and they become simply somewhat ridiculous rebels against a social order that has no genuine need of them and is disposed to tolerate them only when they are not obtrusive. . . .

MARGARET MEAD

Selection from *Coming of Age in Samoa*
1928

The most obvious function performed by social scientists in modern America has been a cognitive one: the advancement of knowledge about society. Another, more subtle function has been a moral one: the articulation and criticism of standards for conduct. The role of the public moralist had long been performed by the clergy and by men and women of letters, but in the twentieth century this role increasingly came to be filled by psychologists, anthropologists, sociologists, and other practitioners of social science. The anthropologist Margaret Mead (1901–78) was perhaps the most influential single example of "the social scientist as public moralist." Mead wrote thirty-four books on a multitude of topics, many of which were only remotely anthropological. She was a formidable presence in American intellectual life for half a century, beginning with her *Coming of Age in Samoa* (1928), from which the selection that follows is taken.

Mead's study of adolescent girls in Samoa was offered frankly as a means of fostering a critical perspective on the growing-up experiences of young people in Mead's own society. In our excerpt she sums up the lessons she wishes readers to derive from her study. Mead was an inveterate enemy of American middle-class provincialism and invited her readers to develop a diverse culture in which individuals could choose between a great variety of ways of life. Although she expressed much sympathy for the homogeneous, easygoing culture she attributed to the people of Samoa, she defended the heterogeneous, complex culture of modern America and sought to foster the knowledge and attitudes that would better equip Americans to take advantage of their opportunities.

A readable, popular biography is Jane Howard, *Margaret Mead: A Life* (New York, 1984). The quality of Mead's fieldwork as an anthropologist has been a matter of dispute, especially in recent years. For a brief, judicious commentary on this controversy see the remarks of James Clifford in the *Times Literary Supplement,* May 13, 1983, 475–76. See also Roy Rappaport, "Desecrating the Holy Woman: Derek Freeman's Attack on Margaret Mead," *American Scholar,* Summer 1986, 313–47. For an analysis of the cultural–critical role played by Mead, Ruth Benedict, and other anthropologists of the school of Franz Boas, see Richard Handler, "Boasian Anthropology and the Critique of American Culture," *American Quarterly* 42 (1990), 252–73. See also John S. Gilkeson, Jr., "The Domestication of 'Culture' in Interwar America, 1919–1941" in JoAnne Brown and David K. van Keuren, eds., *The Estate of Social Knowledge* (Baltimore, 1991), 153–74. On Boas and the larger Boasian tradition, see George W. Stocking, Jr., *The Shaping of American Anthropology* (New York, 1974), esp. 1–20.

For many chapters we have followed the lives of Samoan girls, watched them change from babies to baby tenders, learn to make the oven and weave fine mats, forsake the life of the gang to become more active members of the household, defer marriage through as many years of casual love-making as possible, finally marry and settle down to rearing children who will repeat the same cycle. As far as our material permitted, an experiment has been conducted to discover what the process of development was like in a society very different from our own. Because the length of human life and the complexity of our society did not permit us to make our experiment here, to choose a group of baby girls and bring them to maturity under conditions created for the experiment, it was necessary to go instead to another country where history had set the stage for us. There we found girl children passing through the same process of physical development through which our girls go, cutting their first teeth and losing them, cutting their second teeth, growing tall and ungainly, reaching puberty with their first menstruation, gradually reaching physical maturity, and becoming ready to produce the next generation. It was possible to say: Here are the proper conditions for an experiment; the developing girl is a constant factor in America and in Samoa; the civilisation of America and the civilisation of Samoa are different. In the course of development, the process of growth by which the girl baby becomes a grown woman, are the sudden and conspicuous bodily changes which take place at puberty accompanied by a development which is spasmodic, emotionally charged, and accompanied by an awakened religious sense, a flowering of idealism, a great desire for assertion of self against authority—or not? Is adolescence a period of mental and emotional distress for the growing girl as inevitably as teething is a period of misery for the small baby? Can we think of adolescence as a time in the life history of every girl child which carries with it symptoms of conflict and stress as surely as it implies a change in the girl's body?

Following the Samoan girls through every aspect of their lives we have tried to answer this question, and we found throughout that we had to answer it in the negative. The adolescent girl in Samoa differed from her sister who had not reached puberty in one chief respect, that in the older girl certain bodily changes were present which were absent in the younger girl. There were no other great differences to set off the group passing through adolescence from the group which would become adolescent in two years or the group which had become adolescent two years before.

And if one girl past puberty is undersized while her cousin is tall and able to do heavier work, there will be a difference between them, due to their different physical endowment, which will be far greater than that which is due to puberty. The tall, husky girl will be isolated from her companions, forced to do longer, more adult tasks, rendered shy by a change of clothing, while her cousin, slower to attain her growth, will still be treated as a child and will have to solve only the slightly fewer problems of childhood. The precedent of educators here who recommend special tactics in the treatment of adolescent girls translated into Samoan terms would read: Tall girls are different from short girls of the same age, we must adopt a different method of educating them.

But when we have answered the question we set out to answer we have not finished with the problem. A further question presents itself. If it is proved that adolescence is not necessarily a specially difficult period in a girl's life—and proved it is if we can find any society in which that is so—then what accounts for the presence of storm and stress

Source: Margaret Mead, Coming of Age in Samoa (New York: Morrow, 1955), 195–206, 234–35, 244–48. Copyright 1928, 1955, 1961 by Margaret Mead. Reprinted by permission of William Morrow & Co.

in American adolescents? First, we may say quite simply, that there must be something in the two civilisations to account for the difference. If the same process takes a different form in two different environments, we cannot make any explanations in terms of the process, for that is the same in both cases. But the social environment is very different and it is to it that we must look for an explanation. What is there in Samoa which is absent in America, what is there in America which is absent in Samoa, which will account for this difference?

Such a question has enormous implications and any attempt to answer it will be subject to many possibilities of error. But if we narrow our question to the way in which aspects of Samoan life which irremediably affect the life of the adolescent girl differ from the forces which influence our growing girls, it is possible to try to answer it.

The background of these differences is a broad one, with two important components; one is due to characteristics which are Samoan, the other to characteristics which are primitive.

The Samoan background which makes growing up so easy, so simple a matter, is the general casualness of the whole society. For Samoa is a place where no one plays for very high stakes, no one pays very heavy prices, no one suffers for his convictions or fights to the death for special ends. Disagreements between parent and child are settled by the child's moving across the street, between a man and his village by the man's removal to the next village, between a husband and his wife's seducer by a few fine mats. Neither poverty nor great disasters threaten the people to make them hold their lives dearly and tremble for continued existence. No implacable gods, swift to anger and strong to punish, disturb the even tenor of their days. Wars and cannibalism are long since passed away and now the greatest cause for tears, short of death itself, is a journey of a relative to another island. No one is hurried along in life or punished harshly for slowness of development. Instead the gifted, the precocious, are held back, until the slowest among them have caught the pace. And in personal relations, caring is as slight. Love and hate, jealousy and revenge, sorrow and bereavement, are all matters of weeks. From the first months of its life, when the child is handed carelessly from one woman's hands to another's, the lesson is learned of not caring for one person greatly, not setting high hopes on any one relationship.

And just as we may feel that the Occident penalises those unfortunates who are born into Western civilisation with a taste for meditation and a complete distaste for activity, so we may say that Samoa is kind to those who have learned the lesson of not caring, and hard upon those few individuals who have failed to learn it. Lola and Mala and little Siva, Lola's sister, all were girls with a capacity for emotion greater than their fellows. And Lola and Mala, passionately desiring affection and too violently venting upon the community their disappointment over their lack of it, were both delinquent, unhappy misfits in a society which gave all the rewards to those who took defeat lightly and turned to some other goal with a smile.

In this casual attitude towards life, in this avoidance of conflict, of poignant situations, Samoa contrasts strongly not only with America but also with most primitive civilisations. And however much we may deplore such an attitude and feel that important personalities and great art are not born in so shallow a society, we must recognise that here is a strong factor in the painless development from childhood to womanhood. For where no one feels very strongly, the adolescent will not be tortured by poignant situations. There are no such disastrous choices as those which confronted young people who felt that the service of God demanded forswearing the world forever, as in the

Middle Ages, or cutting off one's finger as a religious offering, as among the Plains Indians. So, high up in our list of explanations we must place the lack of deep feeling which the Samoans have conventionalised until it is the very framework of all their attitudes toward life.

And next there is the most striking way in which all isolated primitive civilisation and many modern ones differ from our own, in the number of choices which are permitted to each individual. Our children grow up to find a world of choices dazzling their unaccustomed eyes. In religion they may be Catholics, Protestants, Christian Scientists, Spiritualists, Agnostics, Atheists, or even pay no attention at all to religion. This is an unthinkable situation in any primitive society not exposed to foreign influence. There is one set of gods, one accepted religious practice, and if a man does not believe, his only recourse is to believe less than his fellows; he may scoff but there is no new faith to which he may turn. Present-day Manu'a approximates this condition; all are Christians of the same sect. There is no conflict in matters of belief although there is a difference in practice between Church-members and non-Church-members. And it was remarked that in the case of several of the growing girls the need for choice between these two practices may some day produce a conflict. But at present the Church makes too slight a bid for young unmarried members to force the adolescent to make any decision.

Similarly, our children are faced with half a dozen standards of morality: a double sex standard for men and women, a single standard for men and women, and groups which advocate that the single standard should be freedom while others argue that the single standard should be absolute monogamy. Trial marriage, companionate marriage, contract marriage—all these possible solutions of a social impasse are paraded before the growing children while the actual conditions in their own communities and the moving pictures and magazines inform them of mass violations of every code, violations which march under no banners of social reform.

The Samoan child faces no such dilemma. Sex is a natural, pleasurable thing; the freedom with which it may be indulged in is limited by just one consideration, social status. Chiefs' daughters and chiefs' wives should indulge in no extra-marital experiments. Responsible adults, heads of households and mothers of families should have too many important matters on hand to leave them much time for casual amorous adventures. Every one in the community agrees about the matter, the only dissenters are the missionaries who dissent so vainly that their protests are unimportant. But as soon as a sufficient sentiment gathers about the missionary attitude with its European standard of sex behaviour, the need for choice, the forerunner of conflict, will enter into Samoan society.

Our young people are faced by a series of different groups which believe different things and advocate different practices, and to each of which some trusted friend or relative may belong. So a girl's father may be a Presbyterian, an imperialist, a vegetarian, a teetotaler, with a strong literary preference for Edmund Burke, a believer in the open shop and a high tariff, who believes that woman's place is in the home, that young girls should wear corsets, not roll their stockings, not smoke, nor go riding with young men in the evening. But her mother's father may be a Low Episcopalian, a believer in high living, a strong advocate of States' Rights and the Monroe Doctrine, who reads Rabelais, likes to go to musical shows and horse races. Her aunt is an agnostic, an ardent advocate of woman's rights, an internationalist who rests all her hopes on Esperanto, is devoted to Bernard Shaw, and spends her spare time in campaigns of anti-vivisection. Her elder brother, whom she admires exceedingly, has just spent two years at Oxford. He is an Anglo-Catholic, an enthusiast concerning all things mediaeval, writes mystical poetry, reads Chesterton, and means to devote his life to seeking for the lost secret of mediaeval stained glass. Her mother's younger brother is an engineer, a strict materialist, who never recovered from reading Haeckel in his youth; he scorns art, believes that science will save the world, scoffs at everything that was said and thought before the nineteenth century, and ruins his health by experiments in the scientific elimination of sleep. Her mother is of a quietistic frame of mind, very much interested in Indian philosophy, a pacifist, a strict non-participator in life, who in spite of her daughter's devotion to her will not make any move to enlist her enthusiasms. And this may be within the girl's own household. Add to it the groups represented, defended, advocated by her friends, her teachers, and the books which she reads by accident, and the list of possible enthusiasms, of suggested allegiances, incompatible with one another, becomes appalling.

The Samoan girl's choices are far otherwise. Her father is a member of the Church and so is her uncle. Her father lives in a village where there is good fishing, her uncle in a village where there are plenty of cocoanut crabs. Her father is a good fisherman and in his house there is plenty to eat; her uncle is a talking chief and his frequent presents of bark cloth provide excellent dance dresses. Her paternal grandmother, who lives with her uncle, can teach her many secrets of healing; her maternal grandmother, who lives with her mother, is an expert weaver of fans. The boys in her uncle's village are admitted younger into the *Aumaga* and are not much fun when they come to call; but there are three boys in her own village whom she likes very much. And her great dilemma is whether to live with her father or her uncle, a frank, straightforward problem which introduces no ethical perplexities, no question of impersonal logic. Nor will her choice be taken as a personal matter, as the American girl's allegiance to the views of one relative might be interpreted by her other relatives. The Samoans will be sure she chose one residence rather than the other for perfectly good reasons, the food was better, she had a lover in one village, or she had quarrelled with a lover in the other village. In each case she was making concrete choices within one recognised pattern of behaviour. She was never called upon to make choices involving an actual rejection of the standards of her social group, such as the daughter of Puritan parents, who permits indiscriminate caresses, must make in our society.

And not only are our developing children faced by a series of groups advocating different and mutually exclusive standards, but a more perplexing problem presents itself to them. Because our civilisation is woven of so many diverse strands, the ideas which any one group accepts will be found to contain numerous contradictions. So if the girl has given her allegiance whole-heartedly to some one group and has accepted in good faith their asseverations that they alone are right and all other philosophies of life are Antichrist and anathema, her troubles are still not over. While the less thoughtful receives her worst blows in the discovery that what father thinks is good, grandfather thinks is bad, and that things which are permitted at home are banned at school, the more thoughtful child has subtler difficulties in store for her. If she has philosophically accepted the fact that there are several standards among which she must choose, she may still preserve a childlike faith in the coherence of her chosen philosophy. Beyond the immediate choice which was so puzzling and hard to make, which perhaps involved hurting her parents or alienating her friends, she expects peace. But she has not reckoned with the fact that each of the philosophies with which she is confronted is itself but the half-ripened fruit of compromise. If she accepts Christianity, she is immediately confused between the Gospel teachings concerning peace and the value of human life and the Church's whole-hearted acceptance of war. The compromise made seventeen centuries ago between the Roman philosophy of war and domination, and the early Church doctrine of peace and humility, is still present to confuse the modern child. If she accepts the philosophic premises upon which the Declaration of Independence of the United States was founded, she finds herself faced with the necessity of reconciling the belief in the equality of man and our institutional pledges of equality and opportunity with our treatment of the Negro and the Oriental. The diversity of standards in present-day society is so striking that the dullest, the most incurious, cannot fail to notice it. And this diversity is so old, so embodied in semi-solutions, in those compromises between different philosophies which we call Christianity, or democracy, or humanitarianism, that it baffles the most intelligent, the most curious, the most analytical.

So for the explanation of the lack of poignancy in the choices of growing girls in Samoa, we must look to the temperament of the Samoan civilisation which discounts strong feeling. But for the explanation of the lack of conflict we must look principally to the difference between a simple, homogeneous primitive civilisation, a civilisation which changes so slowly that to each generation it appears static, and a motley, diverse, heterogeneous modern civilisation. . . .

We have been comparing point for point, our civilisation and the simpler civilisation of Samoa, in order to illuminate our own methods of education. If now we turn from the Samoan picture and take away only the main lesson which we learned there, that adolescence is not necessarily a time of stress and strain, but that cultural conditions make it so, can we draw any conclusions which might bear fruit in the training of our adolescents?

At first blush the answer seems simple enough. If adolescents are only plunged into difficulties and distress because of conditions in their social environment, then by all means let us so modify that environment as to reduce this stress and eliminate this strain and anguish of adjustment. But, unfortunately, the conditions which vex our adolescents are the flesh and bone of our society, no more subject to straightforward manipulation upon our part than is the language which we speak. We can alter a syllable here, a construction there; but the great and far-reaching changes in linguistic structure (as in all parts of culture) are the work of time, a work in which each individual plays an unconscious and inconsiderable part. The principal causes of our adolescents' difficulty are the presence of conflicting standards and the belief that every individual should make his or her own choices, coupled with a feeling that choice is an important matter. Given these cultural attitudes, adolescence, regarded now not as a period of physiological change, for we know that physiological puberty need not produce conflict, but as the beginning of mental and emotional maturity, is bound to be filled with conflicts and difficulties. A society which is clamouring for choice, which is filled with many articulate groups, each urging its own brand of salvation, its own variety of economic philosophy, will give each new generation no peace until all have chosen or gone under, unable to bear the conditions of choice. The stress is in our civilisation, not in the physical changes through which our children pass, but it is none the less real nor the less inevitable in twentieth-century America. . . .

Granting that society presents too many problems to her adolescents, demands too many momentous decisions on a few months' notice, what is to be done about it? One panacea suggested would be to postpone at least some of the decisions, keep the child economically dependent, or segregate her from all contact with the other sex, present her with only one set of religious ideas until she is older, more poised, better able to deal critically with the problems which will confront her. In a less articulate fashion, such an idea is back of various schemes for the prolongation of youth, through raising the working age, raising the school age, shielding school children from a knowledge of controversies like evolution versus fundamentalism, or any knowledge of sex hygiene or birth control. Even if such measures, specially initiated and legislatively enforced, could accomplish the end which they seek and postpone the period of choice, it is doubtful whether such a development would be desirable. It is unfair that very young children should be the battleground for conflicting standards, that their development should be hampered by propagandist attempts to enlist and condition them too young. It is probably equally unfair to culturally defer the decisions too late. Loss of one's fundamental religious faith is more of a wrench at thirty than at fifteen simply in terms of the number of years of acceptance which have accompanied the belief. A sudden knowledge of hitherto unsuspected aspects of sex, or a shattering of all the old conventions concerning sex behaviour, is more difficult just in terms of the strength of the old attitudes. Furthermore, in practical terms, such schemes would be as they are now, merely local, one state legislating against evolution, another against birth control, or one religious group segregating its unmarried girls. And these special local movements would simply unfit groups of young people for competing happily with children who had been permitted to make their choices earlier. Such an educational scheme, in addition to being almost impossible of execution, would be a step backward and would only beg the question.

Instead, we must turn all of our educational efforts to training our children for the choices which will confront them. Education, in the home even more than at school, instead of being a special pleading for one régime, a desperate attempt to form one particular habit of mind which will withstand all outside influences, must be a preparation for those very influences. Such an education must give far more attention to mental and physical hygiene than it has given hitherto. The child who is to choose wisely must be healthy in mind and body, handicapped in no preventable fashion. And even more importantly, this child of the future must have an open mind. The home must cease to plead an ethical cause or a religious belief with smiles or frowns, caresses or threats. The children must be taught how to think, not what to think. And because old errors die slowly, they must be taught tolerance, just as to-day they are taught intolerance. They must be taught that many ways are open to them, no one sanctioned above its alternative, and that upon them and upon them alone lies the burden of choice. Unhampered by prejudices, unvexed by too early conditioning to any one standard, they must come clear-eyed to the choices which lie before them.

For it must be realised by any student of civilisation that we pay heavily for our heterogeneous, rapidly changing civilisation; we pay in high proportions of crime and delinquency, we pay in the conflicts of youth, we pay in an ever-increasing number of neuroses, we pay in the lack of a coherent tradition without which the development of art is sadly handicapped. In such a list of prices, we must count our gains carefully, not to be discouraged. And chief among our gains must be reckoned this possibility of choice, the recognition of many possible ways of life, where other civilisations have recognised only one. Where other civilisations give a satisfactory outlet to only one temperamental type, be he mystic or soldier, business man or artist, a civilisation in which there are many standards offers a possibility of satisfactory adjustment to individuals of many different temperamental types, of diverse gifts and varying interests.

At the present time we live in a period of transition. We have many standards but we still believe that only one standard can be the right one. We present to our children the picture of a battle-field where each group is fully armoured in a conviction of the righteousness of its cause. And each of these groups make forays among the next generation. But it is unthinkable that a final recognition of the great number of ways in which man, during the course of history and at the present time, is solving the problems of life, should not bring with it in turn the downfall of our belief in a single standard. And when no one group claims ethical sanction for its customs, and each group welcomes to its midst only those who are temperamentally fitted for membership, then we shall have realised the high point of individual choice and universal toleration which a heterogeneous culture and a heterogeneous culture alone can attain. Samoa knows but one way of life and teaches it to her children. Will we, who have the knowledge of many ways, leave our children free to choose among them?

JOHN CROWE RANSOM

"Reconstructed but Unregenerate"
1930

"I'll Take My Stand in Dixie," runs the key refrain in a song long popular with southerners nostalgic for the antebellum South and the Confederacy. In 1930, these words were used by the dozen southern writers who contributed to *I'll Take My Stand: The South and the Agrarian Tradition* (New York, 1930). This manifesto, against industrial civilization, science, and liberalism attracted a great deal of attention in the context of the Depression, when even nonsoutherners were ready to listen to its skeptical response to the prevailing order. The deliberately reactionary men who wrote this book appeared, in the political spectrum of the early Depression years, as extreme right-wing counterpoints to the communists on the far Left. The authors became known as the "Nashville Agrarians" because several of them were affiliated with Vanderbilt University, in Nashville, Tennessee. Among these were the poet and critic John Crowe Ransom (1888–1974), who edited *I'll Take My Stand*. "Reconstructed but Unregenerate," which follows, was Ransom's contribution to the collection. He soon lost interest in agrarianism as an economic program, turned his attention to literary criticism, and became one of the most respected scholars in the movement for rigorous textual analysis that came to be called the New Criticism. Ransom also lost interest in the South and, despite the exceedingly romantic description of the Old South he offered in "Reconstructed but Unregenerate," left Nashville in 1939 to live and teach in Ohio. The other contributors to *I'll Take My Stand* also went their separate ways. The best-known of the other agrarians were the poets Alan Tate and Donald Davidson, and Robert Penn Warren, who later wrote one of the most acclaimed novels of the midcentury, *All the King's Men* (New York, 1946). Warren's contribution to *I'll Take My Stand,* "The Briar Patch," was a defense of racial segregation, although so mild in spirit for the times that some of the other agrarians were uncomfortable with its relative liberalism.

For an informative account of the agrarian movement and Ransom's role in it, see Daniel J. Singal, *The War Within: From Victorian to Modernist Thought in the South, 1919–1945* (Chapel Hill, 1982), 198–231. See also the studies of the careers of several of the agrarians in Michael O'Brien, *The Idea of the American South, 1920–1941* (Baltimore, 1979). For an interpretation of Ransom's work, see Kieran Quinlan, *John Crowe Ransom's Secular Faith* (Baton Rouge, (1989).

IT IS out of fashion in these days to look backward rather than forward. About the only American given to it is some unreconstructed Southerner, who persists in his regard for a certain terrain, a certain history, and a certain inherited way of living. He is punished as his crime deserves. He feels himself in the American scene as an anachronism, and knows he is felt by his neighbors as a reproach.

Of course he is a tolerably harmless reproach. He is like some quaint local character of eccentric but fixed principles who is thoroughly and almost pridefully accepted by the village as a rare exhibit in the antique kind. His position is secure from the interference of the police, but it is of a rather ambiguous dignity.

I wish now that he were not so entirely taken for granted, and that as a reproach he might bear a barb and inflict a sting. I wish that the whole force of my own generation in the South would get behind his principles and make them an ideal which the nation at large would have to reckon with. But first I will describe him in the light of the position he seems now to occupy actually before the public.

His fierce devotion is to a lost cause—though it grieves me that his contemporaries are so sure it is lost. They are so far from fearing him and his example that they even in the excess of confidence offer him a little honor, a little petting. As a Southerner I have observed this indulgence and I try to be grateful. Obviously it does not constitute a danger to the Republic; distinctly it is not treasonable. They are good enough to attribute a sort of glamour to the Southern life as it is defined for them in a popular tradition. They like to use the South as the nearest available locus for the scenes of their sentimental songs, and sometimes they send their daughters to the Southern seminaries. Not too much, of course, is to be made of this last gesture, for they do not expose to this hazard their sons, who in our still very masculine order will have to discharge the functions of citizenship, and who must accordingly be sternly educated in the principles of progress at progressive institutions of learning. But it does not seem to make so much difference what principles of a general character the young women acquire, since they are not likely to be impaired by principles in their peculiar functions, such as virtue and the domestic duties. And so, at suitable seasons, and on the main-line trains, one may see them in some numbers, flying south or flying north like migratory birds; and one may wonder to what extent their philosophy of life will be affected by two or three years in the South. One must remember that probably their parents have already made this calculation and are prepared to answer, Not much.

The Southerner must know, and in fact he does very well know, that his antique conservatism does not exert a great influence against the American progressivist doctrine. The Southern idea today is down, and the progressive or American idea is up. But the historian and the philosopher, who take views that are thought to be respectively longer and deeper than most, may very well reverse this order and find that the Southern idea rather than the American has in its favor the authority of example and the approval of theory. And some prophet may even find it possible to expect that it will yet rise again.

I will propose a thesis which seems to have about as much cogency as generalizations usually have: The South is unique on this continent for having founded and defended a culture which was according to the European principles of culture; and the

Source: Twelve Southerners, *I'll Take My Stand* (New York: Harper and Row, 1930), 1–27. Copyright 1930 by the Twelve Southerners. Copyright renewed 1958 by Donald Davidson. Reprinted by permission of Louisiana State University Press.

European principles had better look to the South if they are to be perpetuated in this country.

The nearest of the European cultures which we could examine is that of England; and this is of course the right one in the case, quite aside from our convenience. England was actually the model employed by the South, in so far as Southern culture was not quite indigenous. And there is in the South even today an Anglophile sentiment quite anomalous in the American scene.

England differs from America doubtless in several respects, but most notably in the fact that England did her pioneering an indefinite number of centuries ago, did it well enough, and has been living pretty tranquilly on her establishment ever since, with infrequent upheavals and replacements. The customs and institutions of England seem to the American observer very fixed and ancient. There is no doubt that the English tradition expresses itself in many more or less intangible ways, but it expresses itself most importantly in a material establishment; and by this I mean the stable economic system by which Englishmen are content to take their livelihood from the physical environment. The chief concern of England's half-mythical pioneers, as with pioneers anywhere, was with finding the way to make a living. Evidently they found it. But fortunately the methods they worked out proved transmissible, proved, in fact, the main reliance of the succeeding generations. The pioneers explored the soil, determined what concessions it might reasonably be expected to make of them, housed themselves, developed all their necessary trades, and arrived by painful experiment at a thousand satisfactory recipes by which they might secure their material necessities. Their descendants have had the good sense to consider that this establishment was good enough for them. They have elected to live their comparatively easy and routine lives in accordance with the tradition which they inherited, and they have consequently enjoyed a leisure, a security, and an intellectual freedom that were never the portion of pioneers.

The pioneering life is not the normal life, whatever some Americans may suppose. It is not, if we look for the meaning of European history. The lesson of each of the European cultures now extant is in this—that European opinion does not make too much of the intense practical enterprises, but is at pains to define rather narrowly the practical effort which is prerequisite to the reflective and asthetic life. Boys are very well pleased to employ their muscles almost exclusively, but men prefer to exercise their minds. It is the European intention to live materially along the inherited line of least resistance, in order to put the surplus of energy into the free life of the mind. Thus is engendered that famous, or infamous, European conservatism, which will appear stupid, necessarily, to men still fascinated by materialistic projects, men in a state of arrested adolescence; for instance, to some very large if indefinite fraction of the population of these United States.

I have in mind here the core of unadulterated Europeanism, with its self-sufficient, backward-looking, intensely provincial communities. The human life of English provinces long ago came to terms with nature, fixed its roots somewhere in the spaces between the rocks and in the shade of the trees, founded its comfortable institutions, secured its modest prosperity—and then willed the whole in perpetuity to the generations which should come after, in the ingenuous confidence that it would afford them all the essential human satisfactions. For it is the character of a seasoned provincial life that it is realistic, or successfully adapted to its natural environment, and that as a consequence it is stable, or hereditable. But it is the character of our urbanized, antiprovincial, progressive, and mobile American life that it is in a condition of eternal flux. Affections, and long memories, attach to the ancient bowers of life in the provinces; but they will not attach to what is always changing. Americans, however, are peculiar in being somewhat averse to these affections for natural objects, and to these memories.

Memories of the past are attended with a certain pain called nostalgia. It is hardly a technical term in our sociology or our psychiatry, but it might well be. Nostalgia is a kind of growing-pain, psychically speaking. It occurs to our sorrow when we have decided that it is time for us, marching to some magnificent destiny, to abandon an old home, an old provincial setting, or an old way of living to which we had become habituated. It is the complaint of human nature in its vegetative aspect, when it is plucked up by the roots from the place of its origin and transplanted in foreign soil, or even left dangling in the air. And it must be nothing else but nostalgia, the instinctive objection to being transplanted, that chiefly prevents the deracination of human communities and their complete geographical dispersion as the casualties of an insatiable wanderlust.

Deracination in our Western life is the strange discipline which individuals turn upon themselves, enticed by the blandishments of such fine words as Progressive, Liberal, and Forward-looking. The progressivist says in effect: Do not allow yourself to feel homesick; form no such powerful attachments that you will feel a pain in cutting them loose; prepare your spirit to be always on the move. According to this gospel, there is no rest for the weary, not even in heaven. The poet Browning expresses an ungrateful intention, the moment he shall enter into his reward, to "fight onward, there as here." The progressivist H. G. Wells has outlined very neatly his scheme of progress, the only disheartening feature being that he has had to revise it a good many times, and that the state to which he wants us to progress never has any finality or definition. Browning and Wells would have made very good Americans, and I am sure they have got the most of their disciples on this side of the Atlantic; they have not been good Europeans. But all the true progressivists intend to have a program so elastic that they can always propose new worlds to conquer. If his Utopia were practicable really, and if the progressivist should secure it, he would then have to defend it from further progress, which would mean his transformation from a progressivist into a conservative. Which is unthinkable.

The gospel of Progress is a curious development, which does not reflect great credit on the supposed capacity of our species for formulating its own behavior. Evidently the formula may involve its practitioners in self-torture and suicide just as readily as in the enjoyment of life. In most societies man has adapted himself to environment with plenty of intelligence to secure easily his material necessities from the graceful bounty of nature. And then, ordinarily, he concludes a truce with nature, and he and nature seem to live on terms of mutual respect and amity, and his loving arts, religions, and philosophies come spontaneously into being: these are the blessings of peace. But the latter-day societies have been seized—none quite so violently as our American one—with the strange idea that the human destiny is not to secure an honorable peace with nature, but to wage an unrelenting war on nature. Men, therefore, determine to conquer nature to a degree which is quite beyond reason so far as specific human advantage is concerned, and which enslaves them to toil and turnover. Man is boastfully declared to be a natural scientist essentially, whose strength is capable of crushing and making over to his own desires the brute materiality which is nature; but in his infinite contention with this materiality he is really capitulating to it. His engines transform the face of nature—a little—but when they have been perfected, he must invent new engines that will perform even more heroically. And always the next engine of his invention, even though it be that engine which is to invade the material atom and exploit the most secret treasury of nature's wealth, will be a physical engine; and the man who uses it will be engaged in substantially the same struggle as was the primitive Man with the Hoe.

This is simply to say that Progress never defines its ultimate objective, but thrusts its victims at once into an infinite series. Our vast industrial machine, with its laboratory centers of experimentation, and its far-flung organs of mass production, is like a Prussianized state which is organized strictly for war and can never consent to peace. Or, returning to the original figure, our progressivists are the latest version of those pioneers who conquered the wilderness, except that they are pioneering on principle, or from force of habit, and without any recollection of what pioneering was for.

Along with the gospel of Progress goes the gospel of Service. They work beautifully as a team.

Americans are still dreaming the materialistic dreams of their youth. The stuff these dreams were made on was the illusion of preëminent personal success over a material opposition. Their tone was belligerence, and the euphemism under which it masqueraded was ambition. But men are not lovely, and men are not happy, for being too ambitious. Let us distinguish two forms under which ambition drives men on their materialistic projects; a masculine and a feminine.

Ambitious men fight, first of all, against nature; they propose to put nature under their heel; this is the dream of scientists burrowing in their cells, and then of the industrial men who beg of their secret knowledge and go out to trouble the earth. But after a certain point this struggle is vain, and we only use ourselves up if we prolong it. Nature wears out man before man can wear out nature; only a city man, a laboratory man, a man cloistered from the normal contacts with the soil, will deny that. It seems wiser to be moderate in our expectations of nature, and respectful; and out of so simple a thing as respect for the physical earth and its teeming life comes a primary joy, which is an inexhaustible source of arts and religions and philosophies.

Ambitious men are belligerent also in the way they look narrowly and enviously upon one another; and I do not refer to such obvious disasters as wars and the rumors of wars. Ambition of the first form was primary and masculine, but there is a secondary form which is typically feminine, though the distribution between the sexes may not be without the usual exceptions. If it is Adam's curse to will perpetually to work his mastery upon nature, it is Eve's curse to prompt Adam every morning to keep up with the best people in the neighborhood in taking the measure of his success. There can never be stability and establishment in a community whose every lady member is sworn to see that her mate is not eclipsed in the competition for material advantages; that community will fume and ferment, and every constituent part will be in perpetual physical motion. The good life depends on leisure, but leisure depends on an establishment, and the establishment depends on a prevailing magnanimity which scorns personal advancement at the expense of the free activity of the mind.

The masculine form is hallowed by Americans, as I have said, under the name of Progress. The concept of Progress is the concept of man's increasing command, and eventually perfect command, over the forces of nature; a concept which enhances too readily our conceit, and brutalizes our life. I believe there is possible no deep sense of beauty, no heroism of conduct, and no sublimity of religion, which is not informed by the humble sense of man's precarious position in the universe. The feminine form is likewise hallowed among us under the name of Service. The term has many meanings, but we come finally to the one which is critical for the moderns; service means the function of Eve, it means the seducing of laggard men into fresh struggles with nature. It has special application to the apparently stagnant sections of mankind, it busies itself with the heathen Chinee, with the Roman Catholic Mexican, with the "lower" classes in our own society. Its motive is missionary. Its watchwords are such as Protestantism, Individualism, Democracy, and the point of its appeal is a discontent, generally labeled "divine."

Progress and Service are not European slogans, they are Americanisms. We alone have devoted our lives to ideals which are admirable within their proper limits, but which expose us to slavery when pursued without critical intelligence. Some Europeans are taken in by these ideals, but hardly the American communities on the whole. Herr Spengler, with a gesture of defeat, glorifies the modern American captain of industry when he compares his positive achievements with the futilities of modern poets and artists. Whereupon we may well wish to save Europe from even so formidable a European as Spengler, hoping that he may not convert Europe to his view. And it is hardly likely; Europe is founded on a principle of conservatism, and is deeply scornful of the American and pioneer doctrine of the strenuous life. In 1918 there was danger that Europe might ask to be Americanized, and American missionaries were quite prepared to answer the call. But since then there has been a revulsion in European opinion, and this particular missionary enterprise confronts now an almost solid barrier of hostility. Europe is not going to be Americanized through falling suddenly in love with strenuousness. It only remains to be seen whether Europe may not be Americanized after all through envy, and through being reminded ceaselessly of our superior prosperity. That is an event to be determined by the force of European magnanimity; Europe's problem, not ours.

The Southern states were settled, of course, by miscellaneous strains. But evidently the one which determined the peculiar tradition of the South was the one which came out of Europe most convinced of the virtues of establishment, contrasting with those strains which seem for the most part to have dominated the other sections, and which came out of Europe feeling rebellious toward all establishments. There are a good many faults to be found with the old South, but hardly the fault of being intemperately addicted to work and to gross material prosperity. The South never conceded that the whole duty of man was to increase material production, or that the index to the degree of his culture was the volume of his material production. His business seemed to be rather to envelop both his work and his play with a leisure which permitted the activity of intelligence. On this assumption the South pioneered her way to a sufficiently comfortable and rural sort of establishment, considered that an establishment was something stable, and proceeded to enjoy the fruits thereof. The arts of the section, such as they were, were not immensely passionate, creative, and romantic; they were the eighteenth-century social arts of dress, conversation, manners, the table, the hunt, politics, oratory, the pulpit. These were arts of living and not arts of escape; they were also community arts, in which every class of society could participate after its kind. The South took life easy, which is itself a tolerably comprehensive art.

But so did other communities in 1850, I believe. And doubtless some others do so yet; in part of New England, for example. If there are such communities, this is their token, that they are settled. Their citizens are comparatively satisfied with the life they have inherited, and are careful to look backward quite as much as they look forward. Before the Civil War there must have been many such communities this side of the frontier. The difference between the North and the South was that the South was constituted by such communities and made solid. But solid is only a comparative term here. The South as a culture had more solidity than another section, but there were plenty of gaps in it. The most we can say is that the Southern establishment was completed in a good many of the Southern communities, and that this establishment was an active formative influence on the spaces between, and on the frontier spaces outlying, which had not yet perfected their organization of the economic life.

The old Southern life was of course not so fine as some of the traditionalists like to believe. It did not offer serious competition against the glory that was Greece or the grandeur that was Rome. It hardly began to match the finish of the English, or any other important European civilization. It is quite enough to say that it was a way of life which had been considered and authorized. The establishment had a sufficient economic base, it was meant to be stable rather than provisional, it had got beyond the pioneering stage, it provided leisure, and its benefits were already being enjoyed. It may as well be admitted that Southern society was not an institution of very showy elegance, for the so-called aristocrats were mostly home-made and countrified. Aristocracy is not the word which defines this social organization so well as squirearchy, which I borrow from a recent article by Mr. William Frierson in the *Sewanee Review*. And even the squires, and the other classes, too, did not define themselves very strictly. They were loosely graduated social orders, not fixed as in Europe. Their relations were personal and friendly. It was a kindly society, yet a realistic one; for it was a failure if it could not be said that people were for the most part in their right places. Slavery was a feature monstrous enough in theory, but, more often than not, humane in practice; and it is impossible to believe that its abolition alone could have effected any great revolution in society.

The fullness of life as it was lived in the ante-bellum South by the different social orders can be estimated today only by the application of some difficult sociological technique. It is my thesis that all were committed to a form of leisure, and that their labor itself was leisurely. The only Southerners who went abroad to Washington and elsewhere, and put themselves into the record, were those from the top of the pyramid. They held their own with their American contemporaries. They were not intellectually as seasoned as good Europeans, but then the Southern culture had had no very long time to grow, as time is reckoned in these matters: it would have borne a better fruit eventually. They had a certain amount of learning, which was not as formidable as it might have been: but at least it was classical and humanistic learning, not highly scientific, and not wildly scattered about over a variety of special studies.

Then the North and the South fought, and the consequences were disasrous to both. The Northern temper was one of jubilation and expansiveness, and now it was no longer shackled by the weight of the conservative Southern tradition. Industrialism, the latest form of pioneering and the worst, presently overtook the North, and in due time has now produced our present American civilization. Poverty and pride overtook the South;

poverty to bring her institutions into disrepute and to sap continually at her courage; and a false pride to inspire a distaste for the thought of fresh pioneering projects, and to doom her to an increasing physical enfeeblement.

It is only too easy to define the malignant meaning of industrialism. It is the contemporary form of pioneering; yet since it never consents to define its goal, it is a pioneering on principle, and with an accelerating speed. Industrialism is a program under which men, using the latest scientific paraphernalia, sacrifice comfort, leisure, and the enjoyment of life to win Pyrrhic victories from nature at points of no strategic importance. Ruskin and Carlyle feared it nearly a hundred years ago, and now it may be said that their fears have been realized partly in England, and with almost fatal completeness in America. Industrialism is an insidious spirit, full of false promises and generally fatal to establishments since, when it once gets into them for a little renovation, it proposes never again to leave them in peace. Industrialism is rightfully a menial, of almost miraculous cunning but no intelligence; it needs to be strongly governed or it will destroy the economy of the household. Only a community of tough conservative habit can master it.

The South did not become industrialized; she did not repair the damage to her old establishment, either, and it was in part because she did not try hard enough. Hers is the case to cite when we would show how the good life depends on an adequate pioneering, and how the pioneering energy must be kept ready for call when the establishment needs overhauling. The Southern tradition came to look rather pitiable in its persistence when the twentieth century had arrived, for the establishment was quite depreciated. Unregenerate Southerners were trying to live the good life on a shabby equipment, and they were grotesque in their effort to make an art out of living when they were not decently making the living. In the country districts great numbers of these broken-down Southerners are still to be seen in patched blue-jeans, sitting on ancestral fences, shotguns across their laps and hound-dogs at their feet, surveying their unkempt acres while they comment shrewdly on the ways of God. It is their defect that they have driven a too easy, an unmanly bargain with nature, and that their æstheticism is based on insufficient labor.

But there is something heroic, and there may prove to be yet something very valuable to the Union, in their extreme attachment to a certain theory of life. They have kept up a faith which was on the point of perishing from this continent.

Of course it was only after the Civil War that the North and the South came to stand in polar opposition to each other. Immediately after Appomattox it was impossible for the South to resume even that give-and-take of ideas which had marked her antebellum relations with the North. She was offered such terms that acquiescence would have been abject. She retired within her borders in rage and held the minimum of commerce with the enemy. Persecution intensified her tradition, and made the South more solid and more Southern in the year 1875, or thereabouts, than ever before. When the oppression was left off, naturally her guard relaxed. But though the period of persecution had not been long, nevertheless the Southern tradition found itself then the less capable of uniting gracefully with the life of the Union; for that life in the meantime had been moving on in an opposite direction. The American progressive principle was like a ball rolling down the hill with an increasing momentum, and by 1890 or 1900 it was clear to any intelligent Southerner that it was a principle of boundless aggression against nature which could hardly offer much to a society devoted to the arts of peace.

But to keep on living shabbily on an insufficient patrimony is to decline, both physically and spiritually. The South declined.

And now the crisis in the South's decline has been reached.

Industrialism has arrived in the South. Already the local chambers of commerce exhibit the formidable data of Southern progress. A considerable party of Southern opinion, which might be called the New South party, is well pleased with the recent industrial accomplishments of the South and anxious for many more. Southerners of another school, who might be said to compose an Old South party, are apprehensive lest the section become completely and uncritically devoted to the industrial ideal precisely as the other sections of the Union are. But reconstruction is actually under way. Tied politically and economically to the Union, her borders wholly violable, the South now sees very well that she can restore her prosperity only within the competition of an industrial system.

After the war the Southern plantations were often broken up into small farms. These have yielded less and less of a living, and it said that they will never yield a good living until once more they are integrated into large units. But these units will be industrial units, controlled by a board of directors or an executive rather than a squire, worked with machinery, and manned not by farmers living at home, but by "labor." Even so they will not, according to Mr. Henry Ford, support the population that wants to live on them. In the off seasons the laborers will have to work in factories, which henceforth are to be counted on as among the charming features of Southern landscape. The Southern problem is complicated, but at its center is the farmer's problem, and this problem is simply the most acute version of that general agrarian problem which inspires the despair of many thoughtful Americans today.

The agrarian discontent in America is deeply grounded in the love of the tiller for the soil, which is probably, it must be confessed, not peculiar to the Southern specimen, but one of the more ineradicable human attachments, be the tiller as progressive as he may. In proposing to wean men from this foolish attachment, industrialism sets itself against the most ancient and the most humane of all the modes of human livelihood. Do Mr. Hoover and the distinguished thinkers at Washington see how essential is the mutual hatred between the industrialists and the farmers, and how mortal is their conflict? The gentlemen at Washington are mostly preaching and legislating to secure the fabulous "blessings" of industrial progress; they are on the industrial side. The industrialists have a doctrine which is monstrous, but they are not monsters personally; they are forward-lookers with nice manners, and no American progressivist is against them. The farmers are boorish and inarticulate by comparison. Progressivism is against them in their fight, though their traditional status is still so strong that soft words are still spoken to them. All the solutions recommended for their difficulties are really enticements held out to them to become a little more cooperative, more mechanical, more mobile—in short, a little more industrialized. But the farmer who is not a mere laborer, even the farmer of the comparatively new places like Iowa and Nebraska, is necessarily among the more stable and less progressive elements of society. He refuses to mobilize himself and become a unit in the industrial army, because he does not approve of army life.

I will use some terms which are hardly in his vernacular. He identifies himself with a spot of ground, and this ground carries a good deal of meaning; it defines itself for him as nature. He would till it not too hurriedly and not too mechanically to observe in it the contingency and the infinitude of nature; and so his life acquires its philosophical and even its cosmic consciousness. A man can contemplate and explore, respect and love, an object as substantial as a farm or a native province. But he cannot contemplate nor explore, respect nor love, a mere turnover, such as an assemblage of "natural resources," a pile of money, a volume of produce, a market, or a credit system. It is into precisely these intangibles that industrialism would translate the farmer's farm. It means the dehumanization of his life.

However that may be, the South at last, looking defensively about her in all directions upon an industrial world, fingers the weapons of industrialism. There is one powerful voice in the South which, tired of a long status of disrepute, would see the South made at once into a section second to none in wealth, as that is statistically reckoned, and in progressiveness, as that might be estimated by the rapidity of the industrial turnover. This desire offends those who would still like to regard the South as, in the old sense, a home; but its expression is loud and insistent. The urban South, with its heavy importation of regular American ways and regular American citizens, has nearly capitulated to these novelties. It is the village South and the rural South which supply the resistance, and it is lucky for them that they represent a vast quantity of inertia.

Will the Southern establishment, the most substantial exhibit on this continent of a society of the European and historic order, be completely crumbled by the powerful acid of the Great Progressive Principle? Will there be no more looking backward but only looking forward? Is our New World to be dedicated forever to the doctrine of newness?

It is in the interest of America as a whole, as well as in the interest of the South, that these questions press for an answer. I will enter here the most important items of the situation as well as I can; doubtless they will appear a little over-sharpened for the sake of exhibition.

(1) The intention of Americans at large appears now to be what it was always in danger of becoming: an intention of being infinitely progressive. But this intention cannot permit of an established order of human existence, and of that leisure which conditions the life of intelligence and the arts.

(2) The old South, if it must be defined in a word, practiced the contrary and European philosophy of establishment as the foundation of the life of the spirit. The ante-bellum Union possessed, to say the least, a wholesome variety of doctrine.

(3) But the South was defeated by the Union on the battlefield with remarkable decisiveness, and the two consequences have been dire: the Southern tradition was physically impaired, and has ever since been unable to offer an attractive example of its philosophy in action; and the American progressive principle has developed into a pure industrialism without any check from a Southern minority whose voice ceased to make itself heard.

(4) The further survival of the Southern tradition as a detached local remnant is now unlikely. It is agreed that the South must make contact again with the Union. And in adapting itself to the actual state of the Union, the Southern tradition will have to consent to a certain industrialization of its own.

(5) The question at issue is whether the South will permit herself to be so industrialized as to lose entirely her historic identity, and to remove the last substantial barrier that has stood in the way of American progressivism; or will accept industrialism, but

with a very bad grace, and will manage to maintain a good deal of her traditional philosophy.

The hope which is inherent in the situation is evident from the terms in which it is stated. The South must be industrialized—but to a certain extent only, in moderation. The program which now engages the Southern leaders is to see how the South may handle this fire without being burnt badly. The South at last is to be physically reconstructed; but it will be fatal if the South should conceive it as her duty to be regenerated and get her spirit reborn with a totally different orientation toward life.

Fortunately, the Southern program does not have to be perfectly vague. There are at least two definite lines, along either of which an intelligent Southern policy may move in the right general direction; it may even move back and forth between them and still advance.

The first course would be for the Southern leaders to arouse the sectional feeling of the South to its highest pitch of excitement in defense of all the old ways that are threatened. It might seem ungrateful to the kind industrialists to accept their handsome services in such a churlish spirit. But if one thing is more certain than another, it is that these gentlemen will not pine away in their discouragement; they have an inextinguishable enthusiasm for their rôle. The attitude that needs artificial respiration is the attitude of resistance on the part of the natives to the salesmen of industrialism. It will be fiercest and most effective if industrialism is represented to the Southern people as—what it undoubtedly is for the most part—a foreign invasion of Southern soil, which is capable of doing more devastation than was wrought when Sherman marched to the sea. From this point of view it will be a great gain if the usually-peaceful invasion forgets itself now and then, is less peaceful, and commits indiscretions. The native and the invader will be sure to come to an occasional clash, and that will offer the chance to revive ancient and almost forgotten animosities. It will be in order to proclaim to Southerners that the carpet-baggers are again in their midst. And it will be well to seize upon and advertise certain Northern industrial communities as horrible examples of a way of life we detest—not failing to point out the human catastrophe which occurs when a Southern village or rural community becomes the cheap labor of a miserable factory system. It will be a little bit harder to impress the people with the fact that the new so-called industrial "slavery" fastens not only upon the poor, but upon the middle and better classes of society, too. To make this point it may be necessary to revive such an antiquity as the old Southern gentleman and his lady, and their scorn for the dollar-chasers.

Such a policy as this would show decidedly a sense of what the Germans call *Realpolitik*. It could be nasty and it could be effective.

Its net result might be to give to the South eventually a position in the Union analogous more or less to the position of Scotland under the British crown—a section with a very local and peculiar culture that would, nevertheless, be secure and respected. And Southern traditionalists may take courage from the fact that it was Scottish stubborness which obtained this position for Scotland; it did not come gratuitously; it was the consequence of an intense sectionalism that fought for a good many years before its fight was won.

That is one policy. Though it is not the only one, it may be necessary to employ it, with discretion, and to bear in mind its Scottish analogue. But it is hardly handsome enough for the best Southerners. Its methods are too easily abused; it offers too much room for the professional demagogue; and one would only as a last resort like to have the South stake upon it her whole chance of survival. After all, the reconstruction may be undertaken with some imagination, and not necessarily under the formula of a literal restoration. It does not greatly matter to what extent the identical features of the old Southern establishment are restored; the important consideration is that there be an establishment for the sake of stability.

The other course may not be so easily practicable, but it is certainly more states-manlike. That course is for the South to reënter the American political field with a determination and an address quite beyond anything she has exhibited during her half-hearted national life of the last half a century. And this means specifically that she may pool her own stakes with the stakes of other minority groups in the Union which are circumstanced similarly. There is in active American politics already, to start with, a very belligerent if somewhat uninformed Western agrarian party. Between this party and the South there is much community of interest; both desire to defend home, stability of life, the practice of leisure, and the natural enemy of both is the insidious industrial system. There are also, scattered here and there, numerous elements with the same general attitude which would have some power if united: the persons and even com-munities who are thoroughly tired of progressivism and its spurious benefits, and those who have recently acquired, or miraculously through the generations preserved, a Euro-pean point of view—sociologists, educators, artists, religionists, and ancient New England townships. The combination of these elements with the Western farmers and the old-fashioned South would make a formidable bloc. The South is numerically much the most substantial of these three groups, but has done next to nothing to make the cause prevail by working inside the American political system.

The unifying effective bond between these geographically diverse elements of pub-lic opinion will be the clean-cut policy that the rural life of America must be defended, and the world made safe for the farmers. My friends are often quick to tell me that against the power of the industrial spirit no such hope can be entertained. But there are some protests in these days rising against the industrial ideal, even from the centers where its grip is the stoutest; and this would indicate that our human intelligence is beginning again to assert itself. Of course this is all the truer of the European countries, which have required less of the bitter schooling of experience. Thus Dean Inge declares himself in his Romanes Lecture on "The Idea of Progress":

> I believe that the dissatisfaction with things as they are is caused not only by the failure of nineteenth-century civilization, but partly also by its success. We no longer wish to progress on those lines if we could. Our apocalyptic dream is vanishing into thin air. It may be that the industrial revolution which began in the reign of George the Third has produced most of its fruits, and has had its day. We may have to look forward to such a change as is imagined by Anatole France at the end of his *Isle of Penguins*, when, after an orgy of revolution and destruction, we shall slide back into the quiet rural life of the early modern period. If so, the authors of the revolution will have cut their own throats, for there can be no great manufacturing towns in such a society. Their disappearance will be no great loss. The race will have tried a great experiment, and will have rejected it as unsatisfying.

The South has an important part to play, if she will, in such a counter-revolution. But what pitiful service have the inept Southern politicians for many years been ren-dering to the cause! Their Southern loyalty at Washington has rarely had any more imaginative manifestation than to scramble vigorously for a Southern share in the federal pie. They will have to be miraculously enlightened.

I get quickly beyond my depth in sounding these political possibilities. I will utter one last fantastic thought.

No Southerner ever dreams of heaven, or pictures his Utopia on earth, without providing room for the Democratic party. Is it really possible that the Democratic party can be held to a principle, and that the principle can now be defined as agrarian, conservative, anti-industrial? It may not be impossible, after all. If it proves possible, then the South may yet be rewarded for a sentimental affection that has persisted in the face of many betrayals.

REXFORD G. TUGWELL

Selection from *The Battle for Democracy*
1933

A central figure in the "brain trust" of President Franklin D. Roosevelt was the Columbia University economist Rexford G. Tugwell (1891–1979). Toward the end of 1933, the year in which Roosevelt's New Deal had been launched, Tugwell delivered a major address at his own academic home, Columbia University, designed to clarify the administration's program for economic recovery. The speech was later published in a collection of Tugwell's writings, *The Battle for Democracy* (New York, 1935). The section of the speech reprinted here conveys with unusual cogency several vital, general features of New Deal thought. Tugwell attacked laissez-faire principles and defended economic planning in the public interest by a strong, flexible government. Positioning himself between conservatives and communists, and resisting "doctrinaire," "fanatical" attitudes, he displayed the vaunted pragmatism of the brain trust and of Roosevelt himself. He also expressed the confidence in social scientific expertise and the public-spirited idealism characteristic of intellectuals who worked in Washington in the early years of the New Deal. In a section omitted here, Tugwell outlined in more technical detail the agricultural, industrial, and public works segments of the New Deal program.

Tugwell was among the most consistently social democratic of Roosevelt's advisors. Finding himself substantially to the left of the policies Roosevelt proved willing to support, in 1936 he resigned the position he then held as undersecretary of agriculture. He later wrote an influential study of the president he had tried to serve, *The Democratic Roosevelt* (New York, 1957). For Tugwell's life and career, see Michael Namurato, *Rexford G. Tugwell: A Biography* (New York, 1988).

Perhaps the most important single economic treatise informing the New Deal had been completed by Tugwell's Columbia colleagues, Adolph A. Berle, Jr., and Gardiner C. Means, *The Modern Corporation and Private Property* (New York, 1932) shortly before Roosevelt was elected. This book argued that actual control of corporations was no longer exercised by the people who owned them, but by professional managers in their employ. The separation of control from ownership challenged the traditional free-enterprise ideology that justified private profit on the grounds that owners took risks that deserved to be rewarded by the earnings of their corporations. A splendid anthology of writings by New Deal intellectuals is Howard Zinn, ed., *New Deal Thought* (Indianapolis, 1966).

In the midst of the cross currents of activity in Washington, it is necessary from time to time to stand apart and recall the general outline of the program which is expressing itself in a day-to-day detailed activity. Only as it is considered as a whole will the apparent paradoxes be reconciled and the total effort be comprehended.

The general objective is clear and easily stated—to restore a workable exchangeability among the separate parts of our economic machine and to set it to functioning again; and beyond this to perfect arrangements which may prevent its future disorganization. This means that we must insure adequate income to the farmers, adequate wages to the workers, an adequate return to useful capital, and an adequate remuneration to management. What we want, really, is to provide the opportunity for every individual and every group to work and to be able to consume the product of others' work. This involves a creation of buying power which is coordinate with the creation of goods. We shall not rest nor be diverted to lesser things until that minimum is achieved.

But to outline an objective in such broad terms does not take us far in understanding specific undertakings. What constitutes a workable relationship among income to farmers, wages to workers, and a return to useful capital? Here is a question which we can answer only when we have considered why they are now inadequate.

That they are less than our productive capacity entitles us to, there can be no doubt. Consider what our economic machine could have produced if it had been working in the last four years at the same rate as in 1928 and 1929. If all the labor and equipment which have been idle during the depression could have been converted into houses, every second family in the country could have had a brand new $5,000 house; or we could have scrapped the whole American railroad system and rebuilt it three times over. Such is the waste of the last four years; the waste caused by the failure of the economic machine to function properly, a failure to produce and distribute, which makes inadequate the income of nearly every group in the community. So long as the economic machine fails to operate at its potential capacity the income of each group will continue to be insufficient. So long as our economy provides vastly less to each group in the community than our resources in men and materials make possible, the incomes of everyone will be inadequate.

Consider the reaction of the country to the first three years of depression. Down and down went the curves of business activity. Longer and longer grew the lines of idle workers and the rows of idle machines. The whole constituted a challenge to the American people to act *as a body*, to remedy a ridiculous situation which had developed out of their *acting separately*.

Why was this challenge to American intelligence and action not met in the first three years of depression? We have grown up in a tradition which says that if economic forces are let alone all will come out right in the end. In the past we have regarded social interference in the interest of economic continuity as highly improper. This supremely crucial function we abandoned to private initiative, operating through the price system and controlled by competition. Such a system had worked in the past—haltingly and after a fashion. In the first year of the depression there may have been justification for waiting for recovery in the interest of protecting this principle. In the second year, was there justification? In the third year, with more than a quarter of our

Source: Rexford Guy Tugwell, *The Battle for Democracy* (New York: Columbia University Press, 1935), 78–96. Reprinted with the permission of Columbia University Press.

working population out of work and agricultural income reduced to a third its former size, had not the time come for positive action by the community as a body instead of by individuals alone?

A year ago the people of this country voted on precisely this question. And with an overwhelming majority they chose a President with a mandate for positive action; and he assumed his delegated duty with a gallantry which the whole nation unmistakably approved. The change involved in this was of major importance in the development of this country. It meant a shift from *laissez faire* to positive effort. It implied an effort by the community through its government to restore exchangeability by positive action. It placed directly on the shoulders of the new administration the responsibility for bringing about recovery from one of the deepest depressions this country has ever known.

The immediate reasons for this popular demand for positive action are clear. The terrific waste of depression, the hardships suffered by individuals through no fault of their own, the failure of business leadership to cope with the forces of depression, these all led to the insistent demand for change, a demand which would respect no allegiance to theory or preconceptions. How this demand was to be carried out, what action was to be undertaken, was not clear; but a policy of *laissez faire* was no longer to be countenanced.

What positive measures could be undertaken? Preliminary to their understanding is an assessment of the underlying developments which led to this general demand for governmental activity. This takes us directly into economic analysis. Those people who have so extravagantly praised the beauties of *laissez faire* have always done so on the assumption of highly flexible prices and a degree of freedom in competition. Actually the breakdown came at a time when our economy was a spotted reality of competition and control—with the control entrusted to irresponsible trustees. In 1929 we did not have a system of free competition and flexible prices. True, in some areas, like farming, we have had highly flexible prices and a considerable number of individuals actively competing in both production and price. If prices throughout our economy had been as flexible as those in the farm area were, it is quite possible that the 1929 depression would have been of minor consequence. The truth was, however, that an important part of our economy had prices which were not responsive—as theoretically they should have been—to changes in supply or demand. At the furthest extreme are railroad and public-utility rates, steel rails and many other goods and services whose prices were fixed over very considerable periods of time. In such occupations and areas, the whole impact of changes in demand are taken in the form of changes in production without any changes in price.

Intermediate between the extremes of flexible price and fixed price, lies most of industry. In this area prices are fixed for shorter periods of time but are periodically revised over longer periods of time. Thus, in varying degrees, changes in demand are met by changes in production, and more slowly and over a longer time only, by changes in price.

This matter of temporary or more permanently fixed prices is vitally important. This fixity is a major disturbing influence in a system which is theoretically competitive. Consider a concrete case—the production of automobiles. The manufacturer of cars will set a wholesale price on his cars at the beginning of the season. Presumably he will set a price which he expects will sell as many cars in the year as will make his total profits at that price as large as possible. Once the price is set, any drop in demand for cars will result, not in a drop in price, but in a drop in production. Men will be discharged and machines will become idle. Because of lessening employment and lessening incomes, there is likely to be a further drop in demand for cars. If this condition were typical of all industry the resulting condition would be one which we describe as depression. It is, of course, true that once or twice a year the prices of cars will be revised. But in the intermediate periods, prices are fixed, and changing demand is reflected only in changing production, with a direct effect on the income of consumers. It is this fact which is of major significance. It is this price inflexibility which causes an initial drop in demand to induce unemployment. In this manner, the rigidity of some prices and the flexibility of others tends to make production in our system unstable, deranging the balance between prices and production in different fields. We have a choice, if the situation is to be remedied, of really restoring competition or of extending the areas of rigidity until they include all prices of real social consequence.

Notice how differently the depression has affected different parts of our economy. In the agricultural area, in which prices are highly flexible, the drop in effective demand during the depression has caused a great drop in prices, while production has declined little. The farmers are working as hard as ever, but they get less for their product. Throughout most of industry, the effect of the depression has been essentially different. Prices have dropped relatively little compared to the drop in agricultural prices. The fall in demand has been met for the most part by reduced production. The income of the workers as a body has dropped as rapidly as that of the farm group, not primarily because wages were lower (though that has been important), but because of being out of employment. Thus, while the cash incomes of farmers as a body and of wage workers as a body have fallen off to an almost equal degree, one has fallen because of a fall in prices and the other because of a fall in production.

This difference in the effect of the depression in agriculture and in industry is of great importance because it suggests that quite different methods for restoring balance must be applied in the different fields. Restoration of balance would require a lowering of production and a lifting of prices in agriculture, but a lifting of production and in some cases even a lowering of prices in industry. . . .

Reducing production and raising prices to the farmer, increasing production and raising wages to the industrial worker faster than industrial prices are raised, and the putting into circulation of a new flow of buying power—these are the central core of the recovery drive conceived to be undertaken by the community as a whole. It is, I believe, adequate. It is in many ways unorthodox. It runs counter to the accepted notions of the doctrinaire—convinced believers in *laissez-faire* like it no better than communists. It is tentative, but still carefully hammered out of the iron of reality. We believe it to be the instrument of our present salvation; but we believe in no part of it so fanatically that we are unwilling to change. And this, of course, is the reason for proceeding through permissive powers with a calculated avoidance of any commitment whatever to doctrine.

The sheer hard economics of the situation in which we find ourselves makes certain demands on human nature from which recoil is natural. Sacrifice is demanded. Promise is also offered, of course, but the sacrifice seems much easier to concentrate on than the promise; and those who are squeezed give themselves whole-heartedly to opposition. All the old shibboleths, behind which vested interests have always hidden, are trotted out to do their stuff. The noise is tremendous and all the faint-hearted are quickly intimidated. To pursue a considered program in the midst of this welter of recrimination and special pleading is the task to which we have now to give ourselves.

There is no reason to suppose that our measures are unsound or that any of the experimental procedures have yet failed. They have not achieved utopia; but no one who was intimately concerned with their fashioning supposed that they would. Only the hangers-on, and those whose hopes outran their intelligence, believed that results would be seen before the causes of those results had become operative. There is complaint from many sources; and no administrator can be deaf to it. But what it was hoped to do in two, four or six years, none of us expected to see in eight months. Yet we have, I think, in all modesty, some reasonable ground for pride. The organization necessary to our eventual aims has been, if not perfected, yet set up in measurably competent fashion. And the long-time effort is being pursued by it with singular energy and determination. Besides this, however, it is only just to say that the immediate demands of a population hungry, cold and in despair have been met. We have not turned aside from any responsibility; we have not asked anyone else to do what it seemed possible for us to do.

The most captious critic, I believe, after careful assessment of the efforts of this administration, would be forced to admit that such an outpouring of loyal and devoted effort has seldom before been seen. I wish it were possible for me to describe for you, in any adequate words, the phenomena of sacrifice, of self-imposed discipline, of giving everything which was possessed by heart and hand and brain, which I have seen so intimately among my colleagues in these past months. I have no lack whatever of confidence in the results to come when the time is ripe for them to come; I have, however, a miserable feeling of the inadequacy, in this case, of the test of results. I wish my fellow citizens could have seen the ordeal, got something of its feel and color, so that adequate honor might be paid where it is due. I do not speak of any of those whose names you may have seen in the press or of whom you may have heard reports. It is truly the unknown servants of the Republic who have deserved well of their country in this crisis.

I have called some of them to Washington myself. Others have called more. They have come with fresh minds, clean motives, and unselfish aspirations. Numbers have come from this university [Columbia] at sacrifices known only to themselves. And their only reward will be unspectacular: the personal sense of having served in a crisis to re-create the gigantic strength of America. Those who have come from this and from other universities have come quietly and gone to work in prosaic ways. They have found that what they had to do was really only an extension and an intensification of what they were used to doing. But under the lash of need they have been driven almost unbearably.

I have had a chance to see the truth of the saying that ours is a government of men. The fiction that it is a government of laws would, I think, never have attained its great prestige if the right men had been called to govern. Much has been said lately of the new institutions which have been invented, of the changes which have overtaken hitherto accepted arrangements. It is possible to overemphasize this idea. In fact, a careful examination of the new legislation will disclose that its novel characteristic is its provision of freedom for action by those who have to do the acting. The powers granted are mostly permissive; the rules written are mandates for performance. Everything depends on men.

The center of the present storm is in the economic field. It is natural that economists should be our greatest dependence for guidance as well as for skillful administration. This university and others have not finished their task by thinning the existing ranks and making temporary loans to government. The end of the demand is not in sight; perhaps it never will be. Perhaps it must be assumed as a regular burden from now on. This requires, of course, a return from economics to political economy as the needed discipline. Economics belonged to *laissez-faire;* the world has turned its back on that. The danger is that universities may not find it out, but may continue to turn over and over the sterile dust of free-competitive principles. Men trained in this kind of thinking are handicapped now; it is the greatest single difficulty with economists in government that they can think only of ways to emasculate the government in its dealings with economic phenomena, because they carry in their heads a formula of noninterference. Political economists are what is needed, men not ridden by preconceptions, careful analysts who recognize logical needs and dare to follow them across their concepts to conclusions in simple operating arrangements, even if this requires the government to do novel things. I say this because for a long time I have been saying it and the event has proved the necessity. Some important part of the effort of our universities has gone to stuffing students with preconceptions which are shattered the moment they meet the economic realities of everyday life. The departments of political economy in our universities are not yet conceiving their problem in the terms to which they must ultimately come—or else go the way of the academic classics with which they really belong.

The most grudging consent to our recovery program comes from these departments of economics; they appear to have forgotten how little they liked the logical alternative when they were living with it a year ago. Seemingly they would rather have us fail than to succeed in unorthodox ways. People who find themselves in such a frame of mind belong with the Bourbons, the Malthusians and other historical diehards after whom deluges have come.

It is quite impossible to predict the shape our newly invented economic institutions may take in the future. That seems to me, in any case, unimportant. What is important is that we have undertaken a venture which is theoretically new in the sense that it calls for control rather than drift. In the years to come much ingenuity will be needed in the effort to isolate and strengthen the nerve centers of industrial civilization. We have yet to discover in determinate fashion what efforts are naturally those of common service, and so require a high degree of socialization, and what ones can safely be left to relatively free individual or group contrivance. We are turning away from the entrusting of crucial decisions, and the operation of institutions whose social consequences are their most characteristic feature, to individuals who are motivated by private interests. It will take a long time to learn how this may be done effectively. But the longest step toward its accomplishment was taken when the new and untrod path was entered on. It is my earnest hope that the university which has been my home during so many active years, and from whose encouragement I and others have drawn strength, may enter on these tasks with courage and determination. The link between this institution and that one which I am at the moment serving in Washington is a natural one. The university is a place for learning and for renewal. It is the source on which government must depend for inspiration, for criticism, for expert service; the source, also, of that political economy out of which the new industrial state must be forged.

MERIDEL LE SUEUR

"I Was Marching"
1934

Advocates of concerted, collective political action have often lamented the "bourgeois individualism" prominent in American life. Especially during the 1930s, leftist writers expressed frustration with this individualism and tried to liberate their contemporaries from it. In the personal reporting reprinted here, the journalist and writer Meridel Le Sueur (1900–) attributes to herself those inhibitions that activists then saw as obstacles to disciplined, collective action. She describes the details—strikingly gendered—of her own conversion to a new identity, entailing solidarity with the workers' movement. Le Sueur was not as innocent as she encouraged readers of this piece to believe. In fact, she was the child of socialist parents and had been sufficiently distant from bourgeois sensibilities to have been a member of the Communist party for a decade before the strike of 1934, represented here as the occasion for her renunciation of middle-class inhibitions.

"I Was Marching" is best read the way that Henry Adams's autobiographical writing is generally read: as the account of a semifictional persona created by the author to express certain opinions and achieve a certain artistic effect. So considered, "I Was Marching" is no less arresting as an attack on individualism, no less passionate as a vindication of communal solidarity, and all the more artfully designed as a political argument. "I Was Marching" is one of the period's most insistent statements of faith in the benevolence of even a "machinelike" social organism, if serving the goals of the working class. At almost the same time as this stylized conversion narrative appeared in *The New Masses*, Le Sueur published elsewhere a very different report of the same Minneapolis teamsters' strike, written in the equally stylized voice of a tough, sophisticated analyst arguing that all strikes followed the same logic: see Le Sueur, "What Happens in a Strike," *American Mercury* 33 (1934), 329–35. Le Sueur was unusual among the political writers of the 1930s in that she actually joined the Communist party, and she remained a member of it long after many intellectuals attracted to it had found its discipline too confining and its perspective on the Moscow trials, the Nazi–Soviet pact, and Stalin's leadership too uncritical.

The importance of the Communist party in Le Sueur's career is emphasized by Linda Ray Pratt in "Woman Writer in the CP: The Case of Meridel Le Sueur," *Women's Studies* 14 (1988), 247–64. Le Sueur has preferred not to be regarded as "an intellectual" and has seen her own, continuing commitment to the Communist party as an expression of her solidarity with the masses of humankind. For a study of her work, see Constance Coiner, *Better Red: The Writing and Resistance of Tillie Olsen and Meridel Le Sueur* (New York, 1995).

Minneapolis, 1934

I have never been in a strike before. It is like looking at something that is happening for the first time and there are no thoughts and no words yet accrued to it. If you come from the middle class, words are likely to mean more than an event. You are likely to think about a thing, and the happening will be the size of a pin-point and the words around the happening very large, distorting it queerly. It's a case of "Remembrance of Things Past." When you are in the event, you are likely to have a distinctly individualistic attitude, to be only partly there, and to care more for the happening afterwards than when it is happening. That is why it is hard for a person like myself and others to be in a strike.

Besides, in American life, you hear things happening in a far and muffled way. One thing is said and another happens. Our merchant society has been built upon a huge hypocrisy, a cutthroat competition which sets one man against another and at the same time an ideology mouthing such words as "Humanity," "Truth," the "Golden Rule," and such. Now in a crisis the word falls away and the skeleton of that action shows in terrific movement.

For two days I heard of the strike. I went by their headquarters, I walked by on the opposite side of the street and saw the dark old building that had been a garage and lean, dark young faces leaning from the upstairs windows. I had to go down there often. I looked in. I saw the huge black interior and live coals of living men moving restlessly and orderly, their eyes gleaming from their sweaty faces.

I saw cars leaving filled with grimy men, pickets going to the line, engines roaring out. I stayed close to the door, watching. I didn't go in. I was afraid they would put me out. After all, I could remain a spectator. A man wearing a polo hat kept going around with a large camera taking pictures.

I am putting down exactly how I felt, because I believe others of my class feel the same as I did. I believe it stands for an important psychic change that must take place in all. I saw many artists, writers, professionals, even businessmen and women standing across the street, too, and I saw in their faces the same longings, the same fears.

The truth is I was afraid. Not of the physical danger at all, but an awful fright of mixing, of losing myself, of being unknown and lost. I felt inferior. I felt no one would know me there, that all I had been trained to excel in would go unnoticed. I can't describe what I felt, but perhaps it will come near it to say that I felt I excelled in competing with others and I knew instantly that these people were not competing at all, that they were acting in a strange, powerful trance of movement together. And I was filled with longing to act with them and with fear that I could not. I felt I was born out of every kind of life, thrown up alone, looking at other lonely people, a condition I had been in the habit of defending with various attitudes of cynicism, preciosity, defiance, and hatred.

Looking at the dark and lively building, massed with men, I knew my feelings to be those belonging to disruption, chaos, and disintegration and I felt their direct and awful movement, mute and powerful, drawing them into a close and glowing cohesion like a powerful conflagration in the midst of the city. And it filled me with fear and awe and at the same time hope. I knew this action to be prophetic and indicative of future actions and I wanted to be part of it.

Our life seems to be marked with a curious and muffled violence over America,

Source: New Masses, September 18, 1934, 165–68. Reprinted by permission of International Publishers.

but this action has always been in the dark, men and women dying obscurely, poor and poverty marked lives, but now from city to city runs this violence, into the open, and colossal happenings stand bare before our eyes, the street churning suddenly upon the pivot of mad violence, whole men suddenly spouting blood and running like living sieves, another holding a dangling arm shot squarely off, a tall youngster, running, tripping over his intestines, and one block away, in the burning sun, gay women shopping and a window dresser trying to decide whether to put green or red voile on a manikin.

In these terrible happenings you cannot be neutral now. No one can be neutral in the face of bullets.

The next day, with sweat breaking out on my body, I walked past the three guards at the door. They said, "Let the women in. We need women." And I knew it was no joke.

At first I could not see into the dark building. I felt many men coming and going, cars driving through. I had an awful impulse to go into the office which I passed, and offer to do some special work. I saw a sign which said, "Get your button." I saw they all had buttons with the date and the number of the union local. I didn't get a button. I wanted to be anonymous.

There seemed to be a current, running down the wooden stairs, towards the front of the building, into the street, that was massed with people, and back again. I followed the current up the old stairs packed closely with hot men and women. As I was going up I could look down and see the lower floor, the cars drawing up to await picket call, the hospital roped off on one side.

Upstairs men sat bolt upright in chairs asleep, their bodies flung in attitudes of peculiar violence of fatigue. A woman nursed her baby. Two young girls slept together on a cot, dressed in overalls. The voice of the loudspeaker filled the room. The immense heat pressed down from the flat ceiling. I stood up against the wall for an hour. No one paid any attention to me. The commissary was in back and the women came out sometimes and sat down, fanning themselves with their aprons and listening to the news over the loudspeaker. A huge man seemed hung on a tiny folding chair. Occasionally someone tiptoed over and brushed the flies off his face. His great head fell over and the sweat poured regularly from his forehead like a spring. I wondered why they took such care of him. They all looked at him tenderly as he slept. I learned later he was a leader on the picket line and had the scalps of more cops to his name than any other.

Three windows flankèd the front. I walked over to the windows. A red-headed woman with a button saying, "Unemployed Council," was looking out. I looked out with her. A thick crowd stood in the heat below listening to the strike bulletin. We could look right into the windows of the smart club across the street. We could see people peering out of the windows half hidden.

I kept feeling they would put me out. No one paid any attention. The woman said without looking at me, nodding to the palatial house, "It sure is good to see the enemy plain like that." "Yes," I said. I saw that the club was surrounded by a steel picket fence higher than a man. "They know what they put that there fence there for," she said. "Yes," I said. "Well," she said, "I've got to get back to the kitchen. Is it ever hot?" The thermometer said ninety-nine. The sweat ran off us, burning our skins. "The boys'll be coming in," she said, "for their noon feed." She had a scarred face. "Boy, will it be a mad house?" "Do you need any help?" I said eagerly. "Boy," she said, "some of us have been pouring coffee since two o'clock this morning, steady, without no letup." She started to go. She didn't pay any special attention to me as an individual. She didn't seem to be thinking of me, she didn't seem to see me. I watched her go. I felt rebuffed, hurt. Then I saw instantly she didn't see me because she saw only what she was doing. I ran after her.

I found the kitchen organized like a factory. Nobody asks my name. I am given a large butcher's apron. I realize I have never before worked anonymously. At first I feel strange and then I feel good. The forewoman sets me to washing tin cups. There are not enough cups. We have to wash fast and rinse them and set them up quickly for buttermilk and coffee as the line thickens and the men wait. A little shortish man who is a professional dishwasher is supervising. I feel I won't be able to wash tin cups, but when no one pays any attention except to see that there are enough cups I feel better.

The line grows heavy. The men are coming in from the picket line. Each woman has one thing to do. There is no confusion. I soon learn I am not supposed to help pour the buttermilk. I am not supposed to serve sandwiches. I am supposed to wash tin cups. I suddenly look around and realize all these women are from factories. I know they have learned this organization and specialization in the factory. I look at the round shoulders of the woman cutting bread next to me and I feel I know her. The cups are brought back, washed and put on the counter again. The sweat pours down our faces, but you forget about it.

Then I am changed and put to pouring coffee. At first I look at the men's faces and then I don't look any more. It seems I am pouring coffee for the same tense dirty sweating face, the same body, the same blue shirt and overalls. Hours go by, the heat is terrific. I am not tired. I am not hot. I am pouring coffee. I am swung into the most intense and natural organization I have ever felt. I know everything that is going on. These things become of great matter to me.

Eyes looking, hands raising a thousand cups, throats burning, eyes bloodshot from lack of sleep, body dilated to catch every sound over the whole city. Buttermilk? Coffee?

"Is your man here?" the woman cutting sandwiches asks me.

"No," I say, then I lie for some reason, peering around as if looking eagerly for someone, "I don't see him now."

But I was pouring coffee for living men.

For a long time, about one o'clock, it seemed like something was about to happen. Women seemed to be pouring into headquarters to be near their men. You could hear only lies over the radio. And lies in the papers. Nobody knew precisely what was happening, but everyone thought something would happen in a few hours. You could feel the men being poured out of the hall onto the picket line. Every few minutes cars left and more drew up and were filled. The voice of the loudspeaker was accelerated, calling for men, calling for picket cars.

I could hear the men talking about the arbitration board, the truce that was supposed to be maintained while the board sat with the Governor. They listened to every word over the loudspeaker. A terrible communal excitement ran through the hall like a fire through a forest. I could hardly breathe. I seemed to have no body at all except the body of this excitement. I felt that what had happened before had not been a real movement, these false words and actions had taken place on the periphery. The real action was about to show the real intention.

We kept on pouring thousands of cups of coffee, feeding thousands of men.

The chef with a woman tattooed on his arm was just dishing the last of the stew.

It was about two o'clock. The commissary was about empty. We went into the front hall. It was drained of men. The chairs were empty. The voice of the announcer was excited. "The men are massed at the market," he said. "Something is going to happen." I sat down beside a woman who was holding her hands tightly together, leaning forward listening, her eyes bright and dilated. I had never seen her before. She took my hands. She pulled me towards her. She was crying. "It's awful," she said, "something awful is going to happen. They've taken both my children away from me and now something is going to happen to all those men." I held her hands. She had a green ribbon around her hair.

The action seemed reversed. The cars were coming back. The announcer cried, "This is murder." Cars were coming in. I don't know how we got to the stairs. Everyone seemed to be converging at a menaced point. I saw below the crowd stirring, uncoiling. I saw them taking men out of cars and putting them on the hospital cots, on the floor. At first I felt frightened, the close black area of the barn, the blood, the heavy moment, the sense of myself lost, gone. But I couldn't have turned away now. A woman clung to my hand. I was pressed against the body of another. If you are to understand anything you must understand it in the muscular event, in actions we have not been trained for. Something broke all my surfaces in something that was beyond horror and I was dabbing alcohol on the gaping wounds that buckshot makes, hanging open like crying mouths. Buckshot wounds splay in the body and then swell like a blow. Ness, who died, had thirty-eight slugs in his body, in the chest and in the back.

The picket cars kept coming in. Some men have walked back from the market, holding their own blood in. They move in a great explosion, and the newness of the movement makes it seem like something under ether, moving terrifically towards a culmination.

From all over the city workers are coming. They gather outside in two great half-circles, cut in two to let the ambulances in. A traffic cop is still directing traffic at the corner and the crowd cannot stand to see him. "We'll give you just two seconds to beat it," they tell him. He goes away quickly. A striker takes over the street.

Men, women, and children are massing outside, a living circle close packed for protection. From the tall office building businessmen are looking down on the black swarm thickening, coagulating into what action they cannot tell.

We have living blood on our skirts.

That night at eight o'clock a mass meeting was called of all labor. It was to be in a parking lot two blocks from headquarters. All the women gather at the front of the building with collection cans, ready to march to the meeting. I have not been home. It never occurs to me to leave. The twilight is eerie and the men are saying that the chief of police is going to attack the meeting and raid headquarters. The smell of blood hangs in the hot, still air. Rumors strike at the taut nerves. The dusk looks ghastly with what might be in the next half-hour.

"If you have any children," a woman said to me, "you better not go." I looked at the desperate women's faces, the broken feet, the torn and hanging pelvis, the worn and lovely bodies of women who persist under such desperate labors. I shivered, though it was ninety-six and the sun had been down a good hour.

The parking lot was already full of people when we got there and men swarmed the adjoining roofs. An elegant café stood across the street with water sprinkling from its roof and splendidly dressed men and women stood on the steps as if looking at a show.

The platform was the bullet-riddled truck of the afternoon's fray. We had been told to stand close to this platform, so we did, making the center of a wide massed circle that stretched as far as we could see. We seemed buried like minerals in a mass, packed body to body. I felt again that peculiar heavy silence in which there is the real form of the happening. My eyes burn. I can hardly see. I seem to be standing like an animal in ambush. I have the brightest, most physical feeling with every sense sharpened peculiarly. The movements, the masses that I see and feel I have never known before. I only partly know what I am seeing, feeling, but I feel it is the real body and gesture of a future vitality. I see that there is a bright clot of women drawn close to a bullet-riddled truck. I am one of them, yet I don't feel myself at all. It is curious, I feel most alive and yet for the first time in my life I do not feel myself as separate. I realize then that all my previous feelings have been based on feeling myself separate and distinct from others and now I sense sharply faces, bodies, closeness, and my own fear is not my own alone, nor my hope.

The strikers keep moving up cars. We keep moving back together to let cars pass and form between us and a brick building that flanks the parking lot. They are connecting the loudspeaker, testing it. Yes, they are moving up lots of cars, through the crowd and lining them closely side by side. There must be ten thousand people now, heat rising from them. They are standing silent, watching the platform, watching the cars being brought up. The silence seems terrific like a great form moving of itself. This is real movement issuing from the close reality of mass feeling. This is the first real rhythmic movement I have ever seen. My heart hammers terrifically. My hands are swollen and hot. No one is producing this movement. It is a movement upon which all are moving softly, rhythmically, terribly.

No matter how many times I looked at what was happening I hardly knew what I saw. I looked and I saw time and time again that there were men standing close to us, around us, and then suddenly I knew that there was a living chain of men standing shoulder to shoulder, forming a circle around the group of women. They stood shoulder to shoulder slightly moving like a thick vine from the pressure behind, but standing tightly woven like a living wall, moving gently.

I saw that the cars were now lined one close-fitted to the other with strikers sitting on the roofs and closely packed on the running boards. They could see far over the crowd. "What are they doing that for?" I said. No one answered. The wide dilated eyes of the women were like my own. No one seemed to be answering questions now. They simply spoke, cried out, moved together now.

The last car drove in slowly, the crowd letting them through without command or instruction. "A little closer," someone said. "Be sure they are close." Men sprang up to direct whatever action was needed and then subsided again and no one had noticed who it was. They stepped forward to direct a needed action and then fell anonymously back again.

We all watched carefully the placing of the cars. Sometimes we looked at each other. I didn't understand that look. I felt uneasy. It was as if something escaped me. And then suddenly, on my very body, I knew what they were doing, as if it had been communicated to me from a thousand eyes, a thousand silent throats, as if it had been shouted in the loudest voice.

They were building a barricade.

Two men died from that day's shooting. Men lined up to give one of them a blood transfusion, but he died. Black Friday men called the murderous day. Night and day workers held their children up to see the body of Ness who died. Tuesday, the day of the funeral, one thousand more militia were massed downtown.

It was still over ninety in the shade. I went to the funeral parlors and thousands of men and women were massed there waiting in the terrific sun. One block of women and children were standing two hours waiting. I went over and stood near them. I didn't know whether I could march. I didn't like marching in parades. Besides, I felt they might not want me.

I stood aside not knowing if I would march. I couldn't see how they would ever organize it anyway. No one seemed to be doing much.

At three-forty some command went down the ranks. I said foolishly at the last minute, "I don't belong to the auxiliary—could I march?" Three women drew me in. "We want all to march," they said gently. "Come with us."

The giant mass uncoiled like a serpent and straightened out ahead and to my amazement on a lift of road I could see six blocks of massed men, four abreast, with bare heads, moving straight on and as they moved, uncoiled the mass behind and pulled it after them. I felt myself walking, accelerating my speed with the others as the line stretched, pulled taut, then held its rhythm.

Not a cop was in sight. The cortege moved through the stop-and-go signs, it seemed to lift of its own dramatic rhythm, coming from the intention of every person there. We were moving spontaneously in a movement, natural, hardy, and miraculous.

We passed through six blocks of tenements, through a sea of grim faces, and there was not a sound. There was the curious shuffle of thousands of feet, without drum or bugle, in ominous silence, a march not heavy as the military, but very light, exactly with the heart-beat.

I was marching with a million hands, movements, faces, and my own movement was repeating again and again, making a new movement from these many gestures, the walking, falling back, the open mouth crying, the nostrils stretched apart, the raised hand, the blow falling, and the outstretched hand drawing me in.

I felt my legs straighten. I felt my feet join in that strange shuffle of thousands of bodies moving with direction, of thousands of feet, and my own breath with the gigantic breath. As if an electric charge had passed through me, my hair stood on end, I was marching.

Part Three

To Extend Democracy and to Formulate the Modern

Introduction

The historic, democratic aspirations of the United States were sharpened and articulated anew in the global context of World War II, when Americans found themselves struggling against three of the world's most authoritarian nation-states. Once the governments of Nazi Germany, Fascist Italy, and Imperial Japan had been defeated, moreover, the postwar rivalry with the Soviet Union created another, more enduring setting for Americans to dwell upon democratic ideals. These ideals were said to be at issue in the Cold War no less than in the "hot" war that preceded it. It was fitting, in this international frame, that one of the most influential statements of American democratic ideology written in modern times was produced, not by an American, but a foreign student of American society: the Swedish economist Gunnar Myrdal. Part Three begins with Myrdal's sketch of the "American Creed," which opened his 1944 volume, *An American Dilemma,* addressed to the gap between American ideals and the reality faced by black citizens of the United States.

This particular gap was a major concern of several other contributors to Part Three. Lillian Smith elaborated on the injustice of this gap by exploring the "one drop rule," according to which even the slightest trace of African ancestry served to subject an American to a life of prejudicial treatment that Smith believed wrong for a person of any color. Martin Luther King, Jr., the most influential and widely admired black leader in American history, brought both Christian and democratic principles to bear on the blatant mistreatment of African-Americans.

But it was not only skin color that created a gap between American ideals and American reality. That gender, too, had been allowed to restrict the sphere of life available to individual Americans was an implication of Betty Friedan's complaint about what she called "the feminine mystique." Religious distinctions were also addressed during the midcentury effort to expand the range of American democracy. The Jesuit priest John Courtney Murray argued that the democratic ideals of the United States were more consistent with Catholic teachings than some culturally separatist-leaning Catholics had realized. Murray also implied that Catholics, being fully in tune with American political virtues, did not deserve the suspicion directed toward them by some democracy-affirming Protestant and Jewish Americans. Liberal and conservative versions of an explicitly Christian foundation for American democracy were developed by the theologian Reinhold Niebuhr, and by the brooding ex-communist writer, Whittaker Chambers, respectively.

Some of these discussants of democracy were also answering what Walt Whitman, a century before, had described as the call "to formulate the modern." The concept of a distinctly "modern" culture was highly contested in a variety of contexts. Especially in discussions of literature and the arts did intellectuals advance particular agendas under the sign of "modernism," and quarrel about the character of this apparently multitudinous movement. In Part Three, Clement Greenberg's vindication of avant-garde art introduces this theme. The literary critic Lionel Trilling's anxious reconsideration of the modernist project provides an antiphonal voice. But social scientists, too, were preoccupied with understanding the conditions and problems that defined modernity. The psychologist B. F. Skinner and the sociologists Daniel Bell and C. Wright Mills exemplify this concern in Part Three.

Recommendations for Further Reading

H. Stuart Hughes, *The Sea Change: The Migration of Social Thought, 1930–1965* (New York, 1975); Robert Booth Fowler, *Believing Skeptics* (Westport, Conn., 1978); Carl Pletsch, "The Three Worlds, or the Division of Social Scientific Labor, circa 1950–1975," *Comparative Studies in Society and History* (1981), 565–90; Daniel Joseph Singal, *The War Within: From Victorian to Modernist Thought in the South, 1919–1945* (Chapel Hill, 1982); James Sloan Allen, *The Romance of Commerce and Culture: Capitalism, Modernism, and the Chicago-Aspen Crusade for Cultural Reform* (Chicago, 1983); Christopher Brookeman, *American Culture and Society Since the 1930s* (London, 1984); Richard Pells, *The Liberal Mind in a Conservative Age* (New York, 1985); Martin Jay, *Permanent Exiles: Essays on the Intellectual Migration from Germany to America* (New York, 1986); Terry A. Cooney, *The Rise of the New York Intellectuals: Partisan Review and Its Circle, 1934–1945* (Madison, 1986); Paul S. Boyer, *By the Bomb's Early Light: American Thought and Culture at the Dawn of the Atomic Age* (New York, 1986); Ellen W. Schrecker, *No Ivory Tower: McCarthyism and the Universities* (New York, 1986); Stephen M. Gillon, *Politics and Vision: The ADA and American Liberalism, 1947–1985* (New York, 1987); Spencer Weart, *Nuclear Fear: A History of Images* (Cambridge, 1988); Lary May, ed., *Recasting America: Culture and Politics in the Age of Cold War* (Chicago, 1989); Stephen J. Whitfield, *Cold War Culture* (Baltimore, 1990); Daniel J. Singal, ed., *Modernist Culture in America* (Belmont, Calif., 1991); Thomas Hill Schaub, *American Fiction in the Cold War* (Madison, 1991); Greg Mitman, *The State of Nature: Ecology, Community, and American Social Thought, 1900–1950* (Chicago, 1992); Ronald Numbers, *The Creationists* (New York, 1992); Joan Shelly Rubin, *The Making of Middlebrow Culture* (Chapel Hill, 1992); David A. Hollinger, "How Wide the Circle of the We? American Intellectuals and the Problem of the Ethnos Since World War II," *American Historical Review* (April 1993) 317–37; Wilfred M. McClay, *The Masterless: Self and Society in Modern America* (Chapel Hill, 1994); Joanne Meyerowitz, ed., *Not June Cleaver: Women and Gender in Postwar America, 1945–1960* (New York, 1994); George Marsden, *The Soul of the American University* (New York, 1994); Ron Robin, *The Barbed-Wire College: Reeducating German POWs in the United States During World War II* (Princeton, 1995); Richard Candida Smith, *Utopia and Dissent: Art, Poetry, and Politics in California* (Berkeley, 1995); Ellen Herman, *The Romance of American Psychology: Political Culture in the Age of Experts* (Berkeley, 1995); David A. Hollinger, *Science, Jews, and Secular Culture: Studies in Mid-Twentieth Century American Intellectual History* (Princeton, 1996).

GUNNAR MYRDAL

Selection from *An American Dilemma*
1944

One of the twentieth century's most forthright and influential formulations of traditional American ideals was written by an "outsider," the Swedish economist Gunnar Myrdal (1898–1987). The occasion was the publication in 1944 of a 1483-page analysis of the place of black people in the United States. *An American Dilemma: The Negro Problem and American Democracy* was the product of a six-year effort by a team of researchers assembled by Myrdal in response to a commission from a private foundation, The Carnegie Corporation. Although the bulk of this study consisted of social scientific data and analysis, Myrdal framed the whole report in terms of a gap between American ideals and the reality of how black people lived in the United States. Hence his articulation of "The American Creed" in the opening pages served to cast into bold relief the facts that were to follow: The prejudicial treatment of Negroes was an anomaly, a striking case in which Americans had failed to live up to their ideals.

In trying to reinforce what he took to be the American moral conscience in specific relation to "the Negro Problem," Myrdal exaggerated the extent to which the "Creed" had been accepted, and had been acted upon in other areas of American life. But his formulation of American democratic ideology resonated well beyond the specific policy dilemma that inspired it. It appeared while the United States was engaged in a war against powers who offered not even lip-service to the ideology Myrdal attributed to Americans, and was widely read during the subsequent Cold War era when Americans were preoccupied with distinguishing themselves ideologically from the Soviet Union.

The most comprehensive study of Myrdal's project is Walter A. Jackson, *Gunnar Myrdal and America's Conscience: Social Engineering & Racial Liberalism, 1938–1987* (Chapel Hill, 1990). A valuable account of the reception of *An American Dilemma* is David W. Southern, *Gunnar Myrdal and Black-White Relations: The Use and Abuse of "An American Dilemma," 1944–1969* (Baton Rouge, 1987). A critique influential during the 1960s can be found in Ralph W. Ellison, *Shadow and Act* (New York, 1964), 303–17. For perspectives of the 1990s, see the special issue of *Daedalus* (Winter 1995), "An American Dilemma Revisited." A helpful corrective—reflecting contemporary scholarship—to Myrdal's claim that the "Creed" was largely uncontested in the history of American political ideology is Rogers W. Smith, "Beyond Tocqueville, Myrdal, and Hartz: The Multiple Traditions in America," *American Political Science Review* LXXXVII (1993), 549–66.

It is a commonplace to point out the heterogeneity of the American nation and the swift succession of all sorts of changes in all its component parts and, as it often seems, in every conceivable direction. America is truly a shock to the stranger. The bewildering impression it gives of dissimilarity throughout and of chaotic unrest is indicated by the fact that few outside observers—and, indeed, few native Americans—have been able to avoid the intellectual escape of speaking about America as "paradoxical."

Still there is evidently a strong unity in this nation and a basic homogeneity and stability in its valuations. Americans of all national origins, classes, regions, creeds, and colors, have something in common: a social *ethos,* a political creed. It is difficult to avoid the judgment that this "American Creed" is the cement in the structure of this great and disparate nation.

When the American Creed is once detected, the cacophony becomes a melody. The further observation then becomes apparent: that America, compared to every other country in Western civilization, large or small, has the *most explicitly expressed* system of general ideals in reference to human interrelations. This body of ideals is more widely understood and appreciated than similar ideals are anywhere else. The American Creed is not merely—as in some other countries—the implicit background of the nation's political and judicial order as it functions. To be sure, the political creed of America is not very satisfactorily effectuated in actual social life. But as principles which *ought* to rule, the Creed has been made conscious to everyone in American society.

Sometimes one even gets the impression that there is a relation between the intense apprehension of high and uncompromising ideals and the spotty reality. One feels that it is, perhaps, the difficulty of giving reality to the *ethos* in this young and still somewhat unorganized nation—that it is the prevalence of "wrongs" in America, "wrongs" judged by the high standards of the national Creed—which helps make the ideals stand out so clearly. America is continuously struggling for its soul. These principles of social ethics have been hammered into easily remembered formulas. All means of intellectual communication are utilized to stamp them into everybody's mind. The schools teach them, the churches preach them. The courts pronounce their judicial decisions in their terms. They permeate editorials with a pattern of idealism so ingrained that the writers could scarcely free themselves from it even if they tried. They have fixed a custom of indulging in high-sounding generalities in all written or spoken addresses to the American public, otherwise so splendidly gifted for the matter-of-fact approach to things and problems. Even the stranger, when he has to appear before an American audience, feels this, if he is sensitive at all, and finds himself espousing the national Creed, as this is the only means by which a speaker can obtain human response from the people to whom he talks.

The Negro people in America are no exception to the national pattern. "It was a revelation to me to hear Negroes sometimes indulge in a glorification of American democracy in the same uncritical way as unsophisticated whites often do," relates the Dutch observer, Bertram Schrieke. A Negro political scientist, Ralph Bunche, observes:

> Every man in the street, white, black, red or yellow, knows that this is "the land
> of the free," the "land of opportunity," the "cradle of liberty," the "home of democ-
> racy," that the American flag symbolizes the "equality of all men" and guarantees to

Source: Gunnar Myrdal, *An American Dilemma* (New York: Harper and Row, 1944), 3–12, 24–25. Reprinted by permission of Harper Collins Publishers, Inc.

us all "the protection of life, liberty and property," freedom of speech, freedom of religion and racial tolerance.

The present writer has made the same observation. The American Negroes know that they are a subordinated group experiencing, more than anybody else in the nation, the consequences of the fact that the Creed is not lived up to in America. Yet their faith in the Creed is not simply a means of pleading their unfulfilled rights. They, like the whites, are under the spell of the great national suggestion. With one part of themselves they actually believe, as do the whites, that the Creed is ruling America.

These ideals of the essential dignity of the individual human being, of the fundamental equality of all men, and of certain inalienable rights to freedom, justice, and a fair opportunity represent to the American people the essential meaning of the nation's early struggle for independence. In the clarity and intellectual boldness of the Enlightenment period these tenets were written into the Declaration of Independence, the Preamble of the Constitution, the Bill of Rights and into the constitutions of the several states. The ideals of the American Creed have thus become the highest law of the land. The Supreme Court pays its reverence to these general principles when it declares what is constitutional and what is not. They have been elaborated upon by all national leaders, thinkers and statesmen. America has had, throughout its history, a continuous discussion of the principles and implications of democracy, a discussion which, in every epoch, measured by any standard, remained high, not only quantitatively but also qualitatively. The flow of learned treatises and popular tracts on the subject has not ebbed, nor is it likely to do so. In all wars, including the present one, the American Creed has been the ideological foundation of national morale.

The American Creed is identified with America's peculiar brand of nationalism, and it gives the common American his feeling of the historical mission of America in the world—a fact which just now becomes of global importance but which is also of highest significance for the particular problem studied in this book. The great national historian of the middle nineteenth century, George Bancroft, expressed this national feeling of pride and responsibility:

> In the fulness of time a republic rose in the wilderness of America. Thousands of years had passed away before this child of the ages could be born. From whatever there was of good in the systems of the former centuries she drew her nourishment; the wrecks of the past were her warnings . . . The fame of this only daughter of freedom went out into all the lands of the earth; from her the human race drew hope.

And Frederick J. Turner, who injected the naturalistic explanation into history that American democracy was a native-born product of the Western frontier, early in this century wrote in a similar vein:

> Other nations have been rich and prosperous and powerful. But the United States has believed that it had an original contribution to make to the history of society by the production of a self-determining, self-restrained, intelligent democracy.

Wilson's fourteen points and Roosevelt's four freedoms have more recently expressed to the world the boundless idealistic aspirations of this American Creed. For a century and more before the present epoch, when the oceans gave reality to the Monroe Doctrine, America at least applauded heartily every uprising of the people in any corner of the world. This was a tradition from America's own Revolution. The political revolutionaries of foreign countries were approved even by the conservatives in America. And America wanted generously to share its precious ideals and its happiness in enjoying a society ruled by its own people with all who would come here. James Truslow Adams tells us:

> The American dream that has lured tens of millions of all nations to our shores in the past century has not been a dream of merely material plenty, though that has doubtless counted heavily. It has been much more than that. It has been a dream of being able to grow to fullest development as man and woman, unhampered by the barriers which had slowly been erected in older civilizations, unrepressed by social orders which had developed for the benefit of classes rather than for the simple human being of any and every class. And that dream has been realized more fully in actual life here than anywhere else, though very imperfectly even among ourselves.

This is what the Western frontier country could say to the "East." And even the skeptic cannot help feeling that, perhaps, this youthful exuberant America has the destiny to do for the whole Old World what the frontier did to the old colonies. *American nationalism is permeated by the American Creed,* and therefore becomes international in its essence.

It is remarkable that a vast democracy with so many cultural disparities has been able to reach this unanimity of ideals and to elevate them supremely over the threshold of popular perception. Totalitarian fascism and nazism have not in their own countries—at least not in the short range of their present rule—succeeded in accomplishing a similar result, in spite of the fact that those governments, after having subdued the principal precepts most akin to the American Creed, have attempted to coerce the minds of their people by means of a centrally controlled, ruthless, and scientifically contrived apparatus of propaganda and violence.

There are more things to be wondered about. The disparity of national origin, language, religion, and culture, during the long era of mass immigration into the United States, has been closely correlated with income differences and social class distinctions. Successive vintages of "Old Americans" have owned the country and held the dominant political power; they have often despised and exploited "the foreigners." To this extent conditions in America must be said to have been particularly favorable to the stratification of a rigid class society.

But it has not come to be. On the question of why the trend took the other course, the historians, from Turner on, point to the free land and the boundless resources. The persistent drive from the Western frontier—now and then swelling into great tides as in the Jeffersonian movement around 1800, the Jacksonian movement a generation later, and the successive third-party movements and breaks in the traditional parties—could, however, reach its historical potency only because of the fact that America, from the Revolution onward, had an equalitarian creed as a going national *ethos.* The economic determinants and the force of the ideals can be shown to be interrelated. But the latter should not be relegated to merely a dependent variable. Vernon L. Parrington, the great historian of the development of the American mind, writes thus:

> The humanitarian idealism of the Declaration [of Independence] has always echoed as a battle-cry in the hearts of those who dream of an America dedicated to

democratic ends. It cannot be long ignored or repudiated, for sooner or later it returns to plague the council of practical politics. It is constantly breaking out in fresh revolt. . . . Without its freshening influence our political history would have been much more sordid and materialistic.

Indeed, the new republic began its career with a reaction. Charles Beard, in *An Economic Interpretation of the Constitution of the United States,* and a group of modern historians, throwing aside the much cherished national mythology which had blurred the difference in spirit between the Declaration of Independence and the Constitution, have shown that the latter was conceived in considerable suspicion against democracy and fear of "the people." It was dominated by property consciousness and designed as a defense against the democratic spirit let loose during the Revolution.

But, admitting all this, the Constitution which actually emerged out of the compromises in the drafting convention provided for the most democratic state structure in existence anywhere in the world at that time. And many of the safeguards so skillfully thought out by the conservatives to protect "the rich, the wellborn, and the capable" against majority rule melted when the new order began to function. Other conservative safeguards have fastened themselves into the political pattern. And "in the ceaseless conflict between the man and the dollar, between democracy and property"—again to quote Parrington—property has for long periods triumphed and blocked the will of the people. And there are today large geographical regions and fields of human life which, particularly when measured by the high goals of the American Creed, are conspicuously lagging. But taking the broad historical view, the American Creed has triumphed. It has given the main direction to change in this country. America has had gifted conservative statesmen and national leaders, and they have often determined the course of public affairs. But with few exceptions, only the liberals have gone down in history as national heroes. America is, as we shall point out, conservative in fundamental principles, and in much more than that, though hopefully experimentalistic in regard to much of the practical arrangements in society. But *the principles conserved are liberal* and some, indeed, are radical.

America got this dynamic Creed much as a political convenience and a device of strategy during the long struggle with the English Crown, the London Parliament and the various British powerholders in the colonies. It served as the rallying center for the growing national unity that was needed. Later it was a necessary device for building up a national morale in order to enlist and sustain the people in the Revolutionary War. In this spirit the famous declarations were resolved, the glorious speeches made, the inciting pamphlets written and spread. "The appeal to arms would seem to have been brought about by a minority of the American people, directed by a small group of skillful leaders, who, like Indian scouts, covered their tracks so cleverly, that only the keenest trailers can now follow their course and understand their strategy."

But the Creed, once set forth and disseminated among the American people, became so strongly entrenched in their hearts, and the circumstances have since then been so relatively favorable, that it has succeeded in keeping itself very much alive for more than a century and a half.

The American Creed is a humanistic liberalism developing out of the epoch of Enlightenment when America received its national consciousness and its political structure. The Revolution did not stop short of anything less than the heroic desire for the "emancipation of human nature." The enticing flavor of the eighteenth century, so dear to every intellectual and rationalist, has not been lost on the long journey up to the present time. Let us quote a contemporary exegesis:

> Democracy is a form of political association in which the general control and direction of the commonwealth is habitually determined by the bulk of the community in accordance with understandings and procedures providing for popular participation and consent. Its postulates are:
> 1. The essential dignity of man, the importance of protecting and cultivating his personality on a fraternal rather than upon a differential basis, of reconciling the needs of the personality within the frame-work of the common good in a formula of liberty, justice, welfare.
> 2. The perfectibility of man; confidence in the possibilities of the human personality, as over against the doctrines of caste, class, and slavery.
> 3. That the gains of commonwealths are essentially mass gains rather than the efforts of the few and should be diffused as promptly as possible throughout the community without too great delay or too wide a spread in differentials.
> 4. Confidence in the value of the consent of the governed expressed in institutions, understandings and practices as a basis of order, liberty, justice.
> 5. The value of decisions arrived at by common counsel rather than by violence and brutality.
> These postulates rest upon (1) reason in regarding the essential nature of the political man, upon (2) observation, experience and inference, and (3) the fulfillment of the democratic ideal is strengthened by a faith in the final triumph of ideals of human behavior in general and of political behavior in particular.

For practical purposes the main norms of the American Creed as usually pronounced are centered in the belief in equality and in the rights to liberty. In the Declaration of Independence—as in the earlier Virginia Bill of Rights—equality was given the supreme rank and the rights to liberty are posited as derived from equality. This logic was even more clearly expressed in Jefferson's original formulation of the first of the "self-evident truths": "All men are created equal *and from that equal creation* they derive rights inherent and unalienable, among which are the preservation of life and liberty and the pursuit of happiness."

Liberty, in a sense, was easiest to reach. It is a vague ideal: everything turns around *whose* liberty is preserved, to *what extent* and *in what direction*. In society liberty for one may mean the suppression of liberty for others. The result of competition will be determined by who got a head start and who is handicapped. In America as everywhere else—and sometimes, perhaps, on the average, a little more ruthlessly—liberty often provided an opportunity for the stronger to rob the weaker. Against this, the equalitarianism in the Creed has been persistently revolting. The struggle is far from ended. The reason why American liberty was not more dangerous to equality was, of course, the open frontier and the free land. When opportunity became bounded in the last generation, the inherent conflict between equality and liberty flared up. Equality is slowly winning. The New Deal during the 'thirties was a landslide.

If the European philosophy of Enlightenment was one of the ideological roots of the American Creed, another equally important one was Christianity, particularly as it took the form in the colonies of various lower class Protestant sects, split off from the Anglican Church. "Democracy was envisaged in religious terms long before it assumed a political terminology."

It is true that modern history has relegated to the category of the pious patriotic myths the popular belief that *all* the colonies had been founded to get religious liberty, which could not be had in the Old World. Some of the colonies were commercial adventures and the settlers came to them, and even to the religious colonies later, to improve their economic status. It is also true that the churches in the early colonial times did not always exactly represent the idea of democratic government in America but most often a harsher tyranny over people's souls and behavior than either King or Parliament ever cared to wield.

But the myth itself is a social reality with important effects. It was strong already in the period of the Revolution and continued to grow. A small proportion of new immigrants throughout the nineteenth century came for religious reasons, or partly so, and a great many more wanted to rationalize their uprooting and transplantation in such terms. So religion itself in America took on a spirit of fight for liberty. The Bible is full of support for such a spirit. It consists to a large extent of the tales of oppression and redemption from oppression: in the Old Testament of the Jewish people and in the New Testament of the early Christians. The rich and mighty are most often the wrong-doers, while the poor and lowly are the followers of God and Christ.

The basic teaching of Protestant Christianity is democratic. We are all poor sinners and have the same heavenly father. The concept of natural rights in the philosophy of Enlightenment corresponded rather closely with the idea of moral law in the Christian faith:

> The doctrine of the free individual, postulating the gradual escape of men from external political control, as they learned to obey the moral law, had its counterpart in the emphasis of evangelicism upon the freedom of the regenerated man from the terrors of the Old Testament code framed for the curbing of unruly and sinful generations. The philosophy of progress was similar to the Utopian hopes of the millennarians. The mission of American democracy to save the world from the oppression of autocrats was a secular version of the destiny of Christianity to save the world from the governance of Satan.

But apart from the historical problem of the extent to which church and religion in America actually inspired the American Creed, they became a powerful container and preserver of the Creed when it was once in existence. This was true from the beginning. While in Europe after the Napoleonic Wars the increasing power of the churches everywhere spelled a period of reaction, the great revivals beginning around 1800 in America were a sort of religious continuation of the Revolution.

> In this way great numbers whom the more-or-less involved theory of natural rights had escaped came under the leveling influence of a religious doctrine which held that all men were equal in the sight of God. Throughout the Revival period the upper classes looked upon the movement as "a religious distemper" which spread like a contagious disease, and they pointed out that it made its greatest appeal to "those of weak intellect and unstable emotions, women, adolescents, and Negroes." But to the poor farmer who had helped to win the Revolution only to find himself oppressed as much by the American ruling classes as he had ever been by Crown officials, the movement was "the greatest stir of Religion since the day of Pentecost."

Religion is still a potent force in American life. "They are a religious people," observed Lord Bryce about Americans a half a century ago, with great understanding for the importance of this fact for their national ideology. American scientific observers are likely to get their attentions fixed upon the process of progressive secularization to the extent that they do not see this main fact, that America probably is still the most religious country in the Western world. Political leaders are continuously deducing the American Creed out of the Bible. Vice-President Henry Wallace, in his historic speech of May 8, 1942, to the Free World Association, where he declared the present war to be "a fight between a slave world and a free world" and declared himself for "a people's peace" to inaugurate "the century of the common man," spoke thus:

> The idea of freedom—the freedom that we in the United States know and love so well—is derived from the Bible with its extraordinary emphasis on the dignity of the individual. Democracy is the only true political expression of Christianity.
>
> The prophets of the Old Testament were the first to preach social justice. But that which was sensed by the prophets many centuries before Christ was not given complete and powerful political expression until our Nation was formed as a Federal Union a century and a half ago.

Ministers have often been reactionaries in America. They have often tried to stifle free speech; they have organized persecution of unpopular dissenters and have even, in some regions, been active as the organizers of the Ku Klux Klan and similar "un-American" (in terms of the American Creed) movements. But, on the whole, church and religion in America are a force strengthening the American Creed. The fundamental tenets of Christianity press for expression even in the most bigoted setting. And, again on the whole, American religion is not particularly bigoted, but on the contrary, rather open-minded. The mere fact that there are many denominations, and that there is competition between them, forces American churches to a greater tolerance and ecumenical understanding and to a greater humanism and interest in social problems than the people in the churches would otherwise call for.

I also believe that American churches and their teachings have contributed something essential to the emotional temper of the Creed and, indeed, of the American people. Competent and sympathetic foreign observers have always noted the generosity and helpfulness of Americans. This and the equally conspicuous formal democracy in human contacts have undoubtedly had much to do with the predominantly lower class origin of the American people, and even more perhaps, with the mobility and the opportunities—what de Tocqueville called the "equality of condition"—in the nation when it was in its formative stage. But I cannot help feeling that the Christian neighborliness of the common American reflects, also, an influence from the churches. Apart from its origin, this temper of the Americans is part and parcel of the American Creed. It shows up in the Americans' readiness to make financial sacrifices for charitable purposes. No country has so many cheerful givers as America. It was not only "rugged individualism," nor a relatively continuous prosperity, that made it possible for America to get along without a publicly organized welfare policy almost up to the Great Depression in the 'thirties but it was also the world's most generous private charity.

The third main ideological influence behind the American Creed is English law. The indebtedness of American civilization to the culture of the mother country is nowhere else as great as in respect to the democratic concept of law and order, which it inherited almost without noticing it. It is the glory of England that, after many generations of hard struggle, it established the principles of justice, equity, and equality before the law even in an age when the rest of Europe (except for the cultural islands of Switzerland, Iceland, and Scandinavia) based personal security on the arbitrary police and on *lettres de cachet*.

This concept of a government "of laws and not of men" contained certain fundamentals of both equality and liberty. It will be a part of our task to study how these elemental demands are not nearly realized even in present-day America. But in the American Creed they have never been questioned. And it is no exaggeration to state that the philosophical ideas of human equality and the inalienable rights to life, liberty, and property, hastily sowed on American ground in a period of revolution when they were opportune—even allowing ever so much credit to the influences from the free life on the Western frontier—would not have struck root as they did if the soil had not already been cultivated by English law. . . .

From the point of view of the American Creed the status accorded the Negro in America represents nothing more and nothing less than a century-long lag of public morals. In principle the Negro problem was settled long ago; in practice the solution is not effectuated. The Negro in America has not yet been given the elemental civil and political rights of formal democracy, including a fair opportunity to earn his living, upon which a general accord was already won when the American Creed was first taking form. And this anachronism constitutes the contemporary "problem" both to Negroes and to whites.

If those rights were respected, many other pressing social problems would, of course, still remain. Many Negroes would, together with many whites, belong to groups which would invoke the old ideals of equality and liberty in demanding more effective protection for their social and economic opportunities. But there would no longer be a *Negro* problem. This does not mean that the Negro problem is an easy problem to solve. It is a tremendous task for theoretical research to find out why the Negro's status is what it is. In its unsolved form it further intertwines with all other social problems. It is simple only in the technical sense that in America the value premises—if they are conceived to be the ideals of the American Creed—are extraordinarily specific and definite.

Finally, in order to avoid possible misunderstandings, it should be explained that we have called this Creed "American" in the sense that it is adhered to by the Americans. This is the only matter which interests us in this book, which is focused upon the Negro problem as part of American life and American politics. But this Creed is, of course, no American monopoly. With minor variations, some of which, however, are not without importance, the American Creed is the common democratic creed. "American ideals" are just humane ideals as they have matured in our common Western civilization upon the foundation of Christianity and pre-Christian legalism and under the influence of the economic, scientific, and political development over a number of centuries. The American Creed is older and wider than America itself.

CLEMENT GREENBERG

"Avant-Garde and Kitsch"
1939

The "high" culture produced by an avant-garde of critical artists true to the formal imperatives of their art will resist the manipulations of totalitarian politics, Clement Greenberg (1909–1994) argued in 1939. But such "lower" arts as "magazine covers, illustrations, ads, slick and pulp fiction, comics, Tin Pan Alley music, tap dancing, Hollywood movies, etc." can easily serve the nefarious political purposes of the worst of contemporary political regimes. This association of modernist culture with lofty moral and political purpose proved an inspiration to many artists and critics during the midcentury decades. But in later years it was much resented; Greenberg became a favorite target for antielitists eager to defend "popular culture" against what they saw as the patronizing, arrogant dismissal encouraged by Greenberg.

A suspicion of mass culture on the part of Greenberg and many of his contemporaries was driven, in part, by political experiences of the 1930s involving the communist movement. Leaders of this movement had often defended the use of art as a form of propaganda and had condemned critics who, out of an apparent excess of aesthetic scruple, withheld approval of politically functional art. The *Partisan Review* established its reputation by proclaiming both socialist politics and the autonomy of artists and intellectuals. This combination of commitments informs Greenberg's "Avant-Garde and Kitsch," Harold Rosenberg's "The Fall of Paris" (1940), and a number of other classic *Partisan Review* contributions of the late 1930s and early 1940s. For a study of this magazine and the writers who made it, see Terry A. Cooney, *The Rise of the New York Intellectuals: Partisan Review and Its Circle, 1934–1945* (Madison, 1986). Although socialist politics had dropped out of the work of virtually all of the *Partisan Review* intellectuals by the mid-1940s, the faith in the political and moral efficacy of the independent artist-hero remained a prominent feature of the cultural politics of the Cold War era.

Greenberg was an obscure customshouse clerk when he produced this vindication of modernist high culture. But he soon became one of the most influential art critics of his time, especially in his capacity as a columnist for *The Nation*. The most important of his essays were published in a collection edited by John O'Brien, *Clement Greenberg* (Chicago, 1986). Greenberg's career is the subject of Donald B. Kuspit, *Clement Greenberg: Art Critic* (Madison, 1979).

One and the same civilization produces simultaneously two such different things as a poem by T. S. Eliot and a Tin Pan Alley song, or a painting by Braque and a *Saturday Evening Post* cover. All four are on the order of culture, and ostensibly, parts of the same culture and products of the same society. Here, however, their connection seems to end. A poem by Eliot and a poem by Eddie Guest—what perspective of culture is large enough to enable us to situate them in an enlightening relation to each other? Does the fact that a disparity such as this within the frame of a single cultural tradition, is and has been taken for granted—does this fact indicate that the disparity is a part of the natural order of things? Or is it something entirely new, and particular to our age?

The answer involves more than an investigation in aesthetics. It appears to me that it is necessary to examine more closely and with more originality than hitherto the relationship between aesthetic experience as met by the specific—not generalized—individual, and the social and historical contexts in which that experience takes place. What is brought to light will answer, in addition to the question posed above, other and perhaps more important ones.

A society, as it becomes less and less able, in the course of its development, to justify the inevitability of its particular forms, breaks up the accepted notions upon which artists and writers must depend in large part for communication with their audiences. It becomes difficult to assume anything. All the verities involved by religion, authority, tradition, style, are thrown into question, and the writer or artist is no longer able to estimate the response of his audience to the symbols and references with which he works. In the past such a state of affairs has usually resolved itself into a motionless Alexandrianism, an academicism in which the really important issues are left untouched because they involve controversy, and in which creative activity dwindles to virtuosity in the small details of form, all larger questions being decided by the precedent of the old masters. The same themes are mechanically varied in a hundred different works, and yet nothing new is produced: Statius, mandarin verse, Roman sculpture, Beaux Arts painting, neo-republican architecture.

It is among the hopeful signs in the midst of the decay of our present society that we—some of us—have been unwilling to accept this last phase for our own culture. In seeking to go beyond Alexandrianism, a part of Western bourgeois society has produced something unheard of heretofore: avant-garde culture. A superior consciousness of history—more precisely, the appearance of a new kind of criticism of society, an historical criticism—made this possible. This criticism has not confronted our present society with timeless utopias, but has soberly examined in the terms of history and of cause and effect the antecedents, justifications and functions of the forms that lie at the heart of every society. Thus our present bourgeois social order was shown to be, not an eternal, "natural" condition of life, but simply the latest term in a succession of social orders. New perspectives of this kind, becoming a part of the advanced intellectual conscience of the fifth and sixth decades of the nineteenth century, soon were absorbed by artists and poets, even if unconsciously for the most part. It was no accident, therefore, that the birth of the avant-garde coincided chronologically—and geographically too—with the first bold development of scientific revolutionary thought in Europe.

True, the first settlers of Bohemia—which was then identical with the avant-garde—turned out soon to be demonstratively uninterested in politics. Nevertheless, without the circulation of revolutionary ideas in the air about them, they would never

Source: Partisan Review (Fall 1939), 34–49. Reprinted by permission of the University of Chicago Press.

have been able to isolate their concept of the "bourgeois" in order to define what they were *not*. Nor, without the moral aid of revolutionary political attitudes would they have had the courage to assert themselves as aggressively as they did against the prevailing standards of society. Courage indeed was needed for this, because the avant-garde's emigration from bourgeois society to Bohemia meant also an emigration from the markets of capitalism, upon which artists and writers had been thrown by the falling away of aristocratic patronage. (Ostensibly, at least, it meant this—meant starving in a garret—although, as will be shown later, the avant-garde remained attached to bourgeois society precisely because it needed its money.)

Yet it is true that once the avant-garde had succeeded in "detaching" itself from society, it proceeded to turn around and repudiate revolutionary politics as well as bourgeois. The revolution was left inside society, a part of that welter of ideological struggle which art and poetry find so unpropitious as soon as it begins to involve those "precious," axiomatic beliefs upon which culture thus far has had to rest. Hence it was developed that the true and most important function of the avant-garde was not to "experiment," but to find a path along which it would be possible to keep culture *moving* in the midst of ideological confusion and violence. Retiring from public altogether, the avant-garde poet or artist sought to maintain the high level of his art by both narrowing and raising it to the expression of an absolute in which all relativities and contradictions would be either resolved or beside the point. "Art for art's sake" and "pure poetry" appear, and subject-matter or content becomes something to be avoided like a plague.

It has been in search of the absolute that the avant-garde has arrived at "abstract" or "non-objective" art—and poetry, too. The avant-garde poet or artist tries in effect to imitate God by creating something valid solely on its own terms in the way nature itself is valid, in the way a landscape—not its picture—is aesthetically valid; something *given,* increate, independent of meanings, similars, or originals. Content is to be dissolved so completely into form that the work of art or literature cannot be reduced in whole or in part to anything not itself.

But the absolute is absolute, and the poet or artist, being what he is, cherishes certain relative values more than others. The very values in the name of which he invokes the absolute are relative values, the values of aesthetics. And so he turns out to be imitating, not God—and here I use "imitate" in its Aristotelian sense—but the disciplines and processes of art and literature themselves. This is the genesis of the "abstract." In turning his attention away from subject-matter or common experience, the poet or artist turns it in upon the medium of his own craft. The non-representational or "abstract," if it is to have aesthetic validity, cannot be arbitrary and accidental, but must stem from obedience to some worthy constraint or original. This constraint, once the world of common, extraverted experience has been renounced, can only be found in the very processes or disciplines by which art and literature have already imitated the former. These themselves become the subject matter of art and literature. If, to continue with Aristotle, all art and literature are imitation, then what we have here is the imitation of imitating. To quote Yeats:

> "Nor is there singing school but studying
> Monuments of its own magnificence."

Picasso, Braque, Mondrian, Miro, Kandinsky, Brancusi, even Klee, Matisse and Cezanne, derive their chief inspiration from the medium they work in. The excitement of their art seems to lie most of all in its pure preoccupation with the invention and arrangement of spaces, surfaces, shapes, colors, etc., to the exclusion of whatever is not necessarily implicated in these factors. The attention of poets like Rimbaud, Mallarmé, Valéry, Eluard, Pound, Hart Crane, Stevens, even Rilke and Yeats, appears to be centered on the effort to create poetry and on the "moments" themselves of poetic conversion rather than on experience to be converted into poetry. Of course, this cannot exclude other preoccupations in their work, for poetry must deal with words, and words must communicate. Certain poets, such as Mallarmé and Valéry, are more radical in this respect than others—leaving aside those poets who have tried to compose poetry in pure sound alone. However, if it were easier to define poetry, modern poetry would be much more "pure" and "abstract." . . . As for the other fields of literature—the definition of avant-garde aesthetics advanced here is no Procrustean bed. But aside from the fact that most of our best contemporary novelists have gone to school with the avant-garde, it is significant that Gide's most ambitious book is a novel about the writing of a novel, and that Joyce's *Ulysses* and *Finnegan's Wake* seem to be above all, as one French critic says, the reduction of experience to expression for the sake of expression, the expression mattering more than what is being expressed.

That avant-garde culture is the imitation of imitating—the fact itself—calls for neither approval nor disapproval. It is true that this culture contains within itself some of the very Alexandrianism it seeks to overcome. The lines quoted from Yeats above referred to Byzantium, which is very close to Alexandria; and in a sense this imitation of imitating is a superior sort of Alexandrianism. But there is one most important difference: the avant-garde moves, while Alexandrianism stands still. And this, precisely, is what justifies the avant-garde's methods and makes them necessary. The necessity lies in the fact that by no other means is it possible today to create art and literature of a high order. To quarrel with necessity by throwing about terms like "formalism," "purism," "ivory tower" and so forth is either dull or dishonest. This is not to say, however, that it is to the *social* advantage of the avant-garde that it is what it is. Quite the opposite.

The avant-garde's specialization of itself, the fact that its best artists are artists' artists, its best poets, poets' poets, has estranged a great many of those who were capable formerly of enjoying and appreciating ambitious art and literature, but who are now unwilling or unable to acquire an initiation into their craft secrets. The masses have always remained more or less indifferent to culture in the process of development. But today such culture is being abandoned by those to whom it actually belongs—our ruling class. For it is to the latter that the avant-garde belongs. No culture can develop without a social basis, without a source of stable income. And in the case of the avant-garde this was provided by an elite among the ruling class of that society from which it assumed itself to be cut off, but to which it has always remained attached by an umbilical cord of gold. The paradox is real. And now this elite is rapidly shrinking. Since the avant-garde forms the only living culture we now have, the survival in the near future of culture in general is thus threatened.

We must not be deceived by superficial phenomena and local successes. Picasso's shows still draw crowds, and T. S. Eliot is taught in the universities; the dealers in modernist art are still in business, and the publishers still publish some "difficult" poetry. But the avant-garde itself, already sensing the danger, is becoming more and more timid every day that passes. Academicism and commercialism are appearing in the strangest places. This can mean only one thing: that the avant-garde is becoming unsure of the audience it depends on—the rich and the cultivated.

Is it the nature of avant-garde culture that is alone responsible for the danger it finds itself in? Or is that only a dangerous liability? Are there other, and perhaps more important, factors involved?

Where there is an avant-garde, generally we also find a rear-guard. True enough—simultaneously with the entrance of the avant-garde, a second new cultural phenomenon appeared in the industrial West: that thing to which the Germans give the wonderful name of *Kitsch*: popular, commercial art and literature with their chromeotypes, magazine covers, illustrations, ads, slick and pulp fiction, comics, Tin Pan Alley music, tap dancing, Hollywood movies, etc., etc. For some reason this gigantic apparition has always been taken for granted. It is time we looked into its whys and wherefores.

Kitsch is a product of the industrial revolution which urbanized the masses of Western Europe and America and established what is called universal literacy.

Previous to this the only market for formal culture, as distinguished from folk culture, had been among those who in addition to being able to read and write could command the leisure and comfort that always goes hand in hand with cultivation of some sort. This until then had been inextricably associated with literacy. But with the introduction of universal literacy, the ability to read and write became almost a minor skill like driving a car, and it no longer served to distinguish an individual's cultural inclinations, since it was no longer the exclusive concomitant of refined tastes. The peasants who settled in the cities as proletariat and petty bourgeois learned to read and write for the sake of efficiency, but they did not win the leisure and comfort necessary for the enjoyment of the city's traditional culture. Losing, nevertheless, their taste for the folk culture whose background was the countryside, and discovering a new capacity for boredom at the same time, the new urban masses set up a pressure on society to provide them with a kind of culture fit for their own consumption. To fill the demand of the new market a new commodity was devised: ersatz culture, kitsch, destined for those who, insensible to the values of genuine culture, are hungry nevertheless for the diversion that only culture of some sort can provide.

Kitsch, using for raw material the debased and academicized simulacra of genuine culture, welcomes and cultivates this insensibility. It is the source of its profits. Kitsch is mechanical and operates by formulas. Kitsch is vicarious experience and faked sensations. Kitsch changes according to style, but remains always the same. Kitsch is the epitome of all that is spurious in the life of our times. Kitsch pretends to demand nothing of its customers except their money—not even their time.

The pre-condition for kitsch, a condition without which kitsch would be impossible, is the availability close at hand of a fully matured cultural tradition, whose discoveries, acquisitions and perfected self-consciousness kitsch can take advantage of for its own ends. It borrows from it devices, tricks, strategems, rules of thumb, themes, converts them into a system and discards the rest. It draws its life blood, so to speak, from this reservoir of accumulated experience. This is what is really meant when it is said that the popular art and literature of today were once the daring, esoteric art and literature of yesterday. Of course, no such thing is true. What is meant is that when enough time has elapsed the new is looted for new "twists," which are then watered down and served up as kitsch. Self-evidently, all kitsch is academic, and conversely, all that's academic is kitsch. For what is called the academic as such no longer has an independent existence, but has become the stuffed-shirt "front" for kitsch. The methods of industrialism displace the handicrafts.

Because it can be turned out mechanically, kitsch has become an integral part of our productive system in a way in which true culture could never be except accidentally. It has been capitalized at a tremendous investment which must show commensurate returns; it is compelled to extend as well as to keep its markets. While it is essentially its own salesman, a great sales apparatus has nevertheless been created for it, which brings pressure to bear on every member of society. Traps are laid even in those areas, so to speak, that are the preserves of genuine culture. It is not enough today, in a country like ours, to have an inclination towards the latter; one must have a true passion for it that will give him the power to resist the faked article that surrounds and presses in on him from the moment he is old enough to look at the funny papers. Kitsch is deceptive. It has many different levels, and some of them are high enough to be dangerous to the naive seeker of true light. A magazine like the *New Yorker,* which is fundamentally high-class kitsch for the luxury trade, converts and waters down a great deal of avant-garde material for its own uses. Nor is every single item of kitsch altogether worthless. Now and then it produces something of merit, something that has an authentic folk flavor; and these accidental and isolated instances have fooled people who should know better.

Kitsch's enormous profits are a source of temptation to the avant-garde itself, and its members have not always resisted this temptation. Ambitious writers and artists will modify their work under the pressure of kitsch, if they do not succumb to it entirely. And then those puzzling border-line cases appear, such as the popular novelist, Simenon, in France, and Steinbeck in this country. The net result is always to the detriment of true culture, in any case.

Kitsch has not been confined to the cities in which it was born, but has flowed out over the countryside, wiping out folk culture. Nor has it shown any regard for geographical and national-cultural boundaries. Another mass product of Western industrialism, it has gone on a triumphal tour of the world, crowding out and defacing native cultures in one colonial country after another, so that it is now by way of becoming a universal culture, the first universal culture ever beheld. Today the Chinaman, no less than the South American Indian, the Hindu, no less than the Polynesian, have come to prefer to the products of their native art magazine covers, rotogravure sections and calendar girls. How is this virulence of kitsch, this irresistible attractiveness, to be explained? Naturally, machine-made kitsch can undersell the native handmade article, and the prestige of the West also helps, but why is kitsch a so much more profitable export article than Rembrandt? One, after all, can be reproduced as cheaply as the other.

In his last article on the Soviet cinema in the *Partisan Review,* Dwight Macdonald points out that kitsch has in the last ten years become the dominant culture in Soviet Russia. For this he blames the political regime—not only for the fact that kitsch is the official culture, but also that it is actually the dominant, most popular culture; and he quotes the following from Kurt London's *The Seven Soviet Arts:* ". . . the attitude of the masses both to the old and new art styles probably remains essentially dependent on the nature of the education afforded them by their respective states." Macdonald goes on to say: "Why after all should ignorant peasants prefer Repin (a leading exponent of Russian academic kitsch in painting) to Picasso, whose abstract technique is at least as relevant to their own primitive folk art as is the former's realistic style? No, if the masses crowd into the Tretyakov (Moscow's museum of contemporary Russian art: kitsch) it is largely because they have been conditioned to shun 'formalism' and to admire 'socialist realism'."

In the first place it is not a question of a choice between merely the old and merely the new, as London seems to think—but of a choice between the bad, up-to-date old and the genuinely new. The alternative to Picasso is not Michelangelo, but kitsch. In the second place, neither in backward Russia nor in the advanced West do the masses prefer kitsch simply because their governments condition them towards it. Where state educational systems take the trouble to mention art, we are told to respect the old masters, not kitsch; and yet we go and hang Maxfield Parrish or his equivalent on our walls, instead of Rembrandt and Michelangelo. Moreover, as Macdonald himself points out, around 1925 when the Soviet regime was encouraging avant-garde cinema, the Russian masses continued to prefer Hollywood movies. No, "conditioning" does not explain the potency of kitsch. . . .

All values are human values, relative values, in art as well as elsewhere. Yet there does seem to have been more or less of a general agreement among the cultivated of mankind over the ages as to what is good art and what bad. Taste has varied, but not beyond certain limits: contemporary connoisseurs agree with eighteenth century Japanese that Hokusai was one of the greatest artists of his time; we even agree with the ancient Egyptians that Third and Fourth Dynasty art was the most worthy of being selected as their paragon by those who came after. We may have come to prefer Giotto to Raphael, but we still do not deny that Raphael was one of the best painters of his *time*. There has been an agreement then, and this agreement rests, I believe, on a fairly constant distinction made between those values only to be found in art and the values which can be found elsewhere. Kitsch, by virtue of rationalized technique that draws on science and industry, has erased this distinction in practice.

Let us see for example what happens when an ignorant Russian peasant such as Macdonald mentions stands with hypothetical freedom of choice before two paintings, one by Picasso, the other by Repin. In the first he sees, let us say, a play of lines, colors and spaces that represent a woman. The abstract technique—to accept Macdonald's supposition, which I am inclined to doubt—reminds him somewhat of the icons he has left behind him in the village, and he feels the attraction of the familiar. We will even suppose that he faintly surmises some of the great art values the cultivated find in Picasso. He turns next to Repin's picture and sees a battle scene. The technique is not so familiar—as technique. But that weighs very little with the peasant; for he suddenly discovers values in Repin's picture which seem far superior to the values he has been accustomed to finding in icon art; and the unfamiliar technique itself is one of the sources of those values: the values of the vividly recognizable, the miraculous and the sympathetic. In Repin's picture the peasant recognizes and sees things in the way in which he recognizes and sees things outside of pictures—there is no discontinuity between art and life, no need to accept a convention and say to oneself, that icon represents Jesus because it intends to represent Jesus, even if it does not remind me very much of a man. That Repin can paint so realistically that identifications are self-evident immediately and without any effort on the part of the spectator—that is miraculous. The peasant is also pleased by the wealth of self-evident meanings which he finds in the picture: "it tells a story." Picasso and the icons are so austere and barren in comparison. What is more, Repin heightens reality and makes it dramatic: sunset, exploding shells, running and falling men. There is no longer any question of Picasso or icons. Repin is what the peasant wants, and nothing else but Repin. It is lucky, however, for Repin that the peasant is protected from the products of American capitalism, for he would not stand a chance next to a Saturday Evening Post cover by Norman Rockwell.

Ultimately, it can be said that the cultivated spectator derives the same values from

Picasso that the peasant gets from Repin, since what the latter enjoys in Repin is some-how art too, on however low a scale, and he is sent to look at pictures by the same instincts that send the cultivated spectator. But the ultimate values which the cultivated spectator derives from Picasso are derived at a second remove, as the result of reflection upon the immediate impression left by the plastic values. It is only then that the rec-ognizable, the miraculous and the sympathetic enter. They are not immediately or exter-nally present in Picasso's painting, but must be projected into it by the spectator sen-sitive enough to react sufficiently to plastic qualities. They belong to the "reflected" effect. In Repin, on the other hand, the "reflected" effect has already been included in the picture, ready for the spectator's unreflective enjoyment. Where Picasso paints *cause,* Repin paints *effect.* Repin predigests art for the spectator and spares him effort, provides him with a short cut to the pleasure of art that detours what is necessarily difficult in genuine art. Repin, or kitsch, is synthetic art.

The same point can be made with respect to kitsch literature: it provides vicarious experience for the insensitive with far greater immediacy than serious fiction can hope to do. And Eddie Guest and the *Indian Love Lyrics* are more poetic than T. S. Eliot and Shakespeare.

If the avant-garde imitates the processes of art, kitsch, we now see, imitates its effects. The neatness of this antithesis is more then contrived; it corresponds to and defines the tremendous interval that separates from each other two such simultaneous cultural phenomena as the avant-garde and kitsch. This interval, too great to be closed by all the infinite gradations of popularized "modernism" and "modernistic" kitsch, corresponds in turn to a social interval, a social interval that has always existed in formal culture as elsewhere in civilized society, and whose two termini converge and diverge in fixed relation to the increasing or decreasing stability of the given society. There has always been on one side the minority of the powerful—and therefore the cultivated—and on the other the great mass of the exploited and poor—and therefore the ignorant. Formal culture has always belonged to the first, while the last have had to content themselves with folk or rudimentary culture, or kitsch.

In a stable society which functions well enough to hold in solution the contradic-tions between its classes the cultural dichotomy becomes somewhat blurred. The axioms of the few are shared by the many; the latter believe superstitiously what the former believe soberly. And at such moments in history the masses are able to feel wonder and admiration for the culture, on no matter how high a plane, of its masters. This applies at least to plastic culture, which is accessible to all.

In the Middle Ages the plastic artist paid lip service at least to the lowest common denominators of experience. This even remained true to some extent until the seven-teenth century. There was available for imitation a universally valid conceptual reality, whose order the artist could not tamper with. The subject matter of art was prescribed by those who commissioned works of art, which were not created, as in bourgeois society, on speculation. Precisely because his content was determined in advance, the artist was free to concentrate on his medium. He needed not to be philosopher or visionary, but simply artificer. As long as there was general agreement as to what were the worthiest subjects for art, the artist was relieved of the necessity to be original and inventive in his "matter" and could devote all his energy to formal problems. For him the medium became, privately, professionally, the content of his art, even as today his medium is the public content of the abstract painter's art—with that difference, how-ever, that the medieval artist had to suppress his professional preoccupation in public—

had always to suppress and subordinate the personal and professional in the finished, official work of art. If, as an ordinary member of the Christian community, he felt some personal emotion about his subject matter, this only contributed to the enrichment of the work's public meaning. Only with the Renaissance do the inflections of the personal become legitimate, still to be kept, however, within the limits of the simply and universally recognizable. And only with Rembrandt do "lonely" artists begin to appear, lonely in their art.

But even during the Renaissance, and as long as Western art was endeavoring to perfect its technique, victories in this realm could only be signalized by success in realistic imitation, since there was no other objective criterion at hand. Thus the masses could still find in the art of their masters objects of admiration and wonder. Even the bird who pecked at the fruit in Zeuxes' picture could applaud.

It is a platitude that art becomes caviar to the general when the reality it imitates no longer corresponds even roughly to the reality recognized by the general. Even then, however, the resentment the common man may feel is silenced by the awe in which he stands of the patrons of this art. Only when he becomes dissatisfied with the social order they administer does he begin to criticize their culture. Then the plebeian finds courage for the first time to voice his opinions openly. Every man, from Tammany aldermen to Austrian house-painters, finds that he is entitled to his opinion. Most often this resentment towards culture is to be found where the dissatisfaction with society is a reactionary dissatisfaction which expresses itself in revivalism and puritanism, and latest of all, in fascism. Here revolvers and torches begin to be mentioned in the same breath as culture. In the name of godliness or the blood's health, in the name of simple ways and solid virtues, the statue-smashing commences.

Returning to our Russian peasant for the moment, let us suppose that after he has chosen Repin in preference to Picasso, the state's educational apparatus comes along and tells him that he is wrong, that he should have chosen Picasso—and shows him why. It is quite possible for the Soviet state to do this. But things being as they are in Russia—and everywhere else—the peasant soon finds that the necessity of working hard all day for his living and the rude, uncomfortable circumstances in which he lives do not allow him enough leisure, energy and comfort to train for the enjoyment of Picasso. This needs, after all, a considerable amount of "conditioning." Superior culture is one of the most artificial of all human creations, and the peasant finds no "natural" urgency within himself that will drive him towards Picasso in spite of all difficulties. In the end the peasant will go back to kitsch when he feels like looking at pictures, for he can enjoy kitsch without effort. The state is helpless in this matter and remains so as long as the problems of production have not been solved in a socialist sense. The same holds true, of course, for capitalist countries and makes all talk of art for the masses there nothing but demagogy.

Where today a political regime establishes an official cultural policy, it is for the sake of demagogy. If kitsch is the official tendency of culture in Germany, Italy and Russia, it is not because their respective governments are controlled by philistines, but because kitsch is the culture of the masses in these countries, as it is everywhere else. The encouragement of kitsch is merely another of the inexpensive ways in which totalitarian regimes seek to ingratiate themselves with their subjects. Since these regimes cannot raise the cultural level of the masses—even if they wanted to—by anything short of a surrender to international socialism, they will flatter the masses by bringing all culture down to their level. It is for this reason that the avant-garde is outlawed, and not so much because a superior culture is inherently a more critical culture. (Whether or not the avant-garde could possibly flourish under a totalitarian regime is not pertinent to the question at this point.) As matter of fact, the main trouble with avant-garde art and literature, from the point of view of Fascists and Stalinists, is not that they are too critical, but that they are too "innocent," that it is too difficult to inject effective propaganda into them, that kisch is more pliable to this end. Kitsch keeps a dictator in closer contact with the "soul" of the people. Should the official culture be one superior to the general mass-level, there would be a danger of isolation.

Nevertheless, if the masses were conceivably to ask for avant-garde art and literature, Hitler, Mussolini and Stalin would not hesitate long in attempting to satisfy such a demand. Hitler is a bitter enemy of the avant-garde, both on doctrinal and personal grounds, yet this did not prevent Goebbels in 1932–33 from strenuously courting avant-garde artists and writers. When Gottfried Benn, an Expressionist poet, came over to the Nazis he was welcomed with a great fanfare, although at that very moment Hitler was denouncing Expressionism as *Kulturbolschewismus*. This was at a time when the Nazis felt that the prestige which the avant-garde enjoyed among the cultivated German public could be of advantage to them, and practical considerations of this nature, the Nazis being the skilful politicians they are, have always taken precedence over Hitler's personal inclinations. Later the Nazis realized that it was more practical to accede to the wishes of the masses in matters of culture than to those of their paymasters; the latter, when it came to a question of preserving power, were as willing to sacrifice their culture as they were their moral principles, while the former, precisely because power was being withheld from them, had to be cozened in every other way possible. It was necessary to promote on a much more grandiose style than in the democracies the illusion that the masses actually rule. The literature and art they enjoy and understand were to be proclaimed the only true art and literature and any other kind was to be suppressed. Under these circumstances people like Gottfried Benn, no matter how ardently they support Hitler, become a liability; and we hear no more of them in Nazi Germany.

We can see then that although from one point of view the personal philistinism of Hitler and Stalin is not accidental to the political roles they play, from another point of view it is only an incidentally contributory factor in determining the cultural policies of their respective regimes. Their personal philistinism simply adds brutality and double-darkness to policies they would be forced to support anyhow by the pressure of all their other policies—even were they, personally, devotees of avant-garde culture. What the acceptance of the isolation of the Russian Revolution forces Stalin to do, Hitler is compelled to do by his acceptance of the contradictions of capitalism and his efforts to freeze them. As for Mussolini—his case is a perfect example of the *disponibilité* of a realist in these matters. For years he bent a benevolent eye on the Futurists and built modernistic railroad stations and government-owned apartment houses. One can still see in the suburbs of Rome more modernistic apartments than almost anywhere else in the world. Perhaps Fascism wanted to show its up-to-datedness, to conceal the fact that it was a retrogression; perhaps it wanted to conform to the tastes of the wealthy élite it served. At any rate Mussolini seems to have realized lately that it would be more useful to him to please the cultural tastes of the Italian masses than those of their masters. The masses must be provided with objects of admiration and wonder; the latter can dispense with them. And so we find Mussolini announcing a "new Imperial style." Marinetti, Chirico, et al. are sent into the outer darkness, and the new railroad station in Rome will not be modernistic. That Mussolini was late in coming to this only illustrates again the relative hesitancy with which Italian fascism has drawn the necessary implications of its role. . . .

Capitalism in decline finds that whatever of quality it is still capable of producing becomes almost invariably a threat to its own existence. Advances in culture no less than advances in science and industry corrode the very society under whose aegis they are made possible. Here, as in every other question today, it becomes necessary to quote Marx word for word. Today we no longer look towards socialism for a new culture— as inevitably as one will appear, once we do have socialism. Today we look to socialism *simply* for the preservation of whatever living culture we have right now.

REINHOLD NIEBUHR

Selection from *The Children of Light and the Children of Darkness* 1944

Reinhold Niebuhr (1892–1971) was for several decades the nation's most quoted and respected critic of modern thought's drift away from explicitly Christian foundations. Niebuhr owed much of his influence to the skill with which he—a Protestant preacher and seminary professor—brought the perspectives of liberal theology to bear on the political, social, and cultural issues of the middle third of the twentieth century. An effective polemicist against pacifism, communism, and other utopian projects under attack in the 1940s and 1950s, Niebuhr won a large following among secular intellectuals ("atheists for Niebuhr," such men and women were sometimes called). Although Niebuhr was sometimes associated in the public mind with the neo-orthodox movement led by the Swiss theologian Karl Barth, his most vital engagements were decidedly more worldly and contemporary than Barth's. This was especially true of *Moral Man and Immoral Society* (New York, 1932), which first made Niebuhr famous. This work of political criticism supported collective action by workers against their capitalist oppressors, and it included a critique of Christian pacifism so vehement as to lead some of Niebuhr's ministerial colleagues to accuse him of abandoning the ethics of Jesus for the "tough-minded" views of Pontius Pilate. Niebuhr pulled back from this extremity in *An Interpretation of Christian Ethics* (New York, 1935), but the affairs of civil society always remained at the center of his gaze, and he continued to project a "tougher-than-thou" persona. In *The Children of Light and the Children of Darkness* (New York, 1944), a selection from which follows, Niebuhr criticized the intellectual tradition of the Enlightenment for what he insisted was its prevailing optimism regarding human character. Niebuhr's most theologically ambitious work was *The Nature and Destiny of Man*, 2 vols. (New York, 1943). The most influential book of his later career was an interpretation of the history of the United States in world-historical perspective, *The Irony of American History* (1952).

The best historical study of Niebuhr is Richard Wightman Fox, *Reinhold Niebuhr: A Biography* (New York, 1986), although many of Niebuhr's disciples and surviving friends found this book insufficiently warm in its appreciation for Niebuhr's personality and intellectual contributions. The widespread desire for a more consistently enthusiastic account is well satisfied by Charles C. Brown, *Niebuhr and His Age: Reinhold Niebuhr's Prophetic Role in the Twentieth Century* (Philadelphia, 1992). Niebuhr's brother, H. Richard Niebuhr (1894–1962), was also a distinguished theologian and is often confused with Reinhold Niebuhr. On this second Niebuhr, see Richard Fox, "H. Richard Niebuhr's Divided Kingdom," *American Quarterly* 42 (1990), 93–101. For a general history of American Protestantism during the era of the Niebuhr brothers' rise to prominence, see Martin E. Marty, *Modern American Religion: The Noise of Conflict, 1919–1941* (Chicago, 1991).

We may well designate the moral cynics, who know no law beyond their will and interest, with a scriptural designation of "children of this world" or "children of darkness." Those who believe that self-interest should be brought under the discipline of a higher law could then be termed "the children of light." This is no mere arbitrary device; for evil is always the assertion of some self-interest without regard to the whole, whether the whole be conceived as the immediate community, or the total community of mankind, or the total order of the world. The good is, on the other hand, always the harmony of the whole on various levels. Devotion to a subordinate and premature "whole" such as the nation, may of course become evil, viewed from the perspective of a larger whole, such as the community of mankind. The "children of light" may thus be defined as those who seek to bring self-interest under the discipline of a more universal law and in harmony with a more universal good.

According to the scripture "the children of this world are in their generation wiser than the children of light." This observation fits the modern situation. Our democratic civilization has been built, not by children of darkness but by foolish children of light. It has been under attack by the children of darkness, by the moral cynics, who declare that a strong nation need acknowledge no law beyond its strength. It has come close to complete disaster under this attack, not because it accepted the same creed as the cynics; but because it underestimated the power of self-interest, both individual and collective, in modern society. The children of light have not been as wise as the children of darkness.

The children of darkness are evil because they know no law beyond the self. They are wise, though evil, because they understand the power of self-interest. The children of light are virtuous because they have some conception of a higher law than their own will. They are usually foolish because they do not know the power of self-will. They underestimate the peril of anarchy in both the national and the international community. Modern democratic civilization is, in short, sentimental rather than cynical. It has an easy solution for the problem of anarchy and chaos on both the national and international level of community, because of its fatuous and superficial view of man. It does not know that the same man who is ostensibly devoted to the "common good" may have desires and ambitions, hopes and fears, which set him at variance with his neighbor.

It must be understood that the children of light are foolish not merely because they underestimate the power of self-interest among the children of darkness. They underestimate this power among themselves. The democratic world came so close to disaster not merely because it never believed that Nazism possessed the demonic fury which it avowed. Civilization refused to recognize the power of class interest in its own communities. It also spoke glibly of an international conscience; but the children of darkness meanwhile skilfully set nation against nation. They were thereby enabled to despoil one nation after another, without every civilized nation coming to the defence of each. Moral cynicism had a provisional advantage over moral sentimentality. Its advantage lay not merely in its own lack of moral scruple but also in its shrewd assessment of the power of self-interest, individual and national, among the children of light, despite their moral protestations.

Source: Reinhold Niebuhr, The Children of Light and the Children of Darkness (New York: Scribner's, 1944), 10–22, 31–38. Reprinted by permission of Prentice-Hall, Inc. Copyright renewed 1972 by Ursula Keppel-Compton Niebuhr.

While our modern children of light, the secularized idealists, were particularly foolish and blind, the more "Christian" children of light have been almost equally guilty of this error. Modern liberal Protestantism was probably even more sentimental in its appraisal of the moral realities in our political life than secular idealism, and Catholicism could see nothing but cynical rebellion in the modern secular revolt against Catholic universalism and a Catholic "Christian" civilization. In Catholic thought medieval political universalism is always accepted at face value. Rebellion against medieval culture is therefore invariably regarded as the fruit of moral cynicism. Actually the middle-class revolt against the feudal order was partially prompted by a generous idealism, not unmixed of course with peculiar middle-class interests. The feudal order was not so simply a Christian civilization as Catholic defenders of it aver. It compounded its devotion to a universal order with the special interests of the priestly and aristocratic bearers of effective social power. The rationalization of their unique position in the feudal order may not have been more marked than the subsequent rationalization of bourgeois interests in the liberal world. But it is idle to deny this "ideological taint" in the feudal order and to pretend that rebels against the order were merely rebels against order as such. They were rebels against a particular order which gave an undue advantage to the aristocratic opponents of the middle classes. The blindness of Catholicism to its own ideological taint is typical of the blindness of the children of light.

Our modern civilization, as a middle-class revolt against an aristocratic and clerical order, was irreligious partly because a Catholic civilization had so compounded the eternal sanctities with the contingent and relative justice and injustice of an agrarian-feudal order, that the new and dynamic bourgeois social force was compelled to challenge not only the political-economic arrangements of the order but also the eternal sanctities which hallowed it.

If modern civilization represents a bourgeois revolt against feudalism, modern culture represents the revolt of new thought, informed by modern science, against a culture in which religious authority had fixed premature and too narrow limits for the expansion of science and had sought to restrain the curiosity of the human mind from inquiring into "secondary causes." The culture which venerated science in place of religion, worshipped natural causation in place of God, and which regarded the cool prudence of bourgeois man as morally more normative than Christian love, has proved itself to be less profound than it appeared to be in the seventeenth and eighteenth centuries. But these inadequacies, which must be further examined as typical of the foolishness of modern children of light, do not validate the judgment that these modern rebels were really children of darkness, intent upon defying the truth or destroying universal order.

The modern revolt against the feudal order and the medieval culture was occasioned by the assertion of new vitalities in the social order and the discovery of new dimensions in the cultural enterprise of mankind. It was truly democratic in so far as it challenged the premature and tentative unity of a society and the stabilization of a culture, and in so far as it developed new social and cultural possibilities. The conflict between the middle classes and the aristocrats, between the scientists and the priests, was not a conflict between children of darkness and children of light. It was a conflict between pious and less pious children of light, both of whom were unconscious of the corruption of self-interest in all ideal achievements and pretensions of human culture.

In this conflict the devotees of medieval religion were largely unconscious of the corruption of self-interest in their own position; but it must be admitted that they were not as foolish as their secular successors in their estimate of the force of self-interest in human society. Catholicism did strive for an inner and religious discipline upon inordinate desire; and it had a statesmanlike conception of the necessity of legal and political restraint upon the power of egotism, both individual and collective, in the national and the more universal human community.

Our modern civilization, on the other hand, was ushered in on a wave of boundless social optimism. Modern secularism is divided into many schools. But all the various schools agreed in rejecting the Christian doctrine of original sin. It is not possible to explain the subtleties or to measure the profundity of this doctrine in this connection. But it is necessary to point out that the doctrine makes an important contribution to any adequate social and political theory the lack of which has robbed bourgeois theory of real wisdom; for it emphasizes a fact which every page of human history attests. Through it one may understand that no matter how wide the perspectives which the human mind may reach, how broad the loyalties which the human imagination may conceive, how universal the community which human statecraft may organize, or how pure the aspirations of the saintliest idealists may be, there is no level of human moral or social achievement in which there is not some corruption of inordinate self-love.

This sober and true view of the human situation was neatly rejected by modern culture. That is why it conceived so many fatuous and futile plans for resolving the conflict between the self and the community; and between the national and the world community. Whenever modern idealists are confronted with the divisive and corrosive effects of man's self-love, they look for some immediate cause of this perennial tendency, usually in some specific form of social organization. One school holds that men would be good if only political institutions would not corrupt them; another believes that they would be good if the prior evil of a faulty economic organization could be eliminated. Or another school thinks of this evil as no more than ignorance, and therefore waits for a more perfect educational process to redeem man from his partial and particular loyalties. But no school asks how it is that an essentially good man could have produced corrupting and tyrannical political organizations or exploiting economic organizations, or fanatical and superstitious religious organizations.

The result of this persistent blindness to the obvious and tragic facts of man's social history is that democracy has had to maintain itself precariously against the guile and the malice of the children of darkness, while its statesmen and guides conjured up all sorts of abstract and abortive plans for the creation of perfect national and international communites.

The confidence of modern secular idealism in the possibility of an easy resolution of the tension between individual and community, or between classes, races and nations is derived from a too optimistic view of human nature. This too generous estimate of human virtue is intimately related to an erroneous estimate of the dimensions of the human stature. The conception of human nature which underlies the social and political attitudes of a liberal democratic culture is that of an essentially harmless individual. The survival impulse, which man shares with the animals, is regarded as the normative form of his egoistic drive. If this were a true picture of the human situation man might be, or might become, as harmless as seventeenth- and eighteenth-century thought assumed. Unfortunately for the validity of this picture of man, the most significant distinction between the human and the animal world is that the impulses of the former are "spiritualized" in the human world. Human capacities for evil as well as for good are derived from this spiritualization. There is of course always a natural survival impulse at the core of all human ambition. But this survival impulse cannot be neatly disentangled from two forms of its spiritualization. The one form is the desire to fulfill the potentialities of life and not merely to maintain its existence. Man is the kind of animal who cannot merely live. If he lives at all he is bound to seek the realization of his true nature; and to his true nature belongs his fulfillment in the lives of others. The will to live is thus transmuted into the will to self-realization; and self-realization involves self-giving in relations to others. When this desire for self-realization is fully explored it becomes apparent that it is subject to the paradox that the highest form of self-realization is the consequence of self-giving, but that it cannot be the intended consequence without being prematurely limited. Thus the will to live is finally transmuted into its opposite in the sense that only in self-giving can the self be fulfilled, for: "He that findeth his life shall lose it: and he that loseth his life for my sake shall find it."

On the other hand the will-to-live is also spiritually transmuted into the will-to-power or into the desire for "power and glory." Man, being more than a natural creature, is not interested merely in physical survival but in prestige and social approval. Having the intelligence to anticipate the perils in which he stands in nature and history, he invariably seeks to gain security against these perils by enhancing his power, individually and collectively. Possessing a darkly unconscious sense of his insignificance in the total scheme of things, he seeks to compensate for his insignificance by pretensions of pride. The conflicts between men are thus never simple conflicts between competing survival impulses. They are conflicts in which each man or group seeks to guard its power and prestige against the peril of competing expressions of power and pride. Since the very possession of power and prestige always involves some encroachment upon the prestige and power of others, this conflict is by its very nature a more stubborn and difficult one than the mere competition between various survival impulses in nature. It remains to be added that this conflict expresses itself even more cruelly in collective than in individual terms. Human behaviour being less individualistic than secular liberalism assumed, the struggle between classes, races and other groups in human society is not as easily resolved by the expedient of dissolving the groups as liberal democratic idealists assumed.

Since the survival impulse in nature is transmuted into two different and contradictory spiritualized forms, which we may briefly designate as the will-to-live-truly and the will-to-power, man is at variance with himself. The power of the second impulse places him more fundamentally in conflict with his fellowman than democratic liberalism realizes. The fact he cannot realize himself, except in organic relation with his fellows, makes the community more important than bourgeois individualism understands. The fact that the two impulses, though standing in contradiction to each other, are also mixed and compounded with each other on every level of human life, makes the simple distinctions between good and evil, between selfishness and altruism, with which liberal idealism has tried to estimate moral and political facts, invalid. The fact that the will-to-power inevitably justifies itself in terms of the morally more acceptable will to realize man's true nature means that the egoistic corruption of universal ideals is a much more persistent fact in human conduct than any moralistic creed is inclined to admit.

If we survey any period of history, and not merely the present tragic era of world catastrophe, it becomes quite apparent that human ambitions, lusts and desires, are more inevitably inordinate, that both human creativity and human evil reach greater heights, and that conflicts in the community between varying conceptions of the good and between competing expressions of vitality are of more tragic proportions than was anticipated in the basic philosophy which underlies democratic civilization. . . .

The general confidence of an identity between self-interest and the commonweal, which underlies liberal democratic political theory, is succinctly expressed in Thomas Paine's simple creed: "Public good is not a term opposed to the good of the individual; on the contrary it is the good of every individual collected. It is the good of all, because it is the good of every one; for as the public body is every individual collected, so the public good is the collected good of those individuals." . . .

Perhaps the most remarkable proof of the power of this optimistic creed, which underlies democratic thought, is that Marxism, which is ostensibly a revolt against it, manages to express the same optimism in another form. While liberal democrats dreamed of a simple social harmony, to be achieved by a cool prudence and a calculating egotism, the actual facts of social history revealed that the static class struggle of agrarian societies had been fanned into the flames of a dynamic struggle. Marxism was the social creed and the social cry of those classes who knew by their miseries that the creed of the liberal optimists was a snare and a delusion. Marxism insisted that the increasingly overt social conflict in democratic society would have to become even more overt, and would finally be fought to a bitter conclusion. But Marxism was also convinced that after the triumph of the lower classes of society, a new society would emerge in which exactly that kind of harmony between all social forces would be established, which Adam Smith had regarded as a possibility for any kind of society. The similarities between classical *laissez-faire* theory and the vision of an anarchistic millennium in Marxism are significant, whatever may be the superficial differences. Thus the provisionally cynical Lenin, who can trace all the complexities of social conflict in contemporary society with penetrating shrewdness, can also express the utopian hope that the revolution will usher in a period of history which will culminate in the Marxist millennium of anarchism. "All need for force will vanish," declared Lenin, "since people will grow accustomed to observing the elementary conditions of social existence without force and without subjection." . . .

The Marxists, too, are children of light. Their provisional cynicism does not even save them from the usual stupidity, nor from the fate, of other stupid children of light. That fate is to have their creed become the vehicle and instrument of the children of darkness. A new oligarchy is arising in Russia, the spiritual characteristics of which can hardly be distinguished from those of the American "go-getters" of the latter nineteenth and early twentieth centuries. And in the light of history Stalin will probably have the same relation to the early dreamers of the Marxist dreams which Napoleon has to the liberal dreamers of the eighteenth century.

Democratic theory, whether in its liberal or in its more radical form, is just as stupid in analyzing the relation between the national and the international community as in seeking a too simple harmony between the individual and the national community. Here, too, modern liberal culture exhibits few traces of moral cynicism. The morally autonomous modern national state does indeed arise; and it acknowledges no law beyond its interests. The actual behaviour of the nations is cynical. But the creed of liberal civilization is sentimental. This is true not only of the theorists whose creed was used by the architects of economic imperialism and of the more covert forms of national egotism in the international community, but also of those whose theories were appropriated by the proponents of an explicit national egotism. A straight line runs from Mazzini to Mussolini in the history of Italian nationalism. Yet there was not a touch of moral cynicism in the thought of Mazzini. He was, on the contrary, a pure universalist.

Even the philosophy of German romanticism, which has been accused with some justification of making specific contributions to the creed of German Nazism, reveals the stupidity of the children of light much more than the malice of the children of darkness. There is of course a strong note of moral nihilism in the final fruit of this romantic movement as we have it in Nietzsche; though even Nietzsche was no nationalist. But the earlier romantics usually express the same combination of individualism and universalism which characterizes the theory of the more naturalistic and rationalistic democrats of the western countries. Fichte resolved the conflict between the individual and the community through the instrumentality of the "just law" almost as easily as the utilitarians resolved it by the calculations of the prudent egotist and as easily as Rousseau resolved it by his conception of a "general will," which would fulfill the best purposes of each individual will. This was no creed of a community, making itself the idolatrous end of human existence. The theory was actually truer than the more individualistic and naturalistic forms of the democratic creed; for romanticism understood that the individual requires the community for his fulfillment. Thus even Hegel, who is sometimes regarded as the father of state absolutism in modern culture, thought of the national state as providing "for the reasonable will, insofar as it is in the individual only implicitly the universal will coming to a consciousness and an understanding of itself and being found."

This was not the creed of a collective egotism which negated the right of the individual. Rather it was a theory which, unlike the more purely democratic creed, understood the necessity of social fulfillment for the individual, and which, in common with the more liberal theories, regarded this as a much too simple process.

If the theory was not directed toward the annihilation of the individual, as is the creed of modern religious nationalism, to what degree was it directed against the universal community? Was it an expression of the national community's defiance of any interest or law above and beyond itself? This also is not the case. Herder believed that "fatherlands" might "lie peaceably side by side and aid each other as families. It is the grossest barbarity of human speech to speak of fatherlands in bloody battle with each other." Unfortunately this is something more than a barbarity of speech. Herder was a universalist, who thought a nice harmony between various communities could be achieved if only the right would be granted to each to express itself according to its unique and peculiar genius. He thought the false universalism of imperialism, according to which one community makes itself the standard and the governor of others, was merely the consequence of a false philosophy, whereas it is in fact one of the perennial corruptions of man's collective life.

Fichte, too, was a universalist who was fully conscious of moral obligations which transcend the national community. His difficulty, like that of all the children of light, was that he had a too easy resolution of the conflict between the nation and the community of nations. He thought that philosophy, particularly German philosophy, could achieve a synthesis between national and universal interest. "The patriot," he declared, "wishes the purpose of mankind to be reached first of all in that nation of which he is a member. . . . This purpose is the only possible patriotic goal. . . . Cosmopolitanism is the will that the purpose of life and of man be attained in all mankind, Patriotism is the will that this purpose be attained first of all in that nation of which we are members."

It is absurd to regard such doctrine as the dogma of national egotism, though Fichte could not express it without insinuating a certain degree of national pride into it. The pride took the form of the complacent assumption that German philosophy enabled the German nation to achieve a more perfect relation to the community of mankind than any other nation. He was, in other words, one of the many stupid children of light, who failed to understand the difficulty of the problem which he was considering; and his blindness included failure to see the significance of the implicit denial of an ideal in the thought and action of the very idealist who propounds it. . . .

The preservation of a democratic civilization requires the wisdom of the serpent and the harmlessness of the dove. The children of light must be armed with the wisdom of the children of darkness but remain free from their malice. They must know the power of self-interest in human society without giving it moral justification. They must have this wisdom in order that they may beguile, deflect, harness and restrain self-interest, individual and collective, for the sake of the community.

LILLIAN SMITH

Selection from *Killers of the Dream*
1949

The "one-drop rule," according to which the tiniest quantum of "black blood" made a person black, was prominent among the dogmas of the segregationist South criticized by the liberal, Florida-born writer Lillian Smith (1896–1966). In the autobiographical fragment reprinted here, Smith narrates an incident from her childhood in which an apparently white girl is discovered to possess a black ancestor and is, on that account, rigidly separated from the white society into which the little girl had been mistakenly welcomed.

Smith had already challenged the racism of her milieu through the medium of fiction, especially in *Strange Fruit* (1944), a best-selling novel of interracial love. But the pointed prose and vivid personal testimony of *Killers of the Dream* was too radical for 1949. Not until the Civil Rights era of the 1960s did this collection of critical commentaries on sex and race in the twentieth-century South attain the classic status it has since enjoyed.

The "one-drop rule" was of course designed to serve the interests of slaveholders eager to maximize the number of chattel slaves, and to obscure the widespread sexual exploitation of slave females by the empowered white men who were the fathers, husbands, sons, and employees of the white women whose honor was such a vital element of the culture of slaveholders. This old principle, informally adopted by the nation as a whole, had been criticized as irrational long before Smith's time, most famously in 1894 by Mark Twain in *Puddinhead Wilson*. But not until a century after Twain wrote, and nearly a half-century after Smith's bearing witness against it, did this "rule" for determining who was and was not African-American become the subject of a sustained, critical discourse by scholars and the public in the 1990s. See, for example, the first book-length history of this method of identifying black Americans, F. James Davis, *Who Is Black? One Nation's Definition* (University Park, Pa., 1991), and Lawrence Wright, "One Drop of Blood," *New Yorker* (July 25, 1994).

The atmosphere in which Smith lived and wrote is explored in John Egerton, *Speak Now Against the Day: Prophetic Voices in Yesterday's South* (New York, 1994). A basic introduction to Smith's life and work is Louise Blackwell and Frances Clay, *Lillian Smith* (New York, 1971). The most important of Smith's correspondence has been collected in Margaret Rose Gladney, ed., *How Am I to Be Heard? Letters of Lillian Smith* (New York, 1993).

Even its children knew that the South was in trouble. No one had to tell them; no words said aloud. To them, it was a vague thing weaving in and out of their play, like a ghost haunting an old graveyard or whispers after the household sleeps—fleeting mystery, vague menace to which each responded in his own way. Some learned to screen out all except the soft and the soothing; others denied even as they saw plainly, and heard. But all knew that under quiet words and warmth and laughter, under the slow ease and tender concern about small matters, there was a heavy burden on all of us and as heavy a refusal to confess it. The children knew this "trouble" was bigger than they, bigger than their family, bigger than their church, so big that people turned away from its size. They had seen it flash out and shatter a town's peace, had felt it tear up all they believed in. They had measured its giant strength and felt weak when they remembered.

This haunted childhood belongs to every southerner of my age. We ran away from it but we came back like a hurt animal to its wound, or a murderer to the scene of his sin. The human heart dares not stay away too long from that which hurt it most. There is a return journey to anguish that few of us are released from making.

We who were born in the South called this mesh of feeling and memory "loyalty." We thought of it sometimes as "love." We identified with the South's trouble as if we, individually, were responsible for all of it. We defended the sins and the sorrows of three hundred years as if each sin had been committed by us alone and each sorrow had cut across our heart. We were as hurt at criticism of our region as if our own name had been called aloud by the critic. We knew guilt without understanding it, and there is no tie that binds men closer to the past and each other than that.

It is a strange thing, this umbilical cord uncut. In times of ease, we do not feel its pull, but when we are threatened with change, suddenly it draws the whole white South together in a collective fear and fury that wipe our minds clear of reason and we are blocked from sensible contact with the world we live in.

To keep this resistance strong, wall after wall was thrown up in the southern mind against criticism from without and within. Imaginations closed tight against the hurt of others; a regional armoring took place to ward off the "enemies" who would make our trouble different—or maybe rid us of it completely. For it was a trouble that we did not want to give up. We were as involved with it as a child who cannot be happy at home and cannot bear to tear himself away, or as a grownup who has fallen in love with his own disease. We southerners had identified with the long sorrowful past on such deep levels of love and hate and guilt that we did not know how to break old bonds without pulling our lives down. *Change* was the evil word, a shrill clanking that made us know too well our servitude. *Change* meant leaving one's memories, one's sins, one's ambivalent pleasures, the room where one was born.

In this South I lived as a child and now live. And it is of it that my story is made. I shall not tell, here, of experiences that were different and special and belonged only to me, but those most white southerners born at the turn of the century share with each other. Out of the intricate weaving of unnumbered threads, I shall pick out a few strands, a few designs that have to do with what we call color and race . . . and politics . . . and money and how it is made . . . and religion . . . and sex and the body image . . . and love . . . and dreams of the Good and the killers of dreams.

A southern child's basic lessons were woven of such dissonant strands as these;

Source: Lillian Smith, *Killers of the Dream* (New York, 1949), 25–30, 34–40. Reprinted by permission of W. W. Norton & Co.

sometimes the threads tangled into a terrifying mess; sometimes archaic, startling designs would appear in the weaving; sometimes, a design was left broken while another was completed with minute care. Bewildered teachers, bewildered pupils in home and on the street, driven by an invisible Authority, learned their lessons:

The mother who taught me what I know of tenderness and love and compassion taught me also the bleak rituals of keeping Negroes in their "place." The father who rebuked me for an air of superiority toward schoolmates from the mill and rounded out his rebuke by gravely reminding me that "all men are brothers," trained me in the steel-rigid decorums I must demand of every colored male. They who so gravely taught me to split my body from my mind and both from my "soul," taught me also to split my conscience from my acts and Christianity from southern tradition.

Neither the Negro nor sex was often discussed at length in our home. We were given no formal instruction in these difficult matters but we learned our lessons well. We learned the intricate system of taboos, of renunciations and compensations, of manners, voice modulations, words, feelings, along with our prayers, our toilet habits, and our games. I do not remember how or when, but by the time I had learned that God is love, that Jesus is His Son and came to give us more abundant life, that all men are brothers with a common Father, I also knew that I was better than a Negro, that all black folks have their place and must be kept in it, that sex has its place and must be kept in it, that a terrifying disaster would befall the South if ever I treated a Negro as my social equal and as terrifying a disaster would befall my family if ever I were to have a baby outside of marriage. I had learned that God so loved the world that He gave His only begotten Son so that we might have segregated churches in which it was my duty to worship each Sunday and on Wednesday at evening prayers. I had learned that white southerners are a hospitable, courteous, tactful people who treat those of their own group with consideration and who as carefully segregate from all the richness of life "for their own good and welfare" thirteen million people whose skin is colored a little differently from my own.

I knew by the time I was twelve that a member of my family would always shake hands with old Negro friends, would speak graciously to members of the Negro race unless they forgot their place, in which event icy peremptory tones would draw lines beyond which only the desperate would dare take one step. I knew that to use the word "nigger" was unpardonable and no well-bred southerner was quite so crude as to do so; nor would a well-bred southerner call a Negro "mister" or invite him into the living room or eat with him or sit by him in public places.

I knew that my old nurse who had cared for me through long months of illness, who had given me refuge when a little sister took my place as the baby of the family, who soothed, fed me, delighted me with her stories and games, let me fall asleep on her deep warm breast, was not worthy of the passionate love I felt for her but must be given instead a half-smiled-at affection similar to that which one feels for one's dog. I knew but I never believed it, that the deep respect I felt for her, the tenderness, the love, was a childish thing which every normal child outgrows, that such love begins with one's toys and is discarded with them, and that somehow—though it seemed impossible to my agonized heart—I too, must outgrow these feelings. I learned to use a soft voice to oil my words of superiority. I learned to cheapen with tears and sentimental talk of "my old mammy" one of the profound relationships of my life. I learned the bitterest thing a child can learn: that the human relations I valued most were held cheap by the world I lived in.

From the day I was born, I began to learn my lessons. I was put in a rigid frame too intricate, too twisting to describe here so briefly, but I learned to conform to its slide-rule measurements. I learned it is possible to be a Christian and a white southerner simultaneously; to be a gentlewoman and an arrogant callous creature in the same moment; to pray at night and ride a Jim Crow car the next morning and to feel comfortable in doing both. I learned to believe in freedom, to glow when the word *democracy* was used, and to practice slavery from morning to night. I learned it the way all of my southern people learn it: by closing door after door until one's mind and heart and conscience are blocked off from each other and from reality.

I closed the doors. Or perhaps they were closed for me. One day they began to open again. Why I had the desire or the strength to open them, or what strange accident or circumstance opened them for me would require in the answering an account too long, too particular, too stark to make here. And perhaps I should not have the wisdom that such an analysis would demand of me, nor the will to make it. I know only that the doors opened, a little; that somewhere along that iron corridor we travel from babyhood to maturity, doors swinging inward began to swing outward, showing glimpses of the world beyond, of that bright thing we call "reality."

I believe there is one experience which pushed these doors open, a little. And I am going to tell it here, although I know well that to excerpt from a life and family background one incident and name it as a "cause" of a change in one's life direction is a distortion and often an irrelevance. The hungers of a child and how they are filled have too much to do with the way in which experiences are assimilated to tear an incident out of life and look at it in isolation. Yet, with these reservations, I shall tell it, not because it was in itself a severe trauma, but because it became a symbol of buried experiences that I did not have access to. It is an incident that has rarely happened to other southern children. In a sense, unique. But it was an acting-out, a private production of a little script that is written on the lives of most southern children before they know words. Though they may not have seen it staged this way, each southerner has had his own private showing. . . .

A little white girl was found in the colored section of our town, living with a Negro family in a broken-down shack. This family had moved in a few weeks before and little was known of them. One of the ladies in my mother's club, while driving over to her washerwoman's, saw the child swinging on a gate. The shack, as she said, was hardly more than a pigsty and this white child was living with dirty and sick-looking colored folks. "They must have kidnapped her," she told her friends. Genuinely shocked, the clubwomen busied themselves in an attempt to do something, for the child was very white indeed. The strange Negroes were subjected to a grueling questioning and finally grew evasive and refused to talk at all. This only increased the suspicion of the white group. The next day the clubwomen, escorted by the town marshal, took the child from her adopted family despite their tears.

She was brought to our home. I do not know why my mother consented to this plan. Perhaps because she loved children and always showed concern for them. It was easy for one more to fit into our ample household and Janie was soon at home there. She roomed with me, sat next to me at the table; I found Bible verses for her to say at breakfast; she wore my clothes, played with my dolls and followed me around from morning to night. She was dazed by her new comforts and by the interesting activities of this big lively family; and I was as happily dazed, for her adoration was a new thing to me; and as time passed a quick, childish, and deeply felt bond grew up between us.

But a day came when a telephone message was received from a colored orphanage. There was a meeting at our home. Many whispers. All afternoon the ladies went in and out of our house talking to Mother in tones too low for children to hear. As they passed us at play, they looked at Janie and quickly looked away again, though a few stopped and stared at her as if they could not tear their eyes from her face. When my father came home Mother closed her door against our young ears and talked a long time with him. I heard him laugh, heard Mother say, "But Papa, this is no laughing matter!" And then they were back in the living room with us and my mother was pale and my father was saying, "Well, work it out, Mame, as best you can. After all, now that you know, it is pretty simple."

In a little while my mother called my sister and me into her bedroom and told us that in the morning Janie would return to Colored Town. She said Janie was to have the dresses the ladies had given her and a few of my own, and the toys we had shared with her. She asked me if I would like to give Janie one of my dolls. She seemed hurried, though Janie was not to leave until next day. She said, "Why not select it now?" And in dreamlike stiffness I brought in my dolls and chose one for Janie. And then I found it possible to say, "Why is she leaving? She likes us, she hardly knows them. She told me she had been with them only a month."

"Because," Mother said gently, "Janie is a little colored girl."

"But she's white!"

"We were mistaken. She is colored."

"But she looks—"

"She is colored. Please don't argue!"

"What does it mean?" I whispered.

"It means," Mother said slowly, "that she has to live in Colored Town with colored people."

"But why? She lived here three weeks and she doesn't belong to them, she told me so."

"She is a little colored girl."

"But you said yourself she has nice manners. You said that," I persisted.

"Yes, she is a nice child. But a colored child cannot live in our home."

"Why?"

"You know, dear! You have always known that white and colored people do not live together."

"Can she come to play?"

"No."

"I don't understand."

"I don't either," my young sister quavered.

"You're too young to understand. And don't ask me again, ever again, about this!" Mother's voice was sharp but her face was sad and there was no certainty left there. She hurried out and busied herself in the kitchen and I wandered through that room where I had been born, touching the old familiar things in it, looking at them, trying to find the answer to a question that moaned like a hurt thing. . . .

And then I went out to Janie, who was waiting, knowing things were happening that concerned her but waiting until they were spoken aloud.

I do not know quite how the words were said but I told her she was to return in the morning to the little place where she had lived because she was colored and colored children could not live with white children.

"Are you white?" she said.

"I'm white," I replied, "and my sister is white. And you're colored. And white and colored can't live together because my mother says so."

"Why?" Janie whispered.

"Because they can't," I said. But I knew, though I said it firmly, that something was wrong. I knew my father and mother whom I passionately admired had betrayed something which they held dear. And they could not help doing it. And I was shamed by their failure and frightened, for I felt they were no longer as powerful as I had thought. There was something Out There that was stronger than they and I could not bear to believe it. I could not confess that my father, who always solved the family dilemmas easily and with laughter, could not solve this. I knew that my mother who was so good to children did not believe in her heart that she was being good to this child. There was not a word in my mind that said it but my body knew and my glands, and I was filled with anxiety.

But I felt compelled to believe they were right. It was the only way my world could be held together. And, slowly, it began to seep through me: *I was white. She was colored. We must not be together. It was bad to be together. Though you ate with your nurse when you were little, it was bad to eat with any colored person after that. It was bad just as other things were bad that your mother had told you. It was bad that she was to sleep in the room with me that night. It was bad. . . .*

I was overcome with guilt. For three weeks I had done things that white children were not supposed to do. And now I knew these things had been wrong.

I went to the piano and began to play, as I had always done when I was in trouble. I tried to play my next lesson and as I stumbled through it, the little girl came over and sat on the bench with me. Feeling lost in the deep currents sweeping through our house that night, she crept closer and put her arms around me and I shrank away as if my body had been uncovered. I had not said a word, I did not say one, but she knew, and tears slowly rolled down her little white face. . . .

And then I forgot it. For more than thirty years the experience was wiped out of my memory. But that night, and the weeks it was tied to, worked its way like a splinter, bit by bit, down to the hurt places in my memory and festered there. And as I grew older, as more experiences collected around that faithless time, as memories of earlier, more profound hurts crept closer, drawn to that night as if to a magnet, I began to know that people who talked of love and children did not mean it. That is a hard thing for a child to learn. I still admired my parents, there was so much that was strong and vital and sane and good about them and I never forgot this; I stubbornly believed in their sincerity, as I do to this day, and I loved them. Yet in my heart they were under suspicion. Something was wrong.

Something was wrong with a world that tells you that love is good and people are important and then forces you to deny love and to humiliate people. I knew, though I would not for years confess it aloud, that in trying to shut the Negro race away from us, we have shut ourselves away from so many good, creative, honest, deeply human things in life. I began to understand slowly at first but more clearly as the years passed, that the warped, distorted frame we have put around every Negro child from birth is around every white child also. Each is on a different side of the frame but each is pinioned there. And I knew that what cruelly shapes and cripples the personality of one is as cruelly shaping and crippling the personality of the other. I began to see that though we may, as we acquire new knowledge, live through new experiences, examine old memories, gain the strength to tear the frame from us, yet we are stunted and warped and in our lifetime cannot grow straight again any more than can a tree, put in a steel-like twisting frame when young, grow tall and straight when the frame is torn away at maturity.

As I sit here writing, I can almost touch that little town, so close is the memory of it. There it lies, its main street lined with great oaks, heavy with matted moss that swings softly even now as I remember. A little white town rimmed with Negroes, making a deep shadow on the whiteness. There it lies, broken in two by one strange idea. Minds broken. Hearts broken. Conscience torn from acts. A culture split in a thousand pieces. That is segregation. I am remembering: a woman in a mental hospital walking four steps out, four steps in, unable to go further because she has drawn an invisible line around her small world and is terrified to take one step beyond it. . . . A man in a Disturbed Ward assigning "places" to the other patients and violently insisting that each stay in his place. . . . A Negro woman saying to me so quietly, "We cannot ride together on the bus, you know. It is not legal to be human down here."

Memory, walking the streets of one's childhood . . . of the town where one was born.

WHITTAKER CHAMBERS

Selection from *Witness*
1952

Whittaker Chambers (1904–61) became a national figure in 1948 when he accused a former official of the State Department, Alger Hiss, of having passed classified documents to Chambers while Chambers had been a Soviet agent during the 1930s. A series of dramatic congressional hearings and trials brought the confessed ex-Communist Chambers into sustained public conflict with the all-denying Hiss. Hiss's second trial for perjury ended in conviction early in 1950 when a jury found that Hiss had lied under oath while denying having known and aided Chambers. Immediately after Hiss's conviction, Senator Joseph McCarthy began his reckless campaign against subversion that added the word *McCarthyism* to the American political vocabulary. Chambers himself was not an uncritical supporter of McCarthy's methods, but his own style of anti-Communism was also very sweeping. Chambers believed that secular liberalism was a dangerous step toward Stalin's terror, and he defended simple patriotism and traditional religious faith with a passion that many found eloquent. No one expressed the extreme anti-Communist sensibility of the period with more telling effect than Chambers did in his best-selling autobiography, *Witness* (New York, 1952), the prologue to which is reprinted here. By addressing the American public through the medium of a letter to his own children, Chambers established the persona of the man of experience instructing innocents. By leading them to Golgotha, Chambers invited his readers to see him as a Christ-like martyr, sacrificing himself to save them.

For a sensitive reading of *Witness,* with attention to Chambers's use of Shakespearean and other literary tropes to construct his own narrative of himself, see Eric J. Sundquist, "Witness Recalled," *Commentary,* December 1988, 57–63. The best single work on the Hiss–Chambers case itself is Allen Weinstein, *Perjury* (New York, 1978), which argues that Hiss did pass classified documents to Chambers and that Chambers, for all his melodramatic exaggerations, told in *Witness* a much more accurate story about his own experience as a Communist than had been generally believed. Although most historians now believe that Hiss lied, he has continued to profess his innocence. The critical discussion that the Hiss–Chambers case generated at the time constitutes in itself a formidable and fascinating body of literature, represented by Alastair Cooke in *A Generation on Trial* (New York, 1950), and by Murray Kempton, "A Sheltered Life," in Kempton's *Part of Our Time: Some Monuments and Ruins of the Thirties* (New York, 1955), 13–35.

Beloved Children,

I am sitting in the kitchen of the little house at Medfield, our second farm which is cut off by the ridge and a quarter-mile across the fields from our home place, where you are. I am writing a book. In it I am speaking to you. But I am also speaking to the world. To both I owe an accounting.

It is a terrible book. It is terrible in what it tells about men. If anything, it is more terrible in what it tells about the world in which you live. It is about what the world calls the Hiss-Chambers Case, or even more simply, the Hiss Case. It is about a spy case. All the props of an espionage case are there—foreign agents, household traitors, stolen documents, microfilm, furtive meetings, secret hideaways, phony names, an informer, investigations, trials, official justice.

But if the Hiss Case were only this, it would not be worth my writing about or your reading about. It would be another fat folder in the sad files of the police, another crime drama in which the props would be mistaken for the play (as many people have consistently mistaken them). It would not be what alone gave it meaning, what the mass of men and women instinctively sensed it to be, often without quite knowing why. It would not be what, at the very beginning, I was moved to call it: "a tragedy of history."

For it was more than human tragedy. Much more than Alger Hiss or Whittaker Chambers was on trial in the trials of Alger Hiss. Two faiths were on trial. Human societies, like human beings, live by faith and die when faith dies. At issue in the Hiss Case was the question whether this sick society, which we call Western civilization, could in its extremity still cast up a man whose faith in it was so great that he would voluntarily abandon those things which men hold good, including life, to defend it. At issue was the question whether this man's faith could prevail against a man whose equal faith it was that this society is sick beyond saving, and that mercy itself pleads for its swift extinction and replacement by another. At issue was the question whether, in the desperately divided society, there still remained the will to recognize the issues in time to offset the immense rally of public power to distort and pervert the facts.

At heart, the Great Case was this critical conflict of faiths; that is why it was a great case. On a scale personal enough to be felt by all, but big enough to be symbolic, the two irreconcilable faiths of our time—Communism and Freedom—came to grips in the persons of two conscious and resolute men. Indeed, it would have been hard, in a world still only dimly aware of what the conflict is about, to find two other men who knew so clearly. Both had been schooled in the same view of history (the Marxist view). Both were trained by the same party in the same selfless, semisoldierly discipline. Neither would nor could yield without betraying, not himself, but his faith; and the different character of these faiths was shown by the different conduct of the two men toward each other throughout the struggle. For, with dark certitude, both knew, almost from the beginning, that the Great Case could end only in the destruction of one or both of the contending figures, just as the history of our times (both men had been taught) can end only in the destruction of one or both of the contending forces.

But this destruction is not the tragedy. The nature of tragedy is itself misunderstood. Part of the world supposes that the tragedy in the Hiss Case lies in the acts of disloyalty revealed. Part believes that the tragedy lies in the fact that an able, intelligent man, Alger Hiss, was cut short in the course of a brilliant public career. Some find it

Source: Whittaker Chambers, *Witness* (Washington, D.C.: Regnery-Gateway, 1952), 3–22. Reprinted by permission of Regnery-Gateway Publishers.

tragic that Whittaker Chambers, of his own will, gave up a $30,000-a-year job and a secure future to haunt for the rest of his days the ruins of his life. These are shocking facts, criminal facts, disturbing facts: they are not tragic.

Crime, violence, infamy are not tragedy. Tragedy occurs when a human soul awakes and seeks, in suffering and pain, to free itself from crime, violence, infamy, even at the cost of life. The struggle is the tragedy—not defeat or death. That is why the spectacle of tragedy has always filled men, not with despair, but with a sense of hope and exaltation. That is why this terrible book is also a book of hope. For it is about the struggle of the human soul—of more than one human soul. It is in this sense that the Hiss Case is a tragedy. This is its meaning beyond the headlines, the revelations, the shame and suffering of the people involved. But this tragedy will have been for nothing unless men understand it rightly, and from it the world takes hope and heart to begin its own tragic struggle with the evil that besets it from within and from without, unless it faces the fact that the world, the whole world, is sick unto death and that, among other things, this Case has turned a finger of fierce light into the suddenly opened and reeking body of our time.

My children, as long as you live, the shadow of the Hiss Case will brush you. In every pair of eyes that rests on you, you will see pass, like a cloud passing behind a woods in winter, the memory of your father—dissembled in friendly eyes, lurking in unfriendly eyes. Sometimes you will wonder which is harder to bear: friendly forgiveness or forthright hate. In time, therefore, when the sum of your experience of life gives you authority, you will ask yourselves the question: What was my father?

I will give you an answer: I was a witness. I do not mean a witness for the Government or against Alger Hiss and the others. Nor do I mean the short, squat, solitary figure, trudging through the impersonal halls of public buildings to testify before Congressional committees, grand juries, loyalty boards, courts of law. A man is not primarily a witness *against* something. That is only incidental to the fact that he is a witness *for* something. A witness, in the sense that I am using the word, is a man whose life and faith are so completely one that when the challenge comes to step out and testify for his faith, he does so, disregarding all risks, accepting all consequences.

One day in the great jury room of the Grand Jury of the Southern District of New York, a juror leaned forward slightly and asked me: "Mr. Chambers, what does it mean to be a Communist?" I hesitated for a moment, trying to find the simplest, most direct way to convey the heart of this complex experience to men and women to whom the very fact of the experience was all but incomprehensible. Then I said:

"When I was a Communist, I had three heroes. One was a Russian. One was a Pole. One was a German Jew.

"The Pole was Felix Djerjinsky. He was ascetic, highly sensitive, intelligent. He was a Communist. After the Russian Revolution, he became head of the Tcheka and organizer of the Red Terror. As a young man, Djerjinsky had been a political prisoner in the Paviak Prison in Warsaw. There he insisted on being given the task of cleaning the latrines of the other prisoners. For he held that the most developed member of any community must take upon himself the lowliest tasks as an example to those who are less developed. That is one thing that it meant to be a Communist.

"The German Jew was Eugen Leviné. He was a Communist. During the Bavarian Soviet Republic in 1919, Leviné was the organizer of the Workers and Soldiers Soviets. When the Bavarian Soviet Republic was crushed, Leviné was captured and court-martialed. The court-martial told him: 'You are under sentence of death.' Leviné answered:

'We Communists are always under sentence of death.' That is another thing that it meant to be a Communist.

"The Russian was not a Communist. He was a pre-Communist revolutionist named Kalyaev. (I should have said Sazonov.) He was arrested for a minor part in the assassination of the Tsarist prime minister, von Plehve. He was sent into Siberian exile to one of the worst prison camps, where the political prisoners were flogged. Kalyaev sought some way to protest this outrage to the world. The means were few, but at last he found a way. In protest against the flogging of other men, Kalyaev drenched himself in kerosene, set himself on fire and burned himself to death. That also is what it meant to be a Communist."

That also is what it means to be a witness.

But a man may also be an involuntary witness. I do not know any way to explain why God's grace touches a man who seems unworthy of it. But neither do I know any other way to explain how a man like myself—tarnished by life, unprepossessing, not brave— could prevail so far against the powers of the world arrayed almost solidly against him, to destroy him and defeat his truth. In this sense, I am an involuntary witness to God's grace and to the fortifying power of faith.

It was my fate to be in turn a witness to each of the two great faiths of our time. And so we come to the terrible word, Communism. My very dear children, nothing in all these pages will be written so much for you, though it is so unlike anything you would want to read. In nothing shall I be so much a witness, in no way am I so much called upon to fulfill my task, as in trying to make clear to you (and to the world) the true nature of Communism and the source of its power, which was the cause of my ordeal as a man, and remains the historic ordeal of the world in the 20th century. For in this century, within the next decades, will be decided for generations whether all mankind is to become Communist, whether the whole world is to become free, or whether, in the struggle, civilization as we know it is to be completely destroyed or completely changed. It is our fate to live upon that turning point in history.

The world has reached that turning point by the steep stages of a crisis mounting for generations. The turning point is the next to the last step. It was reached in blood, sweat, tears, havoc and death in World War II. The chief fruit of the First World War was the Russian Revolution and the rise of Communism as a national power. The chief fruit of the Second World War was our arrival at the next to the last step of the crisis with the rise of Communism as a world power. History is likely to say that these were the only decisive results of the world wars.

The last war simplified the balance of political forces in the world by reducing them to two. For the first time, it made the power of the Communist sector of mankind (embodied in the Soviet Union) roughly equal to the power of the free sector of mankind (embodied in the United States). It made the collision of these powers all but inevitable. For the world wars did not end the crisis. They raised its tensions to a new pitch. They raised the crisis to a new stage. All the politics of our time, including the politics of war, will be the politics of this crisis.

Few men are so dull that they do not know that the crisis exists and that it threatens their lives at every point. It is popular to call it a social crisis. It is in fact a total crisis— religious, moral, intellectual, social, political, economic. It is popular to call it a crisis of the Western world. It is in fact a crisis of the whole world. Communism, which claims to be a solution of the crisis, is itself a symptom and an irritant of the crisis.

In part, the crisis results from the impact of science and technology upon mankind which, neither socially nor morally, has caught up with the problems posed by that impact. In part, it is caused by men's efforts to solve those problems. World wars are the military expression of the crisis. World-wide depressions are its economic expression. Universal desperation is its spiritual climate. This is the climate of Communism. Communism in our time can no more be considered apart from the crisis than a fever can be acted upon apart from an infected body.

I see in Communism the focus of the concentrated evil of our time. You will ask: Why, then, do men become Communists? How did it happen that you, our gentle and loved father, were once a Communist? Were you simply stupid? No, I was not stupid. Were you morally depraved? No, I was not morally depraved. Indeed, educated men become Communists chiefly for moral reasons. Did you not know that the crimes and horrors of Communism are inherent in Communism? Yes, I knew that fact. Then why did you become a Communist? It would help more to ask: How did it happen that this movement, once a mere muttering of political outcasts, became this immense force that now contests the mastery of mankind? Even when all the chances and mistakes of history are allowed for, the answer must be: Communism makes some profound appeal to the human mind. You will not find out what it is by calling Communism names. That will not help much to explain why Communism whose horrors, on a scale unparalleled in history, are now public knowledge, still recruits its thousands and holds its millions—among them some of the best minds alive. Look at Klaus Fuchs, standing in the London dock, quiet, doomed, destroyed, and say whether it is possible to answer in that way the simple question: Why?

First, let me try to say what Communism is not. It is not simply a vicious plot hatched by wicked men in a sub-cellar. It is not just the writings of Marx and Lenin, dialectical materialism, the Politburo, the labor theory of value, the theory of the general strike, the Red Army, secret police, labor camps, underground conspiracy, the dictatorship of the proletariat, the technique of the coup d'état. It is not even those chanting, bannered millions that stream periodically, like disorganized armies, through the heart of the world's capitals: Moscow, New York, Tokyo, Paris, Rome. These are expressions of Communism, but they are not what Communism is about.

In the Hiss trials, where Communism was a haunting specter, but which did little or nothing to explain Communism, Communists were assumed to be criminals, pariahs, clandestine men who lead double lives under false names, travel on false passports, deny traditional religion, morality, the sanctity of oaths, preach violence and practice treason. These things are true about Communists, but they are not what Communism is about.

The revolutionary heart of Communism is not the theatrical appeal: "Workers of the world, unite. You have nothing to lose but your chains. You have a world to gain." It is a simple statement of Karl Marx, further simplified for handy use: "Philosophers have explained the world; it is necessary to change the world." Communists are bound together by no secret oath. The tie that binds them across the frontiers of nations, across barriers of language and differences of class and education, in defiance of religion, morality, truth, law, honor, the weaknesses of the body and the irresolutions of the mind, even unto death, is a simple conviction: It is necessary to change the world. Their power, whose nature baffles the rest of the world, because in a large measure the rest of the world has lost that power, is the power to hold convictions and to act on them. It is the same power that moves mountains; it is also an unfailing power to move men.

Communists are that part of mankind which has recovered the power to live or die—to bear witness—for its faith. And it is a simple, rational faith that inspires men to live or die for it.

It is not new. It is, in fact, man's second oldest faith. Its promise was whispered in the first days of the Creation under the Tree of the Knowledge of Good and Evil: "Ye shall be as gods." It is the great alternative faith of mankind. Like all great faiths, its force derives from a simple vision. Other ages have had great visions. They have always been different versions of the same vision: the vision of God and man's relationship to God. The Communist vision is the vision of Man without God.

It is the vision of man's mind displacing God as the creative intelligence of the world. It is the vision of man's liberated mind, by the sole force of its rational intelligence, redirecting man's destiny and reorganizing man's life and the world. It is the vision of man, once more the central figure of the Creation, not because God made man in His image, but because man's mind makes him the most intelligent of the animals. Copernicus and his successors displaced man as the central fact of the universe by proving that the earth was not the central star of the universe. Communism restores man to his sovereignty by the simple method of denying God.

The vision is a challenge and implies a threat. It challenges man to prove by his acts that he is the masterwork of the Creation—by making thought and act one. It challenges him to prove it by using the force of his rational mind to end the bloody meaninglessness of man's history—by giving it purpose and a plan. It challenges him to prove it by reducing the meaningless chaos of nature, by imposing on it his rational will to order, abundance, security, peace. It is the vision of materialism. But it threatens, if man's mind is unequal to the problems of man's progress, that he will sink back into savagery (the A and the H bombs have raised the issue in explosive forms), until nature replaced him with a more intelligent form of life.

It is an intensely practical vision. The tools to turn it into reality are at hand—science and technology, whose traditional method, the rigorous exclusion of all supernatural factors in solving problems, has contributed to the intellectual climate in which the vision flourishes, just as they have contributed to the crisis in which Communism thrives. For the vision is shared by millions who are not Communists (they are part of Communism's secret strength). Its first commandment is found, not in the *Communist Manifesto,* but in the first sentence of the physics primer: "All of the progress of mankind to date results from the making of careful measurements." But Communism, for the first time in history, has made this vision the faith of a great modern political movement.

Hence the Communist Party is quite justified in calling itself the most revolutionary party in history. It has posed in practical form the most revolutionary question in history: God or Man? It has taken the logical next step which three hundred years of rationalism hesitated to take, and said what millions of modern minds think, but do not dare or care to say: If man's mind is the decisive force in the world, what need is there for God? Henceforth man's mind is man's fate.

This vision *is* the Communist revolution, which, like all great revolutions, occurs in man's mind before it takes form in man's acts. Insurrection and conspiracy are merely methods of realizing the vision; they are merely part of the politics of Communism. Without its vision, they, like Communism, would have no meaning and could not rally a parcel of pickpockets. Communism does not summon men to crime or to utopia, as its easy critics like to think. On the plane of faith, it summons mankind to turn its vision into practical reality. On the plane of action, it summons men to struggle against the inertia of the past which, embodied in social, political and economic forms, Communism claims, is blocking the will of mankind to make its next great forward stride. It summons men to overcome the crisis, which, Communism claims, is in effect a crisis of rending frustration, with the world, unable to stand still, but unwilling to go forward along the road that the logic of a technological civilization points out—Communism.

This is Communism's moral sanction, which is twofold. Its vision points the way to the future; its faith labors to turn the future into present reality. It says to every man who joins it: the vision is a practical problem of history; the way to achieve it is a practical problem of politics, which is the present tense of history. Have you the moral strength to take upon yourself the crimes of history so that man at last may close his chronicle of age-old, senseless suffering, and replace it with purpose and a plan? The answer a man makes to this question is the difference between the Communist and those miscellaneous socialists, liberals, fellow travelers, unclassified progressives and men of good will, all of whom share a similar vision, but do not share the faith because they will not take upon themselves the penalties of the faith. The answer is the root of that sense of moral superiority which makes Communists, though caught in crime, berate their opponents with withering self-righteousness.

The Communist vision has a mighty agitator and a mighty propagandist. They are the crisis. The agitator needs no soap box. It speaks insistently to the human mind at the point where desperation lurks. The propagandist writes no Communist gibberish. It speaks insistently to the human mind at the point where man's hope and man's energy fuse to fierceness.

The vision inspires. The crisis impels. The workingman is chiefly moved by the crisis. The educated man is chiefly moved by the vision. The workingman, living upon a mean margin of life, can afford few visions—even practical visions. An educated man, peering from the Harvard Yard, or any college campus, upon a world in chaos, finds in the vision the two certainties for which the mind of man tirelessly seeks: a reason to live and a reason to die. No other faith of our time presents them with the same practical intensity. That is why Communism is the central experience of the first half of the 20th century, and may be its final experience—will be, unless the free world, in the agony of its struggle with Communism, overcomes its crisis by discovering, in suffering and pain, a power of faith which will provide man's mind, at the same intensity, with the same two certainties: a reason to live and a reason to die. If it fails, this will be the century of the great social wars. If it succeeds, this will be the century of the great wars of faith.

You will ask: Why, then, do men cease to be Communists? One answer is: Very few do. Thirty years after the Russian Revolution, after the known atrocities, the purges, the revelations, the jolting zigzags of Communist politics, there is only a handful of ex-Communists in the whole world. By ex-Communists I do not mean those who break with Communism over differences of strategy and tactics (like Trotsky) or organization (like Tito). Those are merely quarrels over a road map by people all of whom are in a hurry to get to the same place.

Nor, by ex-Communists, do I mean those thousands who continually drift into the Communist Party and out again. The turnover is vast. These are the spiritual vagrants of our time whose traditional faith has been leached out in the bland climate of rationalism. They are looking for an intellectual night's lodging. They lack the character for

Communist faith because they lack the character for any faith. So they drop away, though Communism keeps its hold on them.

By an ex-Communist, I mean a man who knew clearly why he became a Communist, who served Communism devotedly and knew why he served it, who broke with Communism unconditionally and knew why he broke with it. Of these there are very few—an index to the power of the vision and the power of the crisis.

History very largely fixes the patterns of force that make men Communists. Hence one Communist conversion sounds much like another—rather impersonal and repetitious, awesome and tiresome, like long lines of similar people all stolidly waiting to get in to see the same movie. A man's break with Communism is intensely personal. Hence the account of no two breaks is likely to be the same. The reasons that made one Communist break may seem without force to another ex-Communist.

It is a fact that a man can join the Communist Party, can be very active in it for years, without completely understanding the nature of Communism or the political methods that follow inevitably from its vision. One day such incomplete Communists discover that the Communist Party is not what they thought it was. They break with it and turn on it with the rage of an honest dupe, a dupe who has given a part of his life to a swindle. Often they forget that it takes two to make a swindle.

Others remain Communists for years, warmed by the light of its vision, firmly closing their eyes to the crimes and horrors inseparable from its practical politics. One day they have to face the facts. They are appalled at what they have abetted. They spend the rest of their days trying to explain, usually without great success, the dark clue to their complicity. As their understanding of Communism was incomplete and led them to a dead end, their understanding of breaking with it is incomplete and leads them to a dead end. It leads to less than Communism, which was a vision and a faith. The world outside Communism, the world in crisis, lacks a vision and a faith. There is before these ex-Communists absolutely nothing. Behind them is a threat. For they have, in fact, broken not with the vision, but with the politics of the vision. In the name of reason and intelligence, the vision keeps them firmly in its grip—self-divided, paralyzed, powerless to act against it.

Hence the most secret fold of their minds is haunted by a terrifying thought: What if we were wrong? What if our inconstancy is our guilt? That is the fate of those who break without knowing clearly that Communism is wrong because something else is right, because to the challenge: *God or Man?*, they continue to give the answer: *Man.* Their pathos is that not even the Communist ordeal could teach them that man without God is just what Communism said he was: the most intelligent of the animals, that man without God is a beast, never more beastly than when he is most intelligent about his beastliness. *"Er nennt's Vernunft,"* says the Devil in Goethe's *Faust,* *"und braucht's allein, nur tierischer als jedes Tier zu sein"*—Man calls it reason and uses it simply to be more beastly than any beast. Not grasping the source of the evil they sincerely hate, such ex-Communists in general make ineffectual witnesses against it. They are witnesses against something; they have ceased to be witnesses for anything.

Yet there is one experience which most sincere ex-Communists share, whether or not they go only part way to the end of the question it poses. The daughter of a former German diplomat in Moscow was trying to explain to me why her father, who, as an enlightened modern man, had been extremely pro-Communist, had become an implacable anti-Communist. It was hard for her because, as an enlightened modern girl, she shared the Communist vision without being a Communist. But she loved her father and the irrationality of his defection embarrassed her. "He was immensely pro-Soviet," she said, "and then—you will laugh at me—but you must not laugh at my father—and then—one night—in Moscow—he heard screams. That's all. Simply one night he heard screams."

A child of Reason and the 20th century, she knew that there is a logic of the mind. She did not know that the soul has a logic that may be more compelling than the mind's. She did not know at all that she had swept away the logic of the mind, the logic of history, the logic of politics, the myth of the 20th century, with five annihilating words: one night he heard screams.

What Communist has not heard those screams? They come from husbands torn forever from their wives in midnight arrests. They come, muffled, from the execution cellars of the secret police, from the torture chambers of the Lubianka, from all the citadels of terror now stretching from Berlin to Canton. They come from those freight cars loaded with men, women and children, the enemies of the Communist State, locked in, packed in, left on remote sidings to freeze to death at night in the Russian winter. They come from minds driven mad by the horrors of mass starvation ordered and enforced as a policy of the Communist State. They come from the starved skeletons, worked to death, or flogged to death (as an example to others) in the freezing filth of sub-arctic labor camps. They come from children whose parents are suddenly, inexplicably, taken away from them—parents they will never see again.

What Communist has not heard those screams? Execution, says the Communist code, is the highest measure of social protection. What man can call himself a Communist who has not accepted the fact that Terror is an instrument of policy, right if the vision is right, justified by history, enjoined by the balance of forces in the social wars of this century? Those screams have reached every Communist's mind. Usually they stop there. What judge willingly dwells upon the man the laws compel him to condemn to death—the laws of nations or the laws of history?

But one day the Communist really hears those screams. He is going about his routine party tasks. He is lifting a dripping reel of microfilm from a developing tank. He is justifying to a Communist fraction in a trade union an extremely unwelcome directive of the Central Committee. He is receiving from a trusted superior an order to go to another country and, in a designated hotel, at a designated hour, meet a man whose name he will never know, but who will give him a package whose contents he will never learn. Suddenly, there closes around that Communist a separating silence, and in that silence he hears screams. He hears them for the first time. For they do not merely reach his mind. They pierce beyond. They pierce to his soul. He says to himself: "Those are not the screams of man in agony. Those are the screams of a soul in agony." He hears them for the first time because a soul in extremity has communicated with that which alone can hear it—another human soul.

Why does the Communist ever hear them? Because in the end there persists in every man, however he may deny it, a scrap of soul. The Communist who suffers this singular experience then says to himself: "What is happening to me? I must be sick." If he does not instantly stifle that scrap of soul, he is lost. If he admits it for a moment, he has admitted that there is something greater than Reason, greater than the logic of mind, of politics, of history, of economics, which alone justifies the vision. If the party senses his weakness, and the party is peculiarly cunning at sensing such weakness, it will humiliate him, degrade him, condemn him, expel him. If it can, it will destroy him.

And the party will be right. For he has betrayed that which alone justifies its faith— the vision of Almighty Man. He has brushed the only vision that has force against the vision of Almighty Mind. He stands before the fact of God.

The Communist Party is familiar with this experience to which its members are sometimes liable in prison, in illness, in indecision. It is recognized frankly as a sickness. There are ways of treating it—if it is confessed. It is when it is not confessed that the party, sensing a subtle crisis, turns upon it savagely. What ex-Communist has not suffered this experience in one form or another, to one degree or another? What he does about it depends on the individual man. That is why no ex-Communist dare answer for his sad fraternity the question: Why do men break with Communism? He can only answer the question: How did you break with Communism? My answer is: Slowly, reluctantly, in agony.

Yet my break began long before I heard those screams. Perhaps it does for everyone. I do not know how far back it began. Avalanches gather force and crash, unheard, in men as in the mountains. But I date my break from a very casual happening. I was sitting in our apartment on St. Paul Street in Baltimore. It was shortly before we moved to Alger Hiss's apartment in Washington. My daughter was in her high chair. I was watching her eat. She was the most miraculous thing that had ever happened in my life. I liked to watch her even when she smeared porridge on her face or dropped it meditatively on the floor. My eye came to rest on the delicate convolutions of her ear— those intricate, perfect ears. The thought passed through my mind: "No, those ears were not created by any chance coming together of atoms in nature (the Communist view). They could have been created only by immense design." The thought was involuntary and unwanted. I crowded it out of my mind. But I never wholly forgot it or the occasion. I had to crowd it out of my mind. If I had completed it, I should have had to say: Design presupposes God. I did not then know that, at that moment, the finger of God was first laid upon my forehead.

One thing most ex-Communists could agree upon: they broke because they wanted to be free. They do not all mean the same thing by "free." Freedom is a need of the soul, and nothing else. It is in striving toward God that the soul strives continually after a condition of freedom. God alone is the inciter and guarantor of freedom. He is the only guarantor. External freedom is only an aspect of interior freedom. Political freedom, as the Western world has known it, is only a political reading of the Bible. Religion and freedom are indivisible. Without freedom the soul dies. Without the soul there is no justification for freedom. Necessity is the only ultimate justification known to the mind. Hence every sincere break with Communism is a religious experience, though the Communist fail to identify its true nature, though he fail to go to the end of the experience. His break is the political expression of the perpetual need of the soul whose first faint stirring he has felt within him, years, months or days before he breaks. A Communist breaks because he must choose at last between irreconcilable opposites— God or Man, Soul or Mind, Freedom or Communism.

Communism is what happens when, in the name of Mind, men free themselves from God. But its view of God, its knowledge of God, its experience of God, is what alone gives character to a society or a nation, and meaning to its destiny. Its culture, the voice of this character, is merely that view, knowledge, experience, of God, fixed by its most intense spirits in terms intelligible to the mass of men. There has never been a society or a nation without God. But history is cluttered with the wreckage of nations that became indifferent to God, and died.

The crisis of Communism exists to the degree in which it has failed to free the peoples that it rules from God. Nobody knows this better than the Communist Party of the Soviet Union. The crisis of the Western world exists to the degree in which it is indifferent to God. It exists to the degree in which the Western world actually shares Communism's materialist vision, is so dazzled by the logic of the materialist interpretation of history, politics and economics, that it fails to grasp that, for it, the only possible answer to the Communist challenge: Faith in God or Faith in Man? is the challenge: Faith in God.

Economics is not the central problem of this century. It is a relative problem which can be solved in relative ways. Faith is the central problem of this age. The Western world does not know it, but it already possesses the answer to this problem—but only provided that its faith in God and the freedom He enjoins is as great as Communism's faith in Man.

My dear children, before I close this foreword, I want to recall to you briefly the life that we led in the ten years between the time when I broke with Communism and the time when I began to testify—the things we did, worked for, loved, believed in. For it was that happy life, which, on the human side, in part made it possible for me to do later on the things I had to do, or endure the things that happened to me.

Those were the days of the happy little worries, which then seemed so big. We know now that they were the golden days. They will not come again. In those days, our greatest worry was how to meet the payments on the mortgage, how to get the ploughing done in time, how to get health accreditation for our herd, how to get the hay in before the rain. I sometimes took my vacation in hay harvest so that I could help work the load. You two little children used to trample the load, drive the hay truck in the fields when you could barely reach the foot pedals, or drive the tractor that pulled up the loaded harpoons to the mow. At evening, you would break off to help Mother milk while I went on haying. For we came of age on the farm when we decided not to hire barn help, but to run the herd ourselves as a family.

Often the ovenlike heat in the comb of the barn and the sweet smell of alfalfa made us sick. Sometimes we fell asleep at the supper table from fatigue. But the hard work was good for us; and you knew only the peace of a home governed by a father and mother whose marriage the years (and an earlier suffering which you could not remember) had deepened into the perfect love that enveloped you.

Mother was a slight, overalled figure forever working for you in the house or beside you in the barns and gardens. Papa was a squat, overalled figure, fat but forceful, who taught John, at nine, the man-size glory of driving the tractor; or sat beside Ellen, at the wheel of the truck, an embodiment of security and power, as we drove loads of cattle through the night. On summer Sundays, you sat between Papa and Mama in the Quaker meeting house. Through the open doors, as you tried not to twist and turn in the long silence, you could see the far, blue Maryland hills and hear the redbirds and ground robins in the graveyard behind.

Only Ellen had a vague, troubled recollection of another time and another image of Papa. Then (it was during the years 1938 and 1939), if for any reason she pattered down the hall at night, she would find Papa, with the light on, writing, with a revolver on the table or a gun against the chair. She knew that there were people who wanted to kill Papa and who might try to kidnap her. But a wide sea of sunlight and of time lay between that puzzling recollection and the farm.

The farm was your kingdom, and the world lay far beyond the protecting walls thrown up by work and love. It is true that comic strips were not encouraged, comic books were banned, the radio could be turned on only by permission which was seldom given (or asked), and you saw few movies. But you grew in the presence of eternal wonders. There was the birth of lambs and calves. You remember how once, when I was away and the veterinarian could not come, you saw Mother reach in and turn the calf inside the cow so that it could be born. There was also the death of animals, sometimes violent, sometimes slow and painful—nothing is more constant on a farm than death.

Sometimes, of a spring evening, Papa would hear that distant honking that always makes his scalp tingle, and we would all rush out to see the wild geese, in lines of hundreds, steer up from the southwest, turn over the barn as over a landmark, and head into the north. Or on autumn nights of sudden cold that set the ewes breeding in the orchard, Papa would call you out of the house to stand with him in the now celebrated pumpkin patch and watch the northern lights flicker in electric clouds on the horizon, mount, die down, fade and mount again till they filled the whole northern sky with ghostly light in motion.

Thus, as children, you experienced two of the most important things men ever know—the wonder of life and the wonder of the universe, the wonder of life within the wonder of the universe. More important, you knew them not from books, not from lectures, but simply from living among them. Most important, you knew them with reverence and awe—that reverence and awe that has died out of the modern world and been replaced by man's monkeylike amazement at the cleverness of his own inventive brain.

I have watched greatness touch you in another way. I have seen you sit, uninvited and unforced, listening in complete silence to the third movement of the Ninth Symphony. I thought you understood, as much as children can, when I told you that that music was the moment at which Beethoven finally passed beyond the suffering of his life on earth and reached for the hand of God, as God reaches for the hand of Adam in Michelangelo's vision of the Creation.

And once, in place of a bedtime story, I was reading Shakespeare to John—at his own request, for I never forced such things on you. I came to that passage in which Macbeth, having murdered Duncan, realizes what he has done to his own soul, and asks if all the water in the world can ever wash the blood from his hand, or will it not rather

The multitudinous seas incarnadine?

At that line, John's whole body twitched. I gave great silent thanks to God. For I knew that if, as children, you could thus feel in your souls the reverence and awe for life and the world, which is the ultimate meaning of Beethoven and Shakespeare, as man and woman you could never be satisfied with less. I felt a great faith that sooner or later you would understand what I once told you, not because I expected you to understand it then, but because I hoped that you would remember it later: "True wisdom comes from the overcoming of suffering and sin. All true wisdom is therefore touched with sadness."

If all this sounds unduly solemn, you know that our lives were not; that all of us suffer from an incurable itch to puncture false solemnity. In our daily lives, we were fun-loving and gay. For those who have solemnity in their souls generally have enough of it there, and do not need to force it into their faces.

Then, on August 3, 1948, you learned for the first time that your father had once been a Communist, that he had worked in something called "the underground," that it was shameful, and that for some reason he was in Washington telling the world about it. While he was in the underground, he testified, he had worked with a number of other Communists. One of them was a man with the odd name of Alger Hiss. Later, Alger Hiss denied the allegation. Thus the Great Case began, and with it our lives were changed forever.

Dear children, one autumn twilight, when you were much smaller, I slipped away from you in play and stood for a moment alone in the apple orchard near the barn. Then I heard your two voices, piping together anxiously, calling to me: "Papa! Papa!" from the harvested cornfield. In the years when I was away five days a week in New York, working to pay for the farm, I used to think of you both before I fell asleep at night. And that is how you almost always came to me—voices of beloved children, calling to me from the gathered fields at dusk.

You called to me once again at night in the same orchard. That was a good many years later. A shadow deeper and more chilling than the autumn evening had closed upon us—I mean the Hiss Case. It was the first year of the Case. We had been doing the evening milking together. For us, one of the few happy results of the Case was that at last I could be home with you most of the time (in life these good things usually come too little or too late). I was washing and disinfecting the cows, and putting on and taking off the milkers. You were stripping after me.

In the quiet, there suddenly swept over my mind a clear realization of our true position—obscure, all but friendless people (some of my great friends had already taken refuge in aloofness; the others I had withdrawn from so as not to involve them in my affairs). Against me was an almost solid line-up of the most powerful groups and men in the country, the bitterly hostile reaction of much of the press, the smiling skepticism of much of the public, the venomous calumnies of the Hiss forces, the all but universal failure to understand the real meaning of the Case or my real purpose. A sense of the enormous futility of my effort, and my own inadequacy, drowned me. I felt a physical cold creep through me, settle around my heart and freeze any pulse of hope. The sight of you children, guiltless and defenseless, was more than I could bear. I was alone against the world; my longing was to be left completely alone, or not to be at all. It was that death of the will which Communism, with great cunning, always tries to induce in its victims.

I waited until the last cow was stripped and the last can lifted into the cooler. Then I stole into the upper barn and out into the apple orchard. It was a very dark night. The stars were large and cold. This cold was one with the coldness in myself. The lights of the barn, the house and the neighbors' houses were warm in the windows and on the ground; they were not for me. Then I heard Ellen call me in the barn and John called: "Papa!" Still calling, Ellen went down to the house to see if I were there. I heard John opening gates as he went to the calf barn, and he called me there. With all the longing of my love for you, I wanted to answer. But if I answered, I must come back to the living world. I could not do that.

John began to call me in the cow stable, in the milk house. He went into the dark side of the barn (I heard him slide the door back), into the upper barn, where at night he used to be afraid. He stepped outside in the dark, calling: "Papa! Papa!"—then, frantically, on the verge of tears: "Papa!" I walked over to him. I felt that I was making the most terrible surrender I should have to make on earth. "Papa," he cried and threw his arms around me, "don't ever go away." "No," I said, "no, I won't ever go away." Both of us knew that the words "go away" stood for something else, and that I had given him my promise not to kill myself. Later on, as you will see, I was tempted, in my wretchedness, to break that promise.

My children, when you were little, we used sometimes to go for walks in our pine woods. In the open fields, you would run along by yourselves. But you used instinctively to give me your hands as we entered those woods, where it was darker, lonelier, and in the stillness our voices sounded loud and frightening. In this book I am again giving you my hands. I am leading you, not through cool pine woods, but up and up a narrow defile between bare and steep rocks from which in shadow things uncoil and slither away. It will be dark. But, in the end, if I have led you aright, you will make out three crosses, from two of which hang thieves. I will have brought you to Golgotha—the place of skulls. This is the meaning of the journey. Before you understand, I may not be there, my hands may have slipped from yours. It will not matter. For when you understand what you see, you will no longer be children. You will know that life is pain, that each of us hangs always upon the cross of himself. And when you know that this is true of every man, woman and child on earth, you will be wise.

Your Father

B. F. SKINNER

Selection from *Beyond Freedom and Dignity*
1971

B. F. Skinner (1904–90) insisted that the survival of our culture depends on the development of a technology of behavior. We must be willing to plan what human beings do, Skinner argued, and we must not flinch at the idea of subjecting human beings to control. In the selection from *Beyond Freedom and Dignity* (New York, 1971) that follows, Skinner defends this social vision against complaints to the effect that so "scientific" a view of human beings serves to diminish their humanity. Skinner developed his ideas in the course of a long and distinguished career as an experimental psychologist, working with laboratory animals as well as with human subjects. Although Skinner speaks here as an essayist and public moralist, his ideas were also set forth in a best-selling utopian novel, *Walden Two* (1948). Skinner also wrote three autobiographical volumes, *Particulars of My Life* (New York, 1976), *The Shaping of a Behaviorist* (New York, 1979), and *A Matter of Consequences* (New York, 1983).

For a study of the intellectual tradition of "behaviorism" of which Skinner became his generation's most distinguished exemplar, see Laurence C. Smith, *Behaviorism and Logical Positivism: A Reassessment of the Alliance* (Stanford, 1980). A contemporary of Skinner's with comparably sweeping, but strikingly different views about politics, society, and the psyche was the Freudian-Marxist Herbert Marcuse, whose *Eros and Civilization* (New York, 1955) can be profitably studied alongside Skinner's writings. For a bold overview of the "therapeutic" mind-set that embraced Freudians, behaviorists, and other psychologically oriented social theorists, see Philip Rieff, *The Triumph of the Therapeutic* (New York, 1966). A sound biography of Skinner himself is Daniel J. Bjork, *B. F. Skinner: A Life* (New York, 1993).

Almost all living things act to free themselves from harmful contacts. A kind of freedom is achieved by the relatively simple forms of behavior called reflexes. A person sneezes and frees his respiratory passages from irritating substances. He vomits and frees his stomach from indigestible or poisonous food. He pulls back his hand and frees it from a sharp or hot object. More elaborate forms of behavior have similar effects. When confined, people struggle ("in rage") and break free. When in danger they flee from or attack its source. Behavior of this kind presumably evolved because of its survival value; it is as much a part of what we call the human genetic endowment as breathing, sweating, or digesting food. And through conditioning similiar behavior may be acquired with respect to novel objects which could have played no role in evolution. These are no doubt minor instances of the struggle to be free, but they are significant. We do not attribute them to any love of freedom; they are simply forms of behavior which have proved useful in reducing various threats to the individual and hence to the species in the course of evolution.

A much more important role is played by behavior which weakens harmful stimuli in another way. It is not acquired in the form of conditioned reflexes, but as the product of a different process called operant conditioning. When a bit of behavior is followed by a certain kind of consequence, it is more likely to occur again, and a consequence having this effect is called a reinforcer. Food, for example, is a reinforcer to a hungry organism; anything the organism does that is followed by the receipt of food is more likely to be done again whenever the organism is hungry. Some stimuli are called negative reinforcers; any response which reduces the intensity of such a stimulus—or ends it—is more likely to be emitted when the stimulus recurs. Thus, if a person escapes from a hot sun when he moves under cover, he is more likely to move under cover when the sun is again hot. The reduction in temperature reinforces the behavior it is "contingent upon"—that is, the behavior it follows. Operant conditioning also occurs when a person simply avoids a hot sun—when, roughly speaking, he escapes from the *threat* of a hot sun.

Negative reinforcers are called aversive in the sense that they are the things organisms "turn away from." The term suggests a spatial separation—moving or running away from something—but the essential relation is temporal. In a standard apparatus used to study the process in the laboratory, an arbitrary response simply weakens an aversive stimulus or brings it to an end. A great deal of physical technology is the result of this kind of struggle for freedom. Over the centuries, in erratic ways, men have constructed a world in which they are relatively free of many kinds of threatening or harmful stimuli—extremes of temperature, sources of infection, hard labor, danger, and even those minor aversive stimuli called discomfort.

Escape and avoidance play a much more important role in the struggle for freedom when the aversive conditions are generated by other people. Other people can be aversive without, so to speak, trying: they can be rude, dangerous, contagious, or annoying, and one escapes from them or avoids them accordingly. They may also be "intentionally" aversive—that is, they may treat other people aversively because of what follows. Thus, a slave driver induces a slave to work by whipping him when he stops; by resuming

Source: B. F. Skinner, *Beyond Freedom and Dignity* (New York: Knopf, 1971), 189–206 (Bantam edition).

work the slave escapes from the whipping (and incidentally reinforces the slave driver's behavior in using the whip). A parent nags a child until the child performs a task; by performing the task the child escapes nagging (and reinforces the parent's behavior). The blackmailer threatens exposure unless the victim pays; by paying, the victim escapes from the threat (and reinforces the practice). A teacher threatens corporal punishment or failure until his students pay attention; by paying attention the students escape from the threat of punishment (and reinforce the teacher for threatening it). In one form or another intentional aversive control is the pattern of most social coordination—in ethics, religion, government, economics, education, psychotherapy, and family life.

A person escapes from or avoids aversive treatment by behaving in ways which reinforce those who treated him aversively until he did so, but he may escape in other ways. For example, he may simply move out of range. A person may escape from slavery, emigrate or defect from a government, desert from an army, become an apostate from a religion, play truant, leave home, or drop out of a culture as a hobo, hermit, or hippie. Such behavior is as much a product of the aversive conditions as the behavior the conditions were designed to evoke. The latter can be guaranteed only by sharpening the contingencies or by using stronger aversive stimuli.

Another anomalous mode of escape is to attack those who arrange aversive conditions and weaken or destroy their power. We may attack those who crowd us or annoy us, as we attack the weeds in our garden, but again the struggle for freedom is mainly directed toward intentional controllers—toward those who treat others aversively in order to induce them to behave in particular ways. Thus, a child may stand up to his parents, a citizen may overthrow a government, a communicant may reform a religion, a student may attack a teacher or vandalize a school, and a dropout may work to destroy a culture.

It is possible that man's genetic endowment supports this kind of struggle for freedom: when treated aversively people tend to act aggressively or to be reinforced by signs of having worked aggressive damage. Both tendencies should have had evolutionary advantages, and they can easily be demonstrated. If two organisms which have been coexisting peacefully receive painful shocks, they immediately exhibit characteristic patterns of aggression toward each other. The aggressive behavior is not necessarily directed toward the actual source of stimulation; it may be "displaced" toward any convenient person or object. Vandalism and riots are often forms of undirected or misdirected aggression. An organism which has received a painful shock will also, if possible, act to gain access to another organism toward which it can act aggressively. The extent to which human aggression exemplifies innate tendencies is not clear, and many of the ways in which people attack and thus weaken or destroy the power of intentional controllers are quite obviously learned.

What we may call the "literature of freedom" has been designed to induce people to escape from or attack those who act to control them aversively. The content of the literature is the philosophy of freedom, but philosophies are among those inner causes which need to be scrutinized. We say that a person behaves in a given way because he possesses a philosophy, but we infer the philosophy from the behavior and therefore cannot use it in any satisfactory way as an explanation, at least until it is in turn explained. The literature of freedom, on the other hand, has a simple objective status. It consists of books, pamphlets, manifestoes, speeches, and other verbal products, designed to induce people to act to free themselves from various kinds of intentional control. It does not impart a philosophy of freedom; it induces people to act.

The literature often emphasizes the aversive conditions under which people live, perhaps by contrasting them with conditions in a freer world. It thus makes the conditions more aversive, "increasing the misery" of those it is trying to rescue. It also identifies those from whom one is to escape or those whose power is to be weakened through attack. Characteristic villains of the literature are tyrants, priests, generals, capitalists, martinet teachers, and domineering parents.

The literature also prescribes modes of action. It has not been much concerned with escape, possibly because advice has not been needed; instead, it has emphasized how controlling power may be weakened or destroyed. Tyrants are to be overthrown, ostracized, or assassinated. The legitimacy of a government is to be questioned. The ability of a religious agency to mediate supernatural sanctions is to be challenged. Strikes and boycotts are to be organized to weaken the economic power which supports aversive practices. The argument is strengthened by exhorting people to act, describing likely results, reviewing successful instances on the model of the advertising testimonial, and so on.

The would-be controllers do not, of course, remain inactive. Governments make escape impossible by banning travel or severely punishing or incarcerating defectors. They keep weapons and other sources of power out of the hands of revolutionaries. They destroy the written literature of freedom and imprison or kill those who carry it orally. If the struggle for freedom is to succeed, it must then be intensified.

The importance of the literature of freedom can scarcely be questioned. Without help or guidance people submit to aversive conditions in the most surprising way. This is true even when the aversive conditions are part of the natural environment. Darwin observed, for example, that the Fuegians seemed to make no effort to protect themselves from the cold; they wore only scant clothing and made little use of it against the weather. And one of the most striking things about the struggle for freedom from intentional control is how often it has been lacking. Many people have submitted to the most obvious religious, governmental, and economic controls for centuries, striking for freedom only sporadically, if at all. The literature of freedom has made an essential contribution to the elimination of many aversive practices in government, religion, education, family life, and the production of goods.

The contributions of the literature of freedom, however, are not usually described in these terms. Some traditional theories could conceivably be said to define freedom as the absence of aversive control, but the emphasis has been on how that condition *feels.* Other traditional theories could conceivably be said to define freedom as a person's condition when he is behaving under nonaversive control, but the emphasis has been upon a state of mind associated with doing what one wants. According to John Stuart Mill, "Liberty consists in doing what one desires." The literature of freedom has been important in changing practice (it has changed practices whenever it has had any effect whatsoever), but it has nevertheless defined its task as the changing of states of mind and feelings. Freedom is a "possession." A person escapes from or destroys the power of a controller in order to feel free, and once he feels free and can do what he desires, no further action is recommended and none is prescribed by the literature of freedom, except perhaps external vigilance lest control be resumed.

The feeling of freedom becomes an unreliable guide to action as soon as would-be controllers turn to nonaversive measures, as they are likely to do to avoid the problems raised when the controllee escapes or attacks. Nonaversive measures are not as conspicuous as aversive and are likely to be acquired more slowly, but they have obvious advantages which promote their use. Productive labor, for example, was once the result of punishment: the slave worked to avoid the consequences of not working. Wages exemplify a different principle; a person is paid when he behaves in a given way so that he will continue to behave in that way. Although it has long been recognized that rewards have useful effects, wage systems have evolved slowly. In the nineteenth century it was believed that an industrial society required a hungry labor force; wages would be effective only if the hungry worker could exchange them for food. By making labor less aversive—for instance, by shortening hours and improving conditions—it has been possible to get men to work for lesser rewards. Until recently teaching was almost entirely aversive: the student studied to escape the consequences of not studying, but nonaversive techniques are gradually being discovered and used. The skillful parent learns to reward a child for good behavior rather than punish him for bad. Religious agencies move from the threat of hellfire to an emphasis on God's love, and governments turn from aversive sanctions to various kinds of inducements, as we shall note again shortly. What the layman calls a reward is a "positive reinforcer," the effects of which have been exhaustively studied in the experimental analysis of operant behavior. The effects are not as easily recognized as those of aversive contingencies because they tend to be deferred, and applications have therefore been delayed, but techniques as powerful as the older aversive techniques are now available.

A problem arises for the defender of freedom when the behavior generated by positive reinforcement has deferred aversive consequences. This is particularly likely to be the case when the process is used in intentional control, where the gain to the controller usually means a loss to the controllee. What are called conditioned positive reinforcers can often be used with deferred aversive results. Money is an example. It is reinforcing only after it has been exchanged for reinforcing things, but it can be used as a reinforcer when exchange is impossible. A counterfeit bill, a bad check, a stopped check, or an unkept promise are conditioned reinforcers, although aversive consequences are usually quickly discovered. The archetypal pattern is the gold brick. Countercontrol quickly follows: we escape from or attack those who misuse conditioned reinforcers in this way. But the misuse of many social reinforcers often goes unnoticed. Personal attention, approval, and affection are usually reinforcing only if there has been some connection with already effective reinforcers, but they can be used when a connection is lacking. The simulated approval and affection with which parents and teachers are often urged to solve behavior problems are counterfeit. So are flattery, back-slapping, and many other ways of "winning friends."

Genuine reinforcers can be used in ways which have aversive consequences. A government may prevent defection by making life more interesting—by providing bread and circuses and by encouraging sports, gambling, the use of alcohol and other drugs, and various kinds of sexual behavior, where the effect is to keep people within reach of aversive sanctions. The Goncourt brothers noted the rise of pornography in the France of their day: "Pornographic literature," they wrote, "serves a Bas-Empire . . . one tames a people as one tames lions, by masturbation."

Genuine positive reinforcement can also be misused because the sheer quantity of reinforcers is not proportional to the effect on behavior. Reinforcement is usually only intermittent, and the schedule of reinforcement is more important than the amount received. Certain schedules generate a great deal of behavior in return for very little reinforcement, and the possibility has naturally not been overlooked by would-be controllers. Two examples of schedules which are easily used to the disadvantage of those reinforced may be noted.

In the incentive system known as piece-work pay, the worker is paid a given amount for each unit of work performed. The system seems to guarantee a balance between the goods produced and the money received. The schedule is attractive to management, which can calculate labor costs in advance, and also to the worker, who can control the amount he earns. This so-called "fixed-ratio" schedule of reinforcement can, however, be used to generate a great deal of behavior for very little return. It induces the worker to work fast, and the ratio can then be "stretched"—that is, more work can be demanded for each unit of pay without running the risk that the worker will stop working. His ultimate condition—hard work with very little pay—may be acutely aversive.

A related schedule, called variable-ratio, is at the heart of all gambling systems. A gambling enterprise pays people for giving it money—that is, it pays them when they make bets. But it pays on a kind of schedule which sustains betting even though, in the long run, the amount paid is less than the amount wagered. At first the mean ratio may be favorable to the bettor; he "wins." But the ratio can be stretched in such a way that he continues to play even when he begins to lose. The stretching may be accidental (an early run of good luck which grows steadily worse may create a dedicated gambler), or the ratio may be deliberately stretched by someone who controls the odds. In the long run the "utility" is negative: the gambler loses all.

It is difficult to deal effectively with deferred aversive consequences because they do not occur at a time when escape or attack is feasible—when, for example, the controller can be identified or is within reach. But the immediate reinforcement is positive and goes unchallenged. The problem to be solved by those who are concerned with freedom is to create immediate aversive consequences. A classical problem concerns "self-control." A person eats too much and gets sick but survives to eat too much again. Delicious food or the behavior evoked by it must be made sufficiently aversive so that a person will "escape from it" by not eating it. (It might be thought that he can escape from it only before eating it, but the Romans escaped afterward through the use of a vomitorium.) Current aversive stimuli may be conditioned. Something of the sort is done when eating too much is called wrong, gluttonous, or sinful. Other kinds of behavior to be suppressed may be declared illegal and punished accordingly. The more deferred the aversive consequences the greater the problem. It has taken a great deal of "engineering" to bring the ultimate consequences of smoking cigarettes to bear on the behavior. A fascinating hobby, a sport, a love affair, or a large salary may compete with activities which would be more reinforcing in the long run, but the run is too long to make countercontrol possible. That is why countercontrol is exerted, if at all, only by those who suffer aversive consequences but are not subject to positive reinforcement. Laws are passed against gambling, unions oppose piece-work pay, and no one is allowed to pay young children to work for them or to pay anyone for engaging in immoral behavior, but these measures may be strongly opposed by those whom they are designed to protect. The gambler objects to antigambling laws and the alcoholic to any kind of prohibition; and a child or prostitute may be willing to work for what is offered.

The literature of freedom has never come to grips with techniques of control which do not generate escape or counterattack because it has dealt with the problem in terms of states of mind and feelings. In his book *Sovereignty*, Bertrand de Jouvenel quotes two important figures in that literature. According to Leibnitz, "Liberty consists in the power to do what one wants to do," and according to Voltaire, "When I can do what I want to do, there is my liberty for me." But both writers add a concluding phrase: Leibnitz,

" . . . or in the power to want what can be got," and Voltaire, more candidly, " . . . but I can't help wanting what I do want." Jouvenel relegates these comments to a footnote, saying that the power to want is a matter of "interior liberty" (the freedom of the inner man!) which falls outside the "gambit of freedom."

A person wants something if he acts to get it when the occasion arises. A person who says "I want something to eat" will presumably eat when something becomes available. If he says "I want to get warm," he will presumably move into a warm place when he can. These acts have been reinforced in the past by whatever was wanted. What a person *feels* when he feels himself wanting something depends upon the circumstances. Food is reinforcing only in a state of deprivation, and a person who wants something to eat may feel parts of that state—for example, hunger pangs. A person who wants to get warm presumably feels cold. Conditions associated with a high probability of responding may also be felt, together with aspects of the present occasion which are similar to those of past occasions upon which behavior has been reinforced. Wanting is not, however, a feeling, nor is a feeling the reason a person acts to get what he wants. Certain contingencies have raised the probability of behavior and at the same time have created conditions which may be felt. Freedom is a matter of contingencies of reinforcement, not of the feelings the contingencies generate. The distinction is particularly important when the contingencies do not generate escape or counterattack.

The uncertainty which surrounds the countercontrol of nonaversive measures is easily exemplified. In the 1930's it seemed necessary to cut agricultural production. The Agricultural Adjustment Act authorized the Secretary of Agriculture to make "rental or benefit payments" to farmers who agreed to produce less—to pay the farmers, in fact, what they would have made on the food they agreed not to produce. It would have been unconstitutional to *compel* them to reduce production, but the government argued that it was merely inviting them to do so. But the Supreme Court recognized that positive inducement can be as irresistible as aversive measures when it ruled that "the power to confer or withhold unlimited benefit is the power to coerce or destroy." The decision was later reversed, however, when the Court ruled that "to hold that motive or temptation is equivalent to coercion is to plunge the law into endless difficulties." We are considering some of these difficulties.

The same issue arises when a government runs a lottery in order to raise revenue to reduce taxes. The government takes the same amount of money from its citizens in both cases, though not necessarily from the same citizens. By running a lottery it avoids certain unwanted consequences: people escape from heavy taxation by moving away or they counterattack by throwing a government which imposes new taxes out of office. A lottery, taking advantage of a stretched variable-ratio schedule of reinforcement, has neither of these effects. The only opposition comes from those who in general oppose gambling enterprises and who are themselves seldom gamblers.

A third example is the practice of inviting prisoners to volunteer for possibly dangerous experiments—for example, on new drugs—in return for better living conditions or shortened sentences. Everyone would protest if the prisoners were forced to participate, but are they really free when positively reinforced, particularly when the condition to be improved or the sentence to be shortened has been imposed by the state?

The issue often arises in more subtle forms. It has been argued, for example, that uncontrolled contraceptive services and abortion do not "confer unrestricted freedom to reproduce or not to reproduce because they cost time and money." Impoverished members of society should be given compensation if they are to have a truly "free choice." If the just compensation exactly offsets the time and money needed to practice birth control, then people will indeed be free of the control exerted by the loss of time and money, but whether or not they then have children will still depend upon other conditions which have not been specified. If a nation generously reinforces the practices of contraception and abortion, to what extent are its citizens free to have or not to have children?

Uncertainty about positive control is evident in two remarks which often appear in the literature of freedom. It is said that even though behavior is completely determined, it is better that a man "feel free" or "believe that he is free." If this means that it is better to be controlled in ways which have no aversive consequences, we may agree, but if it means that it is better to be controlled in ways against which no one revolts, it fails to take account of the possibility of deferred aversive consequences. A second comment seems more appropriate: "It is better to be a conscious slave than a happy one." The word "slave" clarifies the nature of the ultimate consequences being considered: they are exploitative and hence aversive. What the slave is to be conscious of is his misery; and a system of slavery so well designed that it does not breed revolt is the real threat. The literature of freedom has been designed to make men "conscious" of aversive control, but in its choice of methods it has failed to rescue the happy slave.

One of the great figures in the literature of freedom, Jean-Jacques Rousseau, did not fear the power of positive reinforcement. In his remarkable book *Émile* he gave the following advice to teachers:

> Let [the child] believe that he is always in control, though it is always you [the teacher] who really controls. There is no subjugation so perfect as that which keeps the appearance of freedom, for in that way one captures volition itself. The poor baby, knowing nothing, able to do nothing, having learned nothing, is he not at your mercy? Can you not arrange everything in the world which surrounds him? Can you not influence him as you wish? His work, his play, his pleasures, his pains, are not all these in your hands and without his knowing? Doubtless he ought to do only what he wants; but he ought to want to do only what you want him to do; he ought not to take a step which you have not foreseen; he ought not to open his mouth without your knowing what he will say.

Rousseau could take this line because he had unlimited faith in the benevolence of teachers, who would use their absolute control for the good of their students. But . . . benevolence is no guarantee against the misuse of power, and very few figures in the history of the struggle for freedom have shown Rousseau's lack of concern. On the contrary, they have taken the extreme position that all control is wrong. In so doing they exemplify a behavioral process called generalization. Many instances of control are aversive, in either their nature or their consequences, and hence all instances are to be avoided. The Puritans carried the generalization a step further by arguing that most positive reinforcement was wrong, whether or not it was intentionally arranged, just because it occasionally got people into trouble.

The literature of freedom has encouraged escape from or attack upon all controllers. It has done so by making any indication of control aversive. Those who manipulate human behavior are said to be evil men, necessarily bent on exploitation. Control is clearly the opposite of freedom, and if freedom is good, control must be bad. What is overlooked is control which does not have aversive consequences at any time. Many social practices essential to the welfare of the species involve the control of one person by another, and no one can suppress them who has any concern for human achievements. . . . [I]n order to maintain the position that all control is wrong, it has been necessary to disguise or conceal the nature of useful practices, to prefer weak practices just because they can be disguised or concealed, and—a most extraordinary result indeed!—to perpetuate punitive measures.

The problem is to free men, not from control, but from certain kinds of control, and it can be solved only if our analysis takes all consequences into account. How people feel about control, before or after the literature of freedom has worked on their feelings, does not lead to useful distinctions.

Were it not for the unwarranted generalization that all control is wrong, we should deal with the social environment as simply as we deal with the nonsocial. Although technology has freed men from certain aversive features of the environment, it has not freed them from the environment. We accept the fact that we depend upon the world around us, and we simply change the nature of the dependency. In the same way, to make the social environment as free as possible of aversive stimuli we do not need to destroy that environment or escape from it; we need to redesign it. . . .

DANIEL BELL

"The End of Ideology in the West"
1960

In the wake of the violent excesses associated with Hitler and Stalin—two bona fide ideologues—political ideologies came under sharp suspicion during the 1950s. The sociologist
Daniel Bell (1919–   ) was among a host of American intellectuals who gave voice to this
suspicion, who believed that the problems of industrial society defied the solutions offered
by the traditional Right and Left, and who placed their political hopes on a nondoctrinaire
pluralistic consensus of enlightened democratic capitalists. Although the catch phrase for
this anti-ideological impulse was contributed by Bell's book, *The End of Ideology: On the
Exhaustion of Political Ideas in the Fifties* (New York, 1960), Bell's actual formulation of
this impulse was ambivalent. He was troubled by the widespread turning away from systematic political argument that accompanied the rejection of the "terrible simplifiers," the
ideologues. The animated discussion stimulated by Bell is represented in the anthology,
The End of Ideology Debate (New York, 1968), edited by Chaim I. Waxman.

Bell's thought and career during the years leading up to the "end of ideology debate"
is the subject of an excellent historical study: Howard Brick, *Daniel Bell and the Decline of
Intellectual Radicalism: Social Theory and Political Reconciliation in the 1940s* (Madison,
Wis., 1986). For Bell's work as a whole, see Malcolm Waters, *Daniel Bell* (New York, 1995).
Bell's later work includes *The Coming of Postindustrial Society* (New York, 1973), and *The
Cultural Contradictions of Capitalism* (New York, 1976). The debate in which his ideas were
caught up included voices less guarded than Bell's about the prospects for a world in which
perpetual economic growth made social conflict less likely and in which "politics" would
gradually be replaced by "knowledge" and "information" as the basis for decisions made in
the public interest. Among the social science classics of the period engaged by this vision
of "modernization" are those by W. W. Rostow, *The Stages of Economic Growth* (Cambridge,
1960); C. E. Black, *The Dynamics of Modernization* (New York, 1967); and Robert E. Lane,
"The Decline of Politics and Ideology in a Knowledgeable Society," *American Sociological
Review* 31 (1966), 649–62.

Men commit the error of not knowing when to limit their hopes.
—Machiavelli

There have been few periods in history when man felt his world to be durable, suspended surely, as in Christian allegory, between chaos and heaven. In an Egyptian papyrus of more than four thousand years ago, one finds: " . . . impudence is rife . . . the country is spinning round and round like a potter's wheel . . . the masses are like timid sheep without a shepherd . . . one who yesterday was indigent is now wealthy and the sometime rich overwhelm him with adulation." The Hellenistic period as described by Gilbert Murray was one of a "failure of nerve"; there was "the rise of pessimism, a loss of self-confidence, of hope in this life and of faith in normal human effort." And the old scoundrel Talleyrand claimed that only those who lived before 1789 could have tasted life in all its sweetness.

This age, too, can add appropriate citations—made all the more wry and bitter by the long period of bright hope that preceded it—for the two decades between 1930 and 1950 have an intensity peculiar in written history: world-wide economic depression and sharp class struggles; the rise of fascism and racial imperialism in a country that had stood at an advanced stage of human culture; the tragic self-immolation of a revolutionary generation that had proclaimed the finer ideals of man; destructive war of a breadth and scale hitherto unknown; the bureaucratized murder of millions in concentration camps and death chambers.

For the radical intellectual who had articulated the revolutionary impulses of the past century and a half, all this has meant an end to chiliastic hopes, to millenarianism, to apocalyptic thinking—and to ideology. For ideology, which once was a road to action, has come to be a dead end.

Whatever its origins among the French *philosophes,* ideology as a way of translating ideas into action was given its sharpest phrasing by the left Hegelians, by Feuerbach and by Marx. For them, the function of philosophy was to be critical, to rid the present of the past. ("The tradition of all the dead generations weighs like a nightmare on the brain of the living," wrote Marx.) Feuerbach, the most radical of all the left Hegelians, called himself Luther II. Man would be free, he said, if we could demythologize religion. The history of all thought was a history of progressive disenchantment, and if finally, in Christianity, God had been transformed from a parochial deity to a universal abstraction, the function of criticism—using the radical tool of alienation, or self-estrangement—was to replace theology by anthropology, to substitute Man for God. Philosophy was to be directed at life, man was to be liberated from the "specter of abstractions" and extricated from the bind of the supernatural. Religion was capable only of creating "false consciousness." Philosophy would reveal "true consciousness." And by placing Man, rather than God, at the center of consciousness, Feuerbach sought to bring the "infinite into the finite."

If Feuerbach "descended into the world," Marx sought to transform it. And where Feuerbach proclaimed anthropology, Marx, reclaiming a root insight of Hegel, emphasized History and historical contexts. The world was not generic Man, but men; and of men, classes of men. Men differed because of their class position. And truths were class truths. All truths, thus, were masks, or partial truths, but the real truth was the revolutionary truth. And this real truth was rational.

Thus a dynamic was introduced into the analysis of ideology, and into the creation of a new ideology. By demythologizing religion, one recovered (from God and sin) the potential in man. By the unfolding of history, rationality was revealed. In the struggle of classes, true consciousness, rather than false consciousness, could be achieved. But if truth lay in action, one must act. The left Hegelians, said Marx, were only *littérateurs*. (For them a magazine was "practice.") For Marx, the only real action was in politics. But action, revolutionary action as Marx conceived it, was not mere social change. It was, in its way, the resumption of all the old millenarian, chiliastic ideas of the Anabaptists. It was, in its new vision, a new ideology.

Ideology is the conversion of ideas into social levers. Without irony, Max Lerner once entitled a book "Ideas Are Weapons." This is the language of ideology. It is more. It is the commitment to the consequences of ideas. When Vissarion Belinsky, the father of Russian criticism, first read Hegel and became convinced of the philosophical correctness of the formula "what is, is what ought to be," he became a supporter of the Russian autocracy. But when it was shown to him that Hegel's thought contained the contrary tendency, that dialectically the "is" evolves into a different form, he became a revolutionary overnight. "Belinsky's conversion," comments Rufus W. Mathewson, Jr., "illustrates an attitude toward ideas which is both passionate and myopic, which responds to them on the basis of their immediate relevances alone, and inevitably reduces them to tools."

What gives ideology its force is its passion. Abstract philosophical inquiry has always sought to eliminate passion, and the person, to rationalize all ideas. For the ideologue, truth arises in action, and meaning is given to experience by the "transforming moment." He comes alive not in contemplation, but in "the deed." One might say, in fact, that the most important, latent, function of ideology is to tap emotion. Other than religion (and war and nationalism), there have been few forms of channelizing emotional energy. Religion symbolized, drained away, dispersed emotional energy from the world onto the litany, the liturgy, the sacraments, the edifices, the arts. Ideology fuses these energies and channels them into politics.

But religion, at its most effective, was more. It was a way for people to cope with the problem of death. The fear of death—forceful and inevitable—and more, the fear of violent death, shatters the glittering, imposing, momentary dream of man's power. The fear of death, as Hobbes pointed out, is the source of conscience; the effort to avoid violent death is the source of law. When it was possible to believe, really believe, in heaven and hell, then some of the fear of death could be tempered or controlled; without such belief, there is only the total annihilation of the self.

It may well be that with the decline in religious *faith* in the last century and more, this fear of death as total annihilation, unconsciously expressed, has probably increased. One may hypothesize, in fact, that here is a cause of the breakthrough of the irrational, which is such a marked feature of the changed moral temper of our time. Fanaticism, violence, and cruelty are not, of course, unique in human history. But there was a time when such frenzies and mass emotions could be displaced, symbolized, drained away, and dispersed through religious devotion and practice. Now there is only this life, and the assertion of self becomes possible—for some even necessary—in the domination over others. One can challenge death by emphasizing the omnipotence of a movement (as in the "inevitable" victory of communism), or overcome death (as did the "immortality" of Captain Ahab) by bending others to one's will. Both paths are taken, but politics, because it can institutionalize power, in the way that religion once did, becomes the ready avenue for domination. The modern effort to transform the world chiefly or solely through politics (as contrasted with the religious transformation of the self) has meant that all other institutional ways of mobilizing emotional energy would necessarily atrophy. In effect, sect and church became party and social movement.

A social movement can rouse people when it can do three things: simplify ideas, establish a claim to truth, and, in the union of the two, demand a commitment to action. Thus, not only does ideology transform ideas, it transforms people as well. The nineteenth-century ideologies, by emphasizing inevitability and by infusing passion into their followers, could compete with religion. By identifying inevitability with progress, they linked up with the positive values of science. But more important, these ideologies were linked, too, with the rising class of intellectuals, which was seeking to assert a place in society.

The differences between the intellectual and the scholar, without being invidious, are important to understand. The scholar has a bounded field of knowledge, a tradition, and seeks to find his place in it, adding to the accumulated, tested knowledge of the past as to a mosaic. The scholar, qua scholar, is less involved with his "self." The intellectual begins with *his* experience, *his* individual perceptions of the world, *his* privileges and deprivations, and judges the world by these sensibilities. Since his own status is of high value, his judgments of the society reflect the treatment accorded him. In a business civilization, the intellectual felt that the wrong values were being honored, and rejected the society. Thus there was a "built-in" compulsion for the free-floating intellectual to become political. The ideologies, therefore, which emerged from the nineteenth century had the force of the intellectuals behind them. They embarked upon what William James called "the faith ladder," which in its vision of the future cannot distinguish possibilities from probabilities, and converts the latter into certainties.

Today, these ideologies are exhausted. The events behind this important sociological change are complex and varied. Such calamities as the Moscow Trials, the Nazi-Soviet pact, the concentration camps, the suppression of the Hungarian workers, form one chain; such social changes as the modification of capitalism, the rise of the Welfare State, another. In philosophy, one can trace the decline of simplistic, rationalistic beliefs and the emergence of new stoic-theological images of man, e.g. Freud, Tillich, Jaspers, etc. This is not to say that such ideologies as communism in France and Italy do not have a political weight, or a driving momentum from other sources. But out of all this history, one simple fact emerges: for the radical intelligentsia, the old ideologies have lost their "truth" and their power to persuade.

Few serious minds believe any longer that one can set down "blueprints" and through "social engineering" bring about a new utopia of social harmony. At the same time, the older "counter-beliefs" have lost their intellectual force as well. Few "classic" liberals insist that the State should play no role in the economy, and few serious conservatives, at least in England and on the Continent, believe that the Welfare State is "the road to serfdom." In the Western world, therefore, there is today a rough consensus among intellectuals on political issues: the acceptance of a Welfare State; the desirability of decentralized power; a system of mixed economy and of political pluralism. In that sense, too, the ideological age has ended.

And yet, the extraordinary fact is that while the old nineteenth-century ideologies and intellectual debates have become exhausted, the rising states of Asia and Africa are fashioning new ideologies with a different appeal for their own people. These are the ideologies of industrialization, modernization, Pan-Arabism, color, and nationalism. In the distinctive difference between the two kinds of ideologies lies the great political and social problems of the second half of the twentieth century. The ideologies of the nineteenth century were universalistic, humanistic, and fashioned by intellectuals. The mass ideologies of Asia and Africa are parochial, instrumental, and created by political leaders. The driving forces of the old ideologies were social equality and, in the largest sense, freedom. The impulsions of the new ideologies are economic development and national power.

And in this appeal, Russia and China have become models. The fascination these countries exert is no longer the old idea of the free society, but the new one of economic growth. And if this involves the wholesale coercion of the population and the rise of new elites to drive the people, the new repressions are justified on the ground that without such coercions economic advance cannot take place rapidly enough. And even for some of the liberals of the West, "economic development" has become a new ideology that washes away the memory of old disillusionments.

It is hard to quarrel with an appeal for rapid economic growth and modernization, and few can dispute the goal, as few could ever dispute an appeal for equality and freedom. But in this powerful surge—and its swiftness is amazing—any movement that instates such goals risks the sacrifice of the present generation for a future that may see only a new exploitation by a new elite. For the newly risen countries, the debate is not over the merits of communism—the content of that doctrine has long been forgotten by friends and foes alike. The question is an older one: whether new societies can grow by building democratic institutions and allowing people to make choices—and sacrifices—voluntarily, or whether the new elites, heady with power, will impose totalitarian means to transform their countries. Certainly in these traditional and old colonial societies where the masses are apathetic and easily manipulated, the answer lies with the intellectual classes and their conceptions of the future.

Thus one finds, at the end of the fifties, a disconcerting caesura. In the West, among the intellectuals, the old passions are spent. The new generation, with no meaningful memory of these old debates, and no secure tradition to build upon, finds itself seeking new purposes within a framework of political society that has rejected, intellectually speaking, the old apocalyptic and chiliastic visions. In the search for a "cause," there is a deep, desperate, almost pathetic anger. The theme runs through a remarkable book, *Convictions,* by a dozen of the sharpest young Left Wing intellectuals in Britain. They cannot define the content of the "cause" they seek, but the yearning is clear. In the U.S. too there is a restless search for a new intellectual radicalism. Richard Chase, in his thoughtful assessment of American society, *The Democratic Vista,* insists that the greatness of nineteenth-century America for the rest of the world consisted in its radical vision of man (such a vision as Whitman's), and calls for a new radical criticism today. But the problem is that the old politico-economic radicalism (pre-occupied with such matters as the socialization of industry) has lost its meaning, while the stultifying aspects of contemporary culture (e.g., television) cannot be redressed in political terms. At the same time, American culture has almost completely accepted the avant-garde, particularly in art, and the older academic styles have been driven out completely. The irony, further, for those who seek "causes" is that the workers, whose grievances were once the driving energy for social change, are more satisfied with the society than the intellectuals. The workers have not achieved utopia, but their expectations were less than those of the intellectuals, and the gains correspondingly larger.

The young intellectual is unhappy because the "middle way" is for the middle-aged, not for him; it is without passion and is deadening. Ideology, which by its nature is an all-or-none affair, and temperamentally the thing he wants, is intellectually devitalized, and few issues can be formulated any more, intellectually, in ideological terms. The emotional energies—and needs—exist, and the question of how one mobilizes these energies is a difficult one. Politics offers little excitement. Some of the younger intellectuals have found an outlet in science or university pursuits, but often at the expense of narrowing their talent into mere technique; others have sought self-expression in the arts, but in the wasteland the lack of content has meant, too, the lack of the necessary tension that creates new forms and styles.

Whether the intellectuals in the West can find passions outside of politics is moot. Unfortunately, social reform does not have any unifying appeal, nor does it give a younger generation the outlet for "self-expression" and "self-definition" that it wants. The trajectory of enthusiasm has curved East, where, in the new ecstasies for economic utopia, the "future" is all that counts.

The end of ideology is not—should not be—the end of utopia as well. If anything, one can begin anew the discussion of utopia only by being aware of the trap of ideology. The point is that ideologists are "terrible simplifiers." Ideology makes it unnecessary for people to confront individual issues on their individual merits. One simply turns to the ideological vending machine, and out comes the prepared formulae. And when these beliefs are suffused by apocalyptic fervor, ideas become weapons, and with dreadful results.

There is now, more than ever, some need for utopia, in the sense that men need—as they have always needed—some vision of their potential, some manner of fusing passion with intelligence. Yet the ladder to the City of Heaven can no longer be a "faith ladder," but an empirical one: a utopia has to specify *where* one wants to go, *how* to get there, the costs of the enterprise, and some realization of, and justification for the determination of *who* is to pay.

The end of ideology closes the book, intellectually speaking, on an era, the one of easy "left" formulae for social change. But to close the book is not to turn one's back upon it. This is all the more important now when a "new Left," with few memories of the past, is emerging. This "new Left" has passion and energy, but little definition of the future. Its outriders exult that it is "on the move." But where it is going, what it means by Socialism, how to guard against bureaucratization, what one means by democratic planning or workers' control—any of the questions that require hard thought, are only answered by bravura phrases.

It is in attitudes towards Cuba and the new States in Africa that the meaning of intellectual maturity, and of the end of ideology, will be tested. For among the "new Left," there is an alarming readiness to create a *tabula rasa*, to accept the word "Revolution" as an absolution for outrages, to justify the suppression of civil rights and opposition—in short, to erase the lessons of the last forty years with an emotional alacrity that is astounding. The fact that many of these emerging social movements are justified in their demands for freedom, for the right to control their own political and economic destinies, does not mean they have a right to a blank check for everything they choose to do in the name of their emancipation. Nor does the fact that such movements take power in the name of freedom guarantee that they will not turn out to be as imperialist, as grandeur-concerned (in the name of Pan-Africanism or some other ideology), as demanding their turn on the stage of History, as the States they have displaced.

If the end of ideology has any meaning, it is to ask for the end of rhetoric, and rhetoricians, of "revolution" of the day when the young French anarchist Vaillant tossed a bomb into the Chamber of Deputies, and the literary critic Laurent Tailhade declared in his defense: "What do a few human lives matter; it was a *beau geste*." (A *beau geste* that ended, one might say, in a mirthless jest: two years later, Tailhade lost an eye when a bomb was thrown into a restaurant.) Today, in Cuba, as George Sherman, reporting for the *London Observer* summed it up: "The Revolution is law today although nobody has said clearly what that law is. You are expected to be simply for or against it and judge and be judged accordingly. Hatred and intolerance are wiping out whatever middle ground may have existed."

The problems which confront us at home and in the world are resistant to the old terms of ideological debate between"left" and "right," and if "ideology" by now, and with good reason, is an irretrievably fallen word, it is not necessary that "utopia" suffer the same fate. But it will if those who now call loudest for new utopias begin to justify degrading *means* in the name of some Utopian or revolutionary *end,* and forget the simple lessons that if the old debates are meaningless, some old verities are not—the verities of free speech, free press, the right of opposition and of free inquiry.

And if the intellectual history of the past hundred years has any meaning—and lesson—it is to reassert Jefferson's wisdom (aimed at removing the dead hand of the past, but which can serve as a warning against the heavy hand of the future as well), that "the present belongs to the living." This is the wisdom that revolutionists, old and new, who are sensitive to the fate of their fellow men, rediscover in every generation. "I will never believe," says a protagonist in a poignant dialogue written by the gallant Polish philosopher Leszek Kolakowski, "that the moral and intellectual life of mankind follows the law of economics, that is by saving today we can have more tomorrow; that we should use lives now so that truth will triumph or that we should profit by crime to pave the way for nobility."

And these words, written during the Polish "thaw," when the intellectuals had asserted, from their experience with the "future," the claims of humanism, echo the protest of the Russian writer Alexander Herzen, who, in a dialogue a hundred years ago, reproached an earlier revolutionist who would sacrifice the present mankind for a promised tomorrow: "Do you truly wish to condemn all human beings alive today to the sad role of caryatids . . . supporting a floor for others some day to dance on? . . . This alone should serve as a warning to people: an end that is infinitely remote is not an end, but, if you like, a trap; an end must be nearer—it ought to be, at the very least, the labourer's wage or pleasure in the work done. Each age, each generation, each life has its own fullness. . . ."

C. WRIGHT MILLS

Selection from *The Sociological Imagination* 1959

C. Wright Mills (1916–62) agreed with his Columbia colleague Daniel Bell that the inherited ideological traditions were running out of steam, but Mills developed a less hopeful analysis of the prospects of democratic political culture. Mills invoked the figure of "The Cheerful Robot," and sometimes doubted that industrial society had the political capability to prevent the degeneration of human beings into robots, cheerful or gloomy. His fellow social scientists, it seemed to Mills, were facilitating the consolidation of a technocratic social and economic order in which fundamental political issues were never formulated. In a book of 1959, *The Sociological Imagination,* from which we have selected a chapter, Mills called on social scientists and on intellectuals generally to confront the contradictions of modern society and to vindicate once again the values of reason and freedom that were proving to be elusive. Mills's first widely discussed book was *White Collar* (New York, 1951), which served—along with David Riesman's *The Lonely Crowd* (New York, 1950) and William H. Whyte's *The Organization Man* (New York, 1956)—to make the social psychology and politics of middle-class professionals a major preoccupation of a generation of critics, novelists, and researchers. In *The Power Elite* (New York, 1956), Mills insisted that the crucial decisions about the United States were being made not through a democratic give-and-take of competing interest groups but, rather, through the concerted will of a single group of rich men who went to the same schools and served on the same, interlocking boards directing major business, military, and political institutions. This thesis was strongly disputed by a number of political scientists—most notably Robert A. Dahl, in *Who Governs?* (New Haven, 1960)—but *The Power Elite* stimulated a vigorous debate over the character of American "pluralism" and was an important inspiration for many New Left intellectuals of the 1960s.

A cogent and appreciative introduction to Mills's work is Jim Miller, "Democracy and the Intellectual: C. Wright Mills Reconsidered," *Salmagundi* 70–71 (1986), 82–101. Information about Mills's life and career is available in Irving Louis Horowitz, *C. Wright Mills: An American Utopian* (New York, 1983) and in Rick Tillman, *C. Wright Mills: A Native Radical and His American Intellectual Roots* (University Prk, 1984). The most thorough historical study of Mills's thought is found in the various essays by Richard Gillam, for example, "*White Collar* from Start to Finish," *Theory & Society* 10 (1981), 1–30.

The climax of the social scientist's concern with history is the idea he comes to hold of the epoch in which he lives. The climax of his concern with biography is the idea he comes to hold of man's basic nature, and of the limits it may set to the transformation of man by the course of history.

All classic social scientists have been concerned with the salient characteristics of their time—and the problem of how history is being made within it; with "the nature of human nature"—and the variety of individuals that come to prevail within their periods. Marx and Sombart and Weber, Comte and Spencer, Durkheim and Veblen, Mannheim, Schumpeter, and Michels—each in his own way has confronted these problems. In our immediate times, however, many social scientists have not. Yet it is precisely now, in the second half of the twentieth century, that these concerns become urgent as issues, persistent as troubles, and vital for the cultural orientation of our human studies.

Nowadays men everywhere seek to know where they stand, where they may be going, and what—if anything—they can do about the present as history and the future as responsibility. Such questions as these no one can answer once and for all. Every period provides its own answers. But just now, for us, there is a difficulty. We are now at the ending of an epoch, and we have got to work out our own answers.

We are at the ending of what is called The Modern Age. Just as Antiquity was followed by several centuries of Oriental ascendancy, which Westerners provincially call The Dark Ages, so now The Modern Age is being succeeded by a post-modern period. Perhaps we may call it: The Fourth Epoch.

The ending of one epoch and the beginning of another is, to be sure, a matter of definition. But definitions, like everything social, are historically specific. And now our basic definitions of society and of self are being overtaken by new realities. I do not mean merely that never before within the limits of a single generation have men been so fully exposed at so fast a rate to such earthquakes of change. I do not mean merely that we feel we are in an epochal kind of transition, and that we struggle to grasp the outline of the new epoch we suppose ourselves to be entering. I mean that when we try to orient ourselves—if we do try—we find that too many of our old expectations and images are, after all, tied down historically: that too many of our standard categories of thought and of feeling as often disorient us as help to explain what is happening around us; that too many of our explanations are derived from the great historical transition from the Medieval to the Modern Age; and that when they are generalized for use today, they become unwieldy, irrelevant, not convincing. I also mean that our major orientations—liberalism and socialism—have virtually collapsed as adequate explanations of the world and of ourselves.

These two ideologies came out of The Enlightenment, and they have had in common many assumptions and values. In both, increased rationality is held to be the prime condition of increased freedom. The liberating notion of progress by reason, the faith in science as a unmixed good, the demand for popular education and the faith in its political meaning for democracy—all these ideals of The Enlightenment have rested upon the happy assumption of the inherent relation of reason and freedom. Those thinkers who have done the most to shape our ways of thinking have proceeded under this assumption. It lies under every movement and nuance of the work of Freud: To be free, the individual must become more rationally aware; therapy is an aid to giving reason its chance to work freely in the course of an individual's life. The same assumption underpins the main line of marxist work: Men, caught in the irrational anarchy of production, must become rationally aware of their position in society; they must become "class conscious"—the marxian meaning of which is as rationalistic as any term set forth by Bentham.

Liberalism has been concerned with freedom and reason as supreme facts about the individual; marxism, as supreme facts about man's role in the political making of history. The liberals and the radicals of The Modern Period have generally been men who believed in the rational making of history and of his own biography by the free individual.

But what has been happening in the world makes evident, I believe, why the ideas of freedom and of reason now so often seem so ambiguous in both the new capitalist and the communist societies of our time: why marxism has so often become a dreary rhetoric of bureaucratic defense and abuse; and liberalism, a trivial and irrelevant way of masking social reality. The major developments of our time, I believe, can be correctly understood neither in terms of the liberal nor the marxian interpretation of politics and culture. These ways of thought arose as guidelines to reflection about types of society which do not now exist. John Stuart Mill never examined the kinds of political economy now arising in the capitalist world. Karl Marx never analyzed the kinds of society now arising in the communist bloc. And neither of them ever thought through the problems of the so-called underdeveloped countries in which seven out of ten men are trying to exist today. Now we confront new kinds of social structure which, in terms of "modern" ideals, resist analysis in the liberal and in the socialist terms we have inherited.

The ideological mark of The Fourth Epoch—that which sets it off from The Modern Age—is that the ideas of freedom and of reason have become moot; that increased rationality may not be assumed to make for increased freedom.

The role of reason in human affairs and the idea of the free individual as the seat of reason are the most important themes inherited by twentieth-century social scientists from the philosophers of the Enlightenment. If they are to remain the key values in terms of which troubles are specified and issues focused, then the ideals of reason and of freedom must now be re-stated as problems in more precise and solvable ways than have been available to earlier thinkers and investigators. For in our time these two values, reason and freedom, are in obvious yet subtle peril.

The underlying trends are well known. Great and rational organizations—in brief, bureaucracies—have indeed increased, but the substantive reason of the individual at large has not. Caught in the limited milieux of their everyday lives, ordinary men often cannot reason about the great structures—rational and irrational—of which their milieux are subordinate parts. Accordingly, they often carry out series of apparently rational actions without any ideas of the ends they serve, and there is the increasing suspicion that those at the top as well—like Tolstoy's generals—only pretend they know. The growth of such organizations, within an increasing division of labor, sets up more and more spheres of life, work, and leisure, in which reasoning is difficult or impossible. The soldier, for example, "carries out an entire series of functionally rational actions accurately without having any idea as to the ultimate end of this action" or the function of each act within the whole. Even men of technically supreme intelligence may efficiently perform their assigned work and yet not know that it is to result in the first atom bomb.

Science, it turns out, is not a technological Second Coming. That its techniques and its rationality are given a central place in a society does not mean that men live reasonably and without myth, fraud, and superstition. Universal education may lead to technological idiocy and nationalist provinciality—rather than to the informed and independent intelligence. The Mass distribution of historic culture may not lift the level of cultural sensibility, but rather, merely banalize it—and compete mightily with the chance for creative innovation. A high level of bureaucratic rationality and of technology does not mean a high level of either individual or social intelligence. From the first you cannot infer the second. For social, technological, or bureaucratic rationality is not merely a grand summation of the individual will and capacity to reason. The very chance to acquire that will and that capacity seems in fact often to be decreased by it. Rationally organized social arrangements are not necessarily a means of increased freedom—for the individual or for the society. In fact, often they are a means of tyranny and manipulation, a means of expropriating the very chance to reason, the very capacity to act as a free man.

Only from a few commanding positions or—as the case may be—merely vantage points, in the rationalized structure is it readily possible to understand the structural forces at work in the whole which thus affect each limited part of which ordinary men are aware.

The forces that shape these milieux do not originate within them, nor are they controllable by those sunk in them. Moreover, these milieux are themselves increasingly rationalized. Families as well as factories, leisure as well as work, neighborhoods as well as states—they, too, tend to become parts of a functionally rational totality—or they are subject to uncontrolled and irrational forces.

The increasing rationalization of society, the contradiction between such rationality and reason, the collapse of the assumed coincidence of reason and freedom—these developments lie back of the rise into view of the man who is "with" rationality but without reason, who is increasingly self-rationalized and also increasingly uneasy. It is in terms of this type of man that the contemporary problem of freedom is best stated. Yet such trends and suspicions are often not formulated as problems, and they are certainly not widely acknowledged as issues or felt as a set of troubles. Indeed, it is the fact of its unrecognized character, its lack of formulation, that is the most important feature of the contemporary problem of freedom and reason.

From the individual's standpoint, much that happens seems the result of manipulation, of management, of blind drift; authority is often not explicit; those with power often feel no need to make it explicit and to justify it. That is one reason why ordinary men, when they are in trouble or when they sense that they are up against issues, cannot get clear targets for thought and for action; they cannot determine what it is that imperils the values they vaguely discern as theirs.

Given these effects of the ascendant trend of rationalization, the individual "does the best he can." He gears his aspirations and his work to the situation he is in, and from which he can find no way out. In due course, he does not seek a way out: he adapts. That part of his life which is left over from work, he uses to play, to consume, "to have fun." Yet this sphere of consumption is also being rationalized. Alienated from production, from work, he is also alienated from consumption, from genuine leisure. This adaptation of the individual and its effects upon his milieux and self results not only in the loss of his chance, and in due course, of his capacity and will to reason; it also affects his chances and his capacity to act as a free man. Indeed, neither the value of freedom nor of reason, it would seem, are known to him.

Such adapted men are not necessarily unintelligent, even after they have lived and worked and played in such circumstances for quite some time. Karl Mannheim has made the point in a clear way by speaking of "self rationalization," which refers to the way in which an individual, caught in the limited segments of great, rational organizations, comes systematically to regulate his impulses and his aspirations, his manner of life and his ways of thought, in rather strict accordance with "the rules and regulations of the organization." The rational organization is thus an alienating organization: the guiding principles of conduct and reflection, and in due course of emotion as well, are not seated in the individual conscience of the Reformation man, or in the independent reason of the Cartesian man. The guiding principles, in fact, are alien to and in contradiction with all that has been historically understood as individuality. It is not too much to say that in the extreme development the chance to reason of most men is destroyed, as rationality increases and its locus, its control, is moved from the individual to the big-scale organization. There is then rationality without reason. Such rationality is not commensurate with freedom but the destroyer of it.

It is no wonder that the ideal of individuality has become moot: in our time, what is at issue is the very nature of man, the image we have of his limits and possibilities as man. History is not yet done with its exploration of the limits and meanings of "human nature." We do not know how profound man's psychological transformation from the Modern Age to the contemporary epoch may be. But we must now raise the question in an ultimate form: Among contemporary men will there come to prevail, or even to flourish, what may be called The Cheerful Robot?

We know of course that man can be turned into a robot, by chemical and psychiatric means, by steady coercion and by controlled environment; but also by random pressures and unplanned sequences of circumstances. But can he be made to want to become a cheerful and willing robot? Can he be happy in this condition, and what are the qualities and the meanings of such happiness? It will no longer do merely to assume, as a metaphysic of human nature, that down deep in man-as-man there is an urge for freedom and a will to reason. Now we must ask: What in man's nature, what in the human condition today, what in each of the varieties of social structure makes for the ascendancy of the cheerful robot? And what stands against it?

The advent of the alienated man and all the themes which lie behind his advent now affect the whole of our serious intellectual life and cause our immediate intellectual malaise. It is a major theme of the human condition in the contemporary epoch and of all studies worthy of the name. I know of no idea, no theme, no problem, that is so deep in the classic tradition—and so much involved in the possible default of contemporary social science.

It is what Karl Marx so brilliantly discerned in his earlier essays on "alienation"; it is the chief concern of Georg Simmel in his justly famous essay on "The Metropolis"; Graham Wallas was aware of it in his work on The Great Society. It lies behind Fromm's conception of the "automaton." The fear that such a type of man will become ascendant underlies many of the more recent uses of such classic sociological conceptions as "status and contract," "community and society." It is the hard meaning of such notions as Riesman's "other-directed" and Whyte's "social ethic." And of course, most popularly, the triumph—if it may be called that—of such a man is the key meaning of George Orwell's *1984*.

On the positive side—a rather wistful side nowadays—the larger meanings of Freud's "id," Marx's "Freiheit," George Mead's "I," Karen Horney's "spontaneity," lie in the use of such conceptions against the triumph of the alienated man. They are trying to find some center in man-as-man which would enable them to believe that in the end he cannot be made into, that he cannot finally become, such an alien creature—alien to nature, to society, to self. The cry for "community" is an attempt, a mistaken one I believe, to assert the conditions that would eliminate the probability of such a man, and it is because many humanist thinkers have come to believe that many psychiatrists by their practice produce such alienated and self-rationalized men that they reject these adaptive endeavors. Back of all this—and much more of traditional and current worrying and thinking among serious and sensible students of man—there lies the simple and decisive fact that the alienated man is the antithesis of the Western image of the free man. The society in which this man, this cheerful robot, flourishes is the antithesis of the free society—or in the literal and plain meaning of the word, of a democratic society. The advent of this man points to freedom as trouble, as issue, and—let us hope—as problem for social scientists. Put as a trouble of the individual—of the terms and values of which he is uneasily unaware—it is the trouble called "alienation." As an issue for publics—to the terms and values of which they are mainly indifferent—it is no less than the issue of democratic society, as fact and as aspiration.

It is just because this issue and this trouble are not now widely recognized, and so do not in fact exist as explicit troubles and issues, that the uneasiness and the indifference that betoken them are so deep and so wide in meaning and in effect. That is a major part of the problem of freedom today, seen in its political context, and it is a major part of the intellectual challenge which the formulation of the problem of freedom offers to contemporary social scientists.

It is not merely paradoxical to say that the values of freedom and reason are back of the absence of troubles, back of the uneasy feeling of malaise and alienation. In a similar manner, the issue to which modern threats to freedom and reason most typically lead is, above all, the absence of explicit issues—to apathy rather than to issues explicitly defined as such.

The issues and troubles have not been clarified because the chief capacities and qualities of man required to clarify them are the very freedom and reason that are threatened and dwindling. Neither the troubles nor the issues have been seriously formulated as the problems of the kinds of social science I have been criticizing. . . . The promise of classic social science, in considerable part, is that they will be.

The troubles and issues raised up by the crises of reason and freedom cannot of course be formulated as one grand problem, but neither can they be confronted, much less solved, by handling each of them microscopically as a series of small-scale issues, or of troubles confined to a scatter of milieux. They are structural problems, and to state them requires that we work in the classic terms of human biography and of epochal history. Only in such terms can the connections of structure and milieux that effect these values today be traced and casual analysis be conducted. The crisis of individuality and the crisis of history-making; the role of reason in the free individual life and in the making of history—in the re-statement and clarification of these problems lies the promise of the social sciences.

The moral and the intellectual promise of social science is that freedom and reason will remain cherished values, that they will be used seriously and consistently and imaginatively in the formulation of problems. But this is also the political promise of what is loosely called Western culture. Within the social sciences, political crises and intellectual crises of our time coincide: serious work in either sphere is also work in the other. The political traditions of classic liberalism and of classic socialism together exhaust our major political traditions. The collapse of these traditions as ideologies has had to do with the decline of free individuality and the decline of reason in human affairs. Any contemporary political re-statement of liberal and socialist goals must include as central the idea of a society in which all men would become men of substantive reason, whose independent reasoning would have structural consequences for their societies, its history, and thus for their own life fates.

The interest of the social scientist in social structure is not due to any view that the future is structurally determined. We study the structural limits of human decision in an attempt to find points of effective intervention, in order to know what can and what must be structurally changed if the role of explicit decision in history making is to be enlarged. Our interest in history is not owing to any view that the future is inevitable, that the future is bounded by the past. That men have lived in certain kinds of society in the past does not set exact or absolute limits to the kinds of society they may create in the future. We study history to discern the alternatives within which human reason and human freedom can now make history. We study historical social structures, in brief, in order to find within them the ways in which they are and can be controlled. For only in this way can we come to know the limits and the meaning of human freedom.

Freedom is not merely the chance to do as one pleases; neither is it merely the opportunity to choose between set alternatives. Freedom is, first of all, the chance to formulate the available choices, to argue over them—and then, the opportunity to choose. That is why freedom cannot exist without an enlarged role of human reason in human affairs. Within an individual's biography and within a society's history, the social task of reason is to formulate choices, to enlarge the scope of human decisions in the making of history. The future of human affairs is not merely some set of variables to be predicted. The future is what is to be decided—within the limits, to be sure, of historical possibility. But this possibility is not fixed; in our time the limits seem very broad indeed.

Beyond this, the problem of freedom is the problem of how decisions about the future of human affairs are to be made and who is to make them. Organizationally, it is the problem of a just machinery of decision. Morally, it is the problem of political responsibility. Intellectually, it is the problem of what are now the possible futures of human affairs. But the larger aspects of the problem of freedom today concern not only the nature of history and the structural chance for explicit decisions to make a difference in its course; they concern also the nature of man and the fact that the value of freedom cannot be based upon "man's basic nature." The ultimate problem of freedom is the problem of the cheerful robot, and it arises in this form today because today it has become evident to us that *all* men do *not* naturally *want* to be free; that all men are not willing or not able, as the case may be, to exert themselves to acquire the reason that freedom requires.

Under what conditions do men come to *want* to be free and capable of acting freely? Under what conditions are they willing and able to bear the burdens freedom does impose and to see these less as burdens than as gladly undertaken self-transformations? And on the negative side: Can men be made to want to become *cheerful* robots?

In our time, must we not face the possibility that the human mind as a social fact might be deteriorating in quality and cultural level, and yet not many would notice it because of the overwhelming accumulation of technological gadgets? Is not that one meaning of rationality without reason? Of human alienation? Of the absence of any free role for reason in human affairs? The accumulation of gadgets hides these meanings: Those who use these devices do not understand them; those who invent them do not understand much else. That is why we may *not*, without great ambiguity, use technological abundance as the index of human quality and cultural progress.

To formulate any problem requires that we state the values involved and the threat to those values. For it is the felt threat to cherished values—such as those of freedom and reason—that is the necessary moral substance of all significant problems of social inquiry, and as well of all public issues and private troubles.

The values involved in the cultural problem of individuality are conveniently embodied in all that is suggested by the ideal of The Renaissance Man. The threat to that ideal is the ascendancy among us of The Cheerful Robot.

The values involved in the political problem of history making are embodied in the Promethean ideal of its human making. The threat to that ideal is twofold: On the one hand, history making may well go by default, men may continue to abdicate its wilful making, and so merely drift. On the other hand, history may indeed be made—but by narrow elite circles without effective responsibility to those who must try to survive the consequences of their decisions and of their defaults.

I do not know the answer to the question of political irresponsibility in our time or to the cultural and political question of The Cheerful Robot. But is it not clear that no answers will be found unless these problems are at least confronted? Is it not obvious, that the ones to confront them, above all others, are the social scientists of the rich societies? That many of them do not now do so is surely the greatest human default being committed by privileged men in our times.

JOHN COURTNEY MURRAY

Selection from *We Hold These Truths*
1960

No single person did more than the Jesuit priest John Courtney Murray (1904–67) to provide a theoretical basis for the more complete involvement of Catholics in the intellectual life of the United States. In 1960, the year of the successful presidential campaign of the Catholic John F. Kennedy, Murray published a book constructing American democratic ideology in terms that made it seem closer to medieval Catholic doctrines than to the secular philosophers of the Enlightenment. "The American Bill of Rights," Murray insisted in the chapter of *We Hold These Truths: Catholic Reflections on the American Proposition* reprinted here, is "far more the product of Christian history" than of "eighteenth-century rationalist theory." Elsewhere, Murray elaborated an argument that carried great resonance with liberals within and beyond the Catholic community. The Spanish regime of the fascist Francisco Franco, so often defended by American Catholic thinkers of the 1940s and 1950s to the chagrin of their Protestant, Jewish, and agnostic contemporaries, was exactly opposite to true Catholic teaching; this teaching, according to Murray, was more fully expressed in the religious pluralism and sharp separation of church and state found in the United States. Murray's effort to vindicate American democracy on Christian terms bears comparison to the writings of Protestant theologian Reinhold Niebuhr.

Murray's ideas were considered subversive of Catholic authority when he first developed them in writings of the 1950s, some of which were stopped from initial publication by his superiors. But Murray's basic conception of the compatibility of Catholic faith with democratic political culture of the American variety was later to be accepted by more and more lay and clerical voices within the Catholic community of the United States. Murray's use of history was highly selective and has often been criticized as tendentious. But he brought to the study of Catholic history one genuinely historical insight that many Catholic scholars had resisted: the insight that Catholic doctrine, like other ideas and practices of human beings, changed over time.

For an excellent account of Murray's historic role and of his most egregious manipulations of the historical record, see Patrick Allitt, "The Significance of John Courtney Murray," in Mary Segers, ed., *Catholic Polity and American Politics* (New Haven, 1990), 53–67. Murray is also a major character in Allitt's *Catholic Intellectuals and Conservative Politics in America, 1950–1985* (Ithaca, 1993). For probing and informative studies of Catholic intellectual life before and after Murray, see Philip Gleason, *Keeping the Faith: American Catholicism Past and Present* (Notre Dame, 1987).

As it arose in America, the problem of pluralism was unique in the modern world, chiefly because pluralism was the native condition of American society. It was not, as in Europe and in England, the result of a disruption or decay of a previously existent religious unity. This fact created the possibility of a new solution; indeed, it created a demand for a new solution. The possibility was exploited and the demand was met by the American Constitution.

The question here concerns the position of the Catholic conscience in the face of the new American solution to a problem that for centuries has troubled, and still continues to trouble, various nations and societies. A new problem has been put to the universal Church by the fact of America—by the uniqueness of our social situation, by the genius of our newly conceived constitutional system, by the lessons of our singular national history, which has molded in a special way the consciousness and temper of the American people, within whose midst the Catholic stands, sharing with his fellow citizens the same national heritage. The Catholic community faces the task of making itself intellectually aware of the conditions of its own coexistence within the American pluralistic scene. We have behind us a lengthy historical tradition of acceptance of the special situation of the Church in America, in all its differences from the situations in which the Church elsewhere finds herself. But it is a question here of pursuing the subject, not in the horizontal dimension of history but in the vertical dimension of theory. . . .

The first truth to which the American Proposition makes appeal is stated in that landmark of Western political theory, the Declaration of Independence. It is a truth that lies beyond politics; it imparts to politics a fundamental human meaning. I mean the sovereignty of God over nations as well as over individual men. This is the principle that radically distinguishes the conservative Christian tradition of America from the Jacobin laicist tradition of Continental Europe. The Jacobin tradition proclaimed the autonomous reason of man to be the first and the sole principle of political organization. In contrast, the first article of the American political faith is that the political community, as a form of free and ordered human life, looks to the sovereignty of God as to the first principle of its organization. In the Jacobin tradition religion is at best a purely private concern, a matter of personal devotion, quite irrelevant to public affairs. Society as such, and the state which gives it legal form, and the government which is its organ of action are by definition agnostic or atheist. The statesman as such cannot be a believer, and his actions as a statesman are immune from any imperative or judgment higher than the will of the people, in whom resides ultimate and total sovereignty (one must remember that in the Jacobin tradition "the people" means "the party"). This whole manner of thought is altogether alien to the authentic American tradition.

From the point of view of the problem of pluralism this radical distinction between the American and the Jacobin traditions is of cardinal importance. The United States has had, and still has, its share of agnostics and unbelievers. But it has never known organized militant atheism on the Jacobin, doctrinaire Socialist, or Communist model; it has rejected parties and theories which erect atheism into a political principle. In 1799, the year of the Napoleonic *coup d'état* which overthrew the Directory and established a dictatorship in France, President John Adams stated the first of all American first principles in his remarkable proclamation of March 6:

Source: John Courtney Murray, *We Hold These Truths* (New York, 1960), 27–39, 42–43. Reprinted by permission of Sheed & Ward.

... it is also most reasonable in itself that men who are capable of social arts and relations, who owe their improvements to the social state, and who derive their enjoyments from it, should, as a society, make acknowledgements of dependence and obligation to Him who hath endowed them with these capacities and elevated them in the scale of existence by these distinctions. . . .

President Lincoln on May 30, 1863, echoed the tradition in another proclamation:

Whereas the Senate of the United States, devoutly recognizing the supreme authority and just government of Almighty God in all the affairs of men and nations, has by a resolution requested the President to designate and set apart a day for national prayer and humiliation; And whereas it is the duty of nations as well as of men to own their dependence upon the overruling power of God, to confess their sins and trespasses in humble sorrow, yet with the assured hope that genuine repentance will lead to mercy and pardon. . . .

The authentic voice of America speaks in these words. And it is a testimony to the enduring vitality of this first principle—the sovereignty of God over society as well as over individual men—that President Eisenhower in June, 1952, quoted these words of Lincoln in a proclamation of similar intent. There is, of course, dissent from this principle, uttered by American secularism (which, at that, is a force far different in content and purpose from Continental laicism). But the secularist dissent is clearly a dissent; it illustrates the existence of the American affirmation. And it is continually challenged. For instance, as late as 1952 an opinion of the United States Supreme Court challenged it by asserting: "We are a religious people whose institutions presuppose a Supreme Being." Three times before in its history—in 1815, 1892, and 1931—the Court had formally espoused this same principle.

The affirmation in Lincoln's famous phrase, "this nation under God," sets the American proposition in fundamental continuity with the central political tradition of the West. But this continuity is more broadly and importantly visible in another, and related, respect. In 1884 the Third Plenary Council of Baltimore made this statement: "We consider the establishment of our country's independence, the shaping of its liberties and laws, as a work of special Providence, its framers 'building better than they knew,' the Almighty's hand guiding them." The providential aspect of the matter, and the reason for the better building, can be found in the fact that the American political community was organized in an era when the tradition of natural law and natural rights was still vigorous. Claiming no sanction other than its appeal to free minds, it still commanded universal acceptance. And it furnished the basic materials for the American consensus.

The evidence for this fact has been convincingly presented by Clinton Rossiter in his book, *Seedtime of the Republic*, a scholarly account of the "noble aggregate of 'self-evident truths' that vindicated the campaign of resistance (1765–1775), the resolution for independence (1776), and the establishment of the new state governments (1776–1780)." These truths, he adds, "had been no less self-evident to the preachers, merchants, planters, and lawyers who were the mind of colonial America." It might be further added that these truths firmly presided over the great time of study, discussion, and decision which produced the Federal Constitution. "The great political philosophy of the Western world," Rossiter says, "enjoyed one of its proudest seasons in this time of resistance and revolution." By reason of this fact the American Revolution, quite unlike its French counterpart, was less a revolution than a conservation. It conserved, by giving newly vital form to, the liberal tradition of politics, whose ruin in Continental Europe was about to be consummated by the first great modern essay in totalitarianism.

The force for unity inherent in this tradition was of decisive importance in what concerns the problem of pluralism. Because it was conceived in the tradition of natural law the American Republic was rescued from the fate, still not overcome, that fell upon the European nations in which Continental Liberalism, a deformation of the liberal tradition, lodged itself, not least by the aid of the Lodges. There have never been "two Americas," in the sense in which there have been, and still are, "two Frances," "two Italys," "two Spains." Politically speaking, America has always been one. The reason is that a consensus was once established, and it still substantially endures, even in the quarters where its origins have been forgotten.

Formally and in the first instance this consensus was political, that is, it embraced a whole constellation of principles bearing upon the origin and nature of society, the function of the state as the legal order of society, and the scope and limitations of government. "Free government"—perhaps this typically American shorthand phrase sums up the consensus. "A free people under a limited government" puts the matter more exactly. It is a phrase that would have satisfied the first Whig, St. Thomas Aquinas.

To the early Americans government was not a phenomenon of force, as the later legal positivists would have it. Nor was it a "historical category," as Marx and his followers were to assert. Government did not mean simply the power to coerce, though this power was taken as integral to government. Government, properly speaking, was the right to command. It was authority. And its authority derived from law. By the same token its authority was limited by law. In his own way Tom Paine put the matter when he said, "In America Law is the King." But the matter had been better put by Henry of Bracton (d. 1268) when he said, "The king ought not to be under a man, but under God and under the law, because the law makes the king." This was the message of Magna Charta; this became the first structural rib of American constitutionalism.

Constitutionalism, the rule of law, the notion of sovereignty as purely political and therefore limited by law, the concept of government as an empire of laws and not of men—these were ancient ideas, deeply implanted in the British tradition at its origin in medieval times. The major American contribution to the tradition—a contribution that imposed itself on all subsequent political history in the Western world—was the written constitution. However, the American document was not the *constitution octroyée* of the nineteenth-century Restorations—a constitution graciously granted by the King or Prince-President. Through the American techniques of the constitutional convention and of popular ratification, the American Constitution is explicitly the act of the people. It embodies their consensus as to the purposes of government, its structure, the extent of its powers and the limitations on them, etc. By the Constitution the people define the areas where authority is legitimate and the areas where liberty is lawful. The Constitution is therefore at once a charter of freedom and a plan for political order. . . .

Americans agreed to make government constitutional and therefore limited in a new sense, because it is representative, republican, responsible government. It is limited not only by law but by the will of the people it represents. Not only do the people adopt the Constitution; through the techniques of representation, free elections, and frequent rotation of administrations they also have a share in the enactment of all subsequent statutory legislation. The people are really governed; American political theorists did not pursue the Rousseauist will-o'-the-wisp: how shall the individual in society come to obey only himself? Nevertheless, the people are governed because they consent to be governed; and they consent to be governed because in a true sense they govern themselves.

The American consensus therefore includes a great act of faith in the capacity of the people to govern themselves. The faith was not unrealistic. It was not supposed that everybody could master the technical aspects of government, even in a day when these aspects were far less complex than they now are. The supposition was that the people could understand the general objectives of governmental policy, the broad issues put to the decision of government, especially as these issues raised moral problems. The American consensus accepted the premise of medieval society, that there is a sense of justice inherent in the people, in virtue of which they are empowered, as the medieval phrase had it, to "judge, direct, and correct" the processes of government.

It was this political faith that compelled early American agreement to the institutions of a free speech and a free press. In the American concept of them, these institutions do not rest on the thin theory proper to eighteenth-century individualistic rationalism, that a man has a right to say what he thinks merely because he thinks it. The American agreement was to reject political censorship of opinion as unrightful, because unwise, imprudent, not to say impossible. However, the proper premise of these freedoms lay in the fact that they were social necessities. "Colonial thinking about each of these rights had a strong social rather than individualistic bias," Rossiter says. They were regarded as conditions essential to the conduct of free, representative, and responsible government. People who are called upon to obey have the right first to be heard. People who are to bear burdens and make sacrifices have the right first to pronounce on the purposes which their sacrifices serve. People who are summoned to contribute to the common good have the right first to pass their own judgment on the question, whether the good proposed be truly a good, the people's good, the common good. Through the technique of majority opinion this popular judgment becomes binding on government.

A second principle underlay these free institutions—the principle that the state is distinct from society and limited in its offices toward society. This principle too was inherent in the Great Tradition. Before it was cancelled out by the rise of the modern omnicompetent society-state, it had found expression in the distinction between the order of politics and the order of culture, or, in the language of the time, the distinction between *studium* and *imperium*. The whole order of ideas in general was autonomous in the face of government; it was immune from political discipline, which could only fall upon actions, not ideas. Even the medieval Inquisition respected this distinction of orders; it never recognized a crime of opinion, *crimen opinionis;* its competence extended only to the repression of organized conspiracy against public order and the common good. It was, if you will, a Committee on un-Christian Activities; it regarded activities, not ideas, as justiciable.

The American Proposition, in reviving the distinction between society and state, which had perished under the advance of absolutism, likewise renewed the principle of the incompetence of government in the field of opinion. Government submits itself to judgment by the truth of society; it is not itself a judge of the truth in society. Freedom of the means of communication whereby ideas are circulated and criticized, and the freedom of the academy (understanding by the term the range of institutions organized for the pursuit of truth and the perpetuation of the intellectual heritage of society) are immune from legal inhibition or government control. This immunity is a civil right of the first order, essential to the American concept of a free people under a limited government.

"A free people": this term too has a special sense in the American Proposition. America has passionately pursued the ideal of freedom, expressed in a whole system of political and civil rights, to new lengths; but it has not pursued this ideal so madly as to rush over the edge of the abyss, into sheer libertarianism, into the chaos created by the nineteenth-century theory of the "outlaw conscience," *conscientia exlex,* the conscience that knows no law higher than its own subjective imperatives. Part of the inner architecture of the American ideal of freedom has been the profound conviction that only a virtuous people can be free. It is not an American belief that free government is inevitable, only that it is possible, and that its possibility can be realized only when the people as a whole are inwardly governed by the recognized imperatives of the universal moral law.

The American experiment reposes on Acton's postulate, that freedom is the highest phase of civil society. But it also reposes on Acton's further postulate, that the elevation of a people to this highest phase of social life supposes, as its condition, that they understand the ethical nature of political freedom. They must understand, in Acton's phrase, that freedom is "not the power of doing what we like, but the right of being able to do what we ought." The people claim this right, in all its articulated forms, in the face of government; in the name of this right, multiple limitations are put upon the power of government. But the claim can be made with the full resonance of moral authority only to the extent that it issues from an inner sense of responsibility to a higher law. In any phase civil society demands order. In its highest phase of freedom it demands that order should not be imposed from the top down, as it were, but should spontaneously flower outward from the free obedience to the restraints and imperatives that stem from inwardly possessed moral principle. In this sense democracy is more than a political experiment; it is a spiritual and moral enterprise. And its success depends upon the virtue of the people who undertake it. Men who would be politically free must discipline themselves. Likewise institutions which would pretend to be free with a human freedom must in their workings be governed from within and made to serve the ends of virtue. Political freedom is endangered in its foundations as soon as the universal moral values, upon whose shared possession the self-discipline of a free society depends, are no longer vigorous enough to restrain the passions and shatter the selfish inertia of men. The American ideal of freedom as ordered freedom, and therefore an ethical ideal, has traditionally reckoned with these truths, these truisms.

This brings us to the threshold of religion, and therefore to the other aspect of the problem of pluralism, the plurality of religions in America. However, before crossing this threshold one more characteristic of the American Proposition, as implying a consensus, needs mention, namely, the Bill of Rights. The philosophy of the Bill of Rights was also tributary to the tradition of natural law, to the idea that man has certain original responsibilities precisely as man, antecedent to his status as citizen. These responsibilities are creative of rights which inhere in man antecedent to any act of government; therefore they are not granted by government and they cannot be surrendered to government. They are as inalienable as they are inherent. Their proximate source is in nature, and in history insofar as history bears witness to the nature of man; their ultimate source, as the Declaration of Independence states, is in God, the Creator of nature and the Master of history. The power of this doctrine, as it inspired both the Revolution and the form of the Republic, lay in the fact that it drew an effective line of demarcation around the exercise of political or social authority. When government ventures over this line, it collides with the duty and right of resistance. Its authority becomes arbitrary and therefore nil; its act incurs the ultimate anathema, "unconstitutional."

One characteristic of the American Bill of Rights is important for the subject here, namely, the differences that separate it from the Declaration of the Rights of Man in the France of '89. In considerable part the latter was a parchment-child of the Enlightenment, a top-of-the-brain concoction of a set of men who did not understand that a political community, like man himself, has roots in history and in nature. They believed that a state could be simply a work of art, a sort of absolute beginning, an artifact of which abstract human reason could be the sole artisan. Moreover, their exaggerated individualism had shut them off from a view of the organic nature of the human community; their social atomism would permit no institutions or associations intermediate between the individual and the state.

In contrast, the men who framed the American Bill of Rights understood history and tradition, and they understood nature in the light of both. They too were individualists, but not to the point of ignoring the social nature of man. They did their thinking within the tradition of freedom that was their heritage from England. Its roots were not in the top of anyone's brain but in history. Importantly, its roots were in the medieval notion of the *homo liber et legalis,* the man whose freedom rests on law, whose law was the age-old custom in which the nature of man expressed itself, and whose lawful freedoms were possessed in association with his fellows. The rights for which the colonists contended against the English Crown were basically the rights of Englishmen. And these were substantially the rights written into the Bill of Rights.

Of freedom of religion there will be question later. For the rest, freedom of speech, assembly, association, and petition for the redress of grievances, security of person, home, and property—these were great historical as well as civil and natural rights. So too was the right to trial by jury, and all the procedural rights implied in the Fifth- and later in the Fourteenth-Amendment provision for "due process of law." The guarantee of these and other rights was new in that it was written, in that it envisioned these rights with an amplitude, and gave them a priority, that had not been known before in history. But the Bill of Rights was an effective instrument for the delimitation of government authority and social power, not because it was written on paper in 1789 or 1791, but because the rights it proclaims had already been engraved by history on the conscience of a people. The American Bill of Rights is not a piece of eighteenth-century rationalist theory; it is far more the product of Christian history. Behind it one can see, not the philosophy of the Enlightenment but the older philosophy that had been the matrix of the common law. The "man" whose rights are guaranteed in the face of law and government is, whether he knows it or not, the Christian man, who had learned to know his own personal dignity in the school of Christian faith.

Perhaps one day the noble many-storeyed mansion of democracy will be dismantled, levelled to the dimensions of a flat majoritarianism, which is no mansion but a barn, perhaps even a tool shed in which the weapons of tyranny may be forged. Perhaps there will one day be wide dissent even from the political principles which emerge from natural law, as well as dissent from the constellation of ideas that have historically undergirded these principles—the idea that government has a moral basis; that the universal moral law is the foundation of society; that the legal order of society—that is, the state—is subject to judgment by a law that is not statistical but inherent in the nature of man; that the eternal reason of God is the ultimate origin of all law; that this nation in all its aspects—as a society, a state, an ordered and free relationship between governors and governed—is under God. The possibility that widespread dissent from these principles should develop is not foreclosed. If that evil day should come, the results would introduce one more paradox into history. The Catholic community would still be speaking in the ethical and political idiom familiar to them as it was familiar to their fathers, both the Fathers of the Church and the Fathers of the American Republic. The guardianship of the original American consensus, based on the Western heritage, would have passed to the Catholic community, within which the heritage was elaborated long before America was. And it would be for others, not Catholics, to ask themselves whether they still shared the consensus which first fashioned the American people into a body politic and determined the structure of its fundamental law.

What has been said may suffice to show the grounds on which Catholics participate in the American consensus. These grounds are drawn from the materials of the consensus itself. It has been a greatly providential blessing that the American Republic never put to the Catholic conscience the questions raised, for instance, by the Third Republic. There has never been a schism within the American Catholic community, as there was among French Catholics, over the right attitude to adopt toward the established polity. There has never been the necessity for nice distinctions between the regime and the legislation; nor has there ever been the need to proclaim a policy of *ralliement*. In America the *ralliement* has been original, spontaneous, universal. It has been a matter of conscience and conviction, because its motive was not expediency in the narrow sense—the need to accept what one is powerless to change. Its motive was the evident coincidence of the principles which inspired the American Republic with the principles that are structural to the Western Christian political tradition.

LIONEL TRILLING

"On the Teaching of Modern Literature"
1961

Modernism is often identified as the twentieth century's most commanding movement in literature and the arts. Not everyone who has so identified modernism has agreed upon just what defines it, but most celebrants of this multitudinous movement have at least emphasized its self-consciousness, its determination to face the worst as well as the best in the human prospect, and its penchant for aesthetic and moral complexity. The literary critic Lionel Trilling (1905–75) was among the most probing and influential commentators on modernist literature during the midcentury, when the prestige of this distinctive body of writing was at its height. In the essay of 1961 reprinted herein, Trilling reacts to many of the classics of modernism in the specific personal, moral, and professional context of college teaching. Although he expresses his admiration, and even his awe, for the great modernists, he betrays also a dual ambivalence: Is the impact of this literature on students altogether healthy? And is this literature trivialized when one is obliged to address it at the level of a midterm essay?

Trilling's career is ably analyzed in William Chace, *Lionel Trilling: Criticism and Politics* (Stanford, 1980). The special standing accorded to modernist literature by Trilling and his contemporaries is addressed in David A. Hollinger, "The Canon and Its Keepers," in Hollinger's *In the American Province: Studies in the History and Historiography of Ideas* (Bloomington, 1985), 74–91. For a discussion of Trilling in the setting of a comprehensive, critical history of academic literary scholarship, see Gerald Graff, *Professing Literature: An Institutional History* (Chicago, 1987). Cornel West, in *The American Evasion of Philosophy* (Madison, 1989), juxtaposes Trilling with Ralph Waldo Emerson, William James, W.E.B. Du Bois, W.V.O. Quine, C. Wright Mills, and other, diverse American intellectuals whom West believes practiced a distinctive type of cultural criticism. See also the essay by Thomas Bender, "Lionel Trilling and American Culture," *American Quarterly* 42 (1990), 324–47. The perspective, tone, and technique that Trilling displayed in "On the Teaching of Modern Literature" can be compared with features of Paul De Man, "Literary History and Literary Modernity," in De Man's *Blindness and Insight* (New Haven, 1971), perhaps the most influential discussion of literary modernism by any of the "poststructuralist" critics prominent in the generation immediately following Trilling's. Many insights into Trilling's life and work can be gleaned from Diana Trilling, *The Beginning of the Journey: The Marriage of Diana and Lionel Trilling* (New York, 1993).

I propose to consider here a particular theme of modern literature which appears so frequently and with so much authority that it may be said to constitute one of the shaping and controlling ideas of our epoch. I can identify it by calling it the disenchantment of our culture with culture itself—it seems to me that the characteristic element of modern literature, or at least of the most highly developed modern literature, is the bitter line of hostility to civilization which runs through it. It happens that my present awareness of this theme is involved in a personal experience, and I am impelled to speak of it not abstractly but with the husks of the experience clinging untidily to it. I shall go so far in doing this as to describe the actual circumstances in which the experience took place. These circumstances are pedagogic—they consist of some problems in teaching modern literature to undergraduates and my attempt to solve these problems. I know that pedagogy is a depressing subject to all persons of sensibility, and yet I shall not apologize for touching upon it because the emphasis upon the teaching of literature and especially of modern literature is in itself one of the most salient and significant manifestations of the culture of our time. Indeed, if, having in mind Matthew Arnold's lecture, "On the Modern Element in Literature," we are on the hunt for *the* modern element in modern literature, we might want to find it in the susceptibility of modern literature to being made into an academic subject.

For some years I have taught the course in modern literature in Columbia College. I did not undertake it without misgiving and I have never taught it with an undivided mind. My doubts do not refer to the value of the literature itself, only to the educational propriety of its being studied in college. These doubts persist even though I wholly understand that the relation of our collegiate education to modernity is no longer an open question. The unargued assumption of most curriculums is that the real subject of all study is the modern world; that the justification of all study is its immediate and presumably practical relevance to modernity; that the true purpose of all study is to lead the young person to be at home in, and in control of, the modern world. There is really no way of quarreling with the assumption or with what follows upon it, the instituting of courses of which the substance is chiefly contemporary or at least makes ultimate reference to what is contemporary.

It might be asked why anyone should *want* to quarrel with the assumption. To that question I can return only a defensive, eccentric, self-depreciatory answer. It is this: that to some of us who teach and who think of our students as the creators of the intellectual life of the future, there comes a kind of despair. It does not come because our students fail to respond to ideas, rather because they respond to ideas with a happy vagueness, a delighted glibness, a joyous sense of power in the use of received or receivable generalizations, a grateful wonder at how easy it is to formulate and judge, at how little resistance language offers to their intentions. When that despair strikes us, we are tempted to give up the usual and accredited ways of evaluating education, and instead of prizing responsiveness and aptitude, to set store by some sign of personal character in our students, some token of individual will. We think of this as taking the form of resistance and imperviousness, of personal density or gravity, of some power of supposing that ideas are real, a power which will lead a young man to say what Goethe thought was the modern thing to say, "But is this really true—is it true for *me*?" And to say this not in the facile way, not following the progressive educational prescription

Source: Lionel Trilling, *Beyond Culture* (New York: Harcourt Brace Jovanovitch, 1961), 3–27. Copyright © 1961 by Lionel Trilling. Reprinted by permission of the Estate of Lionel Trilling.

to "think for yourself," which means to think in the progressive pieties rather than in the conservative pieties (if any of the latter do still exist), but to say it from his sense of himself as a person rather than as a bundle of attitudes and responses which are all alert to please the teacher and the progressive community.

We can't do anything about the quality of personal being of our students, but we are led to think about the cultural analogue of a personal character that is grave, dense, and resistant—we are led to think about the past. Perhaps the protagonist of Thomas Mann's story, "Disorder and Early Sorrow" comes to mind, that sad Professor Cornelius with his intense and ambivalent sense of history. For Professor Cornelius, who is a historian, the past is dead, is death itself, but for that very reason it is the source of order, value, piety, and even love. If we think about education in the dark light of the despair I have described, we wonder if perhaps there is not to be found in the past that quiet place at which a young man might stand for a few years, at least a little beyond the competing attitudes and generalizations of the present, at least a little beyond the contemporary problems which he is told he can master only by means of attitudes and generalizations, that quiet place in which he can be silent, in which he can *know* something—in what year the Parthenon was begun, the order of battle at Trafalgar, how Linear B was deciphered: almost anything at all that has nothing to do with the talkative and attitudinizing present, anything at all but variations on the accepted formulations about *anxiety,* and *urban society,* and *alienation,* and *Gemeinschaft* and *Gesellschaft,* all the matter of the academic disciplines which are founded upon the modern self-consciousness and the modern self-pity. The modern self-pity is certainly not without its justification; but, if the circumstances that engender it are ever to be overcome, we must sometimes wonder whether this work can be done by minds which are taught in youth to accept these sad conditions of ours as the only right objects of contemplation. And quite apart from any practical consequences, one thinks of the simple aesthetic personal pleasure of having to do with young minds, and maturing minds, which are free of cant, which are, to quote an old poet, "fierce, moody, patient, venturous, modest, shy."

This line of argument I have called eccentric and maybe it ought to be called obscurantist and reactionary. Whatever it is called, it is not likely to impress a Committee on the Curriculum. It was, I think, more or less the line of argument of my department in Columbia College, when, up to a few years ago, it would decide, whenever the question came up, not to carry its courses beyond the late nineteenth century. But our rationale could not stand against the representations which a group of students made to our Dean and which he communicated to us. The students wanted a course in modern literature—very likely, in the way of students, they said that it was a scandal that no such course was being offered in the College. There was no argument that could stand against this expressed desire: we could only capitulate and then with pretty good grace, muster the arguments that justified our doing so. Was not the twentieth century more than half over? Was it not nearly fifty years since Eliot wrote "Portrait of a Lady"? George Meredith had not died until 1909, and even the oldest among us had read one of his novels in a college course—many American universities had been quick to bring into their purview the literature of the later nineteenth century, and even the early twentieth century; there was a strong supporting tradition for our capitulation. Had not Yeats been Matthew Arnold's contemporary for twenty-three years?

Our resistance to the idea of the course had never been based on an adverse judgment of the literature itself. We are a department not only of English but of comparative literature, and if the whole of modern literature is surveyed, it could be said—and we were willing to say it—that no literature of the past surpassed the literature of our time in power and magnificence. Then too, it is a difficult literature, and it is difficult not merely as defenders of modern poetry say that all literature is difficult. We nowadays believe that Keats is a very difficult poet, but his earlier readers did not. We now see the depths and subtleties of Dickens, but his contemporary readers found him as simply available as a plate of oysters on the half shell. Modern literature, however, shows its difficulties at first blush; they are literal as well as doctrinal difficulties—if our students were to know their modern literary heritage, surely they needed all the help that a teacher can give?

These made cogent reasons for our decision to establish, at long last, the course in modern literature. They also made a ground for our display of a certain mean-spirited, last-ditch vindictiveness. I recall that we said something like, "Very well, if they want the modern, let them have it—let them have it, as Henry James says, full in the face. We shall give the course, but we shall give it on the highest level, and if they think, as students do, that the modern will naturally meet them in a genial way, let them have their gay and easy time with Yeats and Eliot, with Joyce and Proust and Kafka, with Lawrence, Mann, and Gide."

Eventually the course fell to me to give. I approached it with an uneasiness which has not diminshed with the passage of time—it has, I think, even increased. It arises, this uneasiness, from my personal relation with the works that form the substance of the course. Almost all of them have been involved with me for a long time—I invert the natural order not out of lack of modesty but taking the cue of W. H. Auden's remark that a real book reads us. I have been read by Eliot's poems and by *Ulysses* and by *Remembrance of Things Past* and by *The Castle* for a good many years now, since early youth. Some of these books at first rejected me; I bored them. But as I grew older and they knew me better, they came to have more sympathy with me and to understand my hidden meanings. Their nature is such that our relationship has been very intimate. No literature has ever been so shockingly personal as that of our time—it asks every question that is forbidden in polite society. It asks us if we are content with our marriages, with our family lives, with our professional lives, with our friends. It is all very well for me to describe my course in the College catalogue as "paying particular attention to the role of the writer as a critic of his culture"—this is sheer evasion: the questions asked by our literature are not about our culture but about ourselves. It asks us if we are content with ourselves, if we are saved or damned—more than with anything else, our literature is concerned with salvation. No literature has ever been so intensely spiritual as ours. I do not venture to call it actually religious, but certainly it has the special intensity of concern with the spiritual life which Hegel noted when he spoke of the great modern phenomenon of the secularization of spirituality.

I do not know how other teachers deal with this extravagant personal force of modern literature, but for me it makes difficulty. Nowadays the teaching of literature inclines to a considerable technicality, but when the teacher has said all that can be said about formal matters, about verse-patterns, metrics, prose conventions, irony, tension, etc., he must confront the necessity of bearing personal testimony. He must use whatever authority he may possess to say whether or not a work is true; and if not, why not; and if so, why so. He can do this only at considerable cost to his privacy. How does one say that Lawrence is right in his great rage against the modern emotions, against the modern sense of life and ways of being, unless one speaks from the intimacies of one's own feelings, and one's own sense of life, and one's own wished-for way of being? How, except with the implication of personal judgment, does one say to students that Gide is perfectly accurate in his representation of the awful boredom and slow corruption of respectable life? Then probably one rushes in to say that this doesn't of itself justify homosexuality and the desertion of one's dying wife, certainly not. But then again, having paid one's *devoirs* to morality, how does one rescue from morality Gide's essential point about the supreme rights of the individual person, and without making it merely historical, academic?

My first response to the necessity of dealing with matters of this kind was resentment of the personal discomfort it caused me. These are subjects we usually deal with either quite unconsciously or in the privacy of our own conscious minds, and if we now and then disclose our thoughts about them, it is to friends of equal age and especial closeness. Or if we touch upon them publicly, we do so in the relative abstractness and anonymity of print. To stand up in one's own person and to speak of them in one's own voice to an audience which each year grows younger as one grows older—that is not easy, and probably it is not decent.

And then, leaving aside the personal considerations, or taking them merely as an indication of something wrong with the situation, can we not say that, when modern literature is brought into the classroom, the subject being taught is betrayed by the pedagogy of the subject? We have to ask ourselves whether in our day too much does not come within the purview of the academy. More and more, as the universities liberalize themselves, and turn their beneficent imperialistic gaze upon what is called Life Itself, the feeling grows among our educated classes that little can be experienced unless it is validated by some established intellectual discipline, with the result that experience loses much of its personal immediacy for us and becomes part of an accredited societal activity. This is not entirely true and I don't want to play the boring academic game of pretending that it *is* entirely true, that the university mind wilts and withers whatever it touches. I must believe and I do believe, that the university study of art is capable of confronting the power of a work of art fully and courageously. I even believe that it can discover and disclose power where it has not been felt before. But the university study of art achieves this end chiefly with works of art of an older period. Time has the effect of seeming to quiet the work of art, domesticating it and making it into a classic, which is often another way of saying that it is an object of merely habitual regard. University study of the right sort can reverse this process and restore to the old work its freshness and force—can, indeed, disclose unguessed-at power. But with the works of art of our own present age, university study tends to accelerate the process by which the radical and subversive work becomes the classic work, and university study does this in the degree that it is vivacious and responsive and what is called non-academic. In one of his poems Yeats mocks the literary scholars, "the bald heads forgetful of their sins," "the old, learned, respectable bald heads," who edit the poems of the fierce and passionate young men.

> Lord, what would they say
> Did their Catullus walk this way?

Yeats, of course, is thinking of his own future fate, and no doubt there is all the radical and comical discrepancy that he sees between the poet's passions and the scholars' close-eyed concentration on the text. Yet for my part, when I think of Catullus, I am moved to praise the tact of all those old heads, from Heinsius and Bentley to Munro and Postgate, who worked on Codex G and Codex O and drew conclusions from them about the lost Codex V—for doing only this and for not trying to realize and demonstrate the true intensity and the true quality and the true cultural meaning of Catullus's passion and managing to bring it somehow into eventual accord with their respectability and baldness. Nowadays we who deal with books in universities live in fear that the World, which we imagine to be a vital, palpitating, passionate, reality-loving World, will think of us as old, respectable, and bald, and we see to it that in our dealings with Yeats (to take him as the example) his wild cry of rage and sexuality is heard by our students and quite thoroughly understood by them as—what is it that we eventually call it?—*a significant expression of our culture.* The exasperation of Lawrence and the subversiveness of Gide, by the time we have dealt with them boldly and straightforwardly, are notable instances of the *alienation of modern man as exemplified by the artist.* "Compare Yeats, Gide, Lawrence, and Eliot in the use which they make of the theme of sexuality to criticize the deficiencies of modern culture. Support your statement by specific references to the work of each author. [Time: one hour.]" And the distressing thing about our examination questions is that they are not ridiculous, they make perfectly good sense—such good sense that the young person who answers them can never again know the force and terror of what has been communicated to him by the works he is being examined on.

Very likely it was with the thought of saving myself from the necessity of speaking personally and my students from having to betray the full harsh meaning of a great literature that I first taught my course in as *literary* a way as possible. A couple of decades ago the discovery was made that a literary work is a structure of words: this doesn't seem a surprising thing to have learned except for its polemical tendency, which is to urge us to minimize the amount of attention we give to the poet's social and personal will, to what he wants to happen outside the poem as a result of the poem; it urges us to fix our minds on what is going on inside the poem. For me this polemical tendency has been of the greatest usefulness, for it has corrected my inclination to pay attention chiefly to what the poet *wants.* For two or three years I directed my efforts toward dealing with the matter of the course chiefly as structures of words, in a formal way, with due attention paid to the literal difficulty which marked so many of the works. But it went against the grain. It went against my personal grain. It went against the grain of the classroom situation, for formal analysis is best carried on by question-and-answer, which needs small groups, and the registration for the course in modern literature in any college is sure to be large. And it went against the grain of the authors themselves—structures of words they may indeed have created, but these structures were not pyramids or triumphal arches, they were manifestly contrived to be not static and commemorative but mobile and aggressive, and one does not describe a quinquereme or a howitzer or a tank without estimating how much *damage* it can do.

Eventually I had to decide that there was only one way to give the course, which was to give it without strategies and without conscious caution. It was not honorable, either to the students or to the authors, to conceal or disguise my relation to the literature, my commitment to it, my fear of it, my ambivalence toward it. The literature had to be dealt with in the terms it announced for itself. As for the students, I have never given assent to the modern saw about "teaching students, not subjects"—I have always thought it right to teach subjects, believing that if one give his first loyalty to the subject, the student is best instructed. So I resolved to give the course with no considerations in mind except my own interests. And since my own interests lead me to see literary situations as cultural situations, and cultural situations as great elaborate fights about moral issues, and moral issues as having something to do with gratuitously chosen images of personal being, and images of personal being as having something to do with literary style, I felt free to begin with what for me was a first concern, the animus of the author, the objects of his will, the things he wants or wants to have happen.

My cultural and non-literary method led me to decide that I would begin the course with a statement of certain themes or issues that might especially engage our attention. I even went so far in non-literariness as to think that my purposes would best be served if I could contrive a "background" for the works we would read—I wanted to propose a history for the themes or issues that I hoped to discover. I did not intend that this history should be either very extensive or very precise. I wanted merely to encourage a *sense* of a history, some general intuition of a past, in students who, as it seems to me, have not been provided with any such thing by their education and who are on the whole glad to be without it. And because there is as yet no adequate general work of history of the culture of the last two hundred years, I asked myself what books of the age just preceding ours had most influenced our literature, or, since I was far less concerned with showing influence than with discerning a tendency, what older books might seem to fall into a line the direction of which pointed to our own literature and thus might serve as a prolegomenon to the course.

It was virtually inevitable that the first work that should have sprung to mind was Sir James Frazer's *The Golden Bough,* not, of course, the whole of it, but certain chapters, those that deal with Osiris, Attis, and Adonis. Anyone who thinks about modern literature in a systematic way takes for granted the great part played in it by myth, and especially by those examples of myth which tell about gods dying and being reborn— the imagination of death and rebirth, reiterated in the ancient world in innumerable variations that are yet always the same, captivated the literary mind at the very moment when, as all accounts of the modern age agree, the most massive and compelling of all the stories of resurrection had lost much of its hold upon the world.

Perhaps no book has had so decisive an effect upon modern literature as Frazer's. It was beautifully to my purpose that it had first been published ten years before the twentieth century began. Yet forty-three years later, in 1933, Frazer delivered a lecture, very eloquent, in which he bade the world be of good hope in the face of the threat to the human mind that was being offered by the Nazi power. He was still alive in 1941. Yet he had been born in 1854, three years before Matthew Arnold gave the lecture "On the Modern Element in Literature." Here, surely, was history, here was the past I wanted, beautifully connected with our present. Frazer was wholly a man of the nineteenth century, and the more so because the eighteenth century was so congenial to him—the lecture of 1933 in which he predicted the Nazi defeat had as its subject Condorcet's *Progress of the Human Mind;* when he took time from his anthropological studies to deal with literature, he prepared editions of Addison's essays and Cowper's letters. He had the old lost belief in the virtue and power of rationality. He loved and counted on order, decorum, and good sense. This great historian of the primitive imagination was in the dominant intellectual tradition of the West which, since the days of the pre-Socratics, has condemned the ways of thought that we call primitive.

It can be said of Frazer that in his conscious intention he was a perfect representative of what Arnold meant when he spoke of a modern age. And perhaps nothing could make clearer how the conditions of life and literature have changed in a hundred years than to note the difference between the way in which Arnold defines the modern element in literature and the way in which we must define it.

Arnold used the word *modern* in a wholly honorific sense. So much so that he seems to dismiss all temporal idea from the word and makes it signify certain timeless intellectual and civic virtues—his lecture, indeed, was about the modern element in the ancient literatures. A society, he said, is a modern society when it maintains a condition of repose, confidence, free activity of the mind, and the tolerance of divergent views. A society is modern when it affords sufficient material well-being for the conveniences of life and the development of taste. And, finally, a society is modern when its members are intellectually mature, by which Arnold means that they are willing to judge by reason, to observe facts in a critical spirit, and to search for the law of things. By this definition Periclean Athens is for Arnold a modern age, Elizabethan England is not; Thucydides is a modern historian, Sir Walter Raleigh is not.

I shall not go into further details of Arnold's definition or description of the modern. I have said enough, I think, to suggest what Arnold was up to, what he wanted to see realized as the desideratum of his own society, what ideal he wanted the works of intellect and imagination of his own time to advance. And at what a distance his ideal of the modern puts him from our present sense of modernity, from our modern literature! To anyone conditioned by our modern literature, Arnold's ideal of order, convenience, decorum, and rationality might well seem to reduce itself to the small advantages and excessive limitations of the middle-class life of a few prosperous nations of the nineteenth century. Arnold's historic sense presented to his mind the long, bitter, bloody past of Europe, and he seized passionately upon the hope of true civilization at last achieved. But the historic sense of our literature has in mind a long excess of civilization to which may be ascribed the bitterness and bloodiness both of the past and of the present and of which the peaceful aspects are to be thought of as mainly contemptible—its order achieved at the cost of extravagant personal repression, either that of coercion or that of acquiescence; its repose otiose; its tolerance either flaccid or capricious; its material comfort corrupt and corrupting; its taste a manifestation either of timidity or of pride; its rationality attained only at the price of energy and passion.

For the understanding of this radical change of opinion nothing is more illuminating than to be aware of the doubleness of mind of the author of *The Golden Bough*. I have said that Frazer in his conscious mind and in his first intention exemplifies all that Arnold means by the modern. He often speaks quite harshly of the irrationality and the orgiastic excesses of the primitive religions he describes, and even Christianity comes under his criticism both because it stands in the way of rational thought and because it can draw men away from intelligent participation in the life of society. But Frazer had more than one intention, and he had an unconscious as well as a conscious mind. If he deplores the primitive imagination, he also does not fail to show it as wonderful and beautiful. It is the rare reader of *The Golden Bough* who finds the ancient beliefs and rituals wholly alien to him. It is to be expected that Frazer's adduction of the many pagan analogues to the Christian mythos will be thought by Christian readers to have an adverse effect on faith, it was undoubtedly Frazer's purpose that it should, yet many readers will feel that Frazer makes all faith and ritual indigenous to humanity, virtually biological; they feel, as De Quincey put it, that not to be at least a *little* superstitious is to lack generosity of mind. Scientific though his purpose was, Frazer had the effect of validating those old modes of experiencing the world which modern men, beginning with the Romantics, have sought to revive in order to escape from positivism and common sense.

The direction of the imagination upon great and mysterious objects of worship is not the only means men use to liberate themselves from the bondage of quotidian fact, and although Frazer can scarcely be held accountable for the ever-growing modern attraction to the extreme mental states—to rapture, ecstasy, and transcendence, which are achieved by drugs, trance, music and dance, orgy, and the derangement of personality—yet he did provide a bridge to the understanding and acceptance of these states, he proposed to us the idea that the desire for them and the use of them for heuristic purposes is a common and acceptable manifestation of human nature.

This one element of Frazer's masterpiece could scarcely fail to suggest the next of my prolegomenal works. It is worth remarking that its author was in his own way as great a classical scholar as Frazer himself—Nietzsche was Professor of Classical Philology at the University of Basel when, at the age of twenty-seven, he published his essay *The Birth of Tragedy*. After the appearance of this stunningly brilliant account of Greek civilization, of which Socrates is not the hero but the villain, what can possibly be left to us of that rational and ordered Greece, that modern, that eighteenth-century, Athens that Arnold so entirely relied on as the standard for judging all civilizations? Professor Kaufmann is right when he warns us against supposing that Nietzsche exalts Dionysus over Apollo and tells us that Nietzsche "emphasizes the Dionysiac only because he feels that the Apolonian genius of the Greeks cannot be fully understood apart from it." But no one reading Nietzsche's essay for the first time is likely to heed this warning. What will reach him before due caution intervenes, before he becomes aware of the portentous dialectic between Dionysus and Apollo, is the excitement of suddenly being liberated from Aristotle, the joy of finding himself acceding to the author's statement that "art rather than ethics constitutes the essential metaphysical activity of man," that tragedy has its source in the Dionysiac rapture, "whose closest analogy is furnished by physical intoxication," and that this rapture, in which "the individual forgets himself completely," was in itself no metaphysical state but an orgiastic display of lust and cruelty, "of sexual promiscuity overriding every form of tribal law." This sadic and masochistic frenzy, Nietzsche is at pains to insist, needs the taming hand of Apollo before it can become tragedy, but it is the primal stuff of the great art, and to the modern experience of tragedy this explanation seems far more pertinent than Aristotle's, with its eagerness to forget its origin in its achievement of a state of noble imperturbability.

Of supreme importance in itself, Nietzsche's essay had for me the added pedagogic advantage of allowing me to establish a historical line back to William Blake. Nothing is more characteristic of modern literature than its discovery and canonization of the primal, non-ethical energies, and the historical point could be made the better by remarking the correspondence of thought of two men of different nations and separated from each other by a good many decades, for Nietzsche's Dionysian orgy and Blake's Hell are much the same thing.

Whether or not Joseph Conrad read either Blake or Nietzsche I do not know, but his *Heart of Darkness* follows in their line. This very great work has never lacked for the admiration it deserves, and it has been given a kind of canonical place in the legend of modern literature by Eliot's having it so clearly in mind when he wrote *The Waste Land* and his having taken from it the epigraph to "The Hollow Men." But no one, to my knowledge, has ever confronted in an explicit way its strange and terrible message of ambivalence toward the life of civilization. Consider that its protagonist, Kurtz, is a progressive and a liberal and that he is the highly respected representative of a society which would have us believe it is benign, although in fact it is vicious. Consider too that he is a practitioner of several arts, a painter, a writer, a musician, and into the bargain a political orator. He is at once the most idealistic and the most practically successful of all the agents of the Belgian exploitation of the Congo. Everybody knows the truth about him which Marlow discovers—that Kurtz's success is the result of a terrible ascendancy he has gained over the natives of his distant station, an ascendancy which is derived from his presumed magical or divine powers, that he has exercised his rule with an extreme of cruelty, that he has given himself to unnamable acts of lust. This is the world of the darker pages of *The Golden Bough*. It is one of the great points of Conrad's story that Marlow speaks of the primitive life of the jungle not as being noble or charming or even free but as being base and sordid—and for *that* reason compelling: he himself feels quite overtly its dreadful attraction. It is to this devilish baseness that Kurtz has yielded himself, and yet Marlow, although he does indeed treat him with hostile irony, does not find it possible to suppose that Kurtz is anything but a hero of the spirit. For me it is still ambiguous whether Kurtz's famous deathbed cry, "The horror! The horror!" refers to the approach of death or to his experience of savage life. Whichever it is, to Marlow the fact that Kurtz could utter this cry at the point of death, while Marlow himself, when death threatens him, can know it only as a weary grayness, marks the difference between the ordinary man and a hero of the spirit. Is this not the essence of the modern belief about the nature of the artist, the man who goes down into that hell which is the historical beginning of the human soul, a beginning not outgrown but established in humanity as we know it now, preferring the reality of this hell to the bland lies of the civilization that has overlaid it?

This idea is proposed again in the somewhat less powerful but still very moving work with which I followed *Heart of Darkness,* Thomas Mann's *Death in Venice.* I wanted this story not so much for its account of an extravagantly Apollonian personality surrendering to forces that, in his Apollonian character, he thought shameful—although this was certainly to my purpose—but rather for Aschenbach's fevered dreams of the erotic past, and in particular that dream of the goat-orgy which Mann, being the kind of writer he is, having the kind of relation to Nietzsche he had, might well have written to serve as an illustration of what *The Birth of Tragedy* means by religious frenzy, the more so, of course, because Mann chooses that particular orgiastic ritual, the killing and eating of the goat, from which tragedy is traditionally said to have been derived.

A notable element of this story in which the birth of tragedy plays an important part is that the degradation and downfall of the protagonist is not represented as tragic in the usual sense of the word—that is, it is not represented as a great deplorable event. It is a commonplace of modern literary thought that the tragic mode is not available even to the gravest and noblest or our writers. I am not sure that this is the deprivation that some people think it to be and a mark of our spiritual inferiority. But if we ask why it has come about, one reason may be that we have learned to think our way back through tragedy to the primal stuff out of which tragedy arose. If we consider the primitive forbidden ways of conduct which traditionally in tragedy lead to punishment by death, we think of them as being the path to reality and truth, to an ultimate self-realization. We have always wondered if tragedy itself may not have been saying just this in a deeply hidden way, drawing us to think of the hero's sin and death as somehow conferring justification, even salvation of a sort—no doubt this is what Nietzsche had in mind when he said that "tragedy denies ethics." What tragedy once seemed to hint, our literature now is willing to say quite explicitly. If Mann's Aschenbach dies at the height of his intellectual and artistic powers, overcome by a passion that his ethical reason condemns, we do not take this to be a defeat, rather a kind of terrible rebirth: at his latter end the artist knows a reality that he had until now refused to admit to consciousness.

Thoughts like these suggested that another of Nietzsche's works, *The Genealogy of Morals,* might be in point. It proposes a view of society which is consonant with the belief that art and not ethics constitutes the essential metaphysical activity of man and with the validation and ratification of the primitive energies. Nietzsche's theory of the social order dismisses all ethical impluse from its origins—the basis of society is to be found in the rationalization of cruelty: as simple as that. Nietzsche has no ultimate Utopian intention in saying this, no hope of revising the essence of the social order, although he does believe that its pain can be mitigated. He represents cruelty as a social necessity, for only by its exercise could men ever have been induced to develop a continuity of will: nothing else than cruel pain could have created in mankind that memory of intention which makes society possible. The method of cynicism which Nietzsche pursued—let us be clear that it is a method and not an attitude—goes so far as to describe punishment in terms of the pleasure derived from the exercise of cruelty: "Compensation," he says, "consists in a legal warrant entitling one man to exercise his cruelty on another." There follows that most remarkable passage in which Nietzsche describes the process whereby the individual turns the cruelty of punishment against himself and creates the bad conscience and the consciousness of guilt which manifests itself as a pervasive anxiety. Nietzsche's complexity of mind is beyond all comparison, for in this book which is dedicated to the liberation of the conscience, Nietzsche makes his defense of the bad conscience as a decisive force in the interests of culture. It is much the same line of argument that he takes when, having attacked the Jewish morality and the priestly existence in the name of the health of the spirit, he reminds us that only by his sickness does man become interesting.

From *The Genealogy of Morals* to Freud's *Civilization and Its Discontents* is but a step, and some might think that, for pedagogic purposes, the step is so small as to make the second book supererogatory. But although Freud's view of society and culture has indeed a very close affinity to Nietzsche's, Freud does add certain considerations which are essential to our sense of the modern disposition.

For one thing, he puts to us the question of whether or not we want to *accept* civilization. It is not the first time that the paradox of civilization has been present to the mind of civilized people, the sense that civilization makes men behave worse and suffer more than does some less developed state of human existence. But hitherto all such ideas were formulated in a moralizing way—civilization was represented at being "corrupt," a divagation from a state of innocence. Freud had no illusions about a primitive innocence, he conceived no practicable alternative to civilization. In consequence, there was a unique force to the question he asked: whether we wished to accept civilization, with all its contradictions, with all its pains—pains, for "discontents" does not accurately describe what Freud has in mind. He had his own answer to the question—his tragic, or stoic, sense of life dictated it: we do well to accept it, although we also do well to cast a cold eye on the fate that makes it our better part to accept it. Like Nietzsche, Freud thought that life was justified by our heroic response to its challenge.

But the question Freud posed has not been set aside or closed up by the answer that he himself gave to it. His answer, like Nietzsche's, is essentially in the line of traditional humanism—we can see this in the sternness with which he charges women not to interfere with men in the discharge of their cultural duty, not to claim men for love and the family to the detriment of their free activity in the world. But just here lies the matter of Freud's question that the world more and more believes Freud himself did not answer. The pain that civilization inflicts is that of the instinctual renunciation that civilization demands, and it would seem that fewer and fewer people wish to say with Freud that the loss of instinctual gratification, emotional freedom, or love, is compensated for either by the security of civilized life or by the stern pleasures of the masculine moral character.

With Freud's essay I brought to a close my list of prolegomenal books for the first term of the course. I shall not do much more than mention the books with which I introduced the second term, but I should like to do at least that. I began with *Rameau's Nephew,* thinking that the peculiar moral authority which Diderot assigns to the envious, untalented, unregenerate protagonist was peculiarly relevant to the line taken by the ethical explorations of modern literature. Nothing is more characteristic of the literature of our time than the replacement of the hero by what has come to be called the anti-hero, in whose indifference to or hatred of ethical nobility there is presumed to lie a special authenticity. Diderot is quite overt about this—he himself in his public character is the deuteragonist, the "honest consciousness," as Hegel calls him, and he takes delight in the discomfiture of the decent, dull person he is by the Nephew's nihilistic mind.

It seemed to me too that there was a particular usefulness in the circumstance that this anti-hero should avow so openly his *envy,* which Tocqueville has called the ruling emotion of democracy, and that, although he envied anyone at all who had access to the creature-comforts and the social status which he lacked, what chiefly animated him was envy of men of genius. Ours is the first cultural epoch in which many men aspire to high achievement in the arts and, in their frustration, form a dispossessed class which cuts across the conventional class lines, making a proletariat of the spirit.

Although *Rameau's Nephew* was not published until fairly late in the century, it was known in manuscript by Goethe and Hegel; it suited the temper and won the admiration of Marx and Freud for reasons that are obvious. And there is ground for supposing that it was known to Dostoevski, whose *Notes from Underground* is a restatement of the essential idea of Diderot's dialogue in terms both more extreme and less genial. The Nephew is still on the defensive—he is naughtily telling secrets about the nature of man and society. But Dostoevski's underground man shouts aloud his envy and hatred and carries the ark of his self-hatred and alienation into a remorseless battle with what he calls "the good and the beautiful," mounting an attack upon every belief not merely of bourgeois society but of the whole humanist tradition. The inclusion of *Notes from Underground* among my prolegomenal books constituted something of a pedagogic risk, for if I wished to emphasize the subversive tendency of modern literature, here was a work which made all subsequent subversion seem like affirmation, so radical and so brilliant was its negation of our traditional pieties and its affirmation of our new pieties.

I hesitated in compunction before following *Notes from Underground* with Tolstoi's *Death of Ivan Ilyitch,* which so ruthlessly and with such dreadful force destroys the citadel of the commonplace life in which we all believe we can take refuge from ourselves and our fate. But I did assign it and then two of Pirandello's plays which, in the atmosphere of the sordidness of the commonplace life, undermine all certitudes of the commonplace, common-sense mind.

From time to time I have raised with myself the question of whether my choice of these prolegomenal works was not extravagant, quite excessively tendentious. I have never been able to believe that it is. And if these works do indeed serve to indicate in an accurate way the nature of modern literature, a teacher might find it worth asking how his students respond to the strong dose.

One response I have already described—the readiness of the students to engage in the process that we might call the socialization of the anti-social, or the acculturation of the anti-cultural, or the legitimization of the subversive. When the term-essays come in, it is plain to me that almost none of the students have been taken aback by what they have read: they have wholly contained the attack. The chief exceptions are the few who simply do not comprehend, although they may be awed by, the categories of our discourse. In their papers, like poor hunted creatures in a Kafka story, they take refuge first in misunderstood large phrases, then in bad grammar, then in general incoherence. After my pedagogical exasperation has run its course, I find that I am sometimes moved to give them a queer respect, as if they had stood up and said what in fact they don't have the wit to stand up and say: "Why do you harry us? Leave us alone. We are not Modern Man. We are the Old People. Ours is the Old Faith. We serve the little Old Gods, the gods of the copybook maxims, the small, dark, somewhat powerful deities of lawyers, doctors, engineers, accountants. With them is neither sensibility not *angst*. With them is no disgust—it is they, indeed, who make ready the way for 'the good and the beautiful' about which low-minded doubts have been raised in this course, that 'good and beautiful' which we do not possess and don't want to possess but which we know justifies our lives. Leave us alone and let us worship our gods in the way they approve, in peace and unawareness." Crass, but—to use that interesting modern word which we have learned from the curators of museums—authentic. The rest, the minds that give me the A papers and the B papers and even the C+ papers, move through the terrors and mysteries of modern literature like so many Parsifals, asking no questions at the behest of wonder and fear. Or like so many seminarists who have been systematically instructed in the constitution of Hell and the ways to damnation. Or like so many *readers*, entertained by moral horror stories. I asked them to look into the Abyss, and, both dutifully and gladly, they have looked into the Abyss, and the Abyss has greeted them with the grave courtesy of all objects of serious study, saying: "Interesting, am I not? And *exciting*, if you consider how deep I am and what dread beasts lie at my bottom. Have it well in mind that a knowledge of me contributes materially to your being whole, or well-rounded, men."

In my distress over the outrage I have conspired to perpetrate upon a great literature, I wonder if perhaps I have not been reading these papers too literally. After all, a term-essay is not a diary of the soul, it is not an occasion for telling the truth. What my students might reveal of their true feelings to a younger teacher they will not reveal to me; they will give me what they conceive to be the proper response to the official version of terror I have given them. I bring to mind their faces, which are not necessarily the faces of the authors of these unperturbed papers, nor are they, not yet, the faces of fathers of families, or of theatergoers, or of buyers of modern paintings: not yet. I must think it possible that in ways and to a degree which they keep secret they have responded directly and personally to what they have read.

And if they have? And if they have, am I the more content?

What form would I want their response to take? It is a teacher's question that I am asking, not a critic's. We have decided in recent years to think of the critic and the teacher of literature as one and the same, and no doubt it is both possible and useful to do so. But there are some points at which the functions of the two do not coincide, or can be made to coincide only with great difficulty. Of criticism we have been told, by Arnold, that "it must be apt to study and praise elements that for fulness of spiritual perfection are wanted, even though they belong to a power which in the practical sphere may be maleficent." But teaching, or at least undergraduate teaching, is not given the same licensed mandate—cannot be given it because the teacher's audience, which stands before his very eyes, as the critic's audience does not, asks questions about "the practical sphere," as the critic's audience does not. For instance, on the very day that I write this, when I had said to my class all I could think of to say about *The Magic Mountain* and invited questions and comments, one student asked, "How would you generalize the idea of the educative value of illness, so that it would be applicable not only to a particular individual, Hans Castorp, but to young people at large?" It makes us smile, but it was asked in all seriousness, and it is serious in its substance, and it had to be answered seriously, in part by the reflection that this idea, like so many ideas encountered in the books of the course, had to be thought of as having reference only to the private life; that it touched the public life only in some indirect or tangential way; that it really ought to be encountered in solitude, even in secrecy, since to talk about it in public and in our academic setting was to seem to propose for it a public practicality and thus to distort its meaning. To this another student replied; he said that, despite the public ritual of the classroom, each student inevitably experienced the books in privacy and found their meaning in reference to his own life. True enough, but the teacher sees the several privacies coming together to make a group, and they propose— no doubt the more because they come together every Monday, Wednesday, and Friday at a particular hour—the idea of a community, that is to say, "the practical sphere."

This being so, the teacher cannot escape the awareness of certain circumstances which the critic, who writes for an ideal, uncircumstanced reader, has no need to take into account. The teacher considers, for example, the social situation of his students— they are not of patrician origin, they do not come from homes in which stubbornness, pride, and conscious habit prevail, nor are they born into a culture marked by these traits, a culture in which other interesting and valuable things compete with and resist ideas; they come, mostly, from "good homes" in which authority and valuation are weak or at least not very salient and bold, so that ideas have for them, at their present stage of development, a peculiar power and preciousness. And in this connection the teacher will have in mind the special prestige that our culture, in its upper reaches, gives to art, and to the ideas that art proposes—the agreement, ever growing in assertiveness, that art yields more truth than any other intellectual activity. In this culture what a shock it is to encounter Santayana's acerb skepticism about art, or Keat's remark, which the critics and scholars never take notice of, presumably because they suppose it to be an aberration, that poetry is "not so fine a thing as philosophy—For the same reason that an eagle is not so fine a thing as a truth." For many students no ideas that they will encounter in any college discipline will equal in force and sanction the ideas conveyed to them by modern literature.

The author of *The Magic Mountain* once said that all his work could be understood as an effort to free himself from the middle class, and this, of course, will serve to describe the chief intention of all modern literature. And the means of freedom which Mann prescribes (the characteristic irony notwithstanding) is the means of freedom which in effect all of modern literature prescribes. It is, in the words of Clavdia Chauchat, *"se perdre et même . . . se laisser dépérir,"* and thus to name the means is to make plain that the end is not merely freedom from the middle class but freedom from society itself. I venture to say that the idea of losing oneself up to the point of self-destruction, of surrendering oneself to experience without regard to self-interest or conventional morality, of escaping wholly from the societal bonds, is an "element" somewhere in the mind of every modern person who dares to think of what Arnold in his unaffected Victorian way called "the fulness of spiritual perfection. But the teacher who undertakes to present modern literature to his students may not allow that idea to remain in the *somewhere* of his mind; he must take it from the place where it exists habitual and unrealized and put it in the conscious forefront of his thought. And if he is committed to an admiration of modern literature, he must also be committed to this chief idea of modern literature. I press the logic of the situation not in order to question the legitimacy of the commitment, or even the propriety of expressing the commitment in the college classroom (although it does seem odd!), but to confront those of us who do teach modern literature with the striking actuality of our enterprise.

MARTIN LUTHER KING, JR.

Selection from "Letter from a Birmingham Jail" 1963

When the civil rights leader Martin Luther King, Jr., (1929–68) was jailed in Birmingham, Alabama, along with twenty-four hundred other antisegregationist demonstrators, a group of local white clergy published an attack on King. The black preacher from Atlanta had broken laws prohibiting blacks from using certain public accommodations and had otherwise promoted "unwise and untimely" demonstrations, according to their statement. King responded from his jail cell. His "Letter from a Birmingham Jail" began as a local document of a local dispute, but when published in *The Christian Century* on June 12, 1963, it quickly became the central text in the nationwide discussion of the theory of civil disobedience. King began his letter with a detailed account of Birmingham city politics and of the process by which the Southern Christian Leadership Conference—of which King was president— had become involved in the struggle to desegregate Birmingham. The selection below begins at the point in the letter when King turns to the issue of just versus unjust laws. Although King's distinctly religious and strictly nonviolent approach was not to the tastes of everyone concerned with civil rights, the argument made in the letter won wide acclaim. The following year, King was awarded the Nobel Peace Prize. King's most important books were *Stride Toward Freedom: The Montgomery Story* (New York, 1958) and *Why We Can't Wait* (New York, 1964).

A comprehensive edition of King's papers is being published by the University of California Press under the editorship of Clay Carson. For a compelling interpretation of American history in the late 1950s and early 1960s treating King as the central figure in the story, see Taylor Branch, *Parting the Waters: America in the King Years, 1954–1963* (New York, 1988).

... You express a great deal of anxiety over our willingness to break laws. This is certainly a legitimate concern. Since we so diligently urge people to obey the Supreme Court's decision of 1954 outlawing segregation in the public schools, at first glance it may seem rather paradoxical for us consciously to break laws. One may well ask, "How can you advocate breaking some laws and obeying others?" The answer lies in the fact that there are two types of laws: just and unjust. I agree with St. Augustine that "an unjust law is no law at all."

Now what is the difference between the two? How does one determine whether a law is just or unjust? A just law is a man-made code that squares with the moral law or the law of God. An unjust law is a code that is out of harmony with the moral law. To put it in the terms of St. Thomas Aquinas, an unjust law is a human law that is not rooted in eternal law and natural law. Any law that uplifts human personality is just. Any law that degrades human personality is unjust. All segregation statutes are unjust because segregation distorts the soul and damages the personality. It gives the segregator a false sense of superiority and the segregated a false sense of inferiority. Segregation, to use the terminology of the Jewish philosopher Martin Buber, substitutes an "I-it" relationship for an "I-thou" relationship and ends up relegating persons to the status of things. Hence segregation is not only politically, economically and sociologically unsound, it is sinful. Paul Tillich has said that sin is separation. Is not segregation an existential expression of man's tragic separation, his awful estrangement, his terrible sinfulness? Thus it is that I can urge men to disobey segregation ordinances, for such ordinances are morally wrong.

Let us consider some of the ways in which a law can be unjust. A law is unjust, for example, if the majority group compels a minority group to obey the statute but does not make it binding on itself. By the same token a law in all probability is just if the majority is itself willing to obey it. Also, a law is unjust if it is inflicted on a minority that, as a result of being denied the right to vote, had no part in enacting or devising the law. Who can say that the legislature of Alabama which set up that state's segregation laws was democratically elected? Throughout Alabama all sorts of devious methods are used to prevent Negroes from becoming registered voters, and there are some counties in which, even though Negroes constitute a majority of the population, not a single Negro is registered. Can any law enacted under such circumstances be considered democratically structured?

Sometimes a law is just on its face and unjust in its application. For instance, I have been arrested on a charge of parading without a permit. Now there is nothing wrong in having an ordinance which requires a permit for a parade. But such an ordinance becomes unjust when it is used to maintain segregation and to deny citizens the First-amendment privilege of peaceful assembly and protest.

I hope you are able to see the distinction I am trying to point out. In no sense do I advocate evading the law, as would the rabid segregationist. That would lead to anarchy. One who breaks an unjust law must do so *openly, lovingly,* and with a willingness to accept the penalty. I submit that an individual who breaks a law that conscience tells him is unjust and who willingly accepts the penalty of imprisonment in order to arouse

Source: The Christian Century, June 12, 1963, 769–75. Copyright © 1963, 1964, by Martin Luther King, Jr. Reprinted by permission of Joan Daves.

the conscience of the community over its injustice is in reality expressing the highest respect for law.

Of course, there is nothing new about this kind of civil disobedience. It was evidenced sublimely in the refusal of Shadrach, Meshach and Abednego to obey the laws of Nebuchadnezzar, on the ground that a higher moral law was at stake. It was practiced superbly by the early Christians who were willing to face hungry lions rather than submit to certain unjust laws of the Roman empire. To a degree, academic freedom is a reality today because Socrates practiced civil disobedience. We should never forget that everything Adolf Hitler did in Germany was "legal" and everything the Hungarian freedom fighters did in Hungary was "illegal." It was "illegal" to aid and comfort a Jew in Hitler's Germany. Even so, I am sure that had I lived in Germany at the time I would have aided and comforted my Jewish brothers. If today I lived in a communist country where certain principles dear to the Christian faith are suppressed, I would openly advocate disobeying that country's antireligious laws.

I must make two honest confessions to you, my Christian and Jewish brothers. First, I must confess that over the past few years I have been gravely disappointed with the white moderate. I have almost reached the regrettable conclusion that the Negro's great stumbling block in his stride toward freedom is not the White Citizen's Counciler or the Klu Klux Klanner but the white moderate who is more devoted to "order" than to justice; who prefers a negative peace which is the absence of tension to a positive peace which is the presence of justice; who constantly says "I agree with you in the goal you seek, but I cannot agree with your methods"; who paternalistically believes he can set the timetable for another man's freedom; who lives by a mythical concept of time and who constantly advises the Negro to wait for a "more convenient season." Shallow understanding from people of good will is more frustrating than absolute misunderstanding from people of ill will. Lukewarm acceptance is much more bewildering than outright rejection.

I had hoped that the white moderate would understand that law and order exist for the purpose of establishing justice and that when they fail in this purpose they block social progress. I had hoped that the white moderate would understand that the present tension in the south is a necessary phase of the transition from an obnoxious negative peace, in which the Negro passively accepted his unjust plight, to a substantive and positive peace, in which all men will respect the dignity and worth of human personality. Actually, we who engage in nonviolent direct action are not the creators of tension. We merely bring to the surface the hidden tension that is already alive. We bring it out in the open where it can be seen and dealt with. Like a boil that can never be cured so long as it is covered up but must be opened with all its pus-flowing ugliness to the natural medicines of air and light, injustice must be exposed, with all the tension its exposure creates, to the light of human conscience and the air of national opinion before it can be cured.

In your statement you assert that our actions, even though peaceful, must be condemned because they precipitate violence. But is this a logical assertion? Isn't this like condemning a robbed man because his possession of money precipitated an act of robbery? Isn't this like condemning Socrates because his unswerving commitment to truth and his philosophical inquiries precipitated the act by the misguided populace in which they made him drink hemlock? Isn't this like condemning Jesus because his unique God-consciousness and never-ceasing devotion to God's will precipitated the evil act of crucifixion? We must come to see that, as the federal courts have consistently affirmed, it is wrong to urge an individual to cease his efforts to gain his basic constitutional rights because the quest may precipitate violence. Society must protect the robbed and punish the robber.

I had also hoped that the white moderate would reject the myth concerning time in relation to the struggle for freedom. I have just received a letter from a white brother in Texas. He writes: "All Christians know that the colored people will receive equal rights eventually, but it is possible that you are in too great a religious hurry. It has taken Christianity almost 2,000 years to accomplish what it has. The teachings of Christ take time to come to earth." Such an attitude stems from a tragic misconception of time, from the strangely irrational notion that there is something in the very flow of time that will inevitably cure all ills. Actually, time itself is neutral; it can be used either destructively or constructively. More and more I feel that the people of ill will have used time much more effectively than have the people of good will. We will have to repent in this generation not merely for the hateful words and actions of the bad people but for the appalling silence of the good people. Human progress never rolls in on wheels of inevitability; it comes through the tireless efforts of men willing to be co-workers with God, and without this hard work time itself becomes an ally of the forces of social stagnation. We must use time creatively, in the knowledge that the time is always ripe to do right. Now is the time to make real the promise of democracy and transform our pending national elegy into a creative psalm of brotherhood. Now is the time to lift our national policy from the quicksand of racial injustice to the solid rock of human dignity.

You speak of our activity in Birmingham as extreme. At first I was rather disappointed that fellow clergymen would see my nonviolent efforts as those of an extremist. I began thinking about the fact that I stand in the middle of two opposing forces in the Negro community. One is a force of complacency made up of Negroes who, as a result of long years of oppression, are so completely drained of self-respect and a sense of "somebodiness" that they have adjusted to segregation, and of a few middle class Negroes who, because of a degree of academic and economic security and because in some ways they profit by segregation, have unconsciously become insensitive to the problems of the masses. The other force is one of bitterness and hatred, and it comes perilously close to advocating violence. It is expressed in the various black nationalist groups that are springing up across the nation, the largest and best-known being Elijah Muhammad's Muslim movement. Nourished by the Negro's frustration over the continued existence of racial discrimination, this movement is made up of people who have lost faith in America, who have absolutely repudiated Christianity, and who have concluded that the white man is an incorrigible "devil."

I have tried to stand between these two forces, saying that we need emulate neither the "do-nothingism" of the complacent nor the hatred of the black nationalist. For there is the more excellent way of love and nonviolent protest. I am grateful to God that, through the influence of the Negro church, the way of nonviolence became an integral part of our struggle.

If this philosophy had not emerged, by now many streets of the south would, I am convinced, be flowing with blood. And I am further convinced that if our white brothers dismiss as "rabble-rousers" and "outside agitators" those of us who employ nonviolent direct action and if they refuse to support our nonviolent efforts, millions of Negroes will, out of frustration and despair, seek solace and security in black nationalist ideologies—a development that would inevitably lead to a frightening racial nightmare.

Oppressed people cannot remain oppressed forever. The yearning for freedom eventually manifests itself, and that is what has happened to the American Negro. Something within has reminded him of his birthright of freedom, and something without has reminded him that it can be gained. Consciously or unconsciously, he has been caught up by the *Zeitgeist,* and with his black brothers of Africa and his brown and yellow brothers of Asia, South America and the Caribbean, the U.S. Negro is moving with a sense of great urgency toward the promised land of racial justice. If one recognizes this vital urge that has engulfed the Negro community, he should readily understand why public demonstrations are taking place. The Negro has many pent-up resentments and latent frustrations, and he must release them. So let him march; let him make prayer pilgrimages to the city hall; let him go on freedom rides—and try to understand why he must do so. If his repressed emotions are not released in nonviolent ways, they will seek expression through violence; this is not a threat but a fact of history. I have not said to my people, "Get rid of your discontent." Rather, I have tried to say that this normal and healthy discontent can be channeled into the creative outlet of nonviolent direct action. And now this approach is being termed extremist.

But though I was initially disappointed at being categorized as an extremist, as I continued to think about the matter I gradually gained a measure of satisfaction from the label. Was not Jesus an extremist for love: "Love your enemies, bless them that curse you, do good to them that hate you, and pray for them which despitefully use you, and persecute you." Was not Amos an extremist for justice: "Let justice roll down like waters and righteousness like an everflowing stream." Was not Paul an extremist for the Christian gospel: "I bear in my body the marks of the Lord Jesus." Was not Martin Luther an extremist: "Here I stand; I can do no other so help me God." And John Bunyan: "I will stay in jail to the end of my days before I make a butchery of my conscience." And Abraham Lincoln: "This nation cannot survive half slave and half free." And Thomas Jefferson: "We hold these truths to be self-evident, that all men are created equal. . . . " So the question is not whether we will be extremists but what kind of extremists we will be. Will we be extremists for hate or for love? Will we be extremists for the preservation of injustice or for the extension of justice? Perhaps the south, the nation and the world are in dire need of creative extremists.

I had hoped that the white moderate would see this need. Perhaps I was too optimistic; perhaps I expected too much. I suppose I should have realized that few members of the oppressor race can understand the deep groans and passionate yearnings of the oppressed race, and still fewer have the vision to see that injustice must be rooted out by strong, persistent and determined action. I am thankful, however, that some of our white brothers have grasped the meaning of this social revolution and committed themselves to it. They are still all too few in quantity, but they are big in quality. Some—such as Ralph McGill, Lillian Smith, Harry Golden and James McBride-Dabbs—have written about our struggle in eloquent and prophetic terms. Others have marched with us down nameless streets of the south. They have languished in filthy, roach-infested jails, suffering the abuse and brutality of policemen who view them as "dirty nigger lovers." Unlike so many of their moderate brothers and sisters, they have recognized the urgency of the moment and sensed the need for powerful "action" antidotes to combat the disease of segregation.

Let me take note of my other major disappointment. Though there are some notable exceptions, I have also been disappointed with the white church and its leadership. I do not say this as one of those negative critics who can always find something wrong with the church. I say this as a minister of the gospel, who loves the church; who was nurtured in its bosom; who has been sustained by its spiritual blessings and who will remain true to it as long as the cord of life shall lengthen.

When I was suddenly catapulted into the leadership of the bus protest in Montgomery, Alabama, a few years ago I felt we would be supported by the white church. I felt that the white ministers, priests and rabbis of the South would be among our strongest allies. Instead, some have been outright opponents, refusing to understand the freedom movement and misrepresenting its leaders; all too many others have been more cautious than courageous and have remained silent and secure behind stained-glass windows.

In spite of my shattered dreams I came to Birmingham with the hope that the white religious leadership of this community would see the justice of our cause and with deep moral concern would serve as the channel through which our just grievances could reach the power structure. But again I have been disappointed.

I have heard numerous southern religious leaders admonish their worshipers to comply with a desegregation decision because it is the *law*, but I have longed to hear white ministers declare, "Follow this decree because integration is morally *right* and because the Negro is your brother." In the midst of blatant injustices inflicted upon the Negro I have watched white churchmen stand on the sideline and mouth pious irrelevancies and sanctimonious trivialities. In the midst of a mighty struggle to rid our nation of racial and economic injustice I have heard many ministers say, "Those are social issues with which the gospel has no real concern," and I have watched many churches commit themselves to a completely otherworldly religion which makes a strange, unbiblical distinction between body and soul, between the sacred and the secular.

We are moving toward the close of the 20th century with a religious community largely adjusted to the status quo—a taillight behind other community agencies rather than a headlight leading men to higher levels of justice.

I have traveled the length and breadth of Alabama, Mississippi and all the other southern states. On sweltering summer days and crisp autumn mornings I have looked at the south's beautiful churches with their lofty spires pointing heavenward, and at her impressive religious education buildings. Over and over I have found myself asking: "What kind of people worship here? Who is their God? Where were their voices when the lips of Governor Barnett dripped with words of interposition and nullification? Where were they when Governor Wallace gave a clarion call for defiance and hatred? Where were their voices of support when bruised and weary Negro men and women decided to rise from the dark dungeons of complacency to the bright hills of creative protest?"

Yes, these questions are still in my mind. In deep disappointment I have wept over the laxity of the church. But be assured that my tears have been tears of love. There can be no deep disappointment where there is not deep love. Yes, I love the church. How could I do otherwise? I am in the rather unique position of being the son, the grandson and the great-grandson of preachers. Yes, I see the church as the body of Christ. But, oh! How we have blemished and scarred that body through social neglect and through fear of being nonconformists.

There was a time when the church was very powerful—in the time when the early Christians rejoiced at being deemed worthy to suffer for what they believed. In those days the church was not merely a thermometer that recorded the ideas and principles of popular opinion; it was a thermostat that transformed the mores of society. Whenever the early Christians entered a town the power structure immediately sought to convict them for being "disturbers of the peace" and "outside agitators." But the Christians pressed on, in the conviction that they were "a colony of heaven," called to obey God rather than man. Small in number, they were big in commitment. By their effort and example they brought an end to such ancient evils as infanticide and gladiatorial contest.

Things are different now. So often the contemporary church is a weak, ineffectual voice with an uncertain sound. So often it is an archdefender of the status quo. Far from being disturbed by the presence of the church, the power structure of the average community is consoled by the church's silent—and often even vocal—sanction of things as they are.

But the judgment of God is upon the church as never before. If today's church does not recapture the sacrificial spirit of the early church, it will lose its authenticity, forfeit the loyalty of millions, and be dismissed as an irrelevant social club with no meaning for the 20th century. Every day I meet young people whose disappointment with the church has turned into outright disgust.

Perhaps I have once again been too optimistic. Is organized religion too inextricably bound to the status quo to save our nation and the world? Perhaps I must turn my faith to the inner spiritual church, the church within the church, as the true *ecclesia* and the hope of the world. But again I am thankful to God that some noble souls from the ranks of organized religion have broken loose from the paralyzing chains of conformity and joined us as active partners in the struggle for freedom. They have left their secure congregations and walked the streets of Albany, Georgia, with us. They have gone down the highways of the south on torturous rides for freedom. Yes, they have gone to jail with us. Some have been kicked out of their churches, have lost the support of their bishops and fellow ministers. But they have acted in the faith that right defeated is stronger than evil triumphant. Their witness has been the spiritual salt that has preserved the true meaning of the gospel in these troubled times. They have carved a tunnel of hope through the dark mountain of disappointment.

I hope the church as a whole will meet the challenge of this decisive hour. But even if the church does not come to the aid of justice, I have no despair about the future. I have no fear about the outcome of our struggle in Birmingham, even if our motives are at present misunderstood. We will reach the goal of freedom in Birmingham and all over the nation, because the goal of America is freedom. Abused and scorned though we may be, our destiny is tied up with America's destiny. Before the pilgrims landed at Plymouth we were here. Before the pen of Jefferson etched across the pages of history the mighty words of the Declaration of Independence, we were here. For more than two centuries our forebears labored in this country without wages; they made cotton king; they built the homes of their masters while suffering gross injustice and shameful humiliation—and yet out of a bottomless vitality they continued to thrive and develop. If the inexpressible cruelties of slavery could not stop us, the opposition we now face will surely fail. We will win our freedom because the sacred heritage of our nation and the eternal will of God are embodied in our echoing demands.

Before closing I feel impelled to mention one other point in your statement that has troubled me profoundly. You warmly commended the Birmingham police force for keeping "order" and "preventing violence." I doubt that you would have so warmly commended the police force if you had seen its angry dogs sinking their teeth into six unarmed, nonviolent Negroes. I doubt that you would so quickly commend the policemen if you were to observe their ugly and inhuman treatment of Negroes here in the city jail; if you were to watch them push and curse old Negro women and young Negro girls; if you were to see them slap and kick old Negro men and young boys; if you were to observe them, as they did on two occasions, refuse to give us food because we wanted to sing our grace together. I cannot join you in your praise of the Birmingham police department.

It is true that the police have exercised discipline in handling the demonstrators. In this sense they have conducted themselves rather "nonviolently" in public. But for what purpose? To preserve the evil system of segregation. Over the past few years I have consistently preached that nonviolence demands that the means we use must be as pure as the ends we seek. I have tried to make clear that it is wrong to use immoral means to attain moral ends. But now I must affirm that it is just as wrong, or perhaps even more so, to use moral means to preserve immoral ends. Perhaps Mr. Connor and his policemen have been rather nonviolent in public, as was Chief Pritchett in Albany, Georgia, but they have used the moral means of nonviolence to maintain the immoral end of racial injustice. As T. S. Eliot has said, there is no greater treason than to do the right deed for the wrong reason.

I wish you had commended the Negro sit-inners and demonstrators of Birmingham for their sublime courage, their willingness to suffer and their amazing discipline in the midst of great provocation. One day the south will recognize its real heroes. They will be the James Merediths, with a noble sense of purpose facing jeering and hostile mobs and the agonizing loneliness that characterizes the life of the pioneer. They will be old, oppressed, battered Negro women, symbolized in a 72-year-old woman in Montgomery, Alabama, who rose up with a sense of dignity and with her people decided not to ride segregated buses, and who responded with ungrammatical profundity to one who inquired about her: "My feet is tired, but my soul is rested." They will be the young high school and college students, the young ministers of the gospel and a host of their elders courageously and nonviolently sitting in at lunch counters and willingly going to jail for conscience' sake. One day the South will know that when these disinherited children of God sat down at lunch counters they were in reality standing up for what is best in the American dream and for the most sacred values in our Judeo-Christian heritage, thereby bringing our nation back to those great wells of democracy which were dug deep by the founding fathers in their formulation of the Constitution and the Declaration of Independence.

Never before have I written so long a letter. I can assure you that it would have been much shorter if I had been writing from a comfortable desk, but what else can one do when he is alone for days in a narrow jail cell, other than write long letters, think long thoughts and pray long prayers?

If I have said anything in this letter that overstates the truth and indicates an unreasonable impatience, I beg you to forgive me. If I have said anything that *under*states the truth and indicates my having a patience that allows me to settle for anything less than brotherhood, I beg God to forgive me.

I hope this letter finds you strong in the faith. I also hope that circumstances will soon make it possible for me to meet each of you, not as an integrationist or a civil rights leader but as a fellow clergyman and a Christian brother. Let us all hope that the dark clouds of racial prejudice will soon pass away and the deep fog of misunderstanding will be lifted from our fear-drenched communities and in some not too distant tomorrow the radiant stars of love and brotherhood will shine over our great nation with all their scintillating beauty.

BETTY FRIEDAN

Selection from *The Feminine Mystique* 1963

An obscure journalist who had written primarily for popular women's magazines created one of the most influential works of social criticism of the entire era since World War II. Betty Friedan (1921–) accused the very magazines for which she wrote of conveying a destructively narrow image of what it meant to be a woman. These magazines shared with the advertising industry, many social scientists, and much of the educational establishment a tendency to mystify certain aspects of femininity, especially the ability to bear children and to stimulate men sexually. Friedan's *The Feminine Mystique* (New York, 1963) called on women to seek rewarding careers without renouncing family life. In the selection from this book reprinted here, Friedan complains audaciously that the writings of even the great Margaret Mead perpetuated—and endowed with quasi-scientific status—many of the same constraining ideas about femininity and masculinity that dominated the popular media. Throughout *The Feminine Mystique,* Friedan promotes an intellectual ideal of womanhood and urges women to seek fulfillment through serious endeavors in philosophy, the sciences, and the arts, as well as in business, politics, and public affairs.

Although most later feminists have praised Friedan for her pioneering accomplishments, the limitations of her analysis have been widely debated in relation to recent feminist theory. Friedan did not try to explain in social–theoretical terms women's subordination to men, nor did she speak to the specific problems of poor and black women. Her perspective, it is often observed, was largely confined to the needs and dilemmas of white middle-class women. Further, Friedan's emphasis on the human characteristics that women share with men contrasts with the emphasis of some later theorists on the differences between men and women.

Recent scholarship has done much to clarify the ideological and personal context of Friedan's work. See Daniel Horowitz, "Rethinking Betty Friedan and *The Feminine Mystique:* Labor Union Radicalism and Feminism in Cold War America," *American Quarterly* XLVIII (1996), 1–42; and Joanne Meyerowitz, "Beyond the Feminine Mystique: A Reassessment of Post War Mass Culture, 1946–1958," *Journal of American History* LXXIX (1993), 1455–82.

. . . Centering primarily on cultural anthropology and sociology and reaching its extremes in the applied field of family-life education, functionalism began as an attempt to make social science more "scientific" by borrowing from biology the idea of studying institutions as if they were muscles or bones, in terms of their "structure" and "function" in the social body. By studying an institution only in terms of its function within its own society, the social scientists intended to avert unscientific value judgments. In practice, functionalism was less a scientific movement than a scientific word-game. "The function is" was often translated "the function should be"; the social scientists did not recognize their own prejudices in functional disguise any more than the analysts recognized theirs in Freudian disguise. By giving an absolute meaning and a sanctimonious value to the generic term "woman's role," functionalism put American women into a kind of deep freeze—like Sleeping Beauties, waiting for a Prince Charming to waken them, while all around the magic circle the world moved on.

The social scientists, male and female, who, in the name of functionalism, drew this torturously tight circle around American women, also seemed to share a certain attitude which I will call "the feminine protest." If there is such a thing as a masculine protest—the psychoanalytic concept taken over by the functionalists to describe women who envied men and wanted to be men and therefore denied that they were women and became more manly than any man—its counterpart can be seen today in a feminine protest, made by men and women alike, who deny what women really are and make more of "being a woman" than it could ever be. The feminine protest, at its most straightforward, is simply a means of protecting women from the dangers inherent in assuming true equality with men. But why should any social scientist, with godlike manipulative superiority, take it upon himself—or herself—to protect women from the pains of growing up?

Protectiveness has often muffled the sound of doors closing against women; it has often cloaked a very real prejudice, even when it is offered in the name of science. If an old-fashioned grandfather frowned at Nora, who is studying calculus because she wants to be a physicist, and muttered, "Woman's place is in the home," Nora would laugh impatiently, "Grandpa, this is 1963." But she does not laugh at the urbane pipe-smoking professor of sociology, or the book by Margaret Mead, or the definitive two-volume reference on female sexuality, when they tell her the same thing. The complex, mysterious language of functionalism, Freudian psychology, and cultural anthropology hides from her the fact that they say this with not much more basis than grandpa.

So our Nora would smile at Queen Victoria's letter, written in 1870: "The Queen is most anxious to enlist everyone who can speak or write to join in checking this mad, wicked folly of 'Woman's Rights' with all its attendant horrors, on which her poor feeble sex is bent, forgetting every sense of womanly feeling and propriety. . . . It is a subject which makes the Queen so furious that she cannot contain herself. God created men and women different—then let them remain each in their own position."

But she does not smile when she reads in *Marriage for Moderns*:

> The sexes are complementary. It is the works of my watch that move the hands and enable me to tell time. Are the works, therefore, more important than the case? . . . Neither is superior, neither inferior. Each must be judged in terms of its own

Source: Betty Friedan, *The Feminine Mystique* (New York: W. W. Norton, 1963), 127–31, 134–37, 145–46. Reprinted with permission of W. W. Norton & Co., Inc. Copyright 1963 by Betty Friedan. Copyright renewed 1991 by Bettery Friedan.

functions. Together they form a functioning unit. So it is with men and women—together they form a functioning unit. Either alone is in a sense incomplete. They are complementary. . . . When men and women engage in the same occupations or perform common functions, the complementary relationship may break down.

This book was published in 1942. Girls have studied it as a college text for the past twenty years. Under the guise of sociology, or "Marriage and Family Life," or "Life Adjustment," they are offered advice of this sort:

> The fact remains, however, that we live in a world of reality, a world of the present and the immediate future, on which there rests the heavy hand of the past, a world in which tradition still holds sway and the mores exert a stronger influence than does the theorist . . . a world in which most men and women do marry and in which most married women are homemakers. To talk about what might be done if tradition and the mores were radically changed or what may come about by the year 2000 may be interesting mental gymnastics, but it does not help the young people of today to adjust to the inevitables of life or raise their marriages to a higher plane of satisfaction.

Of course, this "adjustment to the inevitables of life" denies the speed with which the conditions of life are now changing—and the fact that many girls who so adjust at twenty will still be alive in the year 2000. This functionalist specifically warns against any and all approaches to the "differences between men and women" except "adjustment" to those differences as they now stand. And if, like our Nora, a woman is contemplating a career, he shakes a warning finger.

> For the first time in history, American young women in great numbers are being faced with these questions: Shall I voluntarily prepare myself for a lifelong celibate career? Or shall I prepare for a temporary vocation, which I shall give up when I marry and assume the responsibilities of homemaking and motherhood? Or should I attempt to combine homemaking and a career? . . . The great majority of married women are homemakers. . . .
> If a woman can find adequate self-expression through a career rather than through marriage, well and good. Many young women, however, overlook the fact that there are numerous careers that do not furnish any medium or offer any opportunity for self-expression. Besides they do not realize that only the minority of women, as the minority of men, have anything particularly worthwhile to express.

And so Nora is left with the cheerful impression that if she chooses a career, she is also choosing celibacy. If she has any illusions about combining marriage and career, the functionalist admonishes her:

> How many individuals . . . can successfully pursue two careers simultaneously? Not many. The exceptional person can do it, but the ordinary person cannot. The problem of combining marriage and homemaking with another career is especially difficult, since it is likely that the two pursuits will demand qualities of different types. The former, to be successful, requires self-negation; the latter, self-enhancement. The former demands cooperation; the latter competition. . . . There is greater opportunity for happiness if husband and wife supplement each other than there is when there is duplication of function. . . .

And just in case Nora has any doubts about giving up her career ambitions, she is offered this comforting rationalization:

A woman who is an effective homemaker must know something about teaching, interior decoration, cooking, dietetics, consumption, psychology, physiology, social relations, community resources, clothing, household equipment, housing, hygiene and a host of other things. . . . She is a general practitioner rather than a specialist. . . .

The young woman who decides upon homemaking as her career need have no feeling of inferiority. . . . One may say, as some do, "Men can have careers because women make homes." One may say that women are released from the necessity for wage earning and are free to devote their time to the extremely important matter of homemaking because men specialize in breadwinning. Or one may say that together the breadwinner and the homemaker form a complementary combination second to none.

This marriage textbook is not the most subtle of its school. It is almost too easy to see that its functional argument is based on no real chain of scientific fact. (It is hardly scientific to say "this is what is, therefore this is what should be.") But this is the essence of functionalism as it came to pervade all of American sociology in this period, whether or not the sociologist called himself a "functionalist." In colleges which would never stoop to the "role-playing lessons" of the so-called functional family course, young women were assigned Talcott Parsons' authoritative "analysis of sex-roles in the social structure of the United States," which contemplates no alternative for a woman other than the role of "housewife," patterned with varying emphasis on "domesticity," "glamour," and "good companionship."

It is perhaps not too much to say that only in very exceptional cases can an adult man be genuinely self-respecting and enjoy a respected status in the eyes of others if he does not "earn a living" in an approved occupational role. . . . In the case of the feminine role the situation is radically different. . . . The woman's fundamental status is that of her husband's wife, the mother of his children. . . .

Parsons, a highly respected sociologist and the leading functional theoretician, describes with insight and accuracy the sources of strain in this "segregation of sex roles." He points out that the "domestic" aspect of the housewife role "has declined in importance to the point where it scarcely approaches a full-time occupation for a vigorous person": that the "glamour pattern" is "inevitably associated with a rather early age level" and thus "serious strains result from the problem of adaptation to increasing age," that the "good companion" pattern—which includes "humanistic" cultivation of the arts and community welfare—"suffers from a lack of fully institutionalized status. . . . It is only those with the strongest initiative and intelligence who achieve fully satisfying adaptations in this direction." He states that "it is quite clear that in the adult feminine role there is quite sufficient strain and insecurity so that widespread manifestations are to be expected in the form of neurotic behavior." But Parsons warns:

It is, of course, possible for the adult woman to follow the masculine pattern and seek a career in fields of occupational achievement in direct competition with men of her own class. It is, however, notable that in spite of the very great progress of the emancipation of women from the traditional domestic pattern only a very small fraction have gone very far in this direction. It is also clear that its generalization would only be possible with profound alterations in the structure of the family.

True equality between men and women would not be "functional"; the status quo can be maintained only if the wife and mother is exclusively a homemaker or, at most, has a "job" rather than a "career" which might give her status equal to that of her husband. Thus Parsons finds sexual segregation "functional" in terms of keeping the social structure as it is, which seems to be the functionalist's primary concern. . . .

Functionalism was an easy out for American sociologists. There can be no doubt that they were describing things "as they were," but in so doing, they were relieved of the responsibility of building theory from facts, of probing for deeper truth. They were also relieved of the need to formulate questions and answers that would be inevitably controversial (at a time in academic circles, as in America as a whole, when controversy was not welcome). They assumed an endless present, and based their reasoning on denying the possibility of a future different from the past. Of course, their reasoning would hold up only as long as the future did not change. As C. P. Snow has pointed out, science and scientists are future-minded. Social scientists under the functional banner were so rigidly present-minded that they denied the future; their theories enforced the prejudices of the past, and actually prevented change.

Sociologists themselves have recently come to the conclusion that functionalism was rather "embarrassing" because it really said nothing at all. As Kingsley Davis pointed out in his presidential address on "The Myth of Functional Analysis as a Special Method in Sociology and Anthropology" at the American Sociological Association in 1959:

> For more than thirty years now "functional analysis" has been debated among sociologists and anthropologists. . . . However strategic it may have been in the past, it has now become an impediment rather than a prop to scientific progress. . . . The claim that functionalism cannot handle social change because it posits an integrated static society is true by definition. . . .

Unfortunately, the female objects of functional analysis were profoundly affected by it. At a time of great change for women, at a time when education, science, and social science should have helped women bridge the change, functionalism transformed "what is" for women, or "what was," to "what should be." Those who perpetrated the feminine protest, and made more of being a woman than it can ever be, in the name of functionalism or for whatever complex of personal or intellectual reasons, closed the door of the future on women. In all the concern for adjustment, one truth was forgotten: women were being adjusted to a state inferior to their full capabilities. The functionalists did not wholly accept the Freudian argument that "anatomy is destiny," but they accepted whole-heartedly an equally restrictive definition of woman: woman is what society says she is. And most of the functional anthropologists studied societies in which woman's destiny was defined by anatomy.

The most powerful influence on modern women, in terms both of functionalism and the feminine protest, was Margaret Mead. Her work on culture and personality— book after book, study after study—has had a profound effect on the women in my generation, the one before it, and the generation now growing up. She was, and still is, the symbol of the woman thinker in America. She has written millions of words in the thirty-odd years between *Coming of Age in Samoa* in 1928 and her latest article on American women in the *New York Times Magazine* or *Redbook*. She is studied in college classrooms by girls taking courses in anthropology, sociology, psychology, education, and marriage and family life; in graduate schools by those who will one day teach girls and counsel women; in medical schools by future pediatricians and psychiatrists; even in theological schools by progressive young ministers. And she is read in the women's magazines and the Sunday supplements, where she publishes as readily as in the learned journals, by girls and women of all ages. Margaret Mead is her own best popularizer—and her influence has been felt in almost every layer of American thought.

But her influence, for women, has been a paradox. A mystique takes what it needs from any thinker of the time. The feminine mystique might have taken from Margaret Mead her vision of the infinite variety of sexual patterns and the enormous plasticity of human nature, a vision based on the differences of sex and temperament she found in three primitive societies: the Arapesh, where both men and women were "feminine" and "maternal" in personality and passively sexual, because both were trained to be cooperative, unaggressive, responsive to the needs and demands of others; the Mundugumor, where both husband and wife were violent, aggressive, positively sexed, "masculine"; and the Tchambuli, where the woman was the dominant, impersonal managing partner, and the man the less responsible and emotionally dependent person.

> If those temperamental attitudes which we have traditionally regarded as feminine—such as passivity, responsiveness, and a willingness to cherish children—can so easily be set up as the masculine pattern in one tribe, and in another be outlawed for the majority of women as well as for the majority of men, we no longer have any basis for regarding such aspects of behavior as sex-linked. . . . The material suggests that we may say that many, if not all, of the personality traits which we have called masculine or feminine are as lightly linked to sex, as are the clothing, the manners, and the form of head-dress that a society at a given period assigns to either sex.

From such anthropological observations, she might have passed on to the popular culture a truly revolutionary vision of women finally free to realize their full capabilities in a society which replaced arbitrary sexual definitions with a recognition of genuine individual gifts as they occur in either sex. She had such a vision, more than once:

> Where writing is accepted as a profession that may be pursued by either sex with perfect suitability, individuals who have the ability to write need not be debarred from it by their sex, nor need they, if they do write, doubt their essential masculinity or femininity . . . and it is here that we can find a ground-plan for building a society that would substitute real differences for arbitrary ones. We must recognize that beneath the superficial classifications of sex and race the same potentialities exist, recurring generation after generation, only to perish because society has no place for them.
>
> Just as society now permits the practice of an art to members of either sex, so it might also permit the development of many contrasting temperamental gifts in each sex. It would abandon its various attempts to make boys fight and to make girls remain passive, or to make all children fight. . . . No child would be relentlessly shaped to one pattern of behavior, but instead there should be many patterns, in a world that had learned to allow to each individual the pattern which was most congenial to his gifts.

But this is not the vision the mystique took from Margaret Mead; nor is it the vision that she continues to offer. Increasingly, in her own pages, her interpretation blurs, is subtly transformed, into a glorification of women in the female role—as defined by their sexual biological function. At times she seems to lose her own anthropological awareness of the malleability of human personality, and to look at anthropological data from the Freudian point of view—sexual biology determines all, anatomy is destiny. . . .

As a matter of fact, the lens of "anatomy is destiny" seemed to be peculiarly right for viewing the cultures and personalities of Samoa, Manus, Arapesh, Mundugumor, Tchambuli, Iatmul and Bali; right as perhaps it never was right, in that formulation, for Vienna at the end of the nineteenth century or America in the twentieth.

In the primitive civilizations of the South Sea islands, anatomy was still destiny when Margaret Mead first visited them. Freud's theory that the primitive instincts of the body determined adult personality could find convincing demonstration. The complex goals of more advanced civilizations, in which instinct and environment are increasingly controlled and transformed by the human mind, did not then form the irreversible matrix of every human life. It must have been much easier to see biological differences between men and women as the basic force in life in those unclothed primitive peoples. But only if you go to such an island with the Freudian lens in your eye, accepting before you start what certain irreverent anthropologists call the toilet-paper theory of history, will you draw from observations in primitive civilizations of the role of the unclothed body, male or female, a lesson for modern women which assumes that the unclothed body can determine in the same way the course of human life and personality in a complex modern civilization.

Anthropologists today are less inclined to see in primitive civilization a laboratory for the observation of our own civilization, a scale model with all the irrelevancies blotted out; civilization is just not that irrelevant.

Because the human body is the same in primitive South Sea tribes and modern cities, an anthropologist, who starts with a psychological theory that reduces human personality and civilization to bodily analogies, can end up advising modern women to live through their bodies in the same way as the women of the South Seas. The trouble is that Margaret Mead could not recreate a South Sea world for us to live in: a world where having a baby is the pinnacle of human achievement. . . .

The role of Margaret Mead as the professional spokesman of femininity would have been less important if American women had taken the example of her own life, instead of listening to what she said in her books. Margaret Mead has lived a life of open challenge, and lived it proudly, if sometimes self-consciously, as a woman. She has moved on the frontiers of thought and added to the superstructure of our knowledge. She has demonstrated feminine capabilities that go far beyond childbirth; she made her way in what was still very much a "man's world" without denying that she was a woman; in fact, she proclaimed in her work a unique woman's knowledge with which no male anthropologist could compete. After so many centuries of unquestioned masculine authority, how natural for someone to proclaim a feminine authority. But the great human visions of stopping wars, curing sickness, teaching races to live together, building new and beautiful structures for people to live in, are more than "other ways of having children."

It is not easy to combat age-old prejudices. As a social scientist, and as a woman, she struck certain blows against the prejudicial image of woman that may long outlast her own life. In her insistence that women are human beings—unique human beings, not men with something missing—she went a step beyond Freud. And yet, because her observations were based on Freud's bodily analogies, she cut down her own vision of women by glorifying the mysterious miracle of femininity, which a woman realizes simply by being female, letting the breasts grow and the menstrual blood flow and the baby suck from the swollen breast. In her warning that women who seek fulfillment beyond their biological role are in danger of becoming desexed witches, she spelled out again an unnecessary choice. She persuaded younger women to give up part of their dearly won humanity rather than lose their femininity. In the end she did the very thing that she warned against, re-creating in her work the vicious circle that she broke in her own life. . . .

Part Four

Exploring Diversity and Postmodernity

Introduction

Intellectual history would be a simpler endeavor if there were but a single torch to be passed. Then, one could confidently chart the history of thought from epoch to epoch. The rationalists of the Enlightenment yield to the impetuous and gloomy Romantics, followed by the stolid but anxious Victorians, who are in turn replaced by the bold and austere Moderns. Finally, the torch is passed to the cool and polymorphous Postmoderns. There is something to this familiar sequence of vast and all-encompassing intellectual movements, and to the popular images associated with each, successive movement. But the closer this grand narrative comes to our own time the more cause we have to remind ourselves of the complex and contested character of discourse. The temptation to "name the moment," to sum up in a label or a phrase the prodigious intellectual activities of the last third of the twentieth century, threatens premature closure on a lively debate about contemporary culture.

Hence it is in a highly tentative spirit that *The American Intellectual Tradition* offers *Diversity* and *Postmodernity* as the most useful terms from which a student can begin a study of the recent intellectual history of the United States. That the world is a bigger, more various dispersion of practices, ideas, and human types than had been previously acknowledged has been a "discovery" of many generations. But few generations have proclaimed this discovery of diversity with more excitement, and tried more earnestly to explore its meaning, than have late-twentieth-century thinkers in the United States. That the world is a less stable place than had previously been recognized is also a point made by many generations of intellectuals. But here, again, the intellectuals of the late twentieth century have outdone their predecessors in "postmodern" questioning the basic categories once taken for granted. The exploration of "diversity" and "postmodernity" often overlaps, as in the selections here by Kwame Anthony Appiah on race theory and by Judith Butler on gender theory.

Part Four opens with three sixties classics by Thomas S. Kuhn, Malcolm X, and Susan Sontag that offered bold challenges to prevailing ideas of science, art, and American race relations, respectively. The political meaning of the era of the Vietnam War is addressed by Hannah Arendt and Samuel Huntington. Selections by Richard Rorty, Evelyn Fox Keller, and Michael Walzer join those by Butler and Appiah to represent the explorations of diversity and postmodernity characteristic of the late 1980s and early 1990s.

Suggestions for Further Reading

Andreas Huyssen, *After the Great Divide: Modernism, Mass Culture, Postmodernism* (Bloomington, 1986); David Harvey, *The Condition of Postmodernity* (Cambridge, 1989); Lawrence H. Fuchs, *The American Kaleidoscope: Race, Ethnicity, and the Civic Culture* (Hanover, N. H.,

1990); Brook Thomas, *The New Historicism and Other Old-Fashioned Topics* (Princeton, 1991); Franklin Jameson, *Postmodernism, or, The Cultural Logic of Late Capitalism* (Durham, 1991); Judith Butler and Joan W. Scott, *Feminists Theorize the Political* (New York, 1992); Giles Gunn, *Thinking Across the Grain: Ideology, Intellect, and the New Pragmatism* (Chicago, 1992); James Davison Hunter, *Culture Wars: The Struggle to Define America* (New York, 1992); Pauline Marie Rosenau, *Postmodernism and the Social Sciences* (Princeton, 1992); Linda S. Kauffman, ed., *American Feminist Thought at Century's End* (Cambridge, 1993); John Guillory, *Cultural Capital: The Problem of Literary Canon Formation* (Chicago, 1993); Giovanna Borradori, *The American Philosopher: Conversations with Quine, Davidson, Putnam, Nozick, Danto, Rorty, Cavell, MacIntyre, and Kuhn* (Chicago, 1994); David Farber, *The Age of Great Dreams: America in the 1960s* (New York, 1994); David Farber, ed., *The Sixties: From Memory to History* (Chapel Hill, 1994); Tom Engelhardt, *The End of Victory Culture: Cold War America and the Disillusioning of a Generation* (New York, 1995); Michael Berube and Cary Nelson, eds., *Higher Education Under Fire: Politics, Economics, and the Crisis of the Humanities* (New York, 1995); David A. Hollinger, *Postethnic America: Beyond Multiculturalism* (New York, 1995); Dan Danielsen and Karen Engle, eds., *After Identity: A Reader in Law and Culture* (New York, 1995); Lawrence Cahoone, ed., *From Modernism to Postmodernism* (Cambridge, 1996).

THOMAS S. KUHN

Selection from *The Structure of Scientific Revolutions* 1962

The extraordinary discussion surrounding *The Structure of Scientific Revolutions* is an indicator not only of the insight of its author, the historian of science Thomas S. Kuhn (1922–96), but also of the significance assigned by twentieth-century intellectuals to issues in the theoretical basis of science. This book of 1962 quickly became one of the most widely quoted and earnestly assessed academic works of the past generation. Much of the controversy centers around arguments made by Kuhn in our selection, the penultimate chapter of *Structure*. Here Kuhn places the logical aspect of scientific "proof" in a larger, social, and psychological context. New theories become accepted as true by communities of scientists not because these theories satisfy some absolute criteria of validity, according to Kuhn, but rather because these new theories seem more capable than competing theories of satisfying certain, special needs of these communities. Nothing is more needed by such communities than a framework to guide future scientific work directed at explaining the particular problems upon which the community happens to have focused its immediate attention. When Kuhn speaks in these pages of competing "paradigms," he refers to these general theoretical frameworks that serve to guide specialized scientific work. When the relevant scientific community replaces an old paradigm with another, a "revolution" is constituted, as in several of the historical episodes to which Kuhn alludes: the intellectual innovations we associate with the names of Copernicus, Newton, and Darwin.

An overview of Kuhn's major arguments can be found in Barry Barnes, "Thomas Kuhn," in Quentin Skinner, ed., *The Return of Grand Theory in the Human Sciences* (New York, 1985), 83–100. A collection of critical discussions is Gary Gutting, ed., *Paradigms and Revolutions: Appraisals of Thomas Kuhn's Philosophy of Science* (Notre Dame, 1980). A playful, polemical dramatization of the discourse of philosophy of science in the wake of Kuhn's contribution is Larry Laudan, *Science and Relativism: Some Key Controversies in the Philosophy of Science* (Chicago, 1990), in which four imaginary, composite thinkers debate the issues in a manner calculated to cast doubt on the adequacy of the ideas of Kuhn, Paul Feyerabend, and Richard Rorty. Prominent among Kuhn's historical studies are *The Copernican Revolution* (Cambridge, Mass., 1957), and *Black Body Theory and the Quantum Discontinuity, 1894–1911* (New York, 1978).

For a discussion of *The Structure of Scientific Revolutions* from the viewpoint of the discipline of history, see David A. Hollinger, "T. S. Kuhn's Theory of Science and Its Implications for History," in Hollinger's *In the American Province: Studies in the History and Historiography of Ideas* (Bloomington, 1985), 105–29. The most intensive study of Kuhn's ideas is Paul Hoyningen-Huene, *Reconstructing Scientific Revolutions: Thomas S. Kuhn's Philosophy of Science* tr. Alexander T. Levine (Chicago, 1993).

. . . What is the process by which a new candidate for paradigm replaces its predecessor? Any new interpretation of nature, whether a discovery or a theory, emerges first in the mind of one or a few individuals. It is they who first learn to see science and the world differently, and their ability to make the transition is facilitated by two circumstances that are not common to most other members of their profession. Invariably their attention has been intensely concentrated upon the crisis-provoking problems; usually, in addition, they are men so young or so new to the crisis-ridden field that practice has committed them less deeply than most of their contemporaries to the world view and rules determined by the old paradigm. How are they able, what must they do, to convert the entire profession or the relevant professional subgroup to their way of seeing science and the world? What causes the group to abandon one tradition of normal research in favor of another?

To see the urgency of those questions, remember that they are the only reconstructions the historian can supply for the philosopher's inquiry about the testing, verification, or falsification of established scientific theories. In so far as he is engaged in normal science, the research worker is a solver of puzzles, not a tester of paradigms. Though he may, during the search for a particular puzzle's solution, try out a number of alternative approaches, rejecting those that fail to yield the desired result, he is not testing the *paradigm* when he does so. Instead he is like the chess player who, with a problem stated and the board physically or mentally before him, tries out various alternative moves in the search for a solution. These trial attempts, whether by the chess player or by the scientist, are trials only of themselves, not of the rules of the game. They are possible only so long as the paradigm itself is taken for granted. Therefore, paradigm testing occurs only after persistent failure to solve a noteworthy puzzle has given rise to crisis. And even then it occurs only after the sense of crisis has evoked an alternate candidate for paradigm. In the sciences the testing situation never consists, as puzzle solving does, simply in the comparison of a single paradigm with nature. Instead, testing occurs as part of the competition between two rival paradigms for the allegiance of the scientific community.

Closely examined, this formulation displays unexpected and probably significant parallels to two of the most popular contemporary philosophical theories about verification. Few philosophers of science still seek absolute criteria for the verification of scientific theories. Noting that no theory can ever be exposed to all possible relevant tests, they ask not whether a theory has been verified but rather about its probability in the light of the evidence that actually exists. And to answer that question one important school is driven to compare the ability of different theories to explain the evidence at hand. That insistence on comparing theories also characterizes the historical situation in which a new theory is accepted. Very probably it points one of the directions in which future discussions of verification should go.

In their most usual forms, however, probabilistic verification theories all have recourse to one or another of the pure or neutral observation-languages discussed in Section X. One probabilistic theory asks that we compare the given scientific theory with all others that might be imagined to fit the same collection of observed data. Another demands the construction in imagination of all the tests that the given scientific

Source: Thomas S. Kuhn, *The Structure of Scientific Revolutions* (Chicago: University of Chicago Press, 1962), 143–59. Copyright © 1962 by University of Chicago Press. Reprinted by permission of Thomas S. Kuhn and University of Chicago Press.

theory might conceivably be asked to pass. Apparently some such construction is necessary for the computation of specific probabilities, absolute or relative, and it is hard to see how such a construction can possibly be achieved. If, as I have already urged, there can be no scientifically or empirically neutral system of language or concepts, then the proposed construction of alternate tests and theories must proceed from within one or another paradigm-based tradition. Thus restricted it would have no access to all possible experiences or to all possible theories. As a result, probabilistic theories disguise the verification situation as much as they illuminate it. Though that situation does, as they insist, depend upon the comparison of theories and much widespread evidence, the theories and observations at issue are always closely related to ones already in existence. Verification is like natural selection: it picks out the most viable among the actual alternatives in a particularly historical situation. Whether that choice is the best that could have been made if still other alternatives had been available or if the data had been of another sort is not a question that can usefully be asked. There are no tools to employ in seeking answers to it.

A very different approach to this whole network of problems has been developed by Karl R. Popper who denies the existence of any verificiation procedures at all. Instead, he emphasizes the importance of falsification, i.e., of the test that, because its outcome is negative, necessitates the rejection of an established theory. Clearly, the role thus attributed to falsification is much like the one this essay assigns to anomalous experiences, i.e., to experiences that, by evoking crisis, prepare the way for a new theory. Nevertheless, anomalous experiences may not be identified with falsifying ones. Indeed, I doubt that the latter exist. As has repeatedly been emphasized before, no theory ever solves all the puzzles with which it is confronted at a given time; nor are the solutions already achieved often perfect. On the contrary, it is just the incompleteness and imperfection of the existing data-theory fit that, at any time, define many of the puzzles that characterize normal science. If any and every failure to fit were ground for theory rejection, all theories ought to be rejected at all times. On the other hand, if only severe failure to fit justifies theory rejection, then the Popperians will require some criterion of "improbability" or of "degree of falsification." In developing one they will almost certainly encounter the same network of difficulties that has haunted the advocates of the various probabilistic verification theories.

Many of the preceding difficulties can be avoided by recognizing that both of these prevalent and opposed views about the underlying logic of scientific inquiry have tried to compress two largely separate processes into one. Popper's anomalous experience is important to science because it evokes competitors for an existing paradigm. But falsification, though it surely occurs, does not happen with, or simply because of, the emergence of an anomaly or falsifying instance. Instead, it is a subsequent and separate process that might equally well be called verification since it consists in the triumph of a new paradigm over the old one. Furthermore, it is in that joint verification-falsification process that the probabilist's comparison of theories plays a central role. Such a two-stage formulation has, I think, the virtue of great verisimilitude, and it may also enable us to begin explicating the role of agreement (or disagreement) between fact and theory in the verification process. To the historian, at least, it makes little sense to suggest that verification is establishing the agreement of fact with theory. All historically significant theories have agreed with the facts, but only more or less. There is no more precise answer to the question whether or how well an individual theory fits the facts. But questions much like that can be asked when theories are taken collectively or even in pairs. It makes a great deal of sense to ask which of two actual and competing theories fits the facts *better*. Though neither Priestley's nor Lavoisier's theory, for example, agreed precisely with existing observations, few contemporaries hesitated more than a decade in concluding that Lavoisier's theory provided the better fit of the two.

This formulation, however, makes the task of choosing between paradigms look both easier and more familiar than it is. If there were but one set of scientific problems, one world within which to work on them, and one set of standards for their solution, paradigm competition might be settled more or less routinely by some process like counting the number of problems solved by each. But, in fact, these conditions are never met completely. The proponents of competing paradigms are always at least slightly at cross-purposes. Neither side will grant all the non-empirical assumptions that the other needs in order to make its case. Like Proust and Berthollet arguing about the composition of chemical compounds, they are bound partly to talk through each other. Though each may hope to convert the other to his way of seeing his science and its problems, neither may hope to prove his case. The competition between paradigms is not the sort of battle that can be resolved by proofs.

We have already seen several reasons why the proponents of competing paradigms must fail to make complete contact with each other's viewpoints. Collectively these reasons have been described as the incommensurability of the pre- and postrevolutionary normal-scientific traditions, and we need only recapitulate them briefly here. In the first place, the proponents of competing paradigms will often disagree about the list of problems that any candididate for paradigm must resolve. Their standards or their definitions of science are not the same. Must a theory of motion explain the cause of the attractive forces between particles of matter or may it simply note the existence of such forces? Newton's dynamics was widely rejected because, unlike both Aristotle's and Descartes's theories, it implied the latter answer to the question. When Newton's theory had been accepted, a question was therefore banished from science. That question, however, was one that general relativity may proudly claim to have solved. Or again, as disseminated in the nineteenth century, Lavoisier's chemical theory inhibited chemists from asking why the metals were so much alike, a question that phlogistic chemistry had both asked and answered. The transition to Lavoisier's paradigm had, like the transition to Newton's, meant a loss not only of a permissible question but of an achieved solution. That loss was not, however, permanent either. In the twentieth century questions about the qualities of chemical substances have entered science again, together with some answers to them.

More is involved, however, than the incommensurability of standards. Since new paradigms are born from old ones, they ordinarily incorporate much of the vocabulary and apparatus, both conceptual and manipulative, that the traditional paradigm had previously employed. But they seldom employ these borrowed elements in quite the traditional way. Within the new paradigm, old terms, concepts, and experiments fall into new relationships one with the other. The inevitable result is what we must call, though the term is not quite right, a misunderstanding between the two competing schools. The laymen who scoffed at Einstein's general theory of relativity because space could not be "curved"—it was not that sort of thing—were not simply wrong or mistaken. Nor were the mathematicians, physicists, and philosophers who tried to develop a Euclidean version of Einstein's theory. What had previously been meant by space was necessarily flat, homogeneous, isotropic, and unaffected by the presence of matter. If it had not been, Newtonian physics would not have worked. To make the transition to

Einstein's universe, the whole conceptual web whose strands are space, time, matter, force, and so on, had to be shifted and laid down again on nature whole. Only men who had together undergone or failed to undergo that transformation would be able to discover precisely what they agreed or disagreed about. Communication across the revolutionary divide is inevitably partial. Consider, for another example, the men who called Copernicus mad because he proclaimed that the earth moved. They were not either just wrong or quite wrong. Part of what they meant by "earth" was fixed position. Their earth, at least could not be moved. Correspondingly, Copernicus' innovation was not simply to move the earth. Rather, it was a whole new way of regarding the problems of physics and astronomy, one that necessarily changed the meaning of both "earth" and "motion." Without those changes the concept of a moving earth was mad. On the other hand, once they had been made and understood, both Descartes and Huyghens could realize that the earth's motion was a question with no content for science.

These examples point to the third and most fundamental aspect of the incommensurability of competing paradigms. In a sense that I am unable to explicate further, the proponents of competing paradigms practice their trades in different worlds. One contains constrained bodies that fall slowly, the other pendulums that repeat their motions again and again. In one, solutions are compounds, in the other mixtures. One is embedded in a flat, the other in a curved, matrix of space. Practicing in different worlds, the two groups of scientists see different things when they look from the same point in the same direction. Again, that is not to say that they can see anything they please. Both are looking at the world, and what they look at has not changed. But in some areas they see different things, and they see them in different relations one to the other. That is why a law that cannot even be demonstrated to one group of scientists may occasionally seem intuitively obvious to another. Equally, it is why before they can hope to communicate fully, one group or the other must experience the conversion that we have been calling a paradigm shift. Just because it is a transition between incommensurables, the transition between competing paradigms cannot be made a step at a time, forced by logic and neutral experience. Like the gestalt switch, it must occur all at once (though not necessarily in an instant) or not at all.

How, then, are scientists brought to make this transposition? Part of the answer is that they are very often not. Copernicanism made few converts for almost a century after Copernicus' death. Newton's work was not generally accepted, particularly on the Continent, for more than half a century after the *Principia* appeared. Priestley never accepted the oxygen theory, nor Lord Kelvin the electromagnetic theory, and so on. The difficulties of conversion have often been noted by scientists themselves. Darwin, in a particularly perceptive passage at the end of his *Origin of Species,* wrote: "Although I am fully convinced of the truth of the views given in this volume . . . , I by no means expect to convince experienced naturalists whose minds are stocked with a multitude of facts all viewed, during a long course of years, from a point of view directly opposite to mine. . . . [B]ut I look with confidence to the future,—to young and rising naturalists, who will be able to view both sides of the question with impartiality." And Max Planck, surveying his own career in his *Scientific Autobiography,* sadly remarked that "a new scientific truth does not triumph by convincing its opponents and making them see the light, but rather because its opponents eventually die, and a new generation grows up that is familiar with it."

These facts and others like them are too commonly known to need further emphasis. But the do need re-evaluation. In the past they have most often been taken to indicate that scientists, being only human, cannot always admit their errors, even when confronted with strict proof. I would argue, rather, that in these matters neither proof nor error is at issue. The transfer of allegiance from paradigm to paradigm is a conversion experience that cannot be forced. Lifelong resistance, particularly from those whose productive careers have committed them to an older tradition of normal science, is not a violation of scientific standards but an index to the nature of scientific research itself. The source of resistance is the assurance that the older paradigm will ultimately solve all its problems, that nature can be shoved into the box the paradigm provides. Inevitably, at time of revolution, that assurance seems stubborn and pigheaded as indeed it sometimes becomes. But it is also something more. That same assurance is what makes normal or puzzle-solving science possible. And it is only through normal science that the professional community of scientists succeeds, first, in exploiting the potential scope and precision of the older paradigm and, then, in isolating the difficulty through the study of which a new paradigm may emerge.

Still, to say that resistance is inevitable and legitimate, that paradigm change cannot be justified by proof, is not to say that no arguments are relevant or that scientists cannot be persuaded to change their minds. Though a generation is sometimes required to effect the change, scientific communities have again and again been converted to new paradigms. Furthermore, these conversions occur not despite the fact that scientists are human but because they are. Though some scientists, particularly the older and more experienced ones, may resist indefinitely, most of them can be reached in one way or another. Conversions will occur a few at a time until, after the last holdouts have died, the whole profession will again be practicing under a single, but now a different, paradigm. We must therefore ask how conversion is induced and how resisted.

What sort of answer to that question may we expect? Just because it is asked about techniques of persuasion, or about argument and counterargument in a situation in which there can be no proof, our question is a new one, demanding a sort of study that has not previously been undertaken. We shall have to settle for a very partial and impressionistic survey. In addition, what has already been said combines with the result of the survey to suggest that, when asked about persuasion rather than proof, the question of the nature of scientific argument has no single or uniform answer. Individual scientists embrace a new paradigm for all sorts of reasons and usually for several at once. Some of these reasons—for example, the sun worship that helped make Kepler a Copernican—lie outside the apparent sphere of science entirely. Others must depend upon idiosyncrasies of autobiography and personality. Even the nationality or the prior reputation of the innovator and his teachers can sometimes play a significant role. Ultimately, therefore, we must learn to ask this question differently. Our concern will not then be with the arguments that in fact convert one or another individual, but rather with the sort of community that always sooner or later re-forms as a single group. . . .

Probably the single most prevalent claim advanced by the proponents of a new paradigm is that they can solve the problems that have led the old one to a crisis. When it can legitimately be made, this claim is often the most effective one possible. In the area for which it is advanced the paradigm is known to be in trouble. That trouble has repeatedly been explored, and attempts to remove it have again and again proved vain. "Crucial experiments"—those able to discriminate particularly sharply between the two paradigms—have been recognized and attested before the new paradigm was even invented. Copernicus thus claimed that he had solved the long-vexing problem of the length of the calendar year, Newton that he had reconciled terrestrial and celestial mechanics, Lavoisier that he had solved the problems of gas-identity and of weight relations, and Einstein that he had made electrodynamics compatible with a revised science of motion.

Claims of this sort are particularly likely to succeed if the new paradigm displays a quantitative precision strikingly better than its older competitor. The quantitative superiority of Kepler's Rudolphine tables to all those computed from the Ptolemaic theory was a major factor in the conversion of astronomers to Copernicanism. Newton's success in predicting quantitative astronomical observations was probably the single most important reason for his theory's triumph over its more reasonable but uniformly qualitative competitors. And in this century the striking quantitative success of both Planck's radiation law and the Bohr atom quickly persuaded many physicists to adopt them even though, viewing physical science as a whole, both these contributions created many more problems than they solved.

The claim to have solved the crisis-provoking problems is, however, rarely sufficient by itself. Nor can it always legitimately be made. In fact, Copernicus' theory was not more accurate than Ptolemy's and did not lead directly to any improvement in the calendar. Or again, the wave theory of light was not, for some years after it was first announced, even as successful as its corpuscular rival in resolving the polarization effects that were a principal cause of the optical crisis. Sometimes the looser practice that characterizes extraordinary research will produce a candidate for paradigm that initially helps not at all with the problems that have evoked crisis. When that occurs, evidence must be drawn from other parts of the field as it often is anyway. In those other areas particularly persuasive arguments can be developed if the new paradigm permits the prediction of phenomena that had been entirely unsuspected while the old one prevailed.

Copernicus' theory, for example, suggested that planets should be like the earth, that Venus should show phases, and that the universe must be vastly larger than had previously been supposed. As a result, when sixty years after his death the telescope suddenly displayed mountains on the moon, the phases of Venus, and an immense number of previously unsuspected stars, those observations brought the new theory a great many converts, particularly among non-astronomers. In the case of the wave theory, one main source of professional conversions was even more dramatic. French resistance collapsed suddenly and relatively completely when Fresnel was able to demonstrate the existence of a white spot at the center of the shadow of a circular disk. That was an effect that not even he had anticipated but that Poisson, initially one of his opponents, had shown to be a necessary if absurd consequence of Fresnel's theory. Because of their shock value and because they have so obviously not been "built into" the new theory from the start, arguments like these prove especially persuasive. And sometimes that extra strength can be exploited even though the phenomenon in question had been observed long before the theory that accounts for it was first introduced. Einstein, for example, seems not to have anticipated that general relativity would account with precision for the well-known anomaly in the motion of Mercury's perihelion, and he experienced a corresponding triumph when it did so.

All the arguments for a new paradigm discussed so far have been based upon the competitors' comparative ability to solve problems. To scientists those arguments are ordinarily the most significant and persuasive. The preceding examples should leave no doubt about the source of their immense appeal. But, for reasons to which we shall shortly revert, they are neither individually nor collectively compelling. Fortunately, there is also another sort of consideration that can lead scientists to reject an old paradigm in favor of a new. These are the arguments, rarely made entirely explicit, that appeal to the individual's sense of the appropriate or the aesthetic—the new theory is said to be "neater," "more suitable," or "simpler" than the old. Probably such arguments are less effective in the sciences than in mathematics. The early versions of most new paradigms are crude. By the time their full aesthetic appeal can be developed, most of the community has been persuaded by other means. Nevertheless, the importance of aesthetic considerations can sometimes be decisive. Though they often attract only a few scientists to a new theory, it is upon those few that its ultimate triumph may depend. If they had not quickly taken it up for highly individual reasons, the new candidate for paradigm might never have been sufficiently developed to attract the allegiance of the scientific community as a whole.

To see the reason for the importance of these more subjective and aesthetic considerations, remember what a paradigm debate is about. When a new candidate for paradigm is first proposed, it has seldom solved more than a few of the problems that confront it, and most of those solutions are still far from perfect. Until Kepler, the Copernican theory scarcely improved upon the predictions of planetary position made by Ptolemy. When Lavoisier saw oxygen as "the air itself entire," his new theory could cope not at all with the problems presented by the proliferation of new gases, a point that Priestley made with great success in his counterattack. Cases like Fresnel's white spot are extremely rare. Ordinarily, it is only much later, after the new paradigm has been developed, accepted, and exploited that apparently decisive arguments—the Foucault pendulum to demonstrate the rotation of the earth or the Fizeau experiment to show that light moves faster in air than in water—are developed. Producing them is part of normal science, and their role is not in paradigm debate but in postrevolutionary texts.

Before those texts are written, while the debate goes on, the situation is very different. Usually the opponents of a new paradigm can legitimately claim that even in the area of crisis it is little superior to its traditional rival. Of course, it handles some problems better, has disclosed some new regularities. But the older paradigm can presumably be articulated to meet these challenges as it has met others before. Both Tycho Brahe's earth-centered astronomical system and the later versions of the phlogiston theory were responses to challenges posed by a new candidate for paradigm, and both were quite successful. In addition, the defenders of traditional theory and procedure can almost always point to problems that its new rival has not solved but that for their view are no problems at all. Until the discovery of the composition of water, the combustion of hydrogen was a strong argument for the phlogiston theory and against Lavoisier's. And after the oxygen theory had triumphed, it could still not explain the preparation of a combustible gas from carbon, a phenomenon to which the phlogistonists had pointed as strong support for their view. Even in the area of crisis, the balance of argument and counterargument can sometimes be very close indeed. And outside that area the balance will often decisively favor the tradition. Copernicus destroyed a time-honored explanation of terrestrial motion without replacing it; Newton did the same for an older explanation of gravity, Lavoisier for the common properties of metals, and so on. In short, if a new candidate for paradigm had to be judged from the start by hardheaded people who examined only relative problem-solving ability, the sciences would experience very few major revolutions. Add the counterarguments generated by what we previously called the incommensurability of paradigms, and the sciences might experience no revolutions at all.

But paradigm debates are not really about relative problem-solving ability, though for good reasons they are usually couched in those terms. Instead, the issue is which paradigm should in the future guide research on problems many of which neither competitor can yet claim to resolve completely. A decision between alternate ways of practicing science is called for, and in the circumstances that decision must be based less on past achievement than on future promise. The man who embraces a new paradigm at an early stage must often do so in defiance of the evidence provided by problem solving. He must, that is, have faith that the new paradigm will succeed with the many large problems that confront it, knowing only that the older paradigm has failed with a few. A decision of that kind can only be made on faith.

That is one of the reasons why prior crisis proves so important. Scientists who have not experienced it will seldom renounce the hard evidence of problem solving to follow what may easily prove and will be widely regarded as a will-o'-the-wisp. But crisis alone is not enough. There must also be a basis, though it need be neither rational nor ultimately correct, for faith in the particular candidate chosen. Something must make at least a few scientists feel that the new proposal is on the right track, and sometimes it is only personal and inarticulate aesthetic considerations that can do that. Men have been converted by them at times when most of the articulable technical arguments pointed the other way. When first introduced, neither Copernicus' astronomical theory nor De Broglie's theory of matter had many other significant grounds of appeal. Even today Einstein's general theory attracts men principally on aesthetic grounds, an appeal that few people outside of mathematics have been able to feel.

This is not to suggest that new paradigms triumph ultimately through some mystical aesthetic. On the contrary, very few men desert a tradition for these reasons alone. Often those who do turn out to have been misled. But if a paradigm is ever to triumph it must gain some first supporters, men who will develop it to the point where hard-headed arguments can be produced and multiplied. And even those arguments, when they come, are not individually decisive. Because scientists are reasonable men, one or another argument will ultimately persuade many of them. But there is no single argument that can or should persuade them all. Rather than a single group conversion, what occurs is an increasing shift in the distribution of professional allegiances.

At the start a new candidate for paradigm may have few supporters, and on occasions the supporters' motives may be suspect. Nevertheless, if they are competent, they will improve it, explore its possibilities, and show what it would be like to belong to the community guided by it. And as that goes on, if the paradigm is one destined to win its fight, the number and strength of the persuasive arguments in its favor will increase. More scientists will then be converted, and the exploration of the new paradigm will go on. Gradually the number of experiments, instruments, articles, and books based upon the paradigm will multiply. Still more men, convinced of the new view's fruitfulness, will adopt the new mode of practicing normal science, until at last only a few elderly hold-outs remain. And even they, we cannot say, are wrong. Though the historian can always find men—Priestley, for instance—who were unreasonable to resist for as long as they did, he will not find a point at which resistance becomes illogical or unscientific. At most he may wish to say that the man who continues to resist after his whole profession has been converted has *ipso facto* ceased to be a scientist.

SUSAN SONTAG

"Against Interpretation"
1964

Explorers of the uncertain cultural terrain that separates the "postmodern" from the "modern" have turned increasingly to the early work of Susan Sontag (1933–). In a series of essays written in the mid-1960s, Sontag criticized as a stagnant, academicized establishment a tradition of "modernist" thought about the arts that had long seen itself as a bold, iconoclastic avant-garde. Drawing upon an older, romantic tradition, Sontag insisted that criticism should not try to tell us what art "means," but should show us "the sensuous surface" of art. She endorsed "erotic" rather than "hermeneutic" priorities. The arts now the most alive, Sontag insisted, were popular arts like film, often eschewed as beneath serious scrutiny by the critics of Clement Greenberg's generation.

Although Sontag wrote well before currency of the term *postmodernism,* this label came eventually to stand for the blurring of "high" and "low" art, the liberation of art from political and moral purposes, the focusing on the surfaces instead of the allegedly deep structures of art, and the separation of art objects from large-scale interpretive schemes—all themes of "Against Interpretation," the essay of 1964 reprinted here. Sontag's ideas can be profitably contrasted to those set forth in two "modernist" classics found in this sourcebook, Greenberg's "Avant-Garde and Kitsch" and Lionel Trilling's "On the Teaching of Modern Literature."

Sontag also distinguished herself as a writer of fiction—her best known novel is *Death Kit* (1967)—but her stature as a critical essayist of exceptionally wide range has been sustained not only by *Against Interpretation* (1966), in which our selection was first reprinted, but also by *On Photography* (1977), *Illness as Metaphor* (1979), and *AIDS and Its Metaphors* (1988).

Two studies of her work are Sohnya Sayers, *Susan Sontag: Elegiac Modernist* (New York, 1990), and Liam Kennedy, *Susan Sontag: Mind as Passion* (Manchester, Engl., 1995).

The earliest *experience* of art must have been that it was incantatory, magical; art was an instrument of ritual. (Cf. the paintings in the caves at Lascaux, Altamira, Niaux, La Pasiega, etc.) The earliest *theory* of art, that of the Greek philosophers, proposed that art was mimesis, imitation of reality.

It is at this point that the peculiar question of the *value* of art arose. For the mimetic theory, by its very terms, challenges art to justify itself.

Plato, who proposed the theory, seems to have done so in order to rule that the value of art is dubious. Since he considered ordinary material things as themselves mimetic objects, imitations of transcendent forms or structures, even the best painting of a bed would be only an "imitation of an imitation." For Plato, art is neither particularly useful (the painting of a bed is no good to sleep on), nor, in the strict sense, true. And Aristotle's arguments in defense of art do not really challenge Plato's view that all art is an elaborate *trompe l'oeil*, and therefore a lie. But he does dispute Plato's idea that art is useless. Lie or no, art has a certain value according to Aristotle because it is a form of therapy. Art is useful, after all, Aristotle counters, medicinally useful in that it arouses and purges dangerous emotions.

In Plato and Aristotle, the mimetic theory of art goes hand in hand with the assumption that art is always figurative. But advocates of the mimetic theory need not close their eyes to decorative and abstract art. The fallacy that art is necessarily a "realism" can be modified or scrapped without ever moving outside the problems delimited by the mimetic theory.

The fact is, all Western consciousness of and reflection upon art have remained within the confines staked out by the Greek theory of art as mimesis or representation. It is through this theory that art as such—above and beyond given works of art—becomes problematic, in need of defense. And it is the defense of art which gives birth to the odd vision by which something we have learned to call "form" is separated off from something we have learned to call "content," and to the well-intentioned move which makes content essential and form accessory.

Even in modern times, when most artists and critics have discarded the theory of art as representation of an outer reality in favor of the theory of art as subjective expression, the main feature of the mimetic theory persists. Whether we conceive of the work of art on the model of a picture (art as a picture of reality) or on the model of a statement (art as the statement of the artist), content still comes first. The content may have changed. It may now be less figurative, less lucidly realistic. But it is still assumed that a work of art *is* its content. Or, as it's usually put today, that a work of art by definition *says* something. ("What X is saying is . . . ," "What X is trying to say is . . . ," "What X said is . . ." etc., etc.)

None of us can ever retrieve that innocence before all theory when art knew no need to justify itself, when one did not ask of a work of art what it *said* because one knew (or thought one knew) what it *did*. From now to the end of consciousness, we are stuck with the task of defending art. We can only quarrel with one or another means of defense. Indeed, we have an obligation to overthrow any means of defending and justifying art which becomes particularly obtuse or onerous or insensitive to contemporary needs and practice.

This is the case, today, with the very idea of content itself. Whatever it may have

Source: Susan Sontag, *Against Interpretation* (New York, 1966). Reprinted by permission of Farrar, Straus & Giroux.

been in the past, the idea of content is today mainly a hindrance, a nuisance, a subtle or not so subtle philistinism.

Though the actual developments in many arts may seem to be leading us away from the idea that a work of art is primarily its content, the idea still exerts an extraordinary hegemony. I want to suggest that this is because the idea is now perpetuated in the guise of a certain way of encountering works of art thoroughly ingrained among most people who take any of the arts seriously. What the overemphasis on the idea of content entails is the perennial, never consummated project of *interpretation*. And, conversely, it is the habit of approaching works of art in order to *interpret* them that sustains the fancy that there really is such a thing as the content of a work of art.

Of course, I don't mean interpretation in the broadest sense, the sense in which Nietzsche (rightly) says, "There are no facts, only interpretations." By interpretation, I mean here a conscious act of the mind which illustrates a certain code, certain "rules" of interpretation.

Directed to art, interpretation means plucking a set of elements (the X, the Y, the Z, and so forth) from the whole work. The task of interpretation is virtually one of translation. The interpreter says, Look, don't you see that X is really—or, really means—A? That Y is really B? That Z is really C?

What situation could prompt this curious project for transforming a text? History gives us the materials for an answer. Interpretation first appears in the culture of late classical antiquity, when the power and credibility of myth had been broken by the "realistic" view of the world introduced by scientific enlightenment. Once the question that haunts post-mythic consciousness—that of the *seemliness* of religious symbols— had been asked, the ancient texts were, in their pristine form, no longer acceptable. Then interpretation was summoned, to reconcile the ancient texts to "modern" demands. Thus, the Stoics, to accord with their view that the gods had to be moral, allegorized away the rude features of Zeus and his boisterous clan in Homer's epics. What Homer really designated by the adultery of Zeus with Leto, they explained, was the union between power and wisdom. In the same vein, Philo of Alexandria interpreted the literal historical narratives of the Hebrew Bible as spiritual paradigms. The story of the exodus from Egypt, the wandering in the desert for forty years, and the entry into the promised land, said Philo, was really an allegory of the individual soul's emancipation, tribulations, and final deliverance. Interpretation thus presupposes a discrepancy between the clear meaning of the text and the demands of (later) readers. It seeks to resolve that discrepancy. The situation is that for some reason a text has become unacceptable; yet it cannot be discarded. Interpretation is a radical strategy for conserving an old text, which is thought too precious to repudiate, by revamping it. The interpreter, without actually erasing or rewriting the text, *is* altering it. But he can't admit to doing this. He claims to be only making it intelligible, by disclosing its true meaning. However far the interpreters alter the text (another notorious example is the Rabbinic and Christian "spiritual" interpretations of the clearly erotic Song of Songs), they must claim to be reading off a sense that is already there.

Interpretation in our own time, however, is even more complex. For the contemporary zeal for the project of interpretation is often prompted not by piety toward the troublesome text (which may conceal an aggression), but by an open aggressiveness, an overt contempt for appearances. The old style of interpretation was insistent, but respectful; it erected another meaning on top of the literal one. The modern style of interpretation excavates, and as it excavates, destroys; it digs "behind" the text, to find a sub-text which is the true one. The most celebrated and influential modern doctrines, those of Marx and Freud, actually amount to elaborate systems of hermeneutics, aggressive and impious theories of interpretation. All observable phenomena are bracketed, in Freud's phrase, as *manifest content*. This manifest content must be probed and pushed aside to find the true meaning—the *latent content*—beneath. For Marx, social events like revolutions and wars; for Freud, the events of individual lives (like neurotic symptoms and slips of the tongue) as well as texts (like a dream or a work of art)—all are treated as occasions for interpretation. According to Marx and Freud, these events only seem to be intelligible. Actually, they have no meaning without interpretation. To understand is to interpret. And to interpret is to restate the phenomenon, in effect to find an equivalent for it.

Thus, interpretation is not (as most people assume) an absolute value, a gesture of mind situated in some timeless realm of capabilities. Interpretation must itself be evaluated, within a historical view of human consciousness. In some cultural contexts, interpretation is a liberating act. It is a means of revising, of transvaluing, of escaping the dead past. In other cultural contexts, it is reactionary, impertinent, cowardly, stifling.

Today is such a time, when the project of interpretation is largely reactionary, stifling. Like the fumes of the automobile and of heavy industry which befoul the urban atmosphere, the effusion of interpretations of art today poisons our sensibilities. In a culture whose already classical dilemma is the hypertrophy of the intellect at the expense of energy and sensual capability, interpretation is the revenge of the intellect upon art.

Even more. It is the revenge of the intellect upon the world. To interpret is to impoverish, to deplete the world—in order to set up a shadow world of "meanings." It is to turn *the* world into *this* world. ("This world"! As if there were any other.)

The world, our world, is depleted, impoverished enough. Away with all duplicates of it, until we again experience more immediately what we have.

In most modern instances, interpretation amounts to the philistine refusal to leave the work of art alone. Real art has the capacity to make us nervous. By reducing the work of art to its content and then interpreting *that*, one tames the work of art. Interpretation makes art manageable, comformable.

This philistinism of interpretation is more rife in literature than in any other art. For decades now, literary critics have understood it to be their task to translate the elements of the poem or play or novel or story into something else. Sometimes a writer will be so uneasy before the naked power of his art that he will install within the work itself—albeit with a little shyness, a touch of the good taste of irony—the clear and explicit interpretation of it. Thomas Mann is an example of such an overcooperative author. In the case of more stubborn authors, the critic is only too happy to perform the job.

The work of Kafka, for example, has been subjected to a mass ravishment by no less than three armies of interpreters. Those who read Kafka as a social allegory see case studies of the frustrations and insanity of modern bureaucracy and its ultimate issuance in the totalitarian state. Those who read Kafka as a psychoanalytic allegory see desperate revelations of Kafka's fear of his father, his castration anxieties, his sense of his own impotence, his thralldom to his dreams. Those who read Kafka as a religious allegory explain that K. in *The Castle* is trying to gain access to heaven, that Joseph K. in *The Trial* is being judged by the inexorable and mysterious justice of God. . . .

Another *oeuvre* that has attracted interpreters like leeches is that of Samuel Beckett. Beckett's delicate dramas of the withdrawn consciousness—pared down to essentials, cut off, often represented as physically immobilized—are read as a statement about modern man's alienation from meaning or from God, or as an allegory of psychopathology.

Proust, Joyce, Faulkner, Rilke, Lawrence, Gide . . . one could go on citing author after author; the list is endless of those around whom thick encrustations of interpretation have taken hold. But it should be noted that interpretation is not simply the compliment that mediocrity pays to genius. It is, indeed, the modern way of understanding something, and is applied to works of every quality. Thus, in the notes that Elia Kazan published on his production of *A Streetcar Named Desire,* it becomes clear that, in order to direct the play, Kazan had to discover that Stanley Kowalski represented the sensual and vengeful barbarism that was engulfing our culture, while Blanche Du Bois was Western civilization, poetry, delicate apparel, dim lighting, refined feelings and all, though a little the worse for wear to be sure. Tennessee Williams' forceful psychological melodrama now became intelligible: it was *about* something, about the decline of Western civilization. Apparently, were it to go on being a play about a handsome brute named Stanley Kowalski and a faded mangy belle named Blanche Du Bois, it would not be manageable.

It doesn't matter whether artists intend, or don't intend, for their works to be interpreted. Perhaps Tennessee Williams thinks *Streetcar* is about what Kazan thinks it to be about. It may be that Cocteau in *The Blood of a Poet* and in *Orpheus* wanted the elaborate readings which have been given these films, in terms of Freudian symbolism and social critique. But the merit of these works certainly lies elsewhere than in their "meanings." Indeed, it is precisely to the extent that Williams' plays and Cocteau's films do suggest these portentous meanings that they are defective, false, contrived, lacking in conviction.

From interviews, it appears that Resnais and Robbe-Grillet consciously designed *Last Year at Marienbad* to accommodate a multiplicity of equally plausible interpretations. But the temptation to interpret *Marienbad* should be resisted. What matters in *Marienbad* is the pure, untranslatable, sensuous immediacy of some of its images, and its rigorous if narrow solutions to certain problems of cinematic form.

Again, Ingmar Bergman may have meant the tank rumbling down the empty night street in *The Silence* as a phallic symbol. But if he did, it was a foolish thought. ("Never trust the teller, trust the tale," said Lawrence.) Taken as a brute object, as an immediate sensory equivalent for the mysterious abrupt armored happenings going on inside the hotel, that sequence with the tank is the most striking moment in the film. Those who reach for a Freudian interpretation of the tank are only expressing their lack of response to what is there on the screen.

It is always the case that interpretation of this type indicates a dissatisfaction (conscious or unconscious) with the work, a wish to replace it by something else.

Interpretation, based on the highly dubious theory that a work of art is composed of items of content, violates art. It makes art into an article for use, for arrangement into a mental scheme of categories.

Interpretation does not, of course, always prevail. In fact, a great deal of today's art may be understood as motivated by a flight from interpretation. To avoid interpretation, art may become parody. Or it may become abstract. Or it may become ("merely") decorative. Or it may become non-art.

The flight from interpretation seems particularly a feature of modern painting. Abstract painting is the attempt to have, in the ordinary sense, no content; since there is no content, there can be no interpretation. Pop Art works by the opposite means to the same result; using a content so blatant, so "what it is," it, too, ends by being uninterpretable.

A great deal of modern poetry as well, starting from the great experiments of French poetry (including the movement that is misleadingly called Symbolism) to put silence into poems and to reinstate the *magic* of the word, has escaped from the rough grip of interpretation. The most recent revolution in contemporary taste in poetry—the revolution that has deposed Eliot and elevated Pound—represents a turning away from content in poetry in the old sense, an impatience with what made modern poetry prey to the zeal of interpreters.

I am speaking mainly of the situation in America, of course. Interpretation runs rampant here in those arts with a feeble and negligible avant-garde: fiction and the drama. Most American novelists and playwrights are really either journalists or gentlemen sociologists and psychologists. They are writing the literary equivalent of program music. And so rudimentary, uninspired, and stagnant has been the sense of what might be done with *form* in fiction and drama that even when the content isn't simply information, news, it is still peculiarly visible, handier, more exposed. To the extent that novels and plays (in America), unlike poetry and painting and music, don't reflect any interesting concern with changes in their form, these arts remain prone to assault by interpretation.

But programmatic avant-gardism—which has meant, mostly, experiments with form at the expense of content—is not the only defense against the infestation of art by interpretations. At least, I hope not. For this would be to commit art to being perpetually on the run. (It also perpetuates the very distinction between form and content which is, ultimately, an illusion.) Ideally, it is possible to elude the interpreters in another way, by making works of art whose surface is so unified and clean, whose momentum is so rapid, whose address is so direct that the work can be . . . just what it is. Is this possible now? It does happen in films, I believe. This is why cinema is the most alive, the most exciting, the most important of all art forms right now. Perhaps the way one tells how alive a particular art form is, is by the latitude it gives for making mistakes in it, and still being good. For example, a few of the films of Bergman—though crammed with lame messages about the modern spirit, thereby inviting interpretations—still triumph over the pretentious intentions of their director. In *Winter Light* and *The Silence,* the beauty and visual sophistication of the images subvert before our eyes the callow pseudo-intellectuality of the story and some of the dialogue. (The most remarkable instance of this sort of discrepancy is the work of D. W. Griffith.) In good films, there is always a directness that entirely frees us from the itch to interpret. Many old Hollywood films, like those of Cukor, Walsh, Hawks, and countless other directors, have this liberating anti-symbolic quality, no less than the best work of the new European directors, like Truffaut's *Shoot the Piano Player* and *Jules and Jim,* Godard's *Breathless* and *Vivre Sa Vie,* Antonioni's *L'Avventura,* and Olmi's *The Fiancés.*

The fact that films have not been overrun by interpreters is in part due simply to the newness of cinema as an art. It also owes to the happy accident that films for such a long time were just movies; in other words, that they were understood to be part of mass, as opposed to high, culture, and were left alone by most people with minds. Then, too, there is always something other than content in the cinema to grab hold of, for those who want to analyze. For the cinema, unlike the novel, possesses a vocabulary of forms—the explicit, complex, and discussable technology of camera movements, cutting, and composition of the frame that goes into the making of a film.

What kind of criticism, of commentary on the arts, is desirable today? For I am not saying that works of art are ineffable, that they cannot be described or paraphrased. They can be. The question is how. What would criticism look like that would serve the work of art, not usurp its place?

What is needed, first, is more attention to form in art. If excessive stress on *content* provokes the arrogance of interpretation, more extended and more thorough descriptions of *form* would silence. What is needed is a vocabulary—a descriptive, rather than prescriptive, vocabulary—for forms.* The best criticism, and it is uncommon, is of this sort that dissolves considerations of content into those of form. On film, drama, and painting respectively, I can think of Erwin Panofsky's essay, "Style and Medium in the Motion Pictures," Northrop Frye's essay "A Conspectus of Dramatic Genres," Pierre Francastel's essay "The Destruction of a Plastic Space." Roland Barthes' book *On Racine* and his two essays on Robbe-Grillet are examples of formal analysis applied to the work of a single author. (The best essays in Erich Auerbach's *Mimesis,* like "The Scar of Odysseus," are also of this type.) An example of formal analysis applied simultaneously to genre and author is Walter Benjamin's essay, "The Story Teller: Reflections on the Works of Nicolai Leskov."

Equally valuable would be acts of criticism which would supply a really accurate, sharp, loving description of the appearance of a work of art. This seems even harder to do than formal analysis. Some of Manny Farber's film criticism, Dorothy Van Ghent's essay "The Dickens World: A View from Todgers'," Randall Jarrell's essay on Walt Whitman are among the rare examples of what I mean. These are essays which reveal the sensuous surface of art without mucking about in it.

Transparence is the highest, most liberating value in art—and in criticism—today. Transparence means experiencing the luminousness of the thing in itself, of things being what they are. This is the greatness of, for example, the films of Bresson and Ozu and Renoir's *The Rules of the Game.*

Once upon a time (say, for Dante), it must have been a revolutionary and creative move to design works of art so that they might be experienced on several levels. Now it is not. It reinforces the principle of redundancy that is the principal affliction of modern life.

Once upon a time (a time when high art was scarce), it must have been a revolutionary and creative move to interpret works of art. Now it is not. What we decidedly do not need now is further to assimilate Art into Thought, or (worse yet) Art into Culture.

Interpretation takes the sensory experience of the work of art for granted, and proceeds from there. This cannot be taken for granted, now. Think of the sheer multiplication of works of art available to every one of us, superadded to the conflicting

---

* One of the difficulties is that our idea of form is spatial (the Greek metaphors for form are all derived from notions of space). This is why we have a more ready vocabulary of forms for the spatial than for the temporal arts. The exception among the temporal arts, of course, is the drama; perhaps this is because the drama is a narrative (i.e., temporal) form that extends itself visually and pictorially, upon a stage. . . . What we don't have yet is a poetics of the novel, any clear notion of the forms of narration. Perhaps film criticism will be the occasion of a breakthrough here, since films are primarily a visual form, yet they are also a subdivision of literature.

tastes and odors and sights of the urban environment that bombard our senses. Ours is a culture based on excess, on overproduction; the result is a steady loss of sharpness in our sensory experience. All the conditions of modern life—its material plenitude, its sheer crowdedness—conjoin to dull our sensory faculties. And it is in the light of the condition of our senses, our capacities (rather than those of another age), that the task of the critic must be assessed.

What is important now is to recover our senses. We must learn to *see* more, to *hear* more, to *feel* more.

Our task is not to find the maximum amount of content in a work of art, much less to squeeze more content out of the work than is already there. Our task is to cut back content so that we can see the thing at all.

The aim of all commentary on art now should be to make works of art—and, by analogy, our own experience—more, rather than less, real to us. The function of criticism should be to show *how it is what it is,* even *that it is what it is,* rather than to show *what it means.*

In place of a hermeneutics we need an erotics of art.

MALCOLM X

Selection from "The Ballot or the Bullet"
1964

"Give me liberty, or give me death," Patrick Henry declared in the Virginia House of Burgesses amid the debates of eighteenth-century Americans on how best to deal with the injustices of the British imperial system. Two hundred years later, these violent, revolutionary words were echoed in the black nationalist manifesto reprinted here. Malcolm X (1925–65) addressed a Cleveland, Ohio, gathering of African-Americans looking for ways to sharpen and strengthen the movement to liberate black people from the evils of segregation and from multiple deprivations of basic human rights. "It'll be liberty or it'll be death," proclaimed the thirty-nine-year-old orator, as he set forth what he took to be the alternatives for black people in a nation that still lacked even the Civil Rights Act passed by Congress later in the same year. He was willing to invoke the white firebrand of the American revolution—a sanctioned hero, of course, to generations of American school children—and to remind blacks of the fact that the sympathy of the Supreme Court of the United States was a valuable resource in their struggle. But Malcolm X simultaneously expressed so deep an alienation from things American that he presented himself not as an American but as a victim of an "Americanism" for which he took white Southern racists to be appropriate emblems. In sections of the speech omitted here, Malcolm X detailed the activities of leading segregationists within government, including the Congress of the United States. Whatever help blacks could expect from whites, Malcolm X suggested, would come only if blacks organized among themselves.

Born Malcolm Little, the author of "The Ballot or the Bullet" took on the surname, X, after he had been converted to the Islamic religion while serving a prison term as a young man. Shortly before delivering this speech Malcolm X had broken with Elijah Muhammed and the Nation of Islam, and had begun to establish his own leadership among black nationalists. He was murdered by black gunmen while speaking in New York City in 1965.

Malcolm X's most renowned work is *The Autobiography of Malcolm X* (New York, 1964), assembled by his friend, journalist Alex Haley, from notes taken while Malcolm X spoke about his own life. It was largely through this book that Malcolm X came to exercise in death much greater influence than he had exercised in life. By the 1990s Malcolm X was claimed by proponents of an enormous variety of ideas and practices, many of which are distant from the line of analysis he developed in 1964. Even Clarence Thomas, the conservative Justice of the United States Supreme Court, today counts Malcolm X a hero.

A recent biography is Bruce Perry, *Malcolm: The Life of a Man Who Changed Black America* (New York, 1991). Joe Wood, ed., *Malcolm X: In Our Own Image* (New York, 1992), is an anthology reflecting the many uses to which Malcolm X's memory has been put. The best single book on Malcolm X and his historical significance is Michael Dyson, *Making Malcolm: The Myth and Meaning of Malcolm X* (New York, 1995).

I'm not a politician, not even a student of politics; in fact, I'm not a student of much of anything. I'm not a Democrat, I'm not a Republican, and I don't even consider myself an American. If you and I were Americans, there'd be no problem. Those Hunkies that just got off the boat, they're already Americans; Polacks are already Americans; the Italian refugees are already Americans. Everything that came out of Europe, every blue-eyed thing, is already an American. And as long as you and I have been over here, we aren't Americans yet.

Well, I am one who doesn't believe in deluding myself. I'm not going to sit at your table and watch you eat, with nothing on my plate, and call myself a diner. Sitting at the table doesn't make you a diner, unless you eat some of what's on that plate. Being here in America doesn't make you an American. Being born here in America doesn't make you an American. Why, if birth made you American, you wouldn't need any legislation, you wouldn't need any amendments to the Constitution, you wouldn't be faced with civil-rights filibustering in Washington, D.C., right now. They don't have to pass civil-rights legislation to make a Polack an American.

No, I'm not an American. I'm one of the 22 million black people who are the victims of Americanism. One of the 22 million black people who are the victims of democracy, nothing but disguised hypocrisy. So, I'm not standing here speaking to you as an American, or a patriot, or a flag-saluter, or a flag-waver—no, not I. I'm speaking as a victim of this American system. And I see America through the eyes of the victim. I don't see any American dream; I see an American nightmare.

These 22 million victims are waking up. Their eyes are coming open. They're beginning to see what they used to only look at. They're becoming politically mature. They are realizing that there are new political trends from coast to coast. As they see these new political trends, it's possible for them to see that every time there's an election the races are so close that they have to have a recount. They had to recount in Massachusetts to see who was going to be governor, it was so close. It was the same way in Rhode Island, in Minnesota, and in many other parts of the country. And the same with Kennedy and Nixon when they ran for president. It was so close they had to count all over again. Well, what does this mean? It means that when white people are evenly divided, and black people have a bloc of votes of their own, it is left up to them to determine who's going to sit in the White House and who's going to be in the dog house. . . .

So, where do we go from here? First, we need some friends. We need some new allies. The entire civil-rights struggle needs a new interpretation, a broader interpretation. We need to look at this civil-rights thing from another angle—from the inside as well as from the outside. To those of us whose philosophy is black nationalism, the only way you can get involved in the civil-rights struggle is give it a new interpretation. That old interpretation excluded us. It kept us out. So, we're giving a new interpretation to the civil-rights struggle, an interpretation that will enable us to come into it, take part in it. And these handkerchief-heads who have been dillydallying and pussyfooting and compromising—we don't intend to let them pussyfoot and dillydally and compromise any longer. . . .

Our mothers and fathers invested sweat and blood. Three hundred and ten years we worked in this country without a dime in return—I mean without a *dime* in return.

Source: Malcolm X Speaks, ed. George Breitman (New York, 1965), 25–26, 31–34, 36–44. Reprinted by permission of Betty Shabazz and Pathfinder Press.

You let the white man walk around here talking about how rich this country is, but you never stop to think how it got rich so quick. It got rich because you made it rich.

You take the people who are in this audience right now. They're poor, we're all poor as individuals. Our weekly salary individually amounts to hardly anything. But if you take the salary of everyone in here collectively it'll fill up a whole lot of baskets. It's a lot of wealth. If you can collect the wages of just these people right here for a year, you'll be rich—richer than rich. When you look at it like that, think how rich Uncle Sam had to become, not with this handful, but millions of black people. Your and my mother and father, who didn't work an eight-hour shift, but worked from "can't see" in the morning until "can't see" at night, and worked for nothing, making the white man rich, making Uncle Sam rich.

This is our investment. This is our contribution—our blood. Not only did we give of our free labor, we gave of our blood. Every time he had a call to arms, we were the first ones in uniform. We died on every battlefield the white man had. We have made a greater sacrifice than anybody who's standing up in America today. We have made a greater contribution and have collected less. Civil rights, for those of us whose philosophy is black nationalism, means: "Give it to us now. Don't wait for next year. Give it to us yesterday, and that's not fast enough."

I might stop right here to point out one thing. Whenever you're going after something that belongs to you, anyone who's depriving you of the right to have it is a criminal. Understand that. Whenever you are going after something that is yours, you are within your legal rights to lay claim to it. And anyone who puts forth any effort to deprive you of that which is yours, is breaking the law, is a criminal. And this was pointed out by the Supreme Court decision. It outlawed segregation. Which means segregation is against the law. Which means a segregationist is breaking the law. A segregationist is a criminal. You can't label him as anything other than that. And when you demonstrate against segregation, the law is on your side. The Supreme Court is on your side.

Now, who is it that opposes you in carrying out the law? The police department itself. With police dogs and clubs. Whenever you demonstrate against segregation, whether it is segregated education, segregated housing, or anything else, the law is on your side, and anyone who stands in the way is not the law any longer. They are breaking the law, they are not representatives of the law. Any time you demonstrate against segregation and a man has the audacity to put a police dog on you, kill that dog, kill him, I'm telling you, kill that dog. I say it, if they put me in jail tomorrow, kill—that—dog. Then you'll put a stop to it. Now, if these white people in here don't want to see that kind of action, get down and tell the mayor to tell the police department to pull the dogs in. That's all you have to do. If you don't do it, someone else will.

If you don't take this kind of stand, your little children will grow up and look at you and think "shame." If you don't take an uncompromising stand—I don't mean go out and get violent; but at the same time you should never be nonviolent unless you run into some nonviolence. I'm nonviolent with those who are nonviolent with me. But when you drop that violence on me, then you've made me go insane, and I'm not responsible for what I do. And that's the way every Negro should get. Any time you know you're within the law, within your legal rights, within your moral rights, in accord with justice, then die for what you believe in. But don't die alone. Let your dying be reciprocal. This is what is meant by equality. What's good for the goose is good for the gander. . . .

Right now, in this country, if you and I, 22 million African-Americans—that's what we are—Africans who are in America. You're nothing but Africans. Nothing but Africans. In fact, you'd get farther calling yourself African instead of Negro. Africans don't catch hell. You're the only one catching hell. They don't have to pass civil-rights bills for Africans. An African can go anywhere he wants right now. All you've got to do is tie your head up. That's right, go anywhere you want. Just stop being a Negro. Change your name to Hoogagagooba. That'll show you how silly the white man is. You're dealing with a silly man. A friend of mine who's very dark put a turban on his head and went into a restaurant in Atlanta before they called themselves desegregated. He went into a white restaurant, he sat down, they served him, and he said, "What would happen if a Negro came in here?" And there he's sitting, black as night, but because he had his head wrapped up the waitress looked back at him and says, "Why, there wouldn't no nigger dare come in here."

So, you're dealing with a man whose bias and prejudice are making him lose his mind, his intelligence, every day. He's frightened. He looks around and sees what's taking place on this earth, and he sees that the pendulum of time is swinging in your direction. The dark people are waking up. They're losing their fear of the white man. No place where he's fighting right now is he winning. Everywhere he's fighting, he's fighting someone your and my complexion. And they're beating him. He can't win any more. He's won his last battle. He failed to win the Korean War. He couldn't win it. He had to sign a truce. That's a loss. Any time Uncle Sam, with all his machinery for warfare, is held to a draw by some rice-eaters, he's lost the battle. He had to sign a truce. America's not supposed to sign a truce. She's supposed to be bad. But she's not bad any more. She's bad as long as she can use her hydrogen bomb, but she can't use hers for fear Russia might use hers. Russia can't use hers, for fear that Sam might use his. So, both of them are weaponless. They can't use the weapon because each's weapon nullifies the other's. So the only place where action can take place is on the ground. And the white man can't win another war fighting on the ground. Those days are over. The black man knows it, the brown man knows it, the red man knows it, and the yellow man knows it. So they engage him in guerrilla warfare. That's not his style. You've got to have heart to be a guerrilla warrior, and he hasn't got any heart. I'm telling you now.

I just want to give you a little briefing on guerrilla warfare because, before you know it, before you know it—It takes heart to be a guerrilla warrior because you're on your own. In conventional warfare you have tanks and a whole lot of other people with you to back you up, planes over your head and all that kind of stuff. But a guerrilla is on his own. All you have is a rifle, some sneakers and a bowl of rice, and that's all you need—and a lot of heart. The Japanese on some of those islands in the Pacific, when the American soldiers landed, one Japanese sometimes could hold the whole army off. He'd just wait until the sun went down, and when the sun went down they were all equal. He would take his little blade and slip from bush to bush, and from American to American. The white soldiers couldn't cope with that. Whenever you see a white soldier that fought in the Pacific, he has the shakes, he has a nervous condition, because they scared him to death.

The same thing happened to the French up in French Indochina. People who just a few years previously were rice farmers got together and ran the heavily-mechanized French army out of Indochina. You don't need it—modern warfare today won't work. This is the day of the guerrilla. They did the same thing in Algeria. Algerians, who were nothing but Bedouins, took a rifle and sneaked off to the hills, and de Gaulle and all of his highfalutin' war machinery couldn't defeat those guerrillas. Nowhere on this earth does the white man win in a guerrilla warfare. It's not his speed. Just as guerrilla warfare is prevailing in Asia and in parts of Africa and in parts of Latin America, you've got to be mighty naive, or you've got to play the black man cheap, if you don't think some day he's going to wake up and find that it's got to be the ballot or the bullet.

I would like to say, in closing, a few things concerning the Muslim Mosque, Inc., which we established recently in New York City. It's true we're Muslims and our religion is Islam, but we don't mix our religion with our politics and our economics and our social and civil activities—not any more. We keep our religion in our mosque. After our religious services are over, then as Muslims we become involved in political action, economic action and social and civic action. We become involved with anybody, anywhere, any time and in any manner that's designed to eliminate the evils, the political, economic and social evils that are afflicting the people of our community.

The political philosophy of black nationalism means that the black man should control the politics and the politicians in his own community; no more. The black man in the black community has to be re-educated into the science of politics so he will know what politics is supposed to bring him in return. Don't be throwing out any ballots. A ballot is like a bullet. You don't throw your ballots until you see a target, and if that target is not within your reach, keep your ballot in your pocket. The political philosophy of black nationalism is being taught in the Christian church. It's being taught in the NAACP. It's being taught in CORE meetings. It's being taught in SNCC [Student Nonviolent Coordinating Committee] meetings. It's being taught in Muslim meetings. It's being taught where nothing but atheists and agnostics come together. It's being taught everywhere. Black people are fed up with the dillydallying, pussyfooting, compromising approach that we've been using toward getting our freedom. We want freedom *now*, but we're not going to get it saying "We Shall Overcome." We've got to fight until we overcome.

The economic philosophy of black nationalism is pure and simple. It only means that we should control the economy of our community. Why should white people be running all the stores in our community? Why should white people be running the banks of our community? Why should the economy of our community be in the hands of the white man? Why? If a black man can't move his store into a white community, you tell me why a white man should move his store into a black community. The philosophy of black nationalism involves a re-education program in the black community in regards to economics. Our people have to be made to see that any time you take your dollar out of your community and spend it in a community where you don't live, the community where you live will get poorer and poorer, and the community where you spend your money will get richer and richer. Then you wonder why where you live is always a ghetto or a slum area. And where you and I are concerned, not only do we lose it when we spend it out of the community, but the white man has got all our stores in the community tied up; so that though we spend it in the community, at sundown the man who runs the store takes it over across town somewhere. He's got us in a vise.

So the economic philosophy of black nationalism means in every church, in every civic organization, in every fraternal order, it's time now for our people to become conscious of the importance of controlling the economy of our community. If we own the stores, if we operate the businesses, if we try and establish some industry in our own community, then we're developing to the position where we are creating employment for our own kind. Once you gain control of the economy of your own community, then you don't have to picket and boycott and beg some cracker downtown for a job in his business.

The social philosophy of black nationalism only means that we have to get together and remove the evils, the vices, alcoholism, drug addiction, and other evils that are destroying the moral fiber of our community. We ourselves have to lift the level of our community, the standard of our community to a higher level, make our own society beautiful so that we will be satisfied in our own social circles and won't be running around here trying to knock our way into a social circle where we're not wanted.

So I say, in spreading a gospel such as black nationalism, it is not designed to make the black man re-evaluate the white man—you know him already—but to make the black man re-evaluate himself. Don't change the white man's mind—you can't change his mind, and that whole thing about appealing to the moral conscience of America—America's conscience is bankrupt. She lost all conscience a long time ago. Uncle Sam has no conscience. They don't know what morals are. They don't try and eliminate an evil because it's evil, or because it's illegal, or because it's immoral; they eliminate it only when it threatens their existence. So you're wasting your time appealing to the moral conscience of a bankrupt man like Uncle Sam. If he had a conscience, he'd straighten this thing out with no more pressure being put upon him. So it is not necessary to change the white man's mind. We have to change our own mind. You can't change his mind about us. We've got to change our own minds about each other. We have to see each other with new eyes. We have to see each other as brothers and sisters. We have to come together with warmth so we can develop unity and harmony that's necessary to get this problem solved ourselves. How can we do this? How can we avoid jealousy? How can we avoid the suspicion and the divisions that exist in the community? I'll tell you how.

I have watched how Billy Graham comes into a city, spreading what he calls the gospel of Christ, which is only white nationalism. That's what he is. Billy Graham is a white nationalist; I'm a black nationalist. But since it's the natural tendency for leaders to be jealous and look upon a powerful figure like Graham with suspicion and envy, how is it possible for him to come into a city and get all the cooperation of the church leaders? Don't think because they're church leaders that they don't have weaknesses that make them envious and jealous—no, everybody's got it. It's not an accident that when they want to choose a cardinal [as Pope] over there in Rome, they get in a closet so you can't hear them cussing and fighting and carrying on.

Billy Graham comes in preaching the gospel of Christ, he evangelizes the gospel, he stirs everybody up, but he never tries to start a church. If he came in trying to start a church, all the churches would be against him. So, he just comes in talking about Christ and tells everybody who gets Christ to go to any church where Christ is; and in this way the church cooperates with him. So we're going to take a page from his book.

Our gospel is black nationalism. We're not trying to threaten the existence of any organization, but we're spreading the gospel of black nationalism. Anywhere there's a church that is also preaching and practicing the gospel of black nationalism, join that church. If the NAACP is preaching and practicing the gospel of black nationalism, join the NAACP. If CORE is spreading and practicing the gospel of black nationalism, join CORE. Join any organization that has a gospel that's for the uplift of the black man. And when you get into it and see them pussyfooting or compromising, pull out of it because that's not black nationalism. We'll find another one.

And in this manner, the organizations will increase in number and in quantity and in quality, and by August, it is then our intention to have a black nationalist convention which will consist of delegates from all over the country who are interested in the political, economic and social philosophy of black nationalism. After these delegates convene, we will hold a seminar, we will hold discussions, we will listen to everyone. We want to hear new ideas and new solutions and new answers. And at that time, if we see fit then to form a black nationalist party, we'll form a black nationalist party. If it's necessary to form a black nationalist army, we'll form a black nationalist army. It'll be the ballot or the bullet. It'll be liberty or it'll be death.

It's time for you and me to stop sitting in this country, letting some cracker senators, Northern crackers and Southern crackers, sit there in Washington, D.C., and come to a conclusion in their mind that you and I are supposed to have civil rights. There's no white man going to tell me anything about *my* rights. Brothers and sisters, always remember, if it doesn't take senators and congressmen and presidential proclamations to give freedom to the white man, it is not necessary for legislation or proclamation or Supreme Court decisions to give freedom to the black man. You let that white man know, if this is a country of freedom, let it be a country of freedom; and if it's not a country of freedom, change it.

We will work with anybody, anywhere, at any time, who is genuinely interested in tackling the problem head-on, nonviolently as long as the enemy is nonviolent, but violent when the enemy gets violent. We'll work with you on the voter-registration drive, we'll work with you on rent strikes, we'll work with you on school boycotts—I don't believe in any kind of integration; I'm not even worried about it because I know you're not going to get it anyway; you're not going to get it because you're afraid to die; you've got to be ready to die if you try and force yourself on the white man, because he'll get just as violent as those crackers in Mississippi, right here in Cleveland. But we will still work with you on the school boycotts because we're against a segregated school system. A segregated school system produces children who, when they graduate, graduate with crippled minds. But this does not mean that a school is segregated because it's all black. A segregated school means a school that is controlled by people who have no real interest in it whatsoever.

Let me explain what I mean. A segregated district or community is a community in which people live, but outsiders control the politics and the economy of that community. They never refer to the white section as a segregated community. It's the all-Negro section that's a segregated community. Why? The white man controls his own school, his own bank, his own economy, his own politics, his own everything, his own community—but he also controls yours. When you're under someone else's control, you're segregated. They'll always give you the lowest or the worst that there is to offer, but it doesn't mean you're segregated just because you have your own. You've got to *control* your own. Just like the white man has control of his, you need to control yours.

You know the best way to get rid of segregation? The white man is more afraid of separation than he is of integration. Segregation means that he puts you away from him, but not far enough for you to be out of his jurisdiction; separation means you're gone. And the white man will integrate faster than he'll let you separate. So we will work with you against the segregated school system because it's criminal, because it is absolutely destructive, in every way imaginable, to the minds of the children who have to be exposed to that type of crippling education.

Last but not least, I must say this concerning the great controversy over rifles and shotguns. The only thing that I've ever said is that in areas where the government has proven itself either unwilling or unable to defend the lives and the property of Negroes, it's time for Negroes to defend themselves. Article number two of the constitutional amendments provides you and me the right to own a rifle or a shotgun. It is constitutionally legal to own a shotgun or a rifle. This doesn't mean you're going to get a rifle and form battalions and go out looking for white folks, although you'd be within your rights—I mean, you'd be justified; but that would be illegal and we don't do anything illegal. If the white man doesn't want the black man buying rifles and shotguns, then let the government do its job. That's all. And don't let the white man come to you and ask you what you think about what Malcolm says—why, you old Uncle Tom. He would never ask you if he thought you were going to say, "Amen!" No, he is making a Tom out of you.

So, this doesn't mean forming rifle clubs and going out looking for people, but it is time, in 1964, if you are a man, to let that man know. If he's not going to do his job in running the government and providing you and me with the protection that our taxes are supposed to be for, since he spends all those billions for his defense budget, he certainly can't begrudge you and me spending $12 or $15 for a single-shot, or double-action. I hope you understand. Don't go out shooting people, but any time, brothers and sisters, and especially the men in this audience—some of you wearing Congressional Medals of Honor, with shoulders this wide, chests this big, muscles that big— any time you and I sit around and read where they bomb a church and murder in cold blood, not some grownups, but four little girls while they were praying to the same god the white man taught them to pray to, and you and I see the government go down and can't find who did it.

Why, this man—he can find Eichmann hiding down in Argentina somewhere. Let two or three American soldiers, who are minding somebody else's business way over in South Vietnam, get killed, and he'll send battleships, sticking his nose in their business. He wanted to send troops down to Cuba and make them have what he calls free elections—this old cracker who doesn't have free elections in his own country. No, if you never see me another time in your life, if I die in the morning, I'll die saying one thing: the ballot or the bullet, the ballot or the bullet.

If a Negro in 1964 has to sit around and wait for some cracker senator to filibuster when it comes to the rights of black people, why, you and I should hang our heads in shame. You talk about a march on Washington in 1963, you haven't seen anything. There's some more going down in '64. And this time they're not going like they went last year. They're not going singing "We Shall Overcome." They're not going with white friends. They're not going with placards already painted for them. They're not going with round-trip tickets. They're going with one-way tickets.

And if they don't want that non-nonviolent army going down there, tell them to bring the filibuster to a halt. The black nationalists aren't going to wait. Lyndon B. Johnson is the head of the Democratic Party. If he's for civil rights, let him go into the Senate next week and declare himself. Let him go in there right now and declare himself. Let him go in there and denounce the Southern branch of his party. Let him go in there right now and take a moral stand—right now, not later. Tell him, don't wait until election time. If he waits too long, brothers and sisters, he will be responsible for letting a condition develop in this country which will create a climate that will bring seeds up out of the ground with vegetation on the end of them looking like something these people never dreamed of. In 1964, it's the ballot or the bullet. Thank you.

HANNAH ARENDT

Selection from "Lying in Politics"
1971

How could a government possessed of incalculable resources and an abundance of brilliant technical advisors make the United States into the "pitiful, helpless giant" of Richard Nixon's widely quoted caricature? This question vexed American intellectuals of a great variety of ideological persuasions as the Vietnam War prolonged its poisonous tenure in American and world affairs. The political philosopher Hannah Arendt (1906–75) was among the most deeply troubled discussants of this question in the wake of one portentous event of 1971: the unauthorized release of a forty-seven-volume "History of U.S. Decision-Making Process on Vietnam Policy," popularly known as the Pentagon Papers. This documentary history, commissioned by Secretary of Defense Robert McNamara, remained secret until one of its authors, Daniel Ellsberg, took it upon himself to give a copy to the *New York Times*. Arendt, like many other readers of the Pentagon Papers, was struck with the record of lying and self-deception that had been integral to the course of American involvement in Vietnam.

Arendt had established her reputation with her first and most enduring work, *The Origins of Totalitarianism* (1951). She identified as central to the regimes of Hitler and Stalin a distinctive state of mind induced by a tightly controlled environment of terror. In a varied career as both a systematic theorist and a commentator on contemporary politics, Arendt produced a steady stream of controversial works, including *The Human Condition* (1958), *On Revolution* (1963), and *Eichmann in Jerusalem* (1963).

Born of highly assimilated Jewish parents in Kant's city of Konigsberg, Arendt arrived in the United States in 1941 a refugee from Hitler's Europe. She is one of forty-eight refugee intellectuals whose careers are surveyed in a book that can serve as an introduction to the study of the intellectual migration from Central Europe: Lewis A. Coser, *Refugee Scholars in America: Their Impact and Their Experiences* (New Haven, 1984). As a student in the 1920s Arendt had been involved with her mentor, Martin Heidegger, who later became rector of his university under the authority of the Nazi regime. This intimacy between the most eminent of the German philosophers to side with the Nazis and his Jewish, democracy-affirming student became a matter of renewed discussion twenty years after Arendt's death when it was learned that Arendt had renewed this relationship after World War II. At the center of this discussion was Elzbieta Ettinger, *Hannah Arendt/Martin Heidegger* (New Haven, 1995).

Arendt's influence has increased with time. Today she is one of the most respected and widely studied American intellectuals of the generation that flourished in the third quarter of the twentieth century. Her analysis of totalitarianism, long resisted by thinkers eager to drive a conceptual wedge between the "rightist" Nazis and the "leftist" Stalinists, gained renewed credibility after the collapse of communism in Europe in 1989. For a brief, accessible introduction to Arendt's thought and career, see Tony Judt, "At Home in This Century," *New York Review of Books* (April 6, 1995), 9–14. An excellent book-length study of Arendt's work is Margaret Canovan, *Hannah Arendt: A Reinterpretation of Her Political Thought* (New York, 1992). The best starting point for the study of Arendt is Lewis P. Hinchman and Sandra K. Hinchman, eds., *Hannah Arendt: Critical Essays* (Albany, 1994).

The trouble with lying and deceiving is that their efficiency depends entirely upon a clear notion of the truth that the liar and deceiver wishes to hide. In this sense, truth, even if it does not prevail in public, possesses an ineradicable primacy over all falsehoods.

In the case of the Vietnam war we are confronted with, in addition to falsehoods and confusion, a truly amazing and entirely honest ignorance of the historically pertinent background: not only did the decision-makers seem ignorant of all the well-known facts of the Chinese revolution and the decade-old rift between Moscow and Peking that preceded it, but "no one at the top knew or considered it important that the Vietnamese had been fighting foreign invaders for almost 2,000 years," or that the notion of Vietnam as a "tiny backward nation" without interest to "civilized" nations, which is, unhappily, often shared by the war critics, stands in flagrant contradiction to the very old and highly developed culture of the region. What Vietnam lacks is not "culture," but strategic importance (Indochina is "devoid of decisive military objectives," as a Joint Chiefs of Staff memo said in 1954), a suitable terrain for modern mechanized armies, and rewarding targets for the air force. What caused the disastrous defeat of American policies and armed intervention was indeed no quagmire ("the policy of 'one more step'—each new step always promising the success which the previous *last step* had also *promised* but had unaccountably failed to deliver," in the words of Arthur Schlesinger, Jr., as quoted by Daniel Ellsberg, who rightly denounces the notion as a "myth"), but the willful, deliberate disregard of all facts, historical, political, geographical, for more than twenty-five years.

If the quagmire model is a myth and if no grand imperialist stratagems or will to world conquest can be discovered, let alone interest in territorial gains, desire for profit, or, least of all, concern about national security; if, moreover, the reader is disinclined to be satisfied with such general notions as "Greek tragedy" (proposed by Max Frankel and Leslie H. Gelb) or stab-in-the-back legends, always dear to warmongers in defeat, then the question recently raised by Ellsberg, *"How could they?"*—rather than deception and lying per se—will become the basic issue of this dismal story. For the truth, after all, is that the United States was the richest country and the dominant power after the end of World War II, and that today, a mere quarter of a century later, Mr. Nixon's metaphor of the "pitiful, helpless giant" is an uncomfortably apt description of "the mightiest country on earth."

Unable to defeat, with a "1000-to-1 superiority in fire power," a small nation in six years of overt warfare, unable to take care of its domestic problems and halt the swift decline of its large cities, having wasted its resources to the point where inflation and currency devaluation threaten its international trade as well as its standard of life at home, the country is in danger of losing much more than its claim to world leadership. And even if one anticipates the judgment of future historians who might see this development in the context of twentieth-century history, when the defeated nations in two world wars managed to come out on top in competition with the victors (chiefly because they were compelled by the victors to rid themselves for a relatively long period of the incredible wastefulness of armaments and military expenses), it remains hard to reconcile oneself to so much effort wasted on demonstrating the impotence of bigness—

Source: Hannah Arendt, *Crises of the Republic* (New York, 1971). Reprinted by permission of Harcourt Brace, Inc.

though one may welcome this unexpected, grand-scale revival of David's triumph over Goliath.

The first explanation that comes to mind to answer the question "How could they?" is likely to point to the interconnectedness of deception and self-deception. In the contest between public statements, always overoptimistic, and the truthful reports of the intelligence community, persistently bleak and ominous, the public statements were liable to win simply because they were public. The great advantage of publicly established and accepted propositions over whatever an individual might secretly know or believe to be the truth is neatly illustrated by a medieval anecdote according to which a sentry, on duty to watch and warn the townspeople of the enemy's approach, jokingly sounded a false alarm—and then was the last to rush to the walls to defend the town against his invented enemies. From this, one may conclude that the more successful a liar is, the more people he has convinced, the more likely it is that he will end by believing his own lies.

In the Pentagon papers we are confronted with people who did their utmost to win the minds of the people, that is, to manipulate them; but since they labored in a free country, where all kinds of information were available, they never really succeeded. Because of their relatively high station and their position in government, they were better shielded—in spite of their privileged knowledge of "top secrets"—against this public information, which also more or less told the factual truth, than were those whom they tried to convince and of whom they were likely to think in terms of mere audiences, "silent majorities," who were supposed to watch the scenarists' productions. The fact that the Pentagon papers revealed hardly any spectacular news testifies to the liars' failure to create a convinced audience that they could then join themselves.

Still, the presence of what Ellsberg has called the process of "internal self-deception" is beyond doubt, but it is as though the normal process of self-deceiving were reversed; it was not as though deception ended with self-deception. The deceivers started with self-deception. Probably because of their high station and their astounding self-assurance, they were so convinced of overwhelming success, not on the battlefield, but in the public-relations arena, and so certain of the soundness of their psychological premises about the unlimited possibilities in manipulating people, that they *anticipated* general belief and victory in the battle for people's minds. And since they lived in a defactualized world anyway, they did not find it difficult to pay no more attention to the fact that their audience refused to be convinced than to other facts.

The internal world of government, with its bureaucracy on one hand, its social life on the other, made self-deception relatively easy. No ivory tower of the scholars has ever better prepared the mind for ignoring the facts of life than did the various think tanks for the problem-solvers and the reputation of the White House for the President's advisers. It was in this atmosphere, where defeat was less feared than admitting defeat, that the misleading statements about the disasters of the Tet offensive and the Cambodian invasion were concocted. But what is even more important is that the truth about such decisive matters could be successfully covered up in these internal circles— but nowhere else—by worries about how to avoid becoming "the first American President to lose a war" and by the always present preoccupations with the next election.

So far as problem-solving, in contrast to public-relations managing, is concerned, self-deception, even "internal self-deception," is no satisfactory answer to the question "How could they?" Self-deception still presupposes a distinction between truth and falsehood, between fact and fantasy, and therefore a conflict between the real world and the self-deceived deceiver that disappears in an entirely defactualized world; Washington and its sprawling governmental bureaucracy, as well as the various think tanks in the country, provide the problem-solvers with a natural habitat for mind and body. In the realm of politics, where secrecy and deliberate deception have always played a significant role, self-deception is the danger par excellence; the self-deceived deceiver loses all contact with not only his audience, but also the real world, which still will catch up with him, because he can remove his mind from it but not his body. The problem-solvers who knew all the facts regularly presented to them in the reports of the intelligence community had only to rely on their shared techniques, that is, on the various ways of translating qualities and contents into quantities and numbers with which to calculate outcomes—which then, unaccountably, never came true—in order to eliminate, day in and day out, what they knew to be real. The reason this could work for so many years is precisely that "the goals pursued by the United States government were almost exclusively psychological," that is, matters of the mind.

Reading the memos, the options, the scenarios, the way percentages are ascribed to the potential risks and returns—"too many risks with too little return"—of contemplated actions, one sometimes has the impression that a computer, rather than "decision-makers," had been let loose in Southeast Asia. The problem-solvers did not *judge;* they calculated. Their self-confidence did not even need self-deception to be sustained in the midst of so many misjudgments, for it relied on the evidence of mathematical, purely rational truth. Except, of course, that this "truth" was entirely irrelevant to the "problem" at hand. If, for instance, it can be calculated that the outcome of a certain action is "less likely to be a general war than more likely," it does not follow that we can choose it even if the proportion were eighty to twenty, because of the enormity and *incalculable quality* of the risk; and the same is true when the odds of reform in the Saigon government versus the "chance that we would wind up like the French in 1954" are 70 per cent to 30 per cent. That is a nice outlook for a gambler, not for a statesman, and even the gambler would be better advised to take into account what gain or loss would actually mean for him in daily life. Loss may mean utter ruin and gain no more than some welcome but nonessential improvement of his financial affairs. Only if nothing real is at stake for the gambler—a bit more or less money is not likely to make any difference in his standard of life—can he safely rely on the percentage game. The trouble with our conduct of the war in South Vietnam was that no such control, given by reality itself, ever existed in the minds of either the decision-makers or the problem-solvers.

It is indeed true that American policy pursued no real aims, good or bad, that could limit and control sheer fantasy: "Neither territory nor economic advantage has been pursued in Vietnam. The entire purpose of the enormous and costly effect has been to create a specific state of mind." And the reason such excessively costly means, costly in human lives and material resources, were permitted to be used for such politically irrelevant ends must be sought not merely in the unfortunate superabundance in this country, but in its inability to understand that even great power is *limited* power. Behind the constantly repeated cliché of the "mightiest power on earth," there lurked the dangerous myth of omnipotence.

Just as Eisenhower was the last President who knew he would have to request "Congressional authority to commit American troops in Indochina," so his administration was the last to be aware that "the allocation of more than token U.S. armed forces in that area would be a serious diversion of *limited* U.S. capabilities" (italics added). In spite of all the later calculations of "costs, returns and risks" of certain acts, the calculators remained totally unaware of any absolute, nonpsychological limitation. The limits they perceived were the people's minds, how much they would stand in the loss of American lives, which should not be much larger than, for instance, the loss in traffic accidents. But it apparently never occurred to them that there are limits to the resources that even this country can waste without going bankrupt.

This deadly combination of the "arrogance of power"—the pursuit of a mere image of omnipotence, as distinguished from an aim of world conquest, to be attained by nonexistent unlimited resources—with the arrogance of mind, an utterly irrational confidence in the calculability of reality, becomes the leitmotif of the decision-making processes from the beginning of escalation in 1964. This, however, is not to say that the problem-solvers' rigorous methods of defactualization are at the root of this relentless march into self-destruction.

The problem-solvers, who lost their minds because they trusted the calculating powers of their brains at the expense of the mind's capacity for experience and its ability to learn from it, were preceded by the ideologists of the Cold War period. Anti-Communism—not the old, often prejudiced hostility of America against socialism and communism, so strong in the twenties and still a mainstay of the Republican party during the Roosevelt administration, but the postwar comprehensive ideology—was originally the brain child of former Communists who needed a new ideology by which to explain and reliably foretell the course of history. This ideology was at the root of all "theories" in Washington since the end of World War II. I have mentioned the extent to which sheer ignorance of all pertinent facts and deliberate neglect of postwar developments became the hallmark of established doctrine within the establishment. They needed no facts, no information; they had a "theory," and all data that did not fit were denied or ignored.

The methods of this older generation—the methods of Mr. Rusk as distinguished from those of Mr. McNamara—were less complicated, less brainy, as it were, than those of the problem-solvers, but not less efficacious in shielding men from the impact of reality and in ruining the mind's capacity for judgment and for learning. These men prided themselves on having learned from the past—from Stalin's rule over all Communist parties, hence the notion of "monolithic Communism," and from Hitler's starting a world war after Munich, from which they concluded that every gesture of reconciliation was a "second Munich." They were unable to confront reality on its own terms because they had always some parallels in mind that "helped" them to understand those terms. When Johnson, still in his capacity as Kennedy's Vice-President, came home from an inspection tour in South Vietnam and happily reported that Diem was the "Churchill of Asia," one would have thought that the parallelism game would die from sheer absurdity, but this was not the case. Nor can one say that the left-wing war critics thought in different terms. The extreme fringe had the unhappy inclination of denouncing as "fascist" or "nazi" whatever, often quite rightly, displeased them, and of calling every massacre a genocide, which obviously it was not; this could only help to produce a mentality that was quite willing to condone massacre and other war crimes so long as they were not genocide.

The problem-solvers were remarkably free from the sins of the ideologists; they believed in methods but not in "world views," which, incidentally, is the reason they could be trusted "to pull together the Pentagon's documentary record of the American involvement" in a way that would be both "encyclopedic and objective." But though they did not believe in such generally accepted rationales for policies as the domino theory, these rationales, with their different methods of defactualization, provided the atmosphere and the background against which the problem-solvers then went to work; they had, after all, to convince the cold warriors, whose minds then turned out to be singularly well prepared for the abstract games they had to offer. . . .

Defactualization and problem-solving were welcomed because disregard of reality was inherent in the policies and goals themselves. What did they have to know about Indochina as it really was, when it was no more than a "test case" or a domino, or a means to "contain China" or prove that we *are* the mightiest of the superpowers? Or take the case of bombing North Vietnam for the ulterior purpose of building morale in South Vietnam, without much intention of winning a clear-cut victory and ending the war. How could they be interested in anything as real as victory when they kept the war going not for territorial gain or economic advantage, least of all to help a friend or keep a commitment, and not even for the reality, as distinguished from the image, of power?

When this stage of the game was reached, the initial premise that we should never mind the region or the country itself—inherent in the domino theory—changed into "never mind the enemy." And this in the midst of a war! The result was that the enemy, poor, abused, and suffering, grew stronger while "the mightiest country" grew weaker with each passing year. There are historians today who maintain that Truman dropped the bomb on Hiroshima in order to scare the Russians out of Eastern Europe (with the result we know). If this is true, as it might well be, then we may trace back the earliest beginnings of the disregard for the actual consequences of action in favor of some ulterior calculated aim to the fateful war crime that ended the last world war. The Truman Doctrine, at any rate, "depicted a world full of dominoes," as Leslie H. Gelb has pointed out.

At the beginning of this analysis I tried to suggest that the aspects of the Pentagon papers that I have chosen, the aspects of deception, self-deception, image-making, ideo-logizing, and defactualization, are by no means the only features of the papers that deserve to be studied and learned from. There is, for instance, the fact that this massive and systematic effort at self-examination was commissioned by one of the chief actors, that thirty-six men could be found to compile the documents and write their analysis, quite a few of whom "had helped to develop or to carry out the policies they were asked to evaluate," that one of the authors, when it had become apparent that no one in government was willing to use or even to read the results, went to the public and leaked it to the press, and that, finally, the most respectable newspapers in the country dared to bring material that was stamped "top secret" to the widest possible attention. It has rightly been said by Neil Sheehan that Robert McNamara's decision to find out what went wrong, and why, "may turn out to be one of the most important decisions in his seven years at the Pentagon." It certainly restored, at least for a fleeting moment, this country's reputation in the world. What had happened could indeed hardly have happened anywhere else. It is as though all these people, involved in an unjust war and rightly compromised by it, had suddenly remembered what they owed to their forefathers' "decent respect for the opinions of mankind."

What calls for further close and detailed study is the fact, much commented on, that the Pentagon papers revealed little significant news that was not available to the average reader of dailies and weeklies; nor are there any arguments, pro or con, in the "History of U.S. Decision-Making Process on Vietnam Policy" that have not been debated publicly for years in magazines, television shows, and radio broadcasts. (Personal positions and changes in them aside, the different views of the intelligence community on basic issues were the only matter generally unknown.) That the public had access for years to material that the government vainly tried to keep from it testifies to the integrity and to the power of the press even more forcefully than the way the *Times* broke the story. What has often been suggested has now been established: so long as the press is free and not corrupt, it has an enormously important function to fulfill and can rightly be called the fourth branch of government. Whether the First Amendment will suffice to protect this most essential political freedom, the right to unmanipulated factual information without which all freedom of opinion becomes a cruel hoax, is another question.

There is, finally, a lesson to be learned by those who, like myself, believed that this country had embarked on an imperialist policy, had utterly forgotten its old anticolonial sentiments, and was perhaps succeeding in establishing that Pax Americana that President Kennedy had denounced. Whatever the merits of these suspicions, and they could be justified by our policies in Latin America, if undeclared small wars—aggressive brush-fire operations in foreign lands—are among the necessary means to attain imperialist ends, the United States will be less able to employ them successfully than almost any other great power. For while the demoralization of American troops has by now reached unprecedented proportions—according to *Der Spiegel,* during the past year 89,088 deserters, 100,000 conscientious objectors, and tens of thousands of drug addicts—the disintegration process of the army started much earlier and was preceded by similar developments during the Korean War. One has only to talk to a few of the veterans of this war—or to read Daniel Lang's sober and telling report in *The New Yorker* about the development of a fairly typical case—to realize that in order for this country to carry adventurous and aggressive policies to success there would have to be a decisive change in the American people's "national character." The same could of course be concluded from the extraordinarily strong, highly qualified, and well-organized opposition that has from time to time arisen at home. The North Vietnamese who watched these developments carefully over the years had their hopes always set on them, and it seems that they were right in their assessment.

No doubt all this can change. But one thing has become clear in recent months: the halfhearted attempts of the government to circumvent Constitutional guarantees and to intimidate those who have made up their minds not to be intimidated, who would rather go to jail than see their liberties nibbled away, are not enough and probably will not be enough to destroy the Republic. There is reason to hope, with Mr. Lang's veteran—one of the nation's two and a half million—"that the country might regain its better side as a result of the war. 'I know it's nothing to bet on,' he said, 'but neither is anything else I can think of.' "

SAMUEL HUNTINGTON

Selection from "The Democratic Distemper"
1975

The 1960s and very early 1970s are often celebrated as an era of liberation, in which the arena of human freedom was expanded for Americans. Not everyone agreed with this assessment. Among the skeptics was the Harvard political scientist Samuel Huntington (1927–). Too much democracy, at least of certain kinds, can make the process of governing difficult and can, in turn, damage the prospects of democracy itself, Huntington cautioned. Huntington was one of the first, and ultimately one of the most influential, of the "neo-conservative" intellectuals who were suspicious of "the sixties" and their consequences for American culture and politics. This essay on the "distemper" of contemporary democracy, one of Huntington's most widely quoted works, was published in the neo-conservative journal, *Public Interest*.

Huntington developed further his analyses of the political dilemmas of the United States in *American Politics: The Promise of Disharmony* (Cambridge, 1981). A political scientist of widely ranging engagements, Huntington's other works included *The Soldier and the State* (Cambridge, 1957) and *A Clash of Civilizations?* (Cambridge, 1993).

The governability of a democracy depends upon the relation between the authority of its governing institutions and the power of its opposition institutions. In a parliamentary system, the authority of the cabinet depends upon the balance of power between the governing parties and the opposition parties in the legislature. In the United States, the authority of government depends upon the balance of power between a broad coalition of governing institutions and groups, which includes but transcends the executive and other formal institutions of government, and those institutions and groups which are committed to the opposition. During the 1960's and early 1970's the balance of power between government and opposition shifted significantly. The central governing institution in the political system, the Presidency, declined in power; institutions playing apposition roles in the system, most notably the national media and Congress, significantly increased their power.

"Who governs?" is obviously one of the most important questions to ask concerning any political system. Even more important, however, may be the question, "Does anybody govern?" To the extent that the United States was governed by anyone during the decades after World War II, it was governed by the President acting with the support and cooperation of key individuals and groups in the executive office, the federal bureaucracy, Congress, and the more important businesses, banks, law firms, foundations, and media, which constitute the private sector's "Establishment." In the 20th century, whenever the American political system has moved systematically with respect to public policy, the direction and the initiative have come from the White House. When the President is unable to exercise authority, when he is unable to command the cooperation of key decision-makers elsewhere in society and government, no one else has been able to supply comparable purpose and initiative. To the extent that the United States has been governed on a national basis, it has been governed by the President. During the 1960's and early 1970's, however, the authority of the President declined significantly, and the governing coalition which had, in effect, helped the President to run the country from the early 1940's down to the early 1960's began to disintegrate. . . .

The most notable new source of national power in 1970, as compared to 1950, was the national media—meaning the national television networks, the national news magazines, and the major newspapers with national reach, such as the *Washington Post* and the *New York Times*. It is a long-established and familiar political fact that within a city, and even within a state, the power of the local press serves as a major check on the power of the local government. In the early 20th century, the United States developed an effective national government, making and implementing national policies. Only in recent years, however, has there come into existence a national press with the economic independence and communications reach to play a role with respect to the President that a local newspaper plays with respect to a mayor. This marks the emergence of a very significant check on Presidential power. In the two most dramatic domestic policy conflicts of the Nixon Administration—the Pentagon Papers and Watergate—organs of the national media challenged and defeated the national executive. The press, indeed, played a leading role in bringing about what no other single institution, group, or combination of institutions and groups had done previously in American history: Forcing out of office a President who had been elected less than two years before by an overwhelming popular majority. No future President can or will forget that fact.

Source: The Public Interest (Fall 1975), 23–38. Reprinted by permission of National Affairs, Inc.

The late 1960's and early 1970's also saw a reassertion of the power of Congress. In part, this represented simply the latest phase in the institutionalized constitutional conflict between Congress and President; in part, also, of course, it reflected the fact that after 1968, the Presidency and the Congress were controlled by different parties. In addition, however, these years saw the emergence, first in the Senate and then in the House, of a new generation of Congressional activists willing to challenge established authority in their own chambers as well as in the executive branch.

The increased power of the national opposition, centered in the press and in Congress, undoubtedly is related to and perhaps is a significant cause of the critical attitudes which the public has towards federal, as compared to state and local, government. While data for past periods are not readily available, certainly the impression one gets is that over the years the public often has tended to view state and local government as inefficient, corrupt, inactive, and unresponsive. The federal government, on the other hand, has seemed to command much greater confidence and trust, going all the way from early childhood images of the "goodness" of the President to respect for the Federal Bureau of Investigation, Internal Revenue Service, and other federal agencies having an impact on the population as models of efficiency and integrity. It now would appear that there has been a drastic reversal of this confidence. In 1973, a national sample was asked whether it then had more or less confidence in each of the three levels of government than it had had five years previously. Confidence in all three levels of government declined more than it rose, but the proportion of the public which reported a decline in confidence in the federal government (57 per cent) was far higher than that which reported a decline in confidence in state (26 per cent) or local (30 per cent) government. As one would expect, substantial majorities also went on record in favor of increasing the power of state government (59 per cent) and of local government (61 per cent). But only 32 per cent wanted to increase the power of the federal government, while 42 per cent voted to decrease its power.

The balance between government and opposition depends not only on the relative power of different institutions, but also on their roles in the political system. The Presidency has been the principal national governing institution in the United States; its power has declined. The power of the media and of Congress has increased. Can their roles change? At this point the media are deeply committed to an opposition role. The critical question concerns the role of Congress. In the wake of a declining Presidency, can Congress organize itself to furnish the leadership to govern the country? During most of this century, the trends in Congress have been in the opposite direction. In recent years the increase in the power of Congress has outstripped an increase in its ability to govern. If the institutional balance between government and its opposition is to be redressed, the decline in Presidential power has to be reversed, and the ability of Congress to govern has to be increased.

The vigor of democracy in the United States in the 1960's thus contributed to a democratic distemper involving the expansion of governmental activity on the one hand, and the reduction of governmental authority on the other. This democratic distemper, in turn, had further important consequences for the functioning of the political system. The extent of these consequences, as of 1975, was still unclear, and dependent on the duration and the scope of the democratic surge.

The expansion of governmental activity produced budgetary deficits and a major expansion of total governmental debt from $336 billion in 1960 to $557 billion in 1971. These deficits contributed to inflationary tendencies in the economy. But at the same time that the expansion of governmental activity creates problems of financial solvency for government, the decline in governmental authority reduces still further the ability of government to deal effectively with these problems. The implementation of "hard" decisions imposing constraints on any major economic group is difficult in any democracy and particularly difficult in the United States, where the separation of powers provides economic interest groups with a variety of points of access to governmental decision-making. During the Korean War, for instance, governmental efforts at wage and price control failed miserably, as business and farm groups were able to riddle the legislation with loopholes in Congress, and labor was able to use its leverage with the executive branch to eviscerate wage controls. All this occurred despite the fact that there was a war on and the government was not lacking in authority. The decline in governmental authority in general and of the central leadership in particular during the early 1970's opens new opportunities for special interests to bend governmental behavior to their special purposes.

In the United States, as elsewhere in the industrialized world, domestic problems thus become intractible. The public develops expectations which it is impossible for government to meet. The activities—and expenditures—of government expand, and yet the success of government in achieving its goals seems dubious. In a democracy, however, political leaders in power need to score successes if they are going to stay in power. The natural result is to produce a gravitation to foreign policy, where successes—or seeming successes—are much more easily arranged than they are in domestic policy. Trips abroad, summit meetings, declarations and treaties, and rhetorical aggression all produce the appearance of activity and achievement. The weaker a political leader is at home, the more likely he is to be travelling abroad. The dynamics of this search for foreign policy achievements by democratic leaders who lack authority at home gives to dictatorships (whether Communist party states or oil sheikdoms)—which are free from such compulsions—a major advantage in the conduct of international relations.

The expansion of expenditures and the decrease in authority are also likely to encourage economic nationalism in democratic societies. Each country will have an interest in minimizing the export of some goods in order to keep prices down in its own society. At the same time, other interests are likely to demand protection against the import of foreign goods. In the United States, this has meant embargoes—as on the export of soybeans—on the one hand, and tariffs and quotas on the import of textiles, shoes, and comparable manufactured goods, on the other. A strong government will not necessarily follow more liberal and internationalist economic policies, but a weak government is almost certainly incapable of doing so.

Finally, a government which lacks authority and which is committed to substantial domestic programs will have little ability, short of a cataclysmic crisis, to impose on its people the sacrifices which may be necessary to deal with foreign policy problems and defense. In the early 1970's, as we have seen, spending for all significant foreign policy programs was far more unpopular than spending for any major domestic purpose. The United States government has given up the authority to draft its citizens into the armed forces, and is now committed to providing the monetary incentives to attract volunteers with a stationary or declining percentage of the GNP. . . .

Unlike Japanese society and most European societies, American society is characterized by a broad consensus favoring democratic, liberal, and egalitarian values. For much of the time, the commitment to these values is neither passionate nor intense. During periods of rapid social change, however, these democratic and egalitarian values of the American creed are reaffirmed. The intensity of belief during such "creedal passion periods" leads to the challenging of established authority and to major efforts to change governmental structure to accord more fully with those values. In this respect, as has already been remarked, the democratic surge of the 1960's shares many characteristics with the comparable egalitarian and reform movements of the Jacksonian and Progressive eras. Those "surges," like the contemporary one, also occurred during periods of realignment between party and governmental institutions on the one hand, and social forces on the other. The slogans, goals, values, and targets of all these movements are strikingly similar. Consequently, the implication of this analysis is that in due course the democratic surge and the resulting dual distemper in government will be moderated.

Al Smith once remarked, "The only cure for the evils of democracy is more democracy." Our analysis suggests that applying that cure at the present time could well be adding fuel to the fire. Instead, some of the problems of governance in the United States today stem from an "excess of democracy," in much the same sense in which David Donald used the term to refer to those consequences of the Jacksonian Revolution which helped to precipitate the Civil War. What is needed, instead, is a greater degree of moderation in democracy.

In practice, this moderation has two major areas of application. First, democracy is only one way of constituting authority, and it is not necessarily a universally applicable one. In many situations, the claims of expertise, seniority, experience, and special talents may override the claims of democracy as a way of constituting authority. During the surge of the 1960's, however, the democratic principle was extended to many institutions where it can, in the long run, only frustrate the purposes of those institutions. A university where teaching appointments are subject to approval by students may be a more democratic university, but it is not likely to be a better university. In similar fashion, armies in which the commands of officers have been subject to veto by the collective wisdom of their subordinates have almost invariably come to disaster on the battlefield. The arenas where democratic procedures are appropriate are, in short, limited.

Second, the effective operation of a democratic political system usually requires some measure of apathy and non-involvement on the part of some individuals and groups. In the past, every democratic society has had a marginal population, of greater or lesser size, which has not actively participated in politics. In itself, this marginality on the part of some groups is inherently undemocratic, but it also has been one of the factors which has enabled democracy to function effectively. Marginal social groups, as in the case of the blacks, are now becoming full participants in the political system. Yet the danger of "overloading" the political system with demands which extend its functions and undermine its authority still remains. Less marginality on the part of some groups thus needs to be replaced by more self-restraint on the part of all groups.

The Greek philosophers argued that the best practical state—the "mixed regime"—would combine several different principles of government in its constitution. The Constitution of 1787 was drafted with this insight very much in mind. Over the years, however, the American political system has emerged as a distinctive case of extraordinarily democratic institutions joined to an exclusively democratic value system. Democracy, as a result, can very easily become a threat to itself in the United States. Political authority is never strong here, and it is peculiarly weak during a period of intense commitment to democratic and egalitarian ideals. In the United States, the strength of the democratic ideal poses a problem for the governability of democracy in a way which is not the case elsewhere.

The vulnerability of democratic government in the United States thus comes not primarily from external threats, though such threats are real, nor from internal subversion from the left or the right, although both possibilities could exist, but rather from the internal dynamics of democracy itself in a highly educated, mobilized, and participant society. "Democracy never lasts long," John Adams observed: "It soon wastes, exhausts, and murders itself. There never was a democracy yet that did not commit suicide." That suicide is more likely to be the product of overindulgence than of any other cause. A value which is normally good in itself is not necessarily optimized when it is maximized. We have come to recognize that there are potentially desirable limits to economic growth. There are also potentially desirable limits to the extension of political democracy. Democracy could have a longer life if it has a more balanced existence.

RICHARD RORTY

"Science as Solidarity"
1986

After a distinguished career as an analytic philosopher of the sort often accused of speaking only to a coterie of professional colleagues, Richard Rorty (1931–) became, in the 1980s, a cultural critic and public intellectual. In *Philosophy and the Mirror of Nature* (Princeton, 1979) Rorty complained that philosophers' traditional epistemological preoccupations had proved to be dead ends. It was time to admit that the long-sought "foundation" for knowledge simply did not exist. Philosophers should acknowledge that all discourses, including those of the natural sciences, were culture bound, and they should use their intellect and learning to help people understand one another and to build sustaining communities. In later books and articles, including "Science as Solidarity" (1986), which follows, Rorty developed both his ideal of "social solidarity" and his "antifoundational" perspective on scientific knowledge. In this essay, Rorty drew some conclusions from the work of Thomas Kuhn that were more radical than Kuhn and most of Kuhn's followers were willing to accept. Rorty's most popular and accessible work, *Contingency, Irony and Solidarity* (New York, 1988), also addressed literary and political issues. In his work of the 1990s, Rorty engaged political issues yet more directly, as in his "Human Rights, Rationality, and Sentimentality," *Yale Review* (Autumn 1993), 1–20.

Although Rorty has become the most widely appreciated American philosopher since Dewey, his ideas are often, and even vociferously, contested, especially by the philosophers whose work Rorty believes is a waste of time. An anthology of writings of the 1980s is Alan Malachowski, ed., *Reading Rorty* (Cambridge, 1990). In the 1990s, Rorty's work has stimulated a steady stream of new books and articles, including David Hall, *Richard Rorty: Prophet and Poet of the New Pragmatism* (New York, 1994), and Norman Geras, *Solidarity in the Conversation of Humankind: The Ungroundable Liberalism of Richard Rorty* (New York, 1995). Rorty is the son of James Rorty, a political journalist of the 1930s and 1940s, and is the grandson of the chief leader of the American "social gospel," Walter Rauschenbusch.

In our culture, the notions of "science," "rationality," "objectivity," and "truth" are bound up with one another. Science is thought of as offering "hard," "objective" truth: truth as correspondence to reality, the only sort of truth worthy of the name. Humanists like philosophers, theologians, historians, and literary critics have to worry about whether they are being "scientific"—whether they are entitled to think of their conclusions, no matter how carefully argued, as worthy of the term "true." We tend to identify seeking "objective truth" with "using reason," and so we think of the natural sciences as paradigms of rationality. We also think of rationality as a matter of following procedures laid down in advance, of being "methodical." So we tend to use "methodical," "rational," "scientific," and "objective" as synonyms.

Worries about "cognitive status" and "objectivity" are characteristic of a secularized culture in which the scientist replaces the priest. The scientist is now seen as the person who keeps humanity in touch with something beyond itself. As the universe was depersonalized, beauty (and, in time, even moral goodness) came to be thought of as "subjective." So truth is now thought of as the only point at which human beings are responsible to something nonhuman. A commitment to "rationality" and to "method" is thought to be a recognition of this responsibility. The scientist becomes a moral exemplar, one who selflessly exposes himself again and again to the hardness of fact.

One result of this way of thinking is that any academic discipline which wants a place at the trough, but is unable to offer the predictions and the technology provided by the natural sciences, must either pretend to imitate science or find some way of obtaining "cognitive status" without the necessity of discovering facts. Practitioners of these disciplines must either affiliate themselves with this quasi-priestly order by using terms like "behavioral sciences" or else find something other than "fact" to be concerned with. People in the humanities typically choose the latter strategy. They either describe themselves as concerned with "value" as opposed to facts, or as developing and inculcating habits of "critical reflection."

Neither sort of rhetoric is very satisfactory. No matter how much humanists talk about "objective values," the phrase always sounds vaguely confused. It gives with one hand what it takes back with the other. The distinction between the objective and the subjective was designed to parallel that between fact and value, so an objective value sounds as vaguely mythological as a winged horse. Talk about the humanists' special skill at critical reflection fares no better. Nobody really believes that philosophers or literary critics are better at critical thinking, or at taking big broad views of things, than theoretical physicists or microbiologists. So society tends to ignore both these kinds of rhetoric. It treats humanities as on a par with the arts, and thinks of both as providing pleasure rather than truth. Both are, to be sure, thought of as providing "high" rather than "low" pleasures. But an elevated and spiritual sort of pleasure is still a long way from the grasp of a truth.

These distinctions between hard facts and soft values, truth and pleasure, and objectivity and subjectivity are awkward and clumsy instruments. They are not suited to dividing up culture; they create more difficulties than they resolve. It would be best to find another vocabulary, to start afresh. But in order to do so, we first have to find

Source: John Nelson, Allan Megill, and Donald McCloskey, eds., *The Rhetoric of the Human Sciences* (Madison, Wisc.: University of Wisconsin Press, 1986), 38–52. Reprinted by permission of the University of Wisconsin Press.

a new way of describing the natural sciences. It is not a question of debunking or downgrading the natural scientist, but simply of ceasing to see him as a priest. We need to stop thinking of science as the place where the human mind confronts the world, and of the scientist as exhibiting proper humility in the face of superhuman forces. We need a way of explaining why scientists are, and deserve to be, moral exemplars which does not depend on a distinction between objective fact and something softer, squishier, and more dubious.

To get such a way of thinking, we can start by distinguishing two senses of the term "rationality." In one sense, the one I have already discussed, to be rational is to be methodical: that is, to have criteria for success laid down in advance. We think of poets and painters as using some faculty other than "reason" in their work because, by their own confession, they are not sure of what they want to do before they have done it. They make up new standards of achievement as they go along. By contrast, we think of judges as knowing in advance what criteria a brief will have to satisfy in order to invoke a favorable decision, and of business people as setting well-defined goals and being judged by their success in achieving them. Law and business are good examples of rationality, but the scientist, knowing in advance what would count as disconfirming his hypothesis and prepared to abandon that hypothesis as a result of the unfavorable outcome of a single experiment, seems a truly heroic example. Further, we seem to have a clear criterion for the success of a scientific theory—namely, its ability to predict, and thereby to enable us to control some portion of the world. If to be rational means to be able to lay down criteria in advance, then it is plausible to take natural science as the paradigm of rationality.

The trouble is that in this sense of "rational" the humanities are never going to qualify as rational activities. If the humanities are concerned with ends rather than means, then there is no way to evaluate their success in terms of antecedently specified criteria. If we already knew what criteria we wanted to satisfy, we would not worry about whether we were pursuing the right ends. If we thought we knew the goals of culture and society in advance, we would have no use for the humanities—as totalitarian societies in fact do not. It is characteristic of democratic and pluralistic societies to continually redefine their goals. But if to be rational means to satisfy criteria, then this process of redefinition is bound to be nonrational. So if the humanities are to be reviewed as rational activities, rationality will have to be thought of as something other than the satisfaction of criteria which are statable in advance.

Another meaning for "rational" is, in fact, available. In this sense, the word means something like "sane" or "reasonable" rather than "methodical." It names a set of moral virtues: tolerance, respect for the opinions of those around one, willingness to listen, reliance on persuasion rather than force. These are the virtues which members of a civilized society must possess if the society is to endure. In this sense of "rational," the word means something more like "civilized" than like "methodical." When so construed, the distinction between the rational and the irrational has nothing in particular to do with the difference between the arts and the sciences. On this construction, to be rational is simply to discuss any topic—religious, literary, or scientific—in a way which eschews dogmatism, defensiveness, and righteous indignation.

There is no problem about whether, in this latter, weaker, sense, the humanities are "rational disciplines." Usually humanists display the moral virtues in question. Sometimes they don't, but then sometimes scientists don't either. Yet these moral virtues are felt to be not enough. Both humanists and the public hanker after rationality in the first, stronger sense of the term: a sense which is associated with objective truth, correspondence to reality, and method, and criteria.

We should not try to satisfy this hankering, but rather try to eradicate it. No matter what one's opinion of the secularization of culture, it was a mistake to try to make the natural scientist into a new sort of priest, a link between the human and the nonhuman. So was the idea that some sorts of truths are "objective" whereas others are merely "subjective" or "relative"—the attempt to divide up the set of true sentences into "genuine knowledge" and "mere opinion," or into the "factual" and "judgmental." So was the idea that the scientist has a special method which, if only the humanists would apply it to ultimate values, would give us the same kind of self-confidence about the moral ends as we now have about technological means. I think that we should content ourselves with the second, "weaker" conception of rationality, and avoid the first, "stronger" conception. We should avoid the idea that there is some special virtue in knowing in advance what criteria you are going to satisfy, in having standards by which to measure progress.

One can make these issues somewhat more concrete by taking up the current controversy among philosophers about the "rationality of science." For some twenty years, ever since the publication of Thomas Kuhn's book *The Structure of Scientific Revolutions*, philosophers have been debating whether science is rational. Attacks on Kuhn for being an "irrationalist" are now as frequent and as urgent as were, in the thirties and forties, attacks on the logical positivists for saying that moral judgments were "meaningless." We are constantly being warned of the danger of "relativism," which will beset us if we give up our attachment to objectivity, and to the idea of rationality as obedience to criteria.

Whereas Kuhn's enemies routinely accuse him of reducing science to "mob psychology," and pride themselves on having (by a new theory of meaning, or reference, or verisimilitude) vindicated the "rationality of science," his pragmatist friends (such as myself) routinely congratulate him on having softened the distinction between science and non-science. It is fairly easy for Kuhn to show that the enemies are attacking a straw man. But it is harder for him to save himself from his friends. For he has said that "there is no theory-independent way to reconstruct phrases like 'really there.'" He has asked whether it really helps "to imagine that there is some one full, objective, true account of nature and that the proper measure of scientific achievement is the extent to which it brings us closer to that ultimate goal." We pragmatists quote these passages incessantly in the course of our effort to enlist Kuhn in our campaign to drop the objective-subjective distinction altogether.

What I am calling "pragmatism" might also be called "left-wing Kuhnianism." It has been also rather endearingly called (by one of its critics, Clark Glymour) the "new fuzziness," because it is an attempt to blur just those distinctions between the objective and the subjective and between fact and value which the criterial conception of rationality has developed. We fuzzies would like to substitute the idea of "unforced agreement" for that of "objectivity." We should like to put all of culture on an epistemological level—or, to put it another way, we would like to get rid of the idea of "epistemological level" or "cognitive status." We would like to disabuse social scientists and humanists of the idea that there is something called "scientific status" which is a desirable goal. In our view, "truth" is a univocal term. It applies equally to the judgments of lawyers, anthropologists, physicists, philologists, and literary critics. There is no point in assigning degrees of "objectivity" or "hardness" to such disciplines. For the presence of unforced agreement in all of them gives us everything in the way of "objective truth" which one could possibly want: namely, intersubjective agreement.

As soon as one says that objectivity is intersubjectivity, one is likely to be accused of being a relativist. That is the epithet traditionally applied to pragmatists. But this epithet is ambiguous. It can name any of three different views. The first is the silly and self-refuting view that every belief is as good as every other. The second is the wrong-headed view that "true" is an equivocal term, having as many meanings as there are contexts of justification. The third is the ethnocentric view that there is nothing to be said about either truth or rationality apart from descriptions of the familiar procedures of justification which a given society—*ours*—uses in one or another area of inquiry. The pragmatist does hold this third, ethnocentric, view. But he does not hold the first or the second.

But "relativism" is not an appropriate term to describe this sort of ethnocentrism. For we pragmatists are not holding a positive theory which says that something is relative to something else. Instead, we are making the purely *negative* point that we would be better off without the traditional distinctions between knowledge and opinion, construed as the distinction between truth as correspondence to reality and truth as a commendatory term for well-justified belief. Our opponents call this negative claim "relativistic" because they cannot imagine that anybody would seriously deny that truth has an intrinsic nature. So when we say that there is nothing to be said about truth save that each of us will commend as true those beliefs which he or she finds good to believe, the realist is inclined to interpret this as one more positive theory about the nature of truth: a theory according to which truth is simply the contemporary opinion of a chosen individual or group. Such a theory would, of course, be self-refuting. But we pragmatists do not have a theory of truth, much less a relativistic one. As partisans of solidarity, our account of the value of cooperative human inquiry has only an ethical base, not an epistemological or metaphysical one.

To say that we must be ethnocentric may sound suspicious, but this will only happen if we identify ethnocentrism with pig-headed refusal to talk to representatives of other communities. In my sense of ethnocentrism, to be ethnocentric is simply to work by our own lights. The defense of ethnocentrism is simply that there are no other lights to work by. Beliefs suggested by another individual or another culture must be tested by trying to weave them together with beliefs which we already have. We *can* so test them, because everything which we can identify as a human being or as a culture will be something which shares an enormous number of beliefs with us. (If it did not, we would simply not be able to recognize that it was speaking a language, and thus that it had any beliefs at all.)

This way of thinking runs counter to the attempt, familiar since the eighteenth century, to think of political liberalism as based on a conception of the nature of man. To most thinkers of the Enlightenment, it seemed clear that the access to Nature which physical science had provided should now be followed by the establishment of social, political, and economic institutions which were "in accordance with Nature." Ever since, liberal social thought has centered on social reform as made possible by objective knowledge of what human beings are like—not knowledge of what Greeks or Frenchmen or Chinese are like, but of humanity as such. This tradition dreams of a universal human community which will exhibit a nonparochial solidarity because it is the expression of an ahistorical human nature.

Philosophers who belong to this tradition, who wish to ground solidarity in objectivity, have to construe truth as correspondence to reality. So they must construct an epistemology which had room for a kind of justification which is not merely social but natural, springing from human nature itself, and made possible by a link between that part of nature and the rest of nature. By contrast, we pragmatists, who wish to reduce objectivity to solidarity, do not require either a metaphysics or an epistemology. We do not need an account of a relation between beliefs and objects called "correspondence," nor an account of human cognitive abilities which ensures that our species is capable of entering into that relation. We see the gap between truth and justification not as something to be bridged by isolating a natural and transcultural sort of rationality which can be used to criticize certain cultures and praise others, but simply as the gap between the actual good and the possible better. From a pragmatist point of view, to say that what is rational for us now to believe may not be *true* is simply to say that somebody may come up with a better idea.

On this pragmatist view of rationality as civility, inquiry is a matter of continually reweaving a web of beliefs rather than the application of criteria to cases. Criteria change in just the way other beliefs change, and there is no touchstone which can preserve any criterion from possible revision. That is why the pragmatist is not frightened by the specter of "cultural relativism." Our interchange with other communities and cultures is not to be thought of as a clash between irreconcilable systems of thought, deductively inferred from incompatible first premises. Alternative cultures should not be thought of on the model of alternative geometries—as irreconcilable because they have axiomatic structures and contradictory axioms. Such geometries are *designed* to be irreconcilable. Individual and cultural webs of belief are not so designed, and do not have axiomatic structures.

Cultures can, indeed, protect themselves by institutionalizing knowledge-claims and making people suffer who do not hold certain beliefs. But such institutional backups take the form of bureaucrats and policemen, not of "rules of language" or "criteria of rationality." The criterial conception of rationality has suggested that every distinct culture comes equipped with certain unchallengeable axioms, "necessary truths," and that these form barriers to communication between cultures. So it has seemed as if there could be no conversation between cultures but only subjugation by force. On the pragmatic conception of rationality, there are no such barriers. The distinction between different cultures differs only in degree from the distinction between theories held by members of a single culture. The Tasmanian aborigines and the British colonies, for example, had trouble in communicating, but this trouble was different only in extent from the difficulties in communication experienced by Gladstone and Disraeli. The trouble in all such cases is just the difficulty of explaining why other people disagree with us, and of reweaving our beliefs so as to fit the fact of disagreement together with the other beliefs we hold. The same pragmatist (and, more specifically, Quinean) arguments which dispose of the positivist's distinction between analytic and synthetic truths dispose of the anthropologists' distinction between the intercultural and the intracultural.

Another reason for describing us as "relativistic" is that we pragmatists drop the idea that inquiry is destined to converge to a single point—that Truth is "out there" waiting for human beings to arrive at it. This idea seems to us an unfortunate attempt to carry a religious conception over into a culture. All that is worth preserving of the claim that rational inquiry will converge to a single point is the claim that we must be able to explain why past false views were held in the past, and thus explain how we go about reeducating our benighted ancestors. To say that we think we are heading in the right direction is just to say, with Kuhn, that we can, by hindsight, tell the story of the past as a story of progress.

But the fact that we can trace such a direction and tell such a story does not mean that we have gotten closer to a goal which is out there waiting for us. We cannot, I think, imagine a moment at which the human race could settle back and say, "Well, now that we've finally arrived at the Truth we can relax." Paul Feyerabend is right in suggesting that we should discard the metaphor of inquiry, and human activity generally, as converging rather than proliferating, becoming more unified rather than more diverse. On the contrary, we should relish the thought that the sciences as well as the arts will *always* provide a spectacle of fierce competition between alternative theories, movements, and schools. The end of human activity is not rest, but rather richer and better human activity. We should think of human progress as making it possible for human beings to do more interesting things and be more interesting people, not as heading toward a place which has somehow been prepared for us in advance. To drop the criterial conception of rationality in favor of the pragmatist conception would be to give up the idea of Truth as something to which we were responsible. Instead we should think of "true" as a word which applies to those beliefs upon which we are able to agree, as roughly synonymous with "justified." To say that beliefs can be agreed upon without being true is, once again, merely to say that somebody might come up with a better idea.

Another way of characterizing this line of thought is to say that pragmatists would like to drop the idea that human beings are responsible to a nonhuman power. We hope for a culture in which questions about the "objectivity of value" or the "rationality of science" would seem equally unintelligible. Pragmatists would like to replace the desire for objectivity—the desire to be in touch with a reality which is more than some community with which we identify ourselves—with the desire for solidarity with that community. They think that the habits of relying on persuasion rather than force, of respect for the opinions of colleagues, of curiosity and eagerness for new data and ideas, are the *only* virtues which scientists have. They do not think that there is an intellectual virtue called "rationality" over and above these moral virtues.

On this view there is no reason to praise scientists for being more "objective" or "logical" or "methodical" or "devoted to truth" than other people. But there is plenty of reason to praise the institutions they have developed and within which they work, and to use these as models for the rest of culture. For these institutions give concreteness and detail to the idea of "unforced agreement." Reference to such institutions fleshes out the idea of "a free and open encounter"—the sort of encounter in which truth cannot fail to win. On this view, to say that truth will win in such an encounter is not to make a metaphysical claim about the connection between human reason and the nature of things. It is merely to say that the best way to find out what to believe is to listen to as many suggestions and arguments as you can.

My rejection of traditional notions of rationality can be summed up by saying that the only sense in which science is exemplary is that it is a model of human solidarity. We should think of the institutions and practices which make up various scientific communities as providing suggestions about the way in which the rest of culture might organize itself. When we say that our legislatures are "unrepresentative" or "dominated by special interests," or that the art world is dominated by "fashion," we are contrasting these areas of culture with areas which seem to be in better order. The natural sciences strike us as being such areas. But, on this view, we shall not explain this better order by thinking of the scientists as having a "method" which the rest of us would do well to imitate, nor as benefiting from the desirable hardness of their subjects compared with the undesirable softness of other subjects. If we say that sociology or literary criticism "is not a science," we shall mean merely that the amount of agreement among sociologists or literary critics on what counts as significant work, work which needs following up, is less than among, say, microbiologists.

Pragmatists will not attempt to explain this latter phenomenon by saying that societies or literary texts are squishier than molecules, or that the human sciences cannot be as "value-free" as the natural sciences, or that the sociologists and critics have not yet found their paradigms. Nor will they assume that "a science" is necessarily something which we want sociology to be. One consequence of their view is the suggestion that perhaps "the human sciences" *should* look quite different from the natural sciences. This suggestion is not based on epistemological or metaphysical considerations which show that inquiry into societies must be different from inquiry into things. Instead, it is based on the observation that natural scientists are interested primarily in predicting and controlling the behavior of things, and that prediction and control may not be what we want from our sociologists and our literary critics.

Despite the encouragement he has given it, however, Kuhn draws back from this pragmatist position. He does so when he asks for an explanation of "why science works." The request for such an explanation binds him together with his opponents and separates him from his left-wing friends. Anti-Kuhnians tend to unite in support of the claim that "merely psychological or sociological reasons" will not explain why natural science is so good at predicting. Kuhn joins them when he says that he shares "Hume's itch"—the desire for "an explanation of the viability of the whole language game that involves 'induction' and underpins the form of life we live."

Pragmatists think that one will suffer from Hume's itch only if one has been scratching oneself with what has sometimes been called "Hume's fork"—the distinction between "relations of ideas" and "matters of fact." This distinction survives in contemporary philosophy as the distinction between "questions of language" and "questions of fact." We pragmatists think that philosophers of language such as Wittgenstein, Quine, Goodman, Davidson, and others have shown us how to get along without these distinctions. Once one has lived without them for a while, one learns to live without those between knowledge and opinion, or between subjective and objective, as well. The purposes served by the latter distinctions come to be served by the unproblematic sociological distinction between areas in which unforced agreement is relatively infrequent and areas in which it is relatively frequent. So we do not itch for an explanation of the success of recent Western science any more than for the success of recent Western politics. That is why we fuzzies applaud Kuhn when he says that "one does not know what a person who denies the rationality of learning from experience is trying to say," but are aghast when he goes on to ask *why* "we have no rational alternatives to learning from experience."

On the pragmatist view, the contrast between "relations of ideas" and "matters of fact" is a special case of the bad seventeenth-century contrasts between being "in us" and being "out there," between subject and object, between our beliefs and what those beliefs (moral, scientific, theological, etc.) are trying to get right. Pragmatists avoid this latter contrast by instead contrasting our beliefs with proposed alternative beliefs. They recommend that we worry only about the choice between two hypotheses, rather than about whether there is something which "makes" either true. To take this stance would rid us of questions about the objectivity of value, the rationality of science, and the causes of the viability of our language games. All such theoretical questions would be replaced with practical questions about whether we ought to keep our present values, theories, and practices or try to replace them with others. Given such a replacement, there would be nothing to be responsible to except ourselves.

This may sound like solipsistic fantasy, but the pragmatist regards it as an alternative account of the nature of intellectual and moral responsibility. He is suggesting that instead of invoking anything like the idea-fact, or language-fact, or mind-world, or subject-object distinctions to explicate our intuition that there is something out there to be responsible to, we just drop that intuition. We should drop it in favor of the thought that we might be better than we presently are—in the sense of being better scientific theorists, or citizens, or friends. The backup for this intuition would be the actual or imagined existence of other human beings who were already better (utopian fantasies, or actual experience, of superior individuals or societies). On this account, to be responsible is a matter of what Peirce called "contrite fallibilism" rather than of respect for something beyond. The desire for "objectivity" boils down to a desire to acquire beliefs which will eventually receive unforced agreement in the course of a free and open encounter with people holding other beliefs.

Pragmatists interpret the goal of inquiry (in any sphere of culture) as the attainment of an appropriate mixture of unforced agreement with tolerant disagreement (where what counts as appropriate is determined, within that sphere, by trial and error). Such a reinterpretation of our sense of responsibility would, if carried through, gradually make unintelligible the subject-object model of inquiry, the child-parent model of moral obligation, and the correspondence theory of truth. A world in which those models, and that theory, no longer had any intuitive appeal would be a pragmatist's paradise.

When Dewey urged that we try to create such a paradise, he was said to be irresponsible. For, it was said, he left us bereft of weapons to use against our enemies; he gave us nothing with which to "answer the Nazis." When we new fuzzies try to revive Dewey's repudiation of criteriology, we are said to be "relativistic." We must, people say, believe that every coherent view is as good as every other, since we have no "outside" touchstone for choice among such views. We are said to leave the general public defenseless against the witch doctor, the defender of creationism, or anyone else who is clever and patient enough to deduce a consistent and wide-ranging set of theorems from his "alternative first principles."

Nobody is convinced when we fuzzies say that we can be just as morally indignant as the next philosopher. We are suspected of being contritely fallibilist when righteous fury is called for. Even when we actually display appropriate emotions we get nowhere, for we are told that we have no *right* to these emotions. When we suggest that one of the few things we know (or need to know) about truth is that it is what wins in a free and open encounter, we are told that we have defined "true" as "satisfies the standards of our community." But we pragmatists do not hold this relativist view. We do not infer from "there is no way to step outside communities to a neutral standpoint" that "there is no rational way to justify liberal communities over totalitarian communities." For that inference involves just the notion of "rationality" as a set of ahistorical principles which pragmatists abjure. What we in fact infer is that there is no way to beat totalitarians in argument by appealing to shared common premises, and no point in pretending that a common human nature makes the totalitarians unconsciously hold such premises.

The claim that we fuzzies have no right to be furious at moral evil, no right to commend our views as true unless we simultaneously refute ourselves by claiming that there are objects out there which *make* those views true, begs all the theoretical questions. But it gets to the practical and moral heart of the matter. This is the question of whether notions like "unforced agreement" and "free and open encounter"—descriptions of social situations—can take the place in our moral lives of notions like "the world," "the will of God," "the moral law," "what our beliefs are trying to represent accurately," and "what makes our beliefs true." All the philosophical presuppositions which make Hume's fork seem inevitable are ways of suggesting that human communities must justify their existence by striving to attain a nonhuman goal. To suggest that we can forget about Hume's fork, forget about being responsible to what is "out there," is to suggest that human communities can only justify their existence by comparisons with other actual and possible human communities.

I can make this contrast a bit more concrete by asking whether free and open encounters, and the kind of community which permits and encourages such encounters, are for the sake of truth and goodness, or whether "the quest for truth and goodness" is simply the quest for that kind of community. Is the sort of community which is exemplified by groups of scientific inquirers and by democratic political institutions a means to an end, or is the formation of such communities the only goal we need? Dewey thought that it was the only goal we needed, and I think he was right. But whether he was or not, this question is the one to which the debates about Kuhn's "irrationalism" and the new fuzzies' "relativism" will eventually boil down.

Dewey was accused of blowing up the optimism and flexibility of a parochial and jejune way of life (the American) into a philosophical system. So he did, but his reply was that *any* philosophical system is going to be an attempt to express the ideals of *some* community's way of life. He was quite ready to admit that the virtue of his philosophy was, indeed, nothing more than the virtue of the way of life which it commended. On his view, philosophy does not justify affiliation with a community in the light of something ahistorical called "reason" or "transcultural principles." It simply expatiates on the special advantages of that community over other communities. Dewey's best argument for doing philosophy this way is also the best argument we partisans of solidarity have against partisans of objectivity: it is Nietzsche's argument that the traditional Western metaphysico-epistemological way of firming up our habits is not working anymore.

What would it be like to be less fuzzy and parochial than this? I suggest that it would be to become less genial, tolerant, open-minded, and fallibilist than we are now. In the nontrivial, pejorative, sense of "ethnocentric," the sense in which we congratulate ourselves on being less ethnocentric now than our ancestors were three hundred years ago, the way to avoid ethnocentrism is precisely to abandon the sort of thing we fuzzies are blamed for abandoning. It is to have only the most tenuous and cursory formulations of criteria for changing our beliefs, only the loosest and most flexible standards. Suppose that for the last three hundred years we had been using an explicit algorithm for determining how just a society was, and how good a physical theory was. Would we have developed either parliamentary democracy or relativity physics? Suppose that we had the sort of "weapons" against the fascists of which Dewey was said to deprive us—firm, unrevisable, moral principles which were not merely "ours" but "universal" and "objective." How could we avoid having these weapons turn in our hands and bash all the genial tolerance out of our own heads?

Imagine, to use another example, that a few years from now you open your copy of the *New York Times* and read that the philosophers, in convention assembled, have unanimously agreed that values are objective, science rational, truth a matter of correspondence to reality, and so on. Recent breakthroughs in semantics and meta-ethics, the report goes on, have caused the last remaining noncognitivists in ethics to recant. Similar breakthroughs in philosophy of science have led Kuhn formally to abjure his claim that there is no theory-independent way to reconstruct statements about what is "really there." All the new fuzzies have repudiated all their former views. By way of making amends for the intellectual confusion which the philosophical profession has recently caused, the philosophers have adopted a short, crisp, set of standards of rationality and morality. Next year the convention is expected to adopt the report of the committee charged with formulating a standard of aesthetic taste.

Surely the public reaction to this would not be "Saved!" but rather "Who on earth do these philosophers think they *are?*" It is one of the best things about the form of intellectual life we Western liberals lead that this *would* be our reaction. No matter how much we moan about the disorder and confusion of the current philosophical scene, about the treason of the clerks, we do not really want things any other way. What prevents us from relaxing and enjoying the new fuzziness is perhaps no more than cultural lag, the fact that the rhetoric of the Enlightenment praised the emerging natural sciences in a vocabulary which was left over from a less liberal and tolerant era. This rhetoric enshrined all the old philosophical oppositions between mind and world, appearance and reality, subject and object, truth and pleasure. Dewey thought that it was the continued prevalence of such oppositions which prevented us from seeing that modern science was a new and promising invention, a way of life which had not existed before and which ought to be encouraged and imitated, something which required a new rhetoric rather than justification by an old one.

Suppose that Dewey was right about this, and that eventually we learn to find the fuzziness which results from breaking down such oppositions spiritually comforting rather than morally offensive. What would the rhetoric of the culture, and in particular of the humanities, sound like? Presumably it would be more Kuhnian, in the sense that it would mention particular concrete achievements—paradigms—more, and "method" less. There would be less talk about rigor and more about originality. The image of the great scientist would not be of somebody who got it right but of somebody who made it new. The new rhetoric would draw more on the vocabulary of Romantic poetry and socialist politics, and less on that of Greek metaphysics, religious morality, or Enlightenment scientism. A scientist would rely on a sense of solidarity with the rest of her profession, rather than a picture of herself as battling through the veils of illusion, guided by the light of reason.

If all this happened, the term "science," and thus the oppositions between the humanities, the arts, and the sciences, might gradually fade away. Once "science" was deprived of an honorific sense, we might not need it for taxonomy. We might feel no more need for a term which groups together paleontology, physics, anthropology, and psychology than we do for one which groups together engineering, law, social work, and medicine. The people now called "scientists" would no longer think of themselves as a member of a quasi-priestly order, nor would the public think of themselves as in the care of such an order.

In this situation, "the humanities" would no longer think of themselves as such, nor would they share a common rhetoric. Each of the disciplines which now fall under that rubric would worry as little about its method or cognitive status as do mathematics, civil engineering, and sculpture. It would worry as little about its philosophical foundations. For terms which denoted disciplines would not be thought to divide "subject-matters," chunks of the world which had "interfaces" with each other. Rather, they would be thought to denote communities whose boundaries were as fluid as the interests of their members. In this heyday of the fuzzy, there would be as little reason to be self-conscious about the nature and status of one's discipline as, in the ideal democratic community, about the nature and status of one's race or sex. For one's ultimate loyalty would be to the larger community which permitted and encouraged this kind of freedom and insouciance. This community would serve no higher end than its own preservation and self-improvement, the preservation and enhancement of civilization. It would identify rationality with that effort, rather than with the desire for objectivity. So it would feel no need for a foundation more solid than reciprocal loyalty.

EVELYN FOX KELLER

"Gender and Science: 1990"
1990

The traditional presumption that gender has little or nothing to do with scientific knowledge was challenged by a number of feminist theorists in the late 1970s and 1980s. None of these theorists won more swift and widespread respect than did Evelyn Fox Keller (1936–), who had been a theoretical physicist and then a mathematical biologist before turning to the history and philosophy of science. Keller's *Reflections on Gender and Science* (New Haven, 1985; 2nd. ed., 1995) collected the essays in which she first helped convince many historians, sociologists, and philosophers of science that gender was a matter deserving their attention. Keller is also the author of *A Feeling for the Organism: The Life and Work of Barbara McClintock* (New York, 1983), on which she draws in "Gender and Science: 1990," the essay reprinted here. In this piece, Keller reviews the issues in this rapidly developing discourse from the perspective of 1990 and sharpens ideas developed in her earlier work.

For a discussion of Keller's ideas in relation to those of Jurgen Habermas, Michel Foucault, and other theorists of the politics and ideology of science, see Helen Longino, *Science as Social Knowledge: Values and Objectivity in Scientific Inquiry* (Princeton, 1990), 187–214. Longino's book is in itself an ambitious effort to develop a philosophy of science responsive to feminist insights. Another important treatise on the same issues is Hilary Rose, *Love, Power, and Knowledge: Towards a Feminist Transformation of the Sciences* (Bloomington, 1994). Among the most influential of the many historical studies of science and gender are Donna Haraway, *Primate Visions: Gender, Race, and Nature in the World of Modern Science* (New York, 1989); and two books by Londa Shiebinger, *The Mind Has No Sex? Women in the Origins of Modern Science* (Cambridge, 1989), and *Nature's Body: Gender in the Making of Modern Science* (Boston, 1993).

For Keller's own work of the 1990s, see her *Secrets of Life, Secrets of Death: Essays on Language, Gender, and Science* (New York, 1992).

Schemes for classifying human beings are necessarily multiple and highly variable. Different cultures identify and privilege different criteria in sorting people of their own and other cultures into groups: They may stress size, age, color, occupation, wealth, sanctity, wisdom, or a host of other demarcators. All cultures, however, sort at least many of the human beings that inhabit that culture by sex. What are taken to be the principal indicators of sexual difference as well as the particular importance attributed to this difference undoubtedly vary, but, for obvious reasons, people everywhere engage in the basic act of distinguishing people they call male from those they call female. And for the most part, they even agree about who gets called what. Give or take a few marginal cases, these basic acts of categorization do exhibit, at least when applied to adult human beings of reproductive age, conspicuous cross-cultural consensus: different cultures will sort any given collection of such people into the same two groups. For this reason, we tend to say that there is at least a minimal sense of the term *sex* that denotes categories given to us by nature. One might even say that the universal importance of the reproductive consequences of sexual difference gives rise to as universal a preoccupation with the meaning of this difference.

But for all the cross-cultural consensus we may find around such a minimalist classification, we find equally remarkable cultural variability in what people have made and continue to make of this demarcation; in the significance which they attribute to it; in the properties it connotes; in the role it plays in ordering the human world beyond the immediate spheres of biological reproduction; even in the role it plays in ordering the nonhuman world. It was to underscore this cultural variability that American feminists of the 1970s introduced the distinction between sex and gender, claiming the term *gender* to denote the meaning of "masculinity" and "femininity" a given culture attaches to the categories of male and female.

The initial intent behind this distinction was to highlight the importance of non-biological (i.e., social and cultural) factors shaping the development of adult men and women, to emphasize the truth of Simone de Beauvoir's famous dictum, "One is not born, but rather becomes, a woman." Its function was to facilitate a shift in attention away from the time-honored and perhaps even ubiquitous question of the meaning of sexual difference (i.e., the meanings of masculine and feminine), to the question of how such meanings are constructed. In Donna Haraway's words, "Gender is a concept developed to contest the naturalization of sexual difference."

Very quickly, however, feminists came to see, and, as quickly began to exploit, the considerably larger range of analytic functions that this multipotent category is able to serve. From an original focus on gender as a cultural norm guiding the psychosocial development of individual men and women, the attention of feminists soon turned to gender as a cultural structure organizing social (and sexual) relations between men and women, and finally, to gender as the basis of a sexual division of cognitive and emotional labor that removes women, their work, and the values associated with that work from culturally normative delineations of categories intended as "human": e.g., objectivity, morality, citizenship, power, often even, "human nature" itself. From this perspective, gender and gender norms come to be seen as silent organizers of the mental and discursive maps of the social and natural worlds we simultaneously inhabit and construct—*even of those worlds that women never enter.*

Source: *Great Ideas Today 1990* (Chicago: Encyclopedia Britannica, 1990), 69–93, footnotes omitted. Reprinted by permission of Encyclopedia Britannica, Inc.

This double shift—first, from sex to gender, and second, from the force of gender in shaping the development of adult men and women to its force in delineating the cultural maps of the social and natural worlds these adults inhabit—constitutes the hallmark of contemporary feminist theory. Beginning in the mid-1970s, feminist historians, literary critics, sociologists, political scientists, psychologists, philosophers, and soon, natural scientists as well, sought to supplement earlier feminist thought with an enlarged analysis of the ways in which privately held and publicly shared ideas about gender have shaped the underlying assumptions and operant categories in each of these fields. I have myself described contemporary feminist theory as

> a form of attention, a lens that brings into focus a particular question: What does it mean to describe one aspect of human experience as male and another female? How do such labels affect the ways in which we structure our experimental world, assign value to its different domains, and in turn, acculturate and value actual men and women?

With such questions as these, feminist scholars initiated an intensive investigation of the traces of gender labels evident in many of the fundamental assumptions underlying traditional academic disciplines. While their earliest efforts were confined to the humanities and social sciences, by the late 1970s the lens of feminist inquiry had extended to the natural sciences as well. Those assumptions that posited a dichotomous (and hierarchical) structure tacitly modeled on the prior assumption of a dichotomous (and hierarchical) relation between male and female—e.g., public/private; political/personal; reason/feeling; justice/care; objective/subjective; power/love; and so on—came under particular scrutiny. The object of this endeavor was not to reverse the conventional ordering of these relations, but to undermine the relations themselves—to expose to radical critique a worldview that deploys categories of gender to rend the fabric of human life and thought into a multiplicity of mutually sanctioning, mutually supportive, and mutually defining binary oppositions.

The inclusion of the natural sciences under this broad analytic net posed special opportunities, special difficulties, and special dangers, each of which requires special noting. On the one hand, the presence of gender markings in the root categories of the natural sciences (e.g., mind and nature; reason and feeling; objective and subjective) is, if anything, more conspicuous than in the humanities and social science. At the same time, the central claim of the natural sciences is precisely to a methodology that transcends human particularity, that bears no imprint of individual or collective authorship. As Georg Simmel put it, more than sixty years ago,

> The requirements of . . . correctness in practical judgments and objectivity in theoretical knowledge . . . belong as it were in their form and their claims to humanity in general, but in their actual historical configuration they are masculine throughout. Supposing that we describe these things, viewed as absolute ideas, by the single word "objective," we then find that in the history of our race the equation objective = masculine is a valid one.

Yet Simmel's conclusion, while perhaps unobjectionable as description of a cultural history, alerts us to the particular danger that awaits a feminist critique of the natural sciences. Indeed, Simmel himself appears to have fallen into the very trap that we are seeking to expose: In failing to specify the space in which he claims "validity" for this equation as a *cultural or even ideological space,* his wording invites the reading of it as biological. By referring to its history as a "history of our race" without specifying "our race" as late-modern northern European, he tacitly elides the existence of other cultural histories (as well as other "races") and invites the very conclusion that this cultural history has sought to establish: namely, that "objectivity" really is a privileged possession of the male of the species.

The starting point for a feminist critique of the natural sciences is thus the reframing of this equation as a conundrum: How can the scientific mind be seen at one and the same time as both male and disembodied? How can thinking "objectively," i.e., thinking that is defined as outside the self, impersonal and self-detached, also be understood as "thinking like a man"?

One might suppose that, properly posed (i.e., as a conundrum), such questions have a special urgency for any woman seeking to participate in such a tradition as a scientist. But experience shows otherwise. Women scientists, it turns out, are just as capable of living with submerged contradictions as are other people. Indeed, precisely because of its historical force I would suggest that the cultural equation between "objective" and "masculine" demands of many, if not most, women scientists a quite particular effort to submerge (or deny) the normative contradiction that, for them, such an equation implies.

To take my own case as an example, before I could even *see* this equation as a conundrum in need of analysis, and not simply as a proposition subject to either truth or falsity, I needed to undergo a critical shift in consciousness, as it were acquire another identity, alongside that of a woman scientist. I needed to understand that it was not only things that could have force in the world, but also ideas, beliefs, and even words. Only then could I see the popular association of science, objectivity, and masculinity as a statement about the world that referred not to the bodily and mental capacities of individual men and women but rather to a collective consciousness; as a set of beliefs given existence in the real world not by bodies but by language, and through language granted the force to shape what individual men and women might (or might not) think and do. For me, as for a number of my contemporaries, it took the lens of feminist theory to focus my thinking about science on gender as a cultural rather than biological imperative—as a set of ideas capable of exerting force in their own right, and in their own space, i.e., in the space of ideology and culture.

But this was just a first step. An effective analysis of the role of gender ideals in the history of modern science requires more than a recognition of the social character (and force) of "gender." It requires, as well, recognition of the social character (and force) of the enterprise we call "science."

Although people everywhere, throughout history, have sought reliable knowledge of the world around them, only certain forms of knowledge and certain procedures for acquiring such knowledge have come to count under the general rubric that we, in the late twentieth century, designate as science. Just as "masculine" and "feminine" are categories defined by a culture, and not by biological necessity, so too, "science" is the name we give to a set of practices and a body of knowledge delineated by a community. Even now, in part because of the great variety of practices that the label "science" continues to subsume, the term defies precise definition, obliging us to remain content with a conventional definition—as that which those individuals we call scientists do. Yet, despite conspicuous disciplinary and historical variations, we can nonetheless identify the broad normative dimensions of this venture in its current form—the values, goals, and assumptions that comprise the ideology of modern science; we can even trace their development from the particular upheaval we roughly identify as "the scientific revolution."

For recognition of the conventional character of modern science, feminist theorists have relied heavily on developments over the last three decades in the history, philosophy, and sociology of science. An extensive literature, initially stimulated by the publication of Thomas S. Kuhn's work on scientific revolutions in 1962, has irrevocably altered our understanding of the dynamics of scientific growth. Kuhn's major contribution was to show that the transformations in the history of scientific thought which we call "revolutions" cannot be explained by the arrival of a better theory according to any purely internal criteria. "Ordinarily," he writes, "it is only much later, after the new paradigm has been developed, accepted, and exploited, that apparently decisive arguments are made." Science may be progressive in the sense that the investment of scientific energy is technically productive, but the change in direction that new theories dictate, and the change in worldview they lead to, reflect not logical or empirical necessity but an admixture of scientific and extrascientific needs. The direct implication of such a claim is that, not only different collections of facts and different focal points of scientific attention, but also different organizations of knowledge and different interpretations of the world are both possible and consistent with what we call "science."

Since 1962, an enormous literature has accumulated as historians and sociologists have sought to display the extrascientific forces at work in the definition and growth of scientific knowledge. Throughout almost all of this work, however, two omissions remain notable: one is the contribution of gender, understood now as a social category, and the other, surely related, is the entire dimension of the personal.

Feminism thus makes a unique contribution to both traditional and revisionist studies of science in two respects: It not only focuses our attention on the gender basis of the division of emotional and intellectual labor assumed in traditional scientific discourse, and even in recent social studies of science; it also encourages the inclusion of concerns that have traditionally been assigned to women—not as "a woman's perspective," but as a critical instrument for examining the roots of those dichotomies that isolate such a perspective and deny its legitimacy. Feminism thus seeks to enlarge our understanding of the history, philosophy, and sociology of science through the inclusion of just those domains of human experience that have in the past been relegated to women: namely, the personal, the emotional, and the sexual.

In short, the conjunction of feminist theory and the social studies of science enables us to see that women, men, and science are created together, out of a complex dynamic of interwoven forces. It confronts us with the task of examining the roots, dynamics, and consequences of the interacting network of associations and disjunctions that together constitute what might be called the "science-gender system." It leads us to ask how ideologies of gender and science inform each other in their mutual construction, how that construction functions in our social arrangements, and how it affects men, women, and science. From this perspective the proper subject of gender and science thus becomes the analysis of the web of forces that supports the historic conjunction of science and masculinity, and the equally historic disjunction between science and femininity. It is, in a word, the conjoint making of "men," "women," and "science," or, more precisely, how the making of "men" and "women" has affected the making of "science." . . .

Central to the activity of naming science is the naming (or characterization) of the scientific knower, of that which is to be known, and of the relation between the two that is supposed as making knowledge possible. These acts of naming—of mind, nature, subject and object—inevitably structure the field of scientific inquiry in some degree of consonance with the larger social field such names (underlying images) evoke.

The first step in a feminist analysis of science is thus to call attention to the marks of gender that have been so prevalent throughout the history of scientific discourse and ask how they have functioned in the cognitive and social politics of scientific growth— to ask, in particular, how they have served to delineate and order the domains of mind and nature, reason and feeling, objectivity and subjectivity, which, once delineated and ordered, in turn helped redefine and reorder the domains of masculine and feminine.

Although the naming of material nature as female, and mind as male, was hardly new to seventeenth-century culture, these commonplace metaphors were cast in new relations—relations that fit the rhetorical needs of the founding fathers of modern science as they sought to establish a new cognitive politics in a changing world. When Henry Oldenburg wrote in 1662 that the intention of the Royal Society was "to raise a Masculine Philosophy . . . whereby the Mind of Man may be ennobled with the knowledge of Solid Truths," he was on the one hand drawing on conventional understandings of "Masculine," "Mind," and "Truth," and, on the other hand, contributing to their transformation. Necessarily Oldenburg couched his appeal in language already familiar to his compatriots, thereby contributing to a larger discursive reconfiguration that was by then well under way.

In seventeenth-century England the meanings of "mind" and "knowledge," "man" and "woman," "God" and "nature," as well as the relations obtaining between these various categories, were all under contestation. The self-imposed task of the men who called themselves natural philosophers was both to describe and to prescribe a set of relations that could plausibly claim superiority to those that had obtained in the past. And in this effort the language of gender provided Oldenburg and his colleagues with a central and effectively inexhaustible metaphoric resource. To a considerable degree they were already drawing on the rhetorical accomplishments of their predecessor, Francis Bacon. In the context of Bacon's memorable prose, only a "virile" mind, properly cleansed of all traces of femininity, could effectively consummate his ideal of a "chaste and lawful marriage between Mind and Nature." Bacon envisioned a "chaste, holy, and legal wedlock" with "things themselves" that promised to generate "a blessed race of Heroes and Supermen," a union uniquely capable of "leading [man] to Nature with all her children to bind her to [his] service and make her [his] slave."

What was at issue for both Bacon and his successors was not the identification of nature with woman, wife, or mother, nor the identification of mind with man, husband, or father; in his time, each could be taken for granted. Rather, what was at issue was the relation *between* mind/man and nature/woman that could plausibly promise to yield the kind of knowledge/power imagined as capable of establishing man's dominion over nature, a new science distinctive from that of the "sham philosophers" of old precisely by virtue of its special potency—in Bacon's own words, "A Masculine Birth in Time." Inevitably the character of mind/man and nature/woman—in short, the meanings of "mind," "nature," "masculinity," and "femininity"—were also at issue.

Where Bacon's rhetoric focused on the forms of proper marital congress between mind and nature (e.g., "constraint," "vexation," "hounding," "conquest") that would reveal nature "in her innermost chambers," fifty years later Robert Boyle could presuppose such forms and focus, instead, on the impotence of nature thus revealed. In "A Free Inquiry into the Vulgarly Received Notion of Nature," Boyle argues not only that it is "more consonant to the respect we owe to divine providence, to conceive . . . God [as] a most free, as well as wise agent . . . than to imagine, as we commonly do, that God has appointed an intelligent and powerful Being, called nature, to be as his vicegerent," but also, that his own scientific investigations show that "if there were such a thing, she must be said to act too blindly and impotently, to discharge well the part she is to be trusted with." Furthermore, he adds:

> the veneration, wherewith men are imbued for what they call nature, has been a discouraging impediment to the empire of man over the inferior creatures of God: for many have . . . looked upon it . . . as something of impious to attempt, the removing of those boundaries, which nature seems to have put and settled among her productions. . . .

For Boyle, science and religion conjoin to demand the recasting of "nature" as nothing more venerable than "a great pregnant automaton," a machine whose works it is not only our right but our duty to examine, to emulate, and to excel.

The many social and political factors that informed the philosophical debates attending the institutionalization of modern science in seventeenth-century England constitute a familiar subject for historians of science. But if modern science evolved in, and helped to shape, a particular social and political context, it also evolved in conjunction with, and helped to shape, a particular ideology of gender. We may have become accustomed to the equating of mind, reason, and masculinity, as well as to the dichotomization of mind and nature, reason and feeling, masculine and feminine; but seventeenth-century readers were considerably less so. These conjunctions and disjunctions were in part created by the particular discursive strategy employed by the founding fathers of modern science. And of course, the success of their discourse, in turn, attests to its consonance with concurrent transformations in the larger social, economic, and political arena.

The distinctive features of the role (and meaning) of gender in the rhetoric of men like Bacon, Boyle, and Oldenburg are cast in high relief by juxtaposing their discourse with that of their chief contenders, the Renaissance alchemists. In the decades preceding the founding of the Royal Society, natural philosophers may have been united in their enthusiasm for a "new science," but they were hardly united in their visions of what such a science might mean. Many and sundry interests and beliefs—as yet only partially sorted, and often coexisting in individual minds—might schematically be described in terms of two competing philosophies: the hermetic and the mechanical. In the hermetic tradition, material nature was suffused with spirit; its understanding accordingly required the joint and integrated effort of heart, hand, and mind. By contrast, the mechanical philosophers sought to divorce matter from spirit, and hand and mind from heart. In line with these distinctions, another stands out with prominence: where Bacon's metaphoric ideal was the virile superman, the alchemist's ideal was the hermaphrodite; where Bacon (and Boyle and Oldenburg) sought dominion over nature, the alchemists sought power through "cohabit[ing] with the elements"; where Bacon appealed to conjugal chastity to advocate a disjunction between mind and nature, the alchemists, invoking the same marital metaphor, chose for their root image coition, the conjunction of mind and matter, the merging of male and female.

In hindsight, it is easy to dismiss Renaissance alchemy for its lack of "scientific" merit. But at the time, the very meaning of "scientific" was still under negotiation. If the alchemists had few tangible successes to their credit, the same must be said of the mechanical philosophers of their day. Indeed, the very terms in which the contest between these two competing schools was conducted reveals how inappropriate it may be to apply current standards retroactively. Perhaps especially revealing of the inadequacy of a contemporary perspective are seventeenth-century debates over witchcraft in which, at least in one decisive episode, certain mechanical philosophers insisted on the reality of witches, while the alchemists demurred. For the latter, all phenomena could be interpreted as a manifestation of God, while for the former, some things could only be understood as the work of the Devil: witches, through their omnivorous sexuality, provided direct testimony to Satan's ever-dangerous presence.

At issue for Joseph Glanvill, a participant in this debate and also one of the chief propagandists for the Royal Society, was not simply truth versus falsity but also proper versus improper knowledge. Glanvill warned that true and pious scientists must not be tempted to pursue the "recondite knowledge" that belongs to Satan but must "take care to keep themselves with the Bounds of sober Enquiry." So too, Henry More saw the alchemists' penchant for "tumbling and trying tricks with . . . Matter" as clearly exceeding philosophical propriety. In allowing a kinship between knowledge and erotic sexuality, between experimental and spiritual knowledge, alchemical science not only failed to demarcate Nature adequately; it failed to demarcate the domain of proper knowledge and, accordingly, the domain of "true" knowledge. A century earlier, Paracelsus had written that one "discovers the curative virtues of remedies" by "true love," but now Glanvill wrote, "[W]here the *Will* or *Passion* hath the casting voyce, the case of *Truth is desparate*. . . . The *Woman* in us, still prosecutes a deceit, like that begun in the *Garden*; and our *Understandings* are wedded to an *Eve*, as fatal as the *Mother* of our miseries." Truth has no chance, he concludes, when "the *Affections* wear the breeches and the *Female* rules."

The issues under dispute had little direct relation to the actual politics of sexual domination, but they had a great deal to do with the evaluation of what was regarded as feminine, with the appropriateness of "feminine" traits for men and, perhaps especially, with their place in the new definitions of knowledge—in short, with ideologies of gender and science. Throughout Europe, prevailing concepts of gender had been subtly shifting for over 200 years, and by the end of the seventeenth century the plasticity and fluidity of gender roles that had previously been acceptable was considerably reduced. Definitions of "masculine" and "feminine" were becoming polarized in ways that were eminently well suited to the growing division between work and home required by early industrial capitalism. A new kind of wedge was being driven between the spheres of men and women, to which the rhetoric of the scientific revolution both responded and contributed.

In accordance with the growing division between masculine and feminine, public and private, work and home, modern science opted for an ever-greater polarization of mind and nature, reason and feeling, objective and subjective; in parallel with the gradual desexualization of women; it offered a deanimated, desanctified, and increasingly mechanized conception of nature. In so doing, science itself became an active agent of change. If new criteria of rationality and objectivity, along with new aims to dominate nature, supported the growth of a particular vision of science, they also supported a new definition of manhood. Given the subsequent successes of modern science, now defined in opposition to everything female, fears of both Nature and Woman could subside. With the one reduced to its mechanical substrate, and the other to her asexual virtue, the essence of *Mater* could be tamed and conquered and the Baconian vision of masculine potency confirmed.

A working scientist who happened to read the preceding discussion might well shrug his or her shoulders and say "Well, perhaps, but what does all this have to do with what scientists actually do?" All my observations so far have been about scientific (rather, about metascientific) discourse, and perhaps about subjective motivations, but not about either the practice or theoretical achievements of scientists. Such a reader might also object that, even as discourse, all my examples are dated: they only illustrate the ways in which (some) people have talked about science and nature in the past, not how they talk in the present. These points are well taken, assuming them to have been made in fact, and they need to be addressed.

The second objection can be addressed with relative ease. While it may be true that the prevalence of gender imagery in scientific discourse has considerably abated since the seventeenth century, it has not yet, even today, disappeared. Rather, it might be said that the metaphoric structures the natural philosophers of the seventeenth century helped put in place have so permeated our contemporary world that we hardly notice them anymore. While the basic associations of nature with female, and of mind with male, have been a virtual constant of scientific culture ever since that time, they have come to be so taken for granted as to appear not at all noteworthy. Certainly, norms of gender have undergone considerable variation since the seventeenth century, and at no time have they been either uniform across differences of race and class or entirely binding for particular individuals. The meanings of terms such as *mind, nature, male, female* have been neither invariant nor binding. What matters for the history of our dominant intellectual traditions, however, is the durability, vitality, and force of the metaphoric structure in which they are coupled. The disjunctions between mind and nature, between reason and feeling, between objective and subjective, that were forged with seventeenth-century metaphors of gender are, if anything, stronger and more durable in contemporary scientific culture than they were then. Indeed, so sturdy have they now become that they may no longer need traditional tropes of sex and gender for their maintenance.

In the late twentieth century—in part as a result of contemporary feminism, and in part as a result of internal expansion—science is no longer seen as, and indeed can less and less be said to be, a world of men only. It is a world of men and women (though still mostly men, and predominantly white and middle-class at that) who display certain cognitive facilities—what until very recently we called "thinking like a man" but no longer do because such rhetoric has itself come to be recognized as discriminatory. Despite this twofold (linguistic and occupational) move toward equity, however, the questions put forth by feminist theory still stand: What have *already been* the consequences, for the development of science, of the historic exclusion of those values and human talents which that same history has relegated to the world of women? What have been the consequences of labeling scientific cognition as "thinking like a man" (over the 300 years in which such labels persisted) for the definition and practice of scientific thought? What about the kind of thinking (or whatever mental activity that phrase was intended to bracket) that, as part of their traditional cultural and material work, most women inhabiting such a cultural space perforce had learned to do?

Fifteen years ago, when feminist theorists first began to articulate such questions, the task seemed in some ways easier. To the extent that the occupational and linguistic worlds of the dominant culture were then still divided along the traditional line of sex, to the extent that science in particular remained a bastion not only of masculine virtues but also of male privilege, it seemed possible (although exceedingly problematic just because of its normative implications) to employ the term *women* to connote the values and virtues that had been excluded in their name. It was even possible, then, to hope that the demise of a gendered discourse of science would pave the way for a more human (i.e., "gender-free"), and accordingly more humane, construction of science. In the intervening years, however, it has become abundantly clear how much easier it is to integrate a few women and words than it is to respond substantively to the challenge posed by a different set of values, namely, the values of the culture these women and words necessarily had to leave behind. What was thought to be the problem has proved only to be the symptoms of it. The cure of these, partial though it is, is clearly not enough. Science shows no sign of being changed either by the inclusion of more women, or by our self-conscious attempts to remove the marks of gender from its discourse.

Does this mean that the skepticism of our hypothetical working scientist is justified? That finally (to return now to the first objection), language, the ways in which we talk *about* science and nature, is not relevant to the actual practice and theoretical achievements of science? Hardly. What the lack of change means is that our ordinary ways of speaking do not directly translate into the practice of science, any more than our conventional norms of gender are directly transferred onto the bodies of men and women. It merely underscores the necessity of another level of analysis, moving beyond the exposure of the place and rhetorical function of gender imagery in the history of modern science, to an analysis of how that imagery, along with the cultural norms it conjoins, has affected the actual cognitive and material development of science. More generally yet, it necessitates an analysis of the role of language and ideology in the day-to-day production of scientific theory and practice.

The "doing" of science is a gripping and fully absorbing activity—so much so that it is difficult for anyone so engaged to step outside the demands of the problems under investigation to reflect on the assumptions underlying that investigation, much less on the language in which such assumptions can be said to "make sense." Keeping track of the arguments and data as they unfold, trying always to think ahead, demands total absorption; at the same time, the sense of discovering or even generating a new world yields an intoxication rarely paralleled in other academic fields. The net result is that scientists are probably less reflective of the tacit assumptions that guide their reasoning than any other intellectuals of the modern age.

The success of their enterprise does not, at least in the short run, seem to require such reflectiveness. Some would even argue that that very success demands abstaining from reflection upon matters that do not lend themselves to "clear and distinct" answers. Indeed, they might argue that what distinguishes contemporary science from the more amateurish efforts of their seventeenth-century forebears is precisely its recognition of the dual need to avoid talk *about* science, and to replace "ordinary" language by a technical discourse cleansed of the ambiguity and values that burden ordinary language, as the modern form of the scientific report requires. Let the data speak for themselves, these scientists demand. The problem with this argument is, of course, that data never do speak for themselves.

It is by now a near truism that all data presuppose interpretation. And if an interpretation is to be meaningful—if the data are to be "intelligible" to more than one person—it must be embedded in a community of common practices, a community in which the meaning of terms and their relation to the "objects" to which the terms point is shared. In short, interpretation requires a common language, in science as elsewhere.

Sharing a language means sharing a conceptual universe. It means more than knowing the "right" names by which to call things; it means knowing the "right" syntax in which to pose claims and questions, and even more critically it means sharing a more or less agreed-upon understanding of what questions are legitimate to ask and what can be accepted as meaningful answers. Every question carries with it tacit suppositions and expectations that limit the range of acceptable answers to those which only a properly versed respondent will recognize. To know what kinds of explanation "make sense," and what can be expected to count as "accounting for," is already to be a member of a particular language community.

But if there is one feature that distinguishes scientific from other communities, and is special to scientific discourse, it is the assumption that the universe scientists study is directly accessible, that the "nature" they name as object of inquiry is unmediated by language and can therefore be veridically represented. On this assumption, "laws of nature" are beyond the relativity of language—indeed, they are beyond language, encoded in logical structures that require only the discernment of reason and the confirmation of experiment. Also on this assumption, the descriptive language of science is transparent and neutral; it does not require examination.

Confidence in the transparency and neutrality of scientific language is certainly useful in enabling scientists to get on with their job; it is also wondrously effective in supporting their special claims to truth. It encourages the view that their own language is absolute and, in so doing, helps secure their disciplinary borders against criticism. Language, assumed to be transparent, becomes impervious.

Perforce, then, it falls to others, less enclosed by the demands of science's own self-understanding, to disclose the "thickness" of scientific language, to scrutinize the conventions of practice, interpretation, and shared aspirations on which the truth claims of that language depend, to expose the many forks in the road to knowledge that these very conventions have worked to obscure, and, in that process, finally, to uncover alternatives for the future.

Under careful scrutiny, the hypothesized contrast between ordinary and scientific language gives way to a recognition of disconcerting similarity. Even the most purely technical discourse turns out to depend on metaphor, on ambiguity, on instabilities of meaning—indeed, on the very commonsense understanding of terms from which a technical discourse is supposed to emancipate us. Scientific arguments cannot begin to "make sense," much less be effective, without extensive recourse to shared conventions for controlling these inevitable ambiguities and instabilities. The very term *experimental control* needs to be understood in a far larger sense than has been the custom—describing not only the control of variables but also of the ways of seeing, thinking, acting, and speaking in which an investigator must be extensively trained before he or she can become a contributing member of a discipline.

Even the conventional account scientists offer of their success has been shown by recent work in the history, philosophy, and sociology of science to be itself rooted in metaphor: The very idea of a one-to-one correspondence between theory and reality, or of scientific method as capable of revealing nature "as it is," is based on metaphors of mind as a "glassy essence," and of science as a "mirror of nature." Simple logic, however, suggests that words are far too limited a resource, in whatever combinations, to permit a faithful representation of even our own experience, much less of the vast domain of natural phenomena. The metaphor of science as "mirror of nature" may be both psychologically and politically useful to scientists, but it cannot be taken to be correct. Nor can it be assumed to be particularly useful for a philosophical understanding of how science works; indeed, it has proven to be a positive barrier to our understanding of the development of science in its historical and social context. It is far more useful, and probably even more correct, to suppose, as Mary Hesse suggests, that "[s]cience is successful only because there are sufficient local and particular regularities between things in space-time domains where we can test them. These domains may be very large but it's an elementary piece of mathematics that there is an infinite gap between the largest conceivable number and infinity."

In much the same sense, the idea of "laws of nature" can also be shown to be rooted in metaphor, a metaphor indelibly marked by its political and theological origins. Despite the insistence of philosophers that laws of nature are merely descriptive and not prescriptive, they are historically conceptualized as imposed from above and obeyed from below. "By those who first used the term, [laws of nature] were viewed as commands imposed by the Deity upon matter," the O.E.D. states, "and even writers who do not accept this view often speak of them as 'obeyed' by the phenomena, or as agents by which the phenomena are produced." In this sense the metaphor of "laws of nature" carries into scientific practice the presupposition of an ontological hierarchy, ordering not only mind and matter, but theory and practice, and, of course, the normal and the aberrant. Even in the loosest (most purely descriptive) sense of the term *law*, the kinds of order in nature that laws can accommodate are restricted to those which can be expressed by the language in which laws of nature are codified. All languages are capable of describing regularity, but not all perceived, or even all describable, regularities can be expressed in the existing vocabularies of science. To assume, therefore, that all perceptible regularities can be represented by current (or even by future) theory is to impose a premature limit on what is "naturally" possible, as well as what is potentially understandable.

Nancy Cartwright has suggested that a better way to make sense of theoretical successes of science (as well as its failures) would be to invoke the rather different metaphor of "Nature's Capacities." In apparent sympathy with Hesse, as well as with a number of other contemporary historians and philosophers of science, she suggests that an understanding of the remarkable convergences between theory and experiment that scientists have produced requires attention not so much to the adequacy of the laws that are presumably being tested, but rather to the particular and highly local manipulation of theory and experimental procedure that is required to produce these convergences. Our usual talk of scientific laws, Cartwright suggests, belies (and elides) the conceptual and linguistic work that is required to ground a theory, or "law," to fit a particular set of experimental circumstances, as well as the material work required to construct an experimental apparatus to fit a theoretical claim. Scientific laws may be "true," but the question remains, what exactly are they true of? In Cartwright's account, they are true of highly contrived and local circumstances, reflecting the particular products of human workmanship at least as much as they reflect preexisting invariances of nature.

These philosophical revisions offer us a background against which to return to and reframe the particular concerns of this essay. Our original question about the influence of a gendered discourse on the historical development of modern science can now be reformulated as two separable questions: The first, that of the role of public and private conceptions of gender in the framing of the root metaphors of science, belongs to feminist theory proper, while the second, that of the role of such metaphors in the actual development of scientific theory and practice, belongs to a larger inquiry in the history and philosophy of science. Earlier, I sought to respond to the first question by way of historical examples of explicit appeals to conceptions of gender in the naming of science and nature. By undermining the realism and univocality of scientific discourse, the philosophical groundwork initiated by Kuhn and continued more recently by Hesse, Cartwright, and many others, now makes it possible to respond to the second question, and at least to indicate the kind of analysis that would be necessary to show how such basic acts of naming have helped to shape the actual course of scientific development, obscuring if not foreclosing other possible courses.

The most critical resource for such an inquiry is the de facto plurality of organizing metaphors, theories, and practices evident throughout the history of science. At any given moment, in any given discipline, abundant significant variability can be identified along the following four closely interdependent axes: the aims of scientific inquiry; the questions judged most significant to ask; the theoretical and experimental methodologies deemed most productive for addressing these questions; and, finally, what counts as an acceptable answer or a satisfying explanation. Different metaphors of mind, nature, and the relation between them, reflect different psychological stances of observer to observed; these, in turn, give rise to different cognitive perspectives: to different aims, questions, and even different methodological and explanatory preferences. Such variability is of course always subject to the forces of selection exerted by collective norms, yet there are many moments in scientific history in which alternative visions can survive for long enough to permit identification both of their distinctiveness and of the selective pressures against which they must struggle.

One of the clearest such instances in my own research is provided by the life and work of the cytogeneticist Barbara McClintock. McClintock offers a vision of science premised not on the domination of nature but on "a feeling for the organism." For her, a "feeling for the organism" is simultaneously a state of mind and a resource for knowledge: for the day-to-day work of conducting experiments, observing and interpreting their outcomes—in short, for the "doing" of science. "Nature," to McClintock, is best understood in terms of its largesse and prodigality; accordingly, her conception of the work of science is more consonant with that of exhibiting nature's "capacities" and multiple forms of order, than with pursuing the "laws of nature." "Laws" of nature name nature as blind, obedient, and simple; at the same time, they name their maker as authoritative, generative, and complex. In contrast, I suggest that the conception of nature as "orderly," and not merely as law-bound, permits nature itself to be seen as generative and resourceful—by definition, more complex than we can either describe or prescribe. In this alternative view, nature can come to be seen, as it was by McClintock, as an active partner in a more reciprocal relation to an observer, equally active, but neither omniscient nor omnipotent.

Inevitably, such a relationship between mind and nature suggests a different style of inquiry, no less rigorous but more modest, encouraging one to "listen to what the material has to tell you," rather than assuming that scientific data are self-evident. Following the development of McClintock's research enables one to see, as well, how this quite different naming of nature organizes an entire array of procedural and methodological differences, beginning with differences in the questions she asked, leading to the privileging (and even the perception) of different kinds of data, and ending, finally, with her identification of a radically different mechanism, and principle, of genetic organization. To McClintock, the study of gene structure, and even of the mechanisms of replication and transcription, are subsidiary to questions of function and organization. Genes are neither "beads on a string" nor functionally disjoint pieces of DNA. They are organized functional units whose very function is defined by their position in the organization as a whole. Thus, an adequate understanding must include an account of how genes function in relation to the rest of the cell and, of course, to the organism as a whole. In turn, a conception of cells (or chromosomes) as organized functional units embedded in still larger functional units encourages forms of perception normally reserved for organisms like ourselves. In McClintock's style of research, intimacy and even identification with the objects of scientific research are put to productive "cognitive" use.

McClintock is now widely credited with the "discovery" of genetic transposition, a process of genetic rearrangement that she saw as critical to the organism's developmental and regulatory needs. But before she could be said to have discovered this phenomenon, her mainstream colleagues, employing the different practices and speaking the different language of an increasingly alien community, needed first to concur that such a phenomenon existed.

As it happened, this concurrence took almost forty years. From a historian's point of view, that lag provides an invaluable opportunity to explore the nature of the gap— linguistic, methodological, conceptual—that had impeded consensus; from the point of view of an advocate (as I freely confess to be), it is the fact of ultimate consensus that proves invaluable, that legitimates her story as a resource for us in the first place. History is strewn with dissidents and deviants, not unlike McClintock, whose erasure is readily justified by the conventional narrative of science. Without the validation of the dominant community, her particular claims and the vision of science which had guided them would, equally, be dismissed as mere "mistakes," misguided and false steps in the history of science.

It is also the case, however, that that very validation invites other kinds of misreading: The story of McClintock's life and work is neither a story of error, nor that of a lonely pioneer who was unaccountably able to see directly into nature, to grasp the truth "ahead of her time." Her accomplishments are entirely accountable in terms of the work she performed; the ultimate value of these accomplishments, however—that which we all too casually call "truth"—depended not on her special vision but on their acceptance by the community around her. The philosophical perspective employed here suggests that the arrival of that consensus cannot be understood in terms of self-evident truth claims, but rather must itself be accounted for in terms of greater or lesser convergences of language and practice.

Of greatest importance for this essay, however, is the reminder that this story ought not, indeed cannot, be read as the story of a woman, attached by her sex both to nature and to the arts of "feeling" and "intuition," who, because of that attachment, was able to bring to science the missed virtues of "women's ways of knowing." The details of

McClintock's actual life and work belie all three of these readings, but perhaps especially, they belie this last reading. Instead, they point to a story of diversity, multiplicity, and difference: of a woman rebelling equally against the conventions of science and the conventions of gender. The distinctive resources she brought to science were no more attached to her sex than they were to divine inspiration. They derived instead from a conception of nature and science that called upon many of the human concerns and the cognitive and emotional assets that had been historically excluded from science in the name of "masculinity," but which, by virture of her unconventional naming of "science," "nature," and "woman," she was able to put to productive use as a working scientist. In the face of linguistic conventions that posit nature as the object of masculine prowess, and women and science as mutually exclusive categories, it may well be that McClintock had a particular (sex-based) need to reconceive the categories of "woman," "science," "mind," and "nature," a particular desire to liberate herself and her work from a history of normative constraint. In principle, however, the project and values of such a reconception are available to anyone and have, in fact, been embraced by many others, both male and female.

Still, the largest and most difficult question remains, and I have left it for the conclusion. McClintock's vision of science may be aesthetically and emotionally appealing, and may even have worked well for her, but her success pales before that which has accrued to the history of mainstream science, gendered though it may have been. Indeed, if I were to continue the story about transposition to the present day, I would have to admit that the principal utility of this discovery has proven to lie not in the conceptual revolution she had hoped would come, but in a domain in every way antithetical to McClintock's vision, namely, in genetic engineering. In the last few years, in part thanks to the techniques made possible by genetic transposition, it is the successes and technological prowess of molecular biology rather than of McClintock's vision of science that have captured the scientific and popular imagination. In the process, the very meaning of genetic transposition has been redefined, but against such redefinition, there appears to be little recourse: how, after all, can one argue with success?

By now, we may be well persuaded that the domain of natural phenomena is vastly larger than the domain of scientific theory as we know it, leaving ample room for alternative conceptions of science; that the accumulated body of scientific theory represents only one of the many ways in which human beings, including the human beings we call scientists, have sought to make sense of the world; even that the successes of these theories are highly local and specific. Yet, whatever philosophical accounts we might accept, the fact remains that the particular vision of science that men like Bacon helped articulate has, over the course of time, more than fulfilled Bacon's prophecies, yielding a kind and degree of power that surpasses his wildest dreams. Science as we know it works exceedingly well. The question is, can any other vision of science be reasonably expected to work as well?

Feminist studies of science share with other recent efforts in the history, philosphy, and sociology of science the task of finding a way to integrate the various influences on scientific development of social and political forces, psychological predispositions, experimental constraints, and cognitive demands. Feminist studies also share the task of accounting for the technological efficacy of science. If we can no longer appeal to the simple picture of science as a mirror of nature, if we are to acknowledge the importance of other, extrascientific factors in shaping the development of scientific theory, how then are we to account for the extraordinary degree to which such theories can be said to "work"?

One response has been to challenge the connections between formal theory and practical success that have been claimed for science. I suggest a rather different approach, requiring one further shift in our analytic focus. Until now, the primary focus of our analyses has been on science as representation, rather than as a set of tools for intervention, for materially altering the world around us. Feminist theory may have helped us to re-envision science as a discourse, but not as an agent of change. As such, it tacitly supports the dichotomy between representing and intervening, between scientific truth and its consequences, that is itself part of our scientific heritage. What is needed most urgently, I suggest, is a better understanding of what it means to say that science "works," above all, of what it is that science "works" *at*. What is needed is a reexamination of the meaning of "success."

Scientific theories do undoubtedly impinge on the real, but they do so more loosely and more selectively than we had thought, effecting some kinds of changes rather than others. If scientific theories are produced in a particular discursive tradition, by particular groups of people interacting among themselves, with nonscientists, and with nonhuman subjects, then the effectiveness of the resulting theories must be judged in terms of all the interactions which generate them. These interactions, both social and technical, produce an interlocking system of needs and desires demanding at least partial satisfaction by any theory or research program that is said to "work." But if the efficacy of science, or its consequentiality, is located in the satisfaction of these needs and desires, we must also consider its intentionality, located in the production of this particular system of needs.

A certain amount of the work that a successful theory or research program must do can be described in strictly human terms. It must be able to generate jobs and doable problems; it must offer explanations that provide aesthetic and emotional satisfaction; it must work rhetorically to recruit students, to "win allies," to get grants. In short, it must have the power to persuade a number of different constituencies—the funding agencies, the scientists themselves, potential recruits, the public at large—with interests that are themselves multiple, overlapping, and shifting.

For a research program to survive, however, it must satisfy the desires that motivate it, at least well enough to keep it going. In the short run, a stable network of interests might be well enough satisfied more or less independently of any particular interactions with the nonhuman world: Jobs, satisfying explanations, doable problems might all be generated by the strictly human (and rhetorical) work of a research program. But over the long run, the promises held out must be made good in terms of scientists' direct interactions with their world of nonhuman subjects. By the internal ethic of science, explanations must provide at least some predictive success in order to remain satisfying, and by the social and political ethic justifying their support, this predictive success must enable the production of at least some of the technological "goods" the public thinks it is paying for.

The truly remarkable thing about contemporary science (especially physics and molecular biology) is that it has been able to realize so many of these needs and desires, that it has produced a body of theory that matches the world well enough to satisfy this network of overlapping interests. That success bears testimony, above all, to the resourcefulness of scientists. Out of their interactions with each other, with the public at large, with their own heritage, and with a judiciously culled set of "facts" about the inanimate world, they have succeeded in producing tools which appear to dissolve nature's resistance to our own needs and desires.

But in marveling over their extraordinary success, we need also to consider the almost equally remarkable particularity (perhaps even singularity) of such needs and desires, of our selection of which natural phenomena to engage for experimental and theoretical inquiry (i.e., what it is we seek to know about), and of the social arrangements that facilitate the convergence of these needs and choices. It is only with the recognition of such convergences that we can begin to ask our question about alternatives: How might the unmistakable resourcefulness scientists have displayed be employed toward the fulfillment of other desires, satisfying a convergence of human interests that would be yielded by different social arrangements, producing a science that could be said to "work" differently?

Even so reformulated, however, this question conceals yet another. Feminists have irrevocably undermined our sense of innocence about the aspiration to dominate nature without, however, answering the question of just what it is that is wrong with dominating nature. We know what is wrong with dominating persons—it deprives other subjects of their right to express their own objectivities—and we may indeed worry about the extent to which the motivation to dominate nature reflects a desire for domination of other human beings. But a salient point of a feminist perspective on science derives precisely from the fact that nature is not in fact a woman. A better pronoun for nature is surely "it," rather than "she." And it is not obvious what is wrong with seeking, or even achieving, dominion over things per se.

Perhaps the simplest way to respond to this final objection is to point out that nature, while surely not a woman, is also not a "thing," nor is it even an "it" that can be delineated unto itself, either separate or separable from a speaking and knowing "we." What we know about nature we know only through our interactions with, or rather, our embeddedness in what we call nature. It is precisely because we ourselves are natural beings—beings *in* and *of* nature—that we *can* know. Thus, to represent nature as a "thing" or an "it" is itself a way of talking, undoubtedly convenient, but clearly more appropriate to some ends than to others. And just because there is no one else "out there" capable of choosing, we must acknowledge that these ends represent human choices, for which "we" alone are responsible. The question then becomes: What are the particular ends to which the language of objectification, reification, and domination of nature is particularly appropriate, and perhaps even useful? And to what other ends might a different language—of kinship, embeddedness, and connectivity, of "feeling for the organism"—be equally appropriate and useful?

To ask about alternative aims for science in the late twentieth century is no idle or merely academic pursuit. Scientists have shown themselves to be smart enough to learn what they need to know to get much of what they, or we, thought we wanted, and at least some of us are alarmed. Something has gone terribly wrong. The very prowess of modern science confronts us with the fact that, somehow, we forgot to factor our own survival into our objectives for scientific knowledge. Perhaps it is not too late to reconsider, to rename and redefine the venture that has shown itself to be such a formidable resource; to recast the project of science in language that codifies a commitment to survival—our own as well as that of the world around us—as our first priority.

JUDITH BUTLER

Selection from *Gender Trouble*
1990

"Back in the days when men were men and women were women," begin a variety of complaints about aspects of contemporary life associated with changing social roles for males and females. But what, really, can one mean when one refers to "men," or to "women," in the context of the extensive, probing investigations of gender that took place in the 1970s and 1980s? The feminist philosopher Judith Butler (1956–) was prominent among the thinkers who pursued this question the most relentlessly, refusing to take for granted many of the assumptions about the identity of men and women that were common even among other feminist theorists.

In this selection from the opening chapter of her book of 1990, *Gender Trouble: Feminism and the Subversion of Identity,* Butler insists that even the popular distinction between "gender" as a cultural construction and "sex" as a biological condition attributed too much stability to the identity of women and of men. The very category of "woman," Butler suggests, comes to us from a deep historical and social matrix of language and power that is both heterosexual and "phallogocentric" in orientation. Butler asks for what she calls—inspired by Nietzsche and Foucault—a "genealogical" inquiry into this matrix, meaning the kind of historical investigation that will establish the processes by which the category of "woman" has been produced, and that will identify the interests served by this production. Butler clearly hopes that if people can treat the masculine and the feminine not as "natural" categories, but as "contested sites of meaning," there exists a greater opportunity to change the roles that men and women are expected to play. "The very multiplicity" of constructions of "the regulatory fictions of sex and gender" offer the possibility "of a disruption" of standard ideas of what it means to be a "man" or a "woman."

For a critical perspective on the ideas Butler sketches in the selection from *Gender Trouble* reprinted here, see Selya Benhabib, *Situating the Self: Gender, Community, and Postmodernism in Contemporary Ethics* (New York, 1992), esp. 214–18. Sharp and provocative exchanges between Benhabib, Butler and two other leading feminist theorists of the 1990s, Drucilla Cornell and Nancy Fraser, can be found in a book co-authored by all four, *Feminist Contentions: A Philosophical Exchange* (New York, 1995). This volume, which can serve as an excellent point of entry to contemporary debates among leading feminist theorists, also includes a helpful introduction by Linda Nicholson that clarifies the issues, and underscores the agreements and disagreement displayed by the four in the course their ongoing dialogue.

Butler is also the author of *Bodies that Matter: On the Discursive Limits of "Sex"* (New York, 1993), and is the co-editor, with Joan W. Scott, of an important collection of contemporary feminist writings, *Feminists Theorize the Political* (New York, 1992).

For the most part, feminist theory has assumed that there is some existing identity, understood through the category of women, who not only initiates feminist interests and goals within discourse, but constitutes the subject for whom political representation is pursued. But *politics* and *representation* are controversial terms. On the one hand, *representation* serves as the operative term within a political process that seeks to extend visibility and legitimacy to women as political subjects; on the other hand, representation is the normative function of a language which is said either to reveal or to distort what is assumed to be true about the category of women. For feminist theory, the development of a language that fully or adequately represents women has seemed necessary to foster the political visibility of women. This has seemed obviously important considering the pervasive cultural condition in which women's lives were either misrepresented or not represented at all.

Recently, this prevailing conception of the relation between feminist theory and politics has come under challenge from within feminist discourse. The very subject of women is no longer understood in stable or abiding terms. There is a great deal of material that not only questions the viability of "the subject" as the ultimate candidate for representation or, indeed, liberation, but there is very little agreement after all on what it is that constitutes, or ought to constitute, the category of women. The domains of political and linguistic "representation" set out in advance the criterion by which subjects themselves are formed, with the result that representation is extended only to what can be acknowledged as a subject. In other words, the qualifications for being a subject must first be met before representation can be extended.

Foucault points out that juridical systems of power *produce* the subjects they subsequently come to represent. Juridical notions of power appear to regulate political life in purely negative terms—that is, through the limitation, prohibition, regulation, control and even "protection" of individuals related to that political structure through the contingent and retractable operation of choice. But the subjects regulated by such structures are, by virtue of being subjected to them, formed, defined, and reproduced in accordance with the requirements of those structures. If this analysis is right, then the juridical formation of language and politics that represents women as "the subject" of feminism is itself a discursive formation and effect of a given version of representational politics. And the feminist subject turns out to be discursively constituted by the very political system that is supposed to facilitate its emancipation. This becomes politically problematic if that system can be shown to produce gendered subjects along a differential axis of domination or to produce subjects who are presumed to be masculine. In such cases, an uncritical appeal to such a system for the emancipation of "women" will be clearly self-defeating.

The question of "the subject" is crucial for politics, and for feminist politics in particular, because juridical subjects are invariably produced through certain exclusionary practices that do not "show" once the juridical structure of politics has been established. In other words, the political construction of the subject proceeds with certain legitimating and exclusionary aims, and these political operations are effectively concealed and naturalized by a political analysis that takes juridical structures as their foundation. Juridical power inevitably "produces" what it claims merely to represent; hence, politics must be concerned with this dual function of power: the juridical and

Source: Judith Butler, *Gender Trouble: Feminism and the Subversion of Identity* (New York, 1990), 1–7, 31–33. Reprinted with the permission of Routledge, Chapman & Hall, Inc.

the productive. In effect, the law produces and then conceals the notion of "a subject before the law" in order to invoke that discursive formation as a naturalized foundational premise that subsequently legitimates that law's own regulatory hegemony. It is not enough to inquire into how women might become more fully represented in language and politics. Feminist critique ought also to understand how the category of "women," the subject of feminism, is produced and restrained by the very structures of power through which emancipation is sought.

Indeed, the question of women as the subject of feminism raises the possibility that there may not be a subject who stands "before" the law, awaiting representation in or by the law. Perhaps the subject, as well as the invocation of a temporal "before," is constituted by the law as the fictive foundation of its own claim to legitimacy. The prevailing assumption of the ontological integrity of the subject before the law might be understood as the contemporary trace of the state of nature hypothesis, that foundationalist fable constitutive of the juridical structures of classical liberalism. The performance invocation of a nonhistorical "before" becomes the foundational premise that guarantees a presocial ontology of persons who freely consent to be governed and, thereby, constitute the legitimacy of the social contract.

Apart from the foundationalist fictions that support the notion of the subject, however, there is the political problem that feminism encounters in the assumption that the term *women* denotes a common identity. Rather than a stable signifier that commands the assent of those whom it purports to describe and represent, *women,* even in the plural, has become a troublesome term, a site of contest, a cause for anxiety. As Denise Riley's title suggests, *Am I That Name?* is a question produced by the very possibility of the name's multiple significations. If one "is" a woman, that is surely not all one is; the term fails to be exhaustive, not because a pregendered "person" transcends the specific paraphernalia of its gender, but because gender is not always constituted coherently or consistently in different historical contexts, and because gender intersects with racial, class, ethnic, sexual, and regional modalities of discursively constituted identities. As a result, it becomes impossible to separate out "gender" from the political and cultural intersections in which it is invariably produced and maintained.

The political assumption that there must be a universal basis for feminism, one which must be found in an identity assumed to exist cross-culturally, often accompanies the notion that the oppression of women has some singular form discernible in the universal or hegemonic structure of patriarchy or masculine domination. The notion of a universal patriarchy has been widely criticized in recent years for its failure to account for the workings of gender oppression in the concrete cultural contexts in which it exists. Where those various contexts have been consulted within such theories, it has been to find "examples" or "illustrations" of a universal principle that is assumed from the start. That form of feminist theorizing has come under criticism for its efforts to colonize and appropriate non-Western cultures to support highly Western notions of oppression, but because they tend as well to construct a "Third World" or even an "Orient" in which gender oppression is subtly explained as symptomatic of an essential, non-Western barbarism. The urgency of feminism to establish a universal status for patriarchy in order to strengthen the appearance of feminism's own claims to be representative has occasionally motivated the shortcut to a categorical or fictive universality of the structure of domination, held to produce women's common subjugated experience.

Although the claim of universal patriarchy no longer enjoys the kind of credibility it once did, the notion of a generally shared conception of "women," the corollary to that framework, has been much more difficult to displace. Certainly, there have been plenty of debates: Is there some commonality among "women" that preexists their oppression, or do "women" have a bond by virtue of their oppression alone? Is there a specificity to women's cultures that is independent of their subordination by hegemonic, masculinist cultures? Are the specificity and integrity of women's cultural or linguistic practices always specified against and, hence, within the terms of some more dominant cultural formation? If there is a region of the "specifically feminine," one that is both differentiated from the masculine as such and recognizable in its difference by an unmarked and, hence, presumed universality of "women"? The masculine/feminine binary constitutes not only the exclusive framework in which that specificity can be recognized, but in every other way the "specificity" of the feminine is once again fully decontextualized and separated off analytically and politically from the constitution of class, race, ethnicity, and other axes of power relations that both constitute "identity" and make the singular notion of identity a misnomer.

My suggestion is that the presumed universality and unity of the subject of feminism is effectively undermined by the constraints of the representational discourse in which it functions. Indeed, the premature insistence on a stable subject of feminism, understood as a seamless category of women, inevitably generates multiple refusals to accept the category. These domains of exclusion reveal the coercive and regulatory consequences of that construction, even when the construction has been elaborated for emancipatory purposes. Indeed, the fragmentation within feminism and the paradoxical opposition to feminism from "women" whom feminism claims to represent suggest the necessary limits of identity politics. The suggestion that feminism can seek wider representation for a subject that it itself constructs has the ironic consequence that feminist goals risk failure by refusing to take account of the constitutive powers of their own representational claims. This problem is not ameliorated through an appeal to the category of women for merely "strategic" purposes, for strategies always have meanings that exceed the purposes for which they are intended. In this case, exclusion itself might qualify as such an unintended yet consequential meaning. By conforming to a requirement of representational politics that feminism articulate a stable subject, feminism thus opens itself to charges of gross misrepresentation.

Obviously, the political task is not to refuse representational politics—as if we could. The juridical structures of language and politics constitute the contemporary field of power; hence, there is no position outside this field, but only a critical genealogy of its own legitimating practices. As such, the critical point of departure is *the historical present,* as Marx put it. And the task is to formulate within this constituted frame a critique of the categories of identity that contemporary juridical structures engender, naturalize, and immobilize.

Perhaps there is an opportunity at this juncture of cultural politics, a period that some would call "postfeminist," to reflect from within a feminist perspective on the injunction to construct a subject of feminism. Within feminist political practice, a radical rethinking of the ontological constructions of identity appears to be necessary in order to formulate a representational politics that might revive feminism on other grounds. On the other hand, it may be time to entertain a radical critique that seeks to free feminist theory from the necessity of having to construct a single or abiding ground which is invariably contested by those identity positions or anti-identity positions that it invariably excludes. Do the exclusionary practices that ground feminist theory in a notion of "women" as subject paradoxically undercut feminist goals to extend its claims to "representation"?

Perhaps the problem is even more serious. Is the construction of the category of women as a coherent and stable subject an unwitting regulation and reification of gender relations? And is not such a reification precisely contrary to feminist aims? To what extent does the category of women achieve stability and coherence only in the context of the heterosexual matrix? If a stable notion of gender no longer proves to be the foundational premise of feminist politics, perhaps a new sort of feminist politics is now desirable to contest the very reifications of gender and identity, one that will take the variable construction of identity as both a methodological and normative prerequisite, if not a political goal.

To trace the political operations that produce and conceal what qualifies as the juridical subject of feminism is precisely the task of *a feminist genealogy* of the category of women. In the course of this effort to question "women" as the subject of feminism, the unproblematic invocation of that category may prove to *preclude* the possibility of feminism as a representational politics. What sense does it make to extend representation to subjects who are constructed through the exclusion of those who fail to conform to unspoken normative requirements of the subject? What relations of domination and exclusion are inadvertently sustained when representation becomes the sole focus of politics? The identity of the feminist subject ought not to be the foundation of feminist politics, if the formation of the subject takes place within a field of power regularly buried through the assertion of that foundation. Perhaps, paradoxically, "representation" will be shown to make sense for feminism only when the subject of "women" is nowhere presumed.

Although the unproblematic unity of "women" is often invoked to construct a solidarity of identity, a split is introduced in the feminist subject by the distinction between sex and gender. Originally intended to dispute the biology-is-destiny formulation, the distinction between sex and gender serves the argument that whatever biological intractability sex appears to have, gender is culturally constructed: hence, gender is neither the causal result of sex nor as seemingly fixed as sex. The unity of the subject is thus already potentially contested by the distinction that permits of gender as a multiple interpretation of sex.

If gender is the cultural meanings that the sexed body assumes, then a gender cannot be said to follow from a sex in any one way. Taken to its logical limit, the sex/gender distinction suggests a radical discontinuity between sexed bodies and culturally constructed genders. Assuming for the moment the stability of binary sex, it does not follow that the construction of "men" will accrue exclusively to the bodies of males or that "women" will interpret only female bodies. Further, even if the sexes appear to be unproblematically binary in their morphology and constitution (which will become a question), there is no reason to assume that genders ought also to remain as two. The presumption of a binary gender system implicitly retains the belief in a mimetic relation of gender to sex whereby gender mirrors sex or is otherwise restricted by it. When the constructed status of gender is theorized as radically independent of sex, gender itself becomes a free-floating artifice, with the consequence that *man* and *masculine* might just as easily signify a female body as a male one, and *woman* and *feminine* a male body as easily as a female one.

This radical splitting of the gendered subject poses yet another set of problems. Can we refer to a "given" sex or a "given" gender without first inquiring into how sex and/or gender is given, through what means? And what is "sex" anyway? Is it natural, anatomical, chromosomal, or hormonal, and how is a feminist critic to assess the scientific discourses which purport to establish such "facts" for us? Does sex have a history? Does each sex have a different history, or histories? Is there a history of how the duality of sex was established, a genealogy that might expose the binary options as a variable construction? Are the ostensibly natural facts of sex discursively produced by various scientific discourses in the service of other political and social interests? If the immutable character of sex is contested, perhaps this construct called "sex" is as culturally constructed as gender; indeed, perhaps it was always already gender, with the consequence that the distinction between sex and gender turns out to be no distinction at all.

It would make no sense, then, to define gender as the cultural interpretation of sex, if sex itself is a gendered category. Gender ought not to be conceived merely as the cultural inscription of meaning on a pregiven sex (a juridical conception); gender must also designate the very apparatus of production whereby the sexes themselves are established. As a result, gender is not to culture as sex is to nature; gender is also the discursive/cultural means by which "sexed nature" or "a natural sex" is produced and established as "prediscursive," prior to culture, a politically neutral surface *on which* culture acts. . . .

The "unity" of gender is the effect of a regulatory practice that seeks to render gender identity uniform through a compulsory heterosexuality. The force of this practice is, through an exclusionary apparatus of production, to restrict the relative meanings of "heterosexuality," "homosexuality," and "bisexuality" as well as the subversive sites of their convergence and resignification. That the power regimes of heterosexism and phallogocentrism seek to augment themselves through a constant repetition of their logic, their metaphysic, and their naturalized ontologies does not imply that repetition itself ought to be stopped—as if it could be. If repetition is bound to persist as the mechanism of the cultural reproduction of identities, then the crucial question emerges: What kind of subversive repetition might call into question the regulatory practice of identity itself?

If there is no recourse to a "person," a "sex," or a "sexuality" that escapes the matrix of power and discursive relations that effectively produce and regulate the intelligibility of those concepts for us, what constitutes the possibility of effective inversion, subversion, or displacement within the terms of a constructed identity? What possibilities exist *by virtue of* the constructed character of sex and gender? Whereas Foucault is ambiguous about the precise character of the "regulatory practices" that produce the category of sex, and Wittig appears to invest the full responsibility of the construction to sexual reproduction and its instrument, compulsory heterosexuality, yet other discourses converge to produce this categorial fiction for reasons not always clear or consistent with one another. The power relations that infuse the biological sciences are not easily reduced, and the medicolegal alliance emerging in nineteenth-century Europe has spawned categorial fictions that could not be anticipated in advance. The very complexity of the discursive map that constructs gender appears to hold out the promise of an inadvertent and generative convergence of these discursive and regulatory structures. If the regulatory fictions of sex and gender are themselves multiply contested sites of meaning, then the very multiplicity of their construction holds out the possibility of a disruption of their univocal posturing.

Clearly this project does not propose to lay out within traditional philosophical terms an *ontology* of gender whereby the meaning of *being* a woman or a man is elu-cidated within the terms of phenomenology. The presumption here is that the "being" of gender is *an effect,* an object of a genealogical investigation that maps out the political parameters of its construction in the mode of ontology. To claim that gender is con-structed is not to assert its illusoriness or artificiality, where those terms are understood to reside within a binary that counterposes the "real" and the "authentic" as oppositional. As a genealogy of gender ontology, this inquiry seeks to understand the discursive production of the plausibility of that binary relation and to suggest that certain cultural configurations of gender take the place of "the real" and consolidate and augment their hegemony through that felicitous self-naturalization.

If there is something right in Beauvoir's claim that one is not born, but rather *becomes* a woman, it follows that *woman* itself is a term in process, a becoming, a constructing that cannot rightfully be said to originate or to end. As an ongoing dis-cursive practice, it is open to intervention and resignification. Even when gender seems to congeal into the most reified forms, the "congealing" is itself an insistent and insidious practice, sustained and regulated by various social means. It is, for Beauvoir, never possible finally to become a woman, as if there were a *telos* that governs the process of acculturation and construction. Gender is the repeated stylization of the body, a set of repeated acts within a highly rigid regulatory frame that congeal over time to produce the appearance of substance, of a natural sort of being. A political genealogy of gender ontologies, if it is successful, will deconstruct the substantive appearance of gender into its constitutive acts and locate and account for those acts within the compulsory frames set by the various forces that police the social appearance of gender. . . .

KWAME ANTHONY APPIAH

Selection from *In My Father's House*
1992

Almost everyone now agrees that races do not exist, yet the word "race" is still used to refer to what are said to be socially constructed groups. Black people, for example, are commonly called a "race" rather than an ethnic group because they have shared a social destiny affected by prejudicial ideas now discarded by science. The notion of race was originally developed to refer to deeply structural traits presumed to be immutable, as in the old figure of speech, "the leopard cannot change his spots." Yet now we rely upon the word to denote something virtually antithetical: an identity created not by biology but by social conduct, and conduct we take to be not only changeable, but demanding of change, namely, the conduct that mistreats an individual because of such physical marks of descent as skin color and shape of the face. Thus "race," which once meant the least changable, most "natural" of a person's characteristics, now refers to the end product of a contingent process of social behavior.

In the context of this remarkable linguistic transformation, the Harvard philosopher Kwame Anthony Appiah (1954–) produced the searching critique of the concept of race reprinted here. Appiah's starting point is the work of W.E.B. Du Bois, which he criticizes sympathetically before summarizing the current state of scientific opinion. Appiah then returns to Du Bois, arguing that Du Bois did not complete the logic of his own arguments against racial thinking. Appiah himself carries this logic to what he regards as its proper conclusion, the repudiation, once and for all, of "race" as a term of human difference.

Appiah refers to distinctions made in an earlier chapter of the book from which this selection is taken, *In My Father's House*. Appiah had distinguished between "racialism," "intrinsic racism," and "extrinsic racism." The first is the view that humans have "heritable characteristics" by which they can be divided into groups all members of which "share certain traits and tendencies with each other" not shared "with members of any other race." This "racialism," which Appiah believes false, is presupposed by both "extrinsic" and "intrinsic" racism. The "extrinsic" racist justifies treating members of given races differently on account of the characteristics believed to be essential to a given race. For example, when Jews are said to be avaricious, or blacks lacking in intelligence, an extrinsic racist will regard these claims as a warrant for discriminating on the basis of race. An "intrinsic" racist, by contrast, prefers one person to another simply because one is of the same race with that person, regardless of the traits said to be characteristic of that race. For an intrinsic racist, then, no amount of evidence that other races are as virtuous as one's own can change the initial preference for one's own kind over members of a different race.

Appiah himself is the product of "racial" mixing and a proponent of multiple identities. He is the son of an Englishwoman and of her husband, the late Joe Appiah, an African political leader who knew Du Bois and who was once the comrade and then the imprisoned enemy of Kwame Nkrumah. In an early section of *In My Father's House,* Kwame Anthony Appiah describes his father's multiple identities "as an Asante, as a Ghanaian, as an African, and as a Christian and a Methodist," and observes of himself: "now that my sisters have married a Norwegian and a Nigerian and a Ghanaian, and now that I live in America, I am used to seeing the world as a network of points of affinity." His other works include *Assertions and Conditionals* (1985) and *Necessary Questions* (1989).

In the latter nineteenth century most thinking people (like many even today) believed that what Du Bois called the "grosser differences" were a sign of an inherited racial essence, which accounted for the intellectual and moral deficiency of the "lower" races. In "The Conservation of Races" Du Bois elected, in effect, to admit that color was a sign of a racial essence but to deny that the cultural capacities of the black-skinned, curly-haired members of humankind—the capacities determined by their essence—were inferior to those of the white-skinned, straighter-haired ones. But the collapse of the sciences of racial inferiority led Du Bois to repudiate the connection between cultural capacity and gross morphology, to deny the familiar "impulses and strivings" of his earlier definition. We can find evidence of this change of mind in an article in the August 1911 issue of *The Crisis,* the journal of the American National Association for the Advancement of Colored People, which he edited vigorously through most of the early years of the century.

> The leading scientists of the world have come forward . . . and laid down in categorical terms a series of propositions which may be summarized as follows:
> 1. (a) It is not legitimate to argue from differences in physical characteristics to differences in mental characteristics. . . .
> 2. The civilization of a . . . race at any particular moment of time offers no index to its innate or inherited capacities.

The results have been amply confirmed since then. And we do well, I think, to remind ourselves of the current picture.

The evidence in the contemporary biological literature is, at first glance, misleading. For despite a widespread scientific consensus on the underlying genetics, contemporary biologists are not agreed on the question whether there are any human races. Yet, for our purposes, we can reasonably regard this issue as terminological. What most people in most cultures ordinarily believe about the significance of "racial" difference is quite remote from what the biologists *are* agreed on, and, in particular, it is not consistent with what, in the last essay, I called *racialism.* Every reputable biologist will agree that human genetic variability between the populations of Africa or Europe or Asia is not much greater than that within those populations, though how much greater depends, in part, on the measure of genetic variability the biologist chooses. If biologists want to make interracial difference seem relatively large, they can say that "the proportion of genic variation attributable to racial difference is . . . 9–11%." If they want to make it seem small, they can say that, for two people who are both "Caucasoid," the chances of differing in genetic constitution at one site on a given chromosome have recently been estimated at about 14.3 percent, while for any two people taken at random from the human population the same calculations suggest a figure of about 14.8 percent. The underlying statistical facts about the distribution of variant characteristics in human populations and subpopulations are the same, whichever way you express the matter. Apart from the visible morphological characteristics of skin, hair, and bone, by which we are inclined to assign people to the broadest racial categories—black, white, yellow— there are few genetic characteristics to be found in the population of England that are not found in similar proportions in Zaire or in China, and few too (though more) that

Source: Kwame Anthony Appiah, *In My Father's House: Africa in the Philosophy of Culture* (New York, 1992), 34–45. Reprinted with the permission of Oxford University Press.

are found in Zaire but not in similar proportions in China or in England. All this, I repeat, is part of the consensus.

A more familiar part of the consensus is that the differences between peoples in language, moral affections, aesthetic attitudes, or political ideology—those differences that most deeply affect us in our dealings with each other—are not to any significant degree biologically determined.

This claim will, no doubt, seem outrageous to those who confuse the question whether biological difference accounts for our differences with the question whether biological similarity accounts for our similarities. Some of our similarities as human beings in these broadly cultural respects—the capacity to acquire human languages, for example, or the ability to smile—*are* to a significant degree biologically determined. We can study the biological basis of these cultural capacities, and give biological explanations of features of our exercise of them. But if biological difference between human beings is unimportant in these explanations—and it is—then racial difference, as a species of biological difference, will not matter either. We can see why if we attend to the underlying genetics.

Human characteristics are genetically determined, to the extent that they are determined, by sequences of DNA in the chromosome—in other words, by genes. A region of a chromosome occupied by a gene is called a *locus*. Some loci are occupied in different members of a population by different genes, each of which is called an *allele;* and a locus is said to be *polymorphic* in a population if there is at least a pair of alleles for it. Perhaps as many as half the loci in the human population are polymorphic; the rest, naturally enough, are said to be *monomorphic*.

Many loci have not just two alleles but several, and each has a frequency in the population. Suppose a particular locus has n alleles, which we can just call 1, 2, and so on up to n; then we can call the frequencies of these alleles $x_1, x_2, \ldots, x_n$. If you consider two members of a population chosen at random and look at the same locus on one chromosome of each of them, the probability that they will have the same allele at that locus is just the probability that they will both have the first allele (x_1^2), plus the probability that they'll both have the second (x_2^2) . . . plus the probability that they will both have the nth (x_n^2). We can call this number the *expected homozygosity* at that locus, for it is just the proportion of people in the population who would be homozygous at that locus—having identical alleles at that locus on each of the relevant chromosomes—provided the population was mating at random.

Now if we take the average value of the expected homozygosity for all loci, polymorphic and monomorphic (which geneticists tend to label *J*), we have a measure of the chance that two people, taken at random from the population, will share the same allele at a locus on a chromosome taken at random. This is a good measure of how similar a randomly chosen pair of individuals should be expected to be in their biology, *and* a good guide to how closely—on the average—the members of the population are genetically related.

I can now express simply one measure of the extent to which members of those human populations we call races differ more from each other than they do from members of the same race. For the value of J for "Caucasoids"—estimated, in fact, largely from samples of the English population—is estimated to be about 0.857, while that for the whole human population is estimated at 0.852. The chances, in other words, that two people taken at random from the human population will have the same characteristic at a random locus are about 85.2 percent, while the chances for two (white) people taken from the population of England are about 85.7 percent. And since 85.2 is 100 minus 14.8, and 85.7 is 100 minus 14.3, this is equivalent to what I said previously: the chances of two people who are both "Caucasoid" differing in genetic constitution at one site on a given chromosome are about 14.3 percent, while, for any two people taken at random from the human population, they are about 14.8 percent.

The conclusion is obvious: given only a person's race, it is hard to say what his or her biological characteristics (apart from those that human beings share) will be, except in respect of the "grosser" features of color, hair, and bone (the genetics of which is, in any case, rather poorly understood)—features of "morphological differentiation," as the evolutionary biologist would say. As Nei and Roychoudhury express themselves, somewhat coyly, "The extent of genic differentiation between human races is not always correlated with the degree of morphological differentiation." This may seem relatively untroubling to committed racialists. Race, they might say, is at least important in predicting morphological difference. But that, though true, is not a biological fact but a logical one, for Nei and Roychoudhury's races are defined by their morphology in the first place. The criterion for excluding from an American "Caucasoid" sample people with black skins is just the "gross" morphological fact that their skins are black. But recent immigrants of eastern European ancestry would be included in the sample, while dark-skinned people whose ancestors for the last ten generations had largely lived in the New World would be excluded.

To establish that this notion of race is relatively unimportant in explaining biological differences between people, where biological difference is measured in the proportion of differences in loci on the chromosome, is not yet to show that race is unimportant in explaining cultural difference. It could be that large differences in intellectual or moral capacity are caused by differences at very few loci, and that at these loci, all (or most) black-skinned people differ from all (or most) white-skinned or yellow-skinned ones. As it happens, there is little evidence for any such proposition and much against it. But suppose we had reason to believe it. In the biological conception of the human organism, in which characteristics are determined by the pattern of genes in interaction with environments, it is the presence of the alleles (which give rise to these moral and intellectual capacities) that accounts for the observed differences in those capacities in people in similar environments. So the characteristic racial morphology—skin and hair and bone—could be a sign of those differences only if it were (highly) correlated with those alleles. Since there are no such strong correlations, even those who think that intellectual and moral character are strongly genetically determined must accept that *race* is at best a poor indicator of capacity.

When I defined *racialism* in Chapter 1, I said that it was committed not just to the view that there are heritable characteristics, which constitute "a sort of racial essence," but also to the claim that the essential heritable characteristics account for more than the visible morphology—skin color, hair type, facial features—on the basis of which we make our informal classifications. To say that biological races existed because it was possible to classify people into a small number of classes according to their gross morphology would be to save racialism in the letter but lose it in the substance. The notion of race that was recovered would be of no biological interest—the interesting biological generalizations are about genotypes, phenotypes, and their distribution in geographical populations. We could just as well classify people according to whether or not they were redheaded, or redheaded and freckled, or redheaded, freckled, and broad-nosed too, but nobody claims that this sort of classification is central to human biology.

There are relatively straightforward reasons for thinking that large parts of humanity will fit into no class of people who can be characterized as sharing not only a common superficial morphology but also significant other biological characteristics. The nineteenth-century dispute between monogenesis and polygenesis, between the view that we are descended from one original population and the view that we descend from several, is over. There is no doubt that all human beings descend from an original population (probably, as it happens, in Africa), and that from there people radiated out to cover the habitable globe. Conventional evolutionary theory would predict that as these populations moved into different environments and new characters were thrown up by mutation, some differences would emerge as different characteristics gave better chances of reproduction and survival. In a situation where a group of people was isolated genetically for many generations, significant differences between populations could build up, though it would take a very extended period before the differences led to reproductive isolation—the impossibility of fertile breeding—and thus to the origin of a new pair of distinct species. We know that there is no such reproductive isolation between human populations, as a walk down any street in New York or Paris or Rio will confirm, but we also know that none of the major human population groups have been reproductively isolated for very many generations. If I may be excused what will sound like a euphemism, at the margins there is always the exchange of genes.

Not only has there always been some degree of genetic linkage of this marginal kind; human history contains continued large-scale movements of people—the "hordes" of Attila the Hun, the Mediterranean jihads of the newly Islamized Arabs, the Bantu migrations—that represent possibilities for genetic exchange. As a consequence, all human populations are linked to each other through neighboring populations, *their* neighbors, and so on. We might have ended up as a "ring species," like the gulls of the *Larus argentatus* and *Larus fuscus* groups that circumscribe the North Pole, where there is inbreeding between most neighboring populations but reproductive isolation of the varieties that form the beginning and end of the chain of variation, but we did not.

The classification of people into "races" would be biologically interesting if both the margins and the migrations had not left behind a genetic trail. But they have, and along that trail are millions of us (the numbers obviously depending on the criteria of classification that are used) who can be fitted into no plausible scheme at all. In a sense, trying to classify people into a few races is like trying to classify books in a library: you may use a single property—size, say—but you will get a useless classification, or you may use a more complex system of interconnected criteria, and then you will get a good deal of arbitrariness. No one—not even the most compulsive librarian!—thinks that book classifications reflect deep facts about books. Each of them is more or less useless for various purposes; all of them, as we know, have the kind of rough edges that take a while to get around. And nobody thinks that a library classification can settle which books we should value; the numbers in the Dewey decimal system do not correspond with qualities of utility or interest or literary merit.

The appeal of race as a classificatory notion provides us with an instance of a familiar pattern in the history of science. In the early phases of theory, scientists begin, inevitably, with the categories of their folk theories of the world, and often the criteria of membership of these categories can be detected with the unaided senses. Thus, in early chemistry, color and taste played an important role in the classification of substances; in early natural history, plant and animal species were identified largely by their gross visible morphology. Gradually, as the science develops, however, concepts are developed whose application requires more than the unaided senses; instead of the phenomenal properties of things, we look for "deeper," more theoretical properties. The price we pay is that classification becomes a more specialized activity; the benefit we gain is that we are able to make generalizations of greater power and scope. Few candidates for laws of nature can be stated by reference to the colors, tastes, smells, or touches of objects. It is hard for us to accept that the colors of objects, which play so important a role in our visual experience and our recognition of everyday objects, turn out neither to play an important part in the behavior of matter nor to be correlated with properties that do. Brown, for example, a color whose absence would make a radical difference to the look of the natural world, is hard to correlate in any clear way with the physical properties of reflecting surfaces.

This desire to save the phenomena of our experience by way of objects and properties that are hidden from our direct view is, of course, a crucial feature of the natural sciences. At the heart of this project, as Heisenberg—one of the greatest physicists of our and any time—once pointed out, is a principle that he ascribed to Democritus:

> Democritus' atomic theory . . . realizes that it is impossible to explain rationally the perceptible qualities of matter except by tracing these back to the behaviour of entities which themselves no longer possess these qualities. If atoms are really to explain the origin of colour and smell of visible material bodies, then they cannot possess properties like colour and smell.

The explanation of the phenotypes of organisms in terms of their genotypes fits well into this Democritean pattern. In the same way, nineteenth-century race science sought in a heritable racial essence an explanation of what its proponents took to be the observed phenomena of the differential distribution in human populations both of morphological and of psychological and social traits. What modern genetics shows is that there is no such underlying racial essence. There was nothing wrong with the Democritean impulse, only with the particular form it took and the prejudices that informed— perhaps one should say "deformed"—the theorists' views of the phenomena.

The disappearance of a widespread belief in the biological category of the Negro would leave nothing for racists to have an attitude toward. But it would offer, by itself, no guarantee that Africans would escape from the stigma of centuries. Extrinsic racists could disappear and be replaced by people who believed that the population of Africa had in its gene pool fewer of the genes that account for those human capacities that generate what is valuable in human life; fewer, that is, than in European or Asian or other populations. Putting aside the extraordinary difficulty of defining which genes these are, there is, of course, no scientific basis for this claim. A confident expression of it would therefore be evidence only of the persistence of old prejudices in new forms. But even this view would be, in one respect, an advance on extrinsic racism. For it would mean that each African would need to be judged on his or her own merits. Without some cultural information, being told that someone is of African origin gives you little basis for supposing anything much about them. Let me put the claim at its weakest: in the absence of a racial essence, there could be no guarantee that some particular person was not more gifted—in some specific respect—than any or all others in the populations of other regions.

It was earlier evidence, pointing similarly to the conclusion that "the genic variation within and between the three major races of man . . . is small compared with the intraracial variation" and that differences in morphology were not correlated strongly with intellectual and moral capacity, that led Du Bois in *The Crisis* to an explicit rejection of the claim that biological race mattered for understanding the status of the Negro:

> So far at least as intellectual and moral aptitudes are concerned we ought to speak of civilizations where we now speak of races. . . . Indeed, even the physical characteristics, excluding the skin color of a people, are to no small extent the direct result of the physical and social environment under which it is living. . . . These physical characteristics are furthermore too indefinite and elusive to serve as a basis for any rigid classification or division of human groups.

This is straightforward enough. Yet it would be too swift a conclusion to suppose that Du Bois here expresses his deepest convictions. After 1911 he went on to advocate Pan-Africanism, as he had advocated Pan-Negroism in 1897, and whatever African-Americans and Africans, from Asante to Zulu, share, it is not a single civilization.

Du Bois managed to maintain Pan-Africanism while officially rejecting talk of race as anything other than a synonym for color. We can see how he did this if we turn to his second autobiography, *Dusk of Dawn*, published in 1940.

In *Dusk of Dawn*—the "essay toward the autobiography of a race concept"—Du Bois explicitly allies himself with the claim that race is not a "scientific" concept.

> It is easy to see that scientific definition of race is impossible; it is easy to prove that physical characteristics are not so inherited as to make it possible to divide the world into races; that ability is the monopoly of no known aristocracy; that the possibilities of human development cannot be circumscribed by color, nationality or any conceivable definition of race.

But we need no scientific definition, for

> All this has nothing to do with the plain fact that throughout the world today organized groups of men by monopoly of economic and physical power, legal enactment and intellectual training are limiting with determination and unflagging zeal the development of other groups; and that the concentration particularly of economic power today puts the majority of mankind into a slavery to the rest.

Or, as he puts it pithily a little later, "the black man is a person who must ride 'Jim Crow' in Georgia."

Yet, just a few pages earlier, he has explained why he remains a Pan-Africanist, committed to a political program that binds all this indefinable black race together. This passage is worth citing extensively.

Du Bois begins with Countee Cullen's question—What is Africa to me?—and replies:

> Once I should have answered the question simply: I should have said "fatherland" or perhaps better "motherland" because I was born in the century when the walls of race were clear and straight; when the world consisted of mut[u]ally exclusive races; and even though the edges might be blurred, there was no question of exact definition and understanding of the meaning of the word. . . .
>
> Since [the writing of "The Conservation of Races"] the concept of race has so changed and presented so much of contradiction that as I face Africa I ask myself: what is it between us that constitutes a tie which I can feel better than I can explain?

Africa is of course my fatherland. Yet neither my father nor my father's father ever saw Africa or knew its meaning or cared overmuch for it. My mother's folk were closer and yet their direct connection, in culture and race, became tenuous; still my tie to Africa is strong. On this vast continent were born and lived a large portion of my direct ancestors going back a thousand years or more. The mark of their heritage is upon me in color and hair. These are obvious things, but of little meaning in themselves; only important as they stand for real and more subtle differences from other men. Whether they do or not, I do not know nor does science know today.

But one thing is sure and that is the fact that since the fifteenth century these ancestors of mine and their descendants have had a common history; have suffered a common disaster and have one long memory. The actual ties of heritage between the individuals of this group vary with the ancestors that they have in common with many others: Europeans and Semites, perhaps Mongolians, certainly American Indians. But the physical bond is least and the badge of color relatively unimportant save as a badge; the real essence of this kinship is its social heritage of slavery; the discrimination and insult; and this heritage binds together not simply the children of Africa, but extends through yellow Asia and into the South Seas. It is this unity that draws me to Africa.

This passage is affecting, powerfully expressed. We should like to be able to follow it in its conclusions. But, since it seduces us into error, we should begin distancing ourselves from the appeal of its argument. . . . Color and hair are unimportant save "as they stand for real and more subtle differences," Du Bois says here, and we recall the "subtle forces" that "have generally followed the natural cleavage of common blood, descent and physical peculiarities" of "The Conservation of Races." There it was an essential part of the argument that these subtle forces—impulses and strivings—were the common property of those who shared a "common blood"; here, Du Bois does "not know nor does science" whether this is so. But if it is not so, then, on Du Bois's own admission, these "obvious things" are "of little meaning." And if they are of little meaning, then his mention of them marks, on the surface of his argument, the extent to which he cannot quite escape the appeal of the earlier conception of race.

Du Bois's yearning for the earlier conception that he has now prohibited himself accounts for the pathos of the chasm between the unconfident certainty that Africa is "of course" his fatherland and the concession that it is not the land of his father or his father's father. What use is such a fatherland? What use is a motherland with which even your mother's connection is "tenuous"? What does it matter that a large portion of his ancestors have lived on that vast continent, if there is no subtler bond with them than brute—that is, culturally unmediated—biological descent and its entailed "badge" of hair and color?

Even in the passage that follows his explicit disavowal of the scientific conception of race, the references to "common history"—the "one long memory," the "social heritage of slavery"—only lead us back into the now-familiar move to substitute for the biological conception of race a sociohistorical one. And that, as we have seen, is simply to bury the biological conception below the surface, not to transcend it. Because he never truly "speaks of civilization," Du Bois cannot ask if there is not in American culture—which undoubtedly *is* his—an African residue to take hold of and rejoice in, a subtle connection mediated not by genetics but by intentions, by meaning. Du Bois has no more conceptual resources here for explicating the unity of the Negro race— the Pan-African identity—than he had in "The Conservation of Races" half a century earlier. A glorious non sequitur must be submerged in the depths of the argument. It is easily brought to the surface.

If what Du Bois has in common with Africa is a history of "discrimination and insult," then this binds him, on his own account, to "yellow Asia and . . . the South Seas" also. How can something he shares with the whole nonwhite world bind him to a part of it? Once we interrogate the argument here, a further suspicion arises that the claim to this bond is based on a hyperbolic reading of the facts. The "discrimination and insult" that we know Du Bois experienced in his American childhood and as an adult citizen of the industrialized world were different in character from that experienced by, say, Kwame Nkrumah in colonized West Africa, and were absent altogether in large parts of "yellow Asia." What Du Bois shares with the nonwhite world is not insult but the *badge* of insult, and the badge, without the insult, is just the very skin and hair and bone that it is impossible to connect with a scientific definition of race.

Du Bois's question deserves a more careful answer than he gives it. What *does* cement together people who share a characteristic—the "badge of insult"—on the basis of which some of them have suffered discrimination? We might answer: "Just that; so there is certainly something that the nonwhite people of the world share." But if we go on to ask what harm exactly a young woman in Mali suffers from antiblack race prejudice in Paris, this answer misses all the important details. She *does* suffer, of course, because, for example, political decisions about North-South relations are strongly affected by racism in the metropolitan cultures of the North. But this harm is more systemic, less personal, than the affront to individual dignity represented by racist insults in the postindustrial city. If she is an intellectual, reflecting on the cultures of the North, she may also feel the meditated sense of insult: she may know, after all, that if she were there, in Paris, she would risk being subjected to some of the same discriminations; she may recognize that racism is part of the reason why she could not get a visa to go there; why she would not have a good time if she did.

Such thoughts are certainly maddening, as African and African-American and black European intellectuals will avow, if you ask them how they feel about the racist immigration policies of Europe or the institutionalized racism of apartheid. And they are thoughts that can be had by any nonwhite person anywhere who knows—in a phrase of Chinua Achebe's—"how the world is moving." The thought that if *I* were there now, I would be a victim strikes at you differently, it seems to me, from the thought—which can enrage any decent white human being—that if I were there and *if I were not white,* I would be a victim. Yet we should always remember that this thought, too, has led many to an identification with the struggle against racism.

The lesson, I think, of these reflections must be that there is no one answer to the question what identifications our antiracism may lead us into. Du Bois writes as if he has to choose between Africa, on the one hand, and "yellow Asia and . . . the South Seas," on the other. But that, it seems to me, is just the choice that racism imposes on us—and just the choice we must reject.

I made the claim in Chapter 1 that there are substantial affinities between the racial doctrines of Pan-Africanism and other forms of nationalism rooted in the nineteenth century, in particular, with Zionism. Since we cannot forget what has been done to Jews in the name of race in this century, this claim is bound to invite controversy. I make it only to insist on the ways in which the Pan-Africanism of the African-American creators of black nationalist rhetoric was not untypical of European and American thought of its day, even of the rhetoric of the victims of racism. With Du Bois's position laid out before us, the comparison can be more substantially articulated.

But, given the sensitivity of the issue, I am bound to begin with caveats. It is no part of my brief to argue that Zionism has to be racialist—not the least because, as I shall be arguing finally, the Pan-Africanist impetus can also be given a nonracialist foundation. Nor is it my intention to argue for the claim that the origins of modern Zionism are *essentially* racialist, or that racialism is central to the thought of all the founders of modern Zionism. It seems to me, as I have said, that Judaism—the religion—and the wider body of Jewish practice through which the various communities of the Diaspora have defined themselves allow for a cultural conception of Jewish identity that cannot be made plausible in the case of Pan-Africanism. As evidence of this fact, I would simply cite the way that the fifty or so rather disparate African nationalities in our present world seem to have met the nationalist impulses of many Africans, while Zionism has, of necessity, been satisfied by the creation of a single state.

But despite these differences, it is important to be clear that there were Jewish racialists in the early story of modern Zionism; that they were not marginal figures or fringe madmen; and that they, like Crummell and, later, Du Bois, developed a nationalism rooted in nineteenth-century theories of race. It is important in the practical world of politics because a racialized Zionism continues to be one of the threats to the moral stability of Israeli nationalism; as witness the politics of the late Rabbi Meir Kahane. But it is theoretically important to my argument, because, as I say, it is central to my view that Crummell's inchoate *theoria,* which Du Bois turned to organized theory, was thoroughly conventional.

Now, of course, to establish that Crummell's view was conventional, we should need no more than to cite the historical writings of the first academic historians in the United States, with their charming fantasies of Puritan democracy as part of a continuous tradition derived from the Anglo-Saxon moot, or the works of British Anglo-Saxon historiography, which traced the evolution of British institutions back to Tacitus's Teutonic hordes. . . . But *that* comparison would leave out part of what is so fascinating about the thought of these early nationalists. For, however anachronistic our reaction, our surprise at Crummell and those of his Zionist contemporaries that shared his racialized vision is that they, as victims of racism, endorsed racialist theories.

So that when we read "The Ethics of Zionism" by Horace M. Kallen, published in the *Maccabaean* in New York in August 1906, we may feel the same no-doubt-anachronistic astonishment. Kallen's essay was based on a lecture he had given to a gathering of an American Zionist organization (the *Maccabaean* was its official publication). He says: "It is the race and not the man who, in the greater account of human destiny, struggles, survives or dies, and types of civilization have always reflected the natural character of the dominant races." And we remember Du Bois's "the history of the world is the history, not of individuals . . . but of races." He asks: "What then has the Jew done for civilization? What is his place in the evolution of the human race? What is his moral worth to humanity?" And we are reminded of Du Bois's races each "struggling . . . to develop for civilization its particular message."

There are, of course, instructive differences between Kallen's "ethics" and Du Bois's. Part of the historical divergence between African-American and Jewish-American conceptions of identity is revealed when Kallen explicitly rejects a religious or cultural conception of Jewish identity:

Here is an intensely united people of relatively unmixed blood, and intense race consciousness, sojourning in all parts of the earth, in some manner successfully, and the natural object of hatred of those among whom it lives. To avoid the effect of this hatred many of the race have tried to eliminate all resemblances between themselves and it. Their languages are as various as the countries in which they live; they proclaim their nationalities as Russian, English, French, Austrian, or American and relegate their racial character to a sectarian label. "We", they say, "are not Jews but Judaists.["]

... our duty i[s] to Judaize the Jew.

For this argument presupposes as its antagonist a purely cultural nationalism of a kind that was to develop fully among African-Americans only later. Kallen saw "Cultur-Zionism" of this sort as not "much better than assimilation," which, of course, he actively opposed also. But this resistance to assimilation could not be part of Du Bois's position, either: assimilation, which some took to be a possibility for a brief moment after the American Civil War, did not become more than a theoretical possibility again—save for the few African-Americans who could "pass for white"—until after the civil rights movement, and then, of course, it was largely rejected in favor of a cultural nationalism of *Roots*.

Nevertheless, mutatis mutandis, the operative ideology here is recognizably Du Bois's; American Jewish nationalism—at least in *this* manifestation—and American black nationalism are (unsurprisingly) part of the same scheme of things.

If Du Bois's race concept seems an all-too-American creation, its traces in African rhetoric are legion. When Kwame Nkrumah addressed the Gold Coast Parliament in presenting the "motion of destiny" accepting the independence constitution, he spoke these words:

Honourable Members ... The eyes and ears of the world are upon you; yea, our oppressed brothers throughout this vast continent of Africa and the New World are looking to you with desperate hope, as an inspiration to continue their grim fight against cruelties which we in this corner of Africa have never known—cruelties which are a disgrace to humanity, and to the civilisation which the white man has set himself to teach us.

To a person unencumbered with the baggage of the history of the idea of race, it would surely seem strange that the independence of one nation of black men and women should resonate more with black people than with other oppressed people; strange too that it should be the whiteness of the oppressors—"the white man"—as opposed, say, to their *imperialism,* that should stand out. It should seem a strange idea, even to those of us who live in a world formed by racial ideology, that your freedom from cruelties I have never known should spur me on in my fight for freedom *because we are of the same color*. Yet Du Bois died in Nkrumah's Ghana, led there by the dream of Pan-Africanism and the reality of American racism. If he escaped that racism, he never completed the escape from race. The logic of his argument leads naturally to the final repudiation of race as a term of difference—to speaking "of civilizations where we now speak of races."

MICHAEL WALZER

"What Does It Mean to Be an 'American'?"
1990

Americans have always been quick to talk about what it means to be an American, but during some periods this topic generates an especially active discussion. This has been true since the early 1970s when a variety of ethnic and racial identities were affirmed within a spirit of multiculturalism. Although many discussants have hailed the virtues of diversity within a broad, pluralistic nation, some have worried about the Balkanization of one of the most successful multiethnic societies in the world and have resisted in the name of universalist ideals the new emphasis on descent-based affiliation. In the contribution to this debate reprinted here, the political theorist Michael Walzer (1935–) points to the "negotiated" character of American nationality and to the "radically unfinished" state of American society. In an argument reminiscent in some respects of Randolph Bourne's "Trans-National America," Walzer takes a generous view of the "hyphen" in "Irish-American," "African-American," and so on and hopes that the hyphen can be treated more like a "plus sign" than a dividing line within the self. Of the many other probing discussions of these issues, one cited by Walzer is worthy of special attention: Philip Gleason, "American Identity and Americanization," in Stephen Thernstrom, ed., *The Harvard Encyclopedia of American Ethnic Groups* (Cambridge, Mass., 1980), 31–58. The process of ethnic affiliation in America is the subject of several provocative essays in Werner Sollors, ed., *The Invention of Ethnicity* (New York, 1989). Sollors is also the author of one of the most influential theoretical discussions of ethno-racial identity in the United States, *Beyond Ethnicity: Consent and Descent in American Culture* (New York, 1986). The historical studies of John Higham, available in his *Send These to Me*, 2nd ed. (Baltimore, 1984), remain basic to any study of ethnicity and American national identity. The range of opinion about American and African-American identity among black intellectuals is displayed in a collection of essays of exceptional value, Gerald Early, ed., *Lure and Loathing: Essays on Race, Identity, and the Ambivalence of Assimilation* (New York, 1993). A useful anthology of writings about multiculturalism is David Theo Goldberg, ed., *Multiculturalism: A CriticalReader* (Cambridge, 1994). For an analysis of the multiculturalist movement in its historical context and for a critical evaluation of it, see David A. Hollinger, *Postethnic America: Beyond Multiculturalism* (New York, 1995).

Walzer himself has written a number of acclaimed works of political theory, including *Just and Unjust Wars* (New York, 1977), and *Spheres of Justice: A Defense of Pluralism and Equality* (New York, 1983). For a critique of Walzer's ideas in relation to contemporary debates about nationalism in general and American nationality in particular, see Kenneth Cmiel, "The Fate of the Nation and the Withering of the State," *American Literary History* (Spring 1996), 184–202.

There is no country called America. We live in the United States *of America,* and we have appropriated the adjective "American" even though we can claim no exclusive title to it. Canadians, and Mexicans are also Americans, but they have adjectives more obviously their own, and we have none. Words like "unitarian" and "unionist" won't do; our sense of ourselves is not captured by the mere fact of our union, however important that is. Nor will "statist," even "united statist," serve our purposes; a good many of the citizens of the United States are antistatist. Other countries, wrote the "American" political theorist Horace Kallen, get their names from the people, or from one of the peoples, who inhabit them. "The United States, on the other hand, has a peculiar anonymity." It is a name that doesn't even pretend to tell us who lives here. Anybody can live here, and just about everybody does—men and women from all the world's peoples. (The *Harvard Encyclopedia of American Ethnic Groups* begins with Acadians and Afghans and ends with Zoroastrians.) It is peculiarly easy to become an American. The adjective provides no reliable information about the origins, histories, connections, or cultures of those whom it designates. What does it say, then, about their political allegiance?

American politicians engage periodically in a fierce competition to demonstrate their patriotism. This is an odd competition, surely, for in most countries the patriotism of politicians is not an issue. There are other issues, and this question of political identification and commitment rarely comes up; loyalty to the *patrie,* the fatherland (or motherland), is simply assumed. Perhaps it isn't assumed here because the United States isn't a *patrie.* Americans have never spoken of their country as a fatherland (or a motherland). The kind of natural or organic loyalty that we (rightly or wrongly) recognize in families doesn't seem to be a feature of our politics. When American politicians invoke the metaphor of family they are usually making an argument about our mutual responsibilities and welfarist obligations, and among Americans, that is a controversial argument. One can be an American patriot without believing in the mutual responsibilities of American citizens—indeed, for some Americans disbelief is a measure of one's patriotism.

Similarly, the United States isn't a "homeland" (where a national family might dwell), not, at least, as other countries are, in casual conversation and unreflective feeling. It is a country of immigrants who, however grateful they are for this new place, still remember the old places. And their children know, if only intermittently, that they have roots elsewhere. They, no doubt, are native grown, but some awkward sense of newness here, or of distant oldness, keeps the tongue from calling this land "home." The older political uses of the word "home," common in Great Britain, have never taken root here: home counties, home station, Home Office, home rule. To be "at home" in America is a personal matter: Americans have homesteads and homefolks and hometowns, and each of these is an endlessly interesting topic of conversation. But they don't have much to say about a common or communal home.

Nor is there a common *patrie,* but rather many different ones—a multitude of fatherlands (and motherlands). For the children, even the grandchildren, of the immigrant generation, one's *patrie,* the "native land of one's ancestors," is somewhere else. The term "Native Americans" designates the very first immigrants, who got here centuries before any of the others. At what point do the rest of us, native grown, become

Source: *Social Research* 57 (Fall 1990), 591–614. Reprinted by permission of the New School for Social Research.

natives? The question has not been decided; for the moment, however, the language of nativism is mostly missing (it has never been dominant in American public life), even when the political reality is plain to see. Alternatively, nativist language can be used against the politics of nativism, as in these lines of Horace Kallern, the theorist of an anonymous America:

> Behind [the individual] in time and tremendously in him in quality are his ancestors; around him in space are his relatives and kin, carrying in common with him the inherited organic set from a remoter common ancestry. In all these he lives and moves and has his being. They constitute his, literally, *natio*, the inwardness of his nativity.

But since there are so many "organic sets" (language is deceptive here: Kallen's antinativist nativism is cultural, not biological), none of them can rightly be called "American." Americans have no inwardness of their own; they look inward only by looking backward.

According to Kallen, the United States is less importantly a union of states than it is a union of ethnic, racial, and religious groups—a union of otherwise unrelated "natives." What is the nature of this union? The Great Seal of the United States carries the motto *E pluribus unum*, "From many, one," which seems to suggest that manyness must be left behind for the sake of oneness. Once there were many, now the many have merged or, in Israel Zangwell's classic image, been melted down into one. But the Great Seal presents a different image: the "American" eagle holds a sheaf of arrows. Here there is no merger or fusion but only a fastening, a putting together: many-in-one. Perhaps the adjective "American" describes this kind of oneness. We might say, tentatively, that it points to the citizenship, not the nativity or nationality, of the men and women it designates. It is a political adjective, and its politics is liberal in the strict sense: generous, tolerant, ample, accommodating—it allows for the survival, even the enhancement and flourishing, of manyness.

On this view, appropriately called "pluralist," the word "from" on the Great Seal is a false preposition. There is no movement from many to one, but rather a simultaneity, a coexistence—once again, many-in-one. But I don't mean to suggest a mystery here, as in the Christian conception of a God who is three-in-one. The language of pluralism is sometimes a bit mysterious—thus Kallen's description of America as a "nation of nationalities" or John Rawls's account of the liberal state as a "social union of social unions"—but it lends itself to a rational unpacking. A sheaf of arrows is not, after all, a mysterious entity. We can find analogues in the earliest forms of social organization: tribes composed of many clans, clans composed of many families. The conflicts of loyalty and obligation, inevitable products of pluralism, must arise in these cases too. And yet, they are not exact analogues of the American case, for tribes and clans lack Kallen's "anonymity." American pluralism is, as we shall see, a peculiarly modern phenomenon—not mysterious but highly complex.

In fact, the United States is not a "nation of nationalities" or a "social union of social unions." At least, the singular nation or union is not constituted by, it is not a combination or fastening together of, the plural nationalities or unions. In some sense, it includes them; it provides a framework for their coexistence; but they are not its parts. Nor are the individual states, in any significant sense, the parts that make up the United States. The parts are individual men and women. The United States is an association of citizens. Its "anonymity" consists in the fact that these citizens don't transfer their collective name to the association. It never happened that a group of people called Americans came together to form a political society called America. The people are Americans only by virtue of having come together. And whatever identity they had before becoming Americans, they retain (or, better, they are free to retain) afterward. There is, to be sure, another view of Americanization, which holds that the process requires for its success the mental erasure of all previous identities—forgetfulness or even, as one enthusiast wrote in 1918, "absolute forgetfulness." But on the pluralist view, Americans are allowed to remember who they were and to insist, also, on *what else they are.*

They are not, however, bound to the remembrance or to the insistence. Just as their ancestors escaped the old country, so they can if they choose to escape their old identities, the "inwardness" of their nativity. Kallen writes of the individual that "whatever else he changes, he cannot change his grandfather." Perhaps not; but he can call his grandfather a "greenhorn," reject his customs and convictions, give up the family name, move to a new neighborhood, adopt a new "life-style."

He doesn't become a better American by doing these things (though that is sometimes his purpose), but he may become an American simply, an American and nothing else, freeing himself from the hyphenation that pluralists regard as universal on this side, though not on the other side, of the Atlantic Ocean. But, free from hyphenation, he seems also free from ethnicity: "American" is not one of the ethnic groups recognized in the United States census. Someone who is only an American is, so far as our bureaucrats are concerned, ethnically anonymous. He has a right, however, to his anonymity; that is part of what is means to be an American.

For a long time, British-Americans thought of themselves as Americans simply— and not anonymously: they constituted, so they would have said, a new ethnicity and a new nationality, into which all later immigrants would slowly assimilate. "Americanization" was a political program designed to make sure that assimilation would not be too slow a process, at a time, indeed, when it seemed not to be a recognizable *process* at all. But though there were individuals who did their best to assimilate, that is, to adopt, at least outwardly, the mores of British-Americans, that soon ceased to be a plausible path to an "American" future. The sheer number of non-British immigrants was too great. If there was to be a new nationality, it would have to come out of the melting pot, where the heat was applied equally to all groups, the earlier immigrants as well as the most recent ones. The anonymous American was, at the turn of the century, say, a place-holder for some unknown future person who would give cultural content to the name. Meanwhile, most Americans were hyphenated Americans, more or less friendly to their grandfathers, more or less committed to their manyness. And pluralism was an alternative political program designed to legitimate this manyness and to make it permanent—which would leave those individuals who were Americans and nothing else permanently anonymous, assimilated to a cultural nonidentity.

But though these anonymous Americans were not better Americans for being or for having become anonymous, it is conceivable that they were, and are, better American *citizens.* If the manyness of America is cultural, its oneness is political, and it may be the case that men and women who are free from non-American cultures will commit themselves more fully to the American political system. Maybe cultural anonymity is the best possible grounding for American politics. From the beginning, of course, it has been the standard claim of British-Americans that their own culture is the best grounding. And there is obviously much to be said for that view. Despite the efforts of hyphenated Americans to describe liberal and democratic politics as a kind of United Way to which they have all made contributions, the genealogy of the American political system bears a close resemblance to the genealogy of the Sons and Daughters of the American Revolution—ethnic organizations if there ever were any! But this genealogy must also account for the flight across the Atlantic and the Revolutionary War. The parliamentary oligarchy of eighteenth-century Great Britain wasn't, after all, all that useful a model for America. When the ancestors of the Sons and Daughters described their political achievement as a "new order for the ages," they were celebrating a break with their own ethnic past almost as profound as that which later Americans were called upon to make. British-Americans who refused the break called themselves "Loyalists," but they were called disloyal by their opponents and treated even more harshly than hyphenated Americans from Germany, Russia, and Japan in later episodes of war and revolution.

Citizenship in the "new order" was not universally available, since blacks and women and Indians (Native Americans) were excluded, but it was never linked to a single nationality. "To be or to become an American," writes Philip Gleason, "a person did not have to be of any particular national, linguistic, religious, or ethnic background. All he had to do was to commit himself to the political ideology centered on the abstract ideals of liberty, equality, and republicanism." These abstract ideals made for a politics separated not only from religion but from culture itself or, better, from all the particular forms in which religious and national culture was, and is, expressed—hence a politics "anonymous" in Kallen's sense. Anonymity suggests autonomy too, though I don't want to claim that American politics was not qualified in important ways by British Protestantism, later by Irish Catholicism, later still by German, Italian, Polish, Jewish, African, and Hispanic religious commitments and political experience. But these qualifications never took what might be called a strong adjectival form, never became permanent or exclusive qualities of America's abstract politics and citizenship. The adjective "American" named, and still names, a politics that is relatively unqualified by religion or nationality or, alternatively, that is qualified by so many religions and nationalities as to be free from any one of them.

It is this freedom that makes it possible for America's oneness to encompass and protect its manyness. Nevertheless, the conflict between the one and the many is a pervasive feature of American life. Those Americans who attach great value to the oneness of citizenship and the centrality of political allegiance must seek to constrain the influence of cultural manyness; those who value the many must disparage the one. The conflict is evident from the earliest days of the republic, but I will begin my own account of it with the campaign to restrict immigration and naturalization in the 1850s. Commonly called "nativist" by historians, the campaign was probably closer in its politics to a Rousseauian republicanism. Anti-Irish and anti-Catholic bigotry played a large part in mobilizing support for the American (or American Republican) party, popularly called the Know-Nothings; and the political style of the party, like that of contemporary abolitionists and free-soilers, displayed many of the characteristics of Protestant moralism. But in its self-presentation, it was above all republican, more concerned about the civic virtue of the new immigrants than about their ethnic lineages, its religious critique focused on the ostensible connection between Catholicism and tyranny. The legislative program of the Know-Nothings had to do largely with questions of citizenship at the national level and of public education at the local level. In Congress, where the party had 75 representatives (and perhaps another 45 sympathizers, out of a total of 234) at the peak of its strength in 1855, it seemed more committed to restricting the suffrage than to cutting off immigration. Some of its members would have barred "paupers" from entering the United States, and others would have required an oath of allegiance from all immigrants immediately upon landing. But their energy was directed mostly toward revising the naturalization laws. It was not the elimination of manyness but its disenfranchisement that the Know-Nothings championed.

Something like this was probably the position of most American "nativists" until the last years of the nineteenth century. In 1845, when immigration rates were still fairly low, a group of "native Americans" meeting in Philadelphia declared that they would "kindly receive [all] persons who came to America, and give them every privilege except office and suffrage." I would guess that the nativist view of American blacks was roughly similar. Most of the northern Know-Nothings (the party's greatest strength was in New England) were strongly opposed to slavery, but it did not follow from that opposition that they were prepared to welcome former slaves as fellow citizens. The logic of events led to citizenship, after a bloody war, and the Know-Nothings, by then loyal Republicans, presumably supported that outcome. But the logic of republican principle, as they understood it, would have suggested some delay. Thus a resolution of the Massachusetts legislature in 1856 argued that "republican institutions were especially adapted to an educated and intelligent people, capable of *and accustomed to* self-government. Free institutions could be confined safely only to free men. . . ." The legislators went on to urge a twenty-one-year residence requirement for naturalization. Since it was intended that disenfranchised residents should nonetheless be full members of civil society, another piece of Know-Nothing legislation would have provided that any alien free white person (this came from a Mississippi senator) should be entitled after twelve months residence "to all the protection of the government, and [should] be allowed to inherit, and hold, and transmit real estate . . . in the same manner as though he were a citizen."

Civil society, then, would include a great variety of ethnic and religious and perhaps even racial groups, but the members of these groups would acquire the "inestimable" good of citizenship only after a long period of practical education (but does one learn just by watching?) in democratic virtue. Meanwhile, their children would get a formal education. Despite their name, the Know-Nothings thought that citizenship was a subject about which a great deal had to be known. Some of them wanted to make attendance in public schools compulsory, but, faced with constitutional objections, they insisted only that no public funding should go to the support of parochial schools. It is worth emphasizing that the crucial principle here was not the separation of church and state. The Know-Nothing party did not oppose sabbatarian laws. Its members believed that tax money should not be used to underwrite social manyness—not in the case of religion, obviously, but also not in the case of language and culture. Political identity, singular in form, would be publicly inculcated and defended; the plurality of social identities would have to be sustained in private.

I don't doubt that most nativists hoped that plurality would not, in fact, be sustained. They had ideas, if not sociological theories, about the connection of politics and culture—specifically, as I have said, republican politics and British Protestant culture. I don't mean to underestimate the centrality of these ideas: this was presumably the knowledge that the Know-Nothings were concealing when they claimed to know nothing. Nonetheless, the logic of their position, as of any "American" republican position, pressed toward the creation of a politics independent of all the ethnicities and religions of civil society. Otherwise too many people would be excluded; the political world would look too much like Old England and not at all like the "new order of the ages," not at all like "America." Nor could American nativists challenge ethnic and religious pluralism directly, for both were protected (as the parochial schools were protected) by the constitution to which they claimed a passionate attachment. They could only insist that passionate attachment should be the mark of all citizens—and set forth the usual arguments against the seriousness of love at first sight and in favor of long engagements. They wanted what Rousseau wanted: that citizens should find the greater share of their happiness in public (political) rather than in private (social) activities. And they were prepared to deny citizenship to men and women who seemed to them especially unlikely to do that.

No doubt, again, public happiness came easily to the nativists because they felt so entirely at home in American public life. But we should not be too quick to attribute this feeling to the carry-over of ethnic consciousness into the political sphere. For American politics in the 1850s was already so open, egalitarian, and democratic (relative to European politics) that almost anyone could feel at home in it. Precisely because the United States was no one's *national* home, its politics was universally accessible. All that was necessary in principle was ideological commitment, in practice, a good line of talk. The Irish did very well and demonstrated as conclusively as one could wish that "British" and "Protestant" were not necessary adjectives for American politics. They attached to the many, not to the one.

For this reason, the symbols and ceremonies of American citizenship could not be drawn from the political culture or history of British-Americans. Our Congress is not a Commons; Guy Fawkes Day is not an American holiday; the Magna Carta has never been one of our sacred texts. American symbols and ceremonies are culturally anonymous, invented rather than inherited, voluntaristic in style, narrowly political in content: the flag, the Pledge, the Fourth, the Constitution. It is entirely appropriate that the Know-Nothing party had its origin in the Secret Society of the Star-Spangled Banner. And it is entirely understandable that the flag and the Pledge continue, even today, to figure largely in political debate. With what reverence should the flag be treated? On what occasions must it be saluted? Should we require school children to recite the Pledge, teachers to lead the recitation? Questions like these are the tests of a political commitment that can't be assumed, because it isn't undergirded by the cultural and religious commonalities that make for mutual trust. The flag and the Pledge are, as it were, all we have. One could suggest, of course, alternative and more practical tests of loyalty—responsible participation in political life, for example. But the real historical alternative is the test proposed by the cultural pluralists: one proves one's Americanism, in their view, by living in peace with all the other "Americans," that is, by agreeing to respect social manyness rather than by pledging allegiance to the "one and indivisible" republic. And pluralists are led on by the logic of this argument to suggest that citizenship is something less than an "inestimable" good.

Good it certainly was to be an American citizen. Horace Kallen was prepared to call citizenship a "great vocation," but he clearly did not believe (in the 1910s and '20s, when he wrote his classic essays on cultural pluralism) that one could make a life there. Politics was a necessary, but not a spiritually sustaining activity. It was best understood in instrumental terms; it had to do with the arrangements that made it possible for groups of citizens to "realize and protect" their diverse cultures and "attain the excellence appropriate to their kind." These arrangements, Kallen thought, had to be democratic, and democracy required citizens of a certain sort—autonomous, self-disciplined, capable of cooperation and compromise. "Americanization" was entirely legitimate insofar as it aimed to develop these qualities; they made up Kallen's version of civic virtue, and he was willing to say that they should be common to all Americans. But, curiously perhaps, they did not touch the deeper self. "The common city-life, which depends upon like-mindedness, is not inward, corporate, and inevitable, but external, inarticulate, and incidental . . . not the expression of a homogeneity of heritage, mentality, and interest."

Hence Kallen's program: assimilation "in matters economic and political," dissimilation "in cultural consciousness." The hyphen joined these two processes in one person, so that a Jewish-American (like Kallen) was similar to other Americans in his economic and political activity, but similar only to other Jews at the deeper level of culture. It is clear that Kallen's "hyphenates," whose spiritual life is located so emphatically to the left of the hyphen, cannot derive the greater part of their happiness from their citizenship. Nor, in a sense, should they, since culture, for the cultural pluralists, is far more important than politics and promises a more complete satisfaction. Pluralists, it seems, do not make good republicans—for the same reason that republicans, Rousseau the classic example, do not make good pluralists. The two attend to different sorts of goods.

Kallen's hyphenated Americans can be attentive and conscientious citizens, but on a liberal, not a republican model. This means two things. First, the various ethnic and religious groups can intervene in political life only in order to defend themselves and advance their common interests—as in the case of the NAACP or the Anti-Defamation League—but not in order to impose their culture or their values. They have to recognize that the state is anonymous (or, in the language of contemporary political theorists, neutral) at least in this sense: that it can't take on the character or the name of any of the groups that it includes. It isn't a nation-state of a particular kind and it isn't a Christian republic. Second, the primary political commitment of individual citizens is to protect their protection, to uphold the democratic framework within which they pursue their more substantive activities. This commitment is consistent with feelings of gratitude, loyalty, even patriotism of a certain sort, but it doesn't make for fellowship. There is indeed *union* in politics (and economics) but union of a sort that precludes intimacy. "The political and economic life of the commonwealth," writes Kallen, "is a single unit and serves as the foundation and background for the realization of the distinctive individuality of each *natio*." There pluralism is straightforwardly opposed to republicanism: politics offers neither self-realization nor communion. All intensity lies, or should lie, elsewhere.

Kallen believes, of course, that this "elsewhere" actually exists; his is not a utopian vision; it's not a case of "elsewhere, perhaps." The "organic groups" that make up Kallen's America appear in public life as interest groups only, organized for the pursuit of material and social goods that are universally desired but sometimes in short supply and often unfairly distributed. That is the only appearance countenanced by a liberal and democratic political system. But behind it, concealed from public view, lies the true significance of ethnicity or religion: "It is the center at which [the individual] stands, the point of his most intimate social relations, therefore of his intensest emotional life." I am inclined to say that this is too radical a view of ethnic and religious identification, since it seems to rule out moral conflicts in which the individual's emotions are enlisted, as it were, on both sides. But Kallen's more important point is simply that there is space and opportunity *elsewhere* for the emotional satisfactions that politics can't (or shouldn't) provide. And because individuals really do find this satisfaction, the groups within which it is found are permanently sustainable: they won't melt down, not, at least, in any ordinary (noncoercive) social process. Perhaps they can be repressed, if the repression is sufficiently savage; even then, they will win out in the end.

Kallen wasn't entirely unaware of the powerful forces making for cultural melt-down, even without repression. He has some strong lines on the effectiveness of the mass media—though he knew these only in their infancy and at a time when newspapers were still a highly localized medium and the foreign-language press flourished. In his analysis and critique of the pressure to conform, he anticipated what became by the 1950s a distinctively American genre of social criticism. It isn't always clear whether he sees pluralism as a safeguard against or an antidote for the conformity of ethnic-Americans to that spiritless "Americanism" he so much disliked, a dull protective coloring that destroys all inner brightness. In any case, he is sure that inner brightness will survive, "for Nature is naturally pluralistic; her unities are eventual, not primary. . . ." Eventually, he means, the American union will prove to be a matter of "mutual accommodation," leaving intact the primacy of ethnic and religious identity. In the years since Kallen wrote, his view has gathered a great deal of ideological, but much less of empirical, support. "Pluralist principles . . . have been on the ascendancy," writes a contemporary critic of pluralism, "precisely at a time when ethnic differences have been on the wane." What if the "excellence" appropriate to our "kind" is, simply, an American excellence? Not necessarily civic virtue of the sort favored by nativists, republicans, and contemporary communitarians, but nonetheless some local color, a brightness of our own?

This local color is most visible, I suppose, in popular culture—which is entirely appropriate in the case of the world's first mass democracy. Consider, for example, the movie *American in Paris,* where the hero is an American simply and not at all an Irish- or German- or Jewish-American. Do we drop our hyphens when we travel abroad? But what are we, then, without them? We carry with us cultural artifacts of a quite specific sort: *"une danse americaine,"* Gene Kelly tells the French children as he begins to tap dance. What else could he call it, this melted-down combination of Northern English clog dancing, the Irish jig and reel, and African rhythmic foot stamping, to which had been added, by Kelly's time, the influence of the French and Russian ballet? Creativity of this sort is both explained and celebrated by those writers and thinkers, heroes of the higher culture, that we are likely to recognize as distinctively American: thus Emerson's defense of the experimental life (I am not sure, though, that he would have admired tap dancing), or Whitman's democratic inclusiveness, or the pragmatism of Peirce and James.

"An American nationality," writes Gleason, "does in fact exist." Not just a political status, backed up by a set of political symbols and ceremonies, but a full-blooded nationality, reflecting a history and a culture—exactly like all the other nationalities from which Americans have been, and continue to be, recruited. The ongoing immigration makes it difficult to see the real success of Americanization in creating distinctive types, characters, styles, artifacts of all sorts which, were Gene Kelly to display them to his Parisian neighbors, they would rightly recognize as "American." More important, Americans recognize one another, take pride in the things that fellow Americans have made and done, identify with the national community. So, while there no doubt are people plausibly called Italian-Americans or Swedish-Americans, spiritual (as well as political) life—this is Gleason's view—is lived largely to the right of the hyphen: contrasted with real Italians and real Swedes, these are real Americans.

This view seems to me both right and wrong. It is right in its denial of Kallen's account of America as an anonymous nation of named nationalities. It is wrong in its insistence that America is a nation like all the others. But the truth does not lie, where we might naturally be led to look for it, somewhere between this rightness and this wrongness—as if we could locate America at some precise point along the continuum that stretches from the many to the one. I want to take the advice of that American song, another product of the popular culture, which tells us: "Don't mess with mister in-between." If there are cultural artifacts, songs and dances, styles of life and even philosophies, that are distinctively American, there is also an idea of America that is itself distinct, incorporating oneness and manyness in a "new order" that may or may not be "for the ages" but that is certainly for us, here and now.

The cultural pluralists come closer to getting the new order right than do the nativists and the nationalists and the American communitarians. Nonetheless, there is a nation and a national community and, by now, a very large number of native Americans. Even first- and second-generation Americans, as Gleason points out, have graves to visit and homes and neighborhoods to remember *in this country,* on this side of whatever waters their ancestors crossed to get here. What is distinctive about the nationality of these Americans is not its insubstantial character—substance is quickly acquired—but its nonexclusive character. Remembering the God of the Hebrew Bible, I want to argue that America is not a jealous nation. In this sense, at least, it is different from most of the others.

Consider, for example, a classic moment in the ethnic history of France: the debate over the emancipation of the Jews in 1790 and '91. It is not, by any means, a critical moment; there were fewer than 35,000 Jews in revolutionary France, only 500 in Paris. The Jews were not economically powerful or politically significant or even intellectually engaged in French life (all that could come only after emancipation). But the debate nonetheless was long and serious, for it dealt with the meaning of citizenship and nationality. When the Constituent Assembly voted for full emancipation in September 1791, its position was summed up by Clermont–Tonnerre, a deputy of the Center, in a famous sentence: "One must refuse everything to the Jews as a nation, and give everything to the Jews as individuals.. . . . It would be repugnant to have . . . a nation within a nation." The Assembly's vote led to the disestablishment of Jewish corporate existence in France, which had been sanctioned and protected by the monarchy. "Refusing everything to the Jews as a nation" meant withdrawing the sanction, denying the protection. Henceforth Jewish communities would be voluntary associations, and individual Jews would have rights against the community as well as against the state: Clermont-Tonnerre was a good liberal.

But the Assembly debate also suggests that most of the deputies favoring emancipation would not have looked with favor even on the voluntary associations of the Jews, insofar as these reflected national sensibility or cultural difference. The future Girondin leader Brissot, defending emancipation, predicted that Jews who became French citizens would "lose their particular characteristics." I suspect that he could hardly imagine a greater triumph of French *civisme* than this—as if the secular Second Coming, like the religious version, awaited only the conversion of the Jews. Brissot thought the day was near: "Their eligibility [for citizenship] will regenerate them." Jews could be good citizens only insofar as they were regenerated, which meant, in effect, that they could be good citizens only insofar as they became French. (They must, after all, have some "particular characteristics," and if not their own, then whose?) Their emancipators had, no doubt, a generous view of their capacity to do that but would not have been generous in the face of resistance (from the Jews or from any other of the corporate groups of the old regime). The price of emancipation was assimilation.

This has been the French view of citizenship ever since. Though they have often been generous in granting the exalted status of citizen to foreigners, the successive republics have been suspicious of any form of ethnic pluralism. Each republic really has been "one and indivisible," and it has been established, as Rousseau thought it should be, on a strong national oneness. Oneness all the way down is, on this view, the only guarantee that the general will and the common good will triumph in French politics.

America is very different, and not only because of the eclipse of republicanism in the early nineteenth century. Indeed, republicanism has had a kind of afterlife as one of the legitimating ideologies of American politics. The Minute Man is a republican image of embodied citizenship. Reverence for the flag is a form of republican piety. The Pledge of Allegiance is a republican oath. But emphasis on this sort of thing reflects social disunity rather than unity; it is a straining after oneness where oneness doesn't exist. In fact, America has been, with severe but episodic exceptions, remarkably tolerant of ethnic pluralism (far less so of racial pluralism).[1] I don't want to underestimate the human difficulties of adapting even to a hyphenated Americanism, nor to deny the bigotry and discrimination that particular groups have encountered. But tolerance has been the cultural norm.

Perhaps an immigrant society has no choice; tolerance is a way of muddling through when any alternative policy would be violent and dangerous. But I would argue that we have, mostly, made the best of this necessity, so that the virtues of toleration, in principle though by no means always in practice, have supplanted the singlemindedness of republican citizenship. We have made our peace with the "particular characteristics" of all the immigrant groups (though not, again, of all the racial groups) and have come to regard American nationality as an addition to rather than a replacement for ethnic consciousness. The hyphen works, when it is working, more like a plus sign. "American," then, is a name indeed, but unlike "French" or "German" or "Italian" or "Korean" or "Japanese" or "Cambodian," it can serve as a second name. And as in those modern marriages where two patronymics are joined, neither the first nor the second name is dominant: here the hyphen works more like a sign of equality.

We might go farther than this: in the case of hyphenated Americans, it doesn't matter whether the first or the second name is dominant. We insist, most of the time,

---

1. The current demand of (some) black Americans that they be called African-Americans represents an attempt to adapt themselves to the ethnic paradigm—imitating, perhaps, the relative success of various Asian-American groups in a similar adaptation. But names are no guarantees; nor does antinativist pluralism provide sufficient protection against what is all too often an *ethnic*-American racism. It has been argued that this racism is the necessary precondition of hyphenated ethnicity: the inclusion of successive waves of ethnic immigrants is possible only because of the permanent exclusion of black Americans. But I don't know what evidence would demonstrate *necessity* here. I am inclined to reject the metaphysical belief that all inclusion entails exclusion. A historical and empirical account of the place of blacks in the "system" of American pluralism would require another paper.

that the "particular characteristics" associated with the first name be sustained, as the Know-Nothings urged, without state help—and perhaps they will prove unsustainable on those terms. Still, an ethnic American is someone who can, in principle, live his spiritual life as he chooses, *on either side of the hyphen*. In this sense, American citizenship is indeed anonymous, for it doesn't require a full commitment to American (or to any other) nationality. The distinctive national culture that Americans have created doesn't underpin, it exists alongside of, American politics. It follows, then, that the people I earlier called Americans simply, Americans and nothing else, have in fact a more complicated existence than those terms suggest. They are American-Americans, one more group of hyphenates (not quite the same as all the others), and one can imagine them attending to the cultural aspects of their Americanism and refusing the political commitment that republican ideology demands. They might still be good or bad citizens. And similarly, Orthodox Jews as well as secular (regenerate) Jews, Protestant fundamentalists as well as liberal Protestants, Irish republicans and well as Irish Democrats, black nationalists as well as black integrationists—all these can be good or bad citizens, given the American (liberal rather than republican) understanding of citizenship.

One step more is required before we have fully understood this strange America: it is not the case that Irish-Americans, say, are culturally Irish and politically American, as the pluralists claim (and as I have been assuming thus far for the sake of the argument). Rather, they are culturally Irish-American and politically Irish-American. Their culture has been significantly influenced by American culture; their politics is still, both in style and substance, significantly ethnic. With them, and with every ethnic and religious group except the American-Americans, hyphenation is doubled. It remains true, however, that what all the groups have in common is most importantly their citizenship and what most differentiates them, insofar as they are still differentiated, is their culture. Hence the alternation in American life of patriotic fevers and ethnic revivals, the first expressing a desire to heighten the commonality, the second a desire to reaffirm the difference.

At both ends of this peculiarly American alternation, the good that is defended is also exaggerated and distorted, so that pluralism itself is threatened by the sentiments it generates. The patriotic fevers are the symptoms of a republican pathology. At issue here is the all-important ideological commitment that, as Gleason says, is the sole prerequisite of American citizenship. Since citizenship isn't guaranteed by oneness all the way down, patriots or superpatriots seek to guarantee it by loyalty oaths and campaigns against "un-American" activities. The Know-Nothing party having failed to restrict naturalization, they resort instead to political purges and deportations. Ethnic revivals are less militant and less cruel, though not without their own pathology. What is at issue here is communal pride and power—a demand for political recognition without assimilation, an assertion of interest-group politics against republican ideology, an effort to distinguish this group (one's own) from all the others. American patriotism is always strained and nervous because hyphenation makes indeed for dual loyalty but seems, at the same time, entirely American. Ethnic revivalism is also strained and nervous, because the hyphenates are already Americans, on both sides of the hyphen.

In these circumstances, republicanism is a mirage, and American nationalism or communitarianism is not a plausible option; it doesn't reach to our complexity. A certain sort of communitarianism is available to each of the hyphenate groups—except, it would seem, the American-Americans, whose community, if it existed, would deny the

Americanism of all the others. So Horace Kallen is best described as a Jewish (-American) communitarian and a (Jewish-) American liberal, and this kind of coexistence, more widely realized, would constitute the pattern he called cultural pluralism. But the different ethnic and religious communities are all of them far more precarious than he thought, for they have, in a liberal political system, no corporate form or legal structure or coercive power. And, without these supports, the "inherited organic set" seems to dissipate—the population lacks cohesion, cultural life lacks coherence. The resulting "groups" are best conceived, John Higham suggests, as a core of activists and believers and an expanding periphery of passive members or followers, lost, as it were, in a wider America. At the core, the left side of the (double) hyphen is stronger; along the periphery, the right side is stronger, though never fully dominant. Americans choose, as it were, their own location; and it appears that a growing number of them are choosing to fade into the peripheral distances. They become American-Americans, though without much passion invested in the becoming. But if the core doesn't hold, it also doesn't disappear; it is still capable of periodic revival.

At the same time, continued large-scale immigration reproduces a Kallenesque pluralism, creating new groups of hyphenate Americans and encouraging revivalism among activists and believers in the old groups. America is still a radically unfinished society, and for now, at least, it makes sense to say that this unfinishedness is one of its distinctive features. The country has a political center, but it remains in every other sense decentered. More than this, the political center, despite occasional patriotic fevers, doesn't work against decentering elsewhere. It neither requires nor demands the kind of commitment that would put the legitimacy of ethnic or religious identification in doubt. It doesn't aim at a finished or fully coherent Americanism. Indeed, American politics, itself pluralist in character, *needs* a certain sort of incoherence. A radical program of Americanization would *really* be un-American. It isn't inconceivable that America will one day become an American nation-state, the many giving way to the one, but that is not what it is now; nor is that its destiny. America has no singular national destiny—and to be an "American" is, finally, to know that and to be more or less content with it.

Chronologies

The documents listed in the first column are texts often mentioned in studies of the intellectual history of the United States. The second column shows European works frequently discussed in America. The third column lists some of the significant social, cultural, and political events that took place simultaneously with the publication or production of the works listed in Columns 1 and 2.

Year	American Documents	European Documents	Political, Social, and Cultural Events
1865		J. S. Mill, *Examination of Sir William Hamilton's Philosophy*	Union victory
1866	John Greenleaf Whittier, "Snowbound"	T. H. Huxley, "On the Improving of Natural Knowledge"	
1867	Horatio Alger, *Ragged Dick*	Karl Marx, *Capital* (vol. 1)	
1868	Elizabeth Stuart Phelps, *Gates Ajar*		
1869	Harriet Beecher Stowe, *Oldtown Folks* Louisa May Alcott, *Little Women*	Matthew Arnold *Culture and Anarchy* J. S. Mill, *On the Subjugation of Women*	Transcontinental railway completed
1871	Walt Whitman, *Democratic Vistas* Lewis Henry Morgan, *Systems of Consanguinity and Affinity*	Charles Darwin, *Descent of Man*	Paris Commune

Year	American Documents	European Documents	Political, Social, and Cultural Events
1872	Charles Hodge, *Systematic Theology*		
1873	Mark Twain and C. D. Warner, *The Gilded Age*	Herbert Spencer, *Sociology*	
	Chauncy Wright, "The Evolution of Self-Consciousness"		
	Octavius B. Frothingham, *Religion of Humanity*		
	Whitelaw Reid, "The Scholar in Politics"		
1874	John Fiske, *Outlines of the Cosmic Philosophy*	John Tyndall, "Belfast Address'	
	Charles Hodge, *What Is Darwinism?*		
	John William Draper, *History of the Conflict Between Religion and Science*		
1875	Mary Baker Eddy, *Science and Health*		
1876	Mark Twain, *Tom Sawyer*		American centennial Telephone invented
	Asa Gray, *Darwiniana*		Battle of the Little Big Horn
1877	Henry James, *The American*	W. K. Clifford, "Ethics of Belief"	Great Railway Strike
	Charles S. Peirce, "Fixation of Belief"		End of Reconstruction
1878	Lewis Henry Morgan, *Ancient Society*		
	Charles S. Peirce, "How to Make Our Ideas Clear"		

Year	American Documents	European Documents	Political, Social, and Cultural Events
1879	Henry George, *Progress and Poverty* Newman Smyth, *Old Faiths in New Light* Albion Tourgee, *A Fool's Errand*		
1880	Lew Wallace, *Ben-Hur*		
1881	Oliver Wendell Holmes, Jr., *The Common Law* Joel Chandler Harris, *Uncle Remus* William Graham Sumner, "Sociology" Henry James, *Portrait of a Lady* Helen Hunt Jackson, *Century of Dishonor*		Massive immigration from eastern and southern Europe begins
1882			Edison's electric light becomes widely available
1883	Lester Frank Ward, *Dynamic Sociology* Henry A. Rowland, "A Plea for Pure Science" Charles Augustus Briggs, *Biblical Study* William Graham Sumner, *What Social Classes Owe to Each Other* Theodore Munger, *Freedom of Faith*		
1884	William Dean Howells, *The Rise of Silas Lapham*		

Year	American Documents	European Documents	Political, Social, and Cultural Events
	Lester Frank Ward, "Mind as a Social Factor"		
1885	Mark Twain, *Adventures of Huckleberry Finn*		
	Josiah Royce, *Religious Aspect of Philosophy*		
	John Fiske, *The Idea of God as Affected by Modern Knowledge*		
	Egbert C. Smyth et al., *Progressive Orthodoxy*		
1886	Henry James, *The Bostonians*	Friedrich Nietzsche, *Beyond Good and Evil*	Haymarket riot
	Henry James, *The Princess Cassimassima*		
	Josiah Strong, *Our Country*		
1887	John Dewey, *Psychology*	Friedrich Nietzsche, *Genealogy of Morals*	
	William Dean Howells, "Pernicious Fiction"	Tonnies, *Gemeinschaft und Gesellschaft*	
1888	Edward Bellamy, *Looking Backward, 2000–1887*		
	Russell Conwell, "Acres of Diamonds"		
	James McCosh, *The Religious Aspect of Evolution*		
1889	Robert Ingersoll, "Why I Am an Agnostic"	Ernst Haeckel, *Riddles of the Universe*	

Year	American Documents	European Documents	Political, Social, and Cultural Events
	Andrew Carnegie, "Gospel of Wealth"		
	Mark Twain, *Connecticut Yankee in King Arthur's Court*		
	Ignatious Donnelly, *Caesar's Column*		
	W. C. Brownell, *French Traits*		
1890	William James, *Principles of Psychology* William Dean Howells, *Hazard of New Fortunes* Jacob Riis, *How the Other Half Lives* Emily Dickinson, *Poems* (posthumous) Alfred Thayer Mahan, *Influence of Sea Power on History*	James Frazer, *Golden Bough* Villers de l'Isle Adam, *Axel* Gabriel de Tarde, *Laws of Imitation*	Massacre at Wounded Knee
1891	Hamlin Garland, *Main-Travelled Roads* Joseph LeConte, *Evolution and Its Relation to Religious Thought*		
1892	Charlotte Perkins Gilman, *The Yellow Wallpaper* Elizabeth Cady Stanton, "Solitude of Self"	Karl Pearson, *The Grammar of Science*	Populist Omaha convention
1893	Frederick Jackson Turner, "Significance of Frontier in American History"	T. H. Huxley, *Evolution and Ethics* Emile Durkheim, *Division of Labor in Society*	Chicago World's Fair

Year	American Documents	European Documents	Political, Social, and Cultural Events
	Clarence Darrow, "Realism in Literature and Art"		
	Charles S. Peirce, "Evolutionary Love"		
1894	Henry Demarest Lloyd, *Wealth Against Commonwealth*		Pullman strike
	Mark Twain, *Puddinhead Wilson*		
	Oliver Wendell Holmes, Jr., "Privilege, Malice, and Intent"		
1895	Stephen Crane, *Red Badge of Courage*		
	Booker T. Washington, "Atlanta Address"		
	Oliver Wendell Holmes, Jr., "The Soldier's Faith"		
1896	Andrew Dickson White, *The Warfare of Science with Theology in Christendom*		McKinley defeats Bryan
			Plessy v. Ferguson
	Harold Frederic, *The Damnation of Theron Ware*		
1897	William James, *The Will to Believe*		
	Charles Sheldon, *In His Steps*		
	Oliver Wendell Holmes, Jr., "Path of the Law"		

Year	American Documents	European Documents	Political, Social, and Cultural Events
1898	Charles W. Eliot, "John Gilley of Baker's Island" Josiah Royce, "The Problem of Job" Charlotte Perkins Gilman, *Women and Economics*	Rudyard Kipling, "The White Man's Burden"	Spanish–American War
1899	Thorstein Veblen, *Theory of the Leisure Class* Elbert Hubbard, "Message to Garcia" Kate Chopin, *The Awakening* Edwin Markham, "The Man with the Hoe" John Bates Clark, *Distribution of Wealth*		Dreyfus affair in France
1900	Josiah Royce, *World and Individual* Clarence Stedman, *An American Anthology* Theodore Dreiser, *Sister Carrie*	Rediscovery of Mendel's genetics Sigmund Freud, *The Interpretation of Dreams*	
1901	Frank Norris, *The Octopus* E. A. Ross, *Social Control* Booker T. Washington, *Up from Slavery* George A. Gordon, *New Epoch for Faith*	George Bernard Shaw, *Man and Superman*	

Year	American Documents	European Documents	Political, Social, and Cultural Events
1902	William James, *Varieties of Religious Experience* Jane Addams, *Democracy and Social Ethics* Owen Wister, *The Virginian* Charles Horton Cooley, *Human Nature and Social Order*	Joseph Conrad, *Heart of Darkness* Vladimir Lenin, *What Is to Be Done?* André Gide, *The Immoralist*	
1903	W.E.B. Du Bois, *Souls of Black Folk* John Dewey, *Studies in Logical Theory* Jack London, *Call of the Wild* Helen Thompson Wooley, *Mental Traits of Sex*	Bertrand Russell, *Principles of Mathematics* G. E. Moore, *Principia Ethica*	Wright brothers' first flight
1904	Henry James, *The Golden Bowl* Henry Adams, *Mt.-St. Michel and Chartres* Thorstein Veblen, *Theory of Business Enterprise*	Max Weber, *Protestant Ethic and Spirit of Capitalism*	
1905	Lincoln Steffens, *Shame of the Cities* Thomas Dixon, *The Clansman* Edith Wharton, *House of Mirth* Mary Chesnut, *A Diary from Dixie*	Einstein's special theory of relativity	
1906	Upton Sinclair, *The Jungle*		

Year	American Documents	European Documents	Political, Social, and Cultural Events
	William Graham Sumner, *Folkways*		
	Thorstein Veblen, "The Place of Science in Civilization"		
	George Santayana, *The Life of Reason*		
1907	William James, *Pragmatism*	Henri Bergson, *Creative Evolution*	
	Walter Rauschenbusch, *Christianity and the Social Crisis*		
	Henry James, *The American Scene*		
	Simon Patten, *New Basis for Civilization*		
	The Education of Henry Adams		
1908	Arthur F. Bentley, *Process of Government*	Vladimir Lenin, *Materialism and Empirico-Criticism*	
		Graham Wallas, *Human Nature and Politics*	
1909	Herbert Croly, *Promise of American Life*		
	William James, *A Pluralistic Universe*		
	W. C. Brownell, *American Prose Masters*		
1910	Jane Addams, *Twenty Years at Hull-House*	Sigmund Freud, *Origins and Development of Psychoanalysis*	
	William James, "Moral Equivalent of War"		

Year	American Documents	European Documents	Political, Social, and Cultural Events
1911	Frederick Winslow Taylor, *Principles of Scientific Management* Franz Boas, *Mind of Primitive Man*		
1912	James Harvey Robinson, *The New History* Mary Antin, *The Promised Land* Ezra Pound, *Ripostes* James Weldon Johnson, *The Autobiography of an Ex-Colored Man*	Emile Durkheim, *Elementary Forms of Religious Life*	
1913	Charles Beard, *An Economic Interpretation of the Constitution of the United States* George Santayana, "The Genteel Tradition in American Philosophy" Eleanor Hodgeman Porter, *Pollyana* Walter Lippmann, *A Preface to Politics* Josiah Royce, *Problem of Christianity* Willa Cather, *O Pioneers*	Marcel Proust, *Swann's Way* Sigmund Freud, *Totem and Taboo* Einstein's general theory of relativity	Wilson takes office Armory show
1914	Walter Lippmann, *Drift and Mastery* Louis Brandeis, *Other People's Money*		World War I begins in Europe

Year	American Documents	European Documents	Political, Social, and Cultural Events
	John D. Watson, *Behaviorism*		
1915	Van Wyck Brooks, *America's Coming-of-Age*		
	Wallace Stevens, "Sunday Morning"		
	Charlotte Perkins Gilman, *Herland*		
1916	John Dewey, *Democracy and Education*	James Joyce, *Portrait of the Artist as a Young Man*	
	Randolph Bourne, "Trans-National America"		
	Madison Grant, *The Passing of the Great Race*		
1917	Walter Rauschenbusch, *A Theology for the Social Gospel*	Vladimir Lenin, *Imperialism*	U. S. enters World War I
			Bolshevik revolution
	Randolph Bourne, "Twilight of Idols"		
	Elsie Clews Parsons, *Social Rule*		
	T. S. Eliot, *Prufrock*		
1918	Willa Cather, *My Antonia*	Lytton Strachey, *Eminent Victorians*	Armistice in Europe
	W. I. Thomas and F. Znanicki, *The Polish Peasant in Europe and America*	Oswald Spengler, *Decline of the West* (vol. 1)	
1919	Sherwood Anderson, *Winesburg, Ohio*	J. M. Keynes, *Economic Consequences of the Peace*	Versailles Treaty

Year	American Documents	European Documents	Political, Social, and Cultural Events
	John Reed, *Ten Days That Shook the World*	Max Weber, "Vocation of Science"	
	Irving Babbitt, *Rousseau and Romanticism*	Karl Barth, *Commentary on Romans*	
	T. S. Eliot, "Tradition and the Individual Talent"	H. G. Wells, *Outline of History*	
1920	Sinclair Lewis, *Main Street*		U.S. women obtain right to vote
	T. S. Eliot, *The Sacred Wood*		
	Edith Wharton, *Age of Innocence*		
	Oliver Wendell Holmes, Jr., *Collected Legal Papers*		
	John Dewey, *Reconstruction in Philosophy*		
	F. Scott Fitzgerald, *This Side of Paradise*		
	Ezra Pound, "Hugh Selwyn Mauberley"		
1921	H. L. Mencken, *Prejudices* (first series)		Radio developed
	James Harvey Robinson, *Mind in the Making*		
	Thorstein Veblen, *Engineers and the Price System*		
1922	T. S. Eliot, "The Waste Land"	James Joyce, *Ulysses*	Mussolini seizes power
	Sinclair Lewis, *Babbitt*	Ludwig Wittgenstein, *Tractatus Logico-Philosophicus*	

Year	American Documents	European Documents	Political, Social, and Cultural Events
	John Dewey, *Human Nature and Conduct* Walter Lippmann, *Public Opinion* e. e. cummings, "Enormous Room" W. F. Ogburn, *Social Change* Harold Stearns, ed., *Civilization in the United States*	Oswald Spengler, *Decline of the West* (vol. 2) W. B. Yeats, *Later Poems*	
1923	Robert Frost, *New Hampshire* Thorstein Veblen, *Absentee Ownership* Jean Toomer, *Cane*	D. H. Lawrence, *Studies in Classic American Literature*	
1924	Emma Goldman, *My Disillusionment with Russia* Herman Melville, *Billy Budd* (posthumous) Shailer Mathews, *Faith of Modernism*	Thomas Mann, *Magic Mountain*	Immigration drastically reduced
1925	F. Scott Fitzgerald, *The Great Gatsby* Sinclair Lewis, *Arrowsmith* Alfred North Whitehead, *Science and the Modern World* John Dewey, *Experience and Nature* Alain Locke, ed., *The New Negro*	Franz Kafka, *The Trial* W. B. Yeats, *A Vision* Adolf Hitler, *Mein Kampf*	Scopes trial

Year	American Documents	European Documents	Political, Social, and Cultural Events
	Charles Merriam, *New Aspects of Politics*		
	William Carlos Williams, *In the American Grain*		
	Bruce Barton, *The Man Nobody Knows*		
1926	Ernest Hemingway, *The Sun Also Rises*	Franz Kafka, *The Castle*	
	H. L. Mencken, *Notes on Democracy*	I. A. Richards, *Science and Poetry*	
	Lewis Mumford, *The Golden Day*	Pavlov, *Conditioned Reflexes*	
1927	Sinclair Lewis, *Elmer Gantry*	Virginia Woolf, *To the Lighthouse*	Lindberg's flight to Europe
	Percy C. Bridgman, *The Logic of Modern Physics*	Martin Heidegger, *Being and Time*	
	V. L. Parrington, *Main Currents in American Thought*	Heisenberg's principle of uncertainty	
	Charles and Mary Beard, *The Rise of American Civilization*		
	John Dewey, *The Public and Its Problems*		
1928	Margaret Mead, *Coming of Age in Samoa*	Arthur Eddington, *Nature of the Physical World*	
	Eugene O'Neill, *Strange Interlude*	D. H. Lawrence, *Lady Chatterley's Lover*	
1929	Joseph Wood Krutch, *Modern Temper*	Karl Mannheim, *Ideology and Utopia*	Wall Street crash

Year	American Documents	European Documents	Political, Social, and Cultural Events
	William Faulkner, *The Sound and the Fury*		
	Ernest Hemingway, *Farewell to Arms*		
	Robert and Helen Lynd, *Middletown*		
	Walter Lippmann, *Preface to Morals*		
	John Dewey, *Quest for Certainty*		
	Thomas Wolfe, *Look Homeward, Angel*		
1930	Twelve Southerners, *I'll Take My Stand*	Sigmund Freud, *Civilization and Its Discontents*	
	Jerome Frank, *Law and the Modern Mind*		
	Edith Hamilton, *The Greek Way*		
	Norman Forster, *Humanism in America*		
1931	Edmund Wilson, *Axel's Castle*	Kurt Gödel's proof of the impossibility of a complete mathematical system	Japanese invade Manchuria
	Pearl Buck, *The Good Earth*		
	Lincoln Steffens, *Autobiography*		
	Morris R. Cohen, *Reason and Nature*		
	Constance Rourke, *American Humor*		
1932	Reinhold Niebuhr, *Moral Man and Immoral Society*	Aldous Huxley, *Brave New World*	
	Adolph Berle and Gardiner Means, *Modern Corporation and Private Property*		

Year	American Documents	European Documents	Political, Social, and Cultural Events
	William Faulkner, *Light in August*		
	Carl Becker, "Everyman His Own Historian"		
	James T. Farrell, *Young Lonigan*		
	John Chamberlin, *Farewell to Reform*		
1933	Wesley Mitchell et al., *Recent Social Trends*	John Strachey, *Coming Struggle for Power*	Franklin D. Roosevelt takes office
	J.W.N. Sullivan, *Limitations of Science*	André Malraux, *Man's Fate*	Hitler comes to power
	Sidney Hook, *Toward an Understanding of Karl Marx*		
	Morris R. Cohen, *Law and the Social Order*		
1934	Ruth Benedict, *Patterns of Culture*		
	Malcolm Cowley, *Exile's Return*		
	Lewis Mumford, *Technics and Civilization*		
	Henry Roth, *Call It Sleep*		
	John Dewey, *A Common Faith*		
	John Dewey, *Art as Experience*		
	T. S. Eliot, *After Strange Gods*		
	Matthew Josephson, *The Robber Barons*		

Year	American Documents	European Documents	Political, Social, and Cultural Events
	Charles Beard, "History Written as an Act of Faith"		
	Meridel LeSueur, "I was Marching"		
	George Herbert Mead, *Mind, Self and Society* (posthumous)		
1935	John Dewey, *Liberalism and Social Action*	Karl Popper, *Logic of Scientific Discovery*	Mussolini invades Ethiopia
	Kenneth Burke, *Permanence and Change*	Rudolf Carnap, *Philosophy Logical Syntax*	Soviets call for "Popular Front"
	Thurman Arnold, *Symbols of Government*		
	Reinhold Niebuhr, *An Interpretation of Christian Ethics*		
1936	John Dos Passos, *USA*	A. J. Ayer, *Language, Truth, and Logic*	Spanish Civil War begins
	William Faulkner, *Absalom! Absalom!*	J. M. Keynes, *General Theory of Employment, Interest, and Money*	Moscow trials begin
	H. D. Laswell, *Politics: Who Gets What, When, How?*		
	Arthur O. Lovejoy, *The Great Chain of Being*		
	John Steinbeck, *In Dubious Battle*		
1937	Thurman Arnold, *Folklore of Capitalism*		
	John Dewey et al., *Not Guilty*		

Year	American Documents	European Documents	Political, Social, and Cultural Events
	Zora Neale Hurston, *Their Eyes Were Watching God*		
	Robert and Helen Lynd, *Middletown in Transition*		
	Talcott Parsons, *The Structure of Social Action*		
	Karen Horney, *The Neurotic Personality of Our Time*		
1938	Lewis Mumford, *The Culture of Cities*	George Orwell, *Homage to Catalonia*	Munich pact
	John Dewey, *Logic*	J-P. Sartre, *Nausea*	
	B. F. Skinner, *Behavior of Organisms*		
	Thornton Wilder, *Our Town*		
1939	John Steinbeck, *Grapes of Wrath*	W. H. Auden, "September, 1939"	Nazi–Soviet pact opens World War II in Europe
	John Dewey, *Freedom and Culture*	W. H. Auden, "In Memory of W. B. Yeats"	
	Cleanth Brooks, *Modern Poetry and the Tradition*		
1940	Edmund Wilson, *To the Finland Station*		France falls to Nazi Germany
	Eric Fromm, *Escape from Freedom*		
	Richard Wright, *Native Son*		
	Ernest Hemingway, *For Whom the Bell Tolls*		
	R. P. Blackmur, *The Expense of Greatness*		

Year	American Documents	European Documents	Political, Social, and Cultural Events
	Eugene O'Neill, *Long Day's Journey into Night*		
1941	James Burnham, *The Managerial Revolution*	Arthur Koestler, *Darkness at Noon*	Hitler attacks Soviet Union
	Joseph Davies, *Mission to Moscow*		Japanese bomb Pearl Harbor, bringing U.S. into World War II
	James Agee and Walker Evans, *Let Us Now Praise Famous Men*		
	F. O. Matthiessen, *American Renaissance*		
	W. J. Cash, *The Mind of the South*		
1942	William Faulkner, *Go Down, Moses*	Albert Camus, *The Stranger*	
	Suzanne K. Langer, *Philosophy in a New Key*		
	Alfred Kazin, *On Native Grounds*		
	Joseph Schumpeter, *Capitalism, Socialism, Democracy*		
	Robert K. Merton, "A Note on Science and Democracy"		
	Margaret Mead, *And Keep Your Powder Dry*		
	Carl Hempel, "The Function of General Laws in History"		
	Mary McCarthy, *The Company She Keeps*		
1943	Reinhold Niebuhr, *Nature and Destiny of Man*		

Year	American Documents	European Documents	Political, Social, and Cultural Events
	Wendel Willkie, *One World*		
	C. L. Hull, *Principles of Behavior*		
	Ayn Rand, *The Fountainhead*		
1944	Gunnar Myrdal, *An American Dilemma*	F. A. Hayek, *Road to Serfdom*	Holocaust of European Jews in process
	Reinhold Niebuhr, *The Children of Light and the Children of Darkness*		G.I. Bill
	C. L. Stevenson, *Ethics and Language*		
	Helene Deutsch, *Psychology of Women*		
1945	Dwight Macdonald, "The Responsibility of Peoples"	Karl Popper, *Open Society and Its Enemies*	World War II ends
	Vannevar Bush, *Science—The Endless Frontier*		U.S. drops atomic bombs on Japan
1946	Robert Penn Warren, *All the King's Men*	J-P. Sartre, *Existentialism and Humanism*	
	Hans Morgenthau, *Scientific Man vs. Power Politics*	R. G. Collingwood, *Idea of History* (posthumous)	
	John Hersey, *Hiroshima*		
	James B. Conant, *Understanding Science*		
1947	Lionel Trilling, *Middle of the Journey*	Michael Oakeshott, "Rationalism in Politics"	Truman Doctrine
	Paul Samuelson, *Foundations of Economic Analysis*		

Year	American Documents	European Documents	Political, Social, and Cultural Events
1948	Norman Mailer, *The Naked and the Dead*	George Orwell, *Nineteen Eighty-Four*	Alger Hiss accused of spying
	B. F. Skinner, *Walden Two*		
	Norbert Wiener, *Control and Connection*		
	James Gould Cozzens, *Guard of Honor*		
	Alfred Kinsey, *Sexual Behavior in the Human Male*		
1949	Robert K. Merton, *Social Theory and Social Structure*	Simone de Beauvoir, *Second Sex*	NATO pact
	Morton White, *Social Thought in America*	Fernand Braudel, *Mediterranean in Age of Philip II*	Communist revolution in China
	Arthur Miller, *Death of a Salesman*	Gilbert Ryle, *Concept of Mind*	
	Max Horkheimer and Theodor Adorno, *Dialectic of Enlightenment*		
	Joseph Campbell, *The Hero with a Thousand Faces*		
1950	Lionel Trilling, *The Liberal Imagination*		Korean War begins
	Henry Steele Commager, *The American Mind*		McCarthy claims government is influenced by Communists
	T. W. Adorno et al., *The Authoritarian Personality*		Television becomes widely available
	David Riesman et al., *The Lonely Crowd*		
	Erik Erikson, *Childhood and Society*		

Year	American Documents	European Documents	Political, Social, and Cultural Events
1951	C. Wright Mills, *White Collar*	Albert Camus, *The Rebel*	
	Talcott Parsons, *The Social System*		
	Hannah Arendt, *Origins of Totalitarianism*		
	W.V.O. Quine, "Two Dogmas of Empiricism"		
	J. D. Salinger, *Catcher in the Rye*		
	George Kennan, *American Diplomacy, 1900–1950*		
	Hans Reichenbach, *The Rise of Scientific Philosophy*		
	Kenneth Arrow, *Rational Choice and Individual Values*		
	C. Vann Woodward, *Origins of the New South*		
1952	Ralph Ellison, *Invisible Man*		
	Whittaker Chambers, *Witness*		
	Reinhold Niebuhr, *The Irony of American History*		
	Paul Tillich, *The Courage to Be*		
	Herman Wouk, *The Caine Mutiny*		

Year	American Documents	European Documents	Political, Social, and Cultural Events
1953	Daniel J. Boorstin, *The Genius of American Politics* Saul Bellow, *The Adventures of Augie March* Leo Strauss, *Natural Right and History* Alfred Kinsey, *Sexual Behavior in the Human Female*	Ludwig Wittgenstein, *Philosophical Investigations* (posthumous) Watson–Crick model for DNA C. Milosz, *The Captive Mind* Roland Barthes, *Writing Degree Zero*	Ceasefire in Korea
1954	David Potter, *People of Plenty* Wallace Stevens, *Collected Poems*	Jacques Ellul, *Technological Society* William Golding, *Lord of the Flies*	Oppenheimer hearings Army–McCarthy hearings *Brown v. School Board of Topeka*
1955	Walter Lippmann, *The Public Philosophy* Louis Hartz, *The Liberal Tradition in America* James Baldwin, *Notes of a Native Son* Herbert Marcuse, *Eros and Civilization* C. Vann Woodward, *The Strange Career of Jim Crow* Will Herberg, *Protestant–Catholic–Jew* Edward Steichen, *The Family of Man* Richard Hofstadter, *Age of Reform* Vladimir Nabakov, *Lolita*	Claude Levi-Strauss, *Tristes Tropiques*	

Year	American Documents	European Documents	Political, Social, and Cultural Events
1956	C. Wright Mills, *Power Elite* Alan Ginsberg, *Howl* William H. Whyte, *The Organization Man* Walter Kaufmann, ed., *Existentialism from Dostoevsky to Sartre*		Khrushchev's "secret speech" Soviets crush rebellion in Hungary
1957	James Gould Cozzens, *By Love Possessed* Dwight Macdonald, *Memoirs of a Revolutionist* Mary McCarthy, *Memories of a Catholic Girlhood* Leon Festinger, *A Theory of Cognitive Dissonance* Jack Kerouac, *On the Road*	Milovan Djilas, *New Class* Roland Barthes, *Mythologies*	*Sputnik*
1958	Daniel Lerner, *The Passing of Traditional Society* John Kenneth Galbraith, *The Affluent Society* Martin Luther King, Jr., *Stride Toward Freedom* John Rawls, "Justice as Fairness" William Lederer and Eugene Burdick, *The Ugly American*	Boris Pasternak, *Doctor Zhivago*	

Year	American Documents	European Documents	Political, Social, and Cultural Events
1959	Harold Rosenberg, *Tradition of the New* Norman O. Brown, *Life Against Death* William A. Williams, *The Tragedy of American Diplomacy* C. Wright Mills, *The Sociological Imagination*	C. P. Snow, *The Two Cultures*	
1960	W. W. Rostow, *Stages of Economic Growth* Paul Goodman, *Growing Up Absurd* Daniel Bell, *The End of Ideology* Bruno Bettelheim, *The Informed Heart* Sheldon Wolin, *Politics and Vision* Angus Campbell et al., *The American Voter* S. M. Lipset, *Political Man* John Courtney Murray, *We Hold These Truths*	E. H. Gombrich, *Art and Illusion* Hans Gadamer, *Truth and Method*	F.D.A. approves oral contraception
1961	Lionel Trilling, "On the Teaching of Modern Literature" Ernest Nagel, *The Structure of Science* Robert A. Dahl, *Who Governs?* Joseph Heller, *Catch-22* Erving Goffman, *Asylums*	Michel Foucault, *Madness and Civilization* Franz Fanon, *Wretched of the Earth*	Kennedy takes office

Year	American Documents	European Documents	Political, Social, and Cultural Events
1962	Thomas S. Kuhn, *The Structure of Scientific Revolutions*		Vatican II begins
	Michael Harrington, *The Other America*		
	Ken Kesey, *One Flew over the Cuckoo's Nest*		
	Milton Friedman, *Capitalism and Freedom*		
	Marshall McLuhan, *Gutenberg Galaxy*		
	Rachel Carson, *Silent Spring*		
	SDS, *Port Huron Statement*		
1963	Betty Friedan, *The Feminine Mystique*		Kennedy assassinated
	Mary McCarthy, *The Group*		
	Sylvia Plath, *The Bell Jar*		
	Nathan Glazer and Daniel Moynihan, *Beyond the Melting Pot*		
	Martin Luther King, Jr., "Letter from a Birmingham Jail"		
1964	Saul Bellow, *Herzog*		
	Hannah Arendt, *Eichmann in Jerusalem*		
	Clifford Geertz, "Ideology as a Cultural System"		

Year	American Documents	European Documents	Political, Social, and Cultural Events
	Ralph Ellison, *Shadow and Act*		
	Clark Kerr, *The Uses of the University*		
	Ken Kesey, *Sometimes a Great Notion*		
	Philip E. Converse, "The Nature of Belief Systems in Mass Publics"		
	Martin Luther King, Jr., *Why We Can't Wait*		
1965	Herbert Marcuse, "Repressive Tolerance"	Louis Althusser, *For Marx*	Johnson commits troops to Vietnam
	Lionel Trilling, *Beyond Culture*		Watts riot
	Noam Chomsky, *Aspects of the Theory of Syntax*		Restrictions on immigration sharply reduced
	Malcolm X, *Autobiography*		
	Harvey Cox, *The Secular City*		
1966	Peter Berger and Thomas Luckerman, *The Social Construction of Reality*	Michel Foucault, *The Order of Things*	National Organization for Women founded
		Jacques Lacan, *Écrits*	
	Robert J. Lane, "The Decline of Politics and Ideology in a Knowledgeable Society"		

Year	American Documents	European Documents	Political, Social, and Cultural Events
1967	Harold Cruse, *The Crisis of the Negro Intellectual* John Kenneth Galbraith, *The New Industrial State*	Jacques Derrida, *On Grammatology* Jacques Derrida, *Writing and Difference*	
1968	James D. Watson, *The Double Helix* John Updike, *Couples*	Jurgen Habermas, *Knowledge Human Interests* Jean Piaget, *Structuralism*	King assassinated Abortive revolution in France
1969	Kurt Vonnegut, *Slaughterhouse Five* Theodore Roszak, *Making of a Counter-Culture* Kate Millett, *Sexual Politics*	Michel Foucault, *Archeology of Knowledge*	Stonewall riot Humans walk on moon
1970	Robin Morgan, ed., *Sisterhood Is Powerful* Richard Macksey and Eugenio Donato, eds., *The Structuralist Controversy*		Killings at Kent State University Incursion into Cambodia
1971	John Rawls, *Theory of Justice* B. F. Skinner, *Beyond Freedom and Dignity* E. O. Wilson, *Insect Societies* Wallace Stegner, *Angle of Repose* Paul de Man, *Blindness and Insight*	Antonio Gramsci, *Prison Notebooks* (posthumous)	
1972	Lionel Trilling, *Sincerity and Authenticity*		Watergate break-in

Year	American Documents	European Documents	Political, Social, and Cultural Events
1973	Thomas Pynchon, *Gravity's Rainbow*	Jurgen Habermas, *Legitimation Crisis*	*Roe v. Wade*
	Daniel Bell, *The Coming of Postindustrial Society*		Vietnam War ends
			OPEC-related oil crisis
	Hayden White, *Metahistory*		
1974	Robert Nozick, *Anarchy, State, and Utopia*		Nixon resigns
1975	E. O. Wilson *Sociobiology*	Michel Foucault, *Discipline and Punish*	
1976	Alex Haley, *Roots*	Michel Foucault, *History of Sexuality*	
	Daniel Bell, *The Cultural Contradictions of Capitalism*		
1977	Toni Morison, *Song of Solomon*		